ETHICS AND COMPUTING

Second Edition

Books of Related Interest from IEEE Press

SOCIAL, ETHICAL, AND POLICY IMPLICATIONS OF ENGINEERING: Selected Readings
Edited by Joseph R. Herkert
2000   Softcover   352 pp   IEEE Order No. PP5397   ISBN 0-7803-4712-9

AN EXAMINATION OF HIGH-PERFORMANCE COMPUTING EXPORT CONTROL POLICY IN THE 1990s
Seymour E. Goodman, Peter Wolcott, and Grey E. Burkhart
1996   Softcover   100 pp   IEEE Order No. BR7459   ISBN 0-8186-7459-8

CYBERLAW: The Law of the Internet
Jonathan Rosenoer
1996   Softcover   365 pp   IEEE Order No. BP7776   ISBN 0-387-94832-5

A HISTORY OF COMPUTING TECHNOLOGY, Second Edition
Michael Williams
1997   Hardcover   530 pp   IEEE Order No. BP7739   ISBN 0-8186-7739-2

MICROSOFT RISING . . . AND OTHER TALES OF THE SILICON VALLEY
Ted Lewis
2000   Softcover   350 pp   IEEE Order No. BP0200   ISBN 0-7695-0200-8

ETHICS AND COMPUTING

Living Responsibly in a Computerized World

Second Edition

Edited by

Kevin W. Bowyer
University of South Florida

A Selected Reprint Volume

IEEE PRESS

The Institute of Electrical and Electronics Engineers, Inc., New York

This book and other books may be purchased at a discount
from the publisher when ordered in bulk quantities. Contact:

IEEE Press Marketing
Attn: Special Sales
445 Hoes Lane
P.O. Box 1331
Piscataway, NJ 08855-1331
Fax: +1 732 981 9334

For more information on IEEE Press products, visit the
IEEE Online Catalog & Store: http://www.ieee.org/store.

10   9   8   7   6   5   4   3   2   1

Library of Congress Cataloging-in-Publication Data

Ethics and computing: living responsibly in a computerized world/edited by Kevin W.
Bowyer.—2nd ed.
      p. cm.
      Includes bibliographical references and index.
      ISBN 13: 978-0-7803-6019-8
      1. Computers—Moral and ethical aspects. I. Bowyer, Kevin, 1955–

   QA76.9.M65 B69 2000
   174'.90904—dc21

                                                            00-033594

This book is dedicated to my parents, Mathew and Virginia; my wife, Susan; and our children, Mathew and James.

Contents

Contents

Preface

THIS revised edition incorporates a number of major revisions to the first edition. The Introduction has been rewritten. The Critical Thinking chapter has been heavily revised with substantial new material added. The Professional Codes of Ethics chapter also has been heavily revised and now includes the AITP Code of Ethics and the Software Engineering Code of Ethics. The chapter on Cracking and Computer Security has been rewritten and most of its reprinted articles are replaced to provide up-to-date coverage. Finally, the chapter on Encryption and Law Enforcement has been updated and enhanced. All these chapters have more and better worksheet exercises, and a number of minor revisions at various places in latter chapters have been made. As a result of all these changes, the text has become almost 20% longer.

Becoming a computing *professional* involves more than just learning about how technology works. There is a real need to develop an understanding of the ethical and social implications involved in computing as well. How computing professionals decide to handle such issues as security, privacy, safety-critical systems, whistle blowing, and other issues will greatly affect how they are viewed by the rest of society. The major professional societies involved in the computing industry—AITP, ACM, and IEEE-CS—have their own codes of ethics. Each of the codes touches on most, if not all, of these topics. One result of studying this book is your introduction to the different codes of ethics and how they apply to various issues. However, one theme stressed early in the book is that it is unrealistic to rely on codes of ethics in a simplistic way. It is important that each person be able to reason about the goals, values, and conflicts that are embedded in the codes. Thus strong critical-thinking skills are a prerequisite to effective thinking in ethically challenging situations. Critical thinking is the subject of a complete chapter early in the book (Chapter 2). The theme of having readers *think for themselves* about the issues continues throughout the book.

The text contains original material and selected reprints. The reprints are of several types. Some are "classic" papers by authors with distinguished reputations in their field. Some are more viewpoint-oriented articles or "opinion pieces." In several cases, contrasting viewpoint articles appear one after the other. Yet others are news accounts that present an overview of a case study related to ethics and computing. These augment the real-world case studies presented in the original material.

The text also contains two types of study aids: "worksheets" and "additional assignment" topics. The worksheets call for reading, assimilating, and reasoning about specific material in the chapter, reprints, or references. I recommend that you try to complete all the worksheets that you have time for as you read through the book. This will help you to fully understand the material. Additional assignment topics are more open-ended and often require some library and/or web-based research. They generally would make good topics for term papers or class presentations.

My hope is that you will find the text both informative and challenging. It is of course important that you become better informed through studying this text. But that alone is not enough. It is also important that you are challenged to honestly assess your internal sense of ethics and are motivated to strive for higher ethical standards. My goals will be met if you come away with a deeper understanding of the ethical issues you are likely to confront *and* if you find yourself able to formulate and hold to the highest possible ethical standards.

Kevin W. Bowyer
University of South Florida

Acknowledgments for the First Edition

MANY people deserve thanks for helping to shape the ideas that have gone into this book. I apologize in advance if anyone is forgotten.

First, there are the many students who participated in the course taught at the University of South Florida (USF) while the ideas for this book were taking shape. The interactions with students and the class discussions helped motivate the selection of material and shape the treatment of topics. Especially helpful were interactions with Ronda Caracappa, Mitch Feldman, Hillel Gilboa, Gillian Jean-Baptiste, Bill Labbon, Sherrie Mathis, Cathy Smith, and Hoomam Tahamtani.

Lisa Croy put in word processing effort on portions of the text.

Maha Sallam provided a critique and some excellent suggestions on early drafts of some sections.

Connie Leeper read drafts of several chapters and provided a number of useful comments and suggestions.

Professor Dewey Rundus at USF participated in a number of early discussions about some of the material.

Professor Tom Nartker of the University of Nevada at Las Vegas allowed the reprint of one of the assignments developed for a class he teaches.

Professor Marc Raibert of the Artificial Intelligence Lab at Massachusetts Institute Technology allowed the reprint of "Good Writing" in Appendix A.

Jon Butler, editor in chief of the IEEE Computer Society Press Editorial Board for Advances in Computer Science and Engineering, selected reviewers who made numerous valuable suggestions for correcting and improving different parts of the text. Nancy Talbert did an excellent job as development editor in reshaping portions of the final draft, sharpening the focus, and generally improving the text. Lisa O'Conner organized the printing of the final version. Catherine Harris shepherded the project through its various stages. Thanks to all of them for their efforts.

Unfortunately, even with all of the people who contributed excellent ideas and effort, there are probably still shortcomings, but these are my responsibility!

Finally, I would like to thank Susan Bowyer for enduring my absence for the time it took to write and assemble this book and for reading and critiquing drafts.

Kevin W. Bowyer
University of South Florida

Acknowledgments for the
Second Edition

AGAIN, I have a long list of people to thank. Harold L. Burstyn, patent attorney in the Office of the Staff Judge Advocate at Rome Laboratory in New York pointed out several corrections needed in the chapter on Intellectual Property Issues.

JAN Lee and I have had a number of useful conversations since the first edition of the book appeared, and I appreciate his encouraging comments.

I would like to thank Lotfi Zadeh for allowing me to reprint the text of his commencement address to University of California at Berkeley electrical engineering and computer science graduates. And I would like to thank Walter Elden for allowing me to reprint his article about the responsibilities of state Professional Engineering Boards.

All of the faculty from around the country who participated in my 1998 and 1999 NSF-sponsored workshops on "Teaching Ethics and Computing" provided great interactions and sparked many good ideas. In alphabetical order, this wonderful group of people is as follows: Dennis Anderson, Kathryn Baalman, Gene Bailey, Raj Bandi, Marcelle Bessman, Richard Botting, Wayne Brown, Sheila Castaneda, Gove Effinger, Gerald Engel, Tony Fabbri, Jay Fenwick, Ron Foster, Don Gotterbarn, Nancy Greenwood, Judy Gurka, Cindy Hanchey, Chuck Huff, Joe Kizza, Martha Kosa, Pam Lawhead, Andrea Lawrence, JAN Lee, Diane Martin, John McTaggart, Louise Moses, William Myers, Mary Jane Peters, Jennifer Polack, Sylvia Pulliam, Bill Richards, Wally Roth, Dewey Rundus, Sudeep Sarkar, Melanie Sutton, John Taylor, Elise Turner, Eva Turner, Paul Tymann, Nancy Wahl, Joe Wujek, Bill Yurcik, and Junaid Zubairi.

Jim Eison, director of the Center for Teaching Enhancement at USF, has sharpened my thinking through many valuable discussions about teaching, learning and the design of activities.

Sudeep Sarkar and Robin Murphy read drafts of some of the revised chapters and made useful suggestions.

Kevin W. Bowyer
University of South Florida

Chapter 1

Getting Started

ethics—the study of the general nature of morals and of the specific moral choices to be made by the individual in his relationship with others. the rules or standards governing the conduct of the members of a profession.
moral—of or concerned with the judgment principles of right and wrong in relation to human action and character. teaching or exhibiting goodness or correctness of character and behavior.
right—conforming with or conformable to justice, law or morality. in accordance with fact, reason or truth.
—The American Heritage Dictionary

1.1 Why Study Ethics and Computing?

SINCE you have begun reading this book, you are likely about to devote considerable effort to the study of ethics and computing. In this chapter, I try to set out answers for the why, what, and how questions of this study:

Why study ethics and computing?
What topics are relevant to this study?
How is the material best studied?

The *Why?* question comes first because the answer should set the context for answering the other questions. Why should you study ethics and computing? I assert that there can be just one worthwhile reason:

The goal of studying "ethics and computing" must be to cause you to become a more ethical person, particularly in your career as a computing professional.

If the goal is anything less than this, then the effort spent in this study is wasted!

This statement of the goal for your efforts may seem bold. Perhaps you are tempted to the knee-jerk response of "it isn't *me* that needs to improve *my* ethics." But if you are honest you know that you are far from perfect in your ethical knowledge, judgment, and behavior. Every

person can improve their own personal ethics and do a better job of encouraging ethical behavior in those around them. Once you decide that you want to improve yourself on the ethical dimension, studying this book should help you to realize that desire. If for some reason you do **not** desire to improve yourself ethically, studying this book will at least make you more aware of the ethical norms and expectations that apply to computing professionals.

Also, note that the statement of the goal mentions "person" first and "computing professional" second. There is a reason for this. It is hard to see how one can cultivate ethical behavior as something that is switched on only in your professional life, and is left in neutral in your personal life. It seems more likely that your professional ethics will be closely related to your overall personal ethics.

Our second question is, what topics are relevant to the study of ethics and computing? It should be clear that we do not mean to study all of the field of ethics or all of the field of computing. Our focus is on the practical intersection of these two fields; that is, on studying what constitutes ethical behavior for professionals in information systems, computer science, and software/computer engineering. A prerequisite for success in this study is to have good critical-thinking skills. For this reason, I have included a chapter on critical thinking as the second chapter in this book. The critical-thinking chapter is followed by chapters that address core topics in ethics and computing. The following list of questions should illustrate the range of topics involved in this study.

- What context do professional codes of ethics provide for decision making?
- What ethical and legal issues are involved in computer "cracking" and security?
- How does concern for privacy interact with concern for law enforcement and commerce?
- What are the professional responsibilities in developing safety-critical systems?
- What is the professional responsibility to "blow the whistle" on unethical behavior?
- What are the ethical and legal issues surrounding protection of intellectual property?
- How has the computing industry faced up to issues of use of natural resources?
- What are the standards for ethical interaction with others in the workplace?
- How should ethical concerns interact with how you manage your career?

With some idea of the topics to be covered, the third of the three questions to address in this section is, How is the material best studied? To a large degree, the teaching style of this book is structured around three basic premises. The first premise is that it is useful to get into detailed, real-world case studies as soon as the basic issues of a topic are introduced. The depth of each topic is explored through the various case studies contained in the text, reprints, exercises and worksheets. The second premise is that active learning is better than just reading. For this reason, there are lots of exercises and worksheets included in the book. You should do as many of these, especially the worksheets, as time will allow. You will cheat yourself out of much of the learning experience if you skip doing the exercises and worksheets. The third premise is that it is often useful to read original papers by authors who have distinguished reputations. This can expose you to different viewpoints and styles, and give you a sense of historical context. Reprinted papers that fall into this category include the one by Ken Thompson in the "Cracking and Computer Security" chapter, and those by David Parnas and Nancy Leveson in the "Safety-Critical Systems" chapter.

Two points deserve special emphasis with regard to how to study the material. The first point is that you must learn to suspend your initial reaction and think carefully and completely about a topic or issue. This is the critical-thinking aspect of your study. Without the exercise of strong critical-thinking skills, your study may reduce to a sequence of automatic "Yes!" and "No!" responses that simply reflect whatever initial prejudices you brought to the topic. Conscious application of critical-thinking skills will help you to internalize lessons that may include changes in your own personal ethical framework.

The second point is that you must learn to imagine yourself in the roles of the various persons in each case study. You should try to imagine how you would want to react when you unexpectedly find yourself in a similar situation. This is important. When you are unexpectedly confronted with an ethically challenging situation, and have not previously thought of how you would want to respond, there will be tremendous pressure to take the "path of least resistance." You could find yourself signing off on software that has not been tested as called for, agreeing to keep some important safety problem quiet "for the good of the company," using intellectual property that you know was not legally obtained, or taking any of a variety of other actions that you would regret later. On the other hand, if you have thought deeply about a related situation beforehand, and established in your own mind what an ethical response would be, you are much less likely to give in to the pressures of the moment.

1.2 A Fundamental Prerequisite

For your study of ethics and computing to make sense, it is necessary to accept the existence of good and evil. Most people share a similar informal understanding of these terms. If you need definitions, the American Heritage Dictionary defines "good" as "having positive or desirable qualities" and "evil" as "morally bad or wrong; wicked" [1]. These definitions appropriately suggest abstract concepts that are polar opposites. (If the terms "good" and "evil" are too strong for your taste, perhaps because of strong theological connotations, then substitute the terms "right" and "wrong.")

Why have we digressed into discussing the terms good and evil? The answer is simple. If you accept that concepts of good and evil exist and have meaning, then you can consider how these concepts apply to various decisions, actions, and outcomes. This is necessary in order for our study of ethics and computing to have any substance. In particular, we want to be able to discuss how good and evil relate to decisions, actions, and outcomes that **you** are potentially involved in.

Doesn't everyone automatically agree that concepts of good and evil exist? Actually, no. The framework of "ethical relativism" asserts that good and evil are defined only relative to a particular individual, at a particular time, or in a particular society. In this framework, there are no standards or rules of behavior that can reasonably be applied at all times and in all places. Motivation for this framework comes from the observation that what is considered ethical varies over time within one culture, as well as across different cultures at the same point in time. This observation is certainly correct. For example, at earlier times in the United States, slavery was legally sanctioned, women did not have the right to vote and child-labor practices were essentially unregulated. While these things have all changed in the United States, they are still prevalent in various other cultures around the world.[1] But the fact that different people, societies, or times have endorsed different behaviors as ethical does not prove the absence of absolute ethical standards. It proves only that human beings find it difficult to discover, acknowledge, and adhere to absolute ethical standards. Since ethical relativism denies the existence of universal ethical standards, it leads toward each person deciding for themselves what is moral. With each person's judgment as valid as another person's, there is no right and wrong, only different. The result is moral anarchy. For these reasons, the theory of ethical relativism has received severe criticism. The article by McFarland at the end of this chapter gives a more detailed critique of ethical relativism.

Our study of ethics and computing is explicitly based on the assumption that standards of right and wrong can and do exist. This does not mean that all such standards of right and wrong are known to, or accepted by, all people. Nor does it mean that it will be easy to decide the right and wrong of each situation you encounter. The real world often presents situations in which every available alternative appears to involve some degree of wrong. In fact, these are the situations in which your need for a strong personal ethical foundation is greatest.

1.3 ETHICAL THEORY AND PROFESSIONAL ETHICS

Ethical theory is the study of ethics at a conceptual or philosophical level. *Applied ethics* is aimed at the everyday life of the typical person, while *professional ethics* is aimed at a person engaged in the practice of a particular profession. The study of the theory of ethics is naturally the most general, but in being the most general, it is also necessarily less specific in the details of its application. The study of applied ethics is meant to result in more specific guidelines for use in real-world situations. Of course, the emphasis on specific real situations naturally results in relatively less emphasis on general theories. The study of professional ethics addresses the details of situations and issues that arise specific to some profession, but that might be irrelevant to some other profession.

Our study of ethics and computing is clearly a study of professional ethics. We do not attempt any history, survey, or comparison of ethical theories, even only the "major" and/or "modern" theories. These topics are appropriately the subjects of other books. For those who are interested, MacIntyre provides a short historical perspective on the development of "western" ethical philosophy [8]. Wilkens

provides a short, readable critique of the popular incarnation of a number of different ethical systems [15].

Professional ethics can be different from general ethics to the extent that professional ethics must take into account:

- relations between practicing professionals and their clients,
- relations between the profession and society in general,
- relations among professionals,
- relations between employee and employer, and perhaps most importantly,
- specialized technical details of the profession.

While the context for our study is the computing professions, the basic underlying ethical issues are really not specific to, or generated by, computing technology. I can think of only one ethical issue that might be considered as "new" in the sense of being generated by the development of computing technology. This is the question: How much decision making should be entrusted to a machine? But aside from this question, the core ethical issues are typically as ancient and as simple as basic greed and dishonesty. This is true because a computer is just a tool that lets people solve larger problems faster than they could manually. In this view, the presence of the computer cannot generate new ethical concerns. However, computers may shift the level of practical concern on some ethical issues. Consider the issue of privacy of communications between individuals. The letter carrier has always had the potential to open any envelope and read any letter. But in practice, opening and reading *all* letters is impossible due to the magnitude of the manual effort involved. However, much personal communication now takes place in computer networks. In a computer network, it becomes quite conceivable that literally every communication could be automatically scanned for certain words or phrases. Thus, while the core issue of privacy is not new, computers have turned a mostly theoretical concern into a real one.

1.4 GUIDANCE FOR LIVING ETHICALLY

Since ethical behavior is often in conflict with short-term self-interest, you should not expect ethical behavior to be an easy habit to develop. It is not something that, like a set of facts or equations, you can learn simply from reading a book. (Even this one!) Reading can help you learn about things like codes of ethics and resolutions of particular ethical conflicts, but ethical behavior is a way of life. As such, it is best learned through experience; that is, by continually living ethically yourself. A relevant quote attributed to Aristotle is: *We are what we regularly do. Excellence therefore is not an act, but a habit.* More than "book knowledge" is required to learn to live ethically. It requires that you have a deep desire and conviction to live ethically.

---

[1] For example, around the time this is being written, news accounts have discussed slavery in the Sudan, treatment of women in India and China, and child-labor practices in many countries that manufacture goods sent to the United States.

Fairburn and Watson observe that the primary factor leading us to stray from what we know to be correct ethical behavior is our tendency toward compromise in favor of our own short-term self-interest [5]. Some level of self-interest is perhaps necessary for survival. But an obsession with any particular worldly appetite (money, food, sex, praise, power, etc.) can ruin your life. Fairburn and Watson suggest three steps toward better ethical behavior:

1. Have high standards of ethical conduct.
2. Boldly live with the belief that this is the way to conduct yourself even though you may be giving up more immediate gains.
3. Serve a larger purpose—truth, reason, customers, society, the community, human advancement, God.

Thus the core themes of guidance for living ethically are relatively simple. Most people in most situations can reasonably easily determine what would constitute ethical behavior. But this behavior is quite often in conflict with what we perceive to be our own short-term self-interest. So we are tempted to rationalize and compromise. Therefore, living ethically requires the courage of strong convictions and a substantial degree of self-discipline. The presence or absence of strong ethical convictions and self-discipline is by nature pervasive throughout your life—at work or at play, in your personal or professional life.

As a last motivational quote for this section, consider the following description of the type of person needed in the world today-

> The world needs men [and women] . . . who cannot be bought; whose word is their bond; who put character above wealth; who possess opinions and a will; who are larger than their vocations; who do not hesitate to take chances; who will not lose their individuality in a crowd; who will be as honest in small things as in great things; who will make no compromise with wrong; whose ambitions are not confined to their own selfish desires; who will not say they do it "because everybody else does it"; who are true to their friends through good report and evil report, in adversity as well as in prosperity; who do not believe that shrewdness, cunning, and hardheadedness are the best qualities for winning success; who are not ashamed or afraid to stand for the truth when it is unpopular; who can say "no" with emphasis, although all the rest of the world says "yes."

Charles Swindoll, *Living Above the Level of Mediocrity*, [11]

1.5 CASE STUDY—*Goodearl and Aldred v. Hughes*

The case study presented here involves *whistle blowing.* Whistle blowers are people "who . . . make revelations meant to call attention to negligence, abuses, or dangers that threaten the public interest. They sound an alarm based on their expertise or inside knowledge, often from within the very organization in which they work . . ." [4]. Whistle blowing is the subject of an entire chapter later in the book, but it is useful to have a short introduction and example here. Common examples of situations that lead to whistle blowing are when an employee discovers that their company is knowingly supplying an unsafe product to customers, or when someone discovers that tax dollars are being wasted in a fraudulent or flagrant manner. The particular incident discussed here combines both of these concerns. The description of this incident is adapted from [3]. A time line for the events in this case appears in Figure 1.1.

This case study involves the (lack of) testing of microelectronic chips supplied to the military to be used in weapons systems. The particular chips involved are called

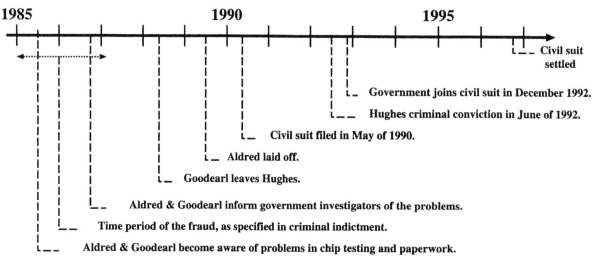

Fig. 1.1 Major events in the Goodearl and Aldred versus Hughes whistle-blowing case.

"hybrids" because they combine analog and digital logic on the same chip. It is standard practice to test chips in various ways before they are delivered to the customer. A contract to supply chips to a customer may state that various tests must be done and the results certified before the chips are to be delivered.

The False Claims Act (31 U.S.C. 3729-31) is a federal law that allows an individual to file a civil suit against a business that defrauds the federal government. The False Claims Act states that a whistle blower may receive between 15 and 25 percent of the recovered funds if the government chooses to participate in the suit. If the government decides not to participate in the suit, the whistle blower may receive between 25 and 30 percent of the recovery, plus legal fees and expenses.

1.5.1 The Cast of Characters

The Micro-electronic Circuits Division of Hughes Aircraft is located in Newport Beach, California. This division manufactured hybrid chips that were supplied to the United States military. The particular chips in question were used in about 75 different weapons programs, including aircraft, missiles and tanks. The results of chip failures in the field could be varied. One scenario that was suggested was that faults in a hybrid chip could cause failure in the radar that a fighter plane uses to direct its weapons! (See Figure 1.2.)

Margaret Goodearl and Ruth Aldred were employees at the Hughes Micro-electronic Circuits Division at the time that the chip-testing fraud occurred.

Donald Anthony LaRue was a shop foreman who also worked at Hughes.

1.5.2 The Sequence of Events

Between 1985 and 1987, Hughes shipped hybrid chips to the U.S. military without performing all of the tests that were required by their contract. Employees were told to omit tests, shorten tests, falsify documents, and otherwise contribute to and cover-up fraud in certifying that chips had passed tests that they in fact had not passed. This resulted in "false claims" being submitted to the government for the chips that were delivered, making Hughes open to criminal charges of fraud and to a civil suit under the False Claims Act.

Goodearl and Aldred's attorney, John Phillips, stated that "When they [Goodearl and Aldred] became aware of the problems with testing procedures at the plant, they tried to bring the matter to the attention of upper management. But they were told to keep quiet and warned that they might get fired if they didn't do so" [14]. It was also alleged that the whistle-blowers were "harassed by means of racial and sexual slurs and verbal comments, in addition to physical gestures and menacing postures," and that one day when Goodearl left work she "found a butchered

Fig. 1.2 F-16 fires an AGM-88 HARM missile. An F-16 Fighting Falcon from the 416th Flight Test Squadron Edwards Air Force Base, Calif., fires an AGM-88 HARM missile during testing. The F-16 is one of the weapons systems in which the hybrid chips were used. Testimony at the criminal trial indicated that chip failure in the field could cause pilots to be unable to aim their weapons. (U.S. Air Force Photo, photo by Tom Reynolds, www.af.mil/photos).

pig's head in a brown paper bag on the hood" of her car [6].

In 1988, Aldred felt that her job had been stripped of real responsibility and she left Hughes. In 1989, Goodearl was laid off from her job at Hughes.

Goodearl and Aldred also informed government officials about their concerns over the falsified chip testing. But they felt that government officials were moving slowly, if at all, to do anything about the incident. Then Goodearl and Aldred found out about the False Claims Act.

The two women filed civil suit against Hughes under the False Claims Act in 1990. The government then joined the civil suit in 1992.

In addition to the civil suit, there was a separate criminal trial against Hughes for the fraud. In the criminal trial, Hughes was convicted in 1992 of criminal conspiracy and fined $3.5 million. Goodearl and Aldred were witnesses in the criminal trial, along with others. Shop foreman Donald Anthony LaRue was charged along with Hughes in the criminal trial. In a comment typical of those directed toward whistle-blowers, it was claimed that LaRue had told Goodearl that she "was not part of the team" [9]. However, LaRue was acquitted in the criminal trial, as he had apparently been pushed to meet production quotas by higher level management.

Hughes lost the civil trial in 1996. This time the settlement was just over $4 million. Under the terms of the False Claims Act, 22% of the civil settlement, or approximately $900,000, went to the whistle-blowers Goodearl and Aldred. Hughes paid an additional $450,000 for the legal costs involved in Goodearl and Aldred bringing the civil suit.

1.5.3 Conclusions and Questions

In terms of the legal resolution, it is tempting to say that Goodearl and Aldred "won" and Hughes "lost." However, this may not accurately describe the situation for Goodearl and Aldred. Their lawyer [Phillips] argued that, "The re-ward is good but not that much considering what they've gone through. We feel good that they will be able to get on with their lives, but it's a long difficult road for anyone who wants to go against their employer with the False Claims Act" [6]. Remember that Aldred and Goodearl left their jobs with Hughes in 1988 and 1989, and the civil suit was not completed until 1996. Aldred was temporarily on welfare before finding a new job in 1991. Goodearl and her husband were forced to file for bankruptcy, and their marriage eventually broke up. Goodearl then moved to Washington, D.C. and worked as a housekeeper. With all of this in context, it is perhaps not so easy to say that Goodearl and Aldred "won."

The incident described here is reasonably typical of the "successful" cases of whistle-blowing. The whistle blowers lost their jobs, went through great turmoil in their personal lives, and were unable to find similar work. Then, after a number of years, their actions were finally vindicated through court decisions. In less successful cases, the whistle-blower may be intimidated into silence or may be worn down and eventually give up.

The dilemma for the whistle blowers is that they discover information that potentially places them in a "no-win" situation. If the management in the company will not address the problem, then the employee is faced with deciding either (1) to become silent and let the problem go on uncorrected or (2) to "blow the whistle" and live with the resulting disruption in their professional and personal lives. It is in some ways a classic case of either giving in to immoral activity in order to preserve monetary benefits or standing up against immoral activity in spite of the cost.

To repeat part of a quote from the previous section, whistle blowers must be people ". . . who cannot be bought . . . who put character above wealth . . . who will make no compromise with wrong . . . who will not say they do it "because everybody else does it" . . . who are not ashamed or afraid to stand for the truth when it is unpopular . . ." [11].

Points to Remember

- You will face a variety of ethically challenging situations in your career.
- Productive use of your knowledge about ethics requires that you accept personal responsibility for your actions.
- Your ability to consistently make appropriate ethical choices will be helped by not focusing on your own self-interest.
- Your ability to consistently make appropriate ethical choices will be greater if you have carefully considered ethical issues before they confront you in the workplace.
- Situations that present a continuing ethical challenge can wear you down. To the extent possible, avoid such situations.

WORKSHEET—"Urgency of Ethical Standards Intensifies"

Read the article by Michael McFarland that is reprinted from *Computer* magazine at the end of this chapter. Then answer the following questions.

1. It is suggested that ". . . if George chooses not to authorize release of the system, it would be done anyway without his approval. So, his sacrifice would have no practical effect." What effects, "practical" or otherwise, could come from George's refusal to authorize release of the system, even if it is then done anyway without his approval?

2. Briefly explain the "two fallacies about ethical knowledge" that McFarland describes.

3. Briefly outline the analogy with Physics that McFarland uses to explain how "ethical knowledge is a dynamic reality."

4. What are the four "meta-ethical principals" that McFarland explains as required in order for an ethical argument to be valid?

5. What is *utilitarianism* and what are the problems that McFarland identifies in it?

6. Reread the description of George's dilemma in the second paragraph of the section "Ethics as a social activity." How accurate is this description? Will you sometimes find yourself in such a situation?

WORKSHEET—"Anatomy of a Fraud" (part 1)

Read the short article titled "Anatomy of a Fraud" that ran in *Business Week* on September 16, 1996. Then answer the following questions.

1. What is Kurzweil Applied Intelligence's area of business?

2. What is an *initial public offering*?

3. What are *receivables* and why were "soaring receivables" a "telltale signal" of the fraud?

4. Who were the direct victims of the fraud?

5. How does the article suggest that the fraud got started?

6. How were the auditors fooled?

7. What was Murray's role in the fraud?

8. What was Campbell's role in the fraud?

9. What was Bradstreet's role in the fraud?

10. What was the role of the "low-level staffers" in the fraud?

WORKSHEET—"Anatomy of a Fraud" (part 2)

Read the short article titled "Anatomy of a Fraud" that ran in *Business Week* on September 16, 1996. Then answer the following questions.

1. Who did the legal system treat most appropriately in the incident? Who least appropriately? How would you change their punishments?

2. What do you see as the main temptation that Bradstreet succumbed to? How can you go about trying to avoid similar temptations?

3. What can you do to avoid becoming a "low-level staffer" who willingly (even enthusiastically) gets caught up in such a fraud?

4. Debra Murray turned herself in, gave detailed testimony against a person that she had worked with for nine years, and pled guilty to charges relating to her own role. Was it out of noble or selfish motivation? If you found yourself involved in a similar incident, would there be a better way to handle it?

5. Make a list of the positive comments that were made about Bernard Bradstreet's moral character by people who knew him. Would your colleagues' comments about you be this positive? more? less?

WORKSHEET—Child Pornography on the Internet

Read the reprinted article from *The Tampa Tribune* titled "Internet pornographer draws long sentence." Then answer the following questions.

1. What was the size of ". . . what investigators believe is the nation's largest documented case of Internet child pornography?"

2. What sentence did Robert Wallace Hudson receive? Is it appropriate, too short, or too long? Why? If they were found guilty, what sentence should the adults in the videos receive?

3. What would you do if you noticed pornographic images on someone else's computer when you were using it? That is, if you found yourself in the position of the consultant hired by Hudson?

4. During the trial, Hudson's defense argued that he ". . . found the child pornography on his hard drive . . . but he did not put it there." Is this at all believable? Do Hudson's comments at sentencing essentially admit that this defense was a lie?

5. Hudson was quoted as saying "I'm not as evil as they paint me to be." So, just how evil do you think he is?

6. Does the Internet make the problem of child pornography any better or worse? How? What measures could you suggest to combat the problem of child pornography being exchanged on the Internet?

7. Is the commercial use of images such as those made (in)famous in Calvin Klein advertising likely to have any effect on the problem of child pornography? What kind of effect? Why?

WORKSHEET—Prioritizing Concerns about Ethical Problems

1. What are the three most important ethical problems that confront you as a student pursuing your education?

2. What are the three most important ethical problems that you expect to confront you as a professional in your career?

3. What are the three most important ethical problems that confront our society in general?

1. **Theodore R. Johnson.** Theodore R. Johnson is not someone you have likely heard about. He worked for United Parcel Service and never earned a big salary, but he invested wisely. When he turned 90, he decided to give $36 million of his $90 million fortune to various charities [10]. Report on how he made his money, who he gave it to, and why.

2. **Inaki Lopez.** In 1993, Inaki Lopez left General Motors Corp. to join Volkswagen. A number of GM executives followed him in switching companies. GM filed suit against VW. Look into the details of this incident. Do you believe Lopez is a positive role model for corporate executives? Does he have the type of reputation you would want to have?

3. **Lawrence Adler.** Lawrence Adler admitted paying a friend to take the SAT exam for him [7]. Report on as many of the specifics of this incident as you can. What is your impression of Adler, the Educational Testing Service, and the judge who heard Adler's case?

4. **The FBI sting at NASA.** The FBI's Operation Lightning Strike was a sting operation at the NASA Johnson Space Center. One corporation and nine individuals were charged as a result of the investigation [12]. Report on as many details of the sting operation and the subsequent charges as you can find.

5. **The U.S. Navy/Solar Turbines Incorporated incident.** The U.S. Navy contracted for $55 million with Solar Turbines Incorporated to develop new equipment. But it appears that some people at the Navy did not want the new technology and developed a strategy to "let Solar Turbines spend so much of its own money on RACER that it would finally throw in the towel" [13]. Report on as many details of this incident as you can find out, especially the roles of the officials involved on the U.S. Navy side.

6. **Arrest for threatening stories on the Internet.** Jake Baker was a student at the University of Michigan who posted a story to a "sex stories" Internet mail group. The story would have been X-rated in any interpretation, as it described the rape, torture, and murder of an individual. In this instance, Baker actually named a real person. Baker was arrested and charged with interstate transmission of a threat [2]. The punishment is up to five years in prison. Look into this case and report on the final decision and your opinion about Baker as an individual.

REFERENCES

[1] *The American Heritage Dictionary*. Houghton Mifflin Company, Boston, Massachusetts, 1982.

[2] Associated Press report, "Student called "ticking bomb" after Internet threat," *The Tampa Tribune,* February 11, 1995.

[3] K. W. Bowyer, Goodearl and Aldred versus Hughes Aircraft: A modern case study in "whistle blowing," *looking.forward* 6 (1998), pp. 2–4.

[4] S. Bok, "The morality of whistle blowing," in *Computers, Ethics & Society,* M. D. Ermann, M. B. Williams, and C. Gutierrez (editors), Oxford University Press, New York, 1990.

[5] D. T. Fairburn and C. E. Watson, "In pursuit of ethics," *Simulation,* June 1992, pp. 427–432.

[6] C. Gewertz, "Whistle-blower suit filed against Hughes," *Los Angeles Times,* February 24, 1990.

[7] V. T. Jennings, "Maryland teen fined $5,000 for SAT lawsuit," *The Washington Post,* June 27, 1992.

[8] A. MacIntyre, *A Short History of Ethics.* MacMillan Publishing Company, New York, 1966.

[9] J. Mathews and S. Pearlstein, "Hughes charged with falsifying test data," *The Washington Post,* December 13, 1991.

[10] A. Moore, "Millionaire donates tuition money for the disabled," *The Orlando Sentinel-Tribune,* February 27, 1992.

[11] C. Swindoll, *Living Above the Level of Mediocrity,* Word Books, Nashville 1990.

[12] "FBI sting nabs NASA employees," *The Tampa Tribune,* February 23, 1994.

[13] "Double cross: How not to do business," *US News & World Report,* July 13, 1992.

[14] H. Weinstein, "Two Hughes whistle-blowers to split $891,000," *Los Angeles Times,* Washington D.C. September 11, 1996.

[15] S. Wilkens, *Beyond Bumper Sticker Ethics.* InterVarsity Press, Downer's Grove, IL, 1995.

STANDARDS

Editor: Fletcher J. Buckley, 103 Wexford Dr., Cherry Hill, NJ 08003, phone (609) 866-6350, fax (609) 866-6289, Compmail+ f.buckley

Urgency of ethical standards intensifies in computer community

Michael C. McFarland

The past several months, George, an electrical engineer working for an aerospace contractor, has been the quality control manager on a project to develop a computerized control system for a new military aircraft. Early simulations of the software for the control system showed that, under certain conditions, instabilities would arise that could cause the plane to crash. The software was subsequently patched to eliminate the specific problems uncovered by the tests. After the repairs were made, the system passed all of the required simulation tests.

George is convinced, however, that these problems were symptomatic of a fundamental design flaw that could only be eliminated by an extensive redesign of the system. Yet, when he brought his concern to his superiors, they assured him that the problems had been resolved, as shown by the tests. Anyway, to reevaluate and possibly redesign the system would introduce delays that would cause the company to miss the delivery date specified in the contract, and that would be very costly.

Now, there's a great deal of pressure on George to sign off on the system and allow it to be flight tested. It has even been hinted that, if he persists in delaying release of the system, the responsibility will be taken away from him and given to someone who is more compliant.

George faces a serious moral dilemma. On the one hand, he feels the pressure to comply with his superiors' orders not only to protect himself and his family from the possible loss of his job but also out of loyalty to his company and deference to the judgment of his superiors. On the other hand, as an engineer and par-

Michael C. McFarland is a professor of computer science at Boston College currently on leave at the AT&T Bell Laboratories in Murray Hill, New Jersey. Also a writer, he specializes in research on ethics in computer science engineering, design automation in VLSI, and system specification and verification. He is a Jesuit priest, and holds a master's degree in social ethics from the Weston School of Theology and a PhD in electrical engineering from Carnegie Mellon University. He has been active in the IEEE Computer Society for more than 10 years. — F. Buckley

ticularly as a quality control manager, he feels responsible for the reliability of the system and the safety of those using it. In his professional judgment, he is not confident the system is safe, so he does not feel it would be justified to say it is.

What makes the situation so difficult for George is that he must choose between conflicting duties: loyalty to self, family, employer, and superiors versus the obligation to tell the truth and to protect others from harm. The situation is complicated by the fact that, even if George chooses not to authorize release of the system, it would be done anyway without his approval. So, his sacrifice would have no practical effect.

This is a hypothetical case, but not unlike those many engineers face.[1-3] In particular, as society becomes more and more dependent on computers in critical applications in such areas as defense, transportation, medical care, and banking, computer scientists and engineers increasingly find themselves encountering difficult ethical dilemmas. These involve not only the reliability and safety of computer systems but also computer security and privacy, ownership of programs and data, the impact of computers on the workplace and education, and the

implications of artificial intelligence research.

How people in the industry handle these dilemmas has implications far beyond their own success and peace of mind; it will affect the welfare of everyone who depends on computer systems in any way. There is, therefore, a growing concern about ethical standards among computer professionals. Many feel we need to work out guidelines on the ethical issues facing the profession. Establishing a set of standards that is accepted and shared by the whole profession is important not only because it can help those facing difficult ethical decisions to make reasonable and fair judgments that serve the best interests of everyone involved, but also because of the sense of support and solidarity such standards can give those making the decisions, making it easier for them to carry through on those decisions with courage and confidence.

The purpose of this article is not so much to propose a set of standards for the profession — we still have much to do before we get to that point — but to provide background material on ethical standards in general. I will discuss where ethical standards come from, how they are arrived at, and how they can be promoted

Reprinted from *IEEE Computer*, Vol. 23, No. 3, pp. 77–81, March 1990.

and applied. I hope this will help prompt a wide-ranging discussion within the profession in general and the IEEE Computer Society in particular that will result in a consensus on a set of standards for the profession.

Two fallacies about ethical knowledge. Ethical standards must be based on some apprehension of what is right and wrong, of what ought to be done, and of what ought not to be done. The first question we must consider, therefore, is "What is ethical knowledge and where does it come from?"

There are two fallacies about the status of ethical knowledge that we must discuss before we can consider what it is. The first and the most prevalent today is called ethical relativism. It holds that there is no objective, shared ethical truth that is knowable by everyone and to which everyone can be held accountable. In this view, each individual is responsible for his or her own ethical judgments and makes them according to his or her own perceptions. This is akin to saying, "What you feel is right, is right for you." No one else has any justification for criticizing it.

This view, of course, is consistent with the observation that intelligent people of good will can hold quite different views on important ethical questions. It also harmonizes well with the great value our culture places on freedom — freedom in the sense of noninterference.

The problem with ethical relativism is that, if applied consistently, it makes it impossible to ever critique another person's behavior. If someone thinks it is right to sexually abuse children, to rob and shoot a taxi driver, or to break into private files on a computer system, that is the individual's decision. It is not for us to decide what is right for that individual.

When the issue is put this way, it is evident that, while ethical relativism may be attractive in individual cases, especially where it seems to spare us painful confrontations on ethical issues, it is simply not tenable as a fundamental ethical principle. If it were taken seriously, there could be no ethical standards and thus no civilization.

Another related view that is seemingly less extreme but in fact just as dangerous is cultural relativism. This states that societies or cultures can come to a consensus on ethical standards that they can impose on their members but that these standards are arbitrary. There is no basis for saying that one set of standards is superior to another.

This view has all the problems of ethical relativism but, if anything, is worse because it operates on a greater scale. If a particular society, for example, decides that it is right to hold people of another race or religion in slavery or to kill them, they are justified in doing so. If we accept cultural relativism, there is no objective basis for opposing such a position.

This form of relativism, often hidden in such cynical phrases as "might makes right" and "the winners write history," must also be rejected. It may allow for the formation of standards, but there is no way of insuring that they have any relation to good. In particular, there is no guarantee of protection for those on the fringes of a society.

In view of the dangers of ethical relativism, it would be nice if we could show that ethical truth is somehow given, as a set of rules or principles that we simply have to look up somewhere. But, of course, we know that there is no commonly accepted source that contains the answers to all our ethical questions.

Even within religious or political traditions that have authoritative statements of ethical rules or principles, such as the Ten Commandments or the Bill of Rights of the US Constitution, it is by no means clear or undisputed what the status and meaning of these texts are and how they are to be applied in all cases. They are important sources of moral wisdom, authoritative for some, but not the definitive answer to every moral problem. Nor is there any philosophical system that offers a clear answer to every dilemma. So, how can there be objective ethical truth if it is not "out there" waiting for us to find it?

I think an analogy with natural science is helpful here. Physics long ago gave up the view that the truth about the structure and dynamics of the universe is an objective reality that exists apart from our asking about it and that can be fully grasped through the mechanical application of known principles. Rather, what is knowable about the physical universe is something dynamic that takes form through our inquiry and experimentation. As much as we know about it, we certainly have not grasped it all and never will.

But that does not mean that there is no truth that can be known about the physical world or that the truth is something completely arbitrary that we invent. If that were true, all science would be in vain, and all attempts to understand physical phenomena would be useless.

Yet, scientists go on experimenting and constructing theoretical models in the belief that these activities can deepen their understanding of the phenomena they study. Their theories may never be complete, but that does not mean that they are useless or arbitrary.

If some theoretical breakthrough should reveal that gravity is not an independent force but part of a larger scheme, everything that past theories of gravity have taught us would not be invalidated. The planets would still move as they always have. It would not be that our previous theories were false, only that they did not give the full picture.

In the same way, ethical knowledge is a dynamic reality, neither totally within our grasp nor totally beyond it. Ethics has its own discipline and its own methodology, just as the physical sciences do. Ethical knowledge emerges from experience and reason, from action, and from reflection on that action.

While they are still provisional and periodically challenged, the principles we have built up over thousands of years have taught us a great deal about how to apprehend and realize the human good. Even if they are someday superseded because we come to a deeper understanding of ethical truth, they will not cease to be useful. Therefore, it is worth learning how to apply them.

Metaethical principles. We do not have a methodology that is precise enough to settle all ethical disputes, but we do have ways of distinguishing sound ethical arguments from fallacious ones and deciding on issues where there is a clear choice between what is right and what is wrong.

There are four conditions that any ethical argument must meet to be valid:

(1) It must be consistent with the facts.
(2) It must be reasonable and logically consistent.
(3) It must be based on sound principles and uphold the highest good.
(4) It must be universalizable. That is, if an argument asserts that action X is justifiable in situation Y, then it must also assert that X is justifiable in every situation Z that does not differ from Y in any way that is morally significant.

The first two conditions are obvious enough, but nevertheless must be emphasized because many ethical arguments fail precisely because they do not respect the facts or do not hold together logically. The third condition requires that we be able to identify and prioritize various human goods and values. In general, this is a very difficult and controverted task, about which I will have more to say later.

Nonetheless, there are many cases where the priority is clear. For example, if someone injects a destructive virus into a computer program because he feels it is more important to show his technical expertise and impress his friends than to respect the needs of those who will lose valuable time and data because of the virus, we can say with some assurance that that is not a valid justification.

The fourth condition provides the most significant and powerful test for ethical arguments. First of all, it insures that ethical standards are applied fairly. I cannot assert that there is one rule for me and another rule for everyone else or that one set of standards applies to one group and a different set to another group that only incidentally differs from the first. For example, I cannot claim that I am justified in copying commercial, copyrighted software without authorization unless I am willing to accept the implications of everyone copying software without paying — which would mean either outrageously overpriced software or the end of commercial software altogether.

Similarly, I cannot claim that it is right for me to misrepresent products or break contracts when they are not to my advantage unless I am willing to accept others lying to me or breaking contracts that give me an advantage over them. This principle always forces us to ask the question, "How would I feel if that were done to me?"

The fourth condition also provides us with a powerful means of testing the validity and applicability of proposed ethical principles or rules of thumb by testing them on a wide range of cases and analogies until we find their limits or see them fall apart. For example, out of concern for the protection of personal information in a large database of credit records, we might propose the rule: "It is wrong to allow any use of personal information in a database without the subject's consent." But then we would have to test the universalizability of this rule by asking whether there are ever situations where we should allow the use of personal information, whether in a database or not, without the subject's consent. Of course there are, for instance in helping to track a dangerous criminal or in investigating cases of child abuse. Therefore, the rule is not universalizable as it is, and we must either reject the rule or, more likely, modify it to allow certain exceptions, such as matters of public safety. But trying to generalize the new version of the rule might show the need to define more clearly which matters of public safety are serious enough to justify the release of public information, who is to decide, and so on. Much ethical argument involves the testing and refining of rules by applying them to analogous cases.

Ethical principles. The methodology sketched in the previous section gives us a way of testing and applying ethical principles, but it does not tell us what those principles are. In this section, I will consider some of the principles that have commonly been found to be important.

The principle of utilitarianism states that, in any given situation, that action is right which produces the greatest net good, that is, the greatest preponderance of good over evil. This assumes that all goods and evils can be quantified in some way and compared on the same scale.

Utilitarianism is probably the ethical principle engineers are most comfortable with. It is the underlying basis for cost-benefit analysis, for example, where all of the consequences of competing strategies are given dollar values, and the strategy with the highest net gain is chosen.

Utilitarianism does have many attractive features. Surely, if we have any ethical obligation at all, it is to do good and avoid evil. Utilitarianism takes that fundamental truth and tries to build a precise calculus around it. Once a method of quantifying goods and evils has been chosen, the system gives definite answers to ethical questions, which is very appealing.

The most difficult ethical choices are those that involve choosing between competing goods or the acceptance of certain evils to avoid others. Utilitarianism offers a definite and seemingly unbiased way of making those choices.

Nevertheless, few ethicists accept utilitarianism as totally adequate in itself.[4,5] There are a number of reasons for this. First, utilitarianism is not as objective as it might appear. Any particular utilitarian calculus contains hidden value judgments, especially in the way the consequences of actions are quantified. For example, how much is a human life worth? $100,000? $1,000,000? $1.98? Who decides?

The method we use for assigning value to human lives embodies some very important judgments about the relative worth of different human beings. If, for instance, we decide to value human beings based on their potential economic productivity over their lifetimes, as some have proposed, we are saying that the elderly and those who are severely handicapped are worth less and deserve less protection and support than others. That conclusion is highly debatable, to say the least, and can lead to severe abuses. Of course, we must make judgments about the relative importance of competing values; that is what ethics is all about. But these decisions must be acknowledged for what they are and worked out openly, not hidden in some supposedly "objective" system.

The second problem with utilitarianism is that, in its pure form, it says nothing about how benefits are to be distributed. Therefore, it does nothing to promote fairness or justice. For example, a cost-benefit analysis might indicate that it is most beneficial overall to place a coal-fired power plant for a major city in a rural area, next to an Indian reservation. There, it would be closer to the sources of coal and would inconvenience far fewer people than it would were it built in a more urban or suburban location. The impact of the plant on the Indians — the strip mining and the pollution that would go with it — would be far more severe than it would be on a more urban or suburban population since the Indians depend much more on the land and nature in general for their economic and spiritual life. But since there are so few of the Indians, the benefits outweigh the costs.

The problem, of course, is that this solution is extremely unfair. Almost all of the benefits of the plant go to a majority urban population that already possesses a disproportionate amount of wealth and power, while those who are already impoverished and discriminated against are forced to bear most of the costs.

The third problem is that, even if utilitarianism were acceptable in theory, it could in practice never adequately account for all the consequences of a possible course of action. For example, it might seem in a particular case that telling a lie would have very little in the way of negative consequences and might bring great benefits. If lying were allowed in every case where it seemed beneficial, however, it would seriously weaken the foundation of trust that society needs to function. It would also weaken the integrity of the one who practices deceit.

Consequences such as these are difficult to foresee and impossible to quantify. For these and other reasons, most ethicists feel that utilitarianism in itself is not an adequate basis for ethics. At the very least, there must be some principle that recognizes an obligation to justice in the distribution of benefits and burdens.

Furthermore, it is generally held that there are some types of actions that are wrong in themselves, so that there is an obligation to avoid them. These include killing or harming innocent human beings, lying, and stealing. Some would argue that these are rules of thumb that can be derived from a consideration of the long-term consequences of the actions in question, while others take them to be fundamental obligations in themselves.

In our culture, these obligations are most often formulated in the language of rights. Every human being is acknowledged to possess certain rights — to life and the means necessary to sustain it, to freedom, to respect, to self-realization, and so on.

The existence of these rights creates obligations in others not to interfere with them. However these obligations are accounted for, in practice there is a great deal of agreement about their content.

The real problems occur when these obligations come into conflict, for example when the only way someone can protect the life of another is by lying, or when the exercise of one person's freedom interferes with the freedom and self-realization of others.

Often such conflicts are settled when, through careful reflection on experience and on the relative importance of the values at stake, people formulate norms or guidelines that minimize or avoid the conflict and distribute the burdens as fairly as possible. These norms often emerge through a long process of argument, testing, and revision, but eventually, as they prove to be sound and workable, they come to be widely accepted as binding on those subject to them.

This is the case, for example, with professional norms, such as those that define the obligations doctors have toward their patients and the obligations lawyers have toward their clients and the legal system.

Ethics as social activity. Returning to George's ethical dilemma, it is clear enough that, if a technical analysis does indeed show that the control system poses a significant risk to the lives of pilots and others and that the risk is avoidable, the company has an obligation to redesign the system. But that does not solve George's problem. Whatever choice he makes will involve some significant evil.

The problem is that he is trying to act ethically in an unethical environment. This does not absolve him of the responsibility of doing what is right as best he can, but it does mean that whatever choice he makes will not be satisfactory. It also means that he will suffer for things that are not his fault.

The social structures George operates in have failed him by not giving him the

To go further

To learn more on this subject or to get involved in this or similar issues, contact

• Ralph Preiss, Chair, IEEE Computer Society Committee on Public Policy, 12 Colburn Dr., Poughkeepsie, NY 12603.

• Computer Professionals for Social Responsibility, PO Box 717, Palo Alto, CA 94301.

support he needs. There are a number of reasons for this:

• There are no clear guidelines to define the responsibilities of George and his coworkers and superiors with regard to the safety of the system. His superiors can argue that as long as the system has passed the required tests, they have fulfilled their responsibilities.

• There is no incentive for George or his company to behave ethically, that is, to make every effort to ensure the safety of the system. In fact, there are strong disincentives in the way the contract is structured.

• There is no structure or procedure that allows George to make his concerns known. If his superiors refuse to consider his concerns, there is nowhere he can go without appearing disloyal to his company.

• The burden of the decision is unfairly placed on George. He will pay a high price no matter what he does, while it is really the responsibility of the whole company to guarantee the safety of the system.

In this case, the problem is not primarily that individuals are acting unethically, although there may be some of that. The main difficulty is that the social structures themselves are not adequate to deal with the problem. And, when that is the case, an individual acting alone cannot hope to correct it.

Even if George, at great personal risk, should blow the whistle by taking his concerns outside the company, he might well be discredited so that his efforts will have no effect. And, he will certainly lose his job. In addition, there is a possibility that he is wrong about the safety of the system, in which case he would be hurting himself and his company for no reason.

Although this case is hypothetical, it is not implausible. In fact, we as computer professionals face many difficult ethical problems, and these problems are inextricably tied to the social systems in which we function. The problem of copying software has to do with the proper functioning of the free market, for example. The privacy issue involves massive databases and the organizations that use them, such as the FBI, the IRS, and credit card companies. There are many other examples.

Individual action will not solve any of these problems. Social problems require social solutions. Computer professionals need to act together to make sure the norms and structures that support ethical activity are in place.

Some of the things needed are

(1) Professional norms. General ex-

hortations to be good and responsible are not sufficient. There must be specific definitions of the rights and duties of computer professionals with respect to the ownership of software and data, security, safety, reliability, and so on.

(2) A forum for discussing ethical problems. Those involved in ethical conflicts or facing ethical dilemmas should have a place where they can discuss the issues and receive the wisdom and support of their peers. It would also be very helpful if there were an independent body that could investigate the claims of those like George who perceive serious threats to the public welfare.

(3) A way of adjudicating conflicts. There must be some way of making members of the profession accountable. The norms referred to in (1) will work only if most members of the profession accept them voluntarily, but there also has to be a system for protecting the members of the profession and others from those who would try to gain an unfair advantage by ignoring the norms. This system must be open and fair and must observe the canons of due process. It must be possible to bring some sanctions against those who violate the norms in an especially destructive or scandalous way.

(4) Support for members who are persecuted for ethical actions. The profession should stand up for members who are willing to take stands on ethical issues where this brings them into conflict with their organizations. This would be easier, of course, if the kind of structure suggested in (2) existed; it could help judge and mediate such conflicts.

The IEEE Computer Society is a professional organization that represents many computer scientists and engineers. As such, it is an obvious vehicle for the kind of organized activity suggested in points (1) through (4) above. In fact, there has been some activity in these areas, although to date it has been rather limited.

IEEE Spectrum has an outstanding record on investigating ethical issues, although for the most part it has avoided taking stands on these issues and has not been involved in the formulation of norms. The IEEE has a code of ethics, but the code is too general to give much guidance on the specific issues facing computer professionals.

Last year, there was a strong effort within the Computer Society Committee on Public Policy to produce a position paper on computer viruses (see *Computer*, July 1989, pp. 83-84) that included some norms. This proposed statement seems to have died, however, when it reached the society's Board of Governors for adoption.

The IEEE does have procedures for

dealing with accusations of unethical conduct, although these are little used and weak when it comes to providing due process.

There are a number of reasons the IEEE and the Computer Society have not done more. Engineers are generally uncomfortable with ethical issues. They feel those issues are outside their competency sphere and are not as well-defined or as susceptible to rigorous analysis as purely technical problems.

Furthermore, becoming involved with ethical problems is risky. The stakes are often very high and feelings run deep, so these issues can lead to confrontations and divisions. I also suspect that the IEEE has never quite figured out if it represents management or the working engineer, so it would rather not get involved in potential conflicts between the two.

Whatever the reasons for the reluctance to get involved in ethical issues, we can no longer afford it. Computer professionals must find a way to take common action on the issues facing the profession if they are to fulfill their responsibilities to society and to themselves. If they do not act on their own, they will find themselves subject to legislation made by people who do not really understand the issues involved.

Let us hope that the IEEE can facilitate the kind of organized action that is needed in the profession. If not, then another context must be found.

References

1. K. Vandivier, "Case Study — The Aircraft Brake Scandal," in *In the Name of Profit*, Doubleday and Co., New York, 1972.

2. T.E. Bell, "The Failure of Space Shuttle Flight 51-L: Deficiencies in Engineering and Management," *IEEE Spectrum*, Feb., 1987, pp. 36-51.

3. P. Faulkner, "Exposing Risks of Nuclear Disaster," in *Whistle Blowing: Loyalty and Dissent in the Corporation*, A.F. Westin, ed., McGraw-Hill, New York, 1981.

4. A. MacIntyre, "Utilitarianism and Cost/ Benefit Analysis: An Essay on the Relevance of Moral Philosophy to Bureaucratic Theory," in *Ethics and the Environment*, D. Scherer and T. Attig, eds., Prentice Hall, Englewood Cliffs, N.J., 1983.

5. W. Frankena, *Ethics*, Prentice Hall, Englewood Cliffs, N.J., 1973.

Internet Pornographer Draws Long Sentence

BARTOW—A man convicted on 328 child pornography charges says he got in "over his head." A judge sentences him to 45 years.

By BILL HEERY
of The Tampa Tribune

The former owner of a video store was sentenced Monday to 45 years in prison in what investigators believe is the nation's largest documented case of Internet child pornography.

A jury last month found Robert Wallace Hudson, 48, guilty of 280 counts of possessing child pornography and 48 counts of distributing it.

Hudson was arrested in April after a computer consultant he had hired told police about the more than 2,000 pornographic pictures of children stored on his home computer hard drive.

The images showed children, the youngest about 6 months old, engaging in explicit sex acts.

Authorities said the children had not been identified.

They said there was no reason to believe the pictures were taken locally.

State sentencing guidelines called for Hudson to receive up to 47 years in prison. But prosecutor Brad Copley asked Circuit Judge Donald Jacobsen for a life sentence.

Lakeland attorney William Kilpatrick, representing Hudson, asked for the minimum 28-year-sentence. He said it was the first time Hudson had been in serious trouble with the law and he had no background of violence.

Hudson, who owned Front Row Video, 8219 U.S. 98 N. in Lakeland, at the time of his arrest, told the judge, "I'm not as evil as they paint me to be. I just got caught up in something and got in way over my head. I tried to get out of it. I just waited too long."

Copley said the pictures and computer videos of grown adults engaging in sex acts with 2-, 3-, 4-, and 5-year-old children represented violence.

"I don't see what could be more violent other than a murder scene. A child was victimized each time those pictures were sent out" on the Internet.

Authorities do not believe Hudson distributed child pornography through his business.

Hudson should have been forewarned when he was convicted in 1991 of three counts of the sale of obscene materials, Copley said.

Kilpatrick countered that those were misdemeanor charges resulting from sales at a video store and had nothing to do with child pornography.

The defense contended during the trial that Hudson found the child pornography on his hard drive, a computer disc that holds vast amounts of data, but he did not put it there.

Following the sentencing on Monday, Hudson's wife of 15 years, Julie, said she didn't believe the charges against her husband.

▶ **Bill Heery covers courts in Polk County and can be reached at (941) 683-6531.**

Chapter 2

Critical-Thinking Skills

Genuine moral integrity requires intellectual character, for bona fide moral decisions require thoughtful discrimination between what is ethically justified and what is merely socially approved. . . . The mere conscious will to do good neither removes prejudices that shape our perceptions nor eliminates the ongoing drive to form prejudices. To minimize our egocentric drives, we must develop critical thinking in a special direction. We need not only intellectual skills but intellectual character as well.
—Richard Paul, from C. A. Barnes's *Critical Thinking: Educational Imperative*

2.1 INTRODUCTION AND OVERVIEW

WHAT does critical thinking have to do with ethics? *Everything*! Ethically difficult situations are difficult precisely because it is hard to reason clearly about them. As discussed in Chapter One, ethically appropriate actions are often in conflict with short-term personal gain. For this reason, it is easy to be led into faulty rationalizations of less-than-ethical behavior. Also as emphasized in Chapter One, real-world ethical dilemmas often leave you no ideal option. In such cases, it is important to be able to weigh alternatives thoughtfully. Strong critical thinking skills can help you to avoid making faulty rationalizations yourself, to detect faulty rationalizations made by others and to think clearly about difficult situations. Strong critical thinking skills can also improve your general ability to communicate clearly and efficiently.

Damer defines critical thinking as "the process of evaluating a claim for the purpose of deciding whether to accept, reject or perhaps suspend judgment about it" [6]. Browne and Keeley present critical thinking as the ability and desire to ask the right questions in analyzing a situation [5]. They suggest a list of critical questions you should ask yourself (I have abbreviated the original questions):

1. What are the issues and the conclusions?
2. What are the reasons?
3. What words or phrases are ambiguous?
4. What are the value conflicts and assumptions?
5. What are the descriptive assumptions?
6. What is the evidence?
7. Are the samples representative and the measurements valid?
8. Are there rival hypotheses?
9. Are there flaws in the statistical reasoning?
10. How relevant are the analogies?
11. Are there errors in reasoning?
12. What significant information is omitted?
13. What conclusions are consistent with the strong reasons?
14. What are my own value preferences in this controversy?

Not all questions on this list necessarily apply in all situations. For example, there is not always a statistical component to the reasoning. But this is a useful list to keep in mind when you reflect over whether or not a situation warrants a particular conclusion.

To better understand the critical thinking process, we will first survey categories of errors that are commonly made in reasoning. Then we will analyze a real incident involving employee privacy as a means of applying and illustrating the critical thinking process.

In common use, the word "argument" means a disagreement, often one that is heated and emotional. But in the context of critical thinking, the word has a more specific technical meaning. An *argument* is a line of reasoning presented with the intent to lead to a certain conclusion. As such, an argument can always take the stylized form of one or more premises followed by a conclusion. A *premise* is simply some statement that serves as a (partial) basis for a line of reasoning. Thus, when confronted with a particular argument you could in principle always rewrite it into the following form.

Since	premise 1, and
	premise 2, . . .
Therefore	conclusion.

In fact, when you are confronted with a confusing argument, it can be quite useful to attempt to restate it in this form. This will often cause the problems in an argument to become more apparent, leading to clearer communication and greater ease in isolating the points of true disagreement or logical weakness.

A "good" (or "valid" or "soundly constructed") argument should have three basic properties: (1) Each premise should be true. (2) Each premise should be relevant to the issue at hand. (3) The collection of premises should be sufficient to establish that the conclusion is true. The reasons for these three properties should be evident. To the extent that a particular argument does not possess these properties, the argument commits some type of *logical fallacy*. Fallacies in reasoning can be categorized in different ways. Here I have summarized nine broadly defined categories of logical fallacies as discussed by Damer [6]:

1. Errors arising from ambiguity.
2. Circular arguments that beg the question.
3. Use of unwarranted assumptions.
4. Fallacies involving missing evidence.
5. Incorrectly identified causation.
6. Premises irrelevant to the stated conclusion.
7. Appeals to emotion/authority/loyalty/etc.
8. Diversion from the main point.
9. Incorrect deductive inference.

Damer provides a complete discussion of these types of fallacies, with common variations of each [6]. Here we need only a short description of some main types in each category to point the way toward clearer thinking.

2.2.1 Errors Arising from Ambiguity

One type of error occurs when people interpret the meaning of some element of an argument differently. This can happen through the use of ambiguous words, ambiguous syntax, selective placement of emphasis on words, or selective wording. An example of ambiguous wording is

Since	computer ABC's speed is 25 megahertz, and
	computer XYZ's speed is 20 megahertz,
Therefore	computer ABC will run your program with greater speed than will XYZ.

The problem here is that "speed" has potentially different meanings in different places in the argument. In the premises, it clearly refers to the clock rate of the CPU chip. But in the conclusion, it subtly shifts to a broader reference, the time required to run a program. There are in fact many possible reasons that a higher CPU clock rate might not translate into a faster program execution—different instruction sets in the two CPUs, different possible memory configurations, and unusual instruction-usage patterns in the program are just a few. So when someone gives you this argument for buying computer ABC, you should realize that the conclusion does not follow automatically from the premises. In a soundly constructed argument, each term has the same meaning in all places, or the use of different meanings at different points is made explicit.

A more subtle example of ambiguity occurs in the following quote from an argument against government ability to wiretap digital communications [2]:

> Even if these are real threats, is enhanced wiretapping the best way to combat them? Apparently, it hasn't been in the past. Over the last 10 years, the average total nationwide number of admissible state and Federal wiretaps has numbered less than 800. Wiretaps are not at present major enforcement tools, and are far less efficient than the informants, witnesses, physical evidence and good old fashioned detective work they usually rely on.

The assertion that "wiretaps are not major enforcement tools" seems to be backed up by the fact that the annual number of admissible wiretaps was less than 800. Many people may feel that the number 800 seems relatively small in this context. But the word "major" is used here in a way that implies more than just a numeric quantity. If even a small fraction of those 800 wiretaps led to preventing or solving a serious crime (kidnap, murder, terrorism) that could not have been prevented or solved otherwise, then most people would consider wiretaps a "major" tool.

A somewhat different type of problem can occur when there is a selected emphasis on the wording of a statement that seems to push you toward drawing a conclusion that is not explicitly stated. If there are three computer models sitting on a table and someone points to a particular one and says "I have never seen *that* one fail," you may infer that the person *has* seen the other two fail. But that was not actually said, nor is it necessarily true.

A related problem occurs when someone uses innuendo to lead you to infer something that was not said. Suppose you are checking the references of a job applicant, Joe Smith, and you ask someone if Joe has any problems regarding the use of alcohol or drugs in the workplace. Perhaps the person giving the reference has some reason to want to hurt Joe Smith, and so replies "Joe Smith was never caught using drugs at work." It may seem that you have been told that Joe Smith did use drugs but just never got caught. Again, however, the person has not actually said this, and it may or may not be true.

2.2.2 Circular Arguments
that Beg the Question

Begging the question is a form of fallacy that occurs when an argument is constructed so that the conclusion is reached by using a premise that is just a disguised form of the conclusion. In essence, the person committing the fallacy is using a *circular argument*. Without the disguise, the argument looks like this:

Since	X is true
Therefore	X is true.

This argument "begs" that you ask whether the premise (the disguised form of the conclusion) is actually true.

Consider the following argument:

Since	The criteria for patentability are originality, novelty, utility, and nonobviousness, and
	My invention is original, novel, useful, and non-obvious,
Therefore	My invention deserves to be patented.

Hopefully the problem with this argument is clear, but it is worth dissecting anyway. The first premise is true by the legal definition of patentability. But the second premise is really only an assertion of the conclusion in a thinly disguised form. Thus, if you accept the second premise as true, you have effectively already accepted the conclusion.

Another version of this type of argument occurs when someone asks a question that presumes the answer to another question, which should have been asked first. A common instance of this is the fund raiser who asks: "How much are you contributing to the Fund for X?" By skipping over the question of *whether* you are going to contribute, the fund raiser hopes to have you focus only on the amount.

2.2.3 Use of Unwarranted Assumptions

An unwarranted assumption is one that is used without explicit justification. One way this can happen is in assuming that some whole composed of a set of parts will automatically have a certain property shared by each part. For example, suppose you are selecting people for a program-ming team. Would you select people independently solely because they were rated excellent individual programmers? That is, would you accept the following argument?

Since	Jane is rated as an excellent programmer, and
	John is rated as an excellent programmer, and
	Mary is rated as an excellent programmer,
Therefore	Jane, John, and Mary would make an excellent programming team.

If you did, you might be disappointed in the outcome. For example, if each person is rated as excellent because of superior coding skills, but no one has superior debugging skills, then they are unlikely to form a superior group. The debugging phase is often crucial and a weakness there is a serious problem. The lesson from this example is that when you are trying to form conclusions about a whole in terms of the properties of its parts, be sure to pay careful attention to interactions among the parts.

An assumption that is in some sense the complement of the one just mentioned is that each part of a whole will naturally possess some property enjoyed by the whole. For example, the best computer company has the best products, the best technical staff, the best sales staff, and the best administrative staff. This is clearly not always the case. The best company may simply be strong in every area, but not the best in any one area.

Another pair of possibly unwarranted assumptions is *what is, ought to be* and *what is new must be better*. An example of the first assumption is the argument against the "look and feel copyrights" (described in detail in a later chapter). In one instance, those against the introduction of these copyrights argue that the software industry has done well for a long time without such a concept and so the concept is not needed. In essence, this argument is

Since	The software industry did not have look and feel copyrights before, and
	The software industry has done fine without them,
Therefore	The software industry doesn't need them.

That the software industry did not have look and feel copyrights previously is not, in and of itself, evidence for or against the use of look and feel copyrights. The second premise of this argument also has problems, as will be pointed out in discussing the next category of fallacy.

The problem with the *what is new must be better* assumption probably needs no explanation. Many new things are definitely not better; in fact, they are sometimes worse. Consider the initial release of any new operating system!

Still another pair of possibly unwarranted assumptions

are *either-or* and *split the difference*. The essence of the first assumption is that the alternatives are either-or; no middle ground is possible. The essence of the second assumption is that a compromise position must necessarily be good. But the following example should point out that there are situations in which compromise is the wrong approach.

Since	Jane feels no additional testing of the control software is needed, and
	John feels another two weeks of testing are required to detect all errors that could potentially lead to catastrophic failures, and
	Compromise is a good idea,
Therefore	We will do one week of additional testing.

It makes no sense in this situation to average the amounts of time that the two people feel should be spent on additional testing. Lives might depend on making this decision. A rational choice would require examining the technical basis for each estimate.

Another kind of unwarranted assumption is that an accumulation of essentially negligible amounts will still be negligible. You sometimes see this sort of failed logic applied in a budgeting process. Independently, any one of many small additional expenses may not cause the budget to be seriously out of balance, but cumulatively their effect can be disastrous.

The last form of unwarranted assumption we will look at is the poor use of analogies. Many analogies seem appropriate at some superficial level, but the "unwarranted" part of this assumption says that an analogy that seems valid at a superficial level is equally valid at a more detailed level. An extreme example of this occurs in the chapter on Cracking and Computer Security, where Richard Stallman makes an analogy between the unauthorized use of the computer and the unauthorized use of a typewriter. The superficial similarity of the two is that they both have a keyboard. The computer, however, is often in shared use by multiple people at the same time and often contains files that belong to a variety of users, to mention just two fundamental differences.

2.2.4 Fallacies Involving Missing Evidence

This type of fallacy involves drawing a conclusion without sufficient evidence to truly justify the conclusion. A common version of this fallacy is to generalize from experience that is too small or is biased in some way. Consider the following suggestion that might be made by a colleague at work. "We shouldn't bother interviewing people at State University this year—the person we hired from there last year didn't know anything about object-oriented programming." The argument apparently being made is:

Since	We need people who know about object-oriented programming, and
	The person we hired from State University last year didn't know anything about object-oriented programming,
Therefore	We shouldn't consider hiring anyone from State University this year.

A sample of one person is not enough to reliably assert that State University doesn't teach its students about object-oriented programming. Also, this one-person sample may be biased. If the former employee was following the electrical engineering curriculum instead of the computer science/engineering or information systems curriculum, then they shouldn't have been expected to know about object-oriented programming.

Another common form of fallacy is to reason speculatively about what would happen in an alternative reality, a world that in some way departs from the world we have experienced. This is sometimes called the *contrary to fact* fallacy. An element of this fallacy can be found in the same argument cited earlier against the look and feel copyrights.

Since	The software industry has never had look and feel copyrights, and
	The software industry has done fine without them,
Therefore	The software industry doesn't need them.

Notice that the second premise implies a comparison between how the software industry developed without look and feel copyrights and how it would have developed with them. The problem, of course, is that the reality in which the software industry developed with look and feel copyrights does not exist, so any claims about it are speculative.

Another common form of this fallacy is to assume that the lack of evidence against (for) some conclusion necessarily means that the conclusion is true (false). Probably all programmers and software users can spot the problem in the following argument:

| Since | The testing process did not reveal any bugs in this piece of software, |
| Therefore | There are no bugs in this piece of software. |

Another common fallacy is the belief in the validity of numeric values that purport to measure something too vaguely defined to be measurable. Probably every student in computing has heard some variation of the following argument: "If you don't keep up with things, half your technical knowledge will be obsolete in five years." Although everyone might agree with the general sentiment, the concepts involved seem too vaguely defined to allow much belief in the exact numbers used in the argument. What experiment can you imagine that would have been conducted to arrive at the values "half" and "five years"? What exactly does it mean to "keep up"? What exactly is your "technical knowledge" and how is it distinguished from your "nontechnical knowledge"?

2.2.5 Incorrectly Identified Causation

This type of fallacy mismatches cause and effect. One form is to assume that an earlier event is the cause of a later event simply because the earlier event precedes the later event. Another form is confusing the cause with the effect. A variation of this is to identify one of a group of effects that are all due to some common cause as being the cause of the other effects. Consider the following argument:

Since	Jane and John had lunch yesterday, and Jane was selecting the new manager of sales, and John was named the new manager of sales today,
Therefore	Jane likes to give promotions to the people with whom she socializes.

The timing of the lunch and the promotion announcement might make you suspect something, but it could be just a confusion of timing with causation. Also, the lunch and the promotion announcement could both be effects of a common cause (promotion decision) that occurred even earlier.

Another form of this type of fallacy is to confuse the necessary and sufficient conditions for something to occur. A *necessary condition* for X is one that must hold for X to be true, but one that does *not* by itself prove that X is true. A *sufficient condition* for X is one that by itself proves X is true.

A third form of this type of fallacy is oversimplifying the cause, or focusing on one among many contributing causes without justifying why it is the predominant cause. You often see an element of this form in the safety-critical system arena, where the failure of some system is attributed to "operator error." (See Chapter 6 for several examples.) In almost all such cases, better system design would have made operator error less likely to occur or easier to recover from.

A fourth form of this type of fallacy is to assume that taking one step in a particular direction must inevitably lead to a sequence of additional steps in the same direction. This is sometimes referred to as the *domino fallacy* or *slippery slope* argument.

Still another form of this type of fallacy is to assume that luck can become a causal factor. This is often referred to as the *gambler's fallacy* and is often expressed as "my luck has to change soon." If each of a sequence of N events is random, the chance of the last event turning out a certain way is the same regardless of what happened in the first N − 1 events. A variation of this faulty reasoning might be "If we bid on enough projects, one of them has to come through." The relative quality of the bid in comparison to those submitted by competitors is obviously a far more important factor in whether the bid wins than is the total number of other bids submitted by the firm.

2.2.6 Premises Irrelevant to the Stated Conclusion

This category of fallacy is committed when one or more of the premises in an argument are not directly relevant to the asserted conclusion, even though they may be relevant to some related possible conclusion. Such an argument is said to "miss the point," though it may in fact have hit some related point. Because the argument may correctly support a related conclusion, this fallacy is sometimes hard to recognize.

The common coping strategy of rationalization is one form of this fallacy type. When something does not turn out as desired, people may attempt to rationalize away the importance of the result by appealing to some collection of reasons that they would not have considered if the event had turned out as desired. Consider the following argument:

Since	Winning that contract would have meant hiring new people, and It would also have meant a lot of overtime work, and We would have been cramped for office space,
Therefore	It is really better that we didn't win the contract.

Clearly, if these factors were known ahead of time and found to be that important, then the bid for the contract should never have been submitted.

Another common form of this fallacy is to attack the motivations of someone making an argument rather than the merits of their argument. Consider the following argument:

Since	Jane proposed the idea of on-site child care, and Jane just recently returned from maternity leave, and Jane would clearly benefit from the company having on-site child care,
Therefore	The company should not consider having on-site child care.

The implication is that the suggestion of having on-site child care should be disregarded because the person suggesting it (Jane) was motivated by self-interest. Note that the facts do support a conclusion that Jane has some self-interest in on-site child care, a point hit by the first two premises. But using the third premise in conjunction with the first two to reach the conclusion misses the asserted point about the value of on-site child care to the company. The fact that Jane would benefit is, in itself, not evidence either for or against the conclusion that the company should have on-site day care.

Another common form of this fallacy is the ad hominem attack on a person. This typically takes the form of attempting to discredit a concept by pointing out personal qualities of someone associated with the concept. Even though the person may have such negative qualities or behavior, they are irrelevant to the value of the concept. Consider the following argument:

Since	John proposed a management reorganization, and
	John is often out drinking too late and too much on the weekends,
Therefore	Our company should not consider the management reorganization.

However much John needs to change his personal habits, the company should consider his proposal solely on its own merits.

The ad hominem attack on an individual is unfortunately common in professional disagreements. In one case, a debate concerning software patents (which I discuss in more depth in Chapter 8), Paul Heckel states that "a nonprofit Marxist economic system is not optimal in promoting innovation in software." The wording would seem to imply that anyone who is against software patents must be a Marxist. A more explicit example is taken from a case that appears in Chapter 7. The famous physicist Edward Teller accuses the whistle blowers in a nuclear power plant incident of "being paid by the Soviets to speak out against nuclear power" [8]. It appears that absolutely no proof was ever offered in support of this claim, and that the motivation was purely to attempt to weaken the credibility of the whistle blowers' technical claims by making false accusations about their motives. Such ad hominem attacks on individuals clearly do not speak to the substance of the disagreement at hand, and they often backfire to weaken the argument of the person making the attack. Someone observing an ad hominem attack might assume that the side being attacked has the stronger argument and that the side making the attack has the weaker ethics.

Another related form of this fallacy is *you do it, too* (or *two wrongs make a right*). That is, when an argument is made that some action is not the best action to take in a situation, the person wanting to take the action responds by saying "you did something wrong as well" or "you would do the same if you were me." An element of this arises in a case detailed in Chapter 7. Chester Walsh's former company (GE) argued that Walsh, the whistle blower, should not receive an award under the False Claims Act because Walsh had not reported the incident promptly to GE. In essence, the argument advanced against Walsh being compensated was as follows:

Since	GE was guilty of fraud in this case, and
	The False Claims Act allows people to receive a portion of the recovered funds, and
	Chester Walsh did not report the fraud internally to GE promptly,
Therefore	Chester Walsh should not receive compensation.

The judge in this case correctly recognized the error in GE's reasoning and awarded Chester Walsh a substantial amount of money.

2.2.7 Irrelevant Appeals to Emotion/ Authority/Loyalty

A good example of this occurs in the argument over cryptography and wiretap. Consider this quote arguing in favor of government ability to wiretap digital communications [11]:

> . . . The law enforcement community views wiretaps as essential. Such surveillance not only provides information not obtainable by other means, it also yields evidence that is considered extremely reliable and probative. According to the FBI, organized crime has had severe setbacks due to the use of wiretap surveillance. The FBI contends the tool is critical for drug cases. Wiretapping is an important investigative technique in cases of governmental corruption and acts of terrorism . . . .

One appeal here is to the authority and prestige of the FBI. Another is to the importance of fighting illegal drugs and terrorism. However, what the FBI thinks would make its job easier is not necessarily constitutional. Also, any gains in fighting drugs and terrorism should be weighed against the costs in other areas (increased cost of communications infrastructure, potential loss of privacy, etc.).

A variation of this fallacy is an appeal to prevailing opinion among some group of people. An instance of this arises in the arguments against look and feel copyrights. The argument given takes essentially the following form:

Since	A survey was taken at a conference of user interface developers, and
	User interface developers do not seem to want user interface copyright,
Therefore	User interface copyright should not exist.

Problems with this argument should be clear. First, there is no way to know if the survey was valid and unbiased without having more information about it. Second, user interface developers are just one group of people affected by the decision. The opinion of any one interest group should not form the basis for the conclusion.

Another common version of this fallacy is an appeal based on flattery or group identification. An example of this could be:

| Since | Your company is a small company, and Our company is also a small company, and You know how difficult it is for small companies to compete, |
| Therefore | You should buy our company's products instead of the big company's. |

Other versions of this fallacy may make the appeal based on intimidation, threat, tradition, or irrelevant or questionable authority.

2.2.8 Diversion from the Main Point

In this type of fallacy, the argument attempts to bring up an irrelevant point that somehow attracts attention away from the relevant line of reasoning. The *straw person* argument is perhaps the most common form of this fallacy. The "straw person" is an uncharitable representation of an opposing point of view, which is brought up specifically because it is easy to refute. This is typically done with the hope that the process of easily refuting the straw person argument will make the opposing point of view seem weaker in general.

The *red herring* argument is another common form of this fallacy. The term "red herring" comes from fox hunting. A herring, which is a type of fish, is drawn across the trail of the fox to draw the dogs off the fox's scent. The purpose of the red herring in an argument is similar. Some strongly stated or emotional side issue is used to divert attention from the main point. Another technique often used to divert attention from the substance of an issue is to make a joke in response to an argument or to ridicule the way in which the argument is stated.

Another fallacy that falls into this category is the use of trivial objections to an argument. The most effective way to refute an argument is to disprove the strongest claims made in the argument. Attacking only the weaker claims may even be taken as a sign that the strong claims are in fact valid.

2.2.9 Incorrect Deductive Inference

Incorrect deductive inference occurs when an argument does not have the connecting structure that it needs to be valid. One set of fallacies involving incorrect deductive inference arises in connection with *categorical syllogisms*.

A syllogism is an argument in which two simple premises are asserted and a conclusion is drawn. A categorical syllogism involves premises and conclusions about the membership of objects in categories. Its generic form is:

| Since | All members of category X are members of category Y, and No member of category Z is a member of category Y, |
| Therefore | No member of category X is a member of category Z. |

This generic example obeys the three rules for a valid syllogism. Failure to observe any one of the three rules leads to a fallacy.

The three rules are fairly simple. Before explaining the rules, several definitions are in order. The first premise in the generic form is called the *major premise*. The second premise is called the *minor premise*. The category term that the two premises have in common (Y in the example) is called the *middle term*. The other two terms (X and Z) are called the *end terms* [6].

The first rule for a valid syllogism is that the middle term must be "distributed" at least once. The middle term is distributed if a premise asserts that it is true of every member of some category. The major premise in the example distributes the middle term Y over every member of the category X.

The second rule is that an end term distributed in the conclusion must also be distributed in one of the premises. In the preceding example, both X and Z are end terms that are distributed. (Lack of membership in X is distributed over every member of Z, and lack of membership in Z is distributed over every member of X.) Thus each end term must be distributed in one of the premises. This rule is satisfied because X is distributed in the major premise and Z is distributed in the minor premise.

The third rule is that the number of negative premises must equal the number of negatives in the conclusion. This is also satisfied because there is one negative premise (the minor premise) and one negative conclusion.

Another set of common fallacies involves *hypothetical reasoning,* reasoning about what would be true if something else were true. The generic structure of a valid hypothetical reasoning argument is:

| Since | If X, then Y, and X, |
| Therefore | Y. |

In this form of reasoning, X is the antecedent condition and Y is the consequent condition.

One fallacy that can occur related to hypothetical reasoning is *denying the antecedent.* This logical error presents itself in the following form:

Since	If X, then Y, and
	Not X,
Therefore	Not Y.

The conclusion of "Not Y" would be valid only if X were known to be the sole possible cause of Y. An example of how this structure for an argument can lead to errors is:

Since	If people were using weak passwords,
	Then we would need to be concerned
	about system security, and
	People are not using weak passwords,
Therefore	We don't need to be concerned about
	system security.

The problem should be clear: weak passwords are not the only reason to be concerned about system security.

Another fallacy that can occur in hypothetical reasoning is *affirming the consequent*. The form of this fallacy is:

Since	If X, then Y, and
	Y,
Therefore	X.

As with the fallacy of denying the antecedent, the conclusion asserted actually requires another premise not stated in the argument (that X is the only possible cause of Y). Here is an example of how this fallacy can lead to problems:

Since	If company ABC had gotten the con-
	tract we were competing for,
	Then they would need to hire more pro-
	grammers, and
	They are currently hiring more pro-
	grammers,
Therefore	They must have gotten the contract we
	were competing for.

Again, the problem should be clear: There can be many other reasons the competing company would be hiring programmers.

2.3 A CRITICAL-THINKING ANALYSIS: WORKPLACE PRIVACY

For a detailed critical-thinking analysis of a real situation, we consider an incident in which a technician discovered pornography on a PC used by the dean of the Harvard School of Divinity [1]. In addition to being a good vehicle for demonstrating the importance of critical thinking, this case study also makes important points about employee privacy in the workplace.

2.3.1 A First Conclusion Based on Incomplete Information

Skimming some of the initial news stories might result in the following understanding of the incident. The Harvard dean of divinity had a collection of *thousands* of pornographic images on the PC in his home office. The pornography was "explicit" but "not illegal." A technician discovered the pornography while working on the dean's PC. The existence of the pornography was reported to the Harvard administration. The dean resigned his position as dean, but was able to keep his position as a tenured faculty member.

We will assume that everyone agrees that the dean showed poor judgment, and that a dean of a divinity school really should not have a pornography habit. Setting aside the dean's role for a moment, let's consider the role of the technician in this incident-*should the technician report the existence of pornography on the dean's PC?* From only this superficial description of the incident, most people conclude that the technician has a responsibility to **not** report the pornography. The argument leading to this conclusion might appear as follows:

Since	Techs have a responsibility to keep per-
	sonal information private, and
	The dean's collection of pornography
	would be embarrassing to him, and
	The tech discovered the pornography
	while working on the dean's PC,
Therefore	The technician should not report the ex-
	istence of the pornography.

However, the superficial description of the incident omits critical elements of the incident. Knowing all of the important facts leads to a rather different conclusion.

2.3.2 A Conclusion Based on More Information

One important element missing in the superficial description is the overall "Harvardness" of the incident. The home and the PC were perks of the dean position. That is, the "dean's PC" was actually owned by Harvard, as was the home that the dean lived in. Also, the technician was not just "a technician" but was a Harvard Divinity School technician. The dean had run short of disk space on the PC in his home office, and requested that a technician come and install a higher-capacity disk drive and transfer the files from the old drive to the new drive. Thus the pornography was discovered when one Harvard employee (the dean) requested that another Harvard employee (the technician) upgrade a piece of Harvard equipment (the PC) supposedly being used for Harvard-related business.

A related consideration is the level of privacy that an employee can reasonably expect in the use of an employer-owned computer. In the absence of any explicit agreement or policy to the contrary, the basic rule is that an employee has no legal expectation of privacy in the use of an employer-owned computer. A 1999 American Management Association survey showed that 27% of the responding companies review employee e-mail [4]. In most cases, the review of e-mail is done on a random basis. In addition, 21% of companies review stored computer files; again, mostly on a random basis. One news story quoted a co-chair of the American Bar Association privacy committee as follows: "In this day and age, I would say that an employee is foolish or naive who allows information to be stored in his or her computer that he or she does not want the employer to be aware of" [4].

Another important consideration is Harvard's policies on use of its computers. The faculty handbook for the Divinity School prohibits "inappropriate, obscene, bigoted or abusive" material on its computers. Policy also restricts computer use to activities "related to the School's mission of education, research and public service." Any "private, commercial, non-Harvard business" use of school computers requires "explicit authorization."

Yet another consideration is how the technician came to report the pornography. Different news reports disagree on some details. One account is that there was a pornographic image on the PC display when the technician arrived to perform the disk upgrade. The dean's lawyer denies this. Another account is that the technician noticed a variety of "unusual" file names during the upgrade, and presumably opened one or more either out of curiosity and/or to verify the contents. The upgrade was performed in three steps: (1) transfer contents of the old disk to a central computer, (2) install a new disk on the PC, and (3) transfer contents of the original disk back to the PC. The upgrade took substantially longer than normal, apparently due to the disk being essentially full and containing lots of image data. At some point, a supervisor asked the technician why the upgrade was taking so long. The technician then reluctantly reported the details of the problem.

Based on this more complete description of this incident, let's revisit the question: *Should the technician report the existence of pornography on the dean's PC?* Based on the additional facts, problems are now apparent with each premise of the earlier argument. Technicians do have a responsibility to maintain the privacy of personal information, but technicians also have a responsibility to their employer to support policies on computer use. The dean's pornography habit is personal in the sense that public knowledge of it would embarrass him, but he chose to keep it on a nonprivate PC owned by Harvard and serviced at Harvard's expense. The technician discovered the porn while working on the "dean's PC," but also while acting as a Harvard employee working on Harvard-owned equipment. The general problem is that the earlier argument was based on the (false) assumption that all relevant facts were considered. With better knowledge of the facts, most people would now reach the opposite conclusion based on a line of reasoning such as the following:

Since	The technician and the dean are both Harvard employees, and The "dean's PC" is a Harvard PC provided as part of his job, and The dean has a responsibility to his employer, and The porn violates several elements of Harvard computer use policy, and The technician has a responsibility to his employer, and The technician is asked by a supervisor about the disk upgrade,
Therefore	The technician should report the existence of the pornography.

Let's also consider a subtle variation of the actual incident: *If not questioned by a supervisor, should the technician still report the pornography?* Based on what we know about the level of privacy that employees can expect in the use of employer-owned computer systems, it is clear that the technician has the right to report the pornography. However, some consideration of the importance of the violation of computer use policy must come into play. For example, an e-mail that contains no mention of any Harvard business would violate the strict letter of the computer use policy. But a technician who looked for and reported all violations of computer use policy, large or small, would have no time left for "real work" and would become a general nuisance. Is the dean's violation of computer use policy big or small? I believe that it is big enough that the technician should report it. Reasons for this include: (1) the dean spent the cost of a disk upgrade and a day of the technician's time on a personal habit, (2) the dean violated policy that he was administratively responsible for upholding, and (3) the nature of the violation is potentially embarrassing to the Divinity school as a whole. At the same time, I expect that many technicians confronted with this situation would decide that the "safe" option is to pretend that they saw nothing.

To clarify the critical elements, we should perhaps consider one more "what if" scenario. Imagine that there was no pornography, but that the technician had accidentally seen an e-mail from a clinic that said that the dean had tested HIV positive. Should the technician reveal this to anyone? Absolutely not! It should be clear that this situation is substantially different from the actual incident. While the e-mail might be considered non-Harvard business and so technically a violation of the computer use policy, the contents of the e-mail are not "inappropriate, obscene, bigoted or abusive" material. Also, one e-mail would not be the driving reason for a disk upgrade, and so the requested work is still legitimate. The technician has witnessed no substantial violation of computer use policy and so has nothing to report. The incidentally learned personal information must be kept confidential.

2.3.3 Roles and Responsibilities of Other Stakeholders

A *stake-holder* is simply someone who has a stake, or personal interest, in the outcome. The technician is not the only stake-holder in this incident. Other stake-holders include the dean, the Harvard president and the reporter who wrote the first story about the incident. In ethically difficult situations, it is often valuable to list the various stake-holders and consider the rights and responsibilities of each.

The dean's primary responsibility is to administer his unit of the university to the best of his ability. The dean was generally considered quite successful. One achievement mentioned in news articles is fundraising; he was able to roughly quadruple the size of the Divinity school endowment. However, the dean's responsibilities also include treating each member of the school with respect, fairly enforcing the policies of the school, and conducting himself in a way that would be supportive of his colleagues and bring credit to the school. Additionally, the dean has personal responsibilities to his wife and two adult daughters. In the specific context of this incident, it is clear that the dean failed in his professional and personal responsibilities.

The Harvard president is a stake-holder because it is his responsibility to handle the report of the dean's misconduct. The president has responsibilities to manage the university as a whole so that it effectively achieves its mission, and to treat each employee fairly and with respect. The president has to consider "higher level" issues than the technician might consider. One consideration is that of possible future sexual harassment or hostile workplace claims. If the president ignores the incident and some other employee is offended by the dean's pornography in the future, that employee would have a stronger claim that Harvard administration condoned a "hostile workplace." The president also has to consider the effect of the incident on the dean's professional credentials. The dean was an ordained pastor in the Evangelical Lutheran Church (ELC), and the ELC has a policy against pornography. When the bishop of the ELC synod that ordained the dean learned of the incident, he commented that he would have to meet with the dean and that one possibility was that the dean would be removed from the list of ordained pastors. On the other hand, the dean had served Harvard well for over twelve years. Also, public knowledge of his pornography habit would embarrass the dean personally and professionally.

The president met with the dean to discuss the incident, and they "agreed that it would be in the best interests of the Divinity School for the dean to resign" [1]. Official Harvard statements at the time made no mention of the pornography. The dean stated that he was taking a sabbatical "to spend time with my family" and cited personal and private reasons and health concerns. At the end of a one-year sabbatical, the dean would return to a position as a regular full professor at Harvard. The resolution protected the integrity and potential liability of Harvard, and at the same time preserved the privacy and the tenured professorship of the (ex-)dean. It seems that the Harvard president resolved the incident about as well as possible.

The president and the dean reached their resolution of the incident in November 1998. The incident only made the news in May 1999. At some point during this time, *Boston Globe* reporter James Bandler became aware of the complete story behind the dean's resignation.

The reporter would also have a set of professional responsibilities. One would be a responsibility to the subjects of his stories to treat them fairly and with respect. Another would be to society as a whole, to deliver truthful and important news. Yet another would be to his employer, a for-profit entity, to write stories that would sell newspapers. It is clear that having the full story appear in the news would result in personal embarrassment to the dean, to Harvard, and possibly also to the ELC. A counterweight to this consideration is that the public would have a right, and possibly a need, to know the full story. Was public knowledge advanced in some way by this story to an extent that would outweigh the damage to the dean's personal privacy? To me, it seems not. The employee/employer workplace privacy issues are not novel. The resolution reached by the president and the dean is not extreme or unusual. It seems that it is only the combination of a divinity dean and pornography that makes this story "newsworthy." And "newsworthy" here seems to be defined primarily in terms of selling newspapers.

An interesting postscript to this case made its way to me just as the revised edition was being finalized. An anonymous, private communication suggested that there were two important facts that had not come out in published accounts of this incident. The first is that the technician involved is a woman. For most people, this probably does not change their analysis of the case. The second suggestion is that the female technician is the one who took the story to the newspaper reporter, after deciding that Harvard's punishment of the dean was not sufficient! This presents more interesting ethical questions. Under what circumstances would the technician be justified in going to the press? Under what circumstances would the technician have a responsibility to "blow the whistle" outside of Harvard?

2.3.4 Examples of Critical-Thinking Lapses

News coverage of this incident provides a number of examples for critical-thinking analysis. We will consider just three of these in detail here. One article included the following comment by Harvard law professor Alan Dershowitz [10]:

. . . Back at Harvard, Frankfurter Professor of Law Alan M. Dershowitz said that, though he did not know the details of the case, what [the dean] chooses to do privately is his own business and only becomes the university's concern if it is illegal. "As long as it's done in private and doesn't hurt anyone it is not the school's business," he said. "I don't think it matters that he is the Divinity School dean."

The argument here appears to be along the following lines.

Since	What the dean does legally and in private is his own business, and the dean's use of pornography was legal and private,
Therefore	It is none of the university's business.

This argument exhibits a number of critical-thinking problems. The first premise basically sets up a circular argument. But by definition, what the dean does on his Harvard-owned PC is not "private." Employers can and do have rules that are more strict than simply "what is legal." Also, the term "in private" is being used ambiguously. In the first premise, "in private" means something that the dean does by himself that he would like to keep from others. In the second premise, the meaning has subtly shifted to mean something that the dean has a right to keep private.

It seems likely that Dershowitz does not really mean to advance the general principle that the technician should report something only if it is illegal. For example, consider the following "what if" scenario. What if it had been a dean of a law school, and this dean was currently nominated to the Supreme Court, and the technician discovered that the dean had been doing *pro bono* legal work for the Ku Klux Klan for the last ten years? There is nothing illegal here. But most people would hope that the technician's sense of responsibility to society would require that the information be made public.

Another article included this comment from an ACLU representative [9]:

"The episode raises questions about the right to privacy and questions about punishing people because they have interests in sexual images," said Sarah Wunsch, an attorney with the American Civil Liberties Union of Massachusetts.

This quote also exhibits several critical-thinking problems. The reference to the "right to privacy" can be seen as an irrelevant appeal to authority. The right to privacy has become something of a motherhood-and-apple-pie concept. But, as already pointed out, there basically is no right to privacy in the use of an employer-owned computer. Also, was the real violation of the dean's privacy done by Harvard or by the *Boston Globe*? The comment about "punishing people because they have interests in sexual images" can be seen as an example of mis-identified causation. It leaves out the critical factors that the dean was pursuing his interest in sexual images on a Harvard computer in violation of Harvard policy, and that it could cost the dean his ordination.

Still another article was titled [15] "Do computer docs need a Hippocratic oath?" This title suggests an analogy between the technician in this incident and our general concept of a personal physician. If you accept this analogy, you tend toward the conclusion that the technician should not report the pornography. But just how valid is the analogy? One way of approaching this question is to diagram the entities and relations involved (see Figure 2.1).

It should be clear that the situation in this incident is really not very similar to the idealized doctor–patient relationship. Good analogies should have diagrams with similar structure and reasonable correspondence between the entities and relations in the diagrams.

2.4 CASE STUDY—A BBS FOR PIRATED SOFTWARE

This case study contains several examples of poor critical thinking. The principal character apparently rationalized to himself that there was nothing really wrong with his

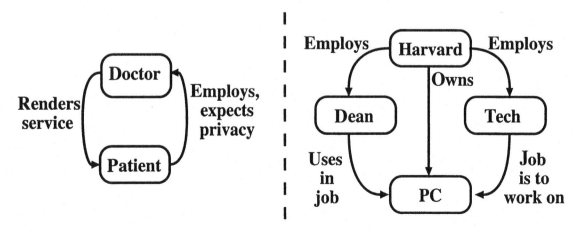

Fig. 2.1 Example diagrams to assess validity of an analogy.

actions. His supporters displayed some unusual logic in defending him. This case study also illustrates how the legal system is being pushed to change in response to situations posed by computer technology.

2.4.1 The Cast of Characters

At the time of this incident, David LaMacchia was 20 years old and a computer science and electrical engineering major at the Massachusetts Institute of Technology.

The Massachusetts Institute of Technology was the owner of the computers used in this incident. MIT had to deal with the misuse of their computers by one of their students.

The Federal Bureau of Investigation plays a relatively minor role in this story. They were called in to investigate the incident.

Donald K. Stern is a US District Attorney for the region, including Boston. He is the prosecutor.

Judge Richard B. Stearns is a US District Court judge in Boston. He decides on the merits of the criminal case presented by the prosecutor.

Harvey Silvergate is the attorney for David LaMacchia.

Laurence Tribe is a well-known professor of law at Harvard University whose role is simply as a commentator on the incident.

2.4.2 The Sequence of Events

David LaMacchia used three computer workstations at MIT to set up and run an Internet bulletin board during the fall of 1993 and the first few months of 1994. The bulletin board was named "cynosure," a word meaning "a center of attention or interest." Information about the bulletin board was apparently widely disseminated on the Internet. It became known as a place where you could post or obtain copies of various copyrighted commercial software packages. Reportedly, as many as 180 people used the system over one 16-hour period [14]. It would later be alleged that over $1 million worth of copies of copyrighted software were made.

MIT discovered that their computers were being used for this purpose and called in the FBI. The FBI investigated. United States attorney Donald Stern obtained an indictment from a federal grand jury on April 7, 1994. LaMacchia was charged with one count of conspiring to violate the federal wire-fraud statute [7]. More specifically, he was accused of setting up the bulletin board, advertising its availability as a source of free software, and transmitting the stolen property by interstate and international wire fraud. LaMacchia was not accused of making any personal financial gain. He was also not accused of making any copies of copyrighted software himself. Penalties for the charge against LaMacchia included jail time and up to $250,000 in fines.

On December 29, 1994, judge Richard B. Stearns ruled that the U.S. Supreme Court decision in *Dowling* v. *the*

United States "precludes LaMacchia's prosecution for criminal copyright infringement under the wire-fraud statute" [7]. The Dowling case involved bootlegged Elvis Presley records. The Supreme Court ruled in the Dowling case that the copyright violation involved in the bootlegged recordings did not constitute theft of property in the sense of the Stolen Property Act. Judge Stearns suggested that criminal penalties "should probably attach to willful, multiple infringements of copyrighted software even absent a commercial motive on the part of the infringer," but noted that "it is the legislature, not the court, which is to define a crime and ordain its punishment" [7]. Even in dismissing the charge, Judge Stearns characterized LaMacchia's actions as "at best heedlessly irresponsible, and at worst nihilistic, self-serving, and lacking in any fundamental sense of values" [7].

United States attorney Donald Stern announced that his office would not appeal the judge's ruling and suggested that new federal legislation was needed. This effectively ended the criminal charges against LaMacchia. It is still conceivable, though unlikely, that some of the companies whose software products were copied could attempt a civil suit against LaMacchia.

Harvey Silvergate, LaMacchia's lawyer, stated that "It is not at all clear that a systems operator who neither controls what is placed on the system nor profits one cent from any copyrighted software that others upload to and download from the system has committed any crime" [7]. Silvergate also suggested that new legislation was needed to protect bulletin-board operators from "excessively harsh liability for the actions of others" [12].

Laurence Tribe's quoted comment on the case was "I am not saying that people have a right to steal software, but using the criminal justice system to police the outer boundaries of property in these gray areas, where it can't be alleged that someone is profiting, is excessive" [13].

2.4.3 Conclusions and Questions

David LaMacchia set up a bulletin board on systems that he did not own to encourage copying of copyrighted software that he did not own. His actions apparently were not quite criminally prosecutable. (That LaMacchia made no personal financial gain and could be characterized as young and idealistic no doubt influenced how hard the U.S. attorney was willing to push the issue of criminal prosecution.) So we have an example of something that is apparently legal but clearly not ethical. Should LaMacchia have been subject to any penalty for his actions? If so, what penalty is appropriate? What sorts of errors in critical thinking must LaMacchia have made to rationalize to himself that his actions were acceptable?

If the story as presented is correct, LaMacchia did none of the copying of copyrighted software. Then there must be a large number of people out there on the Internet who did use the bulletin board as a place to exchange copies of pirated software. Each of these people is more clearly legally liable than LaMacchia. However, it may be essentially impossible to identify any of them.

MIT was presented with the problem of finding that one of their students was using MIT computing equipment to run a bulletin board for pirated software. They chose to call in the FBI. Is it possible that it could have been handled within the university without calling in the FBI? Or would attempting to handle it in this way have been seen as "covering up" and exposing MIT to legal liability?

The district attorney was faced with the problem of trying to find a way to prosecute what appeared to be a massive case of software theft. The route he chose was sufficient to get an indictment from a grand jury but not sufficient for the judge to try the case. Was he trying to "make new law?" Or did he make the best that he could out of an inherently difficult case to prosecute?

The judge ruled that the case could not go forward, but made some disparaging remarks about LaMacchia's actions. Did the judge handle this in the most appropriate manner? Should the judge have let the case go a little further to impress on LaMacchia that he had done something wrong? Or should he have dismissed the case at least as soon as he did and with no comment on LaMacchia's character?

Harvey Silvergate made the observation that "it is not at all clear that LaMacchia has committed any crime." This was actually a fairly trivial observation to make under the circumstances. And it is certainly not a ringing endorsement of his client's morality. Does Silvergate's focus on what is legal, rather than what is right, serve to reinforce negative stereotypes of lawyers?

Professor Laurence Tribe's comments make it sound as if the district attorney was using poor judgment in this case. Tribe's argument appears to be something along the lines of the following:

Since	The property rights in this case are a gray area, and It isn't alleged that the person made any personal financial gain,
Therefore	The person should not be prosecuted.

Does Tribe's argument make sense? Is copyright law really a gray area? Should LaMacchia's lack of personal financial gain be a decisive factor?

Consider a possible analogy. Imagine that Laurence Tribe had just completed writing a new book. LaMacchia sets up a copy machine in his garage. A friend gives LaMacchia a copy of Tribe's new book, and LaMacchia leaves it next to the copy machine. LaMacchia advertises this to everyone that he knows who likes legal books. Nothing of Tribe's is damaged, and LaMacchia does no copying himself. Is this scenario a reasonable analogy to what really happened? Do you think Tribe would have the same opinion of this scenario?

As a postscript to this story, legislation passed in 1997—the "No Electronic Theft (NET) Act"—closed what came to be known as the "LaMacchia loophole." This amendment to the Copyright Act made it clear that someone who willfully infringes a copyright can be prosecuted even if they make no personal financial gain. One of the worksheets in Chapter 8 looks at the first successful prosecution under the NET act.

Points to Remember

- Good critical-thinking skills are a prerequisite to carrying out the intention to act ethically.
- Better critical-thinking skills can lead to clearer thinking, better decision making and better communication with others.
- When confronted with a confusing argument, it can be helpful to attempt to summarize it in the stylized "Since premise, . . . , premise; Therefore conclusion" form.
- When confronted with an argument by analogy, it can be useful to diagram the entities and relations in the two situations in order to assess the validity of the analogy.

WORKSHEET—Critical Thinking in the "Porn On the Dean's PC" Case

Read five or more of the news articles on this case. Rate the articles according to how well they present the critical facts of the incident. Then make your own critical thinking assessment of the following comments offered by different people, plus your favorite other quote from one of the articles that you read.

1. One student was quoted as saying "the way they forced him to resign and the time he resigned was bad."

2. A Harvard divinity graduate was quoted as saying "Is the dean's computer in his home his own? Or because his home and computer are owned by Harvard, is his whole life owned by the Divinity School?"

3. A female Harvard student was quoted as saying the incident was "like getting caught with Playboys under the mattress."

4. The dean's lawyer was quoted as saying "After 13 years of unprecedented success serving as dean of the divinity school, there is a strong feeling that he is now being kicked in the stomach when he's down, while the university continues to protect the privacy of those who have made allegations against the dean."

5. A media critic named Dan Kennedy gave Harvard President Rudenstine a "Muzzle Award" as someone who had "undermine[d] free speech."

WORKSHEET—Who Should Do What About Cheating?

Read the reprinted editorial from *IEEE Potentials* about cheating. Think carefully about it for a moment and then answer the questions. After you answer the worksheet, read the letters that came in response to this editorial and see if you would modify any of your responses.

1. What is the conclusion of the argument being made?

2. What are the reasons offered in support of the conclusion? Rank them, starting with 1, in order of their perceived strength.

3. What are the critical questions you would want to ask?

4. What *should* you do when you witness someone cheating on an assignment?

5. What *do* you do when you witness someone cheating on an assignment? Why?

WORKSHEET—The Quality of Life in Silicon Valley and Our Society

Carefully read the reprinted article by Lotfi Zadeh at the end of this chapter. Then try to outline and assess the underlying argument in the article.

1. The essential first step in a critical-thinking analysis of an article is to identify the *conclusion* of the article. The most common error made when first learning critical-thinking skills is to identify one of the premises as the conclusion. Each premise is, after all, a sort of "minor conclusion" along the way to the "overall conclusion." But the overall conclusion of the article should represent the author's "take-home message" for the audience. It is typically a belief and/or action that is being recommended to the audience. Often this logical conclusion appears near the physical conclusion of the article. Select a quote from the closing paragraph of the article that you feel reasonably represents the conclusion of the article.

2. The next step in a critical-thinking analysis is to identify the major premises of the article. Identify a sequence of three to five short quotes from the article that could represent major premises in support of the conclusion. These quotes may not capture the strongest words or the most controversial statements in the address. Also, there may be several alternative quotes that could be selected to represent a particular point in the argument. But the sequence of quotes you select should reasonably represent a line of argument leading to the conclusion.

3. How would you assess the truth of the individual premises that you identified? How would you assess the collection of premises as "proving" the conclusion?

    What sequence of premises, assuming that they were true, would (better) convince you of the conclusion? That is, could you make a better argument for the conclusion?

WORKSHEET—The Insufficiency of Honesty

Stephen Carter wrote an article titled "The Insufficiency of Honesty," that appeared in *The Atlantic Monthly* in February of 1996. Locate and read a copy of this article. You may notice that it uses a different style of reasoning than what you are used to. Think it over carefully, and answer the questions.

1. What is the definition of "integrity" used in the article?

2. Can two people of integrity (as defined in the article) disagree on an issue? If so, how?

3. What is the conclusion of the argument made in the article?

4. What are some of the premises used in support of this conclusion? Which do you agree with? Which do you disagree with? Why?

5. Carter asserts that ". . . not all moral obligations stem from consent or from a stated intention." Do you agree? Why or why not?

6. Do you agree with the conclusion of the argument made in the article? Why or why not?

1. **Appropriateness of analogies.** Consider the "porn on the dean's PC" incident at the analogy of the technician to a medical doctor. Try to construct a more suitable analogy that involves a medical doctor and a technician. For example, you might consider a scenario as an airline pilot being examined by a doctor.

2. **Comparison of traditional and "web only" information sources.** Pick a recent and/or well-known computer system "cracking" incident. Look up several articles from traditional news sources and an equal number of articles from "web only" sources. Read the different articles carefully and compare them. Excercise your critical-thinking skills to analyze the different treatments of the topic. Is one group more or less informative than the other? More or less biased than the other? More or less clear than the other?

3. **Titles, abstracts, and introductions of current literature.** Locate the current issue of a major technical journal reporting on a topic you are interested in. (If you aren't sure where to start, try browsing through the selection of "*Transactions on . . .*" titles published by the ACM and the IEEE.) Read and critique the title, abstract, and introduction of each article in the issue. Make a list of possible improvements for each article.

4. **Critique of arguments over intellectual property protection.** Chapter 8 discusses several articles that deal with intellectual property protection as it relates to computer software. Any of these would make an excellent case study for critical-thinking. Read one of them before reading the chapter itself, then read the chapter and compare the logical errors you have found with those mentioned in the chapter.

5. **Critique of disagreements over CRT safety.** Chapter 9 discusses several articles dealing with the safety of computer video terminals. Any of these (as well as many of the articles referenced) would make an excellent case study for a critical-thinking review.

REFERENCES

[1] J. Bandler, "Harvard ouster linked to porn; Divinity School dean questioned. *Boston Globe,* May 19, 1999.

[2] J. P. Barlow, Decrypting the Puzzle Palace, *Communications of the ACM,* July 1992, pp. 25–31.

[3] C. A. Barnes, *Critical Thinking: Educational Imperative.* Jossey-Bass Publishers, San Francisco, 1992.

[4] M. Brelis, "PCs: personal, but not private," *Boston Globe,* July 7, 1999.

[5] M. N. Browne and S. M. Keeley, *Asking the right questions: A guide to critical thinking,* Prentice-Hall, Englewood Cliffs, NJ, 1990.

[6] T. E. Damer, *Attacking Faulty Reasoning.* Wadsworth Publishing Company, Belmont, CA, 1987,

[7] C. E. Engler, "Wire fraud case reveals loopholes in U.S. laws protecting software," *The Institute,* March 1995.

[8] K. Fitzgerald, "Whistle blowing: Not always a losing game," *IEEE Spectrum,* December 1990, pp. 49–52.

[9] E. Hayward, "Sources: Divinity school dean resigned over porn," *The Boston Herald,* May 20, 1999.

[10] R. S. Helderman and J. E. Heller, "Porn discovery led to dean's resignation," *Harvard Crimson,* May 21, 1999.

[11] S. Landau, et al., "Crypto policy perspectives," *Communications of the ACM,* August 1994, pp. 115–121.

[12] R. Ranalli, "Feds drop case against MIT computer whiz," *The Boston Herald,* January 28, 1995.

[13] J. Ranowski, "MIT student is called software piracy plotter," *The Boston Globe,* April 8, 1994.

[14] "MIT student charged in pirate bulletin board," *The Tampa Tribune,* April 9, 1994.

[15] M. Wylie, "Do computer docs need a Hippocratic oath?," *Newhouse News Service,* July 6, 1999.

[16] L. A. Zadeh, "Fuzzy Sets," *Information and Control,* volume 8, number 3, pp. 338–353, 1965.

Degrading your degree

Do cheaters lessen its industry value? According to this student, the answer is truthfully, "Yes!"

Gary S. and Vivian Chapman/The Image Bank

In Ethics class, we had a heated discussion about academic cheating here at Cal State. We weren't talking old clichés like "cheaters never prosper" or "cheaters are only cheating themselves." These are all true but trite. We were talking about how a few students' cheating affects the rest of the class and the value of our engineering degrees long after we've gotten them.

Everyone could cite examples of cheating. We had all seen it. Many people knew five or so cohorts who regularly took classes together in order to pass notes during exams and finals. It was reassuring that everyone who knew them wanted something done to stop it. (They were even willing to disclose their names.)

Everyone (about forty students) knew that the immediate effect of cheaters is to lower the grades of everyone else; we all agreed that most classes are graded on a curve. However, beyond the immediate consequences, these few arrogant individuals are degrading the value of the Bachelor of Science degree.

What is your degree worth if anyone can habitually cheat to get through classes - for that matter, to get through the entire engineering program? These shady characters, who graduate without learning even the minimum level of material a reputable engineer should know, go out into industry very possibly lowering your school's reputation among those hiring corporations. Think about your next job interview and realize that your classmates' reputations precedes you. Ultimately, with great enough numbers, the whole engineering profession's reputation will suffer.

One popular misconception held by many students is that the professor should police cheating. This is easy to swallow but an erroneous conclusion. Consider what participants in our Ethics class pointed out. If several people in the class are openly and blatantly cheating by passing notes, there are probably several more individuals covertly holding crib sheets or taping solutions into a book permitted for an exam. What's more, if the rest of the class knowingly condones it by doing nothing, then everyone in the room is actually participating in the act of cheating.

The professor cannot make value judgments for the entire class. If everyone accepts the cheating and its effect on their grades and diplomas, then why should the instructor be required to uphold the moral standards. After all, these virtues are taught to us by our family, our religion and the social associations we make in our lives. These values cannot be changed by the actions of one professor who has an obvious bias against cheating.

One prerequisite of honesty is that it requires an environment of trust to exist. Several people cited examples of well-known universities, such as Cal-Tech and Stanford, where the honor system is so strong that cheating is not tolerated. Exams are typically given without an instructor in the room.

Graduates from these highly esteemed universities are respected and admired because of the self-respect and honesty of everyone involved. They get their degree the hard way, they earn it.

Cheating is a degrading practice that affects us in the classroom and later in industry. Before it can be stopped though, it must be opposed by students, themselves. Students must place value on honesty and start placing peer pressure on those self-serving misfits.

Objections must come from more than one person. One person protesting might be seen as just a complainer; however, several friends sticking together, in the face of lies and deception, can put pressure on the cheaters. To end the corruption, all it takes are words from several students in private with the instructor about who is cheating. When that happens, the only grades the cheaters will devalue will be their own.

Your comments are welcomed.

David Gaines,
California State University, Los Angeles

Reprinted from *IEEE Potentials,* Vol. 11, No. 1, pp. 5, February 1993.

Feedback on student cheating

I am a senior in the Department of Electrical Engineering at the University of Toledo. I am writing in response to the article "Degrading Your Degree" in the February 1993 issue of IEEE Potentials. My reaction to this piece is twofold.

To say that "[moral standards] cannot be changed by the actions of one Professor" is in fact a statement which I contest. Although it is true that no one can change moralistic views except one's own self, there is no reason to assume that a professor cannot be as much of a guiding moral influence as a parent or religious leader. In fact, during four or more years in college, professors may be for many students the only source of moral guidance and model of ethical conduct. Mr. Gaines' ethics class instructor may be one such example and there have certainly been a few in my personal experience. This is not to say that policing students is indeed the responsibility of instructors; however, we must neither excuse our mentors from upholding moral standards nor passively accept a situation. Action should be taken.

The subject of taking action to curb cheating is the focus of my second response. While I fundamentally agree with the view that it is the responsibility of the students to police themselves and the responsibility of the instructors and/or the administration to enact punishment, allow me to propose an alternative to the procedure discussed by Mr. Gaines. It is an unfortunate circumstance in today's educational world that most student bodies disregard an "honor code" at their institution, if in fact, one is still outlined. It is this system which works so well at the "highly esteemed universities" and in other institutions like the military. It is also the system which should be used by those students who wish to curb cheating, even if one is not formally instituted among all students; it can be enforced by only a few effectively.

Because we are all adults and should treat each other as such, the first step in curbing cheating is to have a few words of warning with the offenders, basically along the line of, "See here, friend, we know that you have cheated and be warned: if it occurs again we will take action to see that you are disciplined." If the message is not understood, then after the next incident, the offender is taken aside again and told, "We know you have cheated again. Now we give you the choice of admitting it to the instructor yourself or allowing us to do it for you."

This method not only treats everyone involved as the adults, but is viewed by most faculty and administrators as a more mature, professional method than merely running to the professor at the first sign of cheating like so many children or what some professors irritatingly refer to as "narks." It also lends much more credibility to your claim if you are able to show that you attempted to resolve the situation amongst yourselves instead of immediately throwing it in the professor's lap. This method worked for centuries before, and it is about time we attempt to reestablish the system of the classic university with both guts and conviction.

Alan W. Rudolph
Toledo, OH

I am writing in response to comments made by David Gaines in his recent editorial "Degrading your degree" on pg. 5 of the February Potentials. It was refreshing to see viewpoints concerning academic misconduct in print. I applaud his courage for opening a dialogue on a distasteful and uncomfortable subject matter. I have been a practicing engineer for 12 years and, in the course of my career, have interviewed more than one-hundred engineering grads from a wide variety of backgrounds. With few exceptions, they were (and are) bright, honest, and capable men and women. However, I recently returned to academia to complete my doctorate and was able to witness a bit of cheating from the instructor's perspective. This has led me to believe that the ivory tower has a few cracks.

First let me describe the situation as I see it today. Over the past decade I have seen opportunities for electrical engineers decline: the high tech bust of 1983, DRAM dumping by the Japanese, the end of the cold war, increased global competition. Fortune 500 companies which traditionally provide many of the entry level jobs are scaling back. There have even been recent layoffs at the venerable "Big Blue" (IBM). Since companies that are doing any recruiting at all are cautious and very selective, many students are going to great lengths to make themselves marketable: some are working very hard to make the highest grades possible, some are taking courses in hot technology areas, some are getting a head start with an employer through a co-op program, some are going on to graduate school, and some, as the author correctly points out, are overtly (or covertly) cheating. The pressure to make high grades is tremendous, the costs of failure high. The incentive to cheat is equally high and must not, in my view, go unchecked.

The author's comments about how cheating lessens the value of a degree were largely on track. However, the author prematurely excuses the professor (and effectively the institution that professor represents) from any ethical responsibility at all with, "One popular misconception is that the professor should police cheating."

Is it a "popular misconception" that the person in authority (i.e. the one who passes judgment through grades) can sit idly by while people break the rules and undermine the academic process? If an honest student witnesses cheating, brings it to the professor's attention, and the professor ignores it (or worse yet, becomes perturbed at the honest student), like it or not, that professor has made a value judgment and has sent a clear message to the honest student: "honesty doesn't count, cheating is okay, I do not care."

Ignoring crime and avoiding responsibility is wrong and is all too prevalent in our society today. The feeling that as victims, or bystanders, we can do nothing is a great tragedy that all too often is exacerbated by a criminal justice system (and, in the smaller context, a university administration) that coddles criminals and puts victims on trial.

The author then digs himself in deeper with, "The professor cannot make value judgments for the entire class. If everyone accepts the cheating

Reprinted from *IEEE Potentials,* Vol. 12, No. 3, pp. 11–12, October 1993.

and its effect on their grades and diplomas, then why should the instructor be required to uphold the moral standards?" Why? Because the only way a grade means anything is if it is earned honestly. Because when a professor gives a passing grade it should represent that professor's "seal of approval" (i.e. a genuine achievement) and an assurance that a level of competence has been achieved. One makes the grades, one doesn't steal them. In engineering, where even honest mistakes can cause loss of life, integrity is everything.

The author goes on to say that the honors system works at several premier institutions. That is true, but one could argue that the extremely high admissions standards at these institutions go a long way to weed out the miscreants before they ever get there. It would be a safe conjecture that there are few cheaters with 3.9 grade point averages, near-perfect SATs, sparkling public service records and so forth. Unfortunately, high admission standards cannot be applied everywhere as this would exclude the vast majority of honest students from higher education.

In my heart of hearts, I do not think that honest students accept cheating. This sells them way short. I think honest students abhor cheaters and wish they were kicked out of school. Unfortunately, honest students are busily caught up in their own studies. They hesitate to take actions against cheaters as it could detract from their studies and possibly put them at personal risk. Also, if the professor doesn't have "an obvious bias against cheating," as the author puts it, no meaningful punishment can be exacted anyway!

Additionally, I don't think honest professors and instructors accept cheating either. I just think that the vast majority of them are scared stiff to confront a cheater and know that frequently they would have their hands tied (or their ox gored) if they did. The cheater may take physical retribution. Death threats for a low grade are not unheard of. The administration may not back the professor up for a variety of political reasons. The burden of proof is on the professor. The professor is open to a range of counter-suits from libel to discrimination. Would a professor risk his or her

career over it? Best not rock the boat!!

Well, I think the author is correct when he states that his fellow students can put pressure on cheaters. But, this is not the complete solution. If tolerance of cheating is the status quo, then leadership representing the status quo must reform. The way out of the abyss must come from the top: from the president of the university, to the deans, to the department heads, to the professors, and finally the students. Moral and legal remedies against cheating must be in place, clear, concise, and, most importantly, enforceable. To not take responsibility is terror. We must nurture our bright and honest hopes for the future - and cast out the villains. Any suggestions where we might start?

Dr. Steven J. Apollo
Electrical engineer
Arlington, TX

I am writing in reference to the article "Degrading your degree" in the February 1993 issue. At the University of Southern Maine, I have been intimately involved for a year and a half in the writing of a policy and procedures related to Student Academic Integrity. We began the process by reviewing similar documents from several other universities. Most of the documents that we reviewed started with a list of "thou shalt not" type of statements. We decided to try to take a positive approach as much as possible by stating what is expected of students.

The draft of our document has been approved by our Faculty Senate and is now working its way through our administrative hierarchy. The following is an exact copy of most of the first page of our draft document:

The academic community of the University of Southern Maine recognizes that adherence to high principles of academic integrity is vital to the academic function of the University.

Academic integrity is based upon honesty. All students of the University are expected to be honest in their academic endeveaors. All academic work should be performed in a manner which will provide an honest reflection of the knowledge and abilities of each student. Any breach of academic honesty should be regarded as a serious offense by all members of the academic community.

The entire academic community shares the responsibility for establishing and maintaining standards of academic integrity. Those in charge of academic tasks have an obligation to make known the standards and expectations of acceptable academic conduct. Each student has an obligation to know and understand those standards and expectations. While the academic community recognizes that the responsibility for learning and personal conduct is an individual matter, all students and faculty members are expected to help to maintain academic integrity at the University by refusing to participate in, or tolerate, any dishonesty.

Violations of
Student Academic Integrity
Academic integrity means not lying, cheating, or stealing. To cheat on an examination, to steal the words or ideas of another, or to falsify the results of one's research corrupts the essential process by which knowledge is advanced. Cheating, plagiarism, fabrication of data, giving or receiving unauthorized help on examinations, and other acts of academic dishonesty are contrary to the academic purposes for which the University exists.

Violations of student academic integrity include any actions which attempt to promote or enhance the academic standing of any student by dishonest means. The following is a listing of some, but not necessarily all, actions that are violations of academic integrity :

The list that follows the last statement above includes examples of nine types of violations of academic integrity. The entire document — some twelve pages—continues with other sections to spell out the procedures to be followed and the sanctions that may be imposed.

Since receiving my BS degree in 1951, I have spent a little more than half of my professional career in engineering education, and it is my strong impression that most educational institutions have very similar expectations of student academic integrity. I am appalled to think that there may be some schools where this is not so.

David W. Knudsen, PE
Associate Professor
University of Southern Maine

Editorial
UC-Berkeley Computer Science Commencement Address

ON COMMENCEMENT days such as this one, it is customary to avoid touching upon issues that are contentious or in dissonance with majority-held views. I shall take the liberty of departing from this tradition because there are contentious issues that have to be addressed and serious structural problems in our society that your generation is likely to be called upon to solve.

To put my views in perspective, I should like to note the obvious: I am not a native-born American, as most of you are. Yet, I consider it a privilege to be a citizen of this great country—a country of vast expanse, immense wealth, great diversity, unmatched power, and a world leader in almost every realm of human activity. But what matters most to me is that it is a country in which human rights are taken seriously, governance is ruled by law, and decency, generosity, and fairness are national traits.

To say what I said does not mean that all is well. Our society is faced with serious problems that are visible to all: drug addiction, crime, homelessness, extremes of wealth and poverty, alienation, and ethnic conflicts. But there are other problems that—though less visible—are likely to cause serious damage to the fabric of our society in the long run. My brief remarks will be focused on two linked problems that fall into this category.

Many of you will be taking jobs in Silicon Valley, the heart of our computer industry; the industry that is the driving force behind the economic boom in which we are basking now.

When I ask our graduates who work in Silicon Valley whether they are happy in their jobs, the usual answer is: the pay is good and the work is interesting. But one important element is missing: the sense of security, dignity, and collegiality. In Silicon Valley and, more generally, in the computer industry, the working environment is the environment of cutthroat competition. As they say, "In Silicon Valley if you make the mistake of stopping for lunch, you will be lunch." You are hired today but may be laid off tomorrow, with no farewell parties and no regrets. The bottom line is the stock price and not human welfare.

Something is deeply wrong with our values when elimination of thousands of jobs is greeted with applause by Wall Street, causing the price of stock to go up and, not coincidentally, increasing the value of stock options of company executives. In this climate, executives are not expected to spend sleepless nights when downsizing leads to massive layoffs. Indeed, any company that puts human welfare above profits and efficiency risks serious damage to its competitive

Publisher Item Identifier S 1094-6977(98)01522-3.

position and, possibly, its demise. It is a sobering thought that profits and efficiency have become the driving forces that shape the dynamics of our society, and that money may become the ultimate determinant of values by which we live. Perhaps we should pause and ask ourselves if we are doing the right thing when we exert pressure on other countries to follow our example and abandon their traditions of protection of social rights in the quest for efficiency and stronger competitive position in the global marketplace.

There is a linkage between this state of affairs and the growing intrusion of advertising and commercialism into all aspects of our lives. A disturbing prospect is that as we move further into the information age and the multimedia, the linkage will become stronger and less amenable to control.

To many, advertising is the pillar of free enterprise. Up to a point, advertising serves an essential purpose, but like any good thing that is overdone, unrestrained advertising, with its high content of half-truths and untruths, is becoming a force that is corroding our culture and distorting our goals. The pervasive influence of advertisers on TV and radio programming substitutes the size of audience for genuine concern for program quality. Catering to the least common denominator leads to programming that focuses on crime, violence, sex, sports, scandal, and human interest stories. The amount of time devoted to serious news is declining, and the media, driven by the quest for higher advertising revenue, are abdicating their responsibility to inform, educate, and inspire.

In this climate of media manipulation and commercialism, it is not surprising that our young people have become cynical and materialistic. That calls into question our ability to serve as a positive role model for the young in other countries and other societies. Indeed, it is alarming to observe the degree to which intrusive advertising and commercialism have led to a vulgarization of our culture and an abandonment of moral values that led this country to greatness. The not-so-subtle control of our media by advertisers has led to the emergence of consumerism as the dominant influence shaping our culture, our values, and our perceptions.

What is disconcerting to observe is that the pop culture programs mass produced by the TV, movie, and music industries in the United States are displacing—in the marketplace of other countries—their own products. As in the United States, low-grade programs, intrusive advertising, and rampant commercialism have become the norm in TV programming in Europe and other continents as well. It was a prominent TV personality, who in addressing a European audience had this to say, "We have succeeded in ruining our culture in the United States, and now we are going to ruin your culture."

Reprinted from *IEEE Transactions on Systems, Man, and Cybernetics, Part C: Applications and Reviews*, Vol. 28, No. 1, pp. 7–8, February 1998.

I am touching upon these issues because they have a definite impact on the outlook and aspirations of the young in our society. A telling statistic is that despite the rising demand for computer science graduates, the number of undergraduate degrees in computer science has dropped 43% from 42 000 in 1986 to 24 000 in 1994. What that suggests is that a declining number of students are entering those fields in which hard work is required. A visible facet of this trend is that pursuit of knowledge for its own sake is increasingly being replaced by a quest for education as a ticket to a better-paying job.

I have used harsh expressions to make my points. The picture I have painted is darker than it should be. I have done this with deliberation to underscore that it is our collective responsibility—and especially the responsibility of your generation—the generation that will shape our future—to do whatever can be done in our democratic society to prevent the corrosive forces of commercialism and consumerism from encroaching on our culture and becoming dominant influences in defining our values, our beliefs, and our morals.

LOTFI A. ZADEH
University of California
Berkeley, CA 94720-1776

Chapter 3

Professional Codes of Ethics

These standards expand on the Code of Ethics by providing specific statements of behavior in support of each element of the Code. They are not objectives to be strived for, they are rules that no true professional will violate.

—from the AITP Standards of Conduct

Commitment to ethical professional conduct is expected of every voting, associate, and student member of the ACM. This Code, consisting of 24 imperatives formulated as statements of personal responsibility, identifies the elements of such a commitment. . . .

—preamble to the ACM Code of Ethics

Software engineers shall commit themselves to making the analysis, specification, design, development, testing and maintenance of software a beneficial and respected profession. In accordance with their commitment to the health, safety and welfare of the public, software engineers shall adhere to the following . . .

—preamble to the IEEE-CS/ACM Software Engineering Code of Ethics

We, the members of the IEEE, in recognition of the importance of our technologies in affecting the quality of life throughout the world, and in accepting a personal obligation to our profession, its members and the communities we serve, do hereby commit ourselves to conduct of the highest ethical and professional manner. . . .

—preamble to the IEEE Code of Ethics

3.1 INTRODUCTION

SOME students react with surprise when told that there is even one published code of ethics for the computing disciplines. In fact, almost every professional organization dealing with the field of computing has published its own code of ethics. Influential organizations for computing professionals include the Association of Information Technology Professionals (AITP), the Association for Computing Machinery (ACM), and the Computer Society of the Institute of Electrical and Electronics Engineers (IEEE-CS). Each of these organizations (AITP, ACM, and IEEE) has its own code of ethics. In addition, the ACM and the IEEE-CS jointly sponsor a code of ethics for software engineers. In this chapter, we examine all four of these codes.

A variety of other professional organizations have published codes of ethics that are potentially relevant. Among these are the National Society of Professional Engineers (NSPE), and the Computer Ethics Institute. The NSPE

code is reprinted in Appendix B, because it contains some interesting points of contrast to the other codes.

As you study the codes of ethics presented in this chapter, it will become apparent that a code of ethics is a vehicle for promoting a variety of purposes and goals. Luegenbiehl identifies 12 functions that a professional code of ethics might serve [4]. I summarize these functions here as follows.

1. *Symbolize professionalism.* The fact that a group has its own code of ethics suggests that the group views itself as constituting a profession and that it wishes to be viewed in this way before the public. All four codes have some element of this purpose in them.

2. *Protect group interests.* A code of ethics can also act to promote the economic interests of the group. The Software Engineering code has an element of this in the clause where it states that software engineering

managers and leaders should "offer fair and just remuneration."

3. *Specify membership etiquette.* A code of ethics may also specify standards of professional courtesy, saying how members should treat each other. There is an element of this in each of the codes, but it does not seem to be a large factor.

4. *Inspire good conduct.* The code of ethics for a group may serve to inspire members toward high standards of conduct. There is certainly an element of this in each of the codes, as evidenced by mention of service to the public, responsibility to clients, and other such phrases.

5. *Educate members.* Each of the codes serves some degree of an educational purpose just by its existence. The circulation of a code of ethics naturally serves to teach current members and students about the accepted practices and standards of the profession.

   The ACM code has been published with a set of brief hypothetical case studies that help illustrate how to use the code in making decisions about specific situations. These case studies appear as a reprint at the end of this chapter. This sort of elaboration on the practical meaning of the code seems valuable and possibly should be done in a more comprehensive manner. For example, the American Psychological Association publishes case histories of actual allegations of code violations, important facts determined by a subsequent investigation, and the conclusion reached [2].

6. *Discipline members.* A code of ethics can also be a basis for disciplinary mechanisms. Of the four codes, this purpose is most clear in the IEEE code. An element of this purpose is also evident in the ACM code and the Software Engineering code.

7. *Foster external relations.* Each of the four codes offers some guidance on how members of the profession should relate to clients and others outside the profession.

8. *Enumerate principles.* Each of the codes attempts, to some extent, to enumerate general moral principles that members should respect. For example, the admonition to "reject bribery in all of its forms" (item 4 of the IEEE code) is a statement of general moral principle. Also, one element of the AITP code is "I have an obligation to my country, therefore, in my personal, business and social contacts, I shall uphold my nation and shall honor the chosen way of life of my fellow citizens."

9. *Express ideals.* Each of the codes also has in it some element of expressing ideals that each member should aspire to. The distinction between a principle and an ideal can be a fine one. A *principle* is imagined to be something that you could in fact keep to.

An *ideal,* on the other hand, is more of a goal that may not always be possible. The admonition "to avoid real or perceived conflicts of interest" sounds like a general moral principle, but it is not always possible to achieve it. A conflict may be missed because "perceived" depends in part on who is doing the perceiving. So this admonition is followed by the qualifier "whenever possible" in item 2 of the IEEE code.

10. *Put forth rules.* Rules are much the same as principles, but are meant to address more specific and concrete situations. If "reject bribery in all of its forms" is a general principle, then "when awarding a contract, you may accept no gifts with a total value of more than $50 from any entity competing for the contract" would be a specific rule meant to clarify the meaning of the general principle as applied to a certain situation.

11. *Offer guidelines.* Guidelines are, practically speaking, much the same as rules. A set of "rules" may tend to imply that these are all the do-s and don't-s that you need to worry about. On the other hand, labeling them as guidelines may give more of the feeling that this is not an exhaustive list of do-s and don't-s and that there may be gray areas that require careful interpretation.

12. *Codify rights.* A code of ethics may also serve to enumerate the rights of members as well as their responsibilities.

As you read through the codes of ethics in the next sections, keep in mind the 12 functions just described. Note things that the codes have in common, things that might represent a conflict among them, and things that seem somehow incomplete, incorrect, or just plain inappropriate.

3.2 THE AITP CODE OF ETHICS AND STANDARDS OF CONDUCT

The AITP code of ethics really comes in two parts. The more general of these is labeled the "code of ethics." A more detailed and specific list of guidelines is termed the "standards of conduct." These were updated in August and October of 1997, respectively. The code of ethics is presented as a set of seven obligations that are acknowledged by members of AITP.

3.2.1 Code of Ethics

I acknowledge:

That I have an obligation to management, therefore, I shall promote the understanding of information processing methods and procedures to management using every resource at my command.

That I have an obligation to my fellow members, therefore, I shall uphold the high ideals of AITP as outlined in

Frank & Ernest © NEA

the Association Bylaws. Further, I shall cooperate with my fellow members and shall treat them with honesty and respect at all times.

That I have an obligation to society and will participate to the best of my ability in the dissemination of knowledge pertaining to the general development and understanding of information processing. Further, I shall not use knowledge of a confidential nature to further my personal interest, nor shall I violate the privacy and confidentiality of information entrusted to me or to which I may gain access.

That I have an obligation to my College or University, therefore, I shall uphold its ethical and moral principles.

That I have an obligation to my employer whose trust I hold, therefore, I shall endeavor to discharge this obligation to the best of my ability, to guard my employer's interests, and to advise him or her wisely and honestly.

That I have an obligation to my country, therefore, in my personal, business, and social contacts, I shall uphold my nation and shall honor the chosen way of life of my fellow citizens.

I accept these obligations as a personal responsibility and as a member of this Association. I shall actively discharge these obligations and I dedicate myself to that end.

The AITP code of ethics is supplemented by a statement of standards of conduct. Sections of the standards of conduct relate to the professional's obligations to management, fellow professionals, society and employer. Each section consists of six to eight specific obligations.

3.2.2 Standards of Conduct

These standards expand on the Code of Ethics by providing specific statements of behavior in support of each element of the Code. They are not objectives to be strived for, they are rules that no true professional will violate. It is first of all expected that an information processing professional will abide by the appropriate laws of their country and community. The following standards address tenets that apply to the profession.

In recognition of my obligation to management I shall:

- Keep my personal knowledge up-to-date and insure that proper expertise is available when needed.

- Share my knowledge with others and present factual and objective information to management to the best of my ability.
- Accept full responsibility for work that I perform.
- Not misuse the authority entrusted to me.
- Not misrepresent or withhold information concerning the capabilities of equipment, software or systems.
- Not take advantage of the lack of knowledge or inexperience on the part of others.

In recognition of my obligation to my fellow members and the profession I shall:

- Be honest in all my professional relationships.
- Take appropriate action in regard to any illegal or unethical practices that come to my attention. However, I will bring charges against any person only when I have reasonable basis for believing in the truth of the allegations and without any regard to personal interest.
- Endeavor to share my special knowledge.
- Cooperate with others in achieving understanding and in identifying problems.
- Not use or take credit for the work of others without specific acknowledgment and authorization.
- Not take advantage of the lack of knowledge or inexperience on the part of others for personal gain.

In recognition of my obligation to society I shall:

- Protect the privacy and confidentiality of all information entrusted to me.
- Use my skill and knowledge to inform the public in all areas of my expertise.
- To the best of my ability, insure that the products of my work are used in a socially responsible way.
- Support, respect, and abide by the appropriate local, state, provincial, and federal laws.
- Never misrepresent or withhold information that is germane to a problem or situation of public concern nor will I allow any such known information to remain unchallenged.

49

- Not use knowledge of a confidential or personal nature in any unauthorized manner or to achieve personal gain.

In recognition of my obligation to my employer I shall:

- Make every effort to ensure that I have the most current knowledge and that the proper expertise is available when needed.
- Avoid conflict of interest and insure that my employer is aware of any potential conflicts.
- Present a fair, honest, and objective viewpoint.
- Protect the proper interests of my employer at all times.
- Protect the privacy and confidentiality of all information entrusted to me.
- Not misrepresent or withhold information that is germane to the situation.
- Not attempt to use the resources of my employer for personal gain or for any purpose without proper approval.
- Not exploit the weakness of a computer system for personal gain or personal satisfaction.

Clearly, the obligations listed in the AITP code of ethics are meant to be general statements that set up an ethical framework for AITP members. You can view the obligations in the code as enumerating the typical stakeholders in generic information technology situations: management, fellow professionals, society, university/employer, country and self. The standards of conduct expand on the general statements in the code to give more detail about the relationship to management, fellow professionals, society, and employer.

Probably the main elements of the AITP code that stand out as different are the "obligation to school or university" and the "obligation to country." I believe that the statement of "obligation to school or university" is best read simply as trying to be inclusive of students as members of AITP. If the code mentioned only an obligation to employer, it might seem as if student members were left out. At one level, the obligation to country seems very reasonable. However, this item could clearly lead to conflicts as IT professionals in some other countries try to conform to the code. For example, the federal government in some countries might have a policy toward eavesdropping on computer communications that IT professionals would see as conflicting with privacy and confidentiality obligations. Overall, the content of the AITP code and standards is reasonably comprehensive and, as we shall see, largely similar to that in the other codes.

3.3 THE ACM CODE OF ETHICS

In 1992, the ACM adopted a new code of ethics and professional conduct with supplemental explanations and guidelines. The ACM code of ethics consists of eight general moral imperatives, eight specific professional responsibilities, six organizational leadership imperatives, and two elements for compliance. Appendix B contains the complete code with explanations and guidelines. Here we present just the statement of the basic items of the code.

1. General Moral Imperatives. As an ACM member I will . . .
   - (1.1) Contribute to society and human well-being.
   - (1.2) Avoid harm to others.
   - (1.3) Be honest and trustworthy.
   - (1.4) Be fair and take action not to discriminate.
   - (1.5) Honor property rights including copyrights and patents.
   - (1.6) Give proper credit for intellectual property.
   - (1.7) Respect the privacy of others.
   - (1.8) Honor confidentiality.

2. More Specific Professional Responsibilities. As an ACM computing professional I will . . .
   - (2.1) Strive to achieve the highest quality in both the process and products of professional work.
   - (2.2) Acquire and maintain professional competence.
   - (2.3) Know and respect existing laws pertaining to professional work.
   - (2.4) Accept and provide appropriate professional review.
   - (2.5) Give comprehensive and thorough evaluations of computer systems and their impacts, including analysis of possible risks.
   - (2.6) Honor contracts, agreements, and assigned responsibilities.
   - (2.7) Improve public understanding of computing and its consequences.
   - (2.8) Access computing and communication resources only when authorized to do so.

3. Organizational Leadership Imperatives. As an ACM member and an organizational leader, I will . . .
   - (3.1) Articulate social responsibilities of members of an organizational unit and encourage full acceptance of those responsibilities.
   - (3.2) Manage personnel and resources to design and build information systems that enhance the quality, effectiveness and dignity of working life.
   - (3.3) Acknowledge and support proper and authorized uses of an organization's computing and communications resources.
   - (3.4) Ensure that users and those who will be affected by a computing system have their needs clearly articulated during the assessment and design of requirements. Later the system must be validated to meet requirements.
   - (3.5) Articulate and support policies that protect the dignity of users and others affected by a computing system.

(3.6) Create opportunities for members of the organization to learn the principles and limitations of computer systems.

4. Compliance with the Code. As an ACM member, I will . . .

(4.1) Uphold and promote the principles of this code.

(4.2) Treat violations of this code as inconsistent with membership in the ACM.

A large degree of content overlap in the AITP code/standards and the ACM code should be readily apparent. For example, the themes in the ACM general moral imperatives 1.1, 1.2, and 1.7 appear in the AITP code's obligation to society. The theme of ACM general moral imperative 1.6 appears in the AITP standards of conduct in relation to fellow professionals. The themes of ACM Specific Professional Responsibilities 2.3, 2.5, and 2.7 appear in the AITP standards of conduct in relation to society. You can easily identify a number of other strong similarities.

For the moment it may be more interesting to consider things that seem to be different between the ACM code and the AITP code/standards. The AITP standards of conduct contain explicit statements against several methods of unfair personal gain: "Not take advantage of the lack of knowledge or inexperience on the part of others . . . ," "Not use knowledge of a confidential or personal nature . . . ," "Not attempt to use the resources of my employer . . . ," and "Not exploit the weakness of a computer system . . ." This theme does not appear so strongly in the ACM code. On the other hand the ACM code contains the statement "Be fair and take action not to discriminate." This theme does not appear so explicitly in the AITP code or standards.

3.4 THE SOFTWARE ENGINEERING CODE OF ETHICS

The Software Engineering code of ethics begins with a "short version" overview of the eight general ethical principles. The eight principles represent different areas of concern for the software engineer: public, employer, product, judgment, management, profession, colleagues and self. The short version is followed with a "full version" in which each of the eight general ethical principles is elaborated upon by six to thirteen more specific obligations. The text of the full version appears below, and the complete text of both versions is reprinted in Appendix B.

Preamble.

Computers have a central and growing role in commerce, industry, government, medicine, education, entertainment and society at large. Software engineers are those who contribute by direct participation or by teaching, to the analysis, specification, design, development, certification, maintenance and testing of software systems. Because of their roles in developing software systems, software engi-

neers have significant opportunities to do good or cause harm, to enable others to do good or cause harm, or to influence others to do good or cause harm. To ensure, as much as possible, that their efforts will be used for good, software engineers must commit themselves to making software engineering a beneficial and respected profession. In accordance with that commitment, software engineers shall adhere to the following Code of Ethics and Professional Practice.

The Code contains eight Principles related to the behavior of and decisions made by professional software engineers, including practitioners, educators, managers, supervisors and policy makers, as well as trainees and students of the profession. The Principles identify the ethically responsible relationships in which individuals, groups, and organizations participate and the primary obligations within these relationships. The Clauses of each Principle are illustrations of some of the obligations included in these relationships. These obligations are founded in the software engineer's humanity, in special care owed to people affected by the work of software engineers, and in the unique elements of the practice of software engineering. The Code prescribes these as obligations of anyone claiming to be or aspiring to be a software engineer.

It is not intended that the individual parts of the Code be used in isolation to justify errors of omission or commission. The list of Principles and Clauses is not exhaustive. The Clauses should not be read as separating the acceptable from the unacceptable in professional conduct in all practical situations. The Code is not a simple ethical algorithm that generates ethical decisions. In some situations, standards may be in tension with each other or with standards from other sources. These situations require the software engineer to use ethical judgment to act in a manner which is most consistent with the spirit of the Code of Ethics and Professional Practice, given the circumstances.

Ethical tensions can best be addressed by thoughtful consideration of fundamental principles, rather than blind reliance on detailed regulations. These Principles should influence software engineers to consider broadly who is affected by their work; to examine if they and their colleagues are treating other human beings with due respect; to consider how the public, if reasonably well informed, would view their decisions; to analyze how the least empowered will be affected by their decisions; and to consider whether their acts would be judged worthy of the ideal professional working as a software engineer. In all these judgments, concern for the health, safety and welfare of the public is primary; that is, the "Public Interest" is central to this Code.

The dynamic and demanding context of software engineering requires a code that is adaptable and relevant to new situations as they occur. However, even in this generality, the Code provides support for software engineers and managers of software engineers who need to take positive action in a specific case by documenting the ethical stance of the profession. The Code provides an ethical foundation to which individuals within teams and the team as a whole can appeal. The Code helps to define those actions that are ethically improper to request of a software engineer or teams of software engineers.

The Code is not simply for adjudicating the nature of questionable acts; it also has an important educational function. As this Code expresses the consensus of the profession on ethical issues, it is a means to educate both the public and aspiring professionals about the ethical obligations of all software engineers.

Principles.

1. Public.
   Software engineers shall act consistently with the public interest. In particular, software engineers shall, as appropriate:
   (1.1) Accept full responsibility for their own work.
   (1.2) Moderate the interests of the software engineer, the employer, the client and the users with the public good.
   (1.3) Approve software only if they have a well-founded belief that it is safe, meets specifications, passes appropriate tests, and does not diminish quality of life, diminish privacy or harm the environment. The ultimate effect of the work should be to the public good.
   (1.4) Disclose to appropriate persons or authorities any actual or potential danger to the user, the public, or the environment, that they reasonably believe to be associated with software or related documents.
   (1.5) Cooperate in efforts to address matters of grave public concern caused by software, its installation, maintenance, support or documentation.
   (1.6) Be fair and avoid deception in all statements, particularly public ones, concerning software or related documents, methods and tools.
   (1.7) Consider issues of physical disabilities, allocation of resources, economic disadvantage and other factors that can diminish access to the benefits of software.
   (1.8) Be encouraged to volunteer professional skills to good causes and to contribute to public education concerning the discipline.
2. Client and employer.
   Software engineers shall act in a manner that is in the best interests of their client and employer, consistent with the public interest. In particular, software engineers shall, as appropriate:
   (2.1) Provide service in their areas of competence, being honest and forthright about any limitations of their experience and education.
   (2.2) Not knowingly use software that is obtained or retained either illegally or unethically.
   (2.3) Use the property of a client or employer only in

ways properly authorized, and with the client's or employer's knowledge and consent.
   (2.4) Ensure that any document upon which they rely has been approved, when required, by someone authorized to approve it.
   (2.5) Keep private any confidential information gained in their professional work, where such confidentiality is consistent with the public interest and consistent with the law.
   (2.6) Identify, document, collect evidence and report to the client or the employer promptly if, in their opinion, a project is likely to fail, to prove too expensive, to violate intellectual property law, or otherwise to be problematic.
   (2.7) Identify, document, and report significant issues of social concern, of which they are aware, in software or related documents, to the employer or the client.
   (2.8) Accept no outside work detrimental to the work they perform for their primary employer.
   (2.9) Promote no interest adverse to their employer or client, unless a higher ethical concern is being compromised; in that case, inform the employer or another appropriate authority of the ethical concern.
3. Product.
   Software engineers shall ensure that their products and related modifications meet the highest professional standards possible. In particular, software engineers shall, as appropriate:
   (3.1) Strive for high quality, acceptable cost, and a reasonable schedule, ensuring significant trade-offs are clear to and accepted by the employer and the client, and are available for consideration by the user and the public.
   (3.2) Ensure proper and achievable goals and objectives for any project on which they work or propose.
   (3.3) Identify, define and address ethical, economic, cultural, legal and environmental issues related to work projects.
   (3.4) Ensure that they are qualified for any project on which they work or propose to work, by an appropriate combination of education, training, and experience.
   (3.5) Ensure that an appropriate method is used for any project on which they work or propose to work.
   (3.6) Work to follow professional standards, when available, that are most appropriate for the task at hand, departing from these only when ethically or technically justified.
   (3.7) Strive to fully understand the specifications for software on which they work.
   (3.8) Ensure that specifications for software on which they work have been well documented, satisfy the users' requirements and have the appropriate approvals.

(3.9) Ensure realistic quantitative estimates of cost, scheduling, personnel, quality and outcomes on any project on which they work or propose to work and provide an uncertainty assessment of these estimates.

(3.10) Ensure adequate testing, debugging, and review of software and related documents on which they work.

(3.11) Ensure adequate documentation, including significant problems discovered and solutions adopted, for any project on which they work.

(3.12) Work to develop software and related documents that respect the privacy of those who will be affected by that software.

(3.13) Be careful to use only accurate data derived by ethical and lawful means, and use it only in ways properly authorized.

(3.14) Maintain the integrity of data, being sensitive to outdated or flawed occurrences.

(3.15) Treat all forms of software maintenance with the same professionalism as new development.

4. Judgment.
Software engineers shall maintain integrity and independence in their professional judgment. In particular, software engineers shall, as appropriate:

(4.1) Temper all technical judgments by the need to support and maintain human values.

(4.2) Only endorse documents either prepared under their supervision or within their areas of competence and with which they are in agreement.

(4.3) Maintain professional objectivity with respect to any software or related documents they are asked to evaluate.

(4.4) Not engage in deceptive financial practices such as bribery, double billing, or other improper financial practices.

(4.5) Disclose to all concerned parties those conflicts of interest that cannot reasonably be avoided or escaped.

(4.6) Refuse to participate, as members or advisors, in a private, governmental or professional body concerned with software related issues, in which they, their employers or their clients have undisclosed potential conflicts of interest.

5. Management.
Software engineering managers and leaders shall subscribe to and promote an ethical approach to the management of software development and maintenance. In particular, those managing or leading software engineers shall, as appropriate:

(5.1) Ensure good management for any project on which they work, including effective procedures for promotion of quality and reduction of risk.

(5.2) Ensure that software engineers are informed of standards before being held to them.

(5.3) Ensure that software engineers know the employer's policies and procedures for protecting passwords, files and information that is confidential to the employer or confidential to others.

(5.4) Assign work only after taking into account appropriate contributions of education and experience tempered with a desire to further that education and experience.

(5.5) Ensure realistic quantitative estimates of cost, scheduling, personnel, quality and outcomes on any project on which they work or propose to work, and provide an uncertainty assessment of these estimates.

(5.6) Attract potential software engineers only by full and accurate description of the conditions of employment.

(5.7) Offer fair and just remuneration.

(5.8) Not unjustly prevent someone from taking a position for which that person is suitably qualified.

(5.9) Ensure that there is a fair agreement concerning ownership of any software, processes, research, writing, or other intellectual property to which a software engineer has contributed.

(5.10) Provide for due process in hearing charges of violation of an employer's policy or of this Code.

(5.11) Not ask a software engineer to do anything inconsistent with this Code.

(5.12) Not punish anyone for expressing ethical concerns about a project.

6. Profession.
Software engineers shall advance the integrity and reputation of the profession consistent with the public interest. In particular, software engineers shall, as appropriate:

(6.1) Help develop an organizational environment favorable to acting ethically.

(6.2) Promote public knowledge of software engineering.

(6.3) Extend software engineering knowledge by appropriate participation in professional organizations, meetings and publications.

(6.4) Support, as members of a profession, other software engineers striving to follow this Code.

(6.5) Not promote their own interest at the expense of the profession, client or employer.

(6.6) Obey all laws governing their work, unless, in exceptional circumstances, such compliance is inconsistent with the public interest.

(6.7) Be accurate in stating the characteristics of software on which they work, avoiding not only false claims but also claims that might reasonably be supposed to be speculative, vacuous, deceptive, misleading, or doubtful.

(6.8) Take responsibility for detecting, correcting, and reporting errors in software and associated documents on which they work.

(6.9) Ensure that clients, employers, and supervisors know of the software engineer's commitment to this Code of ethics, and the subsequent ramifications of such commitment.

(6.10) Avoid associations with businesses and organizations which are in conflict with this code.

(6.11) Recognize that violations of this Code are inconsistent with being a professional software engineer.

(6.12) Express concerns to the people involved when significant violations of this Code are detected unless this is impossible, counter-productive, or dangerous.

(6.13) Report significant violations of this Code to appropriate authorities when it is clear that consultation with people involved in these significant violations is impossible, counter-productive or dangerous.

7. Colleagues.
Software engineers shall be fair to and supportive of their colleagues. In particular, software engineers shall, as appropriate:

(7.1) Encourage colleagues to adhere to this Code.

(7.2) Assist colleagues in professional development.

(7.3) Credit fully the work of others and refrain from taking undue credit.

(7.4) Review the work of others in an objective, candid, and properly-documented way.

(7.5) Give a fair hearing to the opinions, concerns, or complaints of a colleague.

(7.6) Assist colleagues in being fully aware of current standard work practices including policies and procedures for protecting passwords, files and other confidential information, and security measures in general.

(7.7) Not unfairly intervene in the career of any colleague; however, concern for the employer, the client or public interest may compel software engineers, in good faith, to question the competence of a colleague.

(7.8) In situations outside of their own areas of competence, call upon the opinions of other professionals who have competence in that area.

8. Self.
Software engineers shall participate in lifelong learning regarding the practice of their profession and shall promote an ethical approach to the practice of the profession. In particular, software engineers shall continually endeavor to:

(8.1) Further their knowledge of developments in the analysis, specification, design, development, maintenance and testing of software and related documents, together with the management of the development process.

(8.2) Improve their ability to create safe, reliable, and useful quality software at reasonable cost and within a reasonable time.

(8.3) Improve their ability to produce accurate, informative, and well-written documentation.

(8.4) Improve their understanding of the software and related documents on which they work and of the environment in which they will be used.

(8.5) Improve their knowledge of relevant standards and the law governing the software and related documents on which they work.

(8.6) Improve their knowledge of this Code, its interpretation, and its application to their work.

(8.7) Not give unfair treatment to anyone because of any irrelevant prejudices.

(8.8) Not influence others to undertake any action that involves a breach of this Code.

(8.9) Recognize that personal violations of this Code are inconsistent with being a professional software engineer.

This code seems easily the longest and most detailed of those presented in this chapter. The eight main Principles in the code are at a level similar to the Specific Professional Responsibilities in the ACM code or the standards of conduct in the AITP code, but each Principle in the Software Engineering code is accompanied by six to thirteen Clauses that elaborate on specific points. However, in the long version of the ACM code (see Appendix B), each item is accompanied by a paragraph of text which gives additional explanation. Including this additional text would make the ACM code similar in length to the Software Engineering code.

Now that you have read the AITP, ACM, and Software Engineering codes, a number of common themes should be clear. Some likely could have been anticipated before reading any of the codes; for example, duty to society. Others may be somewhat surprising; for example, commitment to continuing education or lifelong learning. This appears in the AITP standards under obligations to employer, in the ACM code as Specific Professional Responsibility 2.2 and in the Software Engineering code under Principle 8. Clearly the profession expects that you will continue to learn throughout your career.

The Software Engineering code also contains some other interesting points. Clause 1 of Principle 2 states: "Provide services in their areas of competence, being forthright about any limitations of their experience and education." On a related theme, Clause 4 of Principle 3 states: "Ensure that they are qualified for any project on which the work or propose to work, by an appropriate combination of education, training and experience." If taken seriously, these clauses may well suggest that software engineers specialize in certain types of applications and should not move arbitrarily between areas.

Clause 7 of Principle 6 of the Software Engineering code states: "Be accurate in stating the characteristics of software on which they work, avoiding not only false claims but also claims that might reasonably be supposed to be speculative, vacuous, deceptive, misleading or doubtful." Similar sentiments appear in the AITP and ACM codes. Imagine how this would change advertising about software!

3.4.1 SOFTWARE ENGINEERING AS A LICENSED PROFESSION

The approval of the Software Engineering Code of Ethics is the first in a sequence of steps that lead to "Software Engineering" being a licensed and regulated profession. It became clear that software engineering was destined to be a licensed profession when, in recent years, individual state governments moved toward licensing of software engineers. The worksheet at the end of this chapter dealing with the development of the Software Engineering code mentions the state of Texas as one example. Some people who currently practice (unlicensed, unregulated) software engineering feel that the introduction of licensing for software engineers will have no net beneficial effect on society. However, I tend to agree with those who feel that licensing is inevitable. And, licensing that is driven by the existing professional organizations is far preferable to licensing driven by state legislatures without input from the professional organizations.

The Software Engineering Code of Ethics clearly anticipates the introduction of licensing. Note the wording in the Preamble: "The Clauses of each Principle are illustrations of some of the obligations . . . The Code prescribes these as obligations of anyone claiming to be or aspiring to be a software engineer." This sounds as if the code is meant to apply to anyone who would want to use the title "software engineer." Note also the wording in Principle 1—"Approve software only if they have a well-founded belief that it is safe, meets specifications, passes appropriate tests, ..." This anticipates that licensed software engineers would have to approve specific elements of a software engineering project.

With IEEE-CS and ACM backing of the Software Engineering code, it is almost certain to be the code of ethics that applies to licensed software engineers. When will licensing of software engineers become a reality? This is a difficult question. This type of professional licensing is typically done individually by each state, and so it may be introduced at different times in different states. Licensing is likely to be introduced, at least for software engineers engaged in safety-critical applications, in major states within the next five years. To check on the current state of the joint IEEE-CS/ACM effort in this area, consult the site computer.org/tab/swecc.

3.5 THE IEEE CODE OF ETHICS

The *IEEE Code of Ethics* as set forth in the *IEEE Policy & Procedures Manual,* [3] consists of 10 points, with no ampli-fication or supplemental guidelines. Appendix B contains other sections of the manual with additional information related to ethical issues and IEEE policies, for those interested in examining the IEEE's position on these issues. The IEEE Code of Ethics is as follows.

We, the members of the IEEE, in recognition of the importance of our technologies in affecting the quality of life throughout the world, and in accepting a personal obligation to our profession, its members and the communities we serve, do hereby commit ourselves to conduct of the highest ethical and professional manner and agree:

1. to accept responsibility in making engineering decisions consistent with the safety, health, and welfare of the public, and to disclose promptly factors that might endanger the public or the environment;
2. to avoid real or perceived conflicts of interest whenever possible, and to disclose them to affected parties when they do exist;
3. to be honest and realistic in stating claims or estimates based on available data;
4. to reject bribery in all of its forms;
5. to improve understanding of technology; its appropriate application, and potential consequences;
6. to maintain and improve our technical competence and to undertake technological tasks for others only if qualified by training or experience, or after full disclosure of pertinent limitations;
7. to seek, accept, and offer honest criticism of technical work, to acknowledge and correct errors, and to credit properly the contributions of others;
8. to treat fairly all persons regardless of such factors as race, religion, gender, disability, age, or national origin;
9. to avoid injuring others, their property, reputation, or employment by false or malicious action;
10. to assist colleagues and co-workers in their professional development and to support them in following this code of ethics.

The IEEE code is by far the shortest of the ones we have considered. Even so, at a general level it covers much of the ground covered in the other codes. The IEEE is concerned with a number of engineering disciplines other than computing. As you might expect from this, one "problem" with the IEEE code in relation to computing professionals is the lack of computing-specific content. For example, there is nothing like the ACM code's statement to "access computing and communication resources only when authorized to do so." Nor is there anything like the AITP standard of conduct to "Protect the privacy and confidentiality of all information entrusted to me." And of course there is nothing so specific as the Software Engineering code's statement to "Treat all forms of software maintenance with the same professionalism as new development."

One way to gain perspective on the codes we have examined is to consider how they differ from codes in other professions. I selected two codes from other large and well-known professions. The American Medical Association's *Principles of Medical Ethics* has a long history, originating in the time of Hippocrates, a Greek physician in 377 B.C. [1]. The current code consists of seven basic principles and another six fundamental elements of the patient–physician relationship. The American Psychological Association's *Ethical Principles of Psychologists* [2] consists of 10 multipart principles. The following five points are worth examining for contrasts between the various codes of ethics.

1. **Implied limits to nondiscrimination?** General moral imperative 4 of the ACM code states "be fair and take action not to discriminate" and amplifies this (see Appendix B) with "discrimination on the basis of race, sex, religion, age, disability, national origin, or other such factors is an explicit violation of ACM policy and will not be tolerated." Item 8 of the IEEE code states "to treat fairly all persons regardless of such factors as race, religion, gender, disability, age or national origin." Clause 7 of Principle 8 of the Software Engineering code states—"Not give unfair treatment to anyone because of irrelevant prejudices." Compare these with Part B of Principle 3 in the APA code of ethics—"As employees or employers, psychologists do not engage in or condone practices that are inhumane or that result in illegal or unjustifiable actions. Such practices include, but are not limited to, those based on considerations of race, handicap, age, gender, sexual preference, religion, or national origin in hiring, promotion or training." The difference in wording is small but clear. The APA wording includes the phrase "sexual preference." The codes we have examined do not include any similar explicit phrase. The IEEE code gives a list of categories for nondiscrimination, but does include anything that might be interpreted to include "sexual preference." The "other such factors" wording in the ACM code, and the "any irrelevant prejudices" wording in the Software Engineering code can be ambiguous. Different people might reasonably interpret the wording differently. The AITP code is not really explicit about this issue.

The issue of discrimination on the basis of sexual "preference" or "orientation" is currently a topic of heated debate in our society. Accusations of "special rights for sodomites" and "genocide" are actually some of the more polite things the two sides have said to one another. It is clear from the voting results for laws and ordinances around the country that our society has not reached any consensus and that this debate will continue for some time.

A specific issue to consider here is that the APA code of ethics explicitly says it would be unethical for someone to be fired solely because that person's supervisor or colleagues do not approve of their sexual preference. The AITP, ACM, Software Engineering, and IEEE codes do not. Which is the more appropriate moral stance? Does saying that someone can't be fired for something necessarily imply that society "approves of" the behavior? Should *any* behavior or belief that does not directly impact job performance be protected?

2. **Duty to work to correct laws that are wrong?** The APA and AMA codes suggest that at times people must work for change in the status quo of society. Part d of principle 3 of the APA code states, in part, that "both practitioners and researchers are concerned with the development of such legal and quasi-legal regulations as best serve the public interest, and they work toward changing existing regulations that are not beneficial to the public interest." Principle 3 of the AMA code states "a physician shall respect the law and also recognize a responsibility to seek changes in those requirements which are contrary to the best interests of the patient." The ACM code touches on this topic in its explanation of professional responsibility 2.3 (see Appendix B), where it says ". . . compliance must be balanced with the recognition that sometimes existing laws and rules may be immoral or inappropriate and, therefore, must be challenged." The AITP, Software Engineering and IEEE codes are silent on this issue.

Why do you think the codes differ this way? Consider the existing laws in some areas where computing professionals should have special responsibility; areas such as privacy, communications, encryption, and intellectual property. Can you think of points that computing professionals should work toward improving? If your answer is currently "no," hopefully it will be "yes" before you have finished this text!

3. **Duty to be charitable?** The AMA and APA codes appear to try to convey a greater sense of social and community responsibility than do the ACM, IEEE, and Software Engineering codes. Principle 7 of the AMA code states "a physician shall recognize a responsibility to participate in activities contributing to an improved community." Part d of principle 6 of the APA code states, in part, that psychologists "contribute a portion of their services to work for which they receive little or no financial return."

The ACM, IEEE, and Software Engineering codes are of course centrally concerned with public safety. However, they do not give such specific direction to take actions that benefit those less fortunate and that improve the community as a whole. Clause 8 of Principle 1 of the Software Engineering code is the only thing that comes close to making such a statement: "Be encouraged to volunteer professional skills to good causes and to contribute to public education concerning the discipline." But compare this to the quotes from the AMA and APA codes given above, and to this quote from Professional Obligation 2a of the NSPE code: "Engineers shall seek opportunities to be of constructive service in civic affairs and work for the advancement of the safety, health and well-being of their community."

This omission in the AITP, ACM, and IEEE codes seems rather unfortunate. It can re-reinforce the negative stereotype of "computer people" being concerned with machines and money, but not with people. Certainly people in computing professions can afford to be concerned about, and give to, their communities. This is borne out in the salaries of graduates in the computing disciplines. Many have a starting salary in their first professional job that is greater than the median family income in our country. Think about it—at the beginning of your career, you, one person, will likely have an income larger than that of half the families in the United States.

What do you think is the source of this difference among codes? Might things be different if computing professionals typically dealt with individuals, rather than companies, as clients? What kind of "activities contributing to an improved community" would be natural for computing professionals to participate in?

4. **Duty to police the profession for incompetence?** The AMA code takes a strong position on policing incompetence in the profession. Principle 2 of the AMA code states, in part, that physicians should ". . . strive to expose those physicians deficient in character or competence, or who engage in fraud or deception." The AITP standards of conduct contain something similar but perhaps not as strongly worded: "Take appropriate action in regard to any illegal or unethical practices that come to my attention. However, I will bring charges against any person only when I have reasonable basis for believing in the truth of the allegations and without any regard to personal interest." There is nothing that addresses a similar issue quite so strongly in the ACM, IEEE or Software Engineering codes. Clause 7 of Principle 7 of the Software Engineering code does state: "Not unfairly intervene in the career of any colleague; however, concern for the employer, the client or public interest may compel software engineers, in good faith, to question the competence of a colleague." But this statement is clearly weaker than that in the AMA or AITP codes. It is also much weaker that the corresponding statement in Professional Obligation 8 of the NSPE code: "Engineers who believe others are guilty of unethical or illegal practice shall present such information to the proper authority for action."

Again, what do you think is the source of this difference between the codes? Is there any reason to think that incompetence, fraud, or deception are any less of a problem in computing than they are in medicine? Should the ACM, IEEE, and Software Engineering codes be more vocal on

this point? What exactly should it mean to "expose" those who are incompetent, fraudulent, or deceptive?

5. **Duty not to lend credence to misinformation?** The APA code takes a strong position in this area. Part a of principle 1 states, in part, that psychologists should ". . . plan their research in ways to minimize the possibility that their findings will be misleading . . . ." Part d states that "psychologists have the responsibility to attempt to prevent distortion, misuse, or suppression of psychological findings by the institution or agency of which they are employees." Relevant analogies to these points could be made in the computing profession. Certainly statistical and simulation results of "computer studies that show that X will happen" are often misused or interpreted in incorrect or misleading ways.

Why do the codes dealing with the computing profession not deal directly with this issue? How much responsibility should computing professionals have to prevent misuse of their work?

3.7 PROBLEMS WITH CODES OF ETHICS

We have seen why we cannot count on the legal system to be a complete and correct guide to moral behavior, either for us as individuals in society or as members of a profession. Nor can we expect the professional codes of ethics to be complete, consistent, and correct for all situations. Moreover, the codes of ethics included here are mostly voluntary, in the sense that there is no formal monitoring for compliance and little penalty that can be assessed against violators.

In other words, a person can examine the code and, finding that a certain behavior is not explicitly prohibited, rationalize that the behavior is okay. In addition, a person will eventually encounter situations for which the code makes no explicit recommendations. Even worse, the recommendations of the code may turn out to be inconsistent and conflicting, leaving you to agonize over having no good option.

Codes of ethics suffer the same fundamental problem as ethical theories—goodness cannot be defined through a legalistic enumeration of do-s and don't-s, it must come from the heart. Thus, you must be able to use your internal sense of ethics to fill the holes and resolve the inevitable conflicts. It is my hope that the material in this text will help you develop, refine, and elaborate your internal moral sense.

3.8 CASE STUDY

The description of this incident is drawn from from news accounts [5], [7], [8]. The dominant theme in this incident is conflict of interest. Related secondary themes are greed, plagiarism, bribes, fraud, and whistle blowing. There is also perhaps a less obvious element of poor management oversight. There is not enough space here to reprint the specific codes of ethics for all of the participants in the incident (government employees, university professors, and so on), but try to identify the elements of the codes covered in this chapter that would apply to the actions of the people involved in this incident.

3.8.1 The Cast of Characters

The University of Tennessee Space Institute is located in Tullahoma, Tennessee. It is a state-supported university that specializes in graduate instruction and research.

The U.S. Army Missile and Space Intelligence Center is located in Huntsville, Alabama. Employees at MSIC are able to enroll in graduate programs at UTSI.

The NASA Marshall Space Flight Center is also located in Huntsville, Alabama. Employees at Marshall are also able to enroll in graduate programs at UTSI.

FWG Associates was a private, for-profit company located in Tullahoma. FWG would receive contracts from a variety of government agencies, including MSIC and Marshall.

Walter Frost was a professor at UTSI. One role of a professor is to supervise and mentor graduate students. Another is to bring in contracts and grants that can help support graduate students and research activities. Separate from his job as a professor, Frost founded FWG Associates. FWG made money, so Frost made money by receiving contracts in the same technical area that he worked in as a professor at UTSI.

Dennis Faulkner is a civilian employee at MSIC. One element of his job was to participate in the awarding of contracts to people doing work for the U.S. Army. Earning a graduate degree in a technical area related to his job could be an important element of career advancement for Faulkner.

Peggy Potter is a civilian employee at Marshall. Similar to Faulkner, an element of her job was to participate in the awarding of contracts to people doing work for NASA. Also like Faulkner, she would like to earn a graduate degree to boost her career.

The anonymous whistle blower is a former student at UTSI who was also an employee at FWG.

3.8.2 The Sequence of Events

Walter Frost began work at UTSI in the 1970s. He was apparently quite good at his specialty and developed into something of a star in his field. He supervised a large number of graduate students at UTSI. He was also the principal investigator for a number of grants and contracts awarded to UTSI from from various agencies. Somewhere

along the way he started his own private, for-profit company. FWG Associates then began to receive contracts from agencies for the same type of work that previously might have been done under a contract to UTSI.

Dennis Faulkner enrolled in the graduate program at UTSI. Frost became the faculty supervisor for Faulkner's PhD. Faulkner participated in the awarding of a contract to FWG Associates. Frost provided Faulkner with a technical report that was already completed and allowed or encouraged Faulkner to use the technical report as the basis for Faulkner's doctoral dissertation. Faulkner received his PhD from UTSI in 1990.

Peggy Potter enrolled in the graduate program at UTSI. Frost became the faculty supervisor for Potter's MS. Potter participated in the awarding of a contract to FWG Associates. Frost provided Potter with a technical report and allowed or encouraged Potter to use the technical report as the basis for her research report for her master's thesis. Potter received an MS from UTSI.

[More people may have played roles essentially identical to those of Faulkner and Potter, but a complete listing of them is not essential to the story.]

At some point, a former student at UTSI and an employee at FWG became aware of the similarity between a technical report prepared by Frost and the master's thesis of one of Frost's students. The UTSI administration was notified. An investigation ensued.

Walter Frost took early retirement from UTSI in February 1991. Various contracts to Frost's firm were canceled and others reviewed. NASA demoted Peggy Potter, cut her $55,000 salary by $18,000, and had her pay back the money that NASA had spent for her course work. UTSI took back the degrees of both Faulkner and Potter. Faulkner's appeal process is still in the courts, but has so far been unsuccessful and appears unlikely to succeed. The incident caused NASA to subpoena documents on 80 students who had Frost as their research adviser. Criminal indictments were made against Frost and another faculty member, and against Potter, Faulkner, and two other students.

3.8.3 Conclusions and Questions

The most obvious "bad guy" in the story would appear to be Walter Frost. Founding a for-profit company to accept contracts in the same technical area as his research work for UTSI guaranteed conflicts of interest.

Perhaps this sort of conflict-of-interest situation "happens all the time." If the people involved have strong moral convictions and the institutions involved have clear and well-enforced guidelines, then such situations might operate without the people involved straying outside the boundaries of ethical behavior. That is, people might handle each of their multiple roles in an ethical fashion. But this is asking human beings to be essentially perfect in resisting temptation. In this instance, the people and institutions involved obviously did not handle the conflicts of interest well. It was clearly unethical for Frost to provide students with already completed research reports to reuse and submit as their own. This, by itself, was "only" an incident of conspiring in an act of plagiarism. However, that it was done with people who were in the position of influencing awards to his company has at least the appearance of bribery. Knowing that plagiarism was involved in the acquisition of a degree also becomes a sort of fraud on UTSI and the agencies for which the students worked.

All the blame cannot be placed on Frost alone, however. Faulkner and Potter were capable professionals. Having a major professor at the university whose contracts might pass through their hands at the office clearly had potential for conflict of interest. Faulkner and Potter certainly must have known that copying an existing technical report and presenting it as their research was wrong. They apparently rationalized it as being okay because Frost approved of it, but their clear motive was to get a degree. It is less clear as to whether they sought Frost as an adviser because such an arrangement would then have been possible.

The problems at UTSI and the government agencies are perhaps less obvious, but still should be considered. The potential conflicts of interest involved with Frost's company should have caused administrators on all sides to exercise extra care in avoiding exactly the problems that arose. UTSI, like all universities, should have a policy against professors supervising the work of students with whom they have a business relationship. Marshall and MSIC should have similar policies from their side.

3.8.4 Connections to the Codes of Ethics

One of the AITP standards of conduct in relation to your employer is "avoid conflict of interest and insure that my employer is aware of any potential conflicts." Also, item 4.5 of the Software Engineering code states "disclose to all concerned parties those conflicts of interest that cannot reasonably be avoided or escaped." We can interpret these statements to mean that Frost should disclose to the university and to the other faculty on the MS/PhD committees that the student was a manager of one of his contracts. For the students, it would have meant disclosing to their employer that Frost was supervising their graduate degree.

One of the AITP standards of conduct in relation to fellow members and the profession is "not use or take credit for the work of others without specific acknowledgment and authorization." Item 1.6 of the ACM code states "give proper credit for intellectual property." Item 7.3 of the Software Engineering code states "credit fully the work of others and refrain from taking undue credit." Item 7 of the IEEE code states "to credit properly the contributions of others." Each of these statements provides some warning against the sort of plagiarism allegedly involved in this incident.

No doubt you can identify additional elements of the different codes of ethics that would be relevant to this incident.

Points to Remember

- Each major professional organization in the computing field (AITP, ACM, and IEEE) has its own published code of ethics.
- While the codes we considered have differences in presentation and emphasis, they are in broad agreement on general principles.
- The general principles underlying most ethical dilemmas that you will confront in your career are addressed in the codes.
- Professional codes cannot be counted on for detailed and consistent guidance in all possible situations. You must have your own strong inner sense of what is moral to be able to apply the general principles in specific situations.

WORKSHEET—What Guidance Do the Codes of Ethics Give You?

Return to the "pornography on the dean's PC" case study analyzed in Chapter Two. Focus again on the role of the technician. Consider what guidance the technician might have gotten from the codes covered in this chapter.

1. What items of the AITP code and standards of conduct argue against reporting the existence of the pornography? What items argue for reporting the existence of the pornography?

2. How does the ACM code argue for or against reporting the pornography?

3. How does the Software Engineering code argue for or against reporting?

4. Does the IEEE code provide any basis for arguing either way? If so, what is it?

5. What does this situation with the various codes mean with respect to how an individual can depend on the codes for guidance? Can you locate a paragraph in the preamble to the Software Engineering Code of Ethics that addresses this point?

WORKSHEET—What Guidance Do the Codes of Ethics Give You?

1. What guidance does each of the codes of ethics give you as to your ethical responsibilities in each of the following situations? What would you actually do if this happened to you?

2. You realize that your company has intentionally underestimated the cost of a project in hopes of getting the contract.

3. You have watched your boss take an employment application from a minority applicant and then throw it in the trash after the applicant leaves.

4. You have been told to sign off on the testing phase of the software project because your group is already a week behind schedule, but you haven't tested the software as called for in the specifications.

5. You have been "asked" by your boss to contribute $2,000 to a particular political candidate and told that the company will be keeping track of all employees who make such contributions and giving $2,000 bonuses to each person.

6. A coworker has been fired essentially because her political views were very different from those of the boss, and the person is now suing the company. You have been asked to make a signed written statement about "any and all incidents of poor work habits and poor quality work you may have observed" with regard to this person.

WORKSHEET—Designing the Software Engineering Code of Ethics

Read Don Gotterbarn's reprinted article, "The Ethical Software Engineer," in which he outlines the process behind the development of the IEEE-CS/ACM Software Engineering Code of Ethics. Then answer the following questions.

1. Do you find it unusual that the state of Texas would license software engineers without reference to any code of ethics? What problems could this cause?

2. What are some of the "external pressures not to follow these guidelines" that you expect to encounter in your career?

3. "Ethical tensions can best be addressed through thoughtful consideration of fundamental principles, rather than blind reliance on detailed regulations." Do you agree? Why or why not? When confronted with an ethically difficult situation, are you likely to have time for "thoughtful consideration?"

4. Gotterbarn says that "several large software companies have posted the code as an expected standard of conduct for their employees." Identify some common practices in the software industry that would seem to be in violation of this code. What do you think would happen if an employee were to speak up against these practices?

WORKSHEET—How Should Licensing Boards Support the Public Welfare?

The codes of ethics give primary emphasis to protecting the public welfare. Engineers who conscientiously follow the codes to protect the public welfare may face retaliation from their employer. Those who are unfairly fired may sue in civil court for "wrongful discharge." Walter Elden's article, which follows this worksheet refers to the BART whistle-blowing incident that is an example of this. The incident is also discussed in the whistle-blowing chapter.

Keep in mind that software engineers will likely soon be licensed professionals, and that the licensing may reference the Software Engineering code of ethics. Walter Elden suggests that licensing boards should provide "friend of the court" statements in cases where an employee faces retaliation as a result of following their code of ethics. Read Elden's reprinted article carefully and answer the following questions.

1. What is the sequence of basic premises in Elden's argument?

2. Do you agree with Elden's conclusion? Why/Why not?

3. Why do you think the IEEE provided only one amicus curiae statement in the last 25 years?

4. Why do you think state professional engineering boards have not provided amicus curiae statements more often in court cases?

5. What do you think of the P.E. board official's distinction between "protecting the engineer" and "protecting the public?"

WORKSHEET—What Ethics Help Should a Society Provide Its Members?

The IEEE has a checkered history of providing ethics-related support to engineers who find themselves in trouble with their employers. One high point came when IEEE provided a "friend of the court" statement in the BART whistle-blowing case. This is referred to in the previous worksheet and in the whistle-blowing chapter. However, this seems to be the only instance in which IEEE has provided such a statement. Another high point came when IEEE initiated a volunteer-staffed telephone hot line which members could use to discuss ethics-related problems. However, this hot line was discontinued not long after it was initiated. Stephen Unger's article, reprinted later in this chapter, briefly mentions the hot line. Read Unger's article and answer the following questions.

1. List some of the types of ethics-related help that a professional society could provide its members (telephone hot line, contacts with others in similar situations, friend of the court statements, etc.).

2. Prioritize the types of help listed in the previous question from most valuable to least valuable for the member.

3. Prioritize the types of help listed above from most valuable expensive to least expensive to provide.

4. Based on the combination of priorities, what sorts of help do you think societies like the AITP, ACM, and IEEE should be providing to their members?

(*Note:* for a current "Online Ethics Center Help-Line" see http://onlineethics.org/helpline/)

1. **Something that should not be in the IEEE Code of Ethics?** Unger [6] describes his concerns over item 9 of the IEEE code, which requires members ". . . to avoid injuring others, their property, reputation, or employment by false or malicious action . . ." According to Unger, "the motivation for the provision was to fashion a weapon for use against a well-known member who frequently attacked fellow members, officers, and IEEE staff members, often in a malicious manner—sometimes falsely. Indeed, after passage of the new rule, it was used against that member in the first case in which an IEEE member was formally censured. That member is now deceased, but the rule remains, perhaps to deter some who might otherwise behave maliciously. It is also likely to silence others with legitimate complaints against those in positions of power" [6]. Look more closely into this incident and consider more carefully Unger's objections to this element of the IEEE code. Would you keep this element of the code or remove it? Why?

2. **Evolution of the ACM code.** Look up the previous code of ethics for the Association for Computing Machinery and compare it with the current ACM code. Identify specific changes in the new code and give arguments for why the changes were needed or why they should not have been made.

REFERENCES

[1] *Code of medical ethics: current opinions,* American Medical Association, 1992, 515 North State Street, Chicago, IL 60610.

[2] Ethical principles of psychologists, *American Psychologist,* March 1990, pp. 390–395.

[3] *IEEE Policy and Procedures Manual,* The Institute of Electrical and Electronics Engineers (IEEE), January 1992, 345 East 47th Street, New York, 10017-2394.

[4] H. C. Luegenbiehl, Computer professionals: moral autonomy and a code of ethics, *Journal of Systems and Software,* volume 17, 1992, pp. 61–68.

[5] K. Sawyer, "Amid scandal, NASA studies integrity of degrees awarded to its employees," *The Washington Post,* July 22, 1991.

[6] S. Unger, *Controlling Technology: Ethics and the Responsible Engineer.* John Wiley & Sons, New York, 1984 (second edition).

[7] "A professor swapped degrees for contract, university suspects," *The Wall Street Journal,* July 12, 1991.

[8] "NASA employee accused of plagiarism," *The Washington Times,* April 1, 1992.

ethics

The ethical software engineer

BY DON GOTTERBARN
ACM Ethics Committee Chairman

The Association for Computing Machinery (ACM) and the IEEE Computer Society have adopted the Software Engineering Code of Ethics and Professional Practice (5.2). This is significant, given that the state of Texas has already licensed software engineers without defining any standard of ethical practice. This oversight is dangerous for two reasons. First, licensed software engineers will obey the law, but laws provide inadequate guidance in many critical situations. And second, the failure to connect specific ethical standards to licensing encourages the mistaken view that there is little agreement among software engineers about their professional and moral obligations. The code's development, however, indicates a significant agreement among software engineers about the way they ought to behave.

The code also provides mechanisms to help practitioners make ethical judgments in those situations where the law is silent.

Don Gotterbarn

The code was developed by the joint IEEE-CS/ACM task force on Software Engineering Ethics and Professional Practice (SEEPP). The SEEPP task force is multinational in citizenship and in membership in professional computing organizations. After extensive study of several codes of ethics of computing societies, engineering societies and other professions, SEEPP selected imperatives for the draft code. SEEPP also contributed new imperatives related to its knowledge of software engineering and based on external reviewers' suggestions.

The draft code was reviewed by members of several professional computing societies and went through several revisions. Version 3 appeared with a turnaround ballot in the IEEE-CS's and the ACM's flagship magazines. Most clauses received better than a 90 percent approval rating. Contributed comments led to the development of Version 4 which SEEPP submitted for peer review using the IEEE's formal technical standard review process. Again, the code easily passed this process. Comments were used to develop the final version of the code (www-cs.etsu.edu/seeri/secode.htm) which was approved by the ACM in November and the IEEE-CS in December.

I found the consistently high level of agreement about the behavior expected of a professional software engineer very significant. There is general agreement about our obligations as software engineers, even if some software engineers give in to external pressures not to follow these obligations.

The code aids decision making by overcoming two difficulties with other codes. First, most codes of ethics provide a finite list of principles which are often presented as a complete list and the reader presumes that only things on the list should be of ethical concern for the professional. Second, many codes provide no guidance for situations where rules, having equal priority, appear to conflict. This equal priority leaves the ethical decision maker confused. The software engineering code addresses both of these limitations.

The code explicitly rejects the concept of completeness.

"It is not intended that the individual parts of the Code be used in isolation to justify errors of omission or commission. The list of Principles and Clauses is not exhaustive. The Clauses should not be read as separating the acceptable from the unacceptable in professional conduct in all practical situations. The Code is not a simple ethical algorithm which generates ethical decisions."

The code addresses completeness by providing general guidance for ethical decision making, especially in those areas not explicitly mentioned in the code.

"Ethical tensions can best be addressed by thoughtful consideration of fundamental principles, rather than blind reliance on detailed regulations. These Principles should influence software engineers to consider broadly who is affected by their work; to examine if they and their colleagues are treating other human beings with due respect; to consider how the public, if reasonably well informed, would view their decisions; to analyze how the least empowered will be affected by their decisions; and to consider whether their acts would be judged worthy of the ideal professional working as a software engineer. In all these judgments, concern for the health, safety and welfare of the public is primary; that is, the "Public Interest" is central to this Code."

The first principle asks the developer to consider all stakeholders, not just the software engineer's employer or client. The second principle—due respect—requires a protection of human values. This section states that in all decisions the public interest is the primary concern.

To reinforce the priority of public well-being, the code asserts the priority of concern for the public over loyalty to the employer or profession. It is a professional's obligation to take positive action to address violations of the code. The code addresses both the responsibilities of the practicing professional and of the profession. Several large software companies have posted the code as an expected standard for their employees. Its adoption by two large computing organizations is a positive step because this code is not designed to be self-serving to the profession. The code requires software engineering professionals to be ethically responsible to all of those who are affected by their products.

The IEEE Ethics Committee maintains a Web site at "www.ieee.org/committee/ethics". The author can be reached via e-mail at "gotterbarn@ Access.ETSU.edu".

Reprinted from *IEEE Institute*, February 1999.

Why A State Professional Engineering Board Should Enter an *Amicus Curiae* Brief in a "Wrongful Discharge" Case

WALTER L. ELDEN, P.E. (RETIRED)
w.elden@ieee.org

Synopsis

This paper presents a strong argument as to why, in cases where a terminated licensed Professional Engineer alleges "wrongful discharge" in a suit against a former employer, his/her State or National P.E. Licensed Board should enter an *amicus curiae* (friend of the court) legal brief in the case. The basic premise is the obligation of the P.E. Board to "protect the public," and not necessarily the P.E. directly. The author shows, however, that by a P.E. Board taking such pro-active legal action, the result is the protection of the proper practice of engineering, thus "protecting the public," with an indirect benefit to the P.E.

Wrongful Discharge for Upholding Code of Ethics

The IEEE Member Conduct and Ethics Committees are seeing increasing requests from IEEE members for "ethical support" by having the MCC recommending to the IEEE Executive Committee that IEEE should enter an Amicus Curiae in suits the engineer has brought against a former employer, for alleged "wrongful discharge." This termination generally has resulted from the engineer engaging in actions aimed at "protecting the public" from the improper application of engineering design or technology, by following his/her professional society's Code of Ethics. Some of these members are also licensed Professional Engineers, having been licensed by his/her public Board of P.E. Regulation to "protect the public" from the improper practice of engineering.

IEEE Ethical Support and Amicus Curiae Policies

The IEEE, under By-Law 112, has had a policy for nearly 20 years to offer "ethical support" in situations as described above. Further, as part of this policy, the IEEE provides for the providing of an amicus curiae statement, restricting it to matters of ethical principal, in ethical support requests. Policy 7.13 provides for the preparation of the Amicus Curiae, when approved by the IEEE.

In January 1975, the IEEE entered its first and only Amicus Curiae, in a "wrongful discharge" ethics matter, in the Bay Area Rapid Transit (BART) case. This involved 3 IEEE engineers, who brought suit against the BART District entity for their "wrongful discharge" for actions they took to "protect the public" in matters of engineering design of the automated train control system. Essentially, the IEEE legal brief made these statements of law to the court, in this case:

"In any charge to the jury herein, this court should instruct the jury that if it finds, based upon the evidence, that an engineer has been discharged solely or in substantial part because of his bona fide efforts to conform to recognized ethics of his profession involving his duty to protect the public safety, then such discharge was in breach of an implied term of his contract of employment."

The IEEE brief said that not only should this apply to Public employment bodies, but to private employers too.

What About National/State P.E. Licensing Boards?

Above, we have seen where the IEEE, as a leading international engineering professional society, has had as its policy for the past nearly 20 years, to offer "ethical support" and an amicus curiae to engineers who request it in alleged "wrongful discharge" court cases. It was shown that in 1975, the IEEE did in fact enter one in the BART case. Now, what about National/State P.E. Licensing Boards? What is their policy and history in similar cases to offer Amicus Curiae legal briefs in suits brought by their P.E.s to correct "wrongful discharge" treatment?

The author recently conducted a survey of all State P.E. Boards in the USA which had E-Mail addresses listed for them, asking if they had ever been requested to or actually did enter an Amicus Curiae in alleged "wrongful discharge" cases, involving licensed P.E.s. Many replies were received from these contacted P.E. Boards. Of those who responded, there was not one which had ever entered an Amicus Curiae in such cases. Several contacted their State Attorney General's office to have research done to find out the answer to this question.

One reply was found to be of particular interest to the author. This P.E. Board official who responded offered that in their opinion, "it was not the purpose of the State P.E. Board to protect the P.E. but rather to 'protect the public,' " and therefore, it did not deem it appropriate for them to enter an Amicus Curiae in such cases brought by the P.E. licensed by their Board.

After giving this considerable thought, the author responded with the following argument:

The State P.E. Board licenses an engineer as a P.E. to "protect the public." The P.E. is held legally accountable to know the P.E. law, its Code of Professional Conduct, and to practice in accordance with such Code, to "protect the public." Further, if the P.E.'s actions happen to result in being in conflict with the P.E. law or its Code of Professional Conduct, the State may bring charges against the P.E. and discipline him/her. This is done for the sole purpose of "protecting the public" from the improper practice of engineering.

Now, when a circumstance occurs when a P.E. is terminated from employment (alleged "wrongful discharge") for practicing in accordance with his/her State P.E. law or Code of Professional Conduct, and brings suit against the former employer, why shouldn't the State P.E. Board enter an Amicus Curiae legal brief in this case, to advise the court that such actions of the P.E. as alleged, if provable, were done for the purpose of "protecting the public" and as such, the proper and ethical

practice of engineering by a P.E. should be afforded the protection of the law, in order that the proper practice of engineering be enforced, to "protect the public." The reasoning here is the view that by protecting the proper practice of engineering by a licensed P.E., this action would result directly in the State P.E. Board and the court acting to "protecting the public." It is true, that by taking such protective actions, the court and the P.E. Board's actions may benefit the P.E. in a favorable outcome of his/her suit. But this would not be the primary reason for the P.E. Board or the court to take such action.

After this argument was conveyed to the State P.E. Board official, the author, as yet, has not received a reply to this argument.

CONCLUSION

While the IEEE had had for nearly 20 years a policy to enter an *amicus curiae* in alleged "wrongful discharge" cases, the current practice of State P.E. Licensing Boards in the USA appears not to be the same. By entering such legal briefs in this type of case, however, it has been argued by the author that this would in fact result in the P.E. Board and the court acting to uphold the proper practice of engineering, and thus "protecting the public." The end result here is that National and State P.E. Licensing Boards ought to rethink their practice in this area and move towards a more pro-active position of applying legal protections to the practice of engineering, thus achieving the sole purpose for such regulatory Boards, that being to "protect the public."

Stephen H. Unger

Ethics is a difficult subject to discuss; putting ethics into action can be even more difficult. Everyone is "for" ethics, but tempers often flare when one gets down to the details of what this really means - just the opposite of what well-meaning people intend.

In spite of its complexity and provocative nature, it would seem that this is an era of increased interest in professional ethics. ABET 2000 - the new undergraduate engineering program accreditation criteria - places a renewed emphasis on exposing engineering students to professional ethics. The emergence and growth of the Ethics Officer Association indicates an increased corporate interest in professional ethics. The IEEE Spectrum has recently published two roundtable discussions of engineering ethics (in June 1998 and December 1996).

Steve Unger is one of the founders of SSIT and has remained active in SSIT over the past decades. In addition to his SSIT efforts, Dr. Unger has worked diligently to make and keep IEEE the foremost champion of ethical practice of all the engineering professional societies. He played a principal role in the development of the first IEEE Ethics Code and participated in the revision of this code in the 1990s. His other activities in the ethics support area are detailed in his essay.

Dr. Unger believes that recent actions taken by the IEEE have undone most of the significant progress made over the past four years in developing mechanisms to support the ethical practice of engineering. He presents and defends his position below. We invite other IEEE members to comment on Dr. Unger's essay and to express their own views

We believe that ethical professional practice is a significant topic that is of great interest to most SSIT members. We hope that T&S can contribute modestly to generating a fruitful discourse about what the role of the IEEE should be in supporting ethical conduct of its members.

-Bob Whelchel

T&S Editor

Stephen H. Unger is Chair of the IEEE-SSIT Ethics Committee and was Chair of the IEEE Ethics Committee in 1997 and 1998. He is with the Computer Science Department at Columbia University, New York, NY. Email: s.unger@ieee.org.

The Assault on IEEE Ethics Support

As a life fellow of the IEEE, I am deeply concerned over a number of recent events that I feel have had a devastating effect on IEEE ethics related activities.

1) The IEEE Executive Committee (ExCom) terminated the Ethics Hotline on what appear to be unsubstantiated grounds. This was done without giving the Ethics Committee (EC) a chance to present its case. The ExCom rejected out of hand the clear recommendation of its own specially appointed task force to re-instate the Hotline.

2) After having just been re-elected by the IEEE Board of Directors (BoD) as EC chair, I was not permitted to remain in the room while the IEEE attorney presented his opinions on this matter to the ExCom.

3) I was amazed to be told that the report of the task force, which certainly does not contain any confidential information, will not be released to anybody - my requests for a copy have been to no avail.

I believe that the effect of these events has been the termination of an activity of great value to the IEEE, to its members, to our profession as a whole, to reputable employers of engineers, and to the general public. What follows is an account of what happened, along with my reasons for feeling that the ExCom's actions in the ethics area are misguided.

ORIGINS OF IEEE ETHICS ACTIVITY

The event (around 1972) that motivated IEEE members to demand that the IEEE set up ethics support machinery was the Bay Area Rapid Transit System (BART) case. Three IEEE members working on the development of BART encountered a variety of unsafe and otherwise improper practices on the job. When their efforts to resolve these problems via the normal management chain were repeatedly brushed aside, they took the matter to the BART Board of Directors. Their concerns were rejected and, soon afterward, they were peremptorily fired. Subsequent investigations by various groups, fully validated the points they had made.

This led to calls for the IEEE to intervene on their behalf, and to set up mechanisms for dealing with such cases in the future. One result was an important amicus curiae brief entered by the IEEE in support of

Reprinted from *IEEE Technology and Society*, Vol. 18, No. 1, pp. 36–40, Spring 1999.

the BART engineers' wrongful discharge suit (which is credited with having precipitated an out-of-court settlement). A few years later, the Member Conduct Committee (MCC) was established, with the dual roles of initiating disciplinary proceedings against IEEE members who behave improperly, and of investigating and recommending support for IEEE members who have been punished because of their efforts to adhere to the ethics code.

Shortly after its formation in 1978, the MCC recommended support in the Virginia Edgerton case, which involved computers and New York City's 911 system. Subsequently, probably as a result of an almost complete lack of publicity about the existence of the MCC support function, this mechanism was almost dormant for 18 years. (The disciplinary function was exercised just once during this period.)

EARLY 90S

In the early 90s, the IEEE United States Activities Board Ethics Committee (USAB-EC) developed a program for enhancing IEEE ethics support activity. Consistent with repeated recommendations made by MCC review committees, the USAB-EC called for an ongoing effort to inform IEEE members about the existence of the IEEE Ethics Code and of the mechanisms for supporting it. The overwhelming majority of IEEE members were, at that time, unaware of the existence of either of these. The committee passed a resolution, subsequently endorsed by USAB, calling for a number of measures to strengthen ethics support, including the establishment of a hotline to provide ethics advice and of a support fund to provide financial assistance to those whom the MCC deemed worthy of support because of ethical stances that they had taken. This resolution was brought to the IEEE BoD. Over a two year period, the matter was reviewed extensively by the BoD, which appointed an ad hoc committee to study the proposals. This committee ultimately recommended that the IEEE proceed along the lines of the USAB resolution. In November of 1994, the BoD endorsed the report of its committee, which included the idea of distributing copies of the Ethics Code to members with their membership cards, having articles on ethics published regularly in the Institute or Spectrum, developing an ethics hotline, and developing an ethics support fund. At its January 1995 meeting, the Board voted to establish its own ethics committee (the USAB committee was terminated) to develop mechanisms for implementing the proposals.

WORK OF THE ETHICS COMMITTEE

The accomplishments of the IEEE Ethics Committee (EC) during its initial three years of operation included implementation of the distribution to members of the ethics code on an annual basis, establish-

Guide to Acronyms Used in this Article

This essay of necessity uses many acronyms. In order to help you keep track of who's who, we include this guide. Consult the essay for clarification and further details.

IEEE entities:
    BoD: Board of Directors
    EC: (IEEE) Ethics Committee
    ExCom: Executive Committee
    IC: Insurance Committee
    MCC: Member Conduct Committee
    USAB-EC: United States Activities Board
                    Ethics Committee

Other entities:
    AAUP: American Association of University
                    Professors
    ACLU: American Civil Liberties Union
    AICPA: American Institute of Certified Public
                    Accountants
    EOA: Ethics Officer Association

ment of a bimonthly ethics column in the Institute, and the development and promulgation of a set of guidelines to assist engineers (this term is intended to include all technical professionals in the areas encompassed by the IEEE) in handling ethics related disputes in a constructive manner. The internet was utilized to establish an EC web site (http://www.ieee.org/committee/ethics) and several on-line forums for discussing ethics related issues. A beginning was made on a project to develop a set of guidelines to supplement the ethics code.

Advice and information was supplied to various people both at universities and in industry who were preparing courses or presentations on engineering ethics. More recently, the EC established contact with the Ethics Officer Association (EOA), a group sponsored by industry and comprised of ethics officers of large corporations. Our objective is to find ways in which we can cooperate with the EOA in promoting and encouraging ethical behavior by engineers in industry and to explore the establishments of mechanisms for resolving problems in a cooperative, constructive manner.

A major EC activity was the development of a plan for operating an ethics hotline to provide advice and information for engineers faced with difficult ethics related situations. It was approved by the BoD in November 1995 and went into operation in August 1996. More will be said about this below. Plans for an ethics support fund were also developed to the point where they were placed on the agenda of the BoD, but then certain issues related to taxes were raised and the item was withdrawn pending a satisfactory resolution. This too will be discussed further below.

THE ETHICS HOTLINE

The basic goal of the ethics hotline was to provide immediate support for engineers seeking information, advice, or help regarding ethics related problems. In addition to supplying routine information, or general interpretations of points in the ethics code, the idea was to give engineers an opportunity to discuss ethics related problems with an experienced, sympathetic colleague who might be able to provide useful suggestions or insights. Hotline procedures were fine tuned on the basis of discussions with IEEE attorneys. It was made clear that legal advice would not be given and callers (actually most contacts were via email) were never told what to do. In no case did the hotline purport to speak in the name of the IEEE. Requests of a routine nature were handled directly by IEEE staff, while other calls were routed to EC members who then responded to the callers (our goal, which we generally met, was to respond within a few days). Inquiries from outside the U.S. were generally handed over to EC members from the regions involved.

Aside from the routine questions and occasional comments (including suggestions about the code itself), there were a number of calls pertaining to problems in the publications or conference paper area. These included reports of misuse of papers by reviewers, and failures to credit people for their work. A number of serious cases involving illegalities and threats to safety were reported. Some examples follow:

• A software engineer discovered that his company was basing its products on programs owned by other companies, without obtaining licenses.

• An engineer testing computer chip wafers purchased from another company was instructed by his management to falsify test results so as to defraud the vendor.

• An engineer discovered that a respirator, produced by his company and sold for medical use by infants, had a misplaced relief valve, which, under certain conditions could expose infants to dangerously high lung pressure.

• A software engineer, working for a hospital, reported that the group working on the software interface for a patient monitoring system to be used in an intensive care unit was so far behind schedule that they planned to cut back on testing in an effort to catch up.

• An engineer in the construction and maintenance field reported that he was fired (by a nonengineer official) when he insisted on specifying the installation of emergency exit lights in a university building - which was required by law.

In some cases, after some preliminary exchanges, we advised callers to seek IEEE support via the MCC, or informed them of the possibility (if other means failed) of seeking legal counsel. In other situations, we pointed out to callers that, although they appeared to have been badly treated, the circumstances were such that making a case would be very difficult and

that they would probably be better off dropping the matter and looking for other jobs. In several situations, the results of hotline suggestions resulted in satisfactory resolutions. Note that in two of the cases listed above, the hotline suggested applying for MCC support, this was done, and the results were positive recommendations by the MCC, which were subsequently approved by the IEEE ExCom. This had not happened since the 1978 Edgerton case.

To those of us involved in the operation of the hotline, it is obvious that it served a very valuable function. It provided a direct channel for IEEE members to get help when they were faced with painful professional dilemmas. Our impression is that very few members were aware of this service, but even so, the number of important cases is significant.

THE LIABILITY ISSUE

Total hotline activity amounted to an average of from one to two calls per week (there is some fuzziness because some queries addressed to the EC in connection with the columns that appeared in the Institute were handled via the hotline mechanism). None of these calls resulted in even the slightest hint of trouble for the IEEE. Nevertheless, about a year ago, the specter of law suits against the IEEE was raised, particularly by the IEEE's legal counsel. This issue was never brought directly to the attention of the EC by any member of the ExCom or of the BoD. When we first heard about it, via IEEE staff, we immediately took steps to deal with the problem. (Note that since I responded to many of the hotline calls, I had a special interest in this danger. I would probably be an initial target of any lawsuit and, apart from the financial aspect, I am less than eager to spend my time entangled in legal proceedings.)

We considered two questions. One is, "what is the likelihood of law suits arising from the hotline and how can it be minimized?", and the other is, "can we get liability insurance to cover this contingency?" In order to deal with the second point, we requested, through IEEE staff, a meeting with the IEEE Insurance Committee (IC). Over a period of several months, there was no response at all to this request, which was repeated a number of times.

If we ask the question, "is there any risk of being sued as a consequence of a hotline interaction?", the answer is clearly, "yes". But this answer simply reflects the fact that anybody can sue anybody else about anything. No human activity (or even inactivity!) is risk-free. Virtually everything the IEEE does carries with it some risk of legal liability. It is easy to find instances of risks incurred by IEEE activities that are significantly more plausible than those associated with the hotline. For example, an IEEE periodical might be sued by an author whose paper was rejected.

Or a company might allege that sales of one of their products fell as a result of an erroneous statement in a paper published in an IEEE periodical. An IEEE member whose application for fellow status was denied might sue the IEEE for unfair treatment - perhaps based on gender or race discrimination.

A decision by an IEEE standards committee with respect to some standard might be alleged to damage unfairly the business of some manufacturer. In the "Hydrolevel Case" (1971-1983) the American Society of Mechanical Engineers (ASME) was required to pay $4.74 milion in damages and legal costs resulting from just such a situation.

The relevant question for any activity is, "what is the likelihood of a law suit?" On the basis of our experience with the hotline, our feeling was that this is not a serious risk. But, in order to obtain a more definitive answer, we consulted with a number of other organizations that have had much more extensive experience with hotline type operations. We learned that the American Institute of Certified Public Accountants (AICPA), an organization with about the same number of members as the IEEE, has, for a number of years operated an ethics hotline fielding over 7000 calls annually. No law suits against the AICPA have resulted from this activity. Their legal counsel's response when I mentioned the concerns expressed by the IEEE attorneys was, "did they cite any cases?" It is interesting that the AICPA also has a hotline to assist members on tax related questions. I was told that this service receives over 50 000 queries annually and that no lawsuits have resulted.

Another organization that we checked with is the American Association of University Professors (AAUP). Their legal counsel told us that, for many decades, a major function of the AAUP has been to provide advice to professors (not necessarily AAUP members) about job related problems. No law suits against the AAUP have resulted from this activity.

We also learned that the American Civil Liberties Union (ACLU), both through its national office and via its various state affiliates, responds to queries and gives advice to people requesting help in cases involving civil rights, free speech, etc. An attorney with that organization informed us that, although they field tens of thousands of such calls annually, the ACLU has never been sued by a caller.

I was informed that all of these organizations have reasonably priced liability insurance that covers the operations under discussion.

Which brings us back to the insurance question. One would expect that those concerned about liability risks for the IEEE ethics hotline would check carefully into the availability of appropriate insurance. In the course of our conversations with AICPA people, we learned that their insurance broker is also used by the

IEEE and further, that the IEEE Insurance Committee had actually initiated inquiries about hotline coverage. For further information about this, we were referred to IEEE staff people. I checked and learned from IEEE staff that they had indeed begun negotiations to obtain such coverage. But before these negotiations, which had been proceeding routinely, were concluded, they were instructed by the IEEE ExCom to drop the matter entirely. My efforts to get an explanation of this from various ExCom members were unsuccessful - nobody seemed to know anything about it.

In the course of these conversations I learned something interesting about liability risks in another area. I was told that the standards area is considered so risky by insurance companies, that their premiums for such coverage is excessive. Thus, the IEEE standards operation is "self-insured", i.e., it is not covered at all by liability insurance. During my two years on the IEEE Board of Directors, I do not recall ever having been informed about this very real risk by the IEEE attorneys or by anybody else. (This is not to suggest that I favor terminating IEEE's standards activities, which I consider to be a very important societal service.)

TERMINATION OF THE ETHICS HOTLINE

My first communication from the IEEE Insurance Committee was a July 1997 email from its staff director informing me that the IC was recommending to the IEEE ExCom that the Ethics Hotline be terminated because it was too risky. My protest that this was an inappropriate recommendation and my request for a meeting with the committee were not answered. Subsequently, at its August meeting, the ExCom accepted this recommendation and ordered that the hotline be terminated immediately. At no time was the EC asked to present arguments on this issue, or even informed (other than via the aforementioned note from the IC) that the matter was being considered. Before relating the most recent developments concerning the hotline issue, I will digress to the related issue of the ethics defense fund.

CATCH-22: SQUELCHING THE ETHICS SUPPORT FUND

As mentioned above, during its first two years of operation, the EC developed a proposal for an ethics support fund. The idea with an Ethics Support Fund is to go beyond mere advice and, where it is felt that important issues are at stake, provide some financial support for engineers embattled on behalf of the principles underlying the IEEE ethics code. Our proposal called for this fund to be financed by voluntary contributions from IEEE members - no funding would be sought from the IEEE. We were on the verge of putting this before the BoD in 1996, when we were informed that the IEEE attorney had expressed concerns that this might jeopardize the IEEE's 501(c)(3) tax status (i.e., its status as a charitable, hence tax-exempt organization). In discussions with the attorney, we subsequently learned that the concern is based on the idea that such a fund might be considered by the IRS as a "private inurement", which is strictly prohibited for 501(c)(3) organizations. He did not think this was very likely, but the possibility was sufficient to warrant caution before proceeding. His advice was to have the IEEE seek an "advanced determination letter" from the IRS indicating that such an operation was permissible. This would take a number of months and the legal costs would be of the order of five to ten thousand dollars.

On the face of it, it seemed to me that an operation designed to encourage engineers to behave ethically was so clearly in the public interest as to be at least as appropriate for a tax exempt organization as anything else that the IEEE does. But we withdrew the proposal and proceeded to check out the situation. First, we learned that the AAUP, also a 501(c)(3) organization, has had such a fund for over 40 years (as well as a second such fund for over 20 years) without ever having had its tax status called into question. We were referred to the principal legal reference book on the subject of charitable organizations. We learned that the private inurement prohibition is intended to prevent insiders from siphoning off organization funds into their own pockets through such means as the private use of organization cars or by renting property to the organization at inflated rates. It is quite clear from that book that it would be quite a stretch to construe the proposed fund as a private inurement (particularly since it would be available, not just to IEEE members, but to others in the profession).

Nevertheless, the EC agreed to delay submission of the proposal until the advanced determination letter could be obtained. And here is where Catch-22 comes in. No sooner did we agree to go along with the lawyer's proposal then we were told of a new concern: that requesting the advanced determination letter might call the attention of the IRS to the IEEE and that they might investigate other IEEE activities and find violations of the tax code entirely unrelated to the ethics support fund or any other EC activity. The IEEE lawyer concurred with this concern. When we asked him to find some solution to this impasse, his response was, "We have not been authorized to do further work on these matters".

THE ETHICS TASK FORCE

At its September 1997 meeting, the IEEE ExCom appointed an ethics task force. Its mission was to review the activities of the EC, including the hotline, and to make recommendations to the ExCom early in 1998. At the February 1998 ExCom meeting, the ethics task force reported that, at the instigation of the task force, the

IEEE Insurance Committee (IC) obtained bids from two of its insurance carriers for liability coverage for the hotline. The rates were quite reasonable (for example, about $5000 per year for one million dollars coverage). The report also stated that the Ethics Committee has been doing an excellent job, and the task force recommended that the hotline be reinstated immediately, with perhaps some minor changes in the guidelines.

The IEEE Treasurer then stated that he had been advised by the IC that the proffered policies were not satisfactory, though he did not explain why. He also quoted the July recommendation by the IC referred to above that the hotline be terminated and added that the IEEE's attorneys had advised that the hotline was too risky. I was permitted a brief rejoinder, in which I contrasted the actual experience of our own and of other organizations with the hypothetical arguments of the attorneys. The VP for Technical Activities suggested that the bylaw under which the EC operates may not support such an activity as the hotline. This is an interesting argument, since the hotline was explicitly approved by the same board that passed the bylaw. The only one who spoke in favor of the hotline was the IEEE USA President.

The President of the IEEE then called an executive session to hear from the IEEE attorney. He did not permit me, the newly re-elected EC chair, to remain in the room while a major activity of the EC was being discussed. Following the executive session, without much more in the way of discussion, a motion was made and passed which effectively rejected the recommendations of the ethics task force. Finally, when I later asked for a copy of the report of the Ethics Task Force, I was told that, since it was rejected by the ExCom, it in effect does not exist, and is not to be distributed to anyone.

MY CONCLUSIONS

The IEEE, the world's largest professional society for engineers has, via the action of its Executive Committee, taken a position that it will not offer even informal advice to assist engineers (members or not) in efforts to practice their profession in accordance with the ethical principles that the IEEE espouses via its ethics code. IEEE members are to be denied the opportunity to contribute voluntarily to a fund designed to help those whose careers are jeopardized by their efforts to abide by the ethics code. These actions directly contravene the intent expressed by the IEEE Board of Directors as recently as 1996. The expressed justifications for blocking these efforts to support engineering ethics seem to have no reasonable foundations in either fact or law.

Finally, the behavior of the Executive Committee in squelching proper discussion of the issues and in rejecting and then suppressing the report of its own blue ribbon committee should deeply concern all who take pride in being IEEE members.

Using the New ACM CODE OF ETHICS IN Decision Making

Ronald E. Anderson
Deborah G. Johnson
Donald Gotterbarn
Judith Perrolle

Historically, professional associations have viewed codes of ethics as mechanisms to establish their status as a profession or as a means to regulate their membership and thereby convince the public that they deserve to be self-regulating. Self-regulation depends on ways to deter unethical behavior of the members, and a code, combined with an ethics review board, was seen as the solution. Codes of ethics have tended to list possible violations and threaten sanctions for such violations. ACM's first code, the Code of Professional Conduct, was adopted in 1972 and followed this model. The latest ACM code, the Code of Ethics and Professional Conduct, was adopted in 1992 and takes a new direction.

ACM and many other societies have had difficulties implementing an ethics review system and came to realize that self-regulation depends mostly on the consensus and commitment of its members to ethical behavior. Now the most important rationale for a code of ethics is an embodiment of a set of commitments of that association's members. Sometimes these commitments are expressed as rules and sometimes as ideals, but the essential social function is to clarify and formally state those ethical requirements that are important to the group as a professional association. The new ACM Code of Ethics and Professional Conduct follows this philosophy.

Recent codes of ethics emphasize socialization or education rather than enforced compliance. A code can work toward the collective good even though it may be a mere distillation of collective experience and reflection. A major benefit of an educationally oriented code is its contribution to the group by clarifying the professionals' responsibility to society.

A code of ethics holds the profession accountable to the public. This tends to yield a major payoff in terms of public trust. In Frankel's words, "To the extent that a code confers benefits on clients, it will help persuade the public that professionals are deserving of its confidence and respect, and of increased social and economic rewards" [8].

The final and most important function of a code of ethics is its role as an aid to individual decision making. In the interest of facilitating better ethical decision making, we have developed a set of nine classes that describe situations calling for ethical decision making. These cases address in turn the topics of intellectual property, privacy, confidentiality, professional quality, fairness or discrimination, liability, software risks, conflicts of interest, and unauthorized access to computer systems.

Within each case we begin with a scenario to illustrate a typical ethical decision point and then lay out the different imperatives (principles) of the new Code of Ethics that pertain to that decision. There are 24 principles in the Code and each case analysis calls on at least two or three different principles to evaluate the relevant ethical concerns. Each of the principles is relevant to at least one scenario, and some principles apply to several situations. The purpose of these case analyses is to provide examples of practical applications of the new ACM Code of Ethics.

Case 1: Intellectual Property

Jean, a statistical database programmer, is trying to write a large statistical program needed by her company. Programmers in this company are encouraged to write about their work and to publish their algorithms in professional journals. After months of tedious programming, Jean has found herself stuck on several parts of the program. Her manager, not recognizing the complexity of the problem, wants the job completed within the next few days. Not knowing how to solve the problems, Jean remembers that a coworker had given her source listings from his current work and from an early version of a commercial software package developed at another company. On studying these programs, she sees two areas of code which could be directly incorporated into her own program. She uses segments of code from both her coworker and the commercial software, but does not tell anyone or mention it in the documentation. She completes the project and turns it in a day ahead of time. (Adapted from a scenario by Dave Colantonio and Deborah Johnson.)

The Code addresses questions of intellectual property most explicitly in imperative 1.6: "Give proper credit for intellectual property . . . Specifically, one must not take credit for other's ideas or work . . ." This ethical requirement extends the property rights principle (1.5) that explicitly mentions copyrights, patents, trade secrets and license agreements. These restrictions are grounded in integrity (1.3) and in the need to comply with existing laws (2.3).

Jean violated professional ethics in two areas: failure to give credit for another's work and using code from a commercial package that presumably was copyrighted or in another way protected by law. Suppose that Jean only looked at her coworker's source code for ideas and then com-

pletely wrote her own program; would she still have an obligation to give credit? Our answer is yes, she should have acknowledged credit to her coworker in the documentation. There is a matter of professional discretion here, because if the use of another's intellectual material is truly trivial, then there probably is no need to give formal credit.

Jean's use of commercial software code was not appropriate because she should have checked to determine whether or not her company was authorized to use the source code before using it. Even though it is generally desirable to share and exchange intellectual materials, using bootlegged software is definitely a violation of the Code.

Those interested in additional discussions on this subject should refer to the numerous articles by Pamela Samuelson on intellectual property in *Communications*. Also recommended are [2, 7, 17].

Case 2: Privacy

Three years ago Diane started her own consulting business. She has been so successful that she now has several people working for her and many clients. Their consulting work included advising on how to network microcomputers, designing database management systems, and advising about security.

Presently she is designing a database management system for the personnel office of a medium-sized company. Diane has involved the client in the design process, informing the CEO, the director of computing, and the director of personnel about the progress of the system. It is now time to make decisions about the kind and degree of security to build into the system. Diane has described several options to the client. Because the system is going to cost more than they planned, the client has decided to opt for a less secure system. She believes the information they will be storing is extremely sensitive. It will include performance evaluations, medical records for filing insurance claims, salaries, and so forth.

With weak security, employees working on microcomputers may be able to figure out ways to get access to this data, not to mention the possibilities for on-line access from hackers. Diane feels strongly that the system should be much more secure.

She has tried to explain the risks, but the CEO, director of computing and director of personnel all agree that less security will do. What should she do? Should she refuse to build the system as they request? (Adapted from [14]).

In the Code of Ethics, principle number 1.7 deals with privacy and 1.8 with confidentiality. They are integrally related but the privacy principle here is the most explicit. The Guidelines of the Code say that computer professionals are obligated to preserve the integrity of data about individuals "from unauthorized access or accidental disclosure to inappropriate individuals." The Code also specifies that organizational leaders have obligations to "verify that systems are designed and implemented to protect personal privacy and enhance personal dignity" (3.5), and to assess the needs of all those affected by a system (3.4).

The company officials have an obligation to protect the privacy of their employees, and therefore should not accept inadequate security. Diane's first obligation is to attempt to educate the company officials, which is implied by imperative 2.7 to promote "public understanding of computing and its consequences." If that fails, then Diane needs to consider her contractual obligations as noted under imperative 2.6 on honoring assigned responsibilities. We do not know the details of Diane's contract, but she may have to choose between her contract and her obligation to honor privacy and confidentiality.

Additional perspectives and discussion on the privacy obligations of computer professionals can be found in [5, 6, 14, 23]. We also recommend proceedings of the latest conference on Computers, Freedom and Privacy [13].

Case 3: Confidentiality

Max works in a large state department of alcoholism and drug abuse. The agency administers programs for individuals with alcohol and drug problems, and maintains a huge database of information on the clients who use their services. Some of the data files contain the names and current addresses of clients.

Max has been asked to take a look at the track records of the treatment programs. He is to put together a report that contains the number of clients seen in each program each month for the past five years, length of each client's treatment, number of clients who return after completion of a program, criminal histories of clients, and so on. In order to put together this report, Max has been given access to all files in the agency's mainframe computer. After assembling the data into a new file that includes the client names, he downloads it to the computer in his office.

Under pressure to get the report finished by the deadline, Max decides he will have to work at home over the weekend in order to finish on time. He copies the information onto several disks and takes them home. After finishing the report he leaves the disks at home and forgets about them (adapted from [14]).

This scenario resembles the previous one that dealt with privacy considerations. However, it raises several additional issues. From the Code of Ethics, principles 1.7 on privacy and 1.8 on confidentiality apply. Imperative 2.8 on constraining access to authorized situations is also central to a computer user's decisions in this type of situation. Additionally, the Code specifies that organizational leaders have obligations to "verify that systems are designed and implemented to protect personal privacy and enhance personal dignity," (3.5) and it also states that they should specify appropriate and authorized uses of an organization's resources (3.3).

The government agency should have had policies and procedures that protected the identity of its clients. Max's relatives and friends might accidentally discover the files and inappropriately use the information to harm the reputation of the clients. The files that Max worked with for his report did not need to have any names or other information in the records that made it possible to easily identify individuals. The agency should have removed the identifying information from the files it allowed Max to use. If that procedure had been followed, it would not have mattered that Max copied the file to his computer. Thus the organizational context created many ethical issues for Max, but unfortunately he was not attentive to these ethical issues ahead of time.

Further reading on this subject can be found in [12, 15, 20]. Discus-

sions of computer-related procedures to maintain the confidentiality of data from specific sources also are available from other professional associations such as the American Medical Association and the American Statistical Association.

Case 4: Quality in Professional Work

A computer company is writing the first stage of a more efficient accounting system that will be used by the government. This system will save taxpayers a considerable amount of money every year. A computer professional, who is asked to design the accounting system, assigns different parts of the system to her staff. One person is responsible for developing the reports; another is responsible for the internal processing; and a third for the user interface. The manager is shown the system and agrees that it can do everything in the requirements. The system is installed, but the staff finds the interface so difficult to use that their complaints are heard by upper-level management. Because of these complaints, upper-level management will not invest any more money in the development of the new accounting system and they go back to their original, more expensive system (adapted from [10]).

The Code of Ethics advocates that computer professionals "strive to achieve the highest quality in both process and products" (2.1). Imperative 3.4 elaborates that users and those affected by a system have their needs clearly articulated.

We presume that in this case the failure to deliver a quality product is directly attributable to a failure to follow a quality process. It is likely that most of the problems with this interface would have been discovered in a review process, either with peers or with users, which is promoted by imperative 2.4. When harm results, in this case to taxpayers, the failure to implement a quality process becomes a clear violation of ethical behavior.

For recent discussions of ethics cases that deal with software quality, see [11].

Case 5: Fairness and Discrimination

In determining requirements for an information system to be used in an

employment agency, the client explains that, when displaying applicants whose qualifications appear to match those required for a particular job, the names of white applicants are to be displayed ahead of those of nonwhite applicants, and names of male applicants are to be displayed ahead of those of female applicants (adapted from Donald Gotterbarn and Lionel Diemel).

According to the general moral imperative on fairness, an ACM member will be "fair and take action not to discriminate." In this case the system designer is being asked to build a system that, it appears, will be used to favor white males and discriminate against nonwhites and females. It would seem that the system designer should not simply do what he or she is told but should point out the problematic nature of what is being requested and ask the client why this is being done. Making this inquiry is consistent with 2.3 (to respect existing laws) and 2.5 (to give thorough evaluations) and 4.1 (to uphold and promote the Code of Ethics).

If the client concludes that he or she plans to use the information to favor white males, then the computer professional should refuse to build the system as proposed. To go ahead and build the system would be a violation not only of 1.4 (fairness), but of 2.3 (respecting existing laws) and would be inconsistent with 1.1 (human well-being) and 1.2 (avoiding harm).

For further discussion of the topic of bias see [9, 16, 21].

Case 6: Liability for Unreliability

A software development company has just produced a new software package that incorporates the new tax laws and figures taxes for both individuals and small businesses. The president of the company knows that the program has a number of bugs. He also believes the first firm to put this kind of software on the market is likely to capture the largest market share. The company widely advertises the program. When the company actually ships a disk, it includes a disclaimer of responsibility for errors resulting from the use of the program. The company expects it will receive a number of complaints, queries, and suggestions for modification.

The company plans to use these to make changes and eventually issue updated, improved, and debugged versions. The president argues that this is general industry policy and that anyone who buys version 1.0 of a program knows this and will take proper precautions. Because of bugs, a number of users filed incorrect tax returns and were penalized by the IRS (adapted from scenario V.7 in [18]).

The software company, the president in particular, violated several tenets of the ACM code of ethics. Since he was aware of bugs in the product, he did not strive to achieve the highest quality as called for by 2.1. In failing to inform consumers about bugs in the system, principle 2.5 was also violated.

In this instance the risks to users are great in that they have to pay penalties for mistakes in their income tax which are the result of the program. Companies by law can make disclaimers only when they are "in good conscience." The disclaimer here might not meet this legal test, in which case imperative 2.3 would be violated. As a leader in his organization the president is also violating 3.1, for he is not encouraging his staff to accept their social responsibilities.

Issues of software liability have been discussed by [19, 22].

Case 7: Software Risks

A small software company is working on an integrated inventory control system for a very large national shoe manufacturer. The system will gather sales information daily from shoe stores nationwide. This information will be used by the accounting, shipping, and ordering departments to control all of the functions of this large corporation. The inventory functions are critical to the smooth operation of this system.

Jane, a quality assurance engineer with the software company, suspects that the inventory functions of the system are not sufficiently tested, although they have passed all their contracted tests. She is being pressured by her employers to sign off on the software. Legally she is only required to perform those tests which had been agreed to in the original contract. However, her considerable experience in software testing has led her to be concerned over risks of the

system. Her employers say they will go out of business if they do not deliver the software on time. Jane contends if the inventory subsystem fails, it will significantly harm their client and its employees. If the potential failure were to threaten lives, it would be clear to Jane that she should refuse to sign off. But since the degree of threatened harm is less, Jane is faced by a difficult moral decision (adapted from [10]).

In the Code of Ethics, imperative 1.2 stresses the responsibility of the computing professional to avoid harm to others. In addition, principle 1.1 requires concern for human well-being; 1.3 mandates professional integrity, and 2.1 defines quality as an ethical responsibility. These principles may conflict with the agreements and commitments of an employee to the employer and client.

The ethical imperatives of the Code imply that Jane should not deliver a system she believes to be inferior, nor should she mislead the client about the quality of the product (1.3). She should continue to test, but she has been told that her company will go out of business if she does not sign off on the system now. At the very least the client should be informed about her reservations.

For additional discussion of software risks, [3, 22] are suggested.

Case 8: Conflicts of Interest

A software consultant is negotiating a contract with a local community to design their traffic control system. He recommends they select the TCS system out of several available systems on the market. The consultant fails to mention that he is a major stockholder of the company producing TCS software.

According to the Guidelines, imperative 2.5 means that computer professionals must "strive to be perceptive, thorough and objective when evaluating, recommending, and presenting system descriptions and alternatives." It also says that imperative 1.3 implies a computer professional must be honest about "any circumstances that might lead to conflicts of interest." Because of the special skills held by computing professionals it is their responsibility to ensure that their clients are fully aware of their options and that professional recommendations are not modified for personal gain.

Additional discussion on conflict of interest appears in [1, 25].

Case 9: Unauthorized Access

Joe is working on a project for his computer science course. The instructor has allotted a fixed amount of computer time for this project. Joe has run out of time, but he has not yet finished the project. The instructor cannot be reached. Last year Joe worked as a student programmer for the campus computer center and is quite familiar with procedures to increase time allocations to accounts. Using what he learned last year, he is able to access the master account. Then he gives himself additional time and finishes his project.

The imperative to honor property rights (1.5) has been violated. This general, moral imperative leads to imperative 2.8, which specifies that ACM members should "access communication resources only when authorized to do so." In violating 2.8 Joe also is violating the imperative to "know and respect existing laws" (2.3). As a student member of the ACM he must follow the Code of Ethics even though he may not consider himself a computing professional.

For additional reading see [4, 24,]. The most current material on this subject is likely to be found in [13].

Conclusion

These nine cases illustrate the broad range of issues a computer scientist may encounter in professional practice. While the ACM Code does not precisely prescribe what an individual must do in the situations described, it does identify some decisions as unacceptable. Often in ethical decision making many factors have to be balanced. In such situations computer professionals have to choose among conflicting principles adhering to the *spirit* of the Code as much as to the *letter*.

The ACM Code organizes ethical principles into the four categories: general moral imperatives; more specific professional responsibilities, organizational leadership imperatives, and compliance. Some may find it helpful to sort out the ethical issues involved in other ways. For example, the context of practice is relevant. Those in industry may encounter different issues from those in government or education. Those who are employed in large corporations may experience different tensions than those who work in small firms or who are self-employed. But whether working in private practice or in large organizations, computer professionals must balance responsibilities to employers, to clients, to other professionals, and to society, and these responsibilities can come into conflict. Our range of cases illustrates how one can use the general principles of the Code to deal with these diverse types of situations.

The reader may wonder why we did not have a whistle-blowing case. In a prototypical scenario, a professional has to take action which threatens the employer after concluding that the safety or well-being of some other group must take priority. Three of our cases—5, 6, 7—dealt with whistle-blowing indirectly. In all three cases, the computing professional served an outside client rather than an employer. This adds other dimensions to whistle-blowing. In Case 5, suppose the system designer learns that his client plans to use the database to discriminate and he refuses to design the system. Later he finds that a friend of his designed the system as the client wanted. He would then have to decide whether to "blow the whistle" on his ex-client. These and similar types of situations are indeed important, if not common, for computer professionals. (For more prototypical situations see discussion of the Bart case and [19] on SDI.)

In all of the cases presented, we portrayed individuals acting in constrained situations. Ethical decisions depend on one's institutional context. These environments can facilitate or constrain ethical behavior. Leadership roles can set the tone and create work environments in which computer professionals can express their ethical concerns. It is significant that leadership responsibilities were demonstrated in nearly all of our nine cases. In some instances, the problem could be resolved by following the imperatives in the Code that apply to leaders. In other cases, the problem was created by a lack of ethical leadership, and the individual professional had to make a personal decision on how to proceed.

Several ethical topics were not specifically interpreted in either the **Guidelines** or in our cases. For instance, specific requirements of integrity for research in computing and computer science were not detailed. Nor were specific suggestions offered for maintaining professional development. These should be among the tasks of the ACM leadership to address with future additions to the Guidelines.

Other ethical issues, such as software copyright violation, were addressed but not with sufficient detail relative to their salience to the field of computing. These issues, as well as new issues not yet imagined, will confront the field of computing in the future. Not only will the Guidelines need to be updated, but there will be a need for writing and interpreting more cases typical of the ethical decisions of computing professionals. Those with special ethical computing situations are encouraged to share them with us and with others in order to foster more discussion and attention to exemplary ethical decision-making. ◘

References
1. Bayles, M.D. *Professional Ethics.* Wadsworth, Belmont, Calif., 1981.
2. Bynum, T.W., Maner, W. and Fodor, J., Eds. *Software Ownership and Intellectual Property Rights.* Research Center on Computing and Society, Southern Connecticut State University, New Haven, Conn. 06515, 1992.
3. Clark, D. *Computers at Risk: Safe Computing in the Information Age.* National Research Council, National Academy Press, Washington, D.C., 1990.
4. Denning, P.J., Ed. *Computers under Attack: Intruders, Worms and Viruses.* Addison-Wesley, Inc., Reading, Mass., 1990.
5. Dunlop, C. and Kling, R., Eds. *Computerization and Controversy: Value Conflicts and Social Choices.* Academic Press, New York, N.Y., 1991.
6. Flaherty, D. *Protecting Privacy in Surveillance Societies.* University of North Carolina Press, Chapel Hill, N.C., 1989.
7. Forester, T. Software theft and the problem of intellectual property rights. *Comput. Soc. 20,* 1 (Mar. 1990), 2–11.
8. Frankel, M.S. Professional Codes: Why, How, and with What Impact? *J. Bus. Ethics 8* (2 and 3) (1989), 109–116.
9. Frenkel, K.A. Women and computing. *Commun. ACM 33,* 11 (Nov. 1990), 34–46.
10. Gotterbarn, D. Computer ethics: Responsibility regained. *National Forum* (Summer 1991).
11. Gotterbarn, D. Editor's corner. *J. Syst. Soft. 17* (Jan. 1992), 5–6.
12. Guynes, C.S. Protecting statistical databases: A matter of privacy. *Comput. Soc. 19,* 1 (Mar. 1989), 15–23.
13. IEEE Computer Society Press. *Proceedings of the Second Conference on Computers, Freedom and Privacy.* (Los Alamitos, Calif.), IEEE Computer Society Pres, 1992.
14. Johnson, D.G. *Computer Ethics,* Second Ed. Prentice Hall, Englewood Cliffs, N.J., 1993.
15. Laudon, K.C. *Dossier Society: Value Choices in the Design of National Information Systems.* Columbia University Press, New York, N.Y., 1986.
16. Martin, C.D. and Murche-Beyma, E., Eds. In *Search of Gender Free Paradigms for Computer Science Education.* International Society for Technology in Education, Eugene, Ore., 1992.
17. National Research Council. *Intellectual Property Issues in Software.* National Academy of Sciences, Washington, D.C., 1991.
18. Parker, D., Swope, S. and Baker, B. Ethical conflicts in information and computer science. Techology and Business. Wellesley, Mass. QED Information Sciences, 1990.
19. Parnas, D.L. SDI: A violation of professional responsibility. *Abacus 4,* 2 (Winter 1987), 46–52.
20. Perrolle, J.A. *Computers and Social Change: Information, Property, and Power.* Wadsworth, Belmont, Calif., 1987.
21. Perrolle, J. Conversations and trust in computer interfaces. In *Computers and Controversy.* Dunlop and Kling, Eds., 1991.
22. Pressman, R.S. and Herron, R. *Software Shock: The Danger and the Opportunity.* Dorsett House, 1991.
23. Salpeter, J. Are you obeying copyright law? *Technol. Learning 12,* 8 (1992), 12–23.
24. Spafford, G. Are computer hacker break-ins ethical? *J. Syst. Softw. 17* (Jan. 1992).
25. Stevenson, J.T. *Engineering Ethics: Practices and Principles.* Canadian Scholars Press, Toronto, 1987.

Note: A more extensive list of references for each of the nine specific cases, as well as general discussions of professional ethics, can be obtained by writing Ronald E. Anderson, 909 Social Sciences Bldg., University of Minnesota, Minneapolis, MN 55455. Both the ACM Code of Ethics and the bibliography are available on the Internet from acm.org using anonymous ftp or mailserve. The files are under the SIGCAS Forum and called code_of_ethics.txt and ethics_biblio.txt.

Chapter 4

"Cracking" and Computer Security

Not exploit the weakness of a computer system for personal gain or personal satisfaction.
　　　　　　　　　　　　　　　　　　　—*from the* AITP Standards of Conduct.
Access computing and communications resources only when authorized to do so.
　　　　　　　　　—ACM Code of Ethics, specific professional responsibility 8.
Use the property of a client or employer only in ways properly authorized, and with the client's or employer's knowledge and consent.
　　　　　　　　　—IEEE-CS/ACM Software Engineering Code of Ethics, principle 2.3.

4.1 "CRACKERS" VERSUS "HACKERS"

THE meaning of the word *hacker* has evolved in an unfortunate way. Originally, a hacker meant someone whose motives were essentially positive and productive. A hacker was someone who liked to undertake substantial and difficult computer projects just for the challenge involved. If there were no appropriate project at hand, the hacker was prone to dream one up. These were the people that Steven Levy wrote about in *Hackers—Heroes of the Computer Revolution* [3]. These were people like Dennis Ritchie, Ken Thompson, and Brian Kernighan—people who invented C and Unix as an unofficial project on a spare machine at Bell Labs.

Today, however, the term hacker is also often used to describe people who break into computer systems, either for fun or for more sinister motives. Note that in terms of motivation, technical ability, or emotional maturity, we are talking about two very different types of people. A true hacker would be appalled at the unauthorized use of a computer system. As an example, see Ken Thompson's article at the end of this chapter. On the other hand, a hacker in the second sense of the term might be motivated primarily by the thrill of doing something illicit. A true hacker would be someone creative and technically accomplished. A hacker in this second sense often simply exploits known but unpatched security holes to break into computer systems. True hackers proudly take credit for their accomplishments, accepting both the praise and criticism of their colleagues. Hackers in the new sense generally hide behind nicknames in order to avoid public recognition for their activities. I doubt that anyone knows exactly where and when this second use of the term got started, but we should perhaps apologize to the true hackers for allowing the term to become dirtied.

This problem of divergent meanings of the word "hacker" is well known. It has caused people to suggest alternative terms for the person who breaks into computer systems. One of the more colorful suggestions is "dark-side hacker," but this term seems not to have caught on. Another suggestion is the term "cracker," which has the catchy advantage of rhyming with hacker, and the accuracy advantage of calling to mind the image of a safe cracker. This cracker/hacker distinction in terms does seem to be catching on. For example, it is used in several of the reprinted articles in this chapter. For the revised edition of this book I have settled on using the term *cracker* to refer specifically to people who make various unethical and/or illegal uses of computer systems.[1]

Regrettably, we must focus on crackers in this chapter:

---

[1]The suggestion to use the term *cracker* was made to me by Richard Stallman during preparation of the first edition of this book. I did not take his suggestion at the time, but I have corrected the mistake now. Computer professionals should value using terms that are precise, rather than ambiguous.

what they do, how to recognize them through an understanding of their mindset, how to arrive at a reasonable framework of punishment, and how to protect your systems from the damage they cause.

4.2 EXAMPLES OF "CRACKER" ACTIVITIES

In the narrowest sense, a cracker is someone who breaks into computer systems. But a more general definition is that a cracker is simply a person who makes illegitimate use of computer systems. What is illegitimate use? First, let's consider legitimate use. You are using a computer system in an legitimate manner when (1) you use a valid account assigned for your use by the legitimate administrator of the system, (2) your use is consistent with the established guidelines or policies for the system, and (3) the software you create is not intended to support access to, or use of, a computer system against established guidelines or policies. Other uses of a computer system are illegitimate. Under this definition, there is great variety in cracker activities. The brief tour given below touches on some of the major categories. But keep in mind that the list is by no means complete, and activities may overlap more than one category.

- *"Trojan horse" programs.* The "Trojan horse" name comes from the story by Homer. The Greek army attacks the city of Troy, but cannot get inside the city walls. Then they build a large wooden horse and hide soldiers inside it. The people of Troy find the horse and take it inside the city walls. The Greek soldiers come out of the horse to launch a surprise attack and take the city of Troy. Thus the term "Trojan horse" applies to a program that appears on the surface to be something benign, but in reality hides something dangerous. For example, a Trojan horse login program might be created to take the place of the true login program but also send a list of logins and passwords to the cracker who planted the Trojan horse.

  Ken Thompson walks us through the creation of a Trojan horse in the reprint of his ACM Turing Award acceptance lecture, "Reflections on Trusting Trust." This is the oldest reprinted article in the book, but it is still a classic and deserves careful reading. In the early part of the article, Thompson clearly shows his personal pride in his work and his sense of professionalism. He then moves on to act as the untrustworthy cracker, showing us that "you can't trust code that you did not totally create yourself." This particular Trojan horse is a version of the C compiler that will insert a trap door into the login program and also reinsert the Trojan horse into new versions of the compiler. At the end of the article, Thompson comes down on the press for its glorification of crackers as "whiz kids." The overall theme of the article is that if we can't trust the

technology, we must be able to trust the people behind it. The larger implication for computing professionals is that we must find a way to instill ethical behavior early on.

- *"Virus" programs.* A virus is a program that "infects" a computer by attaching itself to some other program, typically some part of the operating system. Say that you download a program named "GreatGame" from the Internet and run it on your computer. The program may be more than just a great game. As part of its execution it may alter an operating system file on your computer by inserting some extra code. From this point on, the virus code may, for example, be executed each time that the system starts up. It may lie "dormant" for some time, perhaps just checking the date each time it is executed. Then when a certain date arrives, it may delete all the files on the disk. Viruses are common in the personal computer environment. In fact, viruses have become so common that personal computers often come with some version of "antivirus" software.

  The greatest risk of your computer acquiring a virus comes when you use software from a source you cannot trust. Software downloaded from the Internet is a common source of viruses. Early virus programs could generally be detected by comparing the size of all operating system files against their correct size. An overloaded file might indicate that a virus has infected the legitimate code. To hide the virus better, virus writers wrote code that could infect an executable file without changing its size. By rewriting a section of legitimate code in more compact form, space is freed up for the virus within the size of the original legitimate code. Such viruses could still be detected by scanning the disk for a section of code known to be a part of the virus, a virus "signature." Then virus writers wrote "polymorphic" viruses, ones that could automatically alter some of their contents. The reprinted article "Antivirus technology offers new cures" talks about the history of virus technology, presents an overview of some current ideas in the area of anti-virus technology, and gives pointers to some interesting web sites.

  An interesting side story to computer viruses is the "chain e-mail" warnings about computer viruses. These e-mails warn you not to read an e-mail with a certain title (e.g., "Good Times") because it will do something awful to your computer. Traditionally, these warnings were purely jokes, since e-mails did not carry code that could be executed on your computer simply by reading the e-mail. However, as e-mail systems have become more powerful and sophisticated this is no longer the case. See the worksheet and reading on the Melissa virus incident for more information about this topic.

- *"Worm" programs.* A "worm" program is similar to a virus program, in that it "infects" other computers

From BLOOM COUNTY: TOONS FOR OUR TIMES by Berkeley Breathed. Copyright © 1984 by The Washington Post Company. By permission of Little, Brown and Company (Inc).

with a copy of itself. If there is a distinction, then the term "worm" would apply to a program that replicates and transfers itself between computer systems over a network whereas a virus would be less active in transferring itself between computer systems.

The term "worm" became popular in connection with the infamous Internet Worm incident of 1988. This is an incident in which a Cornell University student managed to shut down a large portion of the Internet for several days. The student was apparently experimenting with writing his own virus/worm programs that were intended to be relatively benign and short-lived. The programs took advantage of known security holes in UNIX systems. At some point, a version of the program "got loose" on the Internet and began to replicate itself out of control. Because it would infect systems multiple times, it would create a noticeable load on systems, making them unusable. See the worksheet on this topic to further explore this notorious incident.

• *"Logic bomb" programs.* A logic bomb is a program that watches for a certain condition (date, specified number of executions, etc.) and then disrupts normal system operation in some way (such as altering or erasing files). A virus program may contain a logic bomb. Logic bombs have also occasionally been used by employees or contractors. For example, a programmer might program the payroll system to delete the employee database if their name does not appear. See the Additional Assignments section for a specific incident of a logic bomb left behind by an ex-employee.

• *"Password sniffers."* A password sniffer is a program that monitors network traffic looking for login sequences. When a user logs into a computer over a network, the login and password prompts and the responses to them travel over the network. Normally, the operating system at each computer looks only at packets of information that are addressed to that computer. However, a computer could in principle look at the contents of all packets traveling by it. Once a login prompt is seen, the source and destination computers are noted, and only traffic between them needs to be examined. When the response to the login prompt is seen, the login name is noted. Then the password prompt is seen, and the reply password is noted. The password sniffer now has a login name and password for unauthorized use of a computer. Password sniffers are discussed in the reprinted article "Collaring the cybercrook: An investigator's view."

One author has suggested that password sniffers may be evidence of a planned attack on our network infrastructure by terrorists–"The most interesting evidence of an attack is the continuous seeding of the Internet with well-designed password sniffers by skilled, persistent, and unidentified crackers. Defense officials fear these sniffers are reconnaissance agents sent by an enemy seeking data for use in wartime" [4]. The technology of "cyberwar" is the topic of the reprinted article "Is the US prepared for cyberwar?" Password sniffers, cyberwar and critical infrastructure protection all figure into several of the topics in the Additional Assignments section.

It is not a terribly difficult task to write a primitive password sniffer, and so this particular type of cracking activity has become a serious problem on the Internet [5]. For this reason, organizations that want their employees to be able to log in from remote locations over an insecure network might use "one-time passwords." An employee might carry a small device that is time-synchronized with the main computer. The device is continually generating new pseudo-random passwords, and the main computer is generating the same sequence of passwords. When replying to the password prompt, the employee consults the device for the current valid password.

• *"IP spoofing."* Internet Protocol (IP) spoofing refers to causing a computer system to send traffic on the Internet that represents it as some other computer

83

system. Say that a cracker wants to gain entry to computer A, and discovers that computer B has privileged access to computer A. If the cracker can identify the Internet address of computer B, then he may attempt to gain entry to computer A by masquerading his computer as computer B. IP spoofing is also discussed in the reprinted article "Collaring the cybercrook: An investigator's view."

- *"Denial of service" attacks.* This type of cracker activity has become more common in recent years, as more organizations conduct business on the Internet. A "denial of service" attack aims to prevent an organization from conducting its normal activity over the Internet. This type of attack does not necessarily require breaking into the organization's computer, or even causing their computer to crash. It may simply mean keeping the computer so busy attempting to serve invalid or phantom customers that the real customers cannot get through to be served.

One denial-of-service attack that received a good deal of publicity is described in the reprinted article "Phony connections gag Internet services." This particular attack took the "SYN flooding" approach. A SYN (synchronization) is one particular step in the transmission control protocol (TCP) between machines. The protocol for setting up a connection between machines requires a "three-way handshake." One, computer A sends a SYN to computer B to start the process. Two, computer B responds with a SYN/ACK to computer A. Three, computer A sends an ACK back to computer B. Between steps two and three, computer B has a data structure in memory that represents the requested connection. There is an eventual time-out condition, in case computer A never replies with step three to confirm the connection. The cracker, as computer A, exploits the process by requesting connections as fast as possible but never confirming any request. Computer B then rapidly fills up the available number of "half-open" connections, and can no longer respond to new connection requests. Thus, by "flooding" computer B with "SYN" packets, the cracker can cause computer B to become unable to serve legitimate requests. There are several ways to fight this type of attack, as mentioned in the reprint at the end of the chapter. See the worksheet at the end of the chapter for additional exploration of this topic.

All of the above are examples of activities that are clearly unethical. They are generally also criminal activities. The gentlest interpretation is that the people who do these things are socially maladjusted. Less-forgiving interpretations suggest that people who do these things are a danger to society and need to be put in jail. There has traditionally been a great deal of controversy about what punishment is most appropriate for crackers. People often disagree on how to punish crackers or even if they should be punished

at all. In part, your answer may depend on the assumed motives of the cracker.

4.3 PROFILES OF CRACKER PERSONALITIES

As part of understanding and combating the cracker problem, law enforcement has developed "profiles" for different types of crackers. The reprinted article "Collaring the cybercrook: An investigator's view" mentions two such sets of profiles. One set of profiles uses the categories Novice, Student, Tourist, Crasher, and Thief.

The Novice category represents young, or at least emotionally immature, computer users who have a surface-level fascination with security issues. They would be willing to try out a cracker technique if they came across a "how to" description of it. They would not likely have the attention span or depth of knowledge required to originate new cracker techniques. They might give relatively little thought to the possible consequences before trying out a cracker technique, or before telling others about what they have discovered.

The Student category represents those who have some level of serious technical interest in computer security and might want to experiment with cracker techniques. These people might see themselves as having relatively benign intent, because they are "only trying to learn" or "only trying to educate people." One common view of Robert Morris, the person behind the Internet Worm incident, would be compatible with this category.

The Tourist category represents those with talents like those of the Student, but with more of a "peeping tom" type of motivation. This person would break into a system and look around, but would quickly get bored if they did not find something of interest to them. They might enjoy reading other people's e-mail, browsing personnel records or looking at the tools in the system administrator's account.

The Crasher might have almost any level of technical expertise, and is motivated primarily by the desire to crash a system. They somehow "get their kicks" out of knowing that they have caused a system to crash. We could distinguish a related profile here of the Vandal. Whereas the Crasher would only feel the need to cause the system to crash, the Vandal would feel the need to see more results from their effort, or feel that they have created a larger problem to be fixed. Vandals might take particular interest in cracking systems that support public web pages, in the way that common vandals might deface street signs.

The Thief is in some sense the most explicitly criminal of the categories. The thief has turned to computer cracking, like Willie Sutton robbed banks, because that is where the money is. The Thief might crack into computers to steal credit card numbers, to alter their own credit or banking history, or to steal something that can be sold to another party. There are numerous examples that fall into this category. The "Wily Hacker" [9] was stealing information from Department of Defense computers in the United States to sell to Russian KGB agents. The more recent and infamous U.S. cracker Kevin Mitnick was able to support himself and his activities for years with "no visible means of support." Certainly some part of his cracker activity must have fallen within the Thief category. In fact, Kevin Mitnick may be a good example of how a person could transition between categories. He may have started out in the Student stage, moved through something like a Tourist stage, and ended up in the Thief stage. See the worksheet on the "Wily Hacker" and the Additional Assignments on Kevin Mitnick for further study.

And, of course, this set of profiles is not exhaustive. A variation on the Thief might be the Spy or Terrorist, who is not interested in money per se, but in information that can be used to cause large-scale damage to the normal operation of society. And we might imagine categories such as the Angered Ex-Employee and Spurned Suitor, who might turn to cracker activity as a means of revenge. For example, in January 1997, Adelyn Lee, a former employee of Oracle Corporation and ex-girlfriend of Oracle CEO Larry Ellison was convicted of fabricating an e-mail that incriminated Ellison [1]. The fake e-mail, supposedly from Lee's supervisor to Ellison, said that the supervisor had fired Lee because she refused to have sex with Ellison. The faked e-mail had been used as evidence in a civil trial in which Lee had won $100,000 for wrongful termination.

One theme across all of these profile categories is a lack of proper social adjustment. At the Novice level, it manifests itself mainly as a lack of conscious thought about the consequences. At the Tourist or Crasher level, it is a rationalization that the consequences are less important than short-term personal gratification. At the Thief level, it is explicit antisocial behavior and a hardened lack of concern for others.

4.4 ATTITUDES OF AND TOWARD CRACKERS

Given this broad range of types of people who might commit cracker activities, it should not be surprising that there is disagreement about the appropriate penalties for cracking.

The classic case of Craig Neidorf and the *Phrack* newsletter provides a good vehicle for examining attitudes toward crackers. Neidorf was actually arrested and taken to trial, so there is a substantial record of the facts in this case. The charges against him were dropped due, in essence, to lack of substance, and so this makes a good example for the more benign side of cracker activity. For more information about this case, see the set of articles in the March 1991 issue of the *Communications of the ACM* [6]. In these articles, Dorothy Denning presents an overview of the incident, a variety of authors respond with short position statements, then Denning gives a final rebuttal.

The basics of the incident are as follows. At age 16, Neidorf began an electronic newsletter called *Phrack*. Some of the articles gave instructions on how to gain access to a system or use telecommunications lines at no charge. One article in particular contained a text file that the government claimed was proprietary and sensitive. The value of the document to BellSouth, the company that originated it, was estimated at $23,900. The file, it was claimed, was sensitive and confidential information that contained a "roadmap" of the 911 emergency phone system. Neidorf was charged with six counts of wire fraud, computer fraud, and interstate transportation of stolen property. As the trial began, the defense brought out information that showed that Bellcore sold pamphlets about the 911 emergency system via an 800 number for $13 and $21. These pamphlets contained more information about the 911 system than was contained in the file published in *Phrack*. Also, the defense showed that Neidorf had received the file from another person. This person had downloaded the file from a BellSouth system and sent it to Neidorf for publication in *Phrack*. After the initial testimony, the judge announced the government was dropping the charges and declared a mistrial. Still, Neidorf and his family faced an estimated $100,000 in costs incurred in preparing for the trial [6].

It is a worthwhile exercise in critical thinking about cracking activity to consider the comments given on the Neidorf incident by various personalities and experts in the *CACM* articles [6].

Dorothy Denning suggests that "For many young computer enthusiasts, illegal break-ins and phreaking [manipulating the telephone system, similar to the way "hacking" refers to manipulating computer systems] are a juvenile activity that they outgrow as they see the consequences of their actions in the world. However, a significant number of these crackers may go on to become serious computer criminals." The critical-thinking error here can be seen as one of a circular argument. Note the value judgments about cracker activity that are implicit in the use of the phrases "computer enthusiasts," "juvenile activity" and "outgrow as they see the consequences of their actions." With the incident described in this way, it seems a foregone conclusion that it is a minor activity that should have minimal consequences. On the other hand, you could also easily argue that *all* "young computer enthusiasts" (call them "computer vandals" instead) who engage in "illegal break-ins and phreaking" are *already* "serious computer criminals" and deserve serious punishment.

Steven Levy, author of *Hackers: Heroes of the Computer Revolution*, argues that Neidorf should never have been brought to trial and asks "why the hacker culture—which on balance has been a boon for our economy and intellectual vitality—is seen . . . as something to be stamped out." The critical-thinking error here is one related to ambiguity of terms. Levy seems not to have practiced the distinction between *cracker* and *hacker* here. The hacker culture that "has been a boon for our economy and intellectual vitality" is represented by people like Ken Thompson or Dennis Ritchie. Nobody has suggested that their activities should be stamped out. The cracker culture is represented by people ranging from Craig Neidorf to Kevin Mitnick. People certainly have suggested that our society would be better off without the activities of a person like Mitnick and at least not harmed if the activities of a person like Neidorf were discontinued. The two categories of people and activities are quite different.

Richard Stallman, founder of the Free Software Foundation and the GNU project, argues that unauthorized access in itself should not be a crime. He maintains that the "concept of justice is that only actions that unjustly harm other people should be crimes." The critical-thinking error in this statement may be an instance of ambiguity centered in the phrase "actions that unjustly harm." It sounds like the right principle to use, but without more detail it is too vague to use as a standard. For instance, who gets to decide what constitutes unjust harm? As part of his argument, Stallman also offers the following analogy: "Unauthorized access is sometimes compared with trespassing. They are similar in some respects, but this does not imply they must be judged alike. We do not, for example, have laws against unauthorized use of a typewriter." The critical-thinking error here is one of a faulty analogy. The analogy seems meant to suggest that since there is no need for laws against unauthorized use of a typewriter, there is no need for laws against unauthorized use of a computer. But the analogy is fundamentally flawed. It goes only about as far as the fact that both the computer and the typewriter have a keyboard. What would be the typewriter analogy of what a cracker does when they break into a computer and read through personal records? What would be the typewriter analogy to what a cracker does in a denial-of-service attack? There are no good analogies, and so laws against unauthorized use of a computer may well be needed.

One lingering disagreement about the ethical fundamentals that is highlighted in the discussion of the Neidorf incident is: Is unauthorized access by itself necessarily harmful? There is a small but committed group in the Internet community that believes that there is nothing wrong with breaking into a computer so long as you don't actually do any damage. But would these people be as comfortable with that view if applied to a person who picked the lock of their home, came in, walked around, examined things, and then left? And how do these people know that their "benign" break-in will cause no damage until after they have successfully exited the system without having caused damage? What if they were to break into a system that was running a time-sensitive program at a time when the operator of the system assumed nothing else would be running? Most computer professionals and essentially all people in law enforcement argue that even an attempt to intentionally make unauthorized access is clearly unethical and should be considered criminal. The quotes from the codes of ethics at the beginning of this chapter reflect that sentiment.

4.5 ENHANCING COMPUTER SECURITY

Understanding the types of things crackers do and why they do them is good, but it does nothing by itself to protect your computer system. Those responsible for operating computer systems need to take active measures to monitor and enhance the security of their systems. The importance of preventive measures cannot be overstated. The saying "An ounce of prevention is worth a pound of cure" applies doubly to computer and information security. Unfortunately, management often does not consider computer security to be a concern until after the damage has been done. A study mentioned in the February 1995 issue of *Communications of the ACM* found that even though more than half the 1271 firms surveyed had incurred some loss related to (the lack of) computer security, 42 percent of senior management viewed computer security as only either "somewhat important" or "not important" [2].

The "Collaring the cybercrook" article talks briefly about preventing cracker activity. It mentions risk analysis, audit logs and firewalls as useful tools. "Risk analysis" refers to methodologies for analyzing your computer system to determine where the risks are and how important each is. "Audit logs" refers to keeping track of what commands are executed by what users. Typically not every command is logged, just commands that might represent cracker activity. And, since a successful cracker will typically alter files on a system to hide evidence of their break-in, an audit log is often written to a printer or a write-once device. A "firewall" is a system that stands between your protected systems and the world at large. All traffic to/from the protected systems must pass through the firewall, and it is the firewall's job to shield the protected systems from cracker activity.

Firewalls are becoming an increasingly popular approach to computer security, and so the reprinted article "Firewalls fend off invasions from the net" goes into substantially more detail on the operation of firewall systems. It includes discussion of testing and evaluating firewall systems, and a nice list of pointers to additional information.

The reprinted article "The threat from the net" also discusses firewalls and audit logs. In addition, it mentions several tools available to help systems administrators check on their systems' security: "COPS," "SATAN," and "Tripwire." COPS, which stands for Computerized Oracle and Password System, was an early software package created to help Unix systems administrators detect possible security problems. The SATAN tool package caused a good deal of controversy when it was first publicly released. The worry was that access to the knowledge embedded in SATAN would result in a dramatic increase in cracker attacks. In retrospect, this seems not to have happened.

Perhaps the biggest consistent force for increased computer security on the Internet has been the Computer Emergency Response Team (CERT). CERT was created in 1988 in the aftermath of the Internet Worm incident. CERT is an important resource for administrators of systems on the Internet. Its purpose is to provide help in making computer systems more secure and in tracking down intruders. In the first five and a half years of its existence, CERT responded to nearly 3000 cracker incidents [5]. The article "CERT Incident Response" details a sample incident and the CERT response. It explains current CERT activities and looks at future plans and directions. The article refers to some features and system commands in Unix that may not be familiar to all readers. However, the article is included more to give you an overview of CERT than to explain details of particular Unix operations. Every system administrator should be aware of CERT and its operations.

4.6 Conclusion

Computer security is vitally important. Our financial records, credit histories, and personal information are stored on computers. Our businesses have their customer records and other vital information on computer. We all depend on this information being correct, available when needed, and confidential. Crackers undermine our ability to depend on this. All cracking activity is unethical, and most is also illegal.

How do we go about reducing the level of cracking activity? There is no one answer. Better education about the ethics of computer use should help to some degree. Less sensationalized coverage of cracker incidents by the news media should also help. More consistent and careful attention to computer security by those who operate computer systems is still needed. And, stiffer and more certain punishment may deter some would-be crackers. Combined advances on all of these fronts should make our computerized world more secure.

Points to Remember

- We should recognize a substantial difference in meaning between the terms "cracker" and "hacker."
- The professional codes of ethics clearly state that cracker activities are unethical and unprofessional.
- The legal system is evolving to better handle and better enable the successful prosecution of cracker activities.
- With the emergence of the world-wide-web and e-commerce, cracker activities have greater potential to harm a larger number of people.
- Many organizations are lax in their attention to computer security, and could do a much better job with only a modest additional investment of time and attention.

WORKSHEET—What Makes a Cracker Instead of a Hacker?

1. Describe four personal qualities you would expect to be true of someone called a "hacker" and four qualities you would expect of a "cracker."

2. What should educational institutions do to encourage the development of more hackers and fewer crackers?

3. Can cracker activities be discouraged by stiffer legal penalties? Why or why not?

4. Can cracker activities be discouraged by better system security? Why or why not?

5. Can cracker activities be discouraged by different media coverage? Why or why not?

WORKSHEET—Cracking and Security Concepts and Terminology

1. What is a computer virus?

2. What is a Trojan horse?

3. What is password sniffing?

4. What is a denial-of-service attack?

5. What is a firewall?

6. What is a security audit log?

7. What is CERT?

8. What is SATAN?

WORKSHEET—The "Wily Hacker" Incident

Read the article titled "Stalking the Wily Hacker" by Clifford Stoll in the May 1988 issue of the *Communications of the ACM,* and then answer the following questions.

1. What were the security holes exploited by the cracker?

2. What things did the cracker do to try to avoid detection?

3. What does Stoll describe as the damage caused by the cracker?

4. What was done to increase computer security at LBL after this incident?

5. What was the eventual legal decision in the court case against the cracker? (This can be found in Stoll's book or in the video "The KGB, the Computer and Me.")

6. What do you think happened to the cracker who died before the trial? (Again, this can be found in Stoll's book and in the video.)

WORKSHEET—The "Internet Worm" Incident

Read the article titled "Crisis and Aftermath" by Eugene Spafford in the June 1989 issue of the *Communications of the ACM,* and then answer the following questions.

1. What was the flaw in the **finger** program that was exploited by the worm?

2. What was the flaw in the **sendmail** program that was exploited by the worm?

3. What strategy did the worm use to fish for passwords?

4. What are the reasons for concluding that the worm author had a relatively benign intent?

5. What are the reasons for concluding that the worm author's ultimate intent is unknown?

6. What is Spafford's opinion about the responsibilities of the systems administrators of the infected machines?

7. What is Spafford's opinion about the responsibilities of professional computer scientists and computer engineers?

WORKSHEET—The "Phantomd" Cracker Incident

Read the article titled "Cracker" by David Freeman and Charles Mann in the June 2, 1997 issue of the *US News and World Report,* and then answer the following questions.

1. What were some of the cracker tools used by "Grok?"

2. Has computer security on the Internet changed substantially since the incident described by Stoll?

3. What cracker tools did "Phantomd" and "Jsz" use to get account passwords off the Internet backbone?

4. What was the state of cleanliness in the room where Phantomd worked?

5. What was the state of Phantomd's mental health?

6. What is "RootKit?" Is it dangerous? Should the person placing it on the web be prosecuted? Why/why not?

7. What are the four steps toward greater security suggested at the end of the article?

WORKSHEET—Thompson's "Reflections on Trusting Trust"

Read Ken Thompson's reprinted article titled "Reflections on Trusting Trust" and then answer the following questions.

1. For what technical contribution did Ken Thompson receive the ACM Turing Award?

2. What is the process of teaching the binary version of the compiler to "know" about a particular character code?

3. How does this process relate to installing a "Trojan horse" on a computer?

4. What does Thompson say is the moral to his Trojan horse example?

5. What is Thompson's opinion of press coverage of "hackers?"

6. How appropriate is Thompson's analogy to "breaking into a neighbor's house?"

7. How appropriate is Thompson's analogy to "drunk driving of an automobile?"

WORKSHEET—"SYN flooding" Denial-of-Service Attacks

Read the reprinted article titled "Phony connections gag Internet servers" and then answer the following questions.

1. What was the rate of phony connection requests in the Panix attack? What did this do?

2. What does the article speculate caused/facilitated the attack?

3. Where does the origin of the 75-second time out period trace to? What is suggested as a more reasonable time out period? How does this help?

4. Why does hashing become important in maintaining the request buffer?

5. How does the cracker manage to hide their identity?

6. What does the CERT representative suggest should be done now by Internet Service Providers?

7. Why would ISPs not want to block spoof packets being sent out by their own customers?

8. Would you prefer your ISP to block or not block spoofed packets from being sent? Why or why not?

9. Should it even be legal to send spoofed packets? Why or why not?

WORKSHEET—Distributed Denial-of-Service Attacks

In February 2000, a series of denial-of-service attacks were made against companies such as Amazon.com, Yahoo.com, eBay.com and Buy.com. Read about these attacks and compare them with the attack against Panix described in the reading "Phony connections gag Internet servers" and the Melissa virus incident described in "Melissa Virus Creates a New Type of Threat."

1. What damage was done in the attacks—who was hurt and in what way?

2. If caught, what should the penalty be for the person(s) behind the attacks?

3. How was the attack organized—what types of systems were used? How were they used?

4. Would it help to prevent this type of attack if ISPs block spoofed IP addresses from leaving their systems? Why or why not?

5. Would it help to prevent this type of attack if Amazon.com, Yahoo.com and others used some means of authentication for connection requests? Why or why not?

6. Would it help to prevent this type of attack if more individual systems connected to the Internet used firewalls? Why or why not?

WORKSHEET—The "Melissa Virus" Incident

The Melissa virus caused some major problems in March and April 1999. It is an example of a "MS Word Macro virus." Read the reprinted article titled "Melissa Virus Creates a New Type of Threat" and then answer the following questions.

1. What kinds of systems were affected by this virus?

2. What were the estimates of costs and damage caused by the virus?

3. How quickly was the (alleged) creator of the virus arrested?

4. What are the potential penalties if the person is convicted? Are they appropriate? Too lenient? Too harsh? Why?

5. What is the trade-off between security and functionality that is illustrated by the Melissa virus? Is the added functionality worth the added security risk? Why or why not?

1. **Checking the security of your own system. (!)** Your computer system may be especially vulnerable if you use a *cable modem* or a *digital subscriber line,* since you are essentially on the web whenever your computer is switched on. There are a number of sites on the web that can help you check the security of your computer system; among these are www.grc.com, www.secure-me.net. One site where you can purchase a firewall for your computer is www.networkice.com. (But, as always, you should compare and evaluate products before you buy.) Browse the sites www.grc.com and www.secure-me.net and develop a security report on your computer system.

2. **The "Maxus" credit card extortion incident**. In January 2000, a cracker named "Maxus," apparently based in Eastern Europe, stole over 25,000 credit card numbers from CD Universe. The cracker then contacted CD Universe and threatened to post the numbers on a web site if he or she were not paid $100,000. The company refused to pay, and the cracker posted the numbers. Find as much detail as you can about this incident, including how the cracker managed to get the credit card numbers, what the company did after the credit card numbers were posted to the web and whether the cracker was ever caught.

3. **The case of cracker Kevin Mitnick**. Kevin Mitnick was called "America's most wanted hacker" in an article in *Time* magazine. He was arrested in February 1995. He was released from jail in early 2000. Report on his activities before the arrest and since his release.

4. **Programmer Timothy Lloyd seeding a "logic bomb."** In February 1998, a former programmer for a company which made instruments for the Navy and NASA was charged with creating a logic bomb. The bomb affected the computers at his former place of employment, Omega Engineering Corp., by deleting all of the company's software. Timothy Lloyd had been fired from his job at Omega about a month before this. Report on why Lloyd was fired, the cost to the company of fixing the damage from the logic bomb, and the results of the charges against Lloyd.

5. **Internet Explorer security hole**. In March 1997, Worcester Polytechnic Institute student Paul Greene discovered a security hole in Microsoft's Internet Explorer. The flaw would apparently allow someone to set up a web site that could delete files on the computers of people who use IE to connect to the site. Report on this and any more recent security holes found in web browsers. Are the security holes easily fixed? Are there any documented instances of crackers exploiting the holes? More information on Internet Explorer security issues can be found at www.microsoft.com/ie/security/.

6. **Techniques of information warfare**. Read the book *Information Warfare* by Winn Schwartau. Report on the techniques of information warfare discussed in the book. Which, if any, of these techniques has been reported to be used to date?

7. **Controversy over the SATAN anticracker toolkit**. SATAN is an acronym for Security Administrator Tools for Analyzing Networks. It was released in the Internet in April 1995 by Dan Farmer. Some people felt that the public release of this toolkit would only serve to enable more crackers to break into more systems. Report on the capabilities of SATAN, and the reported uses made of it since its release. Has its release been good or bad for computer security? Why? What other such toolkits are available?

8. **Norwegian Supreme Court ruling on cracking**. In January 1999, Norway's Supreme Court published a controversial ruling to the effect that simply looking for security holes is not a crime. A crime would not occur unless the system was actually broken into. Critics of the ruling suggested that it might make Norway a haven for crackers. Report on the case that led to this ruling, and on whether it resulted in an increase of hacking activity based in Norway.

9. **The Steve Jackson Games incident**. The Steve Jackson Games incident has become a classic case study. It is described in detail, from a certain perspective, by Bruce Sterling in *The Hacker Crackdown* [8]. Report on the facts and the final resolution of this incident.

10. **Levy's book on hackers**. Steve Levy's book, *Hackers– Heroes of the Computer Revolution* [3], contains a chapter, "The Last of the True Hackers." Who are the hackers described in his book? Are they, in general, the kind of people you would want as close friends? How are they different from the people referred to as crackers today? Are there differences in technical accomplishments? Are there differences in motivation? Are there differences in other respects?

REFERENCES

[1] Employment Law Forum of California, "Employee girlfriend of Oracle chief exec may go to prison for perjury," http://www.employlaw.com/HotNews6.htm.

[2] R. Fox, "Newstrack: Losses by numbers," *Communications of the ACM,* February 1995, p. 11.

[3] S. Levy, *Hackers–Heroes of the Computer Revolution.* Dell Publishing Company, New York, 1984.

[4] N. Munro, "Sketching a national information warfare defense plan," *Communications of the ACM,* November 1996, pp. 15–17.

[5] J. A. Osuna, "Internet security questioned," *Computing Research News,* May 1994.

[6] D. E. Denning, D. B. Parker, S. Levy, E. Spafford, M. Rotenberg, J. J. Bloombecker, R. Stallman, "Special section on the Craig Neidorf case," *Communications of the ACM,* March 1991, pp. 24–43.

[7] D. J. Schemo, "Passing the bug got him trouble by the megabyte," *The Roanoke Times & World News,* November 25, 1993.

[8] B. Sterling, *The Hacker Crackdown.* Bantam Books, New York, 1992.

[9] C. Stoll, *The Cuckoo's Egg.* Doubleday Publishing, New York, 1989.

Reflections on Trusting Trust

To what extent should one trust a statement that a program is free of Trojan horses? Perhaps it is more important to trust the people who wrote the software.

KEN THOMPSON

INTRODUCTION

I thank the ACM for this award. I can't help but feel that I am receiving this honor for timing and serendipity as much as technical merit. UNIX[1] swept into popularity with an industry-wide change from central mainframes to autonomous minis. I suspect that Daniel Bobrow [1] would be here instead of me if he could not afford a PDP-10 and had had to "settle" for a PDP-11. Moreover, the current state of UNIX is the result of the labors of a large number of people.

There is an old adage, "Dance with the one that brought you," which means that I should talk about UNIX. I have not worked on mainstream UNIX in many years, yet I continue to get undeserved credit for the work of others. Therefore, I am not going to talk about UNIX, but I want to thank everyone who has contributed.

That brings me to Dennis Ritchie. Our collaboration has been a thing of beauty. In the ten years that we have worked together, I can recall only one case of miscoordination of work. On that occasion, I discovered that we both had written the same 20-line assembly language program. I compared the sources and was astounded to find that they matched character-for-character. The result of our work together has been far greater than the work that we each contributed.

I am a programmer. On my 1040 form, that is what I put down as my occupation. As a programmer, I write

[1] UNIX is a trademark of AT&T Bell Laboratories.

programs. I would like to present to you the cutest program I ever wrote. I will do this in three stages and try to bring it together at the end.

STAGE I

In college, before video games, we would amuse ourselves by posing programming exercises. One of the favorites was to write the shortest self-reproducing program. Since this is an exercise divorced from reality, the usual vehicle was FORTRAN. Actually, FORTRAN was the language of choice for the same reason that three-legged races are popular.

More precisely stated, the problem is to write a source program that, when compiled and executed, will produce as output an exact copy of its source. If you have never done this, I urge you to try it on your own. The discovery of how to do it is a revelation that far surpasses any benefit obtained by being told how to do it. The part about "shortest" was just an incentive to demonstrate skill and determine a winner.

Figure 1 shows a self-reproducing program in the C[3] programming language. (The purist will note that the program is not precisely a self-reproducing program, but will produce a self-reproducing program.) This entry is much too large to win a prize, but it demonstrates the technique and has two important properties that I need to complete my story: 1) This program can be easily written by another program. 2) This program can contain an arbitrary amount of excess baggage that will be reproduced along with the main algorithm. In the example, even the comment is reproduced.

Reprinted with permission from *Communications of the ACM*, K. Thompson, "Reflections on Trusting Trust," Vol. 27, No. 8, pp. 761–763, August 1984. © 1984 by ACM Inc.

```
char s[ ] = |
    '\t',
    '0',
    '\n',
    '|',
    ',',
    '\n',
    '\n',
    '/',
    '.',
    '\n',
    (213 lines deleted)
    0
|;

/*
 * The string s is a
 * representation of the body
 * of this program from '0'
 * to the end.
 */

main( )
|
    int i;

    printf("char\ts[ ] = |\n");
    for(i=0; s[i]; i++)
        printf("\t%d, \n", s[i]);
    printf("%s", s);
|
```
Here are some simple transliterations to allow
a non-C programmer to read this code.

=	assignment
==	equal to .EQ.
!=	not equal to .NE.
++	increment
'x'	single character constant
"xxx"	multiple character string
%d	format to convert to decimal
%s	format to convert to string
\t	tab character
\n	newline character

FIGURE 1.

STAGE II

The C compiler is written in C. What I am about to
describe is one of many "chicken and egg" problems
that arise when compilers are written in their own language. In this case, I will use a specific example from
the C compiler.

C allows a string construct to specify an initialized
character array. The individual characters in the string
can be escaped to represent unprintable characters. For
example,

"Hello world\n"

represents a string with the character "\n," representing
the new line character.

Figure 2.1 is an idealization of the code in the C
compiler that interprets the character escape sequence.
This is an amazing piece of code. It "knows" in a completely portable way what character code is compiled
for a new line in any character set. The act of knowing

then allows it to recompile itself, thus perpetuating the
knowledge.

Suppose we wish to alter the C compiler to include
the sequence "\v" to represent the vertical tab character. The extension to Figure 2.1 is obvious and is presented in Figure 2.2. We then recompile the C compiler, but we get a diagnostic. Obviously, since the binary version of the compiler does not know about "\v,"
the source is not legal C. We must "train" the compiler.
After it "knows" what "\v" means, then our new
change will become legal C. We look up on an ASCII
chart that a vertical tab is decimal 11. We alter our
source to look like Figure 2.3. Now the old compiler
accepts the new source. We install the resulting binary
as the new official C compiler and now we can write
the portable version the way we had it in Figure 2.2.

This is a deep concept. It is as close to a "learning"
program as I have seen. You simply tell it once, then
you can use this self-referencing definition.

STAGE III

Again, in the C compiler, Figure 3.1 represents the high
level control of the C compiler where the routine "com-

```
    . . .
    c = next( );
    if(c != '\\')
        return(c);
    c = next( );
    if(c == '\\')
        return('\\');
    if(c == 'n')
        return('\n');
    . . .
```

FIGURE 2.1.

```
    . . .
    c = next( );
    if(c != '\\')
        return(c);
    c = next( );
    if(c == '\\')
        return('\\');
    if(c == 'n')
        return('\n');
    if(c == 'v')
        return('\v');
    . . .
```

FIGURE 2.2.

```
    . . .
    c = next( );
    if(c != '\\')
        return(c);
    c = next( );
    if(c == '\\')
        return('\\');
    if(c == 'n')
        return('\ n');
    if(c == 'v')
        return(11);
    . . .
```

FIGURE 2.3.

pile" is called to compile the next line of source. Figure 3.2 shows a simple modification to the compiler that will deliberately miscompile source whenever a particular pattern is matched. If this were not deliberate, it would be called a compiler "bug." Since it is deliberate, it should be called a "Trojan horse."

The actual bug I planted in the compiler would match code in the UNIX "login" command. The replacement code would miscompile the login command so that it would accept either the intended encrypted password or a particular known password. Thus if this code were installed in binary and the binary were used to compile the login command, I could log into that system as any user.

Such blatant code would not go undetected for long. Even the most casual perusal of the source of the C compiler would raise suspicions.

The final step is represented in Figure 3.3. This simply adds a second Trojan horse to the one that already exists. The second pattern is aimed at the C compiler. The replacement code is a Stage I self-reproducing program that inserts both Trojan horses into the compiler. This requires a learning phase as in the Stage II example. First we compile the modified source with the normal C compiler to produce a bugged binary. We install this binary as the official C. We can now remove the bugs from the source of the compiler and the new binary will reinsert the bugs whenever it is compiled. Of course, the login command will remain bugged with no trace in source anywhere.

```
compile(s)
char *s;
{
        . . .
}
```
FIGURE 3.1.

```
compile(s)
char *s;
{
        if(match(s, "pattern")) {
                compile("bug");
                return;
        }
        . . .
}
```
FIGURE 3.2.

```
compile(s)
char *s;
{
        if(match(s, "pattern1")) {
                compile ("bug1");
                return;
        }
        if(match(s, "pattern 2")) {
                compile ("bug 2");
                return;
        }
        . . .
}
```
FIGURE 3.3.

MORAL

The moral is obvious. You can't trust code that you did not totally create yourself. (Especially code from companies that employ people like me.) No amount of source-level verification or scrutiny will protect you from using untrusted code. In demonstrating the possibility of this kind of attack, I picked on the C compiler. I could have picked on any program-handling program such as an assembler, a loader, or even hardware microcode. As the level of program gets lower, these bugs will be harder and harder to detect. A well-installed microcode bug will be almost impossible to detect.

After trying to convince you that I cannot be trusted, I wish to moralize. I would like to criticize the press in its handling of the "hackers," the 414 gang, the Dalton gang, etc. The acts performed by these kids are vandalism at best and probably trespass and theft at worst. It is only the inadequacy of the criminal code that saves the hackers from very serious prosecution. The companies that are vulnerable to this activity, (and most large companies are very vulnerable) are pressing hard to update the criminal code. Unauthorized access to computer systems is already a serious crime in a few states and is currently being addressed in many more state legislatures as well as Congress.

There is an explosive situation brewing. On the one hand, the press, television, and movies make heros of vandals by calling them whiz kids. On the other hand, the acts performed by these kids will soon be punishable by years in prison.

I have watched kids testifying before Congress. It is clear that they are completely unaware of the seriousness of their acts. There is obviously a cultural gap. The act of breaking into a computer system has to have the same social stigma as breaking into a neighbor's house. It should not matter that the neighbor's door is unlocked. The press must learn that misguided use of a computer is no more amazing than drunk driving of an automobile.

Acknowledgment. I first read of the possibility of such a Trojan horse in an Air Force critique [4] of the security of an early implementation of Multics. I cannot find a more specific reference to this document. I would appreciate it if anyone who can supply this reference would let me know.

REFERENCES
1. Bobrow, D.G., Burchfiel, J.D., Murphy, D.L., and Tomlinson, R.S. TENEX, a paged time-sharing system for the PDP-10. *Commun. ACM 15*, 3 (Mar. 1972), 135–143.
2. Kernighan, B.W., and Ritchie, D.M. *The C Programming Language*. Prentice-Hall, Englewood Cliffs, N.J., 1978.
3. Ritchie, D.M., and Thompson, K. The UNIX time-sharing system. *Commun. ACM 17*, (July 1974), 365–375.
4. Unknown Air Force Document.

Author's Present Address: Ken Thompson, AT&T Bell Laboratories, Room 2C-519, 600 Mountain Ave., Murray Hill, NJ 07974.

Antivirus Technology Offers New Cures

Lee Garber and Richard Raucci

Work on computer-virus theory began 50 years ago, when John von Neumann described self-replicating systems.

Since then, viruses have become a serious security threat to casual home computer users and large corporate networks alike. The effort to combat this threat has spawned an entire industry.

Over the years, the antivirus industry has had to keep pace as virus writers have become more sophisticated. Antivirus products now not only detect and eliminate viruses, they can even delete or repair infected files, and remove infected sectors from system memory and disk drives.

Researchers have taken many approaches, and some of the newest and most promising antivirus technology is modeled on the way the human body fights viruses.

BIOLOGICAL MODELS

Researchers have been looking into biological models for computer antivirus systems for several years. Some of this research is based on the similarities between human and computer viruses.

Editor: Lee Garber, *Computer*, 10662 Los Vaqueros Circle, PO Box 3014, Los Alamitos, CA 90720-1314; l.garber@computer.org

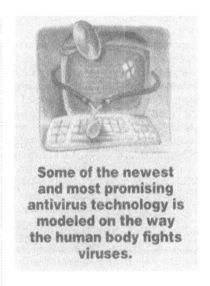

Some of the newest and most promising antivirus technology is modeled on the way the human body fights viruses.

Both types of viruses latch onto a host, use its resources to reproduce, and cause a range of symptoms.

Stephanie Forrest, associate professor at the University of New Mexico's Computer Science Department noted that in her antivirus research, "We were making models of the immune system and thinking about the immune system from an information processing point of view."

Immune System for Cyberspace

One of the most elaborate biologically based systems is IBM's Immune System for Cyberspace (http://www.av.ibm.com/current/FrontPage/), shown in the figure on the next page.

The Immune System will be linked to customers' computer networks via the Internet. It detects viruses using two heuristics, said Jeffrey O. Kephart, manager of IBM's agents and emergent phenomena group

One heuristic uses statistical techniques to create byte-signature fingerprints of uninfected executable files. The system then uses pattern-matching algorithms to compare these fingerprints to subsequent fingerprints of the files, Kephart explained. Changes indicate a possible viral infection. The Immune System then analyzes the changes to determine whether they were actually caused by a virus.

According to Kephart, the Immune System can also use a neural-network technique that quickly identifies short byte sequences that represent instructions for carrying out virus-related tasks. Programs with several of these sequences probably have a viral infection, he said. This technique can detect previously unknown viruses that include these viral instruction patterns, which is an advantage over systems that can recognize only known viruses, he added.

Once an infection has been identified, a copy of the infected program is sent to a central IBM computer. The computer's software provokes a virus into action on a decoy program so that it can be analyzed. The system then compares infected and uninfected decoy programs, using pattern-matching algorithms, to determine a virus' structure and the way it causes infections, Kephart said.

The central computer then develops, tests, and distributes a cure to the infected machine and all computers on the same network. The cure, which would immunize computers against future infection by the same virus, could also be distributed to other organizations that use the Immune System, Kephart said.

In tests, he said, the Immune System completed this process automatically in about three minutes and, in commercial settings, could do so "certainly in less than 10 minutes."

In many ways, the Immune System functions like the human body, which also must recognize that an infectious

Reprinted from *IEEE Computer*, Vol. 31, No. 2, pp. 12–14, June 1997.

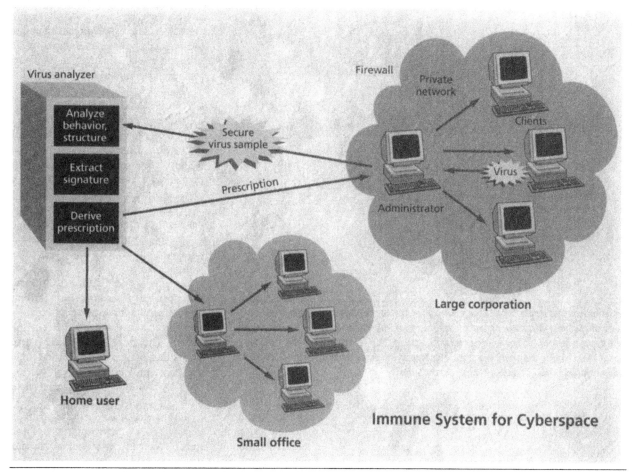

Labels in figure:
Virus analyzer
Analyze behavior, structure
Extract signature
Derive prescription
Secure virus sample
Prescription
Home user
Small office
Firewall
Private network
Clients
Virus
Administrator
Large corporation
Immune System for Cyberspace

IBM's Immune System for Cyberspace uses two types of heuristics to detect viruses. Once a virus is detected in an organization's machine, it is sent to the Immune System. The Immune System provokes the virus into action on an isolated decoy program to study how it works. The system then develops, tests, and distributes a cure to the infected computer, to other machines on the same network, and potentially to other Immune System customers.

agent is present, identify the agent, and then develop and implement a cure. And like the human body, IBM's technology also remembers and stores antibody information, which reduces response time to future infections.

IBM plans to begin a pilot program for selected clients in the near future and to sell Immune System services commercially by the middle of this year, Kephart said.

T-cell model

The University of New Mexico's Forrest has modeled a biologically based approach to antivirus technology on another aspect of the human immune system: T cells.

T cells have many different receptors on their surface, each of which can bind to a different foreign material the cell has not contacted before. This helps the body identify and subsequently fight harmful foreign materials in the body.

Forrest said the algorithm she developed generates random byte patterns, which function like the many receptors on the surface of T cells. The algorithm compares each pattern against existing code in a file, and if there is no match, it stores the pattern. If the pattern shows up later, that means the program has changed. This step is the equivalent of the way the human body uses T cells to identify foreign materials. Forrest said her algorithm uses a partial-matching rule with a threshold that makes sure only changes of a certain extent and nature are analyzed.

Her algorithm is not designed to specifically identify viruses but to determine changes in files, programs, and patterns of activity that could indicate the presence of a virus or some other problem. She said the algorithm will recognize changes even if caused by a virus the

system hasn't seen before.

Because her algorithm is based on the human immune system, which is distributed and parallel, she said, her algorithm makes the most sense in computer settings where you also want distributed protection, such as networked systems or multiple computers that are running the same software. She emphasized that the algorithm is not a full antivirus system but could be used in one.

HISTORY AND PREVALENCE

The development of biological antivirus technologies is the latest step in the history of computer viruses, which began 50 years ago with von Neumann's theories on self-replicating systems.

The first attempts to write programs based on von Neumann's work occurred in the 1960s. A self-replicating program called "Cookie Monster" (ftp://ftp. stratus.com/pub/vos/multics/tvv/cookie.

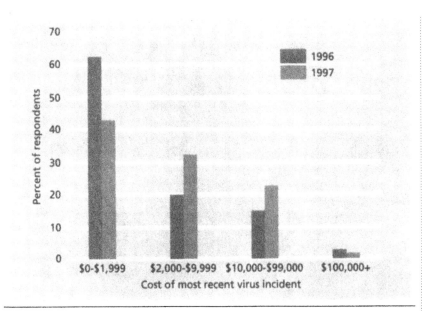

Organizations that responded to surveys conducted the last two years by the International Computer Security Association reported that they experienced a range of costs while coping with damage caused by their most recent virus incident. This reflects the varying levels of damage that viruses can cause due to such factors as lost user productivity and IS staff time. (Source: International Computer Security Association)

html) that some MIT students wrote as a prank for the Multics operating system affected the MIT network in 1970 and spread to other networks. Some observers consider this to be the first computer virus.

Viruses began affecting desktop computers in the 1980s, starting with a harmless virus that infected Apple II systems in 1981. Viruses affected PCs and the Arpanet shortly thereafter. Since the late 1980s, the number of computer viruses has increased rapidly. While some viruses can be relatively benign, some can destroy files and even hard drives, with devastating effects on an organization. The figure above demonstrates the range of damage that viruses can cause.

Last December, the WildList information service (http://www.virusbtn.com/WildLists/199712.html), which works with 46 virus researchers reported that it found 256 different viruses in action currently throughout the world.

The Norton AntiVirus products by Symantec track about 13,000 different virus signatures. Dr. Solomon's Anti-Virus Toolkit tracks more than 15,000 virus fingerprints.

VIRUSES AND THE INTERNET

Viruses have become a particular risk with the advent of Internet technology, which makes it much easier to pass and spread viruses. Such technologies as Java and ActiveX pose important new problems. An ActiveX applet could automatically install itself in the background on a system and load a new file. Antivirus researchers fear a hostile applet could introduce a virus that way.

New viral threats will probably be along these lines, said Shannon Talbott, manager of Network Associate's McAfee Labs. A number of antivirus vendors sell products that block hostile Java applets and ActiveX controls.

ABOUT ANTIVIRUS TECHNOLOGY

Several basic antivirus technologies are used in a variety of products and research projects, including those based on biological models.

Scan-based virus detection

Many antivirus programs scan a system for infected files, either at a preset time (such as system startup) or after certain events (such as a file download).

Many scanning techniques search system memory, boot records, boot sectors, and files for byte strings that match the strings of known viruses stored in a lookup table. To maintain reliability, users must update lookup tables frequently. Viral scanning at the server level or via a LAN manager can help protect against infection being spread through-

out a network.

Other scanning techniques, including the biologically based ones developed by IBM and the University of New Mexico, can also detect unknown viruses.

Behavior-based virus detection

Some antivirus programs monitor a computer system for the type of behavior that a virus causes, such as a file trying to duplicate itself or multiple programs launching at the same time. However, these systems will also give false alarms if legitimate activities produce such behavior, said McAfee's Talbott.

McAfee's products use pattern-matching algorithms to analyze a computer system's behavior.

Symantec's Merritt said Norton Antivirus 4.0 uses a proprietary technology called Bloodhound to look for specific anomalous behaviors. Merritt said Norton Antivirus 4.0 can also execute a suspicious file in a virtual environment shielded from the main system, such as a Word for Windows emulator, to determine if it has a virus infection.

Comparing behavior-based and biologically based antivirus systems, Talbott said, "Basically, it all comes down to heuristics, which all of us in the antivirus community are looking at and implementing."

However, IBM's Kephart said the biological model offers special opportunities to take advantage of the similarities between computer and human viruses.

The University of New Mexico's Forrest agreed and said the key question is "What is it about the [human] immune system that is really important to computing?" Both Forrest and Kephart said it is important to adopt what is useful and discard what is not.

Therefore, to get the best results as research continues into biologically based computer antivirus technology, Forrest said, "We need a rich dialogue between biology and computation." ❖

Lee Garber is a staff editor at Computer magazine. Contact him at l.garber@computer.org.

Richard Raucci is a freelance technology writer based in San Francisco. Contact him at rraucci@well.com.

Collaring the cybercrook:
an investigator's view

In the information age, the cloak is the network
and the dagger is the data packet

Almost 50 years ago, when asked why he robbed banks, master thief Willie Sutton answered famously, "Because that's where the money is." Today, the "money" is in electrons coursing through the computers the world depends on. Over half a billion electronic messages traverse the world's networks each week. Millions of dollars change hands with the flip of a byte. Military might is increasingly a matter of information superiority. Whether to hobbyist cracker, commercial spy, or international terrorist, these transactions expose the soft underbelly of the information age. (A *hacker* is wildly inventive in software techniques, but a *cracker* is a hacker who breaks into computers.)

Just last year the U.S. Federal Computer Incident Response Capability (FedCIRC) reported more than 2500 "incidents," defined as "adverse event[s] in a computer system or networks caused by a failure of a security mechanism, or an attempted or threatened breach of these mechanisms." The Federal Bureau of Investigation's National Computer Crimes Squad, Washington, D.C., estimates that less than 15 percent of all computer crimes are even detected, and only 10 percent of those are reported. And, without solidly built investigative techniques, which would contribute to a public perception of safety, the very stability of today's military and commercial institutions—not to mention the cybermarkets that are envisioned for the Internet—is called into question.

A risky business

Computer crime, broadly put, is damaging someone's interests by means of a computer—stealing computer cycles without having authorized access to the machine; stealing, looking at, or changing the data on that machine; using it to get to other machines (an increasingly common situation in this age of networks), as well as more traditional crimes simply updated: hate e-mail, extortion with threats to computer operations, or, in some cases, even physical theft of machines.

Kevin Mitnick, at one time the most wanted computer criminal in the United States, is shown being arraigned in Raleigh, N.C., two days after his arrest on 15 February 1995.

Investigation of Federal crimes is generally the responsibility of either the Federal Bureau of Investigation (FBI) or the Secret Service, depending on whether the crimes are of an economic or military nature; in addition, a plethora of Department of Defense investigative services may come into play when appropriate.

By now, most people are aware of how dependent society is on computers. National security is in many ways in the lap of the machines, so to speak—from information on the positioning of reconnaissance satellites to technical analyses of weapons systems. Similarly, just as common criminals have learned that computers are where the money is, so espionage agents have learned that computers are where the intelligence is. Espionage is becoming more and more a game of computer break-ins, computer-based cryptography, and message-traffic analysis.

The cloak has become the network, and the dagger, the message data packet. In his 1989 *The Cuckoo's Egg*, a widely popular recounting of an espionage case, Clifford Stoll wrote how a 75-cent commercial accounting imbalance in California led him to a West German cracker extracting information from defense computers in more than 10 nations. The information was then sold to the Soviet intelligence agency.

The type of criminal in Stoll's book is not an isolated phenomenon, nor can his skills be classified as "dangerous to military" vs. "dangerous to economic" interests. Consider Kevin Mitnick [see photo], in some ways the most celebrated cracker of them all, for the number and audacity of his crimes and for his personal cat-and-mouse game with a leading security expert. Mitnick was an equal opportunity criminal. First in trouble with the law at age 16, when he was put on probation for stealing a Pacific Bell technical manual, he then went from strength to strength. By 1988, when he was 25, he was arrested by the FBI for breaking into the Digital Equipment Corp. computer network and stealing a pre-release version of its VMS operating

DAVID J. ICOVE
*Tennessee Valley
Authority*

Reprinted from *IEEE Spectrum*, Vol. 34, No. 6, pp. 31–36, February 1998.

system software; he then stored the software for the time being on a computer at the University of Southern California.

Let out in a supervised release program for his "computer addiction," Mitnick then broke the terms of the release, among other things for. listening in on a Pacific Bell security official's voice mail. By 1994, the U.S. Marshals, the FBI, the California Department of Motor Vehicles, several local police departments, and several telecommunications companies were looking for him. But his pride led to his downfall: he broke into the computer of Internet security expert Tsutomu Shimomura, and went on to dog him in what became a personal test of skills. In 1995, after a chase crossing a plethora of computer systems and data links, he was caught. Mitnick is now facing a sentence in excess of 10 years in prison.

For obvious reasons, the government is loathe to release information on its lapses in security, and inferences must be made from the few cases that have come to light. In 1990, for example, attacks were reported at facilities belonging to the U.S. Department of Energy, which among other things manages much of the United States' nuclear weapons research. The intruders were prevented from obtaining classified information, and an investigation was begun at once. Several weeks later the intruders were identified and located outside the United States.

More recently, a wiretap order was used to trace and identify 21-year-old Julio Cesar Ardita of Buenos Aires, who used a Harvard University computer to gain access to the Navy Research Laboratory, NASA's Jet Propulsion Laboratory and Ames Research Center, the Los Alamos National Laboratory, and the Naval Command Control and Ocean Surveillance Center. Consider that Ardita was essentially acting on his own and not backed by the tremendous resources of an enemy country's national computer facilities or by payments from an enemy country's treasury. It is clear that military and government systems are enduringly attractive targets for computer criminals, whatever their motivation.

Attacks directed against economic resources, by the same token, are wide-ranging both in intent and damage. They can range from strategic attacks against the nation—the corruption of the banking system, say—to vandalism and plain old theft, whether of money or corporate information. Individual computer users, international agencies, or corporations from small offices to conglomerates are all possible victims of computer crime.

Where the money was

Some revealing information on the typology of the crimes has been uncovered by a new study conducted by San Francisco's Computer Security Institute (CSI) in cooperation with the FBI. The "1997 Computer Crime and Security Survey" was aimed at determining the scope of the crime problem, and thereby raising the level of awareness of it among present and potential victims [see To Probe Further, p. 36].

The CSI/FBI survey of 563 organizations of all sizes reinforced what was already suspected—that computer crime is a real and dangerously stealthy threat. Sixty percent of the respondents were able to quantify their total loss due to the crimes, and the figure came to more than US $100 million.

Analysis of the breakdown of the statistics on monetary loss and type of crime is tricky, because not all victim groups were able to report financial losses reliably, nor can their monetary loss be compared with other losses due to criminal acts. Bearing that in mind, the report's summaries are interesting. Of those respondents incurring financial loss, three-quarters reported computer security breaches ranging from fraud (26 respondents and $24 890 000 in losses) and loss of proprietary information (22 respondents, $21 050 000 lost) to telecommunications fraud. The rest of the losses were due to sabotage of data or networks, viruses, unauthorized penetra-

tion by insiders and outsiders, and an old crime updated—the stealing of laptop computers.

It has long been assumed that most computer security problems are internal. But only 43 percent of the respondents reported one to five attacks from the inside, whereas 47 percent reported the same numbers for attacks from the outside.

Classifying the crimes

Computer crimes range from the catastrophic to the merely annoying. A taxonomy commonly adopted for them and of use to investigators groups them in terms of the four classical breaches of security. The first, physical security, covers human access to buildings, equipment, and media. The second, personnel security, involves identification and risk profiling of people within and without an organization.

The third group is the most purely technical of the four: security of communications and data. Finally, the preceding three are shackled if gaps occur in operations security—in the procedures in place that control and manage the security against the preceding areas of attacks, as well as procedures for post-attack recovery.

Physical security concerns itself with the protection of assets. Breaches of physical security include "dumpster diving," in which offenders physically rummage through garbage cans that may hold operating manuals or specifications. Electronic wiretapping, electronic eavesdropping, and denial or degradation of service are also considered physical crimes, because they involve actual access to the computer or cable.

Denial of service covers the physical disabling of equipment or the flooding of communications networks by waves of message traffic. The 1988 Internet Worm, the first Internet criminal event to be reported widely in the public press and the first case prosecuted under the 1986 Computer Fraud and Abuse Act, demonstrated spectacularly the impact of denial of service. This code was released without particular malice in 1988 by its creator, Robert Morris—ironically, as an experiment to enhance security—and was supposed to reproduce itself on one machine after another for a certain time before self-destructing.

But owing to a programming error, like a sorcerer's apprentice the test code continued to multiply on host after host, swamping each in turn until the Internet was basically at a standstill. (In fact, even Morris's e-mailed suggestions for a fix, sent anonymously to system administrators on the first day of the crisis, never made it through the congestion.) Administrators had to shut down computers and network connections, work was halted, electronic mail was lost, and research and other business was delayed. The cost of testing and repairing the affected systems has been estimated at over $100 million. In 1990, Morris was convicted and fined $10 000 (the maximum amount under then-current law), essentially for reckless disregard of the possible damage his code could do, and for using hosts as unwitting guinea pigs—an act of illegal entry no different than any other cracker's.

Personnel security aims at keeping people, both inside and outside the company, from deliberately or accidentally getting at computers or systems for illegal purposes. A common example is termed term social engineering, in which the criminal passes herself off as someone authorized to receive from the legitimate user passwords and access rights.

Breaches in communications and data security are attacks on the end-user's data and the software managing that data. Data attacks, as defined here, lead to the unauthorized copying of end-user data, whereas attacks on the software managing that data could exploit the so-called trap doors in many programs to hijack a session in progress or insert Trojan horses. Trap doors are supposedly secret patches that programmers put in their code so they can remotely get at it for repair or other actions; Trojan horses, like their Homeric namesake, are programs that seem innocuous but conceal damaging contents. Related to Trojan horses is the "salami attack," in which the attacker repeatedly

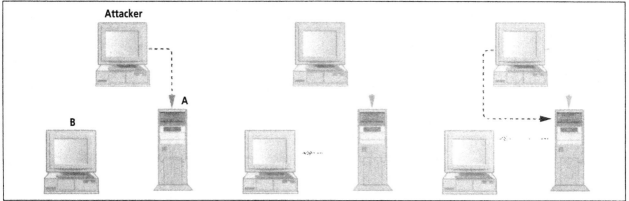

[1] An attacker of secure computers often masquerades as a user of a machine with high-level access rights. With Internet Protocol (IP) spoofing, the attacker's computer assumes another IP address. The scam has four steps. First, the attacker acquires the IP address of say, an Air Force general's computer [Computer A, left panel], perhaps by the simple scam of social engineering—pretending to be someone to whom that address can be released. Under the guise of that address, from a third site he opens a session with Computer B [middle], which contains classified information. Believing the request to be from A, B sends an acknowledgement and signals it is ready for communication. The attacker completes the deception by again mimicking A, in a final acknowledgment of B's signal [right]. As far as B is concerned, the attacker is the Air Force general, who may act in whatever way his access rights allow.

slices off and hangs onto a seemingly insignificant round-off on the fractions of pennies in financial transactions.

To put it at its most succinct, taking care of communications and data security is grounded on checking and rechecking a special trinity: the confidentiality, integrity, and availability of data.

Operations security contends with attacks on procedures already in place for detecting and preventing computer crimes. A case in point is "data diddling"—small but significant changes in data values, such as adding a few zeros to a $10 checking account. IP spoofing uses a method of electronically masquerading as a pre-existing but idle computer on the network and initiating a session under that assumed, perhaps privileged, identity [Fig. 1].

Password sniffing (obtaining passwords) describes the surreptitious monitoring of users' log-in procedures [Fig. 2]. And then there's scanning, the automatic, brute-force attempt at modem access to a computer by successively changing digits in a telephone number or password (scanners are also sometimes called war or demon dialers).

In both IP spoofing and password sniffing, network traffic is monitored by collecting the first 128 or more bytes of each connection, which sometimes contain both the log-in account name and password.

Two other types of computer crimes, one predominantly personal, the other financial, do not fit well into these categories but are serious and must be mentioned: harassment and software piracy. Harassment by sending repeated threatening electronic messages has become the latest form of hate mail. And software piracy is a staggering international economic problem, costing losses of revenues estimated at $4 billion, according to the Business Software Alliance and Software Publishers Association, both in Washington, D.C.

Classifying the crackers

Also for the sake of classification and tracking, it is helpful to have a relatively consistent analysis of the types of crackers. One, proposed by convicted cracker (and now security consultant) Bill Landreth, has five categories, each with fairly self-evident occupants: the Novice (mostly quickly bored young kids), the Student (college-age students with an intellectual curiosity

[2] Rather than fake a two-way communication session from his remote computer using IP spoofing, an attacker may use password sniffing to try to enter a target computer directly. This mode of attack involves monitoring the first 128 or more bytes of each connection, which sometimes contain users' log-in account names and passwords.

in security), the Tourist (who breaks in and persists only if something looks interesting), the Crasher (who delights in simply bringing machines to a halt), and the Thief (the most serious, knowledgeable, and blatantly "criminal" cracker).

For its part, the FBI has established three types of computer criminals: crackers, criminals, and vandals. These so-called offender profiles are based upon interviews of convicted offenders, documented case studies, and scholarly research. (Note that in other contexts these groups are not mutually exclusive: vandalism is legally a criminal act, and so forth.)

Crackers are generally young offenders who seek intellectual stimulation from committing computer crimes. Sadly, this type of behavior has often been reinforced as praiseworthy in popular entertainment. In the movie *Terminator 2*, for example, the boy hero is introduced as he electronically steals money from an automatic teller machine, ostensibly to show how smart he is.

Many offenders are juveniles, who view their computers as the next step up from a video game: for example, in 1989 a 14-year-old boy used a home computer to crack the code of an Air Force satellite-positioning system. He reportedly began his cracking career when he was eight years old.

Criminals, as a profile class, are often adults subgrouped into those who commit fraud or damage systems and those who undertake espionage. Industrial espionage has long been recognized as a shady competitive tactic. Fraud and damage encompasses all forms of traditional crimes—a fertile field for organized crime.

Banks have always tempted computer criminals. As far back as 1988, a seven-member group hatched a plot against a bank in a large mid-western city. They made use of a wire transfer scheme to siphon off about $70 million belonging to three companies first to a New York bank, and then on to two separate banks in Europe. The transfers were authorized over the telephone, and follow-up calls were made by the bank to verify the requests. But, in the group's fatal error, all the follow-up calls were routed to the residence of one of the suspects.

When the deposits did not turn up, needless to say, the three companies called the bank to find out what had happened. Investigators used the telephone records of the verification calls to trace the crime to the suspects.

Vandals usually are not pursuing intellectual stimulation, as when, for example, they deface World Wide Web pages open to the general public. The motivations of electronic vandalism often are rooted in revenge for some real or imagined wrong. A corporation

1. Computer vulnerabilities and countermeasures

Vulnerabilities	Physical threats			
	Intruders	Fire	Other sources	Illicit access to data lines
Software modifications[a]				
Poor auditing				
Ease of illicit access through software				
Easily corrupted/accessible data	●	●	●	
Clear paths for disclosure of information	●			●
Insecure software archives	●			●
Poor configuration control of:				
software				
hardware	●			
communication lines				
Poor physical control of:				
access	●			
environment		●		
personnel and management	●	●		
Poor contingency planning				
Poor communications protection	●			
Poor procedures				
Susceptible to hazards		●	●	
Countermeasures	• Alarms • Guards • I.D. badges • Locks on doors	• Smoke/heat detectors • Sprinkler & alarm systems • Area clear of combustible material • "No smoking" rule	• Water sensors • Anti-static carpet • Uninterruptible power supply • Lightning arrestors • Grounding	• Dedicated communication lines • Monitored access points to computers, networks • Shielded computer enclosures

[a] Includes threats to operating system, applications, and utilities.

undergoing downsizing should be extremely apprehensive of vengeful vandalism by present or past employees.

One of the better known cases in this category is that of Donald Gene Burleson, a systems security analyst at a Texas insurance company who was upset over being fired. Burleson essentially held his employer's computer system hostage. First, he deleted 168 000 of the company's sales commission records. When backup tapes were used to replace the missing files, he then demanded that he be rehired, or else a "logic bomb" in the computer would go off (this destructive software goes into action when triggered by some computational or externally supplied event, such as certain keystrokes or the date). The "bomb" was programmed to take electronic revenge should the employee be terminated. After his arrest and conviction Burleson was fined $11 800 and sentenced to seven years in prison.

Computer crime and the law

Prosecuting computer crimes is usually more complex and demanding than prosecuting other types of crimes. The process requires special technical preparation of the investigators and prosecutors and greater dependence on expert witnesses' testimony. Witnesses testifying for the victims may need to explain why the loss of intangibles—proprietary data, for example—are as serious as losses of tangible goods.

In the United States, the most comprehensive computer crime statute to date was included in the Computer Fraud and Abuse Act of 1986, which added six types of computer crimes to Title 18, United States Code, Section 1030. These newly defined illegal activities include those with traditional, Federal impact, such as unauthorized access aimed at obtaining information on national security; access to a computer used by the Federal government; and, interestingly, unauthorized access to a computer that itself is used to access a Federal government computer.

Equally welcome is the strengthening of the legal defense against economic crimes. Federal law now covers unauthorized interstate or foreign access with intent to defraud or obtain protected financial or credit information; unauthorized access that causes $1000 or more in damage; and fraudulent trafficking in passwords affecting interstate commerce.

Another Federal statute, the Electronic Communications Privacy Act of 1986, is intended to provide security for electronic mail on a par with what users would expect from the U.S. Postal

Procedural threats (on entry, once entry is gained, and in general)		
Illicit entry	Illicit presence	Threats due to sloppiness
●	●	●
●	●	●
●	●	
●	●	●
●	●	●
		●
		●
●	●	
		●
●	●	●
		●
		●
●	●	
		●
		●
		●
		●
• Assign computer passwords • Monitor employee's use vs. access rights • Install rigorous modification & verification routines when data is manipulated • Install rigorous handshaking (agreement) terms between computers before a session is initiated	• Ensure different security control at different levels of access • Install operating system kernel dedicated to security • Remotely monitor status of both physical and logical machines on system	• Peer review of software • Better documentation • Better training • Institute standard operating procedures

Service. As with postal letters on land, it is now a felony to read other people's electronic mail without their permission.

Precisely how does this affect me, you may be wondering. In brief, should your organization, whether public or private, fall victim to a computer crime, it should immediately seek competent legal representation. You may need to pursue legal remedies to what on the surface first appears to be a nuisance offense.

In their *Practical Unix & Internet Security*, Simson Garfinkel and Gene Spafford [see To Probe Further, p. 36] detail the following potential legal scenarios, which often lead to messy results:
• Unauthorized access to classified or sensitive data may require mandatory notification to investigator agencies.
• Being aware of criminal activities without reporting them may make you liable for your inaction.
• Deciding as an executive officer of a company not to make a report and cooperate with law enforcement may lead to your shareholders suing you.
• After filing an insurance claim for damages resulting from computer intrusions, you may be required by the insurance company to pursue legal action against the suspected intruders.

In sum, reporting suspected computer intrusions to the appropriate officials, combined with immediately obtaining competent legal guidance, will substantially reduce your liabilities and increase the likelihood of success by law enforcement in dealing with computer crime.

The prime contact to make after any computer incident is the 24-hour CERT (Computer Emergency Response Team) Coordination Center, which was formed by the U.S. Defense Advanced Research Projects Agency (Darpa) in November 1988 after the Internet Worm disaster. A similar, but private, organization is the Forum of Incidence and Response Security Teams (First), founded in 1993 [for contact information, see To Probe Further, p. 36]. Understanding the computer crime laws is also key to establishing good internal policies for computer crime prevention.

What the offenders teach us

In the late 1980s, the U.S. government started a series of studies designed to better understand the motivations, tools, and techniques of computer criminals. The information most sought after was good motive-based offender profiles, as well as a command of the lessons learned from criminal events, information which could be relayed to the computer security and law enforcement communities. In the end, the FBI prepared a detailed chart of the vulnerabilities of computer systems, possible threats to them, and countermeasures to take against the threats [see a summary of the chart, left].

Consider a member of a cracker group thought responsible for charging more than $30 000 in unauthorized telephone calls through voice mail systems as well as breaking into credit bureau computers to obtain financial information. This individual pleaded no contest to the charges, was sentenced to provide 150 hours of community service, and given a fine of $255 and court costs. The youthful offender was convicted as an adult.

Time and again the offender had accessed credit bureaus and had been quite successful in the art of social engineering, that is, misrepresenting himself as an authorized user or official; he had an outspoken hatred for law enforcement in general; and, when questioned, he had told police only what he believed they already knew.

Further study of the circumstances of the case and the offender's behavior turned up several lessons in security, as well. He had easily gained access to computer systems using default accounts, often even invading the root directory, from which all system-wide administrative procedures can be implemented. He had carefully located known weaknesses in computer systems and had been undeterred by warning calls from security personnel.

Preventive weapons

In the fight against unauthorized access from external sources, or attempts from inside by personnel to exceed their authorized access levels, three distinct computer-crime prevention tools have emerged: firewalls, auditing, and risk assessments.

Firewalls are software programs specifically designed as a

security interface between the Internet and a local host. When correctly installed and maintained, they safeguard against unauthorized access from the Internet, and can control access from within a company network to the Internet. Usually placed upon a secure workstation dedicated only to hosting security software, most firewalls use Unix as their native operating system. An effective firewall also has mandatory file and virus checking to reduce the likelihood of importing malicious computer worms or code.

Auditing data transactions with logs—keeping track of who accesses what and with which processes—is a natural byproduct of a firewall. In addition to providing security, this data record can reveal historical patterns in both internal and external attempts to break into computer systems and data. A critically important security job is timely reviews of the log and user activity, by both trusted human administrators and automatic procedures that take action upon evidence of anomalies.

Risk analysis—establishing a plan for the security and privacy of each computer system—balances the cost of various types of protection against the costs of doing without them. Periodic risk assessment is the best pro-active weapon against computer crimes. Indeed, Section 6 of the Computer Security Act of 1987 (Public Law 100-235) mandates that U.S. Government computer systems containing sensitive information undergo approved risk analyses. [Note: firewalls, auditing, and risk assessments will be discussed in detail in coming issues of *Spectrum*.]

For whom the bell tolls

Computer crime is a grave problem. It threatens national security with opportunities for modern criminals that go far beyond anything previously experienced. Although improvements in security are helping to keep it under control, the criminals are keeping pace with technology.

Surveys, case studies, and observations suggest that major problems will be encountered before the year 2000. Networks will continue to be vulnerable, and financial, medical, and credit reporting networks will endure major outages as a result. Political extremists and terrorists targeting critical services will score successes, as will organized crime. Major international high-technology financial thefts involving electronic fund transfers and "Internet commerce" will take place. To top it all off, court-qualified investigators and laboratory evidence technicians will be in short supply.

But let me put all this as personally as possible. If you are a manager or owner of a business, computer crime can undermine everything you have worked so hard to accomplish within your organization. Computer criminals, masquerading as authorized users, may be able to figure out how to access and steal the business plans you've labored over. Trade secrets about the product on the verge of being released may help a competitor beat you to market. Disclosure of confidential material may also lead to a loss of credibility with your vendors and put your company at risk of not receiving government contracts.

If you are involved in law enforcement, whether as an investigator or a prosecutor, you may have to deal with either a computer crime investigation or a case where computers have been used by those responsible for other crimes. You may have to assist in the preparation of a subpoena for computer crime evidence, participate in the collection of computers and computer media during an arrest or during the execution of a search warrant, or be called upon to conduct a major investigation of a computer crime.

As the victim of a computer crime, you may be asked by law enforcement to assist in tracking a computer trespasser, or in putting together data that will later serve as evidence in the investigation and prosecution of a suspected computer criminal.

If you are an ordinary computer user, realize that you, too, are vulnerable. If you fail to protect your log-in account password, files, disks, and tapes, and other computer equipment and data, they might be subject to attack. Even if what you have is not confidential in any way, having to reconstruct what has been lost could cost hours, days, or longer in productivity and annoyance.

Finally, in this era of networked computers, even if your own data is not a worry, you have a responsibility to protect others. Someone who breaks into your account could use that account to become a privileged user at your site. If you are connected to other machines, the intruder could then use your system's networking facilities to connect to other machines that may contain even more vulnerable information.

The word *responsibility*, at all levels, sums it up. By working together responsibly, far more often than not the good guys can outmatch their adversaries. ◆

To probe further

More detailed techniques and case studies can be found in *Computer Crime: A Crimefighter's Handbook* (O'Reilly & Associates, Cambridge, Mass., 1995), by the author of this article, Karl Seger, and William VonStorch, and in the FBI manual, by the same three authors, on which the book was based: *The Prevention and Investigation of Computer Crime: A Training Manual* (The Federal Bureau of Investigation, 1995).

Kenneth Rosenblatt's *High Technology Crime: Investigating Cases Involving Computers* (KSK Publications, San Jose, Calif., 1995) is also excellent for security personnel. It comes with a disk containing software for search tool kits and sample search warrants.

A good mix of technical and practical knowledge is presented in *Practical Unix & Internet Security*, by Simson Garfinkel and Gene Spafford (O'Reilly & Associates, Cambridge, Mass., 1996).

The most recent survey of the effects of computer crime, and which was highlighted in this article, is discussed in Richard Power's "Computer Security Issues and Trends" (Computer Security Institute, San Francisco, Vol. 3, Spring 1997).

For obvious reasons, the computer security community on the Internet is vast. One well-organized list of resources is at the Library of Congress's Web site, http://lcweb.loc.gov/global/internet /security.html. Another is that of the Coast (Computer operations, audit, and security technology) lab at Purdue University: http://www.cs.purdue.edu/homes/spaf/hotlists/csec.html.

For information explicitly on investigation see the Web site of the High Technology Crime Investigation Association, http://htcia.org/ HTCIA_CH.html.

The 24-hour hotline of the Computer Emergency Response Team Coordination Center (Cert/CC) is 412-268-7090; fax, 412-268-6989; Web, http://www.cert.org; ftp, ftp://info.cert.org/pub/.

Clifford Stoll's *The Cuckoo's Egg: Tracking a Spy through the Maze of Computer Espionage* (1989; reprint, Pocket Books, New York, 1995) first stirred public discussion of the more subtle byways of computer crime.

Good starting points from which to look at security from the cracker's perspective are http://www.digicrime.com and http://www. 2600.com, the home site of 2600 Magazine. A large collection of links to sites of interest to crackers is http://www.ica.net/pages/srusso/hack/ wwwlinks.html.

Spectrum editor: Robert Braham

I n the United States in the late 19th century, when desperadoes rampaged through the Wild West, communication, commerce, and even basic trust in civil authority were threatened. Today's electronic highway is similarly threatened by a new breed of "highwaymen," called crackers, ranging from malicious pranksters to hardened terrorists. For the sake of public trust in the Internet, an infrastructure must be designed to support its safe use; systematic mechanisms and protocols must be developed to prevent breaches of security.

Since the Internet is an international collection of independent networks owned and operated by many organizations, there is no uniform cultural, legal, or legislative basis for addressing misconduct. Because the Internet has no central authority through which it can regulate the behavior of those using it, most organizations connected to the Internet have their own security policies. But these policies vary widely in their objectives and how they are put into effect.

Today most companies have a formal or informal information-security policy—a written or oral statement of objectives for ensuring that a system and the information in it meet with only appropriate treatment. Associated with this statement are those corporate and personal practices that must be implemented to reach the policy's goals. Typical policy objectives include protecting the confidentiality of private information, preventing unauthorized modification of data (that is, ensuring data integrity), and preserving the availability of system resources (such as computer time), in accordance with the needs and expectations of the system's users. In printed form, the policy and practices can range from a single page to manuals of several volumes.

Just as a legal system is designed to stop wrongdoers from harming those who live within its boundaries, a security policy prevents the unacceptable use of an information system's resources and data without impeding legitimate activity. The policy must protect not only the data stored on those company computers connected to the network, but the data contained in the communications relayed by the network as well; electronic mail passed along by network routers must be as sacrosanct as personnel records stored on the corporate mainframe.

A formal security policy may consist of a mathematical model of the system as a collection of all its possible states and operations, plus a set of constraints on when and how they may exist. But just as it is difficult to write laws that precisely define unacceptable behavior, it is hard to write security policies that formally and precisely express which activities are disallowed.

In current practice, security policies are usually stated informally, in ordinary language—which hobbles the task of translating their intent into a computerized form that automates enforcement. Imprecise translation, however, is not the only problem; automated security mechanisms may be configured incorrectly, too. In either case, the problem opens the system to malicious behavior.

Basic to any security policy is prevention of intrusion— that is, denial of access to a system's data or resources by someone not cleared for such access. Even an unintentional intrusion violates security.

As serious as an intrusion is, it is just the start of security problems. Determining what the intruder may have done once he or she gained access is usually more critical. As far back as 1980, the consultant James P. Anderson of Fort Washington, Pa., in his seminal report *Computer Security Threat Monitoring and Surveillance*, defined a still-useful list of the types of mischievous actions an intruder can carry out, which may be summarized as:
• Masquerading (impersonating an authorized user or a system resource, such as an e-mail server).
• Unauthorized use of resources (running a lengthy program that eats up computing cycles and so keeps others from running programs).
• Denial of service (by, say, deliberately overloading a system with messages to keep others from gaining access to it).
• Unauthorized disclosure of information (illicitly reading or copying an individual's personal information, such as a credit card number, or sensitive corporate data, such as business plans).
• Unauthorized alteration of information (tinkering with file data).
A single intrusion can result in a number of these problems.

Ways to detect an intrusion and assess what the intruder did must be well thought out. For the most part, they will rely upon the ability of each system on the Internet to keep a log of events. The logs are invaluable for intrusion

The Threat from the Net

As it stands today, the Internet is not secure, so the only option is to understand how attacks occur and how best to protect against them

detection and analysis; indeed, they are basic to all post-attack analysis. Authors of the security policy must determine what to log (keeping in mind how the desired level of logging will affect system performance) and how the logs should be analyzed. The logs should note who has entered the system as well as what they have done.

Before a detailed examination is made of security methods, the issues affecting security enforcement warrant a broad overview.

An ounce of prevention, a pound of detection
The means of enforcing security policy involves either prevention or detection. Prevention is prophylactic—it

Reprinted from *IEEE Spectrum*, Vol. 34, No. 8, pp. 56–63, August 1997.

seeks to preclude the possibility of malicious behavior. Detection, on the other hand, aims to discover and record any possibly malicious behavior as it occurs.

Among the protection mechanisms are access controls such as permission to access files, cryptography for safeguarding sensitive data such as credit card numbers, and authentication by asking for a password. All these are designed to ensure that only an authorized person can gain access to systems and alter information. Audit mechanisms, on the other hand, are investigative tools that detect and quantify malicious behavior. For example, some tools examine user activities on the system as they occur, while others check the records (called "audit logs") of system behavior.

One class need not be employed exclusively; in fact, most systems employ both. Audit can serve to review the effectiveness of access controls, while audit logs usually have the highest levels of access control to prevent a cracker from covering his or her tracks by altering them.

Even so, policies cannot be enforced exactly because of the limitations inherent in translating policies stated in everyday language into the software that enforces its intent. A case in point: the file protection mechanism of the Unix operating system can limit access to a file, but it cannot prevent any user who has permission to read a file from making a copy of it.

Besides the technological gap, there can be a gap between social policies and information security policies. People can usually distinguish between unintentional mistakes and malicious actions; computers cannot. There is even a gap between policies and actual user behavior: a system can be abused by careless authorized users.

The goal of protection mechanisms is to restrict a user's activities to those allowed by the security policy. A security policy might forbid any external users' viewing of information on an internal Web server, allow all internal users to view the information, but permit only certain corporate users to add to or change information on the server.

When a person tries to access a protected object—be it a text file, a program, or some hardware resource, such as a server—the system's access control mechanism determines whether that person is authorized to do so. If so, the person gains access; if not, the access is denied and an error message may be returned to the user. The decision is usually made during run-time at the beginning of each access. Alternatively, users may be given an electronic token, which they turn in at system start-up prior to making any accesses.

Creating and maintaining a security policy [Fig. 1] is an iterative process, during which the policy's authors must identify the organization's and users' security expectations, set them forth in a policy, enforce the policy, re-assess the system in light of policy violations or intrusions, and modify the original policy specification. During the re-assessment step of each iteration, both the policy and the protection mechanisms may be refined to address new attacks, close vulnerabilities, and update the policy to accommodate new user and organization requirements.

Protection's vulnerabilities

A cracker transgresses a security policy by exploiting the vulnerabilities in the system; if there were none, all attacks would fail. Vulnerabilities exist because the system's

MATT BISHOP, STEVEN CHEUNG,
& CHRISTOPHER WEE
University of California at Davis

designers, implementers, and administrators, when considering the problems would-be intruders might present, make assumptions and tradeoffs—about the environment in which the system will be used, the quality of data on which it will work, and the use to which it will be put. These assumptions stem from personal experience, beliefs about the environment in which the system operates, and the laws and cultural customs of the workplace. Vulnerabilities can be extremely subtle, existing in systems for years before being noticed or exploited; further, the conditions under which they can be exploited may be quite fleeting.

A good example of how assumptions breed vulnerability is to be seen in the development of the Unix operating system. Unix was created by programmers in a friendly environment, in which security mechanisms had to deal only with simple threats, such as one user accidentally deleting another's files. But as the Unix system's popularity grew, it spread into commercial realms, where the threats were very different.

For example, the original design of the Unix system has one all-powerful user (the "super-user"). Now in military and many other environments, the existence of such a user is a serious flaw. In fact, most attackers attempt to gain access in the guise of this user, so they can modify log-in programs or system libraries or even the Unix kernels, to let them return later. So the starting assumptions about security needs, reasonable though they were in the environment in which the Unix system was born, did not generalize well into other environments.

Vulnerabilities also arise when a use is made of systems that was not foreseen when they were built. Suppose a company decided that data from external World Wide Web servers should be barred from the company's network, say, to prevent unauthorized software from being sneaked into the system. To this end, the company could set up a firewall—software that can be configured to block specific types of communications between internal and external networks. To prevent Web traffic, the firewall might be configured to block communications using server port 80, which is the default port used by the Web's hypertext transport protocol (http) to transfer data. However, if someone outside the firewall purposely ran a World Wide Web server that accepted connections on port 25, the firewall would let communications to that server through on port 25. Because this kind of usage is not covered by the assumption (all http communications will go through the firewall at port 80), the site is vulnerable.

Another source of weakness is any flaw in the software system's implementation. A good example here are early server implementations that did not check input data. This allowed attackers to send messages to a Web server and have it execute any instructions in those messages.

Another good example is the initial implementation of Sun Microsystems Computer Corp.'s Java programming language, used to provide downloadable and executable programs called applets. To limit the dangers to the system receiving an applet, the designers restricted the actions the applet could perform, yet a number of implementation flaws allowed the little programs to breach those restrictions.

Also, it was the intent when designing Java to constrain each applet to connect back only to the system from which it was downloaded. To do this, an applet had to be written so that it identified the download system by its alias, or domain name (say www.xyz.com), not its absolute, or network, address (that is, 123.45.6.7), which is the actual address the Internet uses to locate the download system.

The problem, then, was that, when the applet asked to be reconnected to the download system, it had to request the download server's network address over the Internet by sending its domain name to a domain-name server, whose job it was to return the actual network address. If an attacker corrupted the domain-name-to-network-address translation tables in the domain server, it could "lie" and give a false network address.

Java's implementers trusted that the domain-name server's look-up table would be correct and reliable but, under fire from an attacker, it need not be. They later fixed this leak by having applets refer to all systems by addresses, not names.

Errors made when configuring the security system give rise to other vulnerabilities. For example, most World Wide Web servers allow their system administrators to use the address of the client asking for a page to control access to certain Web pages—such as those containing private company data. Should the system administrator mistype an address, or fail to restrict sensitive pages, the company security policy can be violated. Any time a system administrator or user must configure a security-related program—in the specific case noted by typing in a list of allowed-user addresses—a vulnerability exists.

Hardware vulnerabilities, usually more subtle, can also be exploited. Researchers have studied artificially injecting faults into smart cards by varying operating voltages or clock cycles so that the cryptographic keys inserted by the card's issuer could be discovered by comparing good and bad data. Evidently, while the "burning" of keys into hardware is supposed to protect them, it may not protect them well enough.

Vulnerabilities are not confined to end systems like servers. The computers, protocols, software, and hardware along the path to the server—that is, those that make up the Internet itself—have weak points, too. Consider the vulnerability of a router—a computer designed to forward data packets to other routers as those packets traverse the Internet to their final destination.

A router uses a routing table to determine the path along which the packet will be forwarded. Periodically, routers update each other's tables, making it possible to reconfigure the network dynamically as more paths are added to it. If, through design or error, a router were to announce that it were the closest one to all other routers, they all would send it all their packets. The misconfigured router would try to reroute the packets, but all routes would lead back to it. So the packets would never reach their destination—a perfect example of a denial-of-service attack and one that would bring the Internet to its knees.

Whom do you trust?

Central to the problem of vulnerability is the issue of what or whom to trust. Designers and engineers trust a system will be used in a certain way, under certain conditions; design teams trust that the other teams did their jobs correctly so that pieces fit together; program designers trust that the coders do not introduce errors; consumers trust a system will perform as specified. Vulnerabilities arise at every loose link in the chain of trust.

The vast scope of the Internet demands trust. Suppose Robin in Seattle wants to send a love letter via electronic mail to Sam in Tierra del Fuego. Robin types the letter on a computer and uses a mail program to send it to Sam, trusting that:
• The mail message contains the letter as typed, not some other letter.
• The mail program correctly sends the message from the local network to the next network.
• The message is sent on a path, chosen for efficiency by routers, over the Internet to Sam's computer.

• The destination computer's mail-handling program will receive the message, store it, and notify Sam that it has arrived.
• Sam will be able to successfully read the message using a mail-reading program.

For Robin's confidence to be well-placed, multiple pieces of hardware (including computers and dedicated routers) and the transport medium (be it twisted pair, fiber-optic cable, satellite link, or some combination thereof) must operate in the way intended. In addition, numerous pieces of software (including the mail programs, the operating systems, and the software that implements message transportation) must work correctly. In fact, the number of components in the network can become quite large and they must all interact correctly to guarantee that electronic mail is delivered safely. But if one of the components acts in some other way, Robin's trust is misplaced.

The man in the middle

Suppose that an attacker is competing with Robin for Sam's affections, and wants to intercept their e-mail billet-doux. If the messages traveling over the Internet can be modified en route, the message Sam receives need not be the one Robin sent. To do this, the attacker must change the router tables so that all e-mail messages between Robin's and Sam's computers are forwarded to some intermediate system to which the attacker has easy access. The attacker can then read the messages on this intermediate site, change their contents, and forward them to the original destination as if the intermediate site were legitimately on the message's path—a so-called "man in the middle" attack.

Using cryptography to hide the contents of messages, while often seen as the ultimate answer to this problem, is merely a part of the solution, because of a simple yet fundamental problem of trust: how do you distribute cryptographic keys? Public-key cryptographic systems provide each user with both a private key known only to that user and a public key that the user can distribute widely. With this scheme, if Robin wants to send Sam confidential mail, she enciphers a message using Sam's public key and sends the enciphered message to him [Fig. 2]. Only Sam, with his private key, can decipher this message; without that key, the attacker cannot read or change Robin's message.

But suppose the attacker is able to fool Robin into believing that the attacker's public key is Sam's, say by intercepting the unencoded e-mail message that Sam sent giving Robin the public key and substituting his own. Thus, Robin would encipher the message using the attacker's public key and send that message to Sam. The attacker intercepts the message, deciphers it, alters it, and re-encrypts it using Sam's real public key. Sam receives the altered message, deciphers it, and the romance goes sour.

The situation becomes even more complicated with the World Wide Web. Suppose Robin uses a Web browser to view a Web site in Germany. The German Web page, put up by an attacker, has a link on it that says: "Click here to view a graphic image." When she clicks on the link, an applet that scans her system for personal information (such as a credit card number) and invisibly e-mails it to the attacker, is downloaded along with the image. Here, Robin trusted the implied promise of the Web page: that only an image would be downloaded. This trust in implied situations ("this program only does what it says it does") is violated by computer programs containing viruses and Trojan horses. PC users spread viruses by trusting that new programs do only what they are documented to do and have not been altered, so they fail to take necessary precautions.

Auditing's objectives

Auditing, a way of finding such problems, has five main aims:
• To trace any system or file access to an individual, who may then be held accountable for his or her actions.

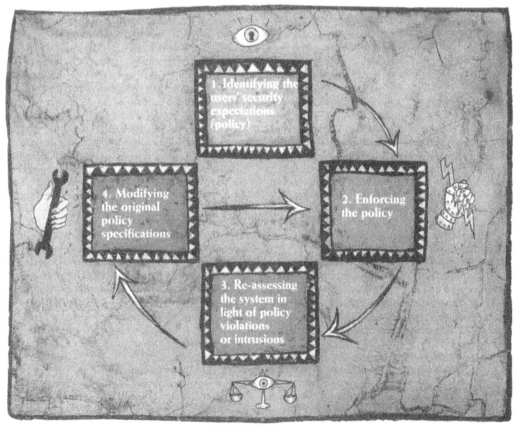

[1] As with most software processes, the creation of a security system is cyclic. Once the policy developers determine what the ultimate users of a system expect and need in the way of security, the cycle of enforcement, reassessment, and modification that makes up its life begins.

114

- To verify the effectiveness of system protection mechanisms and access controls.
- To record attempts that bypass the system's protection mechanisms.
- To detect users with access privileges inappropriate to the user's role within an organization.
- To deter perpetrators (and reassure system users) by making it known that intrusions are recorded, discovered, and acted upon.

While the goals of auditing are clear, they do not dictate that any particular audit scheme, or model, be followed, nor do they indicate how to perform the auditing. Thus current auditing consists of various *ad hoc* practices.

Auditing requires that audit events—such as user accesses to protected files and changes in access privileges—be recorded. A log is a collection of audit events, typically arranged in chronological order, that represents the history of the system; each logged event represents any change in the state of the system that is related to its security.

Because of the complexity of modern computer systems and the inability to target specific actions, audit logs can be voluminous. In fact, the logs are

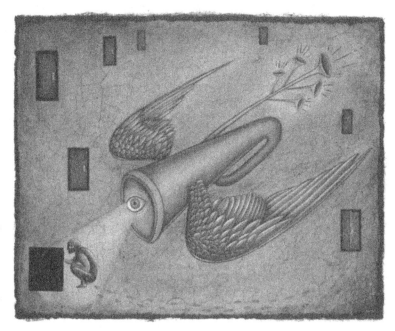

often so large that human analysis is quite time-consuming. It is therefore desirable to have tools that would cull entries of interest from the log. But development of such automated audit tools for all types of computer systems is hampered by three things: a lack of standard formats (such as ASCII or binary) and semantics (the order in which statements occur) for audit logs, and (as mentioned initially) the practice of stating security policies in an ordinary language that does not lend itself to automation.

While some tools have appeared to aid in log analysis, they are difficult to use. As a result, logs are usually inspected manually (often in a cursory manner), or possibly using some audit browsing tools that employ algorithms able to cluster together related data. All too often, they are not reviewed at all.

When the log is reviewed, the auditor compares the users' activities to what the security policy says that user may do and reports any policy violations. An auditor can also use the log to examine the effectiveness of existing protection mechanisms and to detect attempts to bypass the protection or attack the system. The identities of those behind attempts to violate the policy sometimes can be traced in the history of events, provided the audit log contains sufficient detail.

On networked computers, tracing the user may require an audit of logs from several hosts, some quite remote from the system where the intrusion occurred. Law enforcement agencies may want to use these logs as evidence when prosecution of the perpetrators is warranted, and this can spark jurisdictional and other legal disputes.

The Internet's basic design philosophy is to introduce new resources and capabilities at the end points of the network—the client and the server—so as to keep the infrastructure simple, flexible, and robust. The disadvantage of this philosophy is that the Internet Protocol requires only that the network make its best effort to deliver messages; it does not require that messages be delivered at all costs. Nor does it require that records of delivery be kept; as a result, logging on the Internet is merely a function of implementation, not a requirement of the protocols.

In a logging process known as packet sniffing, special software running on each node reads and logs data contained in the packets. Depending on the amount of traffic on the Net, sniffing can use up a lot of processing power and storage space. To minimize this resource drain, sometimes only the header portion of packets—which may contain such information as the packet's source, destination, and the number of packets making up the complete transmission—is logged and the message data in the packet is ignored. Deducing user behavior and the actions caused by the

message from the relatively low-level information obtained by sniffing calls into play many extrapolations and assumptions.

Whereas there is no standard for all types of systems, most World Wide Web servers do use a standard audit log format, so audit tools have been developed for a wide range of Web servers. Also, there is something of a standard for electronic mail: e-mail often has the name of each computer encountered, and some further information, placed in the headers of the message as the mail moves over the Internet. These headers constitute a mini-log of locations and actions that can be analyzed to diagnose problems or to trace the route of the message.

Although prevention mechanisms are designed to prohibit violations of the security policy in the first place, a specter of accountability—the attacker's fear of being discovered—is raised by detection mechanisms and thus serves as a deterrent. An audit, then, may be thought of as a defense against attacks, too, albeit a reactive one, in which clues to the identity and actions of the intruder can be detected.

System check

Fortunately, several tools exist to help administrators check their systems' security. For Unix systems, three popular tools are Satan, tripwire, and Cops; these are available free of charge at many sites on the Internet.

Satan is a World Wide Web–based program that analyzes systems for several known vulnerabilities exploitable only through network attack—such as the ability of a cracker to make available to any server files that are supposed to be restricted. It provides a Web browser interface, and allows scanning of multiple systems simply by clicking on one button. The browser presents a report outlining the vulnerabilities, and provides tutorials on the causes of each, how to close (or mitigate) the security flaw, and where to get hold of more information (such as the Computer Emergency Response Team, or CERT as it is popularly known, a group within Carnegie Mellon University's Software Engineering Institute in Pittsburgh that issues advisories about computer security).

Another means of verifying security is by checking up on the integrity of the system software—such as log-on programs and libraries—by seeing that the software has not somehow been altered without the administrator's knowledge. Tripwire is an integrity checking program that uses a mathematical function to compute a unique number ("hash") based on the contents of each file, be it a document or program. Each hash, along with the name of its corresponding file, is then stored for future reference. At random intervals, a system administrator reruns tripwire and compares the results of the new run with the results of the original one. If any of the hashes differ, the corresponding file has been altered and must be scrutinized more closely.

Cops examines the contents of configuration files and directories and decides if either their contents or settings threaten system security. For example, on Sam's Unix system, the contents of a configuration file might state that Robin need not supply a separate password to use Sam's system. This poses a double security problem at many sites, since anyone who obtains access to Robin's account also obtains access to Sam's system. Tripwire will not detect this problem, as it simply looks for files that changed—and the access control file does not change—but Cops will scan the configuration file, reporting that Robin does not need a password to log in to Sam's system, as part of its analysis of the configuration file's contents.

Intrusion detection

Intrusions can be detected either by manual analysis of logs for any suspicious occurrences or by automated tools that detect certain specific actions. Examples are unusual log-in times or unusual system characteristics, such as a very long run time for one supposedly simple program. Automated methods, of course, process lots of data more quickly and efficiently than humans could. The data comes from either logs or from the current state of the system [Fig. 3].

Human analysis entails looking at all or parts of the logs for a system with a view to uncovering suspicious behavior. The audit data may, though, be at such a low level, as previously mentioned, that events indicating an intrusion or attack may not be readily detectable as such. Here, detecting attacks may require correlating different sets of audit data, possibly gleaned from multiple logs; thus, a change in access privileges from the privilege log might be compared with the log-in log's record of the location from which the user who changed the privileges logged in. The data may span days or weeks and is often voluminous.

Another hindrance is that the person conducting the analysis must have special expertise, both in the hardware and software that constitute the system being audited and the particular way in which it is configured, to understand what may have happened and what actually did occur.

The previously mentioned consultant, James P. Anderson, also made the first serious study of how computers were being used to detect security violations. Modern computers have a capacity to analyze large amounts of data accurately, provided they are programmed to analyze the right data; to correctly detect intrusions, they must be told what to look for.

For this purpose, three methods have been established: anomaly detection, misuse detection, and specification-based detection. Among them, there is no one best approach to detecting intrusions; in practice, the particular combination of approaches used is tailored to an organization's specific needs.

Anomaly detection compares the current behavior of a person using a system to the historical behavior of the person authorized to use the system. The technique presumes that deviations from prior behavior—say, different log-in times or the use of different commands—are symptoms of an intrusion by an unauthorized person using a valid account. Similar reasoning suggests that a program altered to violate the security policy—that is, one changed by a virus so it now writes to other executables or to the boot program—will behave differently than the unaltered version of the program.

An intrusion detection system (IDS) based on anomaly detection must first be trained to know the expected behavior of each user, and there could easily be hundreds of users. This normalcy profile is built using statistical analysis of each user's use of the system and logical rules that define likely behavior for various types of users—programmers, sales managers, support personnel, and so on. Once a normalcy profile is established, the IDS monitors the system by comparing each user's activity to his or her normalcy profile. If some activity deviates markedly from the profile, then the IDS flags it as anomalous and, therefore, a possible intrusion.

Admittedly, a legitimate user can be flagged as an intruder (a false positive) because abnormal behavior is not necessarily an attack; for example, a legitimate user may become more proficient in using a program and thus employ commands not previously invoked. False negatives also occur when an intruder's actions closely resemble the normal behavior of the legitimate user whose log-in they have obtained. Finally, establishing the right time period over which to analyze the user's behavior and how often to retrain the IDS system affects its performance.

One anomaly detection system observes the interaction between a program and the operating system, and builds normalcy profiles of the short sequences of system calls normally made. Activity outside this is presumed to be part of an intrusion. For example, if an attacker tried to exploit a vulnerability in which unusual input, such as an e-mail message sent to a program rather than a person, caused a mail-receiving program to execute unexpected commands, these commands would be detected as anomalous and a warning given.

Unlike anomaly detection, in which normal user behavior is taught so that unusual behavior characteristic of an attack can be distinguished, misuse detection does not require user profiling. Rather it requires a priori specification of the behaviors that constitute attacks; if any observed behavior matches a specified attack pattern, the IDS warns the systems administrator.

The techniques used to describe the attacks vary. One method is to list events expected to be logged during an attack. A graph-based misuse detection IDS employs a set of rules that describe how to construct graphs based on network and host activity—for example, a graph of the connections between the systems involved in an attack, the time at which they became involved, and the duration of their involvement. The rules also describe at

[2] In public-key cryptography, a user sends a public-key–encrypted message, as shown here, that can be decrypted only with the recipient's private key. Many think such a scheme makes communication secure. But an attacker can defeat it by artfully switching the public key.

116

what point such a graph is considered to represent an attack.

Another is to have an expert write a set of rules describing "felonious" behavior. For example, suppose an attacker gave unusual input to a mail-receiving program to change the way it operated. The expected system calls were "read-input; write-file," but the attacker's input would try to change the set to be "read-input; spawn-subprocess; overlay-program." The last two items in the altered set, which tell the system to execute another program, indicate an attack. Were the attacker to try to intrude using that technique, the misuse detection program would detect it.

The misuse detection method can be highly accurate, but, unlike anomaly detection, it cannot detect attacks that fall outside its prepared list of rules describing violations of security. In addition, it depends upon having an expert who is able to specify such rules.

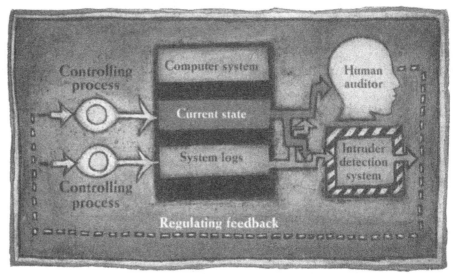

[3] An intrusion detection system (IDS) processes information from both the computer system and its logs and reports any problems to a security auditor. The initial information can also be used to determine what other actions should be taken and what further information should be logged.

While anomaly and misuse detection catch security breaches by focusing on the attacker's behavior, specification-based detection describes breaches in terms of the system's expected behavior. Further, if system behavior has been specified accurately, there are no false alarms. The first step is to formally specify how the system should behave in all circumstances. Once fully profiled, the system is monitored and all its actions compared against the specification; any item of system behavior that falls outside what is specified as correct is flagged as a security violation.

One approach to specification-based detection uses a special policy-specification language to describe the security policy in terms of the access privileges assigned to each program in the system. This language indicates under what conditions certain system calls may be made, and it requires knowledge about privileged programs, what system calls they use, and what directories they access. Depending on the particular system for which the policy is being specified and the specification language used, creating specifications of this kind may require expertise, skill, and some time—although some effort might be automated using program analysis. But if the specifications do not cover all eventualities, false negatives (intrusion alarms) can occur.

Several companies and research groups have developed intrusion detection systems. The authors' group at the Computer Security Laboratory of the University of California, Davis, is designing and developing one such tool, called GrIDS, that will monitor both systems and network traffic, looking for actions indicating misuse. It also supports analysis of attacks conducted from more than one outside source, even when the attack is spread over a large number of systems.

Other, nonresearch systems are less ambitious, but are currently deployed. CMDF from Science Applications International Corp. (SAIC), San Diego, Calif., uses the anomaly approach by building a database of statistical user profiles and looking for deviations from that profile. NetRanger from WheelGroup Corp., San Antonio, Texas, and NetStalker from Haystack Labs Inc., Austin, Texas, detect attacks by comparing system actions to known exploitations of vulnerabilities.

Counterattack and damage assessment

Several responses to security violations are possible, particularly if the attack is detected while it is occurring, typically within a matter of seconds or minutes after an intrusion starts. The simplest reaction is to alert other people, while a more complex, automated detection system might respond autonomously to any violations of policy. The type of response selected depends on the degree of confidence that an attack is actually under way, and upon the nature and severity of the attack.

The first response by a security team to a reported attack is to gather the information needed to analyze the violation and decide how to respond further. Also, additional auditing—of more user accounts or more system resources—may be turned on, possibly only for those users involved in the violation or possibly, if the extent or nature of the violation of policy is not fully understood, for the entire system. Moreover, the system can turn defense into offense, fooling the attacker by countering his activities with misleading or incorrect information; the attacker can even be lured by the security team to a system designed on purpose to monitor intruders.

Another common response to a violation is to determine who is responsible. After that, legal action might be taken, or more direct responses (such as blocking further connections from the attacker's site or automatically logging the attacker off) may be appropriate. However, determining whom to hold accountable can be very difficult, since Internet protocols do not associate users with connections, and the attack might be laundered through multiple stolen accounts and might cross multiple administrative domains, as was the case with the attack described by Clifford Stohl in *The Cuckoo's Egg* (Doubleday, 1989). No formal support infrastructure exists to trace attacks that have been laundered in this way.

Once a violation has been detected, the attacked system needs to be analyzed to determine the immediate cause of the system's vulnerability and the extent of the damage. Knowing the vulnerabilities exploited by the attacker can often help to stop ongoing attacks and stop future ones. If the vulnerability cannot be fixed, knowing its causes helps determine what to monitor.

Security systems that detect deviations in a user's behavior can indicate only that a user may be an attacker, not what weak points were exploited to violate the security policy. Misuse detection systems catch exploitations of known vulnerabilities, but may give only a partial set of those exploited, because the activities that trigger the IDS may not be the root cause of an attack. That is, an attacker may at first use a means to violate the policy that goes undetected; only subsequent violations, based in part on the initial one, are reported.

Successful assessment depends upon the integrity of the audit data and the analysis programs used for the assessment, and a sophisticated attacker may tamper with the audit data or disable or modify the analysis programs to hide the attack. Thus extra resources are needed to secure those data and programs.

For example, where security is of utmost importance, as in military and financial establishments, audit data may be written to write-only devices, such as write-once, read-many (WORM) optical storage disks, and analysis programs may be put on a dedicated machine that does not have ordinary user accounts or network connections and uses the vendor's distribution of the operating system.

Assessment can be approached using event-based or state-based analysis. In event-based analysis, the causal relationships in the events recorded in the log are tracked down. Parent-child processes are a good example: the Unix operating system records each process with an ID that identifies the process that spawned it and the user who started it. Moreover, some versions of Unix record these IDs with the corresponding events in the log.

With the aid of such information, the processes involved in unauthorized events can be pinned down. By tracing the parent-child process relationships, it is often possible to determine the vulnerabilities exploited and assess the damage caused by the attack. Then the user-process associations can be used to identify the user account(s) from which the violation of policy occurred.

The state-based approach constantly analyzes the current state of the system to see if it is secure in accordance with current requirements. A state includes the contents of configuration files and the rights of users to access various files.

Picking up the pieces

Using the information obtained through analysis, the system can be returned to a secure state—a process referred to as recovery. Recovery may mean a number of things. It may include terminating an on-going attack to stop further damage, replacing corrupted files with uncorrupted copies, fixing vulnerabilities to protect the system against future attacks, taking appropriate actions (such as notifying affected parties or aborting planned actions), and restarting system services that have been made unavailable.

Since systems are generally backed up periodically, a common technique used in recovery is rollback—that is, restoring a system to its state before the attack, using the backup files created before the intrusion occurred. A complete backup of all the files in the system may be effected, or else a selective backup in which only copies of recently modified files or critical files are saved. Different levels of backup may be combined—complete system backup once a week, say, and selective backups once a day—depending on the level of integrity a site wishes to maintain and the frequency with which files change significantly.

To reconstruct the pre-attack state of the system, it may be necessary to use the last complete backup plus any later selective backups. So the frequency of the backup is important because, during rollback, every change made since the last backup may be lost. For unchanging programs, backups may not be needed if the program distribution disks are on hand. Note that this rollback technique is useful even if complete damage assessment is not possible.

Another means of returning to a secure state is reconfiguration, in which the system is modified to bring it to a secure state by fixing all configuration files and, if needed, reinstalling all software. Reconfiguration is appropriate when one cannot roll back to a secure state, possibly because backups have not been done recently or the system has been in an insecure state since its inception.

Many vendors aid recovery by distributing "patches" or fixes for software once a vulnerability becomes known. Actually, this can be pre-emptive, because system administrators often receive program patches before the vulnerability has been exploited on their system. But sometimes a weakness cannot be fixed: perhaps the flaw is one of interaction between the software and another component, requiring modification of the operating system, or

perhaps no fix is available. In such cases, administrators may be forced to disable the offending software or service. As an example, if an account's password has been compromised, its owner must change the password before it can be used again. Freezing the account before the password change can prevent future attacks through the compromised account.

A brighter future

As the need for security on the Internet increases, new mechanisms and protocols are being developed and deployed. But a system's security will always be a function of the organization that controls the system. So whether the Internet becomes more secure depends entirely upon the vendors who sell the systems and the organizations that buy them.

Ultimately, people will decide what, how, and how much to trust; and so security is a nontechnical, people problem, deriving its strength from the understanding by specifiers, designers, implementers, configurers, and users of what and how far to trust. ◆

To probe further

A seminal work that introduced the idea of using audit logs to detect security problems is James P. Anderson's *Computer Security Threat Monitoring and Surveillance* (James P. Anderson Co., Fort Washington, Pa., April 1980).

In "Decentralized Trust Management," *Proceedings of the IEEE Conference on Security and Privacy*, May 1996, pp. 164–73, M. Blaze, J. Feigenbaum, and J. Lacy discuss trust and illustrate the complexities of managing it in a distributed environment. Similarly, D. Denning discusses trust and the effect of misplacing it in "A New Paradigm for Trusted Systems," *Proceedings of the Fifteenth National Computer Security Conference*, October 1992, pp. 784–91.

A different take on security analysis is B. Cheswick's "An Evening with Berferd in Which a Cracker is Lured, Endured, and Studied," *Proceedings of the Winter 1992 USENIX Conference*, January 1992, pp. 163–74. This paper presents an encounter with an attacker who attempted to penetrate a Bell Labs system and was spotted. Rather than block the attack, the authors decided to allow the attacker access to a controlled environment to see what he or she would do.

Security problems in various Java implementations and in its design itself, and in downloadable code in general, are discussed in D. Dean, E. Felten, and D. Wallach's "Java Security: From HotJava to Netscape and Beyond," *Proceedings of the 1996 IEEE Symposium on Security and Privacy*, May 1996, pp. 190–200.

Identifying intruders in the first place is very complex, and often impossible. A statistical technique to correlate two connections to see if they belong to the same session is proposed in S. Staniford-Chen and L. T. Heberlein's "Holding Intruders Accountable on the Internet," *Proceedings of the 1995 IEEE Symposium on Security and Privacy*, May 1995, pp. 39–49.

Acknowledgments

Assisting intimately in writing this article were Jeremy Frank, who recently received his Ph.D. from the computer science department at the University of California, Davis, and works at NASA Ames Research, Moffett Field, Calif.; James Hoagland, a Ph.D. candidate at the University of California, Davis, who does research in computer and network security; and Steven Samorodin, a graduate student. Without their invaluable help, it would not have been possible to publish this work.

Spectrum editor: Richard Comerford

The first line of defense against external threats to computer systems and networks is a firewall. Whether a computer is in a corporation, government agency, university, small business, or home, if it is connected by a network to other computers, its resources, plans, and data are at risk—and so is the reputation of its owners. A firewall can help reduce that risk to an acceptable level.

Firewall technology is a set of mechanisms that software that made attempts to connect with them—so many attempts, in fact, that legitimate users were no longer able to access them. The perpetrator was never found, but the attack almost drove one Internet service provider out of business.

Serving as system guardians, firewalls are only part—albeit an important part—of a comprehensive network protection scheme. A balanced approach to security overall rests on well-thought-out strate-

Imperfect but essential, these guardians of computer network security work best if planned carefully and maintained with equal care

Firewalls fend off invasions from the Net

STEVEN W. LODIN
Ernst & Young LLP
&
CHRISTOPH L. SCHUBA
Sun Microsystems Inc.

collectively enforce a security policy on communication traffic entering or leaving a guarded network domain. The security policy is the overall plan for protecting the domain. Embodied in hardware, software, or both, a firewall guards and isolates the domain [Fig. 1]. The name, of course, comes by way of analogy with a structural fire wall that blocks the spread of fire in a building.

Broadly, firewalls attempt to maintain privacy and ensure the authenticity of data communications that pass through their domain's boundaries. Whether data is entering or leaving a domain, it is protected from eavesdropping (passive wiretapping) and change (active wiretapping). But only communication traffic entering or leaving a domain comes under the influence of firewall technology. Traffic that stays inside or outside a domain is unaffected [Fig. 2].

Firewalls do, however, protect other material located in the interior of the domain—the stored data, computation resources, and communication resources. These are guarded against unauthorized access, browsing, leaking, modification, insertion, and deletion. And they provide a measure of protection from "denial of service," in which users inside the domain are prevented from accessing the network by a message that disables communication equipment or by a flood of messages that clogs the internal network.

One such incident made headlines in September 1996, when many Internet sites were attacked by gies to safeguard physical plant, personnel, operations, and communications.

While firewall technology is still very much a developing technology, it is possible to explore its benefits and drawbacks and classify its components. A set of criteria can be established for evaluating firewalls as an aid in designing new firewalls or in determining whether an existing firewall is fulfilling its purpose. Clearly the current challenges to firewalls and the outlook for their future are worth exploring.

Firewall foundations

So far, firewalls have been applied to communication based on the transmission control protocol/Internet protocol (TCP/IP) that governs the public Internet and private intranets. But their concepts are applicable to other network protocols, too. Generally, firewalls provide security for distributed systems and are usually used to protect entire corporate networks.

Not everyone approves of firewalls, however, and discussions of them tend to get emotional. On the one hand, some people strongly favor firewalls because so many computer systems and networked applications simply are not secure and could use them. They argue that firewalls are more than just a retrofit patch for shortcomings in systems and protocols. What's more, even if the host system is secure, firewalls serve as a central focus of security policy and a place to conduct comprehensive security audits.

Moreover, firewalls address some of the problems

Reprinted from *IEEE Spectrum*, Vol. 35, No. 2, pp. 26–34, February 1998.

of network security that security mechanisms in a host do not. Because security functions are combined and concentrated in a firewall, proponents say, installing, configuring, and managing them is simpler. They also make the administration of the system and the management of the network more efficient because they are transparent to users, limit exposure of the internal network, and can accommodate almost any internal network topology. Also, they are widely accepted, readily available, and easily justifiable to purchasing managers.

On the other hand, opponents claim that firewalls generate a false sense of security that leads to laxity in enforcing security measures. This objection was expressed in a now popular analogy to a candy bar: firewalls provide" a hard, crunchy outside with a soft, chewy center" (RFC 1636). [See To Probe Further, p. 34, for more on such requests for com-

Defining terms

ActiveX: a computer scripting language, developed by Microsoft Corp., Redmond, Wash., by which small programs can be downloaded and executed.

Authenticity: the quality of being genuine both in apparent origin and in content.

Datagram: a data packet traveling through the Internet.

Domain: a set of interconnected networks, gateways, and hosts.

Gateway, router, switch: a device that forwards information from one network to another.

Integrity: the quality of being in the original form, without any modifications such as insertions, replacements, or deletions.

Java: a computer language, developed by Sun Microsystems Inc., Palo Alto Calif., for writing small programs that can be downloaded and executed.

Network: a communication system that allows computers and other electronic devices attached to it to exchange data.

Proxy: a technique for relaying data in which a process that allows easy verification is substituted for the original relaying process.

Security policy: the security requirements defined for a given system—a set of standards, rules, and practices.

State: the condition of a process, protocol, or system at a given time.

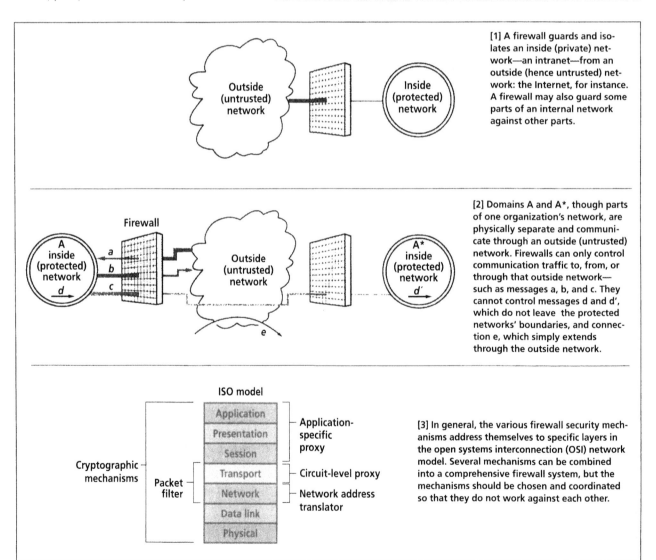

[1] A firewall guards and isolates an inside (private) network—an intranet—from an outside (hence untrusted) network: the Internet, for instance. A firewall may also guard some parts of an internal network against other parts.

[2] Domains A and A*, though parts of one organization's network, are physically separate and communicate through an outside (untrusted) network. Firewalls can only control communication traffic to, from, or through that outside network—such as messages a, b, and c. They cannot control messages d and d', which do not leave the protected networks' boundaries, and connection e, which simply extends through the outside network.

[3] In general, the various firewall security mechanisms address themselves to specific layers in the open systems interconnection (OSI) network model. Several mechanisms can be combined into a comprehensive firewall system, but the mechanisms should be chosen and coordinated so that they do not work against each other.

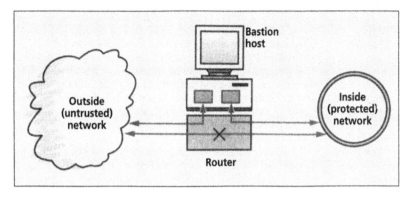

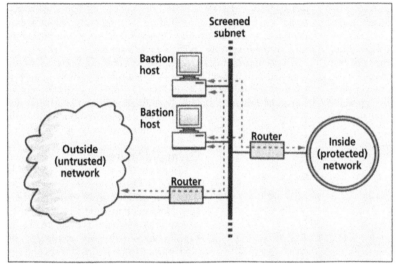

[4] All packet-filter firewalls deny access to traffic that does not meet a set of rules [indicated by a red line with x] and pass traffic that does [green lines with arrowheads].

In a screened-host firewall [top], a router at network level controls access to and from a single host—called a bastion host—through which all traffic to and from the protected network must travel. Direct access to the protected network is denied and the bastion host does not forward packets. The bastion host is a highly defended, secured strongpoint that—one hopes—can resist attack.

In a screened-subnet firewall [above], a pair of routers control access to a small network of bastion hosts. The screened subnet is also called a "demilitarized zone" (DMZ).

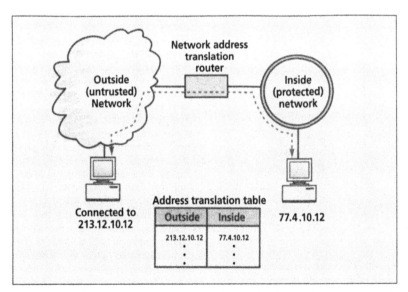

[5] A network address translator hides internal addresses from the outside world. Network address translation (NAT) routers contain a table of outside and inside addresses. They translate the outside address of an incoming message into the hidden inside address, and do the reverse for an outgoing message.

ments (RFCs) and informational bulletins (FYIs), posted on the World Wide Web].

Firewall development typically diverts resources away from improving the security of the computer system behind the firewall. Other criticisms are that firewalls do not provide perfect security; they offer no protection against malicious insiders, for example, and they fail to protect against any connection activities that circumvent them. People can use unauthorized modems attached to computers inside the firewall. They also offer only limited protection against illicit rendezvous (unauthorized connections) and "data-driven" attacks, such as those carried out by malicious executable code in apparently innocent downloaded Java applets or ActiveX controls. But perhaps their most serious limitation is that firewall designers have concentrated so far on acute problems at hand. The reactive nature of firewall design, opponents believe, means that firewalls could be vulnerable to novel attack scenarios of the future.

Nor are firewalls free of operational difficulties. For instance, changes in the firewall system configuration may produce security holes (because, in the usual current practice, the actual configuration is not checked against the security policy). Or the protection mechanisms implemented in the firewall may actually work against each other.

All of these are valid points. Firewalls *do* create a focus for security—but that is a critical advantage. And they *do* suffer from a variety of problems—which, however, are solvable or at least controllable by security policy measures, technological development, and, equally important, theoretical development.

Shortcomings notwithstanding, most computer security experts would agree that a firewall is an important part of security which, in these dangerous times, offers major benefits. In short, a firewall is one of the best available ways to enforce a security policy and keep a site secure.

Defense mechanisms

The various security mechanisms that firewalls employ correspond roughly to certain layers in the open systems interconnection (OSI) model of networking established by ISO the international standardization organization [Fig. 3]. The packet-filtering mechanism, for example, operates primarily on the network and transport layers, while the network address translation mechanism operates solely on the network layer. Operating on the transport level is the circuit-level proxy mechanism while the application-specific proxy mechanism operates on all three top levels.

At all seven layers, cryptographic mechanisms can be applied. For example, at the transport layer, they can provide end-to-end privacy of communications transparently to the user; at the application layer, they can provide application-specific user authentication.

Firewall mechanisms do impose overhead in the form of decreased data throughput, which means, of course, increased delay. But over the years, performance has continuously improved as a direct result of higher processor speeds and software code optimizations.

In general, the lower the mechanism operates in

the OSI layers, the higher its throughput and the lower its delay. Conversely, the stronger the cryptographic mechanism or the more complex the filtering rules, the lower the throughput and the higher the delay.

Checking each packet

In packet-filtering, a router either allows or denies the passage of data after checking its header and contents for conformance to a set of rules that reflect a security policy. In a TCP/IP packet-filtering firewall, the router subjects arriving datagrams (a data packet) to a filtering mechanism that decides whether to forward or discard each datagram. The filter usually examines the source and destination addresses and protocol port numbers contained in the header. The rules operate on datagrams individually, without regard to state information (data on what has previously occurred in the system), so they are viewed separately from other datagrams that are part of the same connection.

A variation on this stateless filtering, called stateful packet-filtering, saves state information for packets that belong to the same connection so that decisions can be made within the context of a particular message. Inbound file transfer protocol (ftp) data connections, for example, can thus be selectively allowed through a firewall if authorized by an ftp control connection. Before stateful packet-filtering, all ftp data connections were allowed through the firewall, which opened networks up to several kinds of attacks.

Packet-filtering gives security personnel the opportunity to examine and verify all data passing through the firewall. But it does not establish a true security association, and the integrity and authenticity of the packets examined cannot be controlled. (In RFC 1825, a security association is defined as "the set of security information relating to a given network connection or a set of connections.")

Verifying each packet naturally induces some delay and jitter, but commercial filtering software designed to minimize delays is available. A more serious objection to verification is the difficulty of developing a set of filtering rules (in low-level specification language) from a statement of security policy (in high-level human language). Even with automated rule-writing tools, graphical user-interfaces, and much experience, generating the accept/reject rules for a complex security policy is a challenge.

Two important examples of packet-filtering firewalls are the screened-host firewall and the screened-subnet firewall. In the first, a router controls access to and from a single host. In the second, a pair of routers protect a "demilitarized zone" network, also referred to as a screened subnet, consisting of one or more bastion hosts [Fig. 4].

Changing addresses

Originally the network address translation (NAT) mechanism was proposed as a short-term solution to the growing shortage of Internet protocol (IP) addresses, not as a security mechanism (RFC 1631). But happily for security administrators, the NAT hides the internal addresses and network topology of its protected domain from the outside. Such obscurity thwarts several methods of attack because little or no target information is available to the outside. Furthermore, hardly any network-based services, except for address translation, connect directly to the outside and therefore the domain is less susceptible to attack than if it were guarded by ordinary routers.

Network address translation devices are placed at the borders of network domains [Fig. 5]. Each NAT device contains a table of address pairs: the local IP address and the corresponding globally unique address. For all outgoing datagrams, the device translates the local address into its associated global address, and for all incoming packets, it translates the global address into its local address.

The address association can be static (not changing, once administratively assigned) or dynamic (the externally visible addresses are taken from a pool of addresses and are automatically assigned to internal addresses on a need basis). The NAT discards the end-to-end significance of addresses, making up for the loss with increased state information in the network.

Like any router, a NAT router keeps messages separate when two inside users send to the same outside destination (an Internet service provider, say, or a much-used Web site) or when two outside sources direct simultaneous messages to the same inside user—that is, the NAT maintains session association. The only difference is that the NAT changes

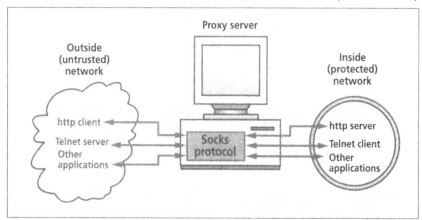

[6] Many firewalls now include built-in support for Socks (the name derives from Unix Sockets), software that allows applications to access a variety of communication protocols. Thus Socks can handle many different types of traffic, routing packets between compatible clients and servers in the untrusted network and the protected one. In effect, it forms a circuit between a client and server; but it acts as a proxy, too, forwarding only those packets deemed acceptable.

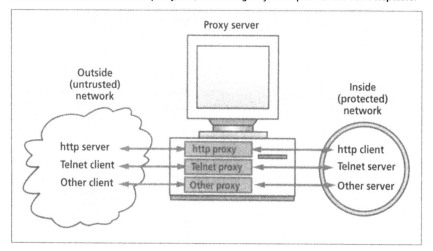

[7] An application-level firewall uses application-specific proxies that can interact with the source and destination of a message to determine whether it meets security standards, and then allows or denies access on the basis of its evaluation. Separate proxies are needed for each application. Further, a so-called "dual-homed" application-level firewall can be built by installing two interfaces, one on each network. So a popular location for such a firewall is a bastion host, in either a screened-host or screened-subnet firewall [see Fig. 4].

addresses belonging to hosts inside the protected network so that they appear different on the outside.

The NAT does not work if higher-layer protocols or applications use and expose the hidden local address. An example is domain name system (DNS) messages; DNS is an Internet protocol and widely distributed database that provides binding resolutions between host names and IP addresses. In some cases, such as electronic mail, though, NAT devices can prevent this problem by rewriting higher-layer–protocol messages with appropriately mapped addresses. Applications that carry and use local addresses across a NAT boundary will not work unless the NAT device is able to detect the addresses imbedded in the packets and correctly translate them.

Circuit-level forwarding

Firewalls that use the circuit-level forwarding mechanism group packets into connections—for example, TCP connections—by maintaining state information across the packets. For example, the firewall may insert a generic transport-layer proxy process into the connection. Inbound as well as outbound connections must connect to the proxy process before they can proceed further. To determine whether the connection should be established or blocked, the proxy makes use of access rules, which can be elaborate, and can require authentication and additional client/proxy protocol message exchanges.

One of the most popular examples of this mechanism is Socks (RFCs 1928, 1929, and 1961) [Fig. 6], which has become the *de facto* standard for proxying on the Internet. Software for Socks firewalls is widely available, and many client programs, both commercial and free, have Socks support built into them.

The generic circuit-level forwarding mechanism can be hidden in low-level libraries; no modification of client/server source code is needed if user interaction is not required. Programs that initiate connections, however, may need to be modified so that they can provide authentication information. Only a few changes are necessary, but there are challenges, such as ensuring the availability of source code, coping with the hetero-

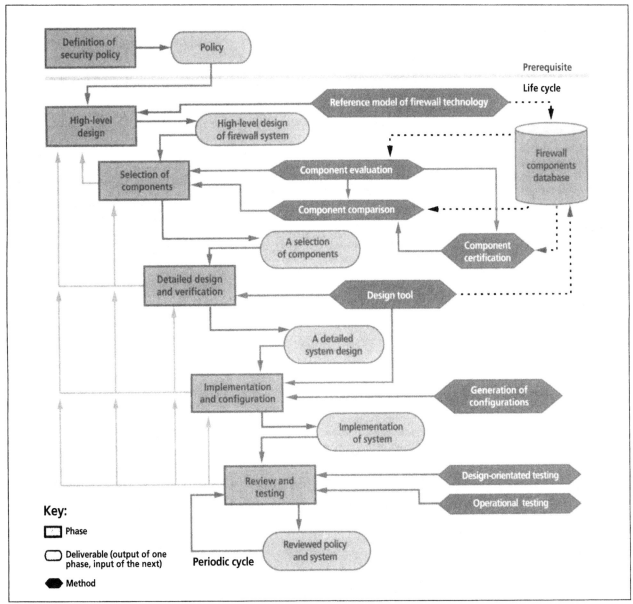

[8] The phases of the firewall's life cycle, shown in blue rectangles, use the methods in the brown hexagonals to the right to produce the results noted in the beige ovals. The life cycle progresses diagonally, beginning with the all important definition of security policy and arriving at implementation, review, and testing after high-level design, selection of components, and detailed design. Even after the firewall is in use, periodic review and testing during the system's lifetime may result in an earlier phase being revisited (indicated by the upward-pointing blue arrows), as when a new, improved firewall component becomes available or when defects in an earlier phase are discovered.

geneity of system platforms, distributing programs, and educating all of the potential users.

Application-level forwarding

In using the application-level proxy forwarding mechanism, firewalls can interpret the data contained in the packets that make up a communication in accordance with the particular application protocols and make security decisions on the basis of that interpretation. This mechanism is similar to circuit-level proxy forwarding, but it can also interact with the communication end points through the application's high-level protocol. It should be noted that this process is, by its nature, application-specific, so for each application, a new forwarding service must be provided.

Among the application-level proxy's many advantages are the fine-grained authentication and access control it offers by virtue of the fact that it interprets the application protocol in use. Also, the mechanism is implemented using small programs that can be more easily scrutinized for vulnerability before deployment than can ordinary server programs. And, if the mechanism does fail, it provides a single point at which the cause can be investigated. An example of a set of software tools and implementation practices for building servers according to the application-specific philosophy is the TIS Internet Firewall Toolkit from Trusted Information Systems (TIS) Inc., Glenwood, Md. (http://www.tis.com/).

But application-specific forwarding has a few drawbacks as well. Like generic circuit-level forwarding, it requires some modification of client software. And it carries protocol processing overhead that reduces its efficiency; it must make two additional round trips through the protocol stack as it interacts with the end points.

The "dual-homed" gateway [Fig. 7] is a representative application-level firewall. Like the bastion host, it generally has two independent network interfaces—one on the external network and one on the internal (protected) network. To insure isolation of the two networks, it does not automatically forward traffic between the two interfaces.

Cryptographic mechanisms

Security mechanisms based on the enciphering and deciphering of messages in secret code are available in great variety. An example is the authentication header (AH) mechanism, which ensures integrity and provides authentication without maintaining confidentiality (RFC 1826). Another is the encapsulating security payload (ESP) mechanism, which guarantees confidentiality and, optionally, integrity and authentication (RFC 1827). Both mechanisms can operate between a set of hosts and/or gateways—that is, end to end, end to intermediate, or intermediate to intermediate, in either unicast or multicast mode (single recipient or many recipients). Both were also standardized by the Internet Engineering Task Force for the IP security (IPsec) protocols.

While these mechanisms protect traffic against eavesdropping, unnoticed modification, insertion, and deletion, they do not protect against analysis of traffic. But their strength lies in their usefulness in building virtual private networks across untrusted networks like the Internet, and in enforcing a variety of security policies.

They are also algorithm-independent, although algorithm identifiers in the security protocol specify standard default algorithms. This provision ensures interoperability of AH and ESP mechanisms in all implementations.

For them to work properly, however, a security association has to be established among the set of hosts and gateways that are party to the protected communications. Of concern, too, are such practical matters as managing the distribution of encryption keys among the hosts and gateways along with minimizing the protocol processing overhead and communication delay introduced by encryption.

Incidentally, encryption, when it is combined with packet-filtering, provides a good illustration of how security mechanisms can work against each other. If the packet filter is not part of the

Firewalls under test

Management and auditors often require that the security of a firewall installation be ensured, so a variety of test and evaluation procedures is available for the job. A big advantage of firewall testing is that it can be applied periodically to renew confidence in an installation—no small comfort to system administrators.

While each of the testing methods has its own advantages and disadvantages, no single method leads to a perfect firewall. They can, however, be applied selectively to suit the occasion.

Two of the most popular approaches to checking out the actual capabilities of firewalls are generally known as design-oriented testing and operational testing.

In design-oriented testing, configurations and release levels of the firewall's components and accessible network services undergo combined manual and automated testing. This method examines firewalls first at a high level and from there passes to lower levels with increasing detail, as far as it is sensible to go.

This approach to testing yields high-quality functional reviews, but it is time-consuming and expensive, requiring the participation of experts in all the components of the firewall system. Often it is not possible to review a product in detail because it is not distributed as an open platform.

The design-oriented testing method is applied after a security policy has been defined and the firewall is deployed and configured. It consists of five steps:
• Comparison of the actual implementation to the owner's plan.
• Manual investigation of the configuration through management interfaces.
• Operation testing, in which the analyst uses tools to probe the firewall and the network behind the firewall for exposed services, determining whether the filtering rules perform the actions they are supposed to.
• Examination of the allowed services to make sure that all available patches to known vulnerabilities are applied.
• Assignment of a periodic review cycle by the same process.

What this method produces are a policy review; an implementation review of firewall configuration and component release levels; an assessment of services, yielding a list of approved services, their configurations, and their release levels; and a review cycle. (To the extent that they contribute to security, services are part of the firewall system and are subject to review as much as the other parts of the system.)

Whenever mismatches between the implementation and the security policy show up, they are resolved by changing either the implementation or the policy. Be forewarned, however, that revamping the policy can be a difficult political process, as it may involve realigning organizational goals to meet security objectives.

The other method of testing—operational testing—is also known by such names as penetration testing and the "tiger team" approach. No matter what it is called, its application requires that the deployed systems be probed by experts for possible vulnerabilities: the firewalls are given a black-box type of evaluation after they have been installed.

Like software testing, this method can ensure proper behavior of the system in certain common scenarios and situations, and can uncover weaknesses. Still, one can never be certain of having tested enough or of not having missed a major flaw. What is more, operational testing also requires a well-thought-out and well-articulated security policy, which is usually difficult to obtain.

—S.W.L. & C.L.S.

Firewall product evaluation: a checklist

Analyzing commercial firewall products is best done by systematically finding answers to a long series of questions. The process helps a designer consider products objectively and choose those that are best for the security problem at hand. A suggested list of questions follows, grouped according to information category.

Identification: Who are the manufacturer and vendor, what is the product version, and what type of firewall mechanism is it? (This information is readily available from manufacturers' brochures and data sheets.)

Education/documentation: Is the product documentation comprehensive, clear, concise, and well organized? Is it in tutorial or manual style or both? Is product training available? Is training included in the purchase price of the product? Is it provided by the manufacturer or by a consultant? Is technical support available? How qualified is the support, and at what hours is it available? Do the technical support people answer questions and address problems promptly and correctly? Are technical support or service contracts included in the purchase price?

Functionality: How does the product integrate with existing systems? Is it essentially a plug and play product, or does it require an extensive setup and adjustment to work well with existing systems? What software platforms, such as operating systems, are compatible? Can the product be readily integrated with other firewall services and support tools? What local network topologies are possible, supported, or required: Internet/intranet, demilitarized zones, virtual private networks, network address translation? What physical network topologies are supported: Ethernet, Fast Ethernet, token ring, asynchronous transfer mode? How does the product interact with other firewall products? How transparent is it to users?

Does the product come as an open system? That is, if it is a software-based firewall, is its source code included in its distribution? What are the application programmer interfaces (APIs) and how extensible are they? Does the product support the content vectoring protocol, an API that allows external programs to operate on a firewall? The answer can help determine what add-on products like virus scanners and World Wide Web filters are compatible.

What protocols are covered? Network protocols such as IP, IPX, Appletalk, XNS, SNA, and X.25 may be of interest. What management protocols are supported—SNMP, SNMP-II, Bridge, OOB? What is the base for the management agent: http, Telnet, SNMP, DECnet, or remote terminal?

Reports and audits: What types of reports are available: usage, operation, incident, summary? Are they available in per-user and per-service formats? Can the data be exported to external databases? Are the reporting mechanisms of the firewall flexible, extensible, and configurable in detail? Is real-time notification possible—by e-mail or paging, for example? What audit media are supported—hard copy, write-once/read-multiple (WORM) drives, remote logging? (WORM technology ensures that audit data, once generated, cannot be erased by intruders to cover their tracks.)

Are audit analysis tools for the reports available or included? Is software for generating and individualizing reports available or included? If intrusion detection is part of the system, how well does it work—what is the number of false positives?

Attacks and responses: What network-based attack scenarios does the product protect against? (Attacks are often based on address spoofing, sequence number prediction, session hijacking, fragmentation, source routing, spoofed naming-service (such as DNS) packets, spoofed routing packets, spoofed control packets, port scanning, "Christmas tree" packets, and/or spoofed multicast and broadcast packets. Usually it is necessary to perform penetration testing—that is, subject the product to an attack—to see how it will behave. Does the product offer counterattack or

cryptographic mechanism's security association, it is unable to perform its function because it is unable to decrypt the higher-layer-protocol headers that it needs to enforce its filtering rules.

Life cycle of a firewall

Like software, firewall systems undergo a gradual development and evolution, called a life cycle, much like the "waterfall" life cycle of software. According to the waterfall model [Fig. 8], the first requirement is to define the network domain security policy. This is perhaps the most difficult phase of the waterfall model because of the vital questions that must be answered. What is the perimeter of the internal network being protected? Which internal services should be available to outside entities? What are those entities and which outside services should be available to users inside the protected domain? What controls are needed? What is the impact of outside services on security? What assumptions are made regarding service and system behavior? Hard as it is to develop, such a well-defined security policy is a prerequisite for the succeeding stages of the model.

The next phase is the decision by the firewall designer on a high-level (general or architectural) structure for the firewall system (ideally, following a reference model for the firewall technology). At this stage, there is no concern about details.

In the third stage, the designer browses through a comprehensive list of firewall products to find components that are likely to be useful, perhaps giving preference to certified products. Before a final selection is made, some unfamiliar products may need to be evaluated.

Using the selected components, the designer can then develop a low-level (detailed) structure for the firewall system. (At this stage, a design tool for firewalls, if one were available, would allow graphical design of firewall systems using descriptions of firewall components from a library, simulations of the behavior of the designed system, and formal verification of certain properties of interest. Such a tool, which is badly needed, could be used to generate configurations and software components for the firewall in its implementation and configuration phase.)

Once these details have been decided upon, the firewall system is built and deployed and the designer has an expert test it. This step ensures that the firewall is capable of enforcing the chosen security policy. Simultaneously, the security policy itself is reviewed.

After it goes into service, the firewall will be tested periodically to revalidate confidence in its installation, and corrections will be made as necessary—a form of preventive maintenance. The system will probably be subject to frequent changes in its internal configuration, network configuration, and security policy.

Checking a firewall's security

Authors Simpson Garfinkel and Gene Spafford in their book *Practical UNIX and Internet Security* [see To probe further, p. 34] note that "a computer is secure if you can depend on it and its software behaves as you expect." By this characterization, natural disasters are as much a threat to computer security as a disgruntled employee or faulty software. Clearly, determining a system's security is hard because the absence of vulnerability must be proved in all possible scenarios [see "Firewalls under test," p. 31]. Nevertheless, some measure of the degree of a system's security is necessary.

A first step in this direction is firewall product certification. The International Computer Security Association (ICSA), Carlisle, Pa.

counterintelligence capability, such as information gathering about the apparent origin sites of malicious packets?

What is the fault tolerance of the product? How does it behave under heavy loads and congestion, after a power failure, and during boot time? (It is known that some firewall products malfunction under some of these conditions.) Does the product contain automated integrity checks, and perhaps congestion control mechanisms?

Does the product recognize data content? Does it determine whether viruses, executable code, Java script or ActiveX code, or mail attachments have been transmitted?

Does the product provide encryption? Which encryption algorithms are available and what are their key lengths? Does it support firewall-to-firewall encryption? Encryption of administrative dial-up connections? User-to-firewall encryption? What is the key-exchange protocol and the frequency of key exchange? How easy is it to exchange keys. Is it compliant with the so-called IPsec protocols developed by the IP Security Working Group of the Internet Engineering Task Force (IETF) ?

Administrative concerns: How secure and flexible is administrative access to the firewall product? Does it support authentication mechanisms like Bellcore S/Key, Security Dynamics

SecurID, Digital Pathways SecureNet Key, CryptoCard RB-1, or Enigma Logic SafeWord? Can security functions be accessed by a dial-up connection? Is there a text-only administrative interface (one that, for security reasons, is not X-Windows–based)? Can the administration separate management tasks and delegate roles?

If your organization has locations outside the country in which it is based, can the firewall product be exported there?

How does the product appear to the external network? Is it network-addressable, or are there no mechanisms for accessing it and attacking it over the network?

How well does it interact with other firewalls? Can loads and bandwidths be balanced among the firewalls? How well does the administrative interface work with multiple firewalls?

What is the product's bandwidth or aggregate throughput, as measured by its packet-forwarding rate? What performance benchmarks are available from independent testing laboratories? How many firewalls are needed to handle saturated T1, T3, or Ethernet traffic? What delay does the product introduce by encryption?

What filters does the product offer? Are input and output filters separated? Are there filters for protocols, addresses, services, and user-defined patterns? What is the filtering rate in packets per

second? Is it easy to specify and implement a filtering policy?

If the product is an application-level gateway, does it offer per-service features for access control, authentication, logging, and auditing? How easy is it to define and implement a user-definable or generic proxy service?

Implementation and afterward: What are the installation requirements? What software is prerequisite? Is third-party code required? What hardware is prerequisite—routers, hosts, electric power, specialized network interfaces? Will any existing routers or hosts have to be replaced or augmented? What administrative infrastructure is needed?

How easy are the hardware and software to install? Do the default settings make sense and are they secure? Are services enabled or disabled by default? Is logging enabled or disabled by default?

Is there a defined upgrade schedule for the product? Does the vendor provide quick fixes for security issues? What is the upgrade distribution mechanism—tapes, diskettes, on-line?

The bottom line: Last but certainly not least, what is the price tag for the hardware, software, extra equipment, installation and migration, training (basic and advanced), service contracts, and ongoing administration? What benefits does the product's warranty provide?

(Web site, http://www.icsa.net), has established a laboratory that evaluates and certifies firewall products and systems. The association's goal is to make the on-line world a safer place and promote its growth by reducing real and perceived risks to computer systems protected by firewalls. The danger in certification, though, is that it can lead to a false sense of security if it simply rubber-stamps products after they have been tested in an artificial laboratory environment. Those labs are generally quite different from real operational environments.

Some organizations offer comparisons of firewall products. For example, the Computer Security Institute, San Francisco, Calif. (http://www.gocsi.com/firewall.htm), periodically publishes a firewall product matrix organized by type and product information, It covers administration and reports, alarms and transparency, authentication and encryption, and proxies, gateways, and servers. While the matrix is neither an evaluation of products nor a comprehensive list of available products (it is primarily generated from marketing brochures), it can serve as a starting point for a review of products.

Another company, Fortified Networks Inc., Carmel, Ind., (http://www.fortified.com/fwcklist.html), offers a firewall evaluation checklist in two versions: a free one and a commercial one that goes into more detail. Both are vendor-neutral; with them, a user can perform a side-by-side comparison of various firewall products.

In addition, various firewall product comparisons have been published by magazines covering security, networking, and PCs. They generally focus on the features and specifications important to the magazine's specialty. For example, PC *Magazine* has evaluated firewall products in terms of their compatibility with Windows NT.

Prospective buyers can also elect to do their own product eval-

uations by systematically seeking answers to the questions in an evaluation checklist [see above]. Some questions can be answered simply by consulting suppliers' marketing information, while others may require research and expert knowledge. An evaluator may assign different weights to each of the categories in the checklist to reflect the company's individual priorities.

Once a firewall product has been selected and installed, a system does not automatically become and stay secure. Keeping the firewall up to date is vital. First and foremost, a firewall owner should sign a maintenance agreement with the supplier so that the latest versions of the firewall software arrive promptly; updates can fix both security and performance problems.

If the firewall is hosted on a standard operating system like Windows NT or Sun Solaris, the user should be sure to install the latest security patches released by the operating system vendor.

Finally, the user should stay in touch with others in the security field to keep abreast of new developments. Recommended mailing lists on the Internet are Firewalls, Firewall Wizards, BugTraq, and NT Security. There are also many Usenet news groups devoted to firewalls and security; they can be found by checking the Usenet comp.security hierarchy on the Web. By staying alert, users can prevent problems instead of having to clean up the mess later.

In the near future, several technological trends are bound to affect firewall users. They should be watched closely and adopted as they develop:
• Advanced network technologies such as asynchronous transfer mode (ATM) will require much faster packet-filtering mechanisms because of their higher speed (155 Mb/s versus 1.5 Mb/s).
• Greater heterogeneity in corporate networks and the Internet is

likely to lead to unforeseen complexity in filtering rules and the necessity for application-level proxies.

• Firewalls will become more integrated with the networks they protect, as routers, mainframes, and PCs start to incorporate firewalls and firewall characteristics.

Remember, too, that all access points of communication traffic to and from a domain have to be guarded. In an age of laptops, wireless communication, easily available Internet service provider subscriptions, desktop modems, and hand-held computing gadgets, the security perimeter is convoluted indeed. Addressing the main arteries and ignoring the nontraditional ones is like securely bolting the front door of a house but leaving the back door open.

A last point worth remembering is that an Internet firewall does not offer any protection from insider threats. It is like a moat around a medieval castle; it helps to keep an outside enemy outside, but it can do nothing to deter an enemy within. ◆

To probe further

In a ground-breaking book, *Firewalls and Internet Security: Repelling the Wily Hacker* (Addison-Wesley, Reading, Mass., 1994), William R. Cheswick and Steven M. Bellovin discuss the processes, issues, and activities surrounding the implementation of an Internet firewall at AT&T Corp.

The classic introduction to transmission control protocol/Internet protocol (TCP/IP) is Douglas E. Comer's *Internetworking with TCP/IP: Principles, Protocols, and Architecture,* third edition (Prentice-Hall, Englewood Cliffs, N.J., 1995). It starts at the physical layer and progresses through the application layer to Internet security and the Next-Generation Internet protocol.

D. Brent Chapman and Elizabeth D. Zwicky, in *Building Internet Firewalls* (O'Reilly & Associates, Sebastopol, Calif., 1995), discuss network security, building firewalls, and keeping a site secure. They include practical examples and specific configuration information for many firewall situations.

Warwick Ford's *Computer Communications Security: Principles, Standard Protocols, and Techniques* (Prentice-Hall, Englewood Cliffs, N.J., 1993) explains modern standardized methods of achieving network security in both TCP/IP and open systems interconnection environments. Ford gives a technical tutorial introduction to computer network security and describes security standards, protocols, and techniques.

A down-to-earth guide, *Practical UNIX and Internet Security,* second edition, by Simpson Garfinkel and Gene Spafford (O'Reilly and Associates, Sebastopol, Calif., 1996), explains dangers to and methods for keeping systems and data secure. It covers computer security basics, user responsibilities, system security, network security, firewalls, and ways of handling security incidents.

Larry J. Hughes Jr., in his *Actually Useful Internet Security Techniques* (New Riders Publishing, Indianapolis, Ind., 1995), discusses computer security basics and specifics of a wide range of Internet security techniques, including firewalls.

In *Implementing Internet Security* (New Riders Publishing, Indianapolis, Ind., 1995) William Stallings and his coauthors discuss the inconsistencies, weaknesses, and breaches in existing computer security implementations and take a comprehensive look at Internet and network security, including firewalls.

Christoph L. Schuba's dissertation "On the modeling, design, and implementation of firewall technology" (Purdue University, Lafayette, Ind., December 1997) describes a reference model for firewall technology and discusses the life cycle model of firewall design in detail.

Karanjit Siyan and Chris Hare, in their *Internet Firewalls and Network Security* (New Riders Publishing, Indianapolis, Ind., 1996) offer guidance about security and the risks involved in connecting to the Internet, building your own firewall, and developing a solid understanding of concepts, passwords, and standards.

For a comprehensive treatment of the many cryptographic mechanisms applicable to firewalls, see Bruce Schneier's *Applied Cryptography,* second edition (John Wiley & Sons, New York, 1995).

For practical and cost-effective solutions to information security protection, including a firewall product matrix and security education and training, contact the Computer Security Institute (CSI), 600 Harrison St., San Francisco, CA 94107; 415-905-2626; Web, http://www.gocsi.com/.

The International Computer Security Association (ICSA), 1200 Walnut Bottom Rd., Carlisle, PA 17013; 717-258-1816; Web, http://www.icsa.net/, is an independent organization that promotes continuous improvement of commercial digital security through the application of its risk framework, and its continuous certification model, to certification, research, and related activities. The ISCA certifies products, systems, and people.

The Computer Operations, Audit, and Security Technology (Coast) Project at Purdue University focuses on real-world needs and limitations, especially those of existing computing systems. It has close ties to researchers and engineers in major companies and government agencies. For further information, check its Web site at http://www.cs.purdue.edu/coast/.

InterNIC Directory and Database Services (http://ds.internic.net/) maintains several archives that contain documents related to the Internet, including Internet requests for comments (RFCs) and informational bulletins (FYIs) and the Internet Engineering Task Force (IETF) activities. The Internet Documentation Repository Web site is http://ds2.internic.net/ds/dspg0intdoc.html. The various RFCs mentioned in this article can be found at that location.

The National Institute of Standards and Technology (NIST) Computer Security Resource Clearinghouse (http://csrc.nist.gov/) pub-lishes national security standards, such as the Data Encryption Standard (DES), and computer security bulletins, such as "Keeping Your Site Comfortably Secure: An Introduction to Internet Firewalls" (NIST Special Publication 800–10, by John P. Wack and Lisa J. Carnahan, 1995).

Check out the Usenet comp.security hierarchy (http://www.liszt.com/ news/comp/security) for security-related mailing lists. To subscribe to a mailing list devoted to discussions of the design, construction, operation, maintenance, and philosophy of firewall systems, send an e-mail to majordomo@greatcircle.com. Archives are available at http://www.greatcircle.com/firewalls. To subscribe to a mailing list about firewalls in the academic environment, send e-mail to majordomo@net.tamu.edu. To get onto a mailing list dealing with Unix and firewall holes in great detail, send an e-mail request to bugtraq-request@fc.net.

Spectrum editor: Richard Comerford

Is the US prepared for cyberwar?

Thomas Kaneshige
Edittech International

The threat posed by high-tech warfare conducted in cyberspace, instead of on the battlefield, was made frighteningly clear recently by a report stating that the US Department of Defense experienced 250,000 computer system attacks last year. In nearly two-thirds of the cases, attackers gained entry to the agency's computer networks, noted the report, which was based on a study conducted for the Defense Department by the Rand Corp., a nonprofit research and analysis institution.

The Defense Department is quick to say that no hacker has found a way to launch a missile. Nonetheless, the number of attacks has been increasing every year. And while technospies are hacking into Pentagon computers, virus developers are looking for ways to render military and vital civilian networks inoperable.

The Defense Department says about 120 governments are currently trying to develop techniques that will bring down its vital computers. US Defense Secretary William Perry said, "We live in an age that is driven by information. Technological breakthroughs . . . are changing the face of war and how we prepare for war."

This concern with strategic information warfare (SIW) is an outgrowth of the US military's relatively recent development of offensive cyberwar capabilities, such as the successful scrambling of the Iraqi army's computer-based communications during the Persian Gulf War.

The race to develop SIW capabilities in the wake of the Gulf War is similar to the nuclear arms race that occurred after the United States dropped two atomic bombs on Japan at the end of World War II, thereby showing that the technology was possible, said Rand Corp. senior researcher Roger Molander, who cowrote the recent SIW report.

The faceless enemy

SIW is extremely difficult to defend against because, unlike classical battlefield warfare, there is no front line, and the enemy's identity is not clear.

US officials can keep track of some known cyberspies. However, in many cases, it can be difficult to determine whether a security breach even came from a foreign government. Individual hackers need only a minimal investment (a PC and an Internet hookup) to attack military computers.

One famous hacker, the Datastream Cowboy, who was apprehended recently, turned out to be a 16-year-old British youth. Datastream Cowboy stole messages containing military orders and passwords from US Air Force Laboratory computers in Rome, New York. US military officials believe Datastream Cowboy passed this information to another source, called Kuji, who remains unidentified and at large. Officials do not know what Kuji did with Datastream Cowboy's information.

Other hackers have sought, for example, critical information about countermeasures to US weapons, details of missions, and top-secret wartime strategies.

Complex viruses that cripple communication networks and wartime operations are another cyberweapon. Many viruses can pose significant threats to computer networks.

For example, the Dark Avenger, who may be based in Bulgaria, uses a polymorphic mutation engine to manufacture viruses that can mutate and hide in different parts of a program. Another type of virus, the macrolanguage WinWord.concept, appeared last year. It was the first virus that was platform-independent and that could travel over the Internet.

A nation could also try to use computer virus warfare to cripple an enemy's electronic commerce, power grid, and air-traffic control and phone systems.

Assessing the threat

Although some industry analysts believe the United States' reliance on computer network infrastructures has turned the nation into an easy target, others feel the predictions of an "Electronic Pearl Harbor" are exaggerated.

The extent of the problem is difficult to quantify because officials do not make public most incidents where hackers have stolen or compromised data in government computers, as they fear there will be a public backlash or national security scare, said the Rand Corp.'s Molander.

"At this stage we don't yet understand how big the threat is or the extent of the vulnerabilities of key infrastructures, and anyone who tells you different from that is lying," he said. "The whole development of this new facet of warfare is really at an embryonic stage."

Fighting back

A Defense Department report recommends that the

Reprinted from *IEEE Computer*, Vol. 29, No. 7, pp. 20–21, July 1996.

agency take a number of steps to fight the threat posed by SIW. For example, the study says, the agency should make better use of encryption and passwords, and should build better firewalls to keep cyberspies and hackers out of its networks.

Meanwhile, federal law enforcement officials helped the effort by identifying an Argentinean man, Julio Cesar Ardita, who allegedly broke into the high-security computer networks of the Defense Department and NASA. Ardita allegedly launched several attacks from universities such as Harvard and the California Institute of Technology via the Internet.

According to US Attorney General Janet Reno and US Attorney Donald Stern, Ardita used illegally obtained account numbers and passwords to enter key networks and retrieve information about government research on satellites, radiation, and energy-related engineering. Reno and Stern said that investigators traced Ardita by using the first wiretap for computer surveillance ever issued in the United States.

Molander added, "By getting serious about building defenses against cyberspace attack, we can build barriers that are at least high enough so that hackers, minor-league mischief makers, small terrorist groups, even 20 angry grad students can't bring down or disrupt key infrastructure systems."

However, he added, the United States may not be able to build barriers that will completely protect against SIW because cyberspies for other countries have the assets and time necessary to overcome many defenses.

Katherine Fithen and Barbara Fraser

CERT Incident Response
and the Internet

In 1988, the Advanced Research Projects Agency (ARPA) established the Computer Emergency Response Team (CERT) Coordination Center in response to the security risks and issues brought to the attention of the Internet community by the Internet Worm [5, 6]. Since that time, CERT, located at Carnegie Mellon University's Software Engineering Institute, has been an active member of the growing Internet community and has watched the Internet grow from less than 100,000 hosts to more than 2.2 million hosts [16].

In this arrangement, CERT draws on and uses a number of Internet services and protocols to accomplish its mission, and provides services to the Internet community as well. As the Internet community is the constituency of CERT, it would be difficult to imagine providing CERT products and services without the use of Internet services and protocols.

Internet Services Used in Support of Incident Response

One way to understand how valuable Internet resources are to CERT is to look at how those resources are used in support of one of the primary activities of CERT: response to computer security incidents. The following scenario describes a sample incident.

CERT was contacted by kathy.org to report that an intruder has compromised an account with an easily guessable password on the host rock.kathy.org. The site, kathy.org, detected the intrusion because users complained of slow response on rock.kathy.org. When the system administrator checked to see what processes were running, he noticed that process "Crack" was being run by user "oldman." When the system administrator checked with the account owner of "oldman," it was dis-

covered that an intruder was using the "oldman" account.

On further investigation, the file "barbara.pass" was found, and it was a password file. The kathy.org contact could not identify the owner of the file. CERT agreed to try to identify and contact the site to which the file belonged.

Prior to sending a password file across a network, we "sanitize" the file by replacing the encrypted passwords. The CERT incident coordinator assigned to this incident sent a script that replaces encrypted passwords in a password file with "deleted," requested that kathy.org run the script on the barbara.pass file, and send the "sanitized" password file to CERT.

After an initial determination of ownership was made, CERT then tried to verify that the passwd file does belong to the particular host by telnetting to the SMTP port (port 25) and using the **vrfy** command. The **vrfy** command verifies that an account name is a valid account on a particular host. This verification is done to ensure that the file is sent to the site to which the file belongs, and not to an incorrect site. This method does not always succeed because some hosts may not allow a telnet connection to the SMTP port, may not allow use of the **vrfy** command, or the **vrfy** command may return whatever was originally entered by the user (e.g., the account name to be verified).

Once the ownership of the password file was determined, CERT then set the "clean" file to the site, or to the Incident Response Team responsible for the site. Follow-up with site included looking for signs of compromise at that site, and checking to see if other sites were involved. If the site was interested in pursuing a legal investigation, CERT would then provide contact information for

the appropriate law enforcement agencies.

Follow-up with the reporting site (kathy.org) would include working to determine:

• If the site has any security incident policies and or procedures, and if not, to encourage the development and implementation of such.
• If the site has installed applicable patches or workarounds from CERT advisories, and if not, to do so.
• If the site is using any security tools (e.g., COPS, TCP wrappers, Tripwire), and if not, to do so.
• To provide documentation on security practices and tools.

Security incidents come in many forms. For example, a valid account could be used by someone other than the account owner, an intruder could gain root access and install a Trojan backdoor, TFTP (Trivial File Transfer Protocol) could be used to obtain a password file, or a product vulnerability could be exploited to gain unauthorized access.

Internet services are useful to CERT when receiving and responding to security incident reports. Even when noncomputer-based methods, such as the telephone, are used for initial contact with CERT, CERT uses Internet services and protocols for related investigation and follow-up. For example, CERT usually receives incident reports in one of two ways:

• A telephone call on the CERT hotline (+1 412-268-7090)
• Email to the cert@cert.org e-mail address

A hotline call is often the original report of an incident, but it is then followed-up using email. The exception to this procedure occurs when root access at a site has been compromised, or if a site is disconnected from the Internet. Communication may then be conducted by telephone or fax transmissions.

In 1993 CERT handled 1,334 incidents [4]. These 1,334 incidents generated 21,267 pieces of email and 2,282 hotline calls. This represents a 73% increase in the number of incidents in 1993 from 1992, and we expect this type of increase in the number of incidents reported to CERT to continue.

Email, FTP, and obtaining site contact information are discussed in further detail in the following sections.

Email

Email is the most prevalent communication mechanism used by CERT. Information received via email allows the Incident Response Group to prioritize its work, so that incident mail and informational requests are separated. Responding to incident mail receives a higher priority than responding to informational requests, although CERT currently strives to respond to informational requests within seven days. This also allows the Incident Response Group to concentrate on the incident email, providing better service to those sites involved in incidents.

The use of Digital Encryption Standard (DES) encrypted mail, Privacy Enhanced Mail (PEM) [5], and Pretty Good Privacy (PGP) [6] allows email to be used even when root has been compromised or when discussing product vulnerabilities with vendors via email.

CERT may exchange DES encryption keys with site contacts by telephone, and then email that has been DES-encrypted can be safely exchanged. Note that there are U.S. export restrictions to which CERT must adhere—DES-encrypted messages can be exchanged, but the DES technology cannot be exported. Other countries have different laws concerning encrypted messages, and CERT must be sensitive to these laws as well.

The concern that email may be read, either by interception or by an intruder reading the clear text copy on-line is of concern. But of greater concern is that email may be altered while en route. PEM provides a mechanism for email signature certification and for encrypted email. This assures sites that email which appears to have been sent by CERT was in-

deed sent by CERT, and that the email has not been altered somewhere en route.

CERT advisories are issued via the cert-advisory mailing list and are also posted to the USENET newsgroup, comp.security.announce. The cert-tools mailing list is moderated by CERT, and the purpose of this mailing list is to encourage the exchange of information on tools and techniques that increase the secure operation of Internet systems.

To keep abreast on security issues, members of CERT read USENET newsgroups and mailing lists. Two examples of this type of information are:

- The comp.security.misc USENET newsgroup, which is a newsgroup for miscellaneous types of discussions on computer security.
- The mailing list "firewalls,"—an unmoderated mailing list for the discussion of firewall hosts. (To subscribe to the firewalls mailing list, send email to: Majordomo@Great-Circle.Com and put "subscribe firewalls" in the body of the message.)

Communication with sites in other time zones is facilitated by the use of email (the email is available when needed and does not depend on coordinating time schedules of contacts from different time zones). Also, the language barrier seems to be smaller and less difficult using text email rather than voice. CERT receives requests to submit articles via email. CERT often emails materials to the requester, as was done with the preparation, review, and subsequent revision of this article.

The Internet Engineering Task Force (IETF) mailing lists and archived information allow members of CERT to follow and participate in the IETF. Much of the IETF information is archived and is available via anonymous FTP.

FIRST, the Forum of Incident Response and Security Teams, communicates via email. CERT is a founding and active member in FIRST. CERT works with FIRST members on incidents and product vulnerabilities. This communication and working relationship assists in resolving incidents and in providing product vulnerability solutions, whether the solu-

tions are patches or "workarounds." CERT also uses DES-encrypted email and PEM with FIRST members when working on incidents and/or product vulnerability reports.

CERT also works closely with FIRST on the Annual FIRST Incident Handling Workshop. Much of this work is done via email. Presentation proposals are submitted, topics discussed, and so forth. This reduces travel costs and time, not only for CERT, but all members of FIRST.

Email is a very valuable communication tool, but there are several considerations and drawbacks one should be aware of:

- Email is easily spoofed.
- Email may be intercepted en route or, if left in clear text on-line, may be seen by an intruder.
- Email to root, hostmaster, postmaster, and other generic system administration accounts or aliases may not be read by anyone at the sites.
- Email may be sent to aliases, and it may be unclear to whom the alias is attributed.
- Email loses voice inflection and the immediacy of phone interaction.
- Email is not normally automatically acknowledged, therefore CERT may not know if the site received the email sent.
- Email sent to the **whois** contact, which may be incorrect (i.e., out-of-date information, incorrect email address), may go unread, may be read by someone else, or may just bounce around the network.
- Services may be interrupted (i.e., a host may be down or there may be network problems).

Spoofing email is discussed in first-term computer classes. The novice user may be unaware of this capability, and may be easily fooled by email that appears to have been sent by root or some other system administrator account.

In addition to the concerns of interception and clear-text on-line email is the concern of email sent to the wrong email address. Since there is no automatic acknowledgement that email has been received (CERT may not receive any response from email sent to a site), there is no way to be certain that the email has been received by the correct addressee.

The loss of voice inflection when using email has improved with the use of "standard" notations, such as the sideways smiley face ":−)". Use of these notations is important to denote such characteristics as humor, sadness, and sarcasm. Without these notations, the reader interprets the email from only their own frame of reference. This can lead to misunderstandings, bad feelings, and/or "flames," which are email responses to a message that scold or chastise the original message sender.

Anonymous FTP

Anonymous FTP (File Transfer Protocol) is used by CERT to receive incident-related files from sites, to provide and to gather information to and from the Internet community. Many sites use anonymous FTP on info.cert.org to send files to CERT for review. CERT has created an incoming directory that is writable, but not readable, on this host. Configuring the incoming directory in this way allows sites to use anonymous FTP to transfer files to CERT, but users can use neither the **ls** nor the **dir** command to list the contents of the directory. The deposit of a file is logged and automatic notification to CERT team members is sent via email.

CERT archives much security-related information, and it is available via anonymous FTP from info. cert.org in the /pub directory. Some of the information archived includes:

• An archive of CERT advisories.
• An archive of virus information.
• An archive of security tools.
• An archive of security papers and technical documents.
• IETF security-related RFCs (Requests for Comments).
• A clipping service (a central archive repository for selected security related USENET News and mailing list postings).

Archived information available via anonymous FTP, whether it is archived by CERT or by another site, is very valuable. For example, some vendor security patches are available via anonymous FTP from ftp.uu. net; if that host is unreachable, then a user can use Archie to obtain a list of other hosts that provide that information via anonymous FTP.

Much of the research done at CERT is based on information provided by the Internet community via either email or anonymous FTP. Research collaboration is also a benefit to CERT and its constituents.

Again, as with email, there are considerations and drawbacks to be considered when using FTP:

• Abuse of anonymous FTP areas can occur.
• Services may be interrupted (i.e., a host may be down or there may be network problems).

The abuse of anonymous FTP areas is a concern of the Internet community where making information freely and easily available is a fundamental belief. Creating anonymous FTP areas for Internet users to share information is considered to be a "good" thing. Unfortunately, some users have used anonymous FTP areas for exchanging pirated commercial software, and for sharing intruder information (e.g., scripts to exploit vulnerabilities, compromised account information). And, Archie information has been exploited to identify sites that provide writable anonymous FTP areas. An intruder could use a listing from an Archie search to create hidden directories in those writable anonymous FTP areas to be used for pirating software.

To prevent the abuse of anonymous FTP areas, CERT has created a document on the suggested configuration of an anonymous FTP area. This document is available via anonymous FTP from info.cert.org and the path for the file is: /pub/tech_tips/anonymous_ftp.

Contact Information

When sending security incident information to a site, CERT generally uses various **whois** databases to find domain contacts for sites. (Note that some sites have designated specific contacts at their sites for security incidents.) Information from the **whois** databases is available via telnet and anonymous FTP:

• rs.internic.net for all domain contacts from the InterNIC **whois** database.
• The WAIS server info.ripe.net (192.87.45.1) for European sites.
• nic.ad.jp (192.41.192.41) for Japa-

nese sites (the .jp domain). You may want to specify that you would like the result of the search in English, as the default is Japanese.
• Files available via anonymous FTP from relay.cdnnet.ca (192.73.5.1) for Canadian sites (the .ca domain).

The InterNIC **whois** information for non-U.S. domains provides the contact information for the entire regional domain (e.g., the contact for "jp-dom" is the contact for the Japan top-level domain [.jp domain]). If a site needs contact information, CERT can provide access assistance.

CERT Future Directions and Plans

With the tremendous growth of the Internet, it is realized that making information available in a variety of ways is important to the success of CERT. CERT is investigating the possibility of providing information via network information resource services such as Wide-Area Information Server (WAIS) and the World-Wide Web (W3 or WWW).

Also important to the success of CERT is the automation of requests for information. CERT receives about 40 informational requests per week. While this may not sound like a large number of requests, in the midst of approximately 500 email messages per week, it is significant. CERT is considering using an automatic mail server, such as LISTSERV, and/or FTP mail, to automate information and mailing list requests and as a second distribution mechanism for lower-level information.

The principal method currently used for dissemination of security-related information from CERT to the Internet community is a CERT advisory. Associated with an advisory is an expected level of urgency for the information in the advisory. CERT recognizes that there are different levels of urgency for security-related information. An example of a way to address these different levels of urgency may be to have several levels of information. A CERT "alert" may contain information of the highest level of urgency, while a CERT "warning" may contain important information, but not as urgent as an alert, while a CERT advisory may contain advisory information or sug-

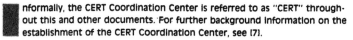

Endnotes

nformally, the CERT Coordination Center is referred to as "CERT" throughout this and other documents. For further background information on the establishment of the CERT Coordination Center, see [7].

- ARPA was formerly DARPA (the Defense Advanced Research Projects Agency).
- For more information on the Internet Worm, there are several books and articles. One suggestion may be [5].
- Note that an incident may involve one site or hundreds (or even thousands) of sites. Also, some incidents may have ongoing activity for long periods of time—up to more than a year.
- For further information on PEM, see RFCs 1113, 1114, and 1319, available via anonymous FTP. There have been several papers and articles published on the topic of PEM; see [2] and [12].
- For further information on PGP contact Viacrypt, Inc.

gestions, which hold little urgency, but yet are still important information to provide to the Internet community. An example of the "advisory" level information is the CA-92: 19.Keystroke.Logging.Banner.Notice advisory. This advisory was a suggestion for a host login screen from the U.S. Department of Justice "as a method of protecting computer systems from unauthorized access."

CERT Future Technology Needs

A few of the short-term technology needs of CERT include:

- Widespread Internet use of PEM, or similar technologies
- Widespread Internet use of one-time passwords
- IP encryption

CERT participated in a beta testing of Trusted Information Systems, Inc. (TIS) PEM, and information has been exchanged with other beta-test sites. CERT sees the need for PEM to be widely distributed to the Internet community to ensure trust that the information that appears to have come from CERT does indeed come from CERT, and that the information has not been altered in any way.

CERT has found one-time password authentication to be a more secure way to connect to hosts via an Internet connection. Even if this one-time password is intercepted, it is not usable by an intruder, since the one-time password is changed each time a login occurs. CERT would like to see this type of technology widely used by the Internet community. Currently,

there are both public and proprietary products available.

The IETF has a working group, the IPSEC working group, investigating and developing IP encryption technologies. The IP encryption technologies being investigated would encrypt the data/contents of the IP packet, but not the header information, and then encapsulate the IP packet to send across the Internet. This will protect the data so that if others "see" the packet as it travels across the Internet, the data is unreadable without the encryption key. CERT supports the development of this capability.

Conclusion

The CERT constituency is the Internet community, and it is natural that CERT uses the Internet to both obtain and provide information and services. In spite of the challenges of working in this huge internet-worked environment, CERT could not provide reasonable service to such a vast constituency without the use of the Internet services and protocols. CERT will continue to encourage the integration of security in the development of the Internet. The relationship between CERT and the Internet continues to be beneficial to both. ▣

References

1. Bishop, M. Privacy-enhanced electronic mail. *J. Internetw. Res. Exp. 2, 4* (Dec. 1991).
2. Bishop, M. Recent changes to privacy-enhanced electronic mail. *J. Internetw. Res. Exp. 4, 1* (Mar. 1993).
3. Comer, D. *Internetworking with TCP/IP*

Vol 1: Principles, Protocols, and Architecture. Second ed. Prentice-Hall, N.Y., 1991.
4. Curry, D.A. Improving the Security of Your UNIX System (Tech. Rep. IT-STD-721-FR-90-21). SRI International, Menlo Park, Calif., Apr. 1990.
5. Curry, D.A. *UNIX System Security: A Guide for Users and System Administrators*. Addison-Wesley, Reading, Mass., 1992.
6. Denning, P.J., Ed. *Computers Under Attack: Intruders, Worms, and Viruses*. ACM Press, New York, 1990.
7. Fraser, B.F. and Pethia, R.D. The CERT/CC Experience: Past, Present, and Future. In *Proceedings of INET'92*. Internet Society, 1992.
8. Galvin, J.M. and Balenson, D.M. *Security Aspects of a UNIX PEM Implementation*. USENIX Security Symposium III, September 14–16, 1992.
9. General Accounting Office of the U.S. *Computer Security: Virus Highlights Need for Improved Internet Management*. United States General Accounting Office (GAO/IMTEC-89-57), 1989.
10. Garfinkel, S. and Spafford, G. *Practical UNIX Security*. O'Reilly and Associates, Inc., 1991.
11. Holbrook, J.P. and Reynolds, J., Eds. *Site Security Handbook*, FYI 8, RFC 1244, CicNet, ISI, July 1991.
12. Kent, S.T. Internet Privacy Enhanced Mail. *Commun. ACM 36*, 8 (Aug. 1993), 48–61.
13. Morris, R.T. and Thompson, K. Password Security: A Case History. *Commun. ACM 22*, 11 (Nov. 1979), 594–597.
14. Pethia, R.D., Crocker, S.D., and Fraser, B.Y. Guidelines for the secure operation of the Internet. RFC 1281, SEI, TIS, Nov. 1991.
15. Scherlis, W.L., Squires, S.L., and Pethia, R.D. Computer emergency response. In P. Denning, Ed., *Computers Under Attack: Intruders, Worms, and Viruses*, ACM Press, New York, 1990, pp. 495–504.
16. SRI International Network Information Systems Center. *Internet Domain Survey*. Jan. 1994.
17. Tardo, J.J. and Alagappan, K. SPX: Global authentication using public key certificates. In *Proceedings of the 1991 IEEE Computer Society Symposium on Research in Security and Privacy*. Oakland, Calif., May 1991, pp. 232–244.

faults & failures

Phony connections gag Internet servers

Providers of Internet services are being besieged by hackers intent on blocking their operations. The earliest reported incident in the current onslaught began on 6 Sept. of last year, when an unknown hacker brought down the servers of Public Access Networks Corp. (Panix), New York City. The company supplies about 6000 subscribers with access to the Internet and hosts 1000 corporate World Wide Web sites. The attacker swamped Panix's e-mail servers by blasting them with up to 150 phony connection requests per second in a technique known as transmission control protocol (TCP) synchronization flooding—SYN flooding, for short.

"Over the next five days, with the help of a lot of friends on the Net, we figured out a way to harden the Unix kernels against this kind of attack," Panix president Alexis Rosen told *IEEE Spectrum*. "It's not a perfect defense, but it is good enough for the kind of attacks that we have suffered. There is no perfect defense, really."

The attack may have been the result of the publication last summer in several hackers' magazines of the code for launching such assaults. "At that point, very few people had ever heard of a SYN attack," said Rosen. "I had known about the concept, but no one that I knew had ever actually seen one."

Since the initial Panix attack, similar incidents have multiplied, at Panix and elsewhere. Rosen has had many requests for help from other administrators. "The problem is not going away," he said. "And it is going to get worse."

The Computer Emergency Response Team Coordination Center (CERT/CC) of Carnegie Mellon University's Software Engineering Institute in Pittsburgh has received 40–50 reports of SYN flooding attacks.

Shaking hands

Vulnerability to SYN flooding attacks originates in the venerable transmission control protocol, which two host computers use when attempting to establish a connection. In the so-called three-way handshake, computer A sends a synchronization packet to computer B. The packet requests a connection to a particular port and includes computer A's return address. In response, computer B sends a synchronization and acknowl-edgment (SYN/ACK) packet back to A acknowledging receipt of A's packet. At this point, the connection is half open. Then, computer A sends an acknowledgment packet (ACK) to B and upon receipt of this second packet, the connection is established.

After B sends its SYN/ACK packet to A, it stores the information contained in A's SYN packet in a buffer and waits up to 75 seconds for A's reply. This is the point at which the hacker works his mischief. He has no intention of actually creating a connection and so never sends A's reply to B. Instead, he simply keeps sending SYN packets fast enough to flood B's buffers so that B can no longer respond to legitimate requests for access.

Fighting back

But Internet service providers are not taking these attacks lying down. Following the lead of Panix, they are taking steps to protect themselves. Companies that supply the server market are also modifying their operating systems to make their machines less vulnerable. First, they are increasing size of the buffer that stores information about the connection requests.

James Ellis, senior member of technical staff of the Computer Emergency Response Team, told *Spectrum* that early systems could store information on a mere eight half-open connections at any one time. In the past, this capacity was adequate. "The half-open state doesn't last long, and no one anticipated that there would be that many connection requests at any one time," he said. "By increasing the buffer space, you can withstand a larger flood. On some systems, you can actually solve the problem in this way if you can make the buffer larger than your bandwidth to the network."

But it does little good to have a large buffer if the information contained in it cannot be located quickly. Hash sorting techniques that distribute the incoming packets into "hash buckets" according to their hash values can help to shorten the search, according to Ellis. (Hashing is a one-way function that takes a message of arbitrary length and computes a shorter number of fixed length.)

A third way to improve the immunity of Internet servers to SYN bombardments is to cut back on the amount of time that the half-open connection state is stored in the buffer. In the old days, when Arpanet was based on a 56-kb/s backbone, 75 seconds was a reasonable amount of time. But since then, the speed of the network has improved, and so 75 seconds is way too long. "If you are under attack, you can afford to cut down the length of time you keep those connections open—under the assumption that most legitimate connections will complete in a second or so," said Ellis. "Only if someone were on a really slow phone link would he be accidentally cut off if the connection remained open for only 5 seconds instead of 75 seconds."

Address spoofing

Crucial to the success of a SYN attack is the ability of the hacker to hide his identity. If the troublemakers could be tracked down, their activities could quickly be stopped. To remain hidden, the hacker pulls another trick out of his bag: Internet protocol (IP) source address spoofing—using a false source address in his SYN message.

What concerns Panix's Rosen is that there are other attacks that use source address spoofing that could cripple large chunks of the Internet, not just one or two sites. "At present, there is really no way to block those at all," he said.

The best defense against source address spoofing would be to have authentication for IP connections, according to the emergency response team's Ellis. With IP authentication, the recipient of a packet would be able to confirm its source and either deny or accept sites depending on their origin. "Authentication is not here yet," he said. "But it's coming. At present, researchers are looking at authentication methods that are lightweight enough to use on individual packets."

So, for the present, the Computer Emergency Response Team advises that Internet service providers throughout the world block spoofed packets that come from their own customers. This only works if all the Internet service providers are cooperating. The reason is that individual service providers cannot tell whether or not a packet is spoofed if it comes in from the outside. But they can tell if the packet comes from one of their own customers. "For an Internet provider to block spoofed packets coming from its customers does not help its customers immediately. It helps everybody else's customers," said Ellis. "But to the extent that all [Internet providers] are doing it, it helps everybody."

LINDA GEPPERT, *Editor*

Reprinted from *IEEE Spectrum*, Vol. 34, No. 2, p. 85, February 1997.

Melissa Virus Creates a New Type of Threat

Lee Garber

The Melissa virus, which tore through computer networks at an astonishing speed in late March, sent a shiver down the spine of the computer industry. There was concern because Melissa spread quickly via infected e-mail attachments that, when opened, sent the virus to people in unsuspecting victims' address books. This meant that Melissa spread very fast throughout the world, overwhelming e-mail servers, before it could be stopped.

Melissa could also send out sensitive documents to people in address books without the user's knowledge. Melissa's approach was particularly insidious because the virus made infected e-mail attachments appear to come from people the recipients knew.

But perhaps the greatest concern about Melissa is what it could mean for the future.

Melissa was relatively easy to create and attacked weaknesses in important and popular technologies that could be exploited again with even more serious results.

For example, Melissa exploited users' widespread and often careless opening of e-mail attachments, which can contain macro viruses.

Editor: Lee Garber, *Computer*, 10662 Los Vaqueros Circle, PO Box 3014, Los Alamitos, CA 90720-1314; l.garber@computer.org

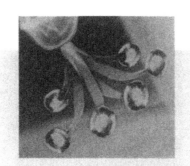

Melissa could be the forerunner of malicious viruses that can spread incredibly fast.

Melissa also took advantage of a potential security threat created by macro languages, in this case Microsoft's Visual Basic for Applications (VBA), which let users program executable functionality into documents. In the case of Melissa, the author programmed malicious functionality into a document used as an e-mail attachment. (See the sidebar "Viruses and Visual Basic for Applications.")

Because of this, the Melissa virus represents a major new development in virus technology, said Peter Tippett, chair and chief technologist at the International Computer Security Association (ICSA), a security consultancy.

Similar viruses in the future could be much more malicious than Melissa, noted Jeff Carpenter, incident response team leader for Carnegie Mellon University's Computer Emergency Response Team.

This could have serious ramifications because many organizations depend on e-mail for mission-critical tasks and because Internet-based commerce is becoming an important economic factor.

At its worst, this type of problem could disrupt Internet-based business operations and cause tens of billions of dollars in losses, said Michael A. Vatis, director of the National Infrastructure Protection Center (NIPC).

MELISSA'S RAMPAGE

Melissa debuted on Friday, 26 March.

Melissa's effects

Users began receiving e-mail messages with

- a subject line that read, "Important Message From ..." followed by the name of the previous victim, who had the recipient's name in an e-mail address book and thus probably knew him or her;
- a text message that said, "Here is that document you asked for ... don't show anyone else ;-)"; and
- an attachment, called list.doc, with a purported list of user names and passwords for pornographic Web sites taken from the alt.sex newsgroup.

Because the message appeared to come from an acquaintance, it encouraged recipients to open the attachment, said Dan Schrader, business manager for security in the Portal Division at Trend Micro, an antivirus software vendor.

If a victim used the Microsoft Outlook e-mail client and either Word 97 or Word 2000, the macro virus' instructions would send the message and infected attachment to the first 50 contacts in each of the victims' e-mail address books. Because a contact could represent a group of people, not just an individual, the virus could be sent to many more than 50 recipients at one time.

The virus also infected Word's normal.dot template, generally used to create documents. New documents would then become infected with Melissa. If users subsequently e-mailed infected documents as attachments, recipients with

Reprinted from *IEEE Computer*, Vol. 32, No. 6, pp. 16–19, June 1999.

Microsoft Outlook would activate the virus upon opening the attachment, thereby sending copies of the infected document to the first 50 contacts in their address books. If the document contained sensitive material, this would cause security problems. Some companies shut down their e-mail servers to keep this from happening.

For Melissa recipients using e-mail clients other than Outlook, the virus infected their Word 97 or Word 2000 normal.dot template and documents subsequently created using the template. However, the virus would not automatically transmit infected documents to people in the victims' address book. Nonetheless, victims could inadvertently send infected documents to other people via e-mail or floppy disk.

If an infection occurred when the number of minutes past the hour of the current time matched the date (for example, at 9:27 a.m. on 27 March), the virus would insert a Bart Simpson quotation from *The Simpsons* television show, "Twenty-two points, plus triple word score, plus 50 points for using all my letters. Game's over. I'm outta here," into a victim's active document.

In Word 97, Melissa disabled the command that would let users receive notification if a document contained a macro and open the document without enabling the macro.

And Melissa set Word 2000 to the lowest macro-virus security level and blocked settings that would let users raise security levels.

As Melissa propagated, it quickly began to overwhelm and force the closure of e-mail servers. This represented a particular hardship for many small organizations that use a single server for e-mail and other important applications.

Millions in losses

Melissa caused serious disruptions at such big organizations as E.I. du Pont de Nemours and Co., Honeywell, Intel, Lockheed-Martin, Lucent Technologies, Microsoft, and the US Marine Corps.

Trend Micro's Schrader said, "Melissa was clearly the fastest spreading virus I've seen, without a doubt."

The ICSA's Tippett estimated that

Viruses and Visual Basic for Applications

The growing popularity of macro languages has fueled concern that macro viruses will become more popular and more dangerous, particularly since the Melissa outbreak.

Macro languages can be used to embed various types of functionality within documents. For example, users could embed a pop-up calendar in an expense report, so they could keep track of travel dates as they fill out the document, noted Neil Charney, Microsoft's group product manager for Office 2000 Developer and Visual Basic for Applications (VBA).

However, virus writers, like the one who wrote Melissa, can use macro languages to embed malicious functionality within documents.

Various application vendors offer macro languages for their products. VBA, first released in 1993, is used with Microsoft's Office, the biggest application platform, so it is the most widely used macro language.

Despite their name, Charney said, macro languages can be used for more than creating macros to automate tasks. He said VBA can serve as a development environment. For example, he said, VBA can be used to customize Microsoft applications, adding features that the vendor did not include.

In addition, VBA can be used to integrate multiple applications' functionality. For example, Charney said, instead of manually entering information from a database into a spreadsheet, VBA could be used to have the spreadsheet automatically pull the appropriate data from the database.

Dan Schrader, business manager for security in the Portal Division at Trend Micro, an antivirus software vendor, agreed that many power users want these capabilities. However, he said, the computer industry must be careful because macro languages can turn documents into executables. Users who open a document just to read its contents can unknowingly activate an embedded program, which could be malicious.

As is generally the case, more functionality leads to less security, noted Roger Thompson, technical director of malicious code research for the International Computer Security Association, a security consultancy. Features like VBA make it easier to do good things and easier to do bad things, he said.

Nonetheless, Schrader said, macro languages are the type of convenient feature that won't go away, so the computer industry must find a way to live safely with them.

Melissa infected about 1.2 million computers and 53,000 servers at 7,800 North American companies that had at least 200 PCs, and it cost between $249 million and $561 million to fix.

ICSA spokesperson Barbara Rose said that of 300 corporations surveyed, the median cost for combating Melissa was $1,750, although some respondents reported costs as high as $100,000.

On 1 April, law enforcement agencies arrested a suspect in the case. (See the sidebar "Melissa Suspect Arrested.")

The fixes

Over the weekend following the Melissa outbreak, IT workers in infected organizations began learning about the virus, shutting down their e-mail servers in many cases, and eliminating the virus from their systems. For example, administrators filtered out all e-mail with Melissa's signature subject line.

Meanwhile, antivirus vendors began their work. "This was a simple virus," said Schrader. "The solution was easy. It took us 20 minutes to develop a pattern to recognize this virus."

Organizations with centralized security-management systems scanned their entire network to get rid of Melissa infections. Other organizations had to scan each desktop.

The variants

In the days following the outbreak,

Melissa Suspect Arrested

As Melissa began spreading through networks on 26 March, law enforcement agencies, including the FBI, began looking for the virus' creator. They eventually tracked the source of the virus to New Jersey.

On 1 April, computer-crime investigators with New Jersey's State Police and Department of Law and Public Safety arrested David L. Smith, 31, a programmer who lived in Aberdeen Township, New Jersey.

David L. Smith (center) attends a court hearing in New Jersey on charges that he created the Melissa virus. He is accompanied by his attorney, Edward F. Borden Jr. (left). AP/Wide World Photo.

Authorities charged Smith, who was released after posting $100,000 bail, with second-degree interruption of public communication, conspiracy to interrupt public communication, and attempted interruption of public communication; and third-degree theft of computer service and damage or wrongful access to computer systems.

Smith's attorney, Edward F. Borden Jr. of Princeton, New Jersey, said his client has pleaded not guilty to all charges.

Smith faces maximum penalties of $480,000 in fines and 40 years in prison, according to Paul Loriquet, spokesperson for the New Jersey Attorney General's Office.

When the ongoing investigation is completed, Loriquet said, the Attorney General's Office can send the case to a state grand jury, which could then decide whether to indict Smith.

virus writers released several Melissa variants, with names like Papa, Mad Cow, Marauder, and Syndicate.

For example, Papa affected Microsoft Excel, which, like Word, supports VBA. When a victim using Microsoft Outlook opened an Excel-based attachment to an e-mail note, the virus would send the note and attachment to the first 60 contacts in the victim's address book.

Roger Thompson, ICSA's technical director of malicious code research, noted that writers may have based their variations on Melissa's code, which was posted on several newsgroups shortly after the virus' outbreak.

However, many antivirus companies expected variants and produced software updates that would recognize them. For example, Schrader said, Trend Micro developed software that catches any macro that, like Melissa, tries to use the Mail API (MAPI) to open Outlook.

Probably because so many users downloaded antivirus updates in the wake of Melissa, he said, comparatively few users were affected by variants.

POTENTIAL FUTURE PROBLEMS

According to Schrader, Melissa represents a significant new type of viral threat, not because its elements were new but because of the way it combined and used its elements.

Also, Melissa was relatively easy to write using VBA. This means that even virus creators with limited programming skills could author similar, more harmful viruses that might not be detected even by current antivirus products.

Such a virus could inflict damage like that caused by the CIH virus, which struck in late April. Although it affected far fewer PCs than Melissa, CIH was more harmful. It could wipe out parts of a hard drive and destroy the flash BIOS, leaving users unable to reboot their computers.

It's not clear that a micro virus alone could cause such problems. However, the ICSA's Thompson said Microsoft's OLE (object linking and embedded) framework for compound documents permits users to embed a binary object within a document. Thus, he said, an author could write a macro virus that, when opened, would call a binary object that causes CIH-like problems.

"The potential effects could be devastating," CERT's Carpenter said.

A Melissa-like virus could also be written to subtly change data in documents or databases. Antivirus software vendors could find ways to detect and block these viruses but couldn't restore the altered data.

Meanwhile, Schrader noted, an author could create an even more infectious version of Melissa by enabling it to strike multiple MAPI-compliant e-mail clients, not just Outlook.

RECOMMENDATIONS

Documents used to be safe to open because they were not executables, but macro languages have changed that, as Melissa shows.

The ICSA's Thompson said macro languages give "the power of programming to people who aren't programmers, including virus writers."

Other word processing programs, such as WordPerfect, have their own macro languages, but VBA is more significant because of Microsoft Word's popularity.

Because of their functionality, Schrader said, macro languages are here to stay. So, he said, "We need to figure out how to deal with it."

Macro safety settings

In past Microsoft Office versions, users who are about to open a document that contains a macro are shown a dialog box that lets them choose whether to enable or disable the macro.

Alan Paller, director of research with the SANS (System Administration, Networking, and Security) Institute, said this is not good enough because most users are not sophisticated or "scared" enough to use such preventive measures properly. Instead, he said, software vendors should send their applications with the capability to receive macros disabled. Users who want the capability can then turn it on, perhaps during the installation process, he explained.

"After all," he said, "shouldn't the guys selling medications put a safety cap on so kids can't get into them?"

The ICSA's Thompson agreed, saying macros present too much of a risk and many users don't need to run them.

The problem is that software vendors like to market products based on a high level of functionality and thus don't want to disable their capabilities, Paller said.

However, Thompson noted, "Security and functionality exist in an inverse relationship."

Neil Charney, Microsoft's group product manager for Office 2000 Developer and VBA, said Office products should not come with macro capabilities disabled. He said many people want to create and use macros and thus don't want to have to spend time and effort enabling those capabilities.

Authentication

Charney said security capabilities that Microsoft has added to its Office 2000 products should protect users.

Microsoft has included an antivirus API that lets antivirus firms integrate their software into Office 2000 products to scan documents before users open them.

Some experts say current default security settings in many applications are not good enough to stop macro viruses.

In addition, Office 2000 users who write VBA 6.0 macros could digitally sign them, certifying the code has come from a trusted source. Users can then configure products or set Word 2000's default setting so the applications will run only macros digitally signed by trusted sources. The default settings for other Office 2000 applications will continue to call the current macro-notification dialog box.

CERT's Carpenter said authentication is a good idea because it verifies that the sender is a trusted source. However, he said, if a trusted source unknowingly passes on a virally infected document, authentication won't help the recipient.

Improved virus protection

Schrader said Melissa's main lesson is the need for antivirus products that scan entire networks, not just individual desktops, as is traditionally the case.

"The antivirus community hasn't owned up to this problem," he said. "The battle has to shift from the desktop to the entry point to your environment."

This could keep viruses like Melissa from getting into a network in the first place. If security is left on the desktop, Schrader said, users may turn it off or use it incorrectly.

Meanwhile, viruses could be cleaned up more easily with centralized antivirus management programs.

The most important place for corporate virus protection is the Internet e-mail gateway, and the second most important is the internal e-mail server, Schrader said.

Currently, though, he said, "We esti-

mate that only about 45 percent of corporations have rolled out virus protection on their e-mail servers."

The ICSA's Thompson cautioned that many organizations don't want to rely solely on network-scanning antivirus software because it won't catch, for example, boot viruses and viruses introduced by floppy disks.

Meanwhile, Schrader said, organizations should use antivirus programs that look for the type of behaviors that a virus causes, even those that appear innocuous, rather than programs that look for specific byte strings from known viruses.

However, Thompson said, the former approach has not been very successful in the marketplace because it has not been supported by corporate help desks. Help desks don't want to respond to the false alarms that occur with the behavior-based approach when legitimate activities cause virus-like behaviors.

Other concerns

Melissa emphasizes that perhaps organizations should stop encrypting all e-mail, Schrader said. When messages are encrypted, antivirus software cannot read their contents and thus cannot determine if they contain e-mail-borne viruses, such as Melissa.

"People need to be more sophisticated," Schrader said. "Is it necessary to encrypt all e-mail? Perhaps they should encrypt only the most critical."

Of course, virus experts also said users should be more careful by, for example, using and regularly updating antivirus software.

CERT's Carpenter said, "While security gets a lot of press attention, I think there are still a lot of people who don't give it the priority they should. Users don't understand the extent of the problem. They don't understand the worth of the assets that need protection."

Schrader agreed and said, "Many people have ignored viruses in the past. But I think Melissa has raised their profile." ❖

Lee Garber is Computer's *news editor. Contact him at l.garber@computer.org.*

Chapter 5

Encryption, Law Enforcement, and Privacy

Protect the privacy and confidentiality of all information entrusted to me.
—*from the* AITP Standards of Conduct
Work to develop software and related documents that respect the privacy of those who will be affected by that software.
—IEEE-CS/ACM Software Engineering Code of Ethics, principle 3.12
The right of the people to be secure in their persons, houses, papers, and effects, against unreasonable searches and seizures, shall not be violated; and no Warrants shall issue, but upon probable cause, supported by Oath or affirmation, and particularly describing the place to be searched, and the persons or things to be seized.
—Fourth Amendment to the Constitution of the United States
No person . . . shall be compelled in any criminal case to be a witness against himself.
—Fifth Amendment to the Constitution of the United States
They that can give up essential liberty to obtain a little temporary safety deserve neither liberty nor safety.
—Benjamin Franklin, Historical Review of Pennsylvania, *1759*

5.1 INTRODUCTION

THE 1990s saw important advances in encryption technology and rapid changes in government proposals, policies, and standards related to encryption. However, despite all of the action, the 1990s ended with the truly major decision(s) yet to be made. It can be difficult to appreciate all of the competing concerns that come crashing together in this area. For context, consider that the world is in transition from a "pre-cyberspace society" to a hoped-for "cyber-utopia." The pre-cyberspace society is the world of, say, 1990. This is before terms like "world-wide web," "global information infrastructure" and "electronic commerce" came into being. The volume of digital communications was small enough that the ability to effectively wiretap them was not a major concern for law enforcement. The Data Encryption Standard (DES) had become time-tested, was considered highly secure, and served as a de facto world standard.

Then the situation changed in multiple ways in the 1990s.

The world-wide web came into existence and gave rise to new business models. Law enforcement began to worry about how to conduct wiretaps of digital communications. Advances in computing power made plain DES clearly insecure. Many different new encryption algorithms were proposed. And the government and the computing industry had repeated confrontations over government regulation of encryption exports.

Through all of the smoke, mirrors, and hype, a vision of a "cyber-utopia" emerged. A dominant element of this cyber-utopia is "e-commerce" that would be global, seamless, and highly secure. For this to happen, among other things, a new encryption standard must emerge. This new standard should somehow allow every interest group to at least maintain their position in the pre-cyberspace society. Individuals should have just as great an assurance of privacy. Law enforcement should have at least the same effective ability to conduct surveillance. The U.S. computing industry should compete at least as effectively in global markets. And, national governments should have no less

ability to regulate what happens inside their nation. So the vision of cyber-utopia is clear. But the ability to achieve it is seriously in doubt. It seems that there are too many conflicting interests for them all to be achieved.

The goal of this chapter is to summarize the general situation that exists as of early 2000.[1] As mentioned earlier, incredibly important decisions remain to be made. Foremost among these is the selection or emergence of a new encryption standard. Based on the outcome of this decision, new laws and/or regulatory mechanisms may be required. To properly understand the importance of the concerns involved, we will spend some time tracing the rise and fall of the Data Encryption Standard, the evolution of wiretapping and the "right to privacy," the development of "public key encryption," and the ups and downs of U.S. government policy toward encryption.

5.2 RISE AND FALL OF THE DATA ENCRYPTION STANDARD

The story of the rise and fall of the Data Encryption Standard is a good place to begin. It starts in the pre-cyberspace world and takes us into the transition era. And it gives us a chance to introduce some of the technical concepts involved in encryption and the social issues involved in regulation of encryption.

5.2.1 Some Basic Concepts

The field of *cryptography* involves the study of methods for encrypting and decrypting information. To *encrypt* (or "encode," or "encipher") a piece of information is to change its appearance so that its meaning is no longer

---

[1] To check up on the latest developments, consult on-line sources such as the Electronic Privacy Information Center (www.epic.org), the Electronic Frontier Foundation (www.eff.org), and the National Institute of Standards and Technology (www.nist.org/aes).

apparent. To *decrypt* (or "decode," or "decipher") a piece of information is to reverse the process.

Traditional methods of encryption can generally be described as *private key* methods. The terms "single key," "secret key," and "symmetric" are also used to describe this class of methods. Encryption is performed using a specified algorithm under the control of a particular key value. Decryption is performed using the same key value. The fact that the same key is used for both encryption and decryption leads to the names "single key" and "symmetric." The fact that the key value must be kept hidden from eavesdroppers leads to the names "private key" and "secret key."

The general approach to private key encryption can be illustrated through the example of a simple substitution cipher. A *substitution cipher* substitutes each character of an alphabet with another character. A key value of 4 could mean to encrypt by substituting each character with the fourth character further along in the alphabet, wrapping around from the last character to the first if necessary. Consider a simple character set in which the blank space comes after Z, so that the encoding algorithm for a key value of 4 is specified as

```
for the letter:   <abcdefghijlkmnopqrstuvwxyz >
   substitute:    <efghijklmnopqrstuvwxyz abcd>
```

In this example, the encoding of the message

```
<secret meeting monday at the usual place>
<wigvixdqiixmrkdqsrhebdexdxlidywyepdtpegi>
```

The normal method of decrypting a message in a private key system is to know both the algorithm and the particular key value used for encrypting the message. In this example, you would have to know that the message was encoded with a substitution cipher on the given alphabet and that the key value was 4. Decryption is then straightforward.

As it turns out, the substitution cipher would be a poor choice of an encryption algorithm. If an eavesdropper obtained a copy of an encrypted message, they could try each possible key value to find the one that turns the gibberish into meaningful information. This brute-force approach to code breaking would succeed in a short amount of time. However, encryption methods can be designed so that the space of possible key values is large enough that the expected time to break an encrypted message is measured in the hundreds of years. Different encryption methods are commonly referred to as weak or strong, based on the expected time required to break an encrypted message.

5.2.2 The Rise of DES

The Data Encryption Standard is a private key encryption algorithm that IBM designed for the federal government in the 1970s. The DES was adopted by the National Bureau of Standards as a Federal Information Processing Standard in 1977. The National Bureau of Standards was the forerunner of the current National Institute of Standards and Technology. DES encrypts data under the control of a 56-bit key, meaning that there are 2^{56} possible key values. The details of the DES algorithm are not so important to cover here. Source code for the algorithm can readily be found on the Internet and in textbooks.

When DES was first adopted as a standard, it was surrounded by controversy. Elements of an early design for the DES were altered, at the instigation of the National Security Agency, before DES was adopted as a standard [8]. This led some people to feel that the National Security Agency did not want DES to provide encryption that even the NSA could not break. There was also initial fear that a *trap door* might exist. In this context, a "trap door" would be a way to break the encryption with much less work than an exhaustive search of the space of possible keys. The more paranoid version of this worry was that the designers intentionally inserted a trap door that only the NSA knew about.

However, concerns about the security of DES faded. The reasons for this reflect the social side of how science is done. The DES algorithm was described in publicly available technical documents and journal articles. Any person could (can) read about the algorithm, reason about how it works, implement it, and conduct experiments with it. Many talented people made a point of examining the DES algorithm to find possible flaws in it. Yet no one ever reported finding any easy way to break DES encryption. As time went on, the weight of the independent examination by numerous experts gave rise to increasing confidence in DES. Due to this confidence and to being a U.S. government standard, DES became the most widely used encryption algorithm in the world. It is (was) widely used in the financial industry, and, in many cases, federal regulations required its use by private companies who conduct sensitive business with the federal government [6]. DES became a de facto worldwide standard for secure encryption.

5.2.3 The Fall of DES

As computers became increasingly more powerful, concern about brute-force attacks on DES became increasingly real. Evidence that plain DES had come to the end of its useful life accumulated throughout the 1990s. One particularly convincing demonstration occurred in 1998 [5]. A firm named Cryptography Research, based in San Francisco, constructed a special-purpose machine to break DES. Their computer was built from 1800 chips, and explored possible keys at a rate of 90 billion per second. The estimated cost of the machine was $250,000. It was reported to take approximately 10 days for the system to evaluate the entire (2^{56})-element DES key space. This incident highlighted the danger in using DES to protect information with a potential value of greater than $250,000 and a useful lifetime of greater than 10 days. These limits of cost and time naturally decrease as computing power continues to increase.

It was clear in the early 1990s that plain DES would become insecure in the foreseeable future. Various alternatives began to be considered. Implementations of "public key encryption" algorithms became popular on the Internet, and were incorporated into some e-mail programs. We will have more to say about public key algorithms in a later section. One obvious alternative was to create a new standard encryption algorithm by repeating a procedure similar to that used to create DES. We will see why the government did not initially take that route in another later section. Yet another alternative is to simply encrypt data by using DES multiple times in succession with different keys. "Double DES" would effectively have 2^{56+56} possible key values, and "triple DES" would effectively have $2^{56+56+56}$ key values. In the absence of an official new standard, "triple DES" becomes an attractive alternative. In fact, at the time of this writing, triple DES is widely recommended and used.

The important elements of the DES story for us are (1) that it showed the importance of public review of an algorithm in establishing trust in the algorithm, and (2) that simple DES came to the end of its useful life without an official successor in sight and at a time when e-commerce badly needed a new encryption standard.

5.3 EVOLUTION OF WIRETAPS AND THE "RIGHT TO PRIVACY"

The United States Constitution contains an explicit list of rights that are guaranteed to U.S. citizens. The purpose of these rights is to protect individuals from the potential abuse of power by government. Since the phrase "right to privacy" is so commonly heard, it may come as a surprise to find out that it is **not** explicitly mentioned in the Constitution. The "right to privacy" emerged as the result of how the U.S. Supreme Court interpreted various decisions involving the Fourth and Fifth Amendments. One effect of these decisions is to prescribe how and when a law enforcement agency may legally eavesdrop on communications. In this chapter, we will use the term "wiretap" generally to refer to law enforcement eavesdropping on a communication without informing the people who are communicating.

In order to make an informed decision about how proposed new encryption systems will affect law enforcement, it is necessary to understand the current situation in law enforcement wiretapping. We will describe the two landmark Supreme Court decisions in this area. Then we will outline 1968 and 1994 legislation related to wiretapping. Finally, we will summarize some facts and figures on the current use of wiretaps.

5.3.1 Olmstead v. United States

The phrase *Olmstead* v. *the United States* refers to a 1928 Supreme Court decision. Recall that the Supreme Court decides whether a particular law or government action is allowed by the United States Constitution. The Olmstead decision is concerned with the protections provided by the Fourth and Fifth Amendments.

Fourth Amendment—*The right of the people to be secure in their persons, houses, papers, and effects, against unreasonable searches and seizures, shall not be violated; and no Warrants shall issue, but upon probable cause, supported by Oath or affirmation, and particularly describing the place to be searched, and the persons or things to be seized.*

Fifth Amendment—*No person . . . shall be compelled in any criminal case to be a witness against himself.*

The Olmstead case took place during the "Prohibition Era." This time period began in 1920, when the 18th Amendment prohibited the production, transportation, and sale of alcoholic beverages. It lasted only until 1933, when the 21st Amendment repealed the 18th Amendment. Olmstead was arrested and convicted in what the Supreme Court characterized as ". . . a conspiracy of amazing magnitude to import, possess and sell liquor unlawfully" [15]. The Supreme Court recognized that he was convicted with the use of wiretap evidence: "The information which led to the discovery of the conspiracy and its nature and extent was largely obtained by intercepting messages on the telephones of the conspirators by four federal prohibition officers. Small wires were inserted along the ordinary telephone wires from the residences of the petitioners. . . . The insertions were made without trespass upon any property of the defendants. They were made in the basement of a large office building. The taps from house lines were made in the streets near the houses" [15]. An important factor is that the officers installed the wiretaps without getting a warrant to do so from a judge. This provided the basis for Olmstead to allege that his Fourth and Fifth Amendment rights had been violated.

If Olmstead's allegation was judged to be true, then the wiretap evidence could not be used against him. This precedent was established in an earlier Supreme Court decision, *Weeks v. United States*. The Olmstead decision explains the reasoning as follows: "The striking outcome of the Weeks Case and those which followed it was the sweeping declaration that the Fourth Amendment, although not referring to or limiting the use of evidence in court, really forbade its introduction, if obtained by government offices through a violation of the amendment. Theretofore many had supposed that under the ordinary common-law rules, if the tendered evidence was pertinent, the method of obtaining it was unimportant" [15].

The Supreme Court ruled that Olmstead's rights were **not** violated. The reasoning of the majority decision went basically as follows. First, they focused on the Fourth Amendment: "There is no room in the present case for applying the Fifth Amendment, unless the Fourth Amendment was first violated" [15]. Then, by appealing to specifics of the case and taking a very literal, physical notion of what the Fourth Amendment protects, they concluded that there was no unreasonable search and seizure. A quote that shows how the Court interpreted the meaning of the amendment in terms of physical things is: "The amendment itself shows that the search is to be of material things—the person, the house, his papers, or his effects. The description of the warrant necessary to make the proceedings lawful is that it must specify the place to be searched and the person or things to be seized" [15]. A quote that shows how this reading was understood in the context of telephone system technology is: "The reasonable view is that one who installs in his house a telephone instrument with connecting wires intends to project his voice to those quite outside, and that the wires beyond his house, and messages while passing over them, are not within the protection of the Fourth Amendment. Here those who intercepted the projected voices were not in the house of either party to the conversation" [15]. Thus the general effect of the Olmstead decision was that law enforcement needed a court order for a wiretap only if installing the wiretap required some physical handling or trespass of the citizen's property.

5.3.2 Dissenting Opinion: Olmstead v. United States

The decision in the Olmstead case was not unanimous. In particular, the dissenting opinion given by Justice Louis Brandeis has become rather famous. A quote from Brandeis that explains the motivation for his nonliteral reading of what is protected by the Fourth Amendment is: "When the Fourth and Fifth Amendments were adopted . . . force and violence were the only means known to man by which a government could directly effect self-incrimination. . . . Subtler and more far-reaching means of invading privacy have become available to the government. Discovery and invention has made it possible for the government . . . to obtain disclosure in courts of what is whispered in the closet. . . . The progress of science in furnishing the government with means of espionage is not likely to stop with wiretapping" [15]. Thus Brandeis attempted to focus on the effect of the amendments in the context of the time that they were passed, and to extrapolate that meaning into the context of his day.

A well-known quote that spells out Brandeis's conclusion is: "The makers of our Constitution undertook to secure conditions favorable to the pursuit of happiness. They recognized the significance of man's spiritual nature, of his feelings and of his intellect. They knew that only a part of the pain, pleasure and satisfactions of life are to be found in material things. They sought to protect Americans in their beliefs, their thoughts, their emotions and their sensations. They conferred, as against the government, the right to be let alone – the most comprehensive of rights and the right most valued by civilized men. To protect that right, every unjustifiable intrusion by the government upon the privacy of the individual, whatever the means employed, must be deemed a violation of the Fourth Amendment. And the use, as evidence in a criminal proceeding, of facts ascertained by such intrusion must be deemed a violation of the Fifth" [15].

Brandeis compellingly describes the notion of a "right to privacy" as something necessarily implied by the amendments of the Constitution. However, it is important to remember that Brandeis was in the minority in this decision. Law enforcement continued to make use of wiretaps, with the Olmstead case providing the controlling legal context. Now we fast-forward approximately 40 years to another Supreme Court decision.

5.3.3 Katz v. United States

The Supreme Court decided the *Katz* v. *United States* case in 1967. Katz was convicted of violating a federal law by transmitting gambling information across state lines by means of telephone. "At trial the Government was permitted, over the petitioner's [Katz] objection, to introduce evidence of the petitioner's end of telephone conversations, overheard by FBI agents who had attached an electronic listening device to the outside of the public telephone booth from which he placed his calls" [16]. The FBI agents did not obtain a court order for their wiretap. However, they did take special care to listen to the wiretap only when Katz was using the phone booth. Also, the government presentation to the Supreme Court stressed that the wiretap did not require any physical trespass into an area occupied by Katz. This point about physical trespass relates to the understanding that the Olmstead decision said a court order was not needed if the wiretap could be accomplished without trespass.

In his appeal, Katz asserted that a public phone booth should be a constitutionally protected area in the context of the Fourth Amendment, and also questioned whether physical trespass was required in order to consider that "search and seizure" had occurred.

The Supreme Court decided in favor of Katz, ruling that the wiretap was a violation of his rights and that the evidence obtained through the wiretap could not be used. This was an important ruling because it explicitly reversed the precedent established in the Olmstead case. This is made clear in the summary of the majority opinion from the ruling [16]:

1. The Government's eavesdropping activities violated the privacy upon which petitioner justifiably relied while using the telephone booth and this constitutes a "search and seizure" within the meaning of the Fourth Amendment.
   (a) The Fourth Amendment governs not only the seizure of tangible items but extends as well to the recording of oral statements.
   (b) Because the Fourth Amendment protects people rather than places, its reach cannot turn on the presence or absence of a physical intrusion into any given enclosure. The "trespass" doctrine of *Olmstead* v. *United States* is no longer controlling.
2. Although the surveillance in this case may have been so narrowly circumscribed that it could constitutionally have been authorized in advance, it was not in fact conducted pursuant to the warrant procedure which is a constitutional precondition of such electronic activity.

With this ruling, the Supreme Court effectively said that the only constitutionally valid wiretap is one that is authorized by the courts.

While this decision greatly strengthened privacy rights, it was not intended to establish the "right to privacy" as advocated by Brandeis. The majority opinion explained this as follows: ". . . the Fourth Amendment cannot be translated into a general constitutional 'right to privacy.' That Amendment protects individual privacy against certain kinds of governmental intrusion, but its protections go further, and often have nothing to do with privacy at all" [16].

5.3.4 Dissenting Opinion in Katz v. United States

The decision in the Katz case was not unanimous. This time Justice Black gave a particularly powerful dissenting opinion. He summarized the basis for his dissent as follows: "My basic objection is twofold: (1) I do not believe that the words of the Amendment will bear the meaning given them by today's decision, and (2) I do not believe that it is the proper role of this Court to rewrite the Amendment in order to bring it into harmony with the times and thus reach a result that many people believe to be desirable" [16].

Black went beyond simply saying that wiretap was not covered by the literal meaning of the words of the Amendment. He argued explicitly that the there was no original intent for the Amendment to cover such things: "Tapping telephone wires, of course, was an unknown possibility at the time the Fourth Amendment was adopted. But eavesdropping (and wiretapping is nothing more than eavesdropping by telephone) was. . . . There can be no doubt that the Framers were aware of this practice, and if they had desired to outlaw or restrict the use of evidence obtained by eavesdropping, I believe that they would have used appropriate language to do so in the Fourth Amendment. They certainly would not have left such a task to the ingenuity of language-stretching judges" [16].

It is difficult today to imagine that the Court would ever decide, for example, that tapping of e-mail without a court order is allowed by the Constitution. However, Black's dissent stands as an example that it is possible to construct a line of reasoning to this end. The "right to privacy" is not an explicit part of the Constitution, but rather something that the Court has read as implied as a logical extension of explicit guarantees.

5.3.5 1968 and 1994 Legislation Related to Wiretaps

The procedures currently followed by law enforcement to conduct authorized wiretaps trace to the 1968 Omnibus Crime Control and Safer Streets Act. In general, the law enforcement agency must present the court with evidence of "probable cause" to believe that a crime is involved, show that the wiretap should produce information relevant to prosecuting the crime, and show that obtaining evidence by means other than the wiretap is not practical. Also, the crime involved must be from a list of serious crimes for which wiretapping is allowed.

The 1968 law also requires that an annual report on wiretap use be made by the U.S. courts to the U.S. Congress. In a later section, we consider some statistics from the most recent annual report [9].

In the early 1990s, the Federal Bureau of Investigation (FBI) began to lobby Congress to pass "digital telephony" legislation. As communications systems began to transfer digital rather than analog data, the old technology for conducting wiretaps was no longer useful. The days of an "alligator clip" on a wire were giving way to the days of a computer which would isolate the selected communications stream. From the FBI's point of view, they simply wanted communications companies to design their equipment to preserve the same level of effective wiretap ability that the FBI had in the pre-cyberspace world.

In the first year that such legislation was submitted to Congress, it gained no sponsors and failed to be introduced for consideration. The proposal also received a great deal of negative comment from Internet privacy advocates. However, in 1994 a revised version of the legislation was sponsored by Patrick Leahy in the Senate and Don Edwards in the House of Representatives. Surprisingly, the Electronic Frontier Foundation, which had been outspoken in opposition to the original bill, worked on the formulation of the revised bill. The EFF, an organization dedicated to protecting individual rights in the context of the new "electronic frontier," described their position as follows: ". . . although we do not support the concept of digital telephony legislation, we believe that if Congress is to pass any version of the bill this year, it should be along the lines of the Edwards/Leahy version" [10].

This legislation passed and became known as the Communications Assistance for Law Enforcement Act (CALEA). The general requirements placed on telecommunications carriers are outlined in section 103 of the Act as follows:

(a) **Capability Requirements:** Except as provided in subsections (b), (c), and (d) of this section and sections 108(a) and 109(b) and (d), a telecommunications carrier shall ensure that its equipment, facilities, or services that provide a customer or subscriber with the ability to originate, terminate, or direct communications are capable of—

1. expeditiously isolating and enabling the government, pursuant to a court order or other lawful authorization, to intercept, to the exclusion of any other communications, all wire and electronic communications carried by the carrier within a service area to or from equipment, facilities, or services of a subscriber of such carrier concurrently with their transmission to or from the subscriber's equipment, facility, or service, or at such later time as may be acceptable to the government;

2. expeditiously isolating and enabling the government, pursuant to a court order or other lawful authorization, to access call-identifying information that is reasonably available to the carrier—(a) before, during, or immediately after the transmission of a wire or electronic communication (or at such later time as may be acceptable to the government); and (b) in a manner that allows it to be associated with the communication to which it pertains, except that, with regard to information acquired solely pursuant to the authority for pen registers and trap and trace devices (as defined in section 3127 of title 18, United States Code), such call-identifying information shall not include any information that may disclose the physical location of the subscriber (except to the extent that the location may be determined from the telephone number);

3. delivering intercepted communications and call-identifying information to the government, pursuant to a court order or other lawful authorization, in a format such that they may be transmitted by means of equipment, facilities, or services procured by the government to a location other than the premises of the carrier; and

4. facilitating authorized communications interceptions and access to call-identifying information unobtrusively and with a minimum of interference with any subscriber's telecommunications service and in a manner that protects— (A) the privacy and security of communica-

tions and call-identifying information not authorized to be intercepted; and (B) information regarding the government's interception of communications and access to call-identifying information. . . . [1]

The law also provides for telecommunications companies to be compensated for the costs of implementing systems to meet the prescribed capabilities. Section 1110 of the law states: "There are authorized to be appropriated to carry out this title a total of $500,000,000 for fiscal years 1995, 1996, 1997, and 1998. Such sums are authorized to remain available until expended" [1]. Clearly the anticipated costs of having digital telephony be wiretap-friendly for law enforcement are large.

The result of this law is to ensure that it is technically feasible for law enforcement to receive the stream of digital data which represents a wiretap. However, from the perspective of law enforcement, the wiretap situation may still be much worse than it was pre-cyberspace. While it was possible in principle for telephone users of the past to encrypt their conversation, or to speak in code, it was so impractical that it was rarely done. By comparison, computer users can encrypt their communications with ease. Thus law enforcement must be concerned not just with the ability to wiretap a communications stream, but also with the ability to decrypt a communications stream that has been encrypted. This is what has motivated some of the government's false starts toward establishing a new encryption standard.

5.3.6 Wiretap Statistics from the Annual Report

At the time of this writing, the most recent wiretap report covers intercepts concluded between January 1, 1998 and December 31, 1998: "From 1997 to 1998, the total number of intercepts authorized by federal and state courts increased 12 percent to 1,329, reflecting continued growth in applications involving the surveillance of narcotics operations (up 10 percent). Following a 2% decrease in 1997, the number of applications for orders by federal authorities remained essentially stable in 1998, dropping one half of one percent. The number of applications reported by state prosecuting officials increased 24 percent over last year, with more jurisdictions providing reports than in previous years. The number of federal intercept applications authorized has grown over the last 10 years, increasing 93% from 1988 to 1998, while state applications have increased 71% since 1988. The number of intercepts employed in drug-related investigations also has experienced significant growth. Drug offenders were targeted in 955 of the interceptions concluded in 1998, compared to 435 in 1988, a 120% increase" [9].

Other interesting facts drawn from the wiretap report include the following.

- The first year in which e-mail taps were authorized was 1998, and there were just five e-mail taps reported.

- In 1998, only two requests for wiretaps were not authorized.
- For 1998, the average length of original authorization was 28 days and that average length of extension was 27 days. (Wiretaps are originally authorized for up to 30 days, but this time may be extended if the authorizing judge is convinced it is warranted.)
- "The average cost of intercept devices installed in 1998 was $57,669. . . ." [9].
- Investigations involving wiretaps resulted in 3450 arrests and 911 convictions in 1998.
- Of the 1329 authorizations in 1998, 53 involved investigation of homicide and assault and 5 involved kidnapping.
- States with no law for their police agencies to conduct wiretaps are Alabama, Arkansas, Kentucky, Maine, Michigan, South Carolina, and Vermont. All other states, the District of Columbia, and the U.S. Virgin Islands have wiretap legislation.

There is often substantial disagreement in how to interpret statistics in the annual wiretap reports. A privacy zealot might point to the fact that only two wiretap applications were denied and conclude that approval of almost any request is automatic. A law-and-order zealot might point to the five wiretaps used in kidnapping cases and ask if you would want law enforcement to use every tool available if one of your children were kidnapped. But there is no disputing the fact that wiretaps are widely used, and that evidence obtained using wiretaps helps to solve crimes and convict criminals.

The important elements of the wiretapping and privacy story for us here are that (1) the move to cyberspace has the potential to reduce the effectiveness of wiretapping in law enforcement, and (2) reducing law enforcement's ability to conduct effective wiretaps will reduce the ability to catch and convict some criminals.

5.4 DEVELOPMENT OF PUBLIC KEY ENCRYPTION

In this section, we take a short diversion to introduce the concept of *public key encryption*. Public key encryption is also sometimes referred to as "asymmetric" encryption. This style of encryption is already in wide use on the Internet (e. g., to send secure e-mail). Regardless of how the government policy toward encryption turns out, it is likely that public key encryption will remain a widely used technology.

There are two major problems with using a private key encryption algorithm in a networked environment. One is that the private key must be distributed ahead of time to the people whom you wish to communicate with. Since the purpose of encryption is to protect against eavesdropping on the network, the private key has to be initially distributed by some trusted means outside of the network.

145

The second is that you want to be able to verify the identity of the person sending the message and ensure that the message has not been altered before you receive it. The concept of public key encryption was put forth by Diffie and Hellman in 1976 as a solution to these problems with private key encryption [4].

The public key encryption concept is both elegant and very practical. The basic idea is as follows. As before, everyone uses the same encryption algorithm. Each person constructs their own **pair** of key values, so that the two values work together in a special way. If you apply the encryption algorithm with the first key value, the result is an encrypted message. Then if you apply the encryption algorithm to the encrypted message using the second key value, the result is the decrypted message. Each person makes their first key value known to the public, which gives rise to the name "public key encryption," and keeps their second key value private.

You can imagine a trusted agent who publishes a "phone book" of the public keys for everyone on the network. If you want to send a message to a person, you look up their public key, use it to encrypt the message, and then send the message on its way. Only the intended receiver knows the proper second key value to use to recover the decrypted message. Of course, it is also important that knowledge of the public key does not make it easy to figure out the corresponding private key.

One major benefit of public key encryption relative to private key encryption is that you don't have to agree ahead of time on a private key. Another nice aspect of public key encryption is the ability to create *digital signatures*. A digital signature allows the recipient of a message to verify the identity of the sender and to determine that the contents of the message have not been altered. The ability to create digital signatures requires one more prop-

erty for the pair of key values. This property is that the pair of keys can be used in either order. That is, whichever is used for encryption, the other then works for decryption. Given this property, digital signatures work in the following way. Assume person A wants to send a signed message to person B. Person A first applies A's private decryption key to the message. Then A applies B's public encryption key to the encrypted message plus a plain message saying that the whole package comes from A. The result is then sent to B. When B decrypts using B's private key, the result is an encrypted message plus a plain message that claims that it came from person A. B can then apply A's public key to the encrypted message. Since only A could have known the key to use ahead of time to cause the message to make sense when encrypted with A's public key, the message must have been received, intact, from A. This process is illustrated in Figure 5.1.

5.4.1 The RSA Algorithm

The benefits of public key encryption should be obvious. But there is still the important detail of how to construct such pairs of encrypt/decrypt keys. Currently the most popular implementation of the public key encryption concept is the RSA algorithm, developed in 1978 by Rivest, Shamir, and Adleman [14]. The encryption and decryption algorithms in the RSA system are based on representing a message as a number, raising it to a power, and then taking the modulus of that result. More formally, the operations are defined as

$$encrypt_A(m) \equiv m^e \bmod n$$
$$decrypt_A(m) \equiv m^d \bmod n$$

Thus, each user has a set of three values to specify: e, d, and n. The pair of values (e, n) is the public encryption

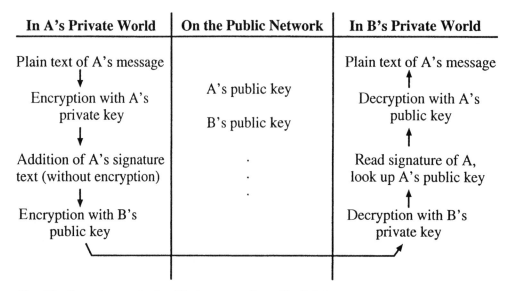

In A's Private World	On the Public Network	In B's Private World
Plain text of A's message ↓ Encryption with A's private key ↓ Addition of A's signature text (without encryption) ↓ Encryption with B's public key	A's public key B's public key · · ·	Plain text of A's message ↑ Decryption with A's public key ↑ Read signature of A, look up A's public key ↑ Decryption with B's private key

Fig. 5.1 General concept of public key encryption with digital signatures.

key. The pair of values (d, n) is the private decryption key. The number n is chosen as the product of two large random primes, p and q. This step is important to the level of security provided. The security of the system rests on the difficulty involved in factoring the value of n after it is made public. The value of d is chosen as a large random integer that is relatively prime to $(p - 1) \times (q - 1)$. Lastly, the value of e is computed as the multiplicative inverse of d modulo $((p - 1) \times (q - 1))$. This guarantees that

$$e \times d \equiv 1 \, modulo \, ((p - 1) \times (q - 1))$$

There are still some important details to consider (such as how to efficiently find good primes or ones of the appropriate size for the level of security needed), but this gives you some idea of how the RSA encryption scheme works.

RSA-style public key encryption is already widely used on the Internet. All encryption methods, private or public key, are subject to brute-force attacks. Given the public key (e, n) one could, in principle, work out the private key (d, n). The security of the RSA encryption algorithm relies on the difficulty of the factoring tasks needed to work out the private key. Choosing larger random prime numbers dramatically increases the amount of work required for a brute-force attack. In principle, one can increase security to any desired level by increasing the size of the numbers. In practice, increasing the size of the numbers also slows down the encryption process. There is another class of methods, referred to as "elliptic curve" methods, that offers promise of both faster encryption and harder brute-force attacks. The method is already being incorporated into some public key encryption systems.

One of the early boosts to the use of this style of encryption for e-mail was the "Pretty Good Privacy" program that was distributed on the Internet. The controversy over this program and its distribution is a good case study in itself, and is the subject of the case study section at the end of this chapter.

Important elements of the public key encryption story for us here are: (1) public key encryption has some inherent advantages over private key encryption in the network environment; (2) public key encryption is already in wide use on the Internet and there are substantial efforts aimed at developing Public Key Infrastructure concepts and standards; and (3) public key encryption can provide arbitrary levels of security, by increasing the size of the key.

5.5 GOVERNMENT POLICY TOWARD ENCRYPTION

The story of federal government involvement in cryptography standards is rather complicated. There are two intertwined elements to the controversy. One element involves how the government has used its power to regulate the export of encryption technology. This power is based on the International Traffic in Arms Regulation (ITAR). The other element involves the government's attempts to create a new encryption standard to replace DES. In general, the position of the computing industry has been that they would like the government to replace DES with a recognizably secure new encryption algorithm and then remove all restrictions on export of encryption technology. On the other side, the position of the government has been that they would like industry to adopt and widely use the proposed encryption algorithms that make it easy for law enforcement to decrypt wiretapped communications. This stalemate occupied a good portion of the 1990s. We will briefly outline the major proposals and issues in this area.

5.5.1 "Escrowed" Encryption

The U.S. government proposed an "Escrowed Encryption Standard" (EES) in early 1993. Skipjack, Clipper, and Capstone are some other names associated with the EES. Clipper and Capstone refer to implementations of the algorithm on a chip. The Capstone chip is meant to make it easy to use the EES with the telephone system, for example. We will use EES to refer generically to this proposal.

The EES is a private key encryption algorithm. As was the case with DES, the National Institute of Standards and Technology and the National Security Agency were involved in the development of the EES. However, unlike DES, the details of the EES algorithm are classified! This fact disturbed many experts in the cryptography community. After all, DES came to be accepted as secure only after it withstood serious analysis by a broad community of experts. There would be no such analysis for the EES.

The "escrowed" element of EES refers to a built-in method of allowing easy decryption by law enforcement. Certain information would be held "in escrow" by some trusted agencies, and turned over when a law enforcement representative presented a court order. The basic scenario for how this would work is as follows. Each EES encryption device would be numbered, and would have a default encryption key. Messages would be encrypted in two stages. In the first stage, the current message would be encrypted with whatever key value is chosen by the user. In the second stage, the encrypted message and the key value for it would be encrypted with the default key for that particular EES device. The message sent would be the results of the second stage encryption plus the EES device number. There would be two escrow agents. Each escrow agent would have a list of EES device numbers, and half of the default key value for each device. When law enforcement obtained a court order for a wiretap, it would be presented to both escrow agents, along with the EES device number. Each escrow agent would return their half of the device key for that device number. The two halves of the device key would be combined. This would allow decrypting the second-stage encryption of the message. This would allow access to the key for decrypting the first-stage encryption.

147

The initial hope of the government was that the EES would be widely accepted and become the same sort of de facto worldwide standard as DES. However, the general response from privacy advocates, the computing industry, and the international community was uncompromisingly negative. Privacy advocates saw too much danger in the databases to be held by the escrow agents. These would clearly be valuable targets for criminals or terrorists. The computing industry felt that supporting EES put them at a clear disadvantage to foreign companies that could offer more trusted encryption algorithms that did not have the escrow feature. The international community generally did not like the idea of a system tailored for the wiretap requirements of U.S. law enforcement.

In the face of unrelenting opposition to EES, the government made some modifications to the original proposal. For example, the particular agencies (NIST, Treasury Department) that play the role of the escrow agents were changed. However, the elements of EES that were the targets of the main objections were (1) that the algorithm itself was classified, and (2) that key values were kept in escrow at all. These elements were seen by the government as necessary. The algorithm needed to be classified to reduce the chance that someone would make encryption devices that acted like real EES devices but did not actually keep track of the message key. And the keys needed to be kept in escrow so that law enforcement could decrypt a wiretapped communication. But the computing industry was simply not going along with the proposal.

5.5.2 "Key Recovery" Systems

By 1996, the government had migrated to a proposal for "key recovery" systems. Basically, the proposal for "key recovery" dropped the requirement for use of the EES encryption algorithm in particular, proposed general licensing of key recovery (escrow) centers, but kept a requirement for there to be some way for the key to be recovered. Thus, in many ways, the "key recovery" concept is just a generalized version of the "escrowed encryption" concept.

In an attempt to make the proposal more attractive to the computing industry, modifications to the encryption export regulations were included. Companies would be allowed to export stronger (56-bit) encryption systems than previously allowed, provided that they were pursuing development of key recovery systems. But eventually only key-recovery systems would be allowed for export.

The response to this proposal was really no warmer than to the original EES proposal. A 1998 report co-authored by eleven experts in encryption and privacy offered this conclusion: "Key recovery systems are inherently less secure, more costly, and more difficult to use than similar systems without a recovery feature. The massive deployment of key-recovery-based infrastructures to meet law enforcement's specifications will require significant sacri-

fices in security and convenience and substantially increase costs to all users of encryption. Furthermore, building the secure infrastructure of the breathtaking scale and complexity that would be required for such a scheme is beyond the experience and current competency of the field, and may well introduce ultimately unacceptable risks and costs" [2].

5.5.3 The Advanced Encryption Standard (AES)

In 1997, the government began a process for selecting a new encryption standard, to be called the "Advanced Encryption Standard." In contrast to the EES effort, the process for selecting the AES is open and highly public. The goal is to design an encryption algorithm that could be used for 20 to 30 years. A call for candidate algorithms was issued in September 1997. In August 1998, at a public conference, fifteen candidate algorithms were announced. The algorithms were proposed by a variety of companies and individuals from around the world. The winner of the competition among these algorithms is projected to be announced in late 2000. The result of this process should be a new encryption algorithm that is available for use worldwide on a royalty-free basis, is faster to use than triple-DES, and is more secure than triple-DES. An archive of documentation on the AES selection process is available at www.nist.gov/aes.

Note that the existence of the AES process does not necessarily mean that government efforts to establish a "key recovery" encryption system are ended. A key recovery system could conceivably be made with the AES as the core encryption algorithm.

5.5.4 Constitutionality of Export Restrictions

The computing industry in the United States is generally unhappy with the export restrictions on encryption technology. These restrictions place U.S. industry at a disadvantage when trying to sell in overseas markets. Many academics and First Amendment advocates are also unhappy with the export restrictions. They see the restrictions as an infringement of the First Amendment right to freedom of speech, and have waged a continuing battle against export restrictions in the Federal courts. One example of this is the case of *Bernstein* v. *Department of Commerce,* which started in 1995. Bernstein is a computer science professor who developed an encryption algorithm and wanted to publicize it and its implementation on the worldwide web. Rather than applying for an export license, he challenged the restrictions in court. Initial rulings went against the government, but as of late 1999 this case was still on appeal in the Ninth Circuit Court. Conflicting decisions in different courts considering different cases may make this an issue to be heard by the Supreme Court in the near future. (See the worksheets at the end of this chapter for additional study on this topic.)

The computing industry has also made its case to Congress. In 1999, Congress was considering a bill titled "Security and Freedom Through Encryption" (SAFE), which would relax export controls on encryption technology. However, Congress also recognizes the problems that encryption may produce for law enforcement. One amendment to the "SAFE" bill as considered by the Commerce Committee of the House of Representatives reads as follows:

> Whoever is required by an order of any court to provide to the court or any other party any information in such person's possession which has been encrypted and who, having possession of the key or such other capability to decrypt such information into the readable or comprehensible format of such information prior to its encryption, fails to provide such information in accordance with the order in such readable or comprehensible form—(1) in the case of a first offense under this section, shall be imprisoned for not more than 5 years, or fined under title 18, U.S. Code, or both; and (2) in the case of a second or subsequent offense under this section, shall be imprisoned for not more than 10 years, or fined under title 18, U.S. Code, or both;

While law enforcement might favor such an amendment, it would almost certainly face a challenge on grounds of violating the Fifth Amendment.

The important elements of the record of government policy on encryption for us here seem to be the following: (1) export controls on encryption technology seem to have little practical value (e.g., many of the candidates for AES originate from outside the United States); (2) the selection of the AES is potentially a very important event; and (3) law enforcement's desire for "escrow" or "recovery" style of encryption systems is fundamentally at odds with the interests of the computing industry and privacy advocates.

5.6 Current Social Conflicts and Ethical Issues

Where do these various lines of development leave us? Unfortunately, we seem to be left well short of the hoped-for cyber-utopia. A number of ethical/legal/social issues remain to be resolved. Among these are the following:

- *What is the best technology for a highly secure long-term encryption standard?* The AES development process is an attempt to answer this question. The goal of achieving both greater security and greater speed than triple-DES is a good one. The process seems to include consideration of some well-regarded algorithms, and so there is reason to be hopeful.
- *What should be the government's ability to regulate encryption export?* This issue is currently being dealt with on all sides: by new regulations from the government, by new laws under consideration in Congress, and by challenges through the court system. At the moment, it appears that the government's ability to legally restrict export of encryption technology is destined to be substantially reduced. However, in practical terms, highly secure encryption products have been readily available outside the United States for some time now.
- *Is any sort of "escrow" or "recovery" facility an acceptable risk?* Concern has been raised over the level of security required of the key escrow databases. These databases would certainly seem to be attractive targets for criminals and terrorists. They could be compromised either technically or through more traditional means of somehow recruiting an accomplice "on the inside." Is the compromise of an escrow database so catastrophic that such facilities simply should not be contemplated?
- *How can law enforcement capabilities best be preserved?* It seems almost inevitable that law enforcement will have a poorer capability for wiretapping in cyberspace than it did in the pre-cyberspace world. There are many highly secure encryption algorithms readily available on the Internet. And it is much easier for computer users to use their own encryption on their digital messages than it was for the typical phone system users to encrypt their own analog voice communications. Even if some form of "key recovery" system is eventually adopted, it seems unlikely that it could become the only form of encryption that is widely used. It is tempting to want to make it illegal to fail to provide the decrypted version of a message when asked for it by a court order. But this will likely run afoul of the Fifth Amendment protection against self-incrimination. This is perhaps the area where some unusual compromise is most likely to emerge.

5.7 Case Study

The history of the "Pretty Good Privacy" (PGP) program is interesting and relevant to the issues in this chapter. The program is now available for free to noncommercial users in the United States at the site web.mit.edu/network/pgp.html. It is also a part of commercial security packages (see www.nai.com). PGP uses the RSA public key encryption algorithm (see www.rsa.com).

5.7.1 The Cast of Characters

Philip Zimmermann is a 40-something, "twice-jailed peace activist" [13] turned computer programmer.

Rivest, Shamir, and Adleman are the co-inventors of the RSA public key encryption algorithm. RSA Data Security, Inc., is the company named after the developers of the algorithm. This company controls the patent rights to the algorithm.

MIT is, of course, the Massachusetts Institute of Technology. Their role in this story is pretty much just that of a "name" institution used to provide credibility.

The U.S. government enters this story as an agency interested in enforcing export restrictions on munitions.

The "distributor" is alleged to be an anonymous friend of Philip Zimmermann.

Viacrypt is a company that has a license for the RSA algorithm.

5.7.2 The Sequence of Events

Rivest, Shamir, and Adleman introduced the RSA algorithm in 1978. RSA Data Security was formed to exploit the patent rights to the RSA algorithm. United States government export restrictions on munitions allow RSA to sell their encryption products to U.S. citizens but not to foreigners.

Somewhere around 1990, Philip Zimmermann spent about six months developing the Pretty Good Privacy software package. PGP allows the secure exchange of e-mail through the use of the RSA algorithm.

Zimmermann did not initially obtain a license for the RSA algorithm. This led RSA Data Security president James Bidzos to joke that PGP actually stood for "Pretty Good Piracy." RSA Data Security would send letters to users of the original PGP warning them about patent-license violations.

The "distributor" posted the source code for Zimmermann's unlicensed PGP on a bulletin board on the Internet. This meant that PGP was open to anonymous distribution at no cost to individuals around the world. This, of course, did nothing to make RSA Data Security happier about patent-license violations. It also caused the U.S. government to become interested and to consider charging Zimmermann with a violation of export-restriction laws. The charge could mean a 15-month jail term.

Viacrypt used their RSA license and a royalty agreement with Zimmermann to market an entirely legal version of PGP. Americans and Canadians can purchase the MS-DOS version for $100 and the Unix version for $150. Viacrypt would be interested in selling the product abroad as well, but is prevented from doing so by export restrictions.

In May 1994, RSA Data Security and MIT worked out a way to provide a legal version of PGP available at no cost to noncommercial users. PGP 6.5.1 source code is distributed by MIT along with a valid license from RSA. This may not be as altruistic on the part of RSA as it first seems. With MIT supplying the free PGP to noncommercial users, chances are that users of old versions of PGP will switch over to the new version, and a customer base is created for commercial users. Establishing control over a widely used "standard" version of PGP should have some value in opening up a market for sales to commercial users.

5.7.3 Conclusions and Questions

Whoever posted the original version of PGP to the Internet clearly violated at least the spirit of the export-restriction laws. Since Zimmermann claims that he personally did not do it, and since he made no financial gain from the action, many people view him as a "white hat" who has been unfairly persecuted by the government. Consider this more carefully. Did Zimmermann make anything available to U.S. citizens that they could not have bought from RSA Data Security? If not, wasn't the true short-term impact of PGP simply to damage the market for RSA Data Security products? Could it be that the creation of PGP was just an over-zealous idealist's way of doing harm to a perceived "big brother" government? If Zimmermann did give PGP to a friend with the intention that the friend would post it to the Internet, is Zimmermann just as guilty as the friend?

To go back and question the basics of the patent issue, what exactly should RSA Data Security be allowed to have patent protection for? A particular implementation of an algorithm? Any use of an algorithm? Any use of any algorithm to implement the public key encryption concept? Did RSA push any ethical boundaries by writing letters to users of Zimmermann's original PGP?

Finally, what about the government's role in enforcing export restrictions? Can applying the restrictions to encryption products be justified on ethical grounds?

Points to Remember

- The ability of law enforcement agencies to conduct telephone wiretaps is subject to detailed regulations. Currently, those same procedures are being used to authorize wiretaps on e-mail and other forms of communication.
- Plain DES encryption has reached the end of its useful life in terms of providing secure encryption, and a new standard algorithm is badly needed. Initial government attempts at a new standard that includes escrow or recovery features failed to gain acceptance, but the new AES process seems promising.
- There is still strong sentiment in law enforcement and government for preserving the ability to wiretap in cyberspace. This could take the form of standards for escrow or recovery. It could also take the form of laws that make it a crime to fail to decrypt a message when asked by a court order.
- The "right to privacy" as we know it is not explicitly spelled out in the Constitution, but rather results from interpretations made by the Supreme Court.

WORKSHEET—Review of Encryption Concepts

1. How does private key encryption work?

2. How does public key encryption work?

3. What is the Data Encryption Standard?

4. How does escrowed encryption work?

5. What is the primary advantage of public key encryption over private key encryption?

6. What is the primary advantage of escrowed encryption over nonescrowed encryption?

WORKSHEET—Legal Challenges to Encryption Export Regulations

In 1998, Judge James Gwin of the District Court in Cleveland ruled against Peter Junger. Junger is a faculty member at Case Western Reserve University. He challenged the government's export restrictions in court, with the claim that they violated his right to free speech. In 1997, Judge Marilyn Patel of the District Court in San Francisco ruled in favor of Daniel Bernstein. Bernstein is a faculty member at the University of Chicago who had brought a similar suit against the government's export restrictions, also claiming that they violated his right to free speech. Obtain and read copies of the two court decisions, or of newspaper articles that describe the decisions.

1. Summarize the government's argument in the two cases.

2. Summarize the arguments of Junger and Bernstein.

3. Summarize the reasoning behind Judge Gwin's ruling.

4. Summarize the reasoning behind Judge Patel's ruling.

5. What did Gwin have to say about Patel's ruling?

6. Which judge's ruling do you feel is correct and why?

7. Follow up to see what rulings have been made on appeal in these cases.

153

WORKSHEET—The Importance of Not Being Different

Read Bruce Schneier's article at the end of this chapter. Then answer the following questions.

1. Explain Schneier's opening analogy about a doctor and antibiotics. How accurate does the analogy seem to you?

2. Schneier says, "Most cryptography products on the market are insecure. Some don't work as advertised. Some are obviously flawed. . . ." What does this imply for the importance of a standard like the AES? How likely is the AES to suffer from such problems? Why?

3. Schneier says, "Security has nothing to do with functionality." Explain what he means by this.

4. What does Schneier say are the reasons for the flaws he sees in Microsoft's Point-To-Point Tunneling Protocol?

5. Why does Schneier suggest that there is great confidence in the correctness of DES, RSA, and PGP?

WORKSHEET—Is Staying With the Herd Really Best?

Read Terry Ritter's article at the end of this chapter. (If you have not already read Schneier's article, read it also.) Then answer the following questions.

1. Ritter asserts that ". . . anyone concerned with real security probably should consider using something other than the same cipher as everyone else." What is his reasoning for this conclusion? What practical problems would you foresee with "using something other than the same cipher as everyone else?" Based on Schneier's article, what do you think would be Schneier's counter-argument? Who do you think is more correct, and why?

2. Ritter asserts that ". . . most crypto experts probably would agree that just because 20 years of analysis of the U.S. Data Encryption Standard has not found an easy break does not mean that no easy break exists. . . . In practice, even extensive review is not a rational or scientific indication of strength." Do you agree? Why or why not?

3. Ritter asserts that "Since no one can prove that any cipher is secure, absolute confidence is simply not available. Any cipher can fail at any time." Do you agree? Why or why not? Does Ritter's assertion imply that all cipher algorithms are equally (un)reliable?

4. Is "strength against unknown attack" the only property of interest in a cipher algorithm? Why or why not?

5. Who would you hire as your encryption security consultant, Ritter or Schneier? Why?

ADDITIONAL ASSIGNMENTS

1. **Development of Internet wiretap capability.** While the phone systems are wiretap-capable to some reasonable degree, the Internet is not so wiretap-friendly. In October 1999, the FBI encouraged the Internet Engineering Task Force to consider the issue of making the Internet more wiretap-capable. In January 2000, the executive committee of the IETF decided that they would not consider the requirements for wiretapping in the development of Internet protocols. Report on the issues involved, including what the FBI would like to see happen and why the IETF declined to move in this direction.

2. **Development of Public Key Infrastructure.** Report on the current status of industry and government efforts aimed at developing a Public Key Infrastructure. The Internet Engineering Task Force (ietf.org) and the National Institute of Standards may be good places to begin studying this topic.

3. **The "Cyberspace Electronic Security Act" proposed in 1999.** Report on the proposed "Cyberspace Electronic Security Act" described at

   www.epic.org/crypto/legislation/cesa_release.html.

   How would adoption of this law change the situation with monitoring of Internet communications as it compares to wiretap of traditional telephone communications?

4. **Choosing a key length for public key encryption.** How big should your RSA encryption key be? Study some of the documents on the sites:

   http://www.rsasecurity.com/rsalabs/challenges/
   http://www.counterpane.com/keylength.html.

   Report on the recommended key length for use in RSA public key encryption. Then check what key length is used in some of your favorite on-line stores. Are you satisfied with the level of security? Why or why not?

5. **Illegal wiretapping in modern times.** Stories of illegal wiretaps in the 1960s (e.g., targeted at Martin Luther King, Jr.) are well known. Most people assume that reforms have been effective and therefore such abuses are relatively rare today. The Los Angeles Police Department made the news in 1999 over charges of "widespread" illegal wiretapping. Report on the allegations, investigation and eventual outcome of this story.

6. **The "Echelon" eavesdropping controversy.** In late 1999, several news stories appeared about the "Echelon" intelligence gathering system. For example, see

   http://www.wired.com/news/print/0,1294,32302,00.html.

   Read several of these stories and report on the allegations made and the facts admitted. What truly new information was revealed in these stories?

7. **Elliptic-curve cryptography.** Report in more detail on the relative merits of elliptic-curve versus RSA-style public key encryption. Possible places to start include:

   http://www.certicom.com/ecc/enter/index.htm
   http://www.cryptosavvy.com

8. **Bruce Schneier's Crypto-Gram newsletter.** Back issues of the Crypto-Gram newsletter are available at

   http://www.counterpane.com

   Read through the last few issues and report on the most interesting recent development in encryption and security.

9. **The Electronic Communications Privacy Act and the privacy of e-mail.** One of the touchiest issues in today's workplace is whether employers should monitor their employees' e-mail. Some people have suggested that the Electronic Communications Privacy Act of 1986 gives employers the right to monitor e-mail sent on company computers. Others have suggested that the law is not so clear. Perhaps most unsettling is that only 18 percent of companies are estimated to have a written policy on the matter [3]. Look into the Electronic Communications Privacy Act to find out exactly what it says, and see if you can find instances of both good and bad company monitoring of e-mail.

REFERENCES

[1] Communications Assistance for Law Enforcement Act, H.R. 4922, 1994. Online version available at www.epic.org.

[2] H. Abelson et al., The risks of key recovery, key escrow and trusted third part encryption, on-line version available at www.epic.org.

[3] R. Britt, Employers have the right to read e-mail, *The Tampa Tribune,* June 8, 1994.

[4] W. Diffie and M. Hellman, New directions in cryptography, *IEEE Transactions on Information Theory,* November 1976, pp. 644–654.

[5] Richard Folkers, Jimmying the Internet, U.S. News and World Report, September 14, 1998, pp. 45–46.

[6] J. E. Katz, "Social aspects of telecommunications policy," *IEEE Technology and Society Magazine,* June/July 1990, pp. 16–24.

[7] S. T. Kent, Internet privacy enhanced mail, *Communications of the ACM,* August 1993, pp. 48–60.

[8] S. Landau, S. Kent, C. Brooks, S. Charney, D. Denning, W. Diffie, A. Lauck, D. Miller, P. Neumann, and D. Sobel, "Codes, keys and conflicts: Issues in US crypto policy," *ACM US Public Policy Committee Report,* June 1994. (ftp://info.acm.org/reports/acm_crypto_study/)

[9] L. R. Mecham Report of the Director of the Administrative Office of the United States Courts on Applications for Orders Authorizing or Approving the Interception of Wire, Oral, or Electronic Communications, April 1999. Online version available at www.epic.org.

[10] J. A. Osuna, House, Senate pass wiretap legislation, *Computing Research News,* November 1994, pp. 7–8.

[11] "Digital disclosure needs a new privacy ethic," *PC Week,* September 21, 1992.

[12] M. Puente, "A step closer to era of ID cards," *USA Today,* August 31, 1994.

[13] C. Reed, "Code breaking: privacy on parade," *The Guardian,* May 26, 1994.

[14] R. L. Rivest, A. Shamir and L. Adleman, "A method for obtaining digital signatures and public-key cryptosystems," *Communications of the ACM,* February 1978, pp. 120–126.

[15] U.S. Supreme Court, Olmstead v. U.S., 277 U.S. 438, 1928. Online version available at www.findlaw.com.

[16]V U.S. Supreme Court, Katz v. U.S., 389 U.S. 347, 1967. Online version available at www.findlaw.com.

Cryptography: The Importance of Not Being Different

Bruce Schneier, Counterpane Systems

Suppose your doctor said, "I realize we have antibiotics that are good at treating your kind of infection without harmful side effects, and that there are decades of research to support this treatment. But I'm going to give you tortilla-chip powder instead, because, uh, it *might* work." You'd get a new doctor.

Practicing medicine is difficult. The profession doesn't rush to embrace new drugs; it takes years of testing before benefits can be proven, dosages established, and side effects cataloged. A good doctor won't treat a bacterial infection with a medicine he just invented when proven antibiotics are available. And a smart patient wants the same drug that cured the last person, not something different.

Cryptography is difficult, too. It combines mathematics, computer science, sometimes electrical engineering, and a twisted mindset that can figure out how to get around rules, break systems, and subvert the designers' intentions. Even very smart, knowledgeable, experienced people invent bad cryptography. In the crypto community, people aren't even all

Editor: Ron Vetter, University of North Carolina at Wilmington, Department of Computer Science, 601 South College Rd., Wilmington, NC 28403; voice (910) 962-3667; fax (910) 962-7107; vetterr@uncwil.edu

The best security methods leverage the collective analytical ability of the cryptographic community.

that embarrassed when their algorithms and protocols are broken. That's how hard it is.

REUSING SECURE COMPONENTS

Building cryptography into products is hard, too. Most cryptography products on the market are insecure. Some don't work as advertised. Some are obviously flawed. Others are more subtly flawed. Sometimes people discover the flaws quickly, while other times it takes years (usually because no one bothered to look for them). Sometimes a decade goes by before someone invents new mathematics to break something.

This difficulty is made even more serious for several reasons. First, flaws can appear anywhere. They can be in the trust model, the system design, the algorithms and protocols, the implementations, the source code, the human-computer interface, the procedures, the underlying computer system. Anywhere.

Second, these flaws cannot be found through normal beta testing. Security has nothing to do with functionality. A cryptography product can function normally and be completely insecure. Flaws remain undiscovered until someone looks for them explicitly.

Third, and most importantly, a single flaw breaks the security of the entire system. If you think of cryptography as a chain, the system is only as secure as its weakest link. This means that everything has to be secure. It's not enough to make the algorithms and protocols perfect if the implementation has problems. A great product with a broken algorithm is useless. And a great algorithm, protocol, and implementation can be ruined by a flawed random-number generator. If there is a security flaw in the code, the rest of it doesn't matter.

Given this harsh reality, the most rational design decision is to use as few links as possible, and as high a percentage of strong links as possible. Since it is impractical for a system designer (or even a design team) to analyze a completely new system, a smart designer reuses components that are generally believed to be secure, and only invents new cryptography where absolutely necessary.

TRUSTING THE KNOWN

Consider IPSec, the Internet IP security protocol (described in the sidebar "About IPSec"). Beginning in 1992, it was designed in the open by committee and was the subject of considerable public scrutiny from the start. Everyone knew it was an important protocol, and people spent a lot of effort trying to get it right. Security technologies were proposed, broken, and then modified. Versions were codified and analyzed. The first draft of the standard was published in 1995. Aspects were debated on security merits and on performance, ease of implementation, upgradability, and use.

In November 1998, the committee published a pile of RFCs—one in a series of steps to make IPSec an Internet standard. And it is still being studied.

Reprinted from *IEEE Computer*, Vol. 32, No. 3, pp. 108–109 & 112, March 1999.

Cryptographers at the Naval Research Laboratory recently discovered a minor implementation flaw. The work continues, in public, by anyone and everyone who is interested.

On the other hand, Microsoft developed its own Point-to-Point Tunneling Protocol (PPTP) to do much the same thing. They invented their own authentication protocol, their own hash functions, and their own key-generation algorithm. Every one of these items was badly flawed. They used a known encryption algorithm, but they used it in such a way as to negate its security. They made implementation mistakes that weakened the system even further. But since they did all this work internally, no one knew that their PPTP was weak.

Microsoft fielded PPTP in Windows NT and 95, and used it in their virtual private network (VPN) products. It wasn't until summer of 1998 that Counterpane Systems published a paper describing the flaws we found. Microsoft quickly posted a series of fixes, which we have since evaluated and found wanting. They don't fix things nearly as well as Microsoft would like people to believe.

And then there is a company like TriStrata, which claimed to have a proprietary security solution without telling anyone how it works (because it's patent pending). You have to trust them. They claimed to have a new algorithm and new set of protocols that are much better than any that exist today. And even if they make their system public, the fact that they've patented it and retain proprietary control means that many cryptographers won't bother analyzing their claims.

LEVERAGING THE COLLECTIVE STRENGTH

You can choose any of these three systems to secure your virtual private network. Although it's possible for any of them to be flawed, you want to minimize your risk. If you go with IPSec, you have a much greater assurance that the algorithms and protocols are strong. Of course, the product could still be flawed—there could be an implementation bug or a bug in any of the odd little corners of the code not covered in the IPSec standards—but at least you know

that the algorithms and protocols have withstood a level of analysis and review that the Microsoft and TriStrata options have not.

Choosing the TriStrata system is like going to a doctor who has no medical

> **No single organization (outside the military) has the financial resources necessary to evaluate a new cryptographic algorithm.**

degree and whose novel treatments (which he refuses to explain) have no support by the AMA. Sure, it's possible (although highly unlikely) that he's discovered a totally new branch of medicine, but do you want to be the guinea pig?

The point here is that the best security methods leverage the collective analytical ability of the cryptographic community. No single company (outside the military) has the financial resources necessary to evaluate a new cryptographic algorithm or shake the design flaws out of a complex protocol. The same holds true in cryptographic libraries. If you write your own, you will probably make mistakes. If you use one that's public and has been around for a while, some of the mistakes will have been found and corrected.

It's hard enough making strong cryptography work in a new system; it's just plain lunacy to use new cryptography when viable, long-studied alternatives exist. Yet most security companies, and even otherwise smart and sensible people, exhibit acute neophilia and are easily blinded by shiny new pieces of cryptography.

FOLLOWING THE CROWD

At Counterpane Systems, we analyze dozens of products a year. We review all sorts of cryptography, from new algorithms to new implementations. We break the vast majority of proprietary systems, and, with no exception, the best products are the ones that use existing cryptography as much as possible. Not only are the conservative choices generally smarter, but they mean we can actu-

ally analyze the system. We can review a simple cryptography product in a couple of days if it reuses existing algorithms and protocols, in a week or two if it uses newish protocols and existing algorithms. If it uses new algorithms, a week is barely enough time to get started.

This doesn't mean that everything new is lousy. What it does mean is that everything new is suspect. New cryptography belongs in academic papers, and then in demonstration systems. If it is truly better, then eventually cryptographers will

About IPSec

IPSec is a set of protocols being developed by the IETF to support secure packet exchange at the IP layer. Once it's completed, IPSec is expected to be deployed widely to implement Virtual Private Networks. The current IPSec standards include three algorithm-independent base specifications that are currently standards-track RFCs. These three RFCs are in the process of being revised (according to the usual IETF procedures), and the revisions will take into account a number of security issues with the current specifications.

The IP Security Architecture (ftp://ds.internic.net/rfc/rfc1825.txt) defines the overall architecture and specifies elements common to both the IP Authentication Header and the IP Encapsulating Security Payload.

The IP Authentication Header (ftp://ds.internic.net/rfc/rfc1826.txt) defines an algorithm-independent mechanism for providing exportable cryptographic authentication without encryption to IPv4 and IPv6 packets.

The IP Encapsulating Security Payload (ftp://ds.internic.net/rfc/rfc1827.txt) defines an algorithm-independent mechanism for providing encryption to IPv4 and IPv6 packets.

For more information on IPSec, see the IETF's IPSec charter (http://www.ietf.cnri.reston.va.us/html.charters/ipsec-charter.html).

come to trust it. And only then does it make sense to use it in real products. This process can take five to ten years for an algorithm, less for protocols or source code libraries. Look at the length of time it is taking elliptic curve systems to be accepted, and even now they are only accepted when more-trusted alternatives can't meet performance requirements.

In cryptography, there is security in following the crowd. A homegrown algorithm can't possibly be subjected to the hundreds of thousands of hours of cryptanalysis that DES and RSA have seen. A company, or even an industry association, can't begin to mobilize the resources that have been brought to bear against the Kerberos authentication protocol, for example. No one can duplicate the confidence that PGP offers, after years of people going over the code, line by line, looking for implementation flaws. By following the crowd you can leverage the cryptanalytic expertise of the worldwide community, not just a few weeks of some analyst's time.

And beware the doctor who says, "I invented and patented this totally new treatment that consists of tortilla-chip powder. It has never been tried before, but I just know it is much better and I'm going to give it to you." There's a good reason we call new cryptography "snake oil."❖

Cryptography: Is Staying with the Herd Really Best?

Terry Ritter, Ritter Software Engineering

A recent Internet Watch column argues that new cryptography is bad cryptography. Drawing an analogy to the medical profession, it says, "A good doctor won't treat a bacterial infection with a medicine he just invented when proven antibiotics are available." That certainly sounds reasonable. But, in a very real and practical sense, there *is* no proven cryptography. And this is not just an issue of mathematical proof: The cryptographic profession simply can't tell whether or not a cipher really is protecting data. It is as though medical doctors were telling us about their cures when in reality they couldn't even tell if their patients were alive or dead.

It is not that we want to avoid cryptanalysis; indeed, we want all the analysis we can get. And it is true that a brand new cipher has had scant time for analysis. But the result of even deep analysis is not a proven design; it is just something that we don't positively know to be weak. This slight shift of meaning is the

Editor: Ron Vetter, University of North Carolina at Wilmington, Department of Computer Science, 601 South College Rd., Wilmington, NC 28403; voice (910) 962-3667, fax (910) 962-7107; vetterr@uncwil.edu.

There is neither proof nor a test of overall strength for either new or old cryptosystems.

basis for understanding what cryptography can and can't do. For one thing, it means that any cipher—no matter how deeply analyzed—could be weak in practice. And that means that anyone concerned with real security probably should consider using something other than the same cipher as everyone else. One possibility is using new cryptography in new ways, which is the exact opposite of what that previous column suggests.

Surely, we all would like to have a fully reviewed library or cipher in the same way that we would like to have a fully debugged program. But not even lengthy review or analysis guarantees either cryp-

tographic strength (the ability to resist attack) or a lack of program bugs. For example, most crypto experts probably would agree that just because 20 years of analysis of the US Data Encryption Standard has not found an easy break doesn't mean that no easy break exists. And if a break does exist, it may have been actively exploited for years without our knowing. We certainly couldn't call that a strong cipher. In practice, even extensive review is not a rational or scientific indication of strength.

This is not an issue of perfection versus reality, and it isn't like software where we tolerate various bugs and still get real work done. In software, the bugs are generally peripheral to our goals, and we usually know if we are getting what we want. But in cryptography, we have no idea whether or not someone can break our cipher, even if there are no bugs at all in the program.

CONFIDENCE IN CIPHERS

Perhaps the central problem in cryptography is how we can have confidence in a cryptographic design. Ways often mentioned to gain confidence in ciphers include mathematical proof, practical tests, open cryptanalysis, and long use.

Mathematical proof and practical tests

Despite more than 50 years of mathematical cryptography, there is no complete mathematical proof of strength for any practical cipher, at least not in the open literature. (A one-time pad is often assumed to be secure, but is impractical in most cases.)

Likewise, there is no set of tests that measures all possible weaknesses in a cipher. The very feature we need—strength against unknown attack—is something we can't measure. This is like a publisher who can measure the quality of paper, printing, and binding yet still not know the quality of a book or articles. The essence of a cipher is not the measurable ciphering process itself, but rather the effect that process has on confounding each opponent. Cipher quality is necessarily contextual, and we can't know the context.

Reprinted from *IEEE Computer*, Vol. 32, No. 8, pp. 94–95, March 1999.

Cryptanalysis

Cryptanalysis is the art of trying to find an easy way around a security design's cryptographic protections. While many specific attacks are known in an expanding literature, the number of possibilities is essentially unbounded. There is no exhaustive theory of cryptanalysis. Without such a theory, cryptanalysis that does not find a problem does not testify that no problems exist. Cryptanalysis gives us an upper bound for strength, but not the lower bound that describes the minimum effort needed to break a cipher.

Nor does cryptanalysis provide evidence that our cipher is strong. Surely we use only ciphers we can't break. But predicting what an opponent can do on the basis of what we can do is at the very essence of weak cryptography. The classic examples occurred in Germany and Japan in World War II, but every broken system is a failed assumption of strength. We can either learn from history or repeat it on the losing side.

Long use

Our opponents operate in secrecy and do not reveal their successes. If they break our cipher and take some care to protect the results, we will continue to use that broken cipher, all the while assuming our data is protected. Confidence from long use is a self-delusion that springs from not specifically being told that our cipher has failed. We hope that our lack of knowledge means that our cipher has not been broken. But if hope were enough, we wouldn't need cryptography.

THE CRISIS OF CIPHER CONFIDENCE

There is no known proof, measurement, or analysis that provides confidence in cipher strength. Cryptosystems both new and old are in exactly the same boat: Against unknown attack, even an extensively reviewed system may not be as strong as one not reviewed at all. An implied problem with a new cryptosystem is that we can't know that it is strong. But the real problem is that we can't know that the old system is strong—and that is the system we are actually using.

If academics refuse to address patented cipher designs on a rational, technical basis, they won't develop the background to understand or compare the new cryptographic technologies. It is even possible that there may be a practical security advantage to a patented cipher: Since no one can prove that any cipher is secure, absolute confidence is simply not available. Any cipher can fail at any time. But if a patented cipher fails, we may be able to prove that someone used an unlicensed deciphering program and take legal steps to recover our losses.

> There is no known proof, measurement, or analysis that provides confidence in cipher strength.

WHAT CHOICES DO WE HAVE?

Even if we consider every cipher as possibly insecure, we do have alternatives. Instead of reacting to rumor or waiting for academic breakthroughs, we can proactively use new approaches and new technology. We can, as a matter of course, multicipher our data: We can use one cipher on the plaintext, a different cipher on the resulting ciphertext, and yet another cipher on that result. In general, if even one of the three ciphers is strong, our data is protected. And even if each cipher has a weakness, it may be impossible to exploit those weaknesses in the multiciphering context. For example, multiciphering protects individual ciphers from known plaintext attacks.

Another alternative is to use a wide variety of structurally different ciphers and to randomly select ciphers by automatic negotiation. In addition to terminating any existing break, this spreads our information among many different ciphers, thus reducing the reward for breaking any particular one. Another step is to continually add to the set of ciphers used. This increases costs for our opponents, who must somehow acquire, analyze, and construct software (or even hardware) to break each new cipher. But new ciphers would be only a modest cost for us.

Absent a mathematical theory to assure a high cost of cipher-breaking, experimentation is the main way to test a cipher's strength, but real designs are far too large to know in any depth. So another alternative is to construct scalable designs that produce both tiny toy ciphers (which can be broken and deeply examined experimentally) and large serious ciphers from the same specification.

Despite the frequent cryptography articles in IEEE journals, cryptography is an art, not an engineering discipline: The property we seek to produce—strength against unknown attack—is not measurable, and so it is literally out of control. But if we avoid new technology, we help our opponents, who certainly don't want to deal with a wide array of new ciphers.

Not applying new technology is wrong—wrong for an innovator who seeks compensation, wrong for the user who wants the best systems, and wrong for those who want the field to mature. It is necessary, therefore, to take recommendations against using new cryptography along with a healthy dose of reality. ❖

For More About Cryptography

Additional information about related topics can be found on Ritter's Web site (http://www.io.com/~ritter/), including a basic introduction to cryptography (http://www.io.com/~ritter/LEARNING.HTM), an extensive crypto glossary (http://www.io.com/~ritter/GLOSSARY.HTM), literature surveys, Usenet conversations, crypto links, and his own work.

Chapter 6

Computers in Safety-Critical Systems

To the best of my ability, insure that the products of my work are used in a socially responsible way.
—from the AITP Standards of Conduct

Give comprehensive and thorough evaluations of computer systems and their impacts, including analysis of possible risks.
—ACM Code of Ethics, specific professional responsibility 5

Ensure adequate testing, debugging, and review of software and related documents on which they work.
—IEEE-CS/ACM Software Engineering Code of Ethics, principles 3.10

Accept responsibility in making engineering decisions consistent with the safety, health, and welfare of the public . . .

—IEEE Code of Ethics, item 1

6.1 INTRODUCTION

THE design, development, and maintenance of safety-critical systems is one of the most important areas in computer science and engineering. When human welfare is at stake, the price for haphazard practices is severe, and computing professionals must exercise extreme care to ensure that a system is safe. This implies that two requirements must be satisfied: One is to have some idea of the techniques needed to develop computer systems that are as safe as is practically possible. The other is to be able to arrive at a reasonably objective assessment of exactly what that level of safety is.

What makes safety-critical systems so difficult to cover in any text is the extreme reliance on professional ethics intertwined with the demand for a high degree of professional competence. As Nancy Leveson and Clarke Turner state in "An Investigation of the Therac-25 Accidents" at the end of this chapter:

> Most accidents involving complex technology are caused by a combination of organizational, managerial, technical, and, sometimes, sociological or political factors. Preventing accidents requires paying attention to *all* the root causes, . . .

On the one hand, the social and political considerations that come into play can be deeply subjective. At the same time, the technical material is as complex as that of any other chapter. For these reasons, rather than attempt to distill the range of topics in this area, I have selected a set of reprints I believe reflects the most important issues.

6.2 TERMINOLOGY RELATED TO SAFETY-CRITICAL SYSTEMS

The phrase "safety-critical systems" is sometimes taken narrowly to mean systems with a component of real-time control that can have a direct life-threatening impact. Examples of this type of safety-critical system appear in aircraft/air traffic control, nuclear-reactor control, missile systems, and medical-treatment systems. In this text, I take a broader view that encompasses the software used in the design of physical systems and structures whose failure can have massive life-threatening impact. Examples of this type of safety-critical software appear in bridge and building design, selection of waste-disposal sites, and analytical models of medical treatment and other applications.

The first reprinted article, "Managing Murphy's Law: Engineering a Minimum-Risk System," gives a high-level overview of the issues and terminology involved in conducting a thorough risk assessment of a system. Here, the

ARLO & JANIS © NEA

word *system* is meant in a very general sense as some process that may involve humans, computers, other man-made devices and even natural phenomena. The article gives you an idea of the broad view that must be taken by making distinctions among the terms *risk, hazard,* and *reliability.* Indeed, terminology is not standard throughout all fields related to software safety. Nancy Leveson's article, which appears later in the collection, and a letter to the editor that follows it show how professionals can disagree on terminology. In "Managing Murphy's Law," *reliability* is used to indicate the probability that a particular system component will function according to specifications over a given time (and perhaps also over a specified range of conditions). *Hazard* is used to indicate a potential for injury or danger. Combining these two terms, we can see that for a particular system component over a given time there is a (1–*reliability*) probability of a particular set of hazards being generated. This leads to the definition of *risk* as "the combination of the probability of an undesired event with the magnitude of each and every foreseeable consequence (damage to property, loss of money, injury to people, and so on)."

The article also has a table that compares the basic properties of some of the major risk-analysis techniques. For more on the problems involved in risk assessment, see Kristin Shrader-Frechette's article, "The Conceptual Risks of Risk Assessment" [12].

6.3 Correspondence Between Models and Reality

The reprinted article, "How Engineers Lose Touch," emphasizes the need to verify that the system analyzed on paper corresponds well to the one in the field. An inherent danger when dealing with computer models is that you may come to believe that the system in the real world is simply a realization of the model. The more appropriate view is that the computer model is an abstraction of the real system. The difference may seem subtle, but it can be important. If you view the model as the abstraction of the real system, there is an implied warning that not all aspects

of the world are necessarily accurately represented in the model. The other view implicitly assumes that the model accurately represents the real system and its environment.

6.4 Evaluating Software

The fifth reprint, "Evaluation of Safety-Critical Software," is longer and more detailed, and is an excellent way to gain insight into the many factors involved in evaluating software in this area. The article begins with a mandate to developers of safety-critical software:

> . . . computers now have safety-critical functions in both military and civilian aircraft, in nuclear plants, and in medical devices. It is incumbent upon those responsible for programming, purchasing, installing and licensing these systems to determine whether or not the software is ready to be used.

The article considers questions such as: What standards must a software product satisfy if it is to be used in safety-critical applications? What documentation should be required? How much testing is needed? How should the software be structured? Some of these issues should be familiar to those who have had a strong software-engineering course. However, the level of intellectual rigor suggested by the article is certainly beyond what is routinely practiced in software engineering today. As you read the article, reflect carefully on the ethics of "undertaking technological tasks only if qualified" and "striving to achieve the highest quality in both the process and products of professional work." If you wish to read further in this area, review the references at the end of the chapter, especially [7], [8], [9].

6.5 Case Studies of Safety-Critical Failures

The reprint, "An Investigation of the Therac-25 Accidents," presents a detailed analysis of what has become a classic case study. Several instances of failure in a radiation-therapy system were traced to errors in special timing-dependent sequences of events in the user interface. These could easily be considered software errors. However, appropriate hardware/software interlocks could have prevented the hazards that resulted from this event. This article is followed by two pages of letters to the editor written in response to the article. These letters bring up a number of interesting questions and points of view. One reader asks about the role of the MDs in the incident. Another seems to suggest that we simply should not create systems that use software in a safety-critical application. A third letter argues over the use of standard terminology. The last letter emphasizes that the system in question lacked sufficient redundancy checks on safety.

The two short reprints "Design By Contract: The Lessons of Ariane" and "Ariane 5: Who Dunnit?" both deal with the spectacular failure of an Ariane 5 rocket in June 1996. While no human life was lost in the accident, the economic loss was estimated at $500 million. The immediate cause of the accident was an exception condition that was improperly handled. The two articles consider a variety of views on how the problem could have been avoided.

Points to Remember

- Risk analysis—assessing and quantifying the risks in a system—is a difficult task that has an inherently subjective component.
- Assumptions about the logical independence of different types of failures are often not fully supported by the physical realization of the system.
- A software model of a real-world physical system can never perfectly represent all relevant aspects of the system. Over-reliance on computer models that are not properly validated and verified for the specific application at hand is an invitation to disaster.
- Disregarding the contribution of the software in a safety-critical system is a mistake. Software components do contribute to risk and failure.
- Focusing only on the software component (or any one type of component) of a safety-critical system is a mistake. Most failures have multiple contributing causes and could have been prevented by improving any of several system components.
- While there are not yet widely accepted formal standards to be followed in the development of safety-critical software, there are many advanced techniques for software design, evaluation, review, and testing that you can use to help produce higher quality software. Professionals engaged in the development of safety-critical software should know and use such techniques.

WORKSHEET—Review of Risk-Analysis Concepts

1. What is the meaning of risk analysis?

2. What is the difference between independent failure modes and common failure modes? Give one example from the readings of a system that had a common failure mode.

3. What is the difference between logical redundancy and physical redundancy? Give one example from the readings of a system that had logical but not physical redundancy.

4. Explain the relation of the terms "failure," "risk," "hazard," and "reliability" as Trudy Bell uses them in "Managing Murphy's Law: Engineering a Minimum-Risk System."

5. Explain the meaning of "hubris" as used in "How Engineers Lose Touch."

WORKSHEET—Review of Safety-Critical Software

1. According to the article "Evaluation of Safety-Critical Software," how is software different from other controller technologies?

2. What are the important implications of the limitations on software testing as a method of assuring correctness?

3. According to the same article, what reviews of software are needed to help ensure correctness?

4. What are the three classes of programs identified in the article, and what is suggested as necessary in order to establish reliability estimates for programs in each class?

5. The article asserts that "The safety and trustworthiness of the system will rest on a tripod. . . ." What are the elements of the tripod? Which of these do you think is the weakest element? Why?

WORKSHEET—Review of the Therac-25 Incident: General

1. How many Therac-25 accidents were recognized over what period of time?

2. How did the level of computer control change from the CGR Sagittaire to the AECL/CGR Therac-20 to the AECL Therac-25?

3. What is the apparent reuse of existing software between the Therac-6, Therac-20 and Therac-25?

4. What was the estimated failure rate for "computer selects wrong energy?"

5. What is a "RAD?" What was the level of overdose received by the patient in the 1985 Kennestone ROC accident?

6. What is the difference between a Therac-25 "treatment suspend" and a "treatment pause?" Which is more convenient for the operator, and which is safer for the patient?

7. What are the three basic positions of the Therac-25 turntable assembly, and what is in the beam path in each one?

8. What was the status of the audio and video monitors during the March 1986 east Texas Cancer Center accident?

9. What does Leveson mean by "most accidents are systems accidents?"

WORKSHEET—Review of the Therac-25 Incident: Software Design

1. What are the four major components of the Therac-25 real-time operating system?

2. What is the importance of the fact that "the software allows concurrent access to shared memory?"

3. What was the meaning of the "dose input 2" error message?

4. Who eventually identified the cause of a "Malfunction 54" message, and what was the cause?

5. What was the problem with the "bending magnet flag" in the "Magnet" and the "Ptime" routines? Where was the clearing of the "bending magnet flag" moved?

6. What is the logical meaning of the "Class3" variable? What is the physical realization of the variable? What operation is performed on "Class3" by the "SetUpTest" routine? How did this cause a problem? What was the fix?

WORKSHEET—Review of the Therac-25 Incident: People

1. What was focused on by AECL as the potential cause of the 1985 accident at the Ontario Cancer Foundation?

2. What did the independent consultant hired by the Ontario Cancer Foundation recommend?

3. What did the letter sent out by AECL on April 15, 1986 suggest that the Therac-25 users should do?

4. How many people were involved in the Therac-25 software development, and what is known about them?

5. List as many people as you can who were involved in some degree of ethical lapse and who could have prevented or mitigated the sequence of accidents. Consider the manufacturer and its employees, the hospitals and their employees, the regulatory agencies and their employees, and the patients along with their families and legal representatives.

1. **ADA, exception handling, and the Ariane 5 failure.** The Ariane 5 failure is described in two reprinted articles. Both mention the role of exception handling in the language ADA. One of the articles observes that "Ada's exception mechanism has been criticized in the literature, but in this case it *could* have been used to catch the exception." (italics added) Read Tony Hoare's ACM Turing Award Lecture paper in the February 1981 issue of the *Communications of the ACM*. Was the problem with the use of exception handling in the Ariane 5 accident the type of problem that Hoare had predicted would happen?

2. **The Patriot antimissile system failure.** The Patriot antimissile system received an enormous amount of favorable publicity during the Gulf War with Iraq. Postwar accounts of the system's performance were not nearly so favorable. One spectacular incident of failure was traced to a timing-related problem in the system's control software. Report on this failure, its consequences, and how it could have been prevented [6].

3. **The "lost satellite" incident.** A viewpoint article by Norman [11] provides a pointer to what may be the source of the "lost satellite" story. The essence of the story is that a satellite was lost because of a one-character typographical error in one line of a program. Look into this incident to determine precisely what happened and what safeguards could have been in place to detect and correct the problem without losing the satellite.

4. **The Aegis/Vincennes defensive weapons system incident.** The Aegis system was developed by the U.S. Navy to allow ships to monitor the airspace around them. An overview of the original hopes for the system appears in the June 1988 issue of *IEEE Spectrum* [1]. In July 1988, the USS Vincennes, equipped with the Aegis system, accidentally shot down an Iranian passenger airliner, killing 290 people. A contributing element to this accident was the poor design of the user interface. Look into this incident to find out exactly what flaws were later identified in the user interface and how they can be (or have been) corrected [6].

5. **The North Staffordshire Hospital radiation-therapy incident.** The North Staffordshire Hospital is located near London, England. From 1982 through 1991, a computer program used in calculating the doses of radiation used in therapy contained an error that caused patients to receive up to 35 percent less radiation than prescribed [13]. Look into this incident to find out exactly what the software error was, how it was eventually detected, and what was done to prevent such an error from occurring again.

6. **Computer models predicting catastrophes.** Walter Karplus is a well-known academic researcher in computer modeling and simulation. His book *The Heavens Are Falling* explores the (mis)use of computer models in predicting a variety of catastrophes that some have said will occur in the near future [5]. Write a brief paper summarizing Karplus's discussion of simulation methodology and the distinction between scientific and unscientific predictions.

7. **Software error that caused telephone system outages.** The cause of this incident was three faulty computer instructions that were hidden in software changes that were sent out without major testing because the company judged that the changes were "too small to require it." It's hard to understand how any company could judge any modification to any safety-critical software to be too small to require testing. But amazing as it seems, this actually happened in 1991 [3]. Phone service was affected in Washington, Pittsburgh, Los Angeles, and San Francisco. Report on exactly what caused the problem and on the measures that have since been taken in the telephone industry to prevent such problems from recurring.

REFERENCES

[1] J. A. Adam, "Pinning defense hopes on the Aegis," *IEEE Spectrum,* June 1988, pp. 24–27.

[2] P. V. Bhansali, "Survey of software standards shows diversity," *Computer,* January 1993, pp. 88–89.

[3] J. Burgess, "Tiny bug caused phone blackouts," *The Washington Post,* July 10, 1991.

[4] Special issue: "Three Mile Island and the future of nuclear power," *IEEE Spectrum,* November 1979.

[5] W. K. Karplus, *The Heavens Are Falling.* Plenum Press, New York, 1992.

[6] L. Lee, *The Day The Phones Stopped.* Primus Books, New York, 1992.

[7] N. G. Leveson, "Software safety: Why, what and how," *ACM Computing Surveys,* June 1986, pp. 125–163.

[8] N. G. Leveson, "Software safety in embedded computer systems," *Communications of the ACM,* February 1991, pp. 34–46.

[9] B. Littlewood and L. Stringini, "Validation of ultrahigh dependability for software-based systems," *Communications of the ACM,* November 1993, pp. 69–80.

[10] D. H. Meadows, D. L. Meadows, J. Randers, and W. W. Behrens, *The Limits to Growth* (second edition). Signet Books, New York, 1975.

[11] D. A. Norman, "Commentary: Human errors and the design of computer systems," *Communications of the ACM,* January 1990, pp. 4–7.

[12] K. S. Shrader-Frechette, "The conceptual risks of risk assessment," *IEEE Technology and Society Magazine,* June 1986, pp. 4–11.

[13] "Computer errors blamed in cancer deaths," *The Tampa Tribune,* September 30, 1993.

SPECIAL REPORT:

Managing Murphy's law: engineering a minimum-risk system

How can hardware faults and human lapses be dealt with in systems so complex that not all potential fault paths may be foreseen?

Whatever can go wrong, will. Murphy's law is an ironic joke in engineering. But it also happens to be true for complex systems intended to run for years or decades.

In designing, building, and operating any large system, engineers must face up to such questions as: what can go wrong, and how likely is it to happen? What range of consequences might there be, when, and how could they be averted or mitigated? How much risk should be tolerated, or accepted, during normal operation, and how can it be measured, reduced, and managed?

Then there's the human element. What could human operators do to the system, for better or for worse? Or can their responses even be predicted? And if health, quality of life, or human life itself is at stake, how safe is "safe enough"?

Formal risk analysis attempts to pin down and, wherever possible, to quantify the answers to those questions. In new systems, it is coming to be accepted in engineering as a way of comparing the risks inherent in alternative designs, spotlighting the high-risk portions of a system, and pointing up techniques for mitigating those risks. For older systems, risk analyses conducted after they have been built and operated have often revealed crucial design faults. One such fault cost the lives of 167 workers on the British oil production platform Piper Alpha in the North Sea last year [see illustration opposite].

Risk analysts define risk as a combination of the probability of an undesirable event with the magnitude of each and every foreseeable consequence (damage to property, loss of money, injury to people, lives lost, and so on). The consequences considered range in seriousness all the way from "'no, never mind' to the catastrophic," said Joseph R. Fragola, vice president of a risk analysis consulting firm, Science Applications International Corp. (SAIC), in New York City.

Reliability, while related to risk, is only part of the picture. "Reliability is the probability of a component or system performing its mission over a certain length of time," Fragola said. The concept excludes both the consequences of failure and any causes that happen to be external to the component or system.

Most risk experts also distinguish between risk and hazard. To them, a hazard represents only the potential for injury or

Trudy E. Bell   Senior Editor

danger—for example, the toxic materials or radioactive fuel that a chemical or nuclear plant must manipulate—while risk adds in the likelihood of that injury or danger occurring. To them, therefore, a hazards analysis is just one step in a risk analysis.

Confusingly, not all industries accept these definitions. For example, in one article about the risks of chemical plants, the author stated: "The word 'risk' can refer either to a hazard or to the chance of loss." Another author in the chemical industry defined risk as pertaining only to "methods of determining the commercial risks of a project." The National Aeronautics and Space Administration (NASA), until last year, officially defined risk as "the chance (qualitative) of loss of personnel capability, loss of system, or damage to or loss of equipment or property."

For consistency's sake, the risk analysts' definitions of risk and hazard are the ones adopted in this special report.

Assessing and quantifying risk

A complete risk analysis of any system requires "a 'cradle-to-grave' systems approach to safety that foresees waste disposal and end users' risk" right from the start, in the design stage, observed Aviva Brecher of the Safety and Security Systems Division of the Department of Transportation's Transportation Systems Center in Cambridge, Mass. Safety is to be viewed not as an add-on but as another design objective, on a par with operability, security, privacy, or maintainability.

The first step is to tabulate the different stages or phases of the system's mission and "list the risk sensitivities in each phase," said SAIC's Fragola, pointing out that the time at which a failure occurs may exacerbate or mitigate its consequences. For example, a failure in an air traffic control system at a major airport would disrupt local air traffic far more at weeknight rush hour than on a Sunday morning. Similarly, a failure in a chemical processing plant would be more dangerous if it interfered with an intermediate reaction that produced a toxic chemical than if it occurred at a stage when the byproducts were more benign.

Next, for each phase of the mission, the system's operation should be diagrammed and the logical relationships of the components and subsystems during that phase determined. The most useful techniques for the job are failure modes and effects analysis (FMEA), event tree analysis, and fault tree analysis [see table, pp. 26-27]. The three complement one another, and when used together, help engineers to identify the hazards in a system, potential interactions between parts of a system, and the range of potential consequences. The interactions are particularly important because one piece of equipment might be caused to fail by another's failure to, say, supply fuel or current.

Some industries call a halt after this qualitative analysis. But if a quantitative risk assessment is the goal, the next step is quantifying the probability that any particular failure will occur in each mission phase. This probability may vary from phase to phase, because in some the critical piece of equipment may be functioning and in others it may be idle. When an accident involves the failure of one or more system components, its probability will depend in part on test data about the components' reliability under various operating conditions.

Also to be anticipated are destructive outside forces. Thus, a risk analysis for siting a nuclear power plant may factor into the equation such natural hazards as earthquakes. This kind of event may cause unrelated system elements to fail simultaneously.

For engineers and their managers, the chief purpose of a risk analysis—defining the stages of a mission, examining the relationships between system parts, and quantifying failure probabilities—is to highlight any weaknesses in a system design and identify those that contribute most heavily to risk. The pro-

Reprinted from *IEEE Spectrum*, Vol. 26, No. 6, pp. 24-27, June 1989.

Computer simulation of the July 6, 1988, explosion due to a gas leak within the $3 billion British Piper Alpha offshore oil-drilling platform in the North Sea reveals in part what cost 167 workers their lives in the oil industry's worst disaster. The platform had a vertical structure, and no risk analysis was done of the design. Workers' accommodations were on top [top blue box, second column from the right], above the control room and several stories above the lower compartments, which housed equipment for separating oil from natural gas. The accommodations were believed to be protected by the steel structure and therefore immune to any mishap. But as the computer simulation reveals, the energy from the explosion in a lower level coupled to the platform's frame. Stress waves were dissipated effectively into the water below, but reflections at the steel-air interface at the upper levels in short order expanded, weakened, and shattered the structure. The simulation employed finite-difference analysis and was run on a Cray-2 supercomputer. The color values reflect the steel's density throughout the structure 100 milliseconds after the explosion. In contrast, Norwegian platforms [not shown], which are designed with Government-mandated risk analysis, are long and horizontal like aircraft carriers, with the workers' accommodations at the opposite end of the platform to the processing facilities and insulated from them by steel doors.

PIPER ALPHA EXPLOSION

cess may even suggest ways of minimizing or mitigating the risk.

A case in point is the probabilistic risk analysis on the space shuttle's auxiliary power units, completed for NASA in December 1987 by the independent engineering consulting firm Pickard; Lowe & Garrick Inc. of Newport Beach, Calif. The auxiliary power units, among other tasks, throttle the orbiter's main engines and operate its wing ailerons. NASA engineers and managers, using qualitative techniques, had formerly judged fuel leaks in the three auxiliary fuel units "unlikely" and the risks acceptable, without fully understanding the magnitude of the risks they accepted, even though a worst-case consequence could be the loss of the vehicle, said the study's principal investigator, Michael Frank, now head of Safety Factor Associates in Encinitas, Calif. One of the problems with the qualitative assessment "is that subjective interpretation of words such as 'likely' and 'un-

likely' allows opportunity for errors in judgment about risk," Frank said. For example, NASA had applied the word "unlikely" to risks whose chances ranged from 1 in 250 to 1 in 20 000.

The probabilistic risk analysis revealed that although the probability of individual leaks was low, there were so many places where leaks could occur that five had in fact occurred in the first 24 shuttle missions. Moreover, in the ninth mission, on Nov. 28, 1983, the escaping fuels self-ignited while the orbiter was hurtling back to earth, and exploded after the orbiter had landed. If the explosion had occurred before landing, "many NASA experts believe the orbiter wouldn't have made it," Frank observed.

The probabilistic analysis pinpointed the fact that an explosion was more likely to occur during landing than during launch, when the auxiliary power units are purged with nitrogen to remove combustible atmospheric oxygen. The analysis also sug-

Defining terms

Accident: an undesired consequence, often associated with an unwanted transfer of energy due to lack or failure of barriers and/or controls, inflicting injury on persons or damage on property or process.

Common cause: a cause, such as an earthquake, that affects more than one component or subsystem, so that their failures are not independent.

Event: an internal or external occurrence involving equipment performance or human action that causes a system upset.

Failure: the inability of a system, subsystem, or component to perform its required function.

Failure modes: the various ways in which failures occur.

Hazard: an intrinsic property or condition that has the potential to cause an accident.

Initiating event: an event that will result in an accident unless systems or operators intervene.

Intermediate event: an event in an accident event sequence that helps propagate the accident or helps prevent the accident or mitigate the consequences.

Quality assurance: the probability that a system, subsystem, or component will perform its intended function when tested.

Reliability: the probability that a system, subsystem, or component will perform its intended function for a specified period of time under normal conditions.

Risk: the combination of the probability of an abnormal event or failure and the consequence(s) of that event or failure to a system's operators, users, or its environment.

Risk assessment: the process and procedures of identifying, characterizing, quantifying, and evaluating risks and their significance.

Risk management: any techniques used either to minimize the probability of an accident or to mitigate its consequences with, for instance, good operating practice, preventive maintenance, and evacuation plans.

Uncertainty: a measure of the limits of knowledge in a technical area, expressed as a distribution of probabilities around a point estimate. The four principal elements of uncertainty are statistical confidence (a measure of sampling accuracy), tolerance (a measure of the relevance of available information to the problem at hand), incompleteness and inaccuracy of the input data, and ambiguity in the modeling of the problem.

gested several ways of reducing the risk, such as changing the fuels or placing fire barriers between the power units.

Accepting and managing risk

Once the risks are determined, engineers and managers must decide what levels of risk are acceptable—in other words, make a social and political judgment call. The decision can be controversial because it necessarily involves subjective judgments about the costs and benefits of the system, the worth of the surrounding natural environment, the value (monetary or otherwise) of human life, and potential liability (monetary or otherwise) in case of an accident.

Risk is often tolerated at a higher level in the workplace, such as a chemical or nuclear plant where employees work voluntarily and may receive "hazard pay," than outside among the populace at large, which has no choice but to be exposed to potentially harmful technology.

Whatever the level of risk finally judged acceptable, it is compared with and, if necessary, used to adjust the risks calculated to be inherent in the system design. The probability of failure may be further reduced by redundant or standby subsystems, safety shut-down systems, containment vessels, shielding, or escape systems. Also, system managers may prepare to counter the consequences of a failure by devising emergency procedures and evacuation plans.

Coping with uncertainty

Two other sources of uncertainty still need to be considered—one intrinsic in probability theory and the other born of all too human error.

Major risk-analysis techniques for evaluating the design and operation of large systems, from least to most quantitative

Name	Purpose	When to use	Procedure	Type of results	
Preliminary hazard analysis (PHA)	Early identification of hazards to provide design engineers with guidance in final design stage	Early design phase, when only basic system elements and raw materials are defined	Examine the design specifications to ascertain hazards related to raw materials, system equipment, components, interfaces, operating environment, operations and maintenance procedures, safety equipment	List of hazards with recommendations for their reduction in the final design	
Hazard and operability studies (HazOp)	Identification of hazard and operability problems that could compromise a system's ability to achieve intended productivity	Late design phase, when design is nearly firm and documented; also for an existing system when a major redesign is planned	Examine instrument diagrams and operation flowcharts; at each critical node identify potential operational deviations, possible causes of such deviations, and possible consequences	List of hazards and operating problems, potential deviations from intended functions, potential consequences, potential causes, and suggested changes in design or procedures	
Failure modes and effects analysis with critical items list (FMEA/CIL)	Identification of all the ways a piece of equipment can fail, and each failure mode's potential effect(s) on the system	Design, construction, operation	Collect up-to-date design data about equipment and its functional relationship to rest of system; list all conceivable malfunctions; describe intermediate and ultimate effects of failure on other equipment or rest of system; rank each failure mode and its effect by each failure mode's severity	List of identified failure modes, their potential effects, existing or required compensation or control procedures, and potential consequences for the system (including worst-case consequences of single-point failures)	
Event tree analysis (ETA)	Identification of potential accidents by means of "forward thinking" from an initiating event (equipment failure, human error, process upset)	Design, operation	Design a decision tree that shows accident sequences and defines chronological relationships between initiating and subsequent events; rank the accidents to determine the most important risks	A graphic decision tree illustrating the way a malfunction can propagate through a system, accounting for both the successes and failures of safety functions as the breakdown progresses	
Human reliability analysis	Identification of risk contribution of human interaction with hardware design features and operational procedures	Design, construction, operation	Examine plant drawings and procedures to identify events initiated or mitigated by humans; classify the probabilities of events to determine significance; determine interaction of events with equipment; see if event is related to a procedure or time-critical decision; ascertain if system can recover from the event	List of events where human interaction contributes significant risk	
Common-cause, common-mode, correlated-failure analyses	Supplementing independent failure analyses to determine hidden interface failures	Design, construction, operation	Examine physical, environmental, and procedural interconnections between systems and their components for single factors (such as power supply, support system, lubricating oil, seismic potential) that could cause failure of multiple components or subsystems	Probability distribution or list of events highlighting common causes	
Fault tree analysis (FTA)	Deduction of various causes of failure by means of "reverse thinking" starting from a postulated failure of a system; discovery of hidden failure modes that result from subsystem interactions and combinations of malfunctions	Design, operation	Construct a diagram using logic symbols to show the logical interrelationships between components, causes, and the accident	List of sets of equipment and/or operator failures that can result in a specific malfunction, ranked qualitatively by importance	

Sources: Aviva Brecher, "An Overview of Formal Methods of Risk Assessment," *IEEE Electro*, 1988; Center for Chemical Process Safety, *Guidelines for Hazard Evaluations Procedures*, American Institute of Chemical Engineers, New York, N.Y. 1985; Joseph R. Fragola, Science Applications International Corp., New York City; Ernst G. Frankel, *Systems Reliability and Risk Analysis*, Martinus Nijhoff Publishers, Boston, 1984; A.E. Green (ed.), *High Risk Safety Technology*, John Wiley & Sons, New York, 1982

First, the laws of chance exclude the prediction of when and where a particular failure may occur. That remains true even if enough statistical information about the system's operation exists for a reliable estimate of how likely it is to fail. Then the probability of failure itself is surrounded by a halo of uncertainty, which expands or shrinks depending on how much data is available and how well the system is understood. This statistical level of confidence is expressed as a standard deviation about a mean or some other statistical measure. Finally, if the system is so new that little or no data is available on it, and dissimilar but related information must be used to get a handle on potential risks, there is the uncertainty over how well the estimate resembles the actual case. "The job of risk analysis is to balance these sources of uncertainty, recognizing that the uncertainty can never be eliminated," Fragola said.

Nature of results	Data requirements	Limitations, other comments
Qualitative only	Available system design criteria, equipment specifications, raw materials specifications	Is poor at showing the effects of mitigation or assigning priorities to potential causes of one undesired event; is most useful for system where past experience gives little or no insight into potential problems
Qualitative with quantitative potential	Detailed system descriptions (drawings, procedures, flow charts), knowledge of system's instrumentation and operation	Resembles FMEA/CIL but often integrated with probabilistic analysis of considered conditions; depends heavily for its success on data completeness and accuracy of drawings
Qualitative, although can be quantified if failure probabilities for components are known; can be used to derive percentages of failures by mode	System equipment list; knowledge of equipment function; knowledge of system function	Is poor at identifying interactive combinations of equipment failures that lead to accidents; is not useful for examining operator errors, common-cause failures, or dependent failures
Qualitative, although the expected probability of the sequences can be quantified if the event probabilities are known	Knowledge of initiating events, the system's functions, and safety system functions	Is poor at handling partial failures or time delays; is well suited for analyzing events that can have varied outcomes
Qualitative or quantitative with a ranking based on risk	Knowledge of system procedures, layout, functions, tasks, human factors, and cognitive psychology	Cannot ensure discovery of all possibilities; suffers from lack of data about human reliability and difficulty of validating models of human interaction with the system
Qualitative list of causes with their quantitative contributions to risk	An even more detailed understanding of the system than fault tree analysis requires	Cannot guarantee anticipation of every interaction; no standard technique exists for evaluating residual, ineradicable common causes
Qualitative with quantitative potential if probabilistic data on components and subsystems are available	Complete understanding of the system's functions, its failure modes, and their effects; this information could be obtained from an FMEA/CIL	Readily demonstrates the effects of mitigation or redesign; enables identification and quantitative examination of critical factors and interrupt modes for chains of failures; requires careful consideration to be given to independence or mutual interdependence of events entering a particular logic gate so as to ensure correct choice of probability methods (conditional, joint, mutually exclusive)

At the human interface, the challenge is to design a system so that it will not only operate as it should but also leave the operator little room for erroneous judgment. Additional risk can be introduced if a designer cannot anticipate what information an operator may need to digest and interpret under the daily pressures of actual operation, especially when an emergency starts to develop.

Poor operational design can introduce greater risk, sometimes with tragic consequences. After the U.S.S. *Vincennes* on July 3, 1988, mistook Iran Air Flight 655 for an enemy F-14 and shot down the airliner over international waters in the Persian Gulf, Rear Admiral Eugene La Roque (USN, ret.) blamed the calamity on the bewildering complexity of the Aegis radar system. "We have scientists and engineers capable of devising complicated equipment without any thought of how it will be integrated into a combat situation or that it might be too complex to operate," La Roque was quoted as saying in the April 1989 issue of *Aerospace America*, the journal of the American Institute of Aeronautics and Astronautics. "These machines produce too much information, and don't sort the important from the unimportant. There's a disconnection between technical effort and combat use."

Physiological factors such as fatigue also need factoring in. A study published early this year in *Sleep*, the journal of the American Society of Sleep Research, revealed that many major disasters—including the Chernobyl nuclear accident and the decision to launch the space shuttle Challenger—have started after midnight, when "the danger of an error due to sudden overwhelming sleepiness increases progressively with continued sleep loss or 'sleep debt.'"

All told, human behavior is not nearly as predictable as an engineered system's. Some people rise to a crisis and quickly bring ingenuity and creativity to bear on it. Others foul things up. Today there are many techniques for quantifying the probability of slips, lapses, and misperceptions with fair reliability. Still, remaining uncertainty in the prediction of individual behavior contributes to residual risk in systems touched by human hands.

These uncertainties and often the sheer lack of data fuel heated controversy in some quarters. At issue is the applicability or value of quantitative risk assessment techniques as opposed to qualitative engineering judgment—NASA having been one of the greater skeptics of probabilistic methods for its space programs. Other industries, such as nuclear power, have been leaders in applying quantitative techniques.

Neither the existence of uncertainty nor the sparsity of data, however, robs a numerical risk analysis of all value, as long as the uncertainties are recognized, said Robert K. Weatherwax, president of Sierra Energy & Risk Assessment Inc., Roseville, Calif. "A probabilistic risk assessment can 'highlight' the most frequent set of failures that cause problems," he said, "so you have a good understanding where to put the limited bucks you have to make things better." ◆

178

Early in the century MIT students learned about electricity by operating the same kinds of machines that industrial companies of the day used.

How Engineers

Engineering students have been taught
to rely far too completely on computer models,
and their lack of old-fashioned, direct
hands-on experience can be disastrous

by Eugene S. Ferguson

Until the 1960s a student in an American engineering school was expected by his teachers to use his mind's eye to examine things that engineers had designed—to look at them, listen to them, walk around them, and thus develop an intuitive "feel" for the way the material world works and sometimes doesn't work. Students developed a sense of form

Reprinted with permission from *American Heritage of Invention and Technology,* E. S. Ferguson, "How Engineers Lose Touch," pp. 16–24, Winter 1993. Adapted from "Engineering and the Mind's Eye" by E. S. Ferguson, The MIT Press, Cambridge, Mass., 1992. © 1993 by MIT Press.

Present-day researchers in MIT's Media Lab create computer-driven design and information tools. But will users understand their limitations?

Lose Touch

and proportion by drawing and redrawing. They acquired a knowledge of materials in testing laboratories, foundries, and metalworking shops. Students took field trips to power plants, steel mills, heavy machine shops, automobile assembly plants, and chemical works, where company engineers with operating experience helped them grasp the subtleties of the real world of engineering.

These young engineers' picture of the material world continued to be enlarged after graduation. As working engineers they routinely looked carefully at many features of the built world as they expanded and refined their repertoire of nonverbal and tacit knowledge.

They also seized opportunities to see unusual structures or machines being erected, and they studied accidents and equipment failures on the spot.

By the 1980s engineering curricula had shifted to analytical approaches, and visual and other sensual knowledge of the world seemed much less relevant. Computer programs spewed out wonderfully rapid and precise solutions of obviously complicated problems, making it possible for students and teachers to believe that civilization had at last reached a state in which

Design flaws led to the famous Tacoma Narrows Bridge collapse on November 7, 1940. In the sequence at right, the deck undulates up and down as the center span twists; then a huge section finally gives way. In the aftermath of the collapse, one of the side spans sags like a piece of lasagna; the next day a ship passes beneath what remains of the bridge—two lonely towers.

all technical problems were readily solvable.

As faculties dropped engineering drawing and shop practice from their curricula and deemed plant visits unnecessary, students had no reason to believe that curiosity about the physical meaning of the subjects they were studying was necessary. With the National Science Foundation and the Department of Defense offering apparently unlimited funds for scientific research projects, working knowledge

neers steeped in the understanding of existing engineering systems as well as in the new systems being designed.

The science writer James Gleick, in relating the development of the "new science" of "chaos," points out that computer simulations "break reality into chunks, as many as possible but always too few," and that "a computer model is just a set of arbitrary rules, chosen by programmers." You, the programmer, have the choice, he says: "You can make your model more com-

Judgment is brought to bear as designers repeatedly modify their means to reach desired ends. Design is thus a contingent process. It is also a creative process that Robert W. Mann, a leader in engineering-design education, observes, "is, virtually by definition, unpredictable. The sequence of the steps is never known at the beginning. If it were, the whole process could be accomplished by the computer since the information prerequisite to the computer program would be available. Indeed, the creative process is the process of learning how to accomplish the desired result."

Bad design results from errors of engineering judgment, which is not reducible to science or mathematics.

of the material world disappeared from faculty agendas and therefore from student agendas, and the nonverbal, tacit, and intuitive understanding essential to engineering design atrophied. In this new era, with engineering guided by science, the process of design would be freed from messy nonscientific decisions, subtle judgments, and, of course, human error.

Despite the enormous effort and money that have been poured into creating analytical tools to add rigor and precision to the design of complex systems, a paradox remains. There has been a harrowing succession of flawed designs with fatal results—the *Challenger*, the *Stark*, the Aegis system in the *Vincennes*, and so on. Those failures exude a strong scent of inexperience or hubris or both and reflect an apparent ignorance of, or disregard for, the limits of stress in materials and people under chaotic conditions. Successful design still requires expert tacit knowledge and intuitive "feel" based on experience; it requires engi-

plex and more faithful to reality, or you can make it simpler and easier to handle." For engineers a central discovery in the formal study of chaos is that a tiny change in the initial conditions of a dynamic system can result in a major unexpected departure from the calculated final conditions. It was long believed that a highly complex system, such as all automobile traffic in the United States, is in principle fully predictable and thus controllable. "Chaos" has proved this belief wrong.

Alan Colquhoun, a British architect, argues convincingly that no matter how rigorously the laws of science are applied in solving a design problem, the designer must still have a mental picture of the desired outcome. "[Scientific] laws are not found in nature," he declares. "They are constructs of the human mind; they are models which are valid as long as events do not prove them wrong." A successful new design combines formal knowledge and experience and always contains more judgment than certainty.

Engineering design is usually carried on in an atmosphere of optimistic enthusiasm, tempered by the recognition that every mistake or misjudgment must be rooted out before any plans are turned over to the shops for fabrication.

Despite all the care engineers exercise and all their systems for ensuring correct engineering choices, evidence of faulty judgment shows up again and again in some of the most expensive and (at least on paper or on a computer screen) most carefully designed and tested machines of the twentieth century.

Of course there is nothing new about wrong choices and faulty judgments in engineering design. More than a hundred years ago the editors of *Engineering News* tried to track down the reasons for failures of bridges and buildings so that civil engineers might learn from others' mistakes. "We could easily," they wrote, "if we had the facilities, publish the most interesting, the most instructive and the most valued engineering journal in the world, by devoting it to only

one particular class of facts, the records of failures. . . . For the whole science of engineering, properly so-called, has been built up from such records."

Such a journal of failures was never published; however, *Engineering News* and its successors have presented many valuable reports of engineering failures. One of these reports—careful, comprehensive, knowledgeable, and fair to all parties—was published in *Engineering News* just a week after a cantilever railway bridge being built over the St. Lawrence River near Quebec City collapsed on August 29, 1907, killing seventy-four workmen (see "A Disaster in the Making," *Invention & Technology*, Spring 1986).

"Long and careful inspection of the wreck," wrote the reporter, "shows that the material was of excellent quality; that the workmanship was remarkably good." But because the members were much larger than those used in ordinary bridges, he questioned the judgment that led to the design of the built-up compression members: "We step up from the ordinary columns of ordinary construction, tried out in multiplied practice, to enormous, heavy, thick-plated pillars of steel, and we apply the same rules. Have we the confirmation of experiment as a warranty? Except in the light of theory, these structures are virtually unknown. We know the material that goes into their make-up, but we do not know the composite, the structure."

Whereas with the Quebec Bridge disaster the fault was found to lie in a lack of experience supporting the analytic theory behind the structure, there is today an unfortunate belief that the newer analytic techniques available to designers will prevent failures in the future. The report in *Science* of the collapse of a twenty-seven-year-old radio telescope, three hundred feet in diameter, in Green Bank, West Virginia, in 1989 implied that such a failure could not occur in a radio telescope designed today. The "cause" of the collapse was pinpointed in "the fracture of a single highly stressed steel plate" (which had survived for more than twenty-five years). "An independent panel appointed by the National Science Foundation" declared that "parts of the telescope were under far higher stresses than would be permitted today" and that "computerized stress analysis would identify potential failure points in telescopes built today, but these methods were not available when the instrument was built in 1962." One wonders what explanation will be given for the collapse, some years hence, of a structure designed today with the help of a "computerized stress analysis."

A much more sensible and realistic outlook on design failures may be found in a book titled *To Engineer Is Human: The Role of Failure in Successful Design*, written by Henry Petroski, a professor of civil engineering who graduated from engineering school in the early 1960s. Toward the end of his book, Petroski has a chapter called "From Slide Rule to Computer: Forgetting How It Used to Be Done." He describes the Keuffel & Esser Log Log Duplex Decitrig slide rule that he purchased when he entered engineering school in 1959 to emphasize that the limits of a slide rule's accuracy—generally three significant figures—are no disadvantage, because the data on which the calculations depend are seldom better than approximations.

Petroski uses the 1978 collapse of the modern "space-frame" roof of the Hartford Civic Center under a snow load as an example of the limitations of computerized design. The roof failed a few hours after a basketball game that had been attended by several thousand people, and providentially nobody was hurt in the collapse. Petroski explains the complexity of a space frame, which suggests mammoth Tinkertoys, with long, straight steel rods arranged vertically, horizontally, and diagonally. To design a space frame using a slide rule or a mechanical calculator was a laborious process with too many uncertainties for nearly any engineer, so space frames were seldom built before computer programs became available. With a computer model, however, analyses can be made quickly. The computer's apparent precision, says Petroski—to six or more significant figures—can give engineers "an unwarranted confidence in the validity of the resulting numbers."

Who makes the computer model of a proposed structure is of more than passing interest. If the model is worked out on a commercially available analytical program, the designer will have no easy way of discovering all the assumptions made by the programmer. Consequently, the designer must either accept on faith the program's results or check the results—experimentally, graphically, and numerically—in sufficient depth to be satisfied that the programmer did not make dangerous assumptions or omit critical factors and that the program reflects fully the subtleties of the designer's own unique problem.

To underline the hazards of using a program written by somebody else, Petroski quotes a Canadian structural engineer on the use of commercial software: "Because structural analysis and detailing programs are com-

The Hartford Civic Center's roof collapsed under a load of snow on January 18, 1978. Its design relied heavily on computer modeling.

plex, the profession as a whole will use programs written by a few. These few will come from the ranks of structural 'analysts' . . . and not from the structural 'designers.' Generally speaking, their design and construction-site experience and background will tend to be limited. It is difficult to envision a mechanism for ensuring that the products of such a person will display the experience and intuition of a competent designer. . . . More than ever before, the challenge to the profession and to educators is to develop designers who will be able to stand up to and reject or modify the results of a computer aided analysis and design."

The engineers who can "stand up to" a computer will be those who understand that software incorporates many assumptions that cannot be easily detected by its users but that affect the validity of the results. There are a thousand points of doubt in every complex computer program. Successful computer-aided design re-

quires vigilance and the same visual knowledge and intuitive sense of fitness that successful designers have always depended on when making critical design decisions.

Engineers need to be continually reminded that nearly all engineering failures result from faulty judgments rather than faulty calculations. For instance, in the 1979 accident in the nuclear power plant at Three Mile Island, the level of the coolant in the reactor vessel was low because an automatic relief valve remained open while, for more than two hours after the accident began, an indicator on the control panel said it was shut. The relief valve was opened by energizing a solenoid; it was closed by a simple spring when the solenoid was shut off. The designer who specified the controls and indicators on the control panel assumed that there would never be a problem with the valve's closing properly, so he chose to show

on the panel not the valve position but merely whether the solenoid was on or off. When the solenoid was off, he assumed, the valve would be closed. The operators of the plant assumed, quite reasonably, that the indicator told them directly, not by inference, whether the valve was open or closed.

The choice made in this case may have seemed so simple and sensible as to be overlooked in whatever checking the design underwent. It might have been re-examined had the checker had experience with sticky relief valves or comprehension of the life-and-death importance of giving a nuclear power plant's operators direct and accurate information. This was not a failure of calculation but a failure of judgment.

A cluster of newspaper articles that appeared in the first half of 1990 (a similar crop may be harvested in any half-year) has fattened my "failure" file folder and has led me to expect only more of the same under the accepted regimen of abstract, high-tech design. The magnitude of the errors of judgment in some of the reported failures suggests that engineers of the new breed have climbed to the tops of many bureaucratic ladders and are now making decisions that should be made by people with more common sense and experience.

The first oil spill that year occurred on January 1, when a transfer line from the Exxon Bayway refinery in Linden, New Jersey, spilled more than 500,000 gallons into the Arthur Kill, which separates New Jersey from Staten Island. A few feet of a side seam had split in a section of pipe, and an automatic alarm valve, intended to shut off the flow, detected the leak but had been wedged open for twelve years because the shut-down alarm was "too sensitive" and kept interrupting flow in the

sors ignored the significant difference in performance requirements between air conditioners and refrigerators. In air conditioners a convenient stream of air keeps the body of the compressor, and thus the lubricating oil sealed inside, cool. Refrigerators lack an equivalent airstream, and none was provided to cool the new compressors.

A consultant suggested a joint venture with a Japanese firm experienced in rotary-compressor design. Although the designers had had little experience with rotary compressors, they rejected the advice and proceeded to develop a design that required tolerances smaller than those found in mass-produced machines of any kind. According to one of his former associates, the chief design engineer "figured you didn't need previous compressor-design experience to design a new compressor."

cating compressors at a cost of about $450 million.

In May of 1990 the National Aeronautics and Space Administration returned to the front pages with two blunders less chilling than the *Challenger* explosion but likely to waste hundreds of millions of dollars. The Hubble space telescope, launched on April 24, had been confidently advertised as the answer to the problem of the atmosphere's interference with extremely faint light waves from far-distant heavenly bodies. The space telescope was expected to increase the diameter of the known universe by a factor of seven. The first pictures were to be transmitted to earth a week after the launch. But several unexpected happenings postponed the expected first transmission to the end of the year, about eight months behind schedule. Most significantly, an error had been made in grinding the large mirror, and it was impossible to bring any heavenly body into sharp focus. Computer experts fell back on proposing programs that would "enhance" the distorted images.

It is a gross insult to harried users of the Aegis system to attribute the *Vincennes* tragedy to "operator error."

pipeline. In all those years, according to Exxon, the pipe had never leaked.

On May 7 the *Wall Street Journal* gave a careful account of the expensive problems that poor design judgment and unreasonable production deadlines had caused when General Electric introduced a new and insufficiently tested compressor in its domestic refrigerators in 1986. The new refrigerators featured rotary compressors rather than the reciprocating compressors that had been employed since the 1920s.

Rotary compressors, common in air conditioners, were attractive to GE managers because they were expected to be much cheaper to build. Many engineers learn in school a bit of folklore about the invariable superiority of rotating machinery over reciprocating machinery. Rotating gas compressors, however, require substantially more power than reciprocating compressors, and their high rotative speeds make them difficult to cool and lubricate.

The designers of the new compres-

The first of the new compressors were to be tested for the assumed lifetime of a refrigerator; however, the tests were cut short long before a lifetime had elapsed, and the misgivings voiced by the experienced technician who ran the tests were disregarded. This senior technician—who had worked in the testing lab for thirty years—reported that although the compressors did not actually fail in the truncated testing program, "they didn't look right, either." Discoloration from high temperatures, bearing surfaces that looked worn, and a black, oily crust on some parts pointed to eventual trouble with overheating, wear, and a breakdown of the sealed-in lubricating oil. The experience-based assessment was discounted because it came from a mere technician.

The new refrigerators sold well, and trouble didn't begin for almost a year. After the dimensions of the design debacle began to be clear, the company found itself replacing more than a million rotary compressors with recipro-

The first smaller-scale mishap occurred when the satellite carrying the telescope was launched from the shuttle vehicle. An electrical cable, connecting an adjustable antenna dish to the television transmitter, was kinked as it exited the shuttle, causing a significant reduction in the antenna's adjustability. Transmission to earth was interrupted by the inability to point the antenna continuously at the receiving station.

A few days later newspaper readers learned that the telescope could not be pointed accurately at stars and planets. The controlling computer program had been based on an outdated star chart and introduced a pointing error of about half a degree. Furthermore, the telescope developed a tendency to drift and to pick up other nearby stars just slightly brighter or dimmer than those it was supposed to hold in focus.

Finally, vibrations of the entire telescope satellite raised questions about its ability to obtain any information that is not available to ordinary telescopes on the ground. An unanticipated (i.e., unthought of in the design) cycle of expansion and contraction of the solar-panel supports, as the spacecraft moved into and out of the earth's shadow, caused the panels to sway "like the slowly flapping wings of a great bird," as a newspaper report put it. The computer program for stabilizing the spacecraft, confused by the unexpected vibrations, called for corrective measures that only exacerbated the vibration.

Further deficiencies turned up in Hubble's second year in orbit. Two gyroscopes (of six) have failed, and two others exhibit signs of incipient failure. The Goddard high-resolution spectograph may have to be shut down because of intermittent loss of connection with its data computer. The flapping solar panels are attached to booms that have developed a jerky motion that may lead to their collapse and a catastrophic power loss. Although NASA hopes to send repair missions to Hubble in 1994, one wonders whether the repair missions will be able to keep ahead of the failures of one component after another. These blunders resulted not from mistaken calculations but from the inability to visualize realistic conditions. They suggest that although a great deal of hard thinking may have been done to accomplish the stated missions of Hubble, the ability to imagine the mundane things that can go wrong remains sadly deficient at NASA.

R ichard P. Feynman, the maverick physicist who served on the official panel reviewing the *Challenger* explosion, argued that more failures and embarrassing surprises

Aegis system operators get too much information thrown at them in too little time.

would be inevitable if NASA did not radically change the way its big projects were designed. He accused the space agency of "top-down design" and contrasted this with sensible "bottom-up" design, which has been normal engineering practice for centuries.

In bottom-up design the various components of a system are designed, tested, and, if necessary, modified before the design of the entire system has been set in concrete. In the top-down mode (invented by the military), the whole system is designed at once, before resolving the many questions and conflicts that are normally ironed out in a bottom-up design. The system is then built before there is time to test all its components, so that deficient and incompatible ones must ultimately be located (often a difficult problem in itself), redesigned, and rebuilt—an expensive and uncertain process.

Furthermore, as Feynman pointed out, the political problems faced by NASA encourage, if not force, it to "exaggerate" when explaining its needs for large sums of money. It was, he wrote, "*apparently* necessary [in the case of the shuttle] to exaggerate: to exaggerate how economical the shuttle would be, to exaggerate how often it could fly, to exaggerate how safe it would be, to exaggerate the big scientific facts that would be discovered. 'The shuttle can make so-and-so many flights and it'll cost such-and-such; we went to the moon, so we can *do* it!'"

Until the foolishness of top-down design has been dropped in a fit of common sense, the harrowing succes-

sion of flawed designs in high-tech, high-cost public projects will continue.

In the mid-1960s a prominent British structural engineer, Sir Alfred Pugsley, made a wise and important prescription for the design of pioneering projects. He said that in such projects the chief engineer should be given a "sparring partner," a senior engineer who would be privy to essentially all the information available to the chief engineer and whose status would be such that the chief could not ignore his comments and recommendations. This sparring partner would be given ample time to follow the design work and to study and think about the implications of details as well as the "big" decisions made by the chief engineer.

T he hazards of permitting a chief engineer to determine all aspects of a complex project, without critical review, are insidious and far-reaching, but Pugsley also warned against an even worse commonplace hazard: the adoption of a faulty doctrine by a whole profession.

Pugsley cited as an example of misplaced enthusiasm for a new doctrine the collapse of the Tacoma Narrows suspension bridge in 1940, the "major lesson" of which was "the unwisdom of allowing a particular profession to become too inward looking and so screened from relevant knowledge growing up in other fields around it." Had the designers of the Tacoma Narrows Bridge known more of aerodynamics, he thought, the collapse might have been averted. It is fairly certain, however, that if the relevance of aerodynamics to that design had been suggested by a person outside the network of "leading structural engineers," the advice would have been considered an attack on the profession of civil engineering.

The experience of two engineers

who published historical articles on the collapse of the bridge supports my surmise. The professional reaction to an article in *Engineering News-Record* by James Kip Finch of Columbia University prompted him to virtually retract its contents. David Billington, an unorthodox professor of civil engineering at Princeton University, was excoriated by several prominent bridge engineers when his paper on events leading to the collapse was published in a journal of the American Society of Civil Engineers.

Billington, in a historical study of suspension bridges, argues convincingly that a design decision made in the 1920s by O. H. Ammann, designer of the George Washington Bridge over the Hudson River, "led directly to the failure of the Tacoma Narrows bridge." Ammann decided that the deck of his

Billington's article was characteristically greeted by engineers as "an attack on the leading figures of the period and especially upon O. H. Ammann" (in the words of Herbert Rothman, one of Ammann's defenders). Rebuttal was necessary, he continued, in order to "remove the undeserved blame" leveled at several bridge designers and to "preserve their proper position in the history of engineering."

The need to justify the way engineers do things is unfortunately often felt even when ill-considered systems lead them to make fatally wrong judgments. The missile cruiser USS *Vincennes* was equipped with a billion-dollar "state-of-the-art" air defense system called Aegis. On July 3, 1988, the ship shot down an

The designer of the Aegis, which is the prototype system for the Strategic Defense Initiative, greatly underestimated the demands that their designs would place on the operators, who often lack the knowledge of the idiosyncrasies and limitations built into the system. Disastrous errors of judgment are inevitable so long as operator error rather than designer error is routinely considered the cause of disasters. Hubris and an absence of common sense in the design process set the conditions that produce the confusingly overcomplicated tasks that the equipment demands of operators. Human abilities and limitations need to be designed into systems, not designed out.

If we are to avoid calamitous design errors—as well as those that are merely irritating or expensive—it is necessary for engineers to understand that such errors are not errors of mathematics or calculation but errors of engineering judgment, of judgment that is not reducible to engineering science or to mathematics.

Computer programs have made too many people believe that all technical problems are readily solvable.

bridge could be built without vertical stiffening, and he omitted the stiffening trusses that John Roebling and other suspension-bridge engineers had felt were necessary to keep winds from causing undulation of the bridge deck. Ammann's reasoning appealed to many in the civil engineering profession, and they applied it to several long, narrower, lighter, and disturbingly flexible suspension bridges they built in the 1930s, including the Golden Gate Bridge, which was stiffened after a harrowing experience with crosswinds in 1951.

After the Tacoma Narrows Bridge fell, structural engineers found that a sense of history might have tempered their enthusiastic acceptance and extension of Ammann's design precept. They learned, as Billington points out, that published records of suspension bridges in Europe and America "described nineteenth-century failures that were amazingly similar to what they saw in the motion pictures of the Tacoma collapse."

Iranian civilian airliner, killing 290 people. The Aegis system had received IFF (Identification, Friend or Foe) signals for both military and civilian planes, yet the ship's radar indicated only one plane, and the decision was made to destroy it. (No radar or any other existing equipment will identify a plane by its physical shape and size alone.) Later the Navy decided that an enlisted man had misinterpreted the signals on his visual display and that therefore the captain was not at fault for ordering the destruction of the civilian airplane.

As with most "operator errors" that have led to major disasters, the operators aboard the *Vincennes* had been deluged with more information than they could assimilate in the few seconds before a crucial decision had to be made. It is a gross insult to the operators who have to deal with such monstrous systems to say, as the Navy did, that the Aegis system worked perfectly and that the tragedy was due to "operator error."

Here, indeed, is the crux of all arguments about the nature of the education that an engineer requires. Necessary as the analytical tools of science and mathematics most certainly are, more important is the development in student and neophyte engineers of sound judgment and an intuitive sense of fitness and adequacy.

No matter how vigorously a "science" of design may be pushed, the successful design of real things in a contingent world will always be based more on art than on science. Unquantifiable judgments and choices are the elements that determine the way a design comes together. Engineering design is simply that kind of process. It always has been. It always will be. ★

*Dependable
Computing*

*John Rushby
Editor*

Evaluation of Safety-Critical Software

*Methods and approaches for testing the reliability and trustworthiness of
software remain among the most controversial issues facing this age of high
technology. The authors present some of the crucial questions faced by
software programmers and eventual users.*

David L. Parnas, A. John van Schouwen, and Shu Po Kwan

It is increasingly common to use programmable computers in applications where their failure could be life-threatening and could result in extensive damage. For example, computers now have safety-critical functions in both military and civilian aircraft, in nuclear plants, and in medical devices. It is incumbent upon those responsible for programming, purchasing, installing, and licensing these systems to determine whether or not the software is ready to be used. This article addresses questions that are simple to pose but hard to answer. What standards must a software product satisfy if it is to be used in safety-critical applications such as those mentioned? What documentation should be required? How much testing is needed? How should the software be structured?

This article differs from others concerned with software in safety-critical applications, in that it does not attempt to identify *safety* as a property separate from reliability and trustworthiness. In other words, we do not attempt to separate safety-critical code from other code in a product used in a safety-critical application. In our experience, software exhibits *weak-link* behavior, that is failures in even the unimportant parts of the code can have unexpected repercussions elsewhere. For a discussion of another viewpoint, we suggest the work of N. G. Leveson [6, 7, 8].

We favor keeping safety-critical software as small and simple as possible by moving any functions that are not safety critical to other computers. This further justifies our assumption that all parts of a safety-critical software product must be considered safety critical.

WHY IS SOFTWARE A SPECIAL CONCERN?
Within the engineering community software systems have a reputation for being undependable, especially in the first years of their use. The public is aware of a few spectacular stories such as the Space Shuttle flight that was delayed by a software timing problem, or the Ve-

This work was supported by the National Science and Engineering Research
Board of Canada as well as the Atomic Energy Control Board of Canada.

nus probe that was lost because of a punctuation error. In the software community, the problem is known to be much more widespread.

A few years ago, David Benson, professor of Computer Science at Washington State University, issued a challenge by way of several electronic bulletin board systems. He asked for an example of a real-time system that functioned adequately when used for the first time by people other than its developers for a purpose other than testing. Only one candidate for this honor was proposed, but even that candidate was controversial. It consisted of approximately 18,000 instructions, most of which had been used for several years before the "first use." The only code that had not been used before that first use was a simple sequence of 200 instructions that simulated a simple analogue servomechanism. That instruction sequence had been tested extensively against an analogue model. All who have looked at this program regard it as exceptional. If we choose to regard this small program as one that worked in its first real application, it is the proverbial "exception that proves the rule."

As a rule software systems do not work well until they have been used, and have failed repeatedly, in real applications. Generally, many uses and many failures are required before a product is considered reliable. Software products, including those that have become relatively reliable, behave like other products of evolution-like processes; they often fail, even years after they were built, when the operating conditions change.

While there are errors in many engineering products, experience has shown that errors are more common, more pervasive, and more troublesome, in software than in other technologies. This information must be understood in light of the fact it is now standard practice among software professionals to have their product go through an extensive series of carefully planned tests before real use. The products fail in their first real use because the situations that were not anticipated by the programmers were also overlooked by the test planners. Most major computer-using organizations, both military and civilian, are investing heavily in searching for ways to improve the state of the art in software. The problem remains serious and there is no sign of a "silver bullet." The most promising development is the work of Harlan Mills and his colleagues at IBM on a software development process known as "clean room" [3, 9, 12]. Mills uses randomly selected tests, carried out by an independent testing group. The use of randomly generated test data reduces the likelihood of shared oversights. We will discuss this approach in more detail later in this article.

WHY IS SOFTWARE USED?

If software is so untrustworthy, one might ask why engineers do not avoid it by continuing to use hard-wired digital and analogue hardware. Here, we list the three main advantages of replacing hardware with software:

1. Software technology makes it practical to build more *logic* into the system. Software-controlled computer systems can distinguish a large number of situations and provide output appropriate to each of them. Hard-wired systems could not obtain such behavior without prohibitive amounts of hardware. Programmable hardware is less expensive than the equivalent hard-wired logic because it is regular in structure and it is mass produced. The economic aspects of the situation also allow software-controlled systems to perform more checking; reliability can be increased by periodic execution of programs that check the hardware.
2. Logic implemented in software is, in theory, easier to change than logic implemented in hardware. Many changes can be made without adding new components. When a system is replicated or located in a physical position that is hard to reach, it is far easier to make changes in software than in hardware.
3. Computer technology and software flexibility make it possible to provide more information to operators and to provide that information in a more useful form. The operator of a modern software-controlled system can be provided with information that would be unthinkable in a pure hardware system. All of this can be achieved using less space and power than was used by noncomputerized systems.

These factors explain the replacement of hard-wired systems with software-controlled systems in spite of software's reputation as an unreliable technology.

HOW ARE SOFTWARE CONTROLLERS LIKE OTHER CONTROLLERS?

In the next section we will argue that software technology requires some refinements in policies and standards because of differences between software and hardware technology. However, it is important to recognize some common properties of software and hardware control systems.

In the design and specification of control systems,

engineers have long known how to use a black box mathematical model of the controller. In such models, (1) the inputs to the controller are described as mathematical functions of certain observable environmental state variables, (2) the outputs of the controller are described as mathematical functions of the inputs, (3) the values of the controlled environmental variables are described as mathematical functions of the controller's outputs, and (4) the required relation between the controlled variables and observed variables is described. It is then possible to confirm that the behavior of the controller meets its requirements.

It is important to recognize that, in theory, software-implemented controllers can be described in exactly the same way as black box mathematical models. They can also be viewed as black boxes whose output is a mathematical function of the input. In practice, they are not viewed this way. One reason for the distinction is that their functions are more complex (i.e. harder to describe) than the functions that describe the behavior of conventional controllers. However, [4] and [17] provide ample evidence that requirements for real systems can be documented in this way. We return to this theme later.

HOW IS SOFTWARE DIFFERENT FROM OTHER CONTROLLER TECHNOLOGIES?

Software problems are often considered growing pains and ascribed to the adolescent nature of the field. Unfortunately there are fundamental differences between software and other approaches that suggest these problems are here to stay.

Complexity: The most immediately obvious difference between software and hardware technologies is their complexity. This can be observed by considering the size of the most compact descriptions of the software. Precise documentation, in a reasonably general notation, for small software systems can fill a bookcase. Another measure of complexity is the time it takes for a programmer to become closely familiar with a system. Even with small software systems, it is common to find that a programmer requires a year of working with the program before he/she can be trusted to make improvements on his/her own.

Error Sensitivity: Another notable property of software is its sensitivity to small errors. In conventional engineering, every design and manufacturing dimension can be characterized by a tolerance. One is not required to get things exactly right; being within the specified *tolerance* of the right value is good enough. The use of a tolerance is justified by the assumption that small errors have small consequences. It is well known that in software, trivial clerical errors can have major consequences. No useful interpretation of tolerance is known for software. A single punctuation error can be disastrous, even though fundamental oversights sometimes have negligible effects.

Hard to Test: Software is notoriously difficult to test

adequately. It is common to find a piece of software that has been subjected to a thorough and disciplined testing regime has serious flaws. Testing of analogue devices is based on interpolation. One assumes that devices that function well at two close points will function well at points in-between. In software that assumption is not valid. The number of cases that must be tested in order to engender confidence in a piece of software is usually extremely large. Moreover, as Harlan Mills has pointed out, "testing carried out by selected test cases, no matter how carefully and well-planned, can provide nothing but anecdotes" [3, 9, 12].

These properties are fundamental consequences of the fact that the mathematical functions implemented by software are not continuous functions, but functions with an arbitrary number of discontinuities. The lack of continuity constraints on the functions describing program effects makes it difficult to find compact descriptions of the software. The lack of such constraints gives software its flexibility, but it also allows the complexity. Similarly, the sensitivity to small errors, and the testing difficulties, can be traced to fundamental mathematical properties; we are unlikely to discover a miracle cure. Great discipline and careful scrutiny will always be required for safety-critical software systems.

Correlated Failures: Many of the assumptions normally made in the design of high-reliability hardware are invalid for software. Designers of high-reliability hardware are concerned with manufacturing failures and wear-out phenomena. They can perform their analysis on the assumption that failures are not strongly correlated and simultaneous failures are unlikely. Those who evaluate the reliability of hardware systems should be, and often are, concerned about design errors and correlated failures; however in many situations the effects of other types of errors are dominant.

In software there are few errors introduced in the manufacturing (compiling) phase; when there are such errors they are systematic, not random. Software does not wear out. The errors with which software reliability experts must be concerned are design errors. These errors cannot be considered statistically independent. There is ample evidence that, even when programs for a given task are written by people who do not know of each other, they have closely related errors [6, 7, 8].

In contrast to the situation with hardware systems, one cannot obtain higher reliability by duplication of software components. One simply duplicates the errors. Even when programs are written independently, the oversights made by one programmer are often shared by others. As a result, one cannot count on increasing the reliability of software systems simply by having three computers where one would be sufficient [6, 7, 8].

Lack of Professional Standards: A severe problem in the software field is that, strictly speaking, there are no software engineers. In contrast to older engineering fields, there is no accrediting agency for professional software engineers. Those in software engineering have not agreed on a set of skills and knowledge that should be possessed by every software engineer. Anyone with a modicum of programming knowledge can be called a software engineer. Often, critical programming systems are built by people with no postsecondary training about software. Although they may have useful knowledge of the field in which the software will be applied, such knowledge is not a substitute for understanding the foundations of software technology.

SOFTWARE TESTING CONCERNS

Some engineers believe one can design black box tests without knowledge of what is inside the box. This is, unfortunately, not completely true. If we know that the contents of a black box exhibit linear behavior, the number of tests needed to make sure it would function as specified could be quite small. If we know that the function can be described by a polynomial of order "N," we can use that information to determine how many tests are needed. If the function can have a large number of discontinuities, far more tests are needed. That is why a shift from analogue technology to software brings with it a need for much more testing.

Built-in test circuitry is often included in hardware to perform testing while the product is in use. Predetermined values are substituted for inputs, and the outputs are compared to normative values. Sometimes this approach is imitated in software designs and the claim is made that built-in online testing can substitute for black box testing. In hardware, built-in testing tests for decay or damage. Software does not decay and physical damage is not our concern. Software can be used to test the hardware, but its value for testing itself is quite doubtful. Software self-testing does increase the complexity of the product and, consequently, the likelihood of error. Moreover, such testing does not constitute adequate testing because it usually does not resemble the conditions of actual use.

The fundamental limitations on testing mentioned earlier have some very practical implications.

We cannot test software for correctness: Because of the large number of states (and the lack of regularity in its structure), the number of states that would have to be tested to assure that software is correct is preposterous. Testing can show the presence of bugs, but, except for toy problems, it is not practical to use testing to show that software is free of design errors.

It is difficult to make accurate predictions of software reliability and availability: Mathematical models show that it is practical to predict the reliability of software, provided that one has good statistical models of the actual operating conditions. Unfortunately, one usually gains that information only after the system is installed. Even when a new system replaces an existing one, differences in features may cause changes in the input distribution. Nonetheless, in safety-critical situations, one must attempt to get and use the necessary statistical data. The use of this data is discussed later in this article.

Predictions of availability are even more difficult; estimates of availability depend on predictions of the time it will take to correct a bug in the software. We never know what that amount of time will be in advance; data from earlier bugs is not a good predictor of the time it will take to find the next bug.

It is not practical to measure the trustworthiness of software: We consider a product to be trustworthy if we believe that the probability of it having a potentially catastrophic flaw is acceptably low. Whereas reliability is a measure of the probability of a problem occurring while the system is in service, trustworthiness is a measure of the probability of a serious flaw remaining after testing and review. In fact, inspection and testing can increase the trustworthiness of a product without affecting its reliability.

Software does not need to be correct in order to be trustworthy. We will trust imperfect software if we believe its probability of having a serious flaw is very low. Unfortunately, as we will show, the amount of testing necessary to establish high confidence levels for most software products is impractically large. The number of states and possible input sequences is so large that the probability of an error having escaped our attention will remain high even after years of testing. Methods other than testing must be used to increase our trust in software.

There is a role for testing: A number of computer scientists, aware of the limitations on software testing, would argue that one should not test software. They would argue that the effort normally put into testing should, instead, be put into a form of review known as mathematical verification. A program is a mathematical object and can be proven correct. Unfortunately, such mathematical inspections are based on mathematical models that may not be accurate. No amount of mathematical analysis will reveal discrepancies between the model being used and the real situation; only testing can do that. Moreover, errors are often made in proofs. In mature engineering fields, mathematical methods and testing are viewed as complementary and mutually supportive.

There is a need for an independent validation agency: It is impossible to test software completely and difficult to test one's own design in an unbiased way. A growing number of software development projects involve independent verification and validation (V&V). The V&V contractor is entirely independent of the development contractor. Sometimes a competitor of the development contractor is given the V&V contract. The testers work from the specification for the software and attempt to develop tests that will show the software to be faulty. One particularly interesting variation of this approach has been used within the IBM Federal Systems Division. In IBM's *clean room* development approach the authors of the software are not allowed

to execute their programs. All testing is done by an independent tester and test reports are sent to the developer's supervisors. The test cases are chosen using random number generators and are intended to yield statistically valid data. It was hypothesized that the software would be written far more carefully under these conditions and would be more reliable. Early reports support the hypothesis [3, 9, 12].

It is important that these validation tests not be made available to the developers before the software is submitted for testing. If the developers know what tests will be performed, they will use those tests in their debugging. The result is likely to be a program that will pass the tests but is not reliable in actual use.

SOFTWARE REVIEWABILITY CONCERNS

Why is reviewability a particular concern for software?

Traditionally, engineers have approached software as if it were an art form. Each programmer has been allowed to have his own style. Criticisms of software structure, clarity, and documentation were dismissed as "matters of taste."

In the past, engineers were rarely asked to examine a software product and certify that it would be trustworthy. Even in systems that were required to be trustworthy and reliable, software was often regarded as an unimportant component, not requiring special examination.

In recent years, however, manufacturers of a wide variety of equipment have been substituting computers controlled by software for a wide variety of more conventional products. We can no longer treat software as if it were trivial and unimportant.

In the older areas of engineering, safety-critical components are inspected and reviewed to assure the design is consistent with the safety requirements. To make this review possible, the designers are required to conform to industry standards for the documentation, and even the structure, of the product. The documentation must be sufficiently clear and well organized that a reviewer can determine whether or not the design meets safety standards. The design itself must allow components to be inspected so the reviewer can verify they are consistent with the documentation. In construction, inspections take place during the process—while it is still possible to inspect and correct work that will later be hidden.

When software is a safety-critical component, analogous standards should be applied. In software, there is no problem of physical visibility but there is a problem of clarity. Both practical experience and planned experiments have shown that it is common for programs with major flaws to be accepted by reviewers. In one particularly shocking experiment, small programs were deliberately flawed and given to a skilled reviewer team. The reviewers were unable to find the flaws in spite of the fact they were certain such flaws were present. In theory, nothing is invisible in a program—

it is all in the listing; in practice, poorly structured programs hide a plethora of problems.

In safety-critical applications we must reject the "software-as-art-form" approach. Programs and documentation must conform to standards that allow reviewers to feel confident they understand the software and can predict how it will function in situations where safety depends on it. However, we must, equally strongly, reject standards that require a mountain of paper that nobody can read. The standards must insure clear, precise, and concise documentation.

It is symptomatic of the immaturity of the software profession that there are no widely accepted software standards assuring the reviewability essential to licensing of software products that must be seen as trustworthy. The documentation standards name and outline certain documents, but they only vaguely define the contents of those documents. Recent U.S. military procurement regulations include safety requirements; while they require that safety checks be done, they neither describe how to do them nor impose standards that make those checks practicable. Most standards for code documentation are so vague and syntactic in nature that a program can meet those standards in spite of being incomprehensible.

In the next section we derive some basic standards by considering the reviews that are needed and the information required by the reviewers.

What reviews are needed?

Software installed as a safety-critical component in a large system should be subjected to the following reviews:

a. Review for correct intended function. If the software works as the programmers intend, will it meet the actual requirements?
b. Review for maintainable, understandable, well documented structure. Is it easy to find portions of the software relevant to a certain issue? Are the responsibilities of the various modules clearly defined? If all of the modules work as required, will the whole system work as intended? If changes are needed in the future, can those changes be restricted to easily identified portions of the code?
c. Review each module to verify the algorithm and data structure design are consistent with the specified behavior. Is the data structure used in the module appropriate for representing the information maintained by that module? If the programs are correctly coded, will the modules perform as required? Will the algorithms selected perform as required? These reviews must use mathematical methods; one cannot rely on intuitive approaches. We have found a formal review based on functional semantics, [10], to be practical and effective.
d. Review the code for consistency with the algorithm and data structure design. Is the actual source code consistent with the algorithms and data structures described by the designers? Have the assemblers,

compilers, and other support tools been used correctly?
e. Review test adequacy. Was the testing sufficient to provide sound confidence in the proper functioning of the software?

The structure of this set of reviews is consistent with modern approaches to software engineering. Because we are unable to comprehend all the critical details about a software product at once, it is necessary to provide documentation that allows programmers and reviewers to focus on one aspect at a time and to zoom in on the relevant details.

Developing and presenting these views in the sequence listed is the analogue of providing inspections during a construction project. Just as construction is inspected before further work obscures what has been done, the early specifications should be reviewed before subsequent coding hides the structure in a sea of detail.

The set of reviews also reflects the fact that reviewers of a software product have a variety of skills. Those who have a deep understanding of the requirements are not usually skilled software designers. It follows that the best people to review the functional behavior of the software are not the ones who should study the software. Similarly, within the software field we have people who are good at algorithm design, but not particularly good finding an architecture for software products. Skilled algorithm designers are not necessarily experts on a particular compiler or machine language. Those intimately familiar with a compiler or assembly language are not always good at organizing large programs. When the software is safety critical, it is important that each of the five reviews be conducted by those best qualified to review that aspect of the work.

Within this framework, all code and documentation supplied must be of a quality that facilitates review and allows the reviewers to be confident of their conclusions. It is the responsibility of the designers to present their software in a way that leaves no doubt about their correctness. It is not the responsibility of the reviewers to guess the designers' intent. Discrepancies between code and documentation must be treated as seriously as errors in the code. If the designers are allowed to be sloppy with their documentation, quality control will be ineffective.

In the following sections of this article, we will describe the documentation that must be provided for each of these reviews. This documentation should not be created merely for review purposes. It should be used throughout the development to record and propagate design decisions. When separate review documents are produced, projects experience all the problems of keeping two sets of books. Because of the complexity of software products, it is unlikely that both records would be consistent. Moreover, the documents described below from the reviewers' viewpoint are invaluable to the designers as well [5, 13, 16].

What documentation is required to review the functional requirements?

The software can be viewed as a control system whose output values respond to changes in the states of variables of interest in its environment. For many real-time systems, the desired outputs approximate piece-wise continuous functions of time and the history of the relevant environmental parameters. For other systems, the outputs are functions of a snapshot of the environmental parameters taken at some point in time. Some systems provide both reports and continuous outputs.

The reviewers at this stage should be engineers and scientists who understand the situation being monitored and the devices to be controlled. They may not be computer specialists and should not be expected to read and understand programs. Because the requirements could, in theory, be fulfilled by a completely hardware design, the description should use the mathematics of control systems, not the jargon and notation of computer programming. The functional requirements can be stated precisely by giving three mathematical relations: (1) The required values of the controlled environmental variables in terms of the values of the relevant observable environmental parameters, (2) the computer inputs in terms of those observable environmental variables, and (3) the values of the controlled environmental variables in terms of the computer outputs.

These requirements can be communicated as a set of tables and formulae describing the mathematical functions to be implemented [4]. We should not describe a sequence of computations anywhere in this document. The use of natural language, which inevitably introduces ambiguity, should be minimized. Documents of this form have been written for reasonably complex systems and are essential when safety-critical functions are to be performed. Our experience has shown that documents written this way can be thoroughly and effectively reviewed by engineers who are not programmers. Some suggestions for organizing the reviews are contained in [19]. A complete example of such a document has been published as a model for other projects [17].

What documentation is required to review the software structure?

For this review we require documents that describe the breakdown of the program into modules. Each module is a unit that should be designed, written and reviewed independently of other modules. Each module is a collection of programs; the programs that can be invoked from other modules are called access programs. The purpose of this review is to make sure that: (1) the structure is one that allows independent development and change; (2) all programs that are needed are included once and only once in the structure; (3) the interfaces to the modules are precisely defined; (4) the modules are compatible and will, to-

gether, constitute a system that meets the functional requirements.

For this review three types of documents are required. The first is the requirements specification, which should have been approved by an earlier review. The second is an informal document describing the responsibilities of each module. The purpose of this *module guide* is to allow a reviewer to find all the modules relevant to a particular aspect of system design [1]. The third type of document is known as a module specification. It provides a complete black box description of the module interface. There should be one specification for each module mentioned in the module guide [2, 14].

Reviewers of these documents must be experienced software engineers. Some of them should have had experience with similar systems. This experience is necessary to note omissions in the module structure. Discussions of these documents and how to organize the reviews are contained in [14, 19].

What documentation is required to review the module's internal design?

The first step in designing the module should be to describe the data structures that will be used and each proposed program's effect on the data. This information can be described in a way that is, except for the data types available, independent of the programming language being used.

The design documentation is a description of two types of mathematical functions: program functions and abstraction functions. This terminology was used in IBM's Federal Systems Division, the IBM branch responsible for U.S. Government systems. These concepts are described more fully elsewhere [11, 13]. The program functions, one for each module access program, give the mapping from the state before the program is executed to the state after the program terminates. The abstraction functions are used to define the "meaning" of the data structure; they give the mapping between the data states and abstract values visible to the users of the module. It is well-known that these functions provide sufficient information for a formal review of correctness of the design before the programs are implemented.

Programs that cannot be described on a single page must be presented in a hierarchical way; each page must present a small program, calling other programs whose functions are specified on that page. This type of presentation allows the algorithm to be understood and verified one page at a time.

If the module embodies a physical model (i.e., a set of equations that allows us to compute nonobservables from observables), the model must be described and its limitations documented.

If the module performs numerical calculations in which accuracy will be a concern, numerical analysis justifying the design must be included.

If the module is hardware-dependent, the documentation must include either a description of the hardware or a reference to such a description.

If the module is responsible for certain parts of the functional specification, a cross reference must be provided.

The reviewers of each internal module design document will include experienced software engineers and other specialists. For example, if a physical model is involved, a physicist or engineer with expertise in that area must be included as a reviewer. If the information is presented in a notation that is independent of the programming language, none of the reviewers needs to be an expert in the programming language involved. Numerical analysts will be needed for some modules, device specialists for others.

What documentation is required to review the code?

While it is important that the algorithms and data structures be appropriate to the task, this will be of little help if the actual code is not faithful to the abstract design. Because of the previous reviews, those who review the code do not need to examine the global design of the system. Instead, they examine the correspondence between the algorithms and the actual code. These reviewers must be experienced users of the hardware and compilers involved; of course, they must also understand the notation used to specify the algorithms.

What documentation is required for the Test Plan Review?

Although these reviews, if carried out rigorously, constitute a mathematical verification of the code, testing is still required. Sound testing requires that a test plan (a document describing the way test cases will be selected) be developed and approved in advance. In addition to the usual engineering practice of normal case and limiting case checks, it is important that the reliability of safety-critical systems be estimated by statistical methods. Reliability estimation requires statistically valid random testing; careful thought must be given to the distribution from which the test cases will be drawn. It is important for the distribution of inputs to be typical of situations in which the correct functioning of the system is critical. A more detailed discussion of statistical testing can be found in the upcoming section, Reliability Assessment for Safety-Critical Software.

The test plan should be described in a document that is not available to the designers. It should be reviewed by specialists in software testing, and specialists in the application area, who compare it with the requirements specification to make certain the test coverage is adequate.

Reviewing the relationship between these documents

The hierarchical process described is designed to allow reviews to be conducted in an orderly way, focusing on one issue at a time. To make this "separation of concerns" work, it is important that the required relationships between the documents be verified.

a. The module guide must show clearly that each of the mathematical functions described in the re-

quirements specification is the responsibility of a specific module. There must be no ambiguity about the responsibilities of the various modules. The module specifications must be consistent with the module guide and the requirements specification.

b. Each module design document should include argumentation showing that the internal design satisfies the module specification. If the module specification is mathematical [18], mathematical verification of the design correctness is possible [11].

c. The module design document, which describes the algorithms, must be clearly mapped onto the code. The algorithms may be described in an abstract notation or via hierarchically structured diagrams.

d. The test plan must show how the tests are derived and how they cover the requirements. The test plan must include black box module tests as well as black box system tests.

Why is configuration management essential for rigorous reviews?

Because of the complexity of software, and the amount of detail that must be taken into consideration, there is always a tremendous amount of documentation. Some of the most troublesome software errors occur when documents are allowed to get out-of-date while their authors work with pencil notes on their own copies.

For the highly structured review process outlined earlier to succeed, all documents must be kept consistent when changes are made. If a document is changed, it, and all documents related to it, must be reviewed again. A careful review of the software may take weeks or months. Each reviewer must be certain that the documents given to him are consistent and up-to-date. The time and energy of reviewers should not be wasted, comparing different versions of the same document.

A process known in the profession as *configuration management*, supported by a configuration control mechanism, is needed to ensure that every designer and reviewer has the latest version of the documents and is informed of every change in a document that might affect the review.

We should be exploiting computer technology to make sure that programmers, designers, and reviewers do not need to retain paper copies of the documents at all. Instead, they use online documentation. If a change must be made, all who have used the affected document should be notified of the change by the computer system. When a change is being considered, but is not yet approved, users of the document should receive a warning. The online versions must be kept under strict control so they cannot be changed without authorization. Every page must contain a version identifier that makes it easier for a reviewer to verify that the documents he has used represent a consistent snapshot.

MODULAR STRUCTURE

Modern software engineering standards call for software to be organized in accordance with a principle known variously as "Information Hiding," "Object-Oriented Programming," "Separation of Concerns," "Encapsulation," "Data Abstraction," etc. This principle is designed to increase the cohesion of the modules while reducing the "coupling" between modules. Several new textbooks, well-known programming languages such as ADA, practical languages such as MESA, PROTEL, and MODULA, are designed to support such an organization.

Any large program must be organized into programmer work assignments known as modules. In information-hiding designs, each module hides a secret, a fact, or closely related set of facts, about the design that does not need to be known by the writers and reviewers of other modules. Each work assignment becomes much simpler than in an old-fashioned design because it can be completed and understood without knowing much about the other modules. When changes are needed, they do not ripple through an unpredictable number of other modules, as they frequently do in more conventional software designs.

A number of practical systems illustrate the benefits of information hiding even when the designers did not use that abstract principle but depended on their own intuition. For example, the widely used UNIX operating system gains much of its flexibility from hiding the difference between files and devices.

The thought of hiding information from others often strikes engineers as unnatural and wrong. In engineering projects, careful scrutiny by others working on the project is considered an important part of quality control. However, information hiding occurs naturally in large multidisciplinary projects. An electrical engineer may use a transformer without understanding its molecular structure or knowing the size of the bolts that fasten it to a chassis. The circuit designer works with a specification that specifies such abstractions as voltage ratio, hysteresis curve, and linearity. Designers of large mechanical structures work with abstract descriptions of the girders and other components, not with the detailed molecular structures that are the concern of materials engineers. Large engineering projects would be impossible if every engineer on the project had to be familiar with all the details of every component of the product.

Large software projects have the complexity of huge multidisciplinary projects, but there is only one discipline involved. Consequently, information hiding does not occur naturally and must be introduced as an engineering discipline. Software engineers should be trained to provide and use abstract mathematical specifications of components just as other engineers do.

The criterion of information hiding does not determine the software structure. Software engineers try to minimize the information that one programmer must have about another's work. They also try to minimize the expected cost of a system over the period of its use. Both information and expected cost are probabilistic measures. For maximum benefit, one should hide those details most likely to change but does not need to hide facts that are fundamental and unlikely to change. Further, decisions likely to be changed and reviewed together should be hidden in the same module. This implies that to apply the principle, one must make assumptions about the likelihood of various types of changes. If two designers apply the information-hiding principle, but make different assumptions about the likelihood of changes, they will come up with different structures.

RELIABILITY ASSESSMENT FOR SAFETY-CRITICAL SOFTWARE

Should we discuss the reliability of software at all?

Manufacturers, users, and regulatory agencies are often concerned about the reliability of systems that include software. Over many decades, reliability engineers have developed sophisticated methods of estimating the reliability of hardware systems based upon estimates of the reliability of their components. Software is often viewed as one of those components and an estimate of the reliability of that component is deemed essential to estimating the reliability of the overall system.

Reliability engineers are often misled by their experience with hardware. They are usually concerned with the reliability of devices that work correctly when new, but wear out and fail as they age. In other cases, they are concerned with mass-produced components where manufacturing techniques introduce defects that affect only a small fraction of the devices. Neither of these situations applies to software. Software does not wear out, and the errors introduced when software is copied have not been found to be significant.

As a result of these differences, it is not uncommon to see reliability assessments for large systems based on an estimated software reliability of 1.0. Reliability engineers argue that the correctness of a software product is not a probabilistic phenomenon. The software is either correct (reliability 1.0) or incorrect (reliability 0). If they assume a reliability of 0, they cannot get a useful reliability estimate for the system containing the software. Consequently, they assume correctness. Many consider it nonsense to talk about "reliability of software."

Nonetheless, our practical experience is that software appears to exhibit stochastic properties. It is quite useful to associate reliability figures such as MTBF (Mean Time Between Failures) with an operating system or other software product. Some software experts attribute the apparently random behavior to our ignorance. They believe that all software failures would be predictable if we fully understood the software, but our failure to understand our own creations justifies the treatment of software failures as random. However, we know that if we studied the software long enough, we could obtain a complete description of its response to inputs. Even then, it would be useful to talk about the MTBF of the product. Hence, ignorance should not satisfy us as a philosophical justification.

When a program first fails to function properly, it is because of an input sequence that had not occurred before. The reason that software appears to exhibit random behavior, and the reason that it is useful to talk about the MTBF of software, is because the input sequences are unpredictable. When we talk about the failure rate of a software product, we are predicting the probability of encountering an input sequence that will cause the product to fail.

Strictly speaking, we should not consider software as a component in systems at all. The software is simply the initial data in the computer and it is the initialized computer that is the component in question. However, in practice, the reliability of the hardware is high and failures caused by software errors dominate those caused by hardware problems.

What should we be measuring?

What we intuitively call "software reliability" is the probability of not encountering a sequence of inputs that leads to failure. If we could accurately characterize the sequences that lead to failure we would simply measure the distribution of input histories directly. Because of our ignorance of the actual properties of the software, we must use the software itself to measure the frequency with which failure-inducing sequences occur as inputs.

In safety-critical applications, particularly those for which a failure would be considered catastrophic, we may wish to take the position that design errors that would lead to failure are always unacceptable. In other technologies we would not put a system with a known design error in service. The complexity of software, and its consequent poor track record, means we seldom have confidence that software is free of serious design errors. Under those circumstances, we may wish to evaluate the probability that serious errors have been missed by our tests. This gives rise to our second probabilistic measure of software quality, *trustworthiness*.

In the sequel we shall refer to the probability that an input will not cause a failure as the reliability of the software. We shall refer to the probability that no serious design error remains after the software passes a set of randomly chosen tests as the trustworthiness of the software. We will discuss how to obtain estimates of both of these quantities.

Some discussions about software systems use the terms *availability* and *reliability* as if they were interchangeable. Availability usually refers to the fraction of time that the system is running and assumed to be ready to function. Availability can depend strongly on the time it takes to return a system to service once it has failed. If a system is truly safety-critical (e.g., a shutdown system in a nuclear power station), we would not depend on it during the time it was unavailable. The nuclear reactor would be taken out of service while its shutdown system was being repaired. Con-

sequently, reliability and availability can be quite different.

For systems that function correctly only in rare emergencies, we wish to measure the reliability in those situations where the system must take corrective action, and not include data from situations in which the system is not needed. The input sequence distributions used in reliability assessment should be those that one would encounter in emergency situations, and not those that characterize normal operation.

Much of the literature on software reliability is concerned with estimation and prediction of error-rates, the number of errors per line of code. For safety purposes, such rates are both meaningless and unimportant. Error counts are meaningless because we cannot find an objective way to count errors. We can count the number of lines in the code that are changed to eliminate a problem, but there usually are many ways to alleviate that problem. If each approach to repairing the problem involves a different number of lines (which is usually the case), the number of errors in the code is a subjective, often arbitrary, judgment. Error counts are unimportant because a program with a high error count is not necessarily less reliable than one with a low error count. In other words, even if we could count the number of errors, reliability is not a function of the error count. If asked to evaluate a safety-critical software product, there is no point in attempting to estimate or predict the number of errors remaining in a program.

Other portions of the literature are concerned with reliability growth models. These attempt to predict the reliability of the next (corrected) version on the basis of reliability data collected from previous versions. Most assume the failure rate is reduced whenever an error is corrected. They also assume the reductions in failure rates resulting from each correction are predictable. These assumptions are not justified by either theoretical or empirical studies of programs. Reliability growth models may be useful for management and scheduling purposes, but for safety-critical applications one must treat each modification of the program as a new program. Because even small changes can have major effects, we should consider data obtained from previous versions of the program to be irrelevant.

We cannot predict a software failure rate from failure rates for individual lines or subprograms.

The essence of system-reliability studies is the computation of the reliability of a large system when given the reliability of the parts. It is tempting to try to do the same thing for software, but the temptation should be resisted. The lines or statements of a program are not analogous to the components of a hardware system. The components of a hardware system function independently and simultaneously. The lines of a computer program function sequentially and the effect of one execution depends on the state that results from the earlier executions. One failure at one part of a program may lead to many problems elsewhere in the code.

When evaluating the reliability of a safety-critical software product, the only sound approach is to treat the whole computer, hardware and software, as a black box.

The finite state machine model of programs

The following discussion is based on the simplest and oldest model of digital computing. Used for more than 50 years, this model recognizes that every digital computer has a finite number of states and there are only a finite number of possible input and output signals at any moment in time. Each machine is described by two functions: *next-state*, and *output*. Both have a domain consisting of (state, input) pairs. The range of the next-state function is the set of states. The range of the output function is a set of symbols known as the output alphabet. These functions describe the behavior of a machine that starts in a specified initial state and periodically selects new states and outputs in accordance with the functions.

In this model, the software can be viewed as part of the initial data. It determines the initial state of the programmed machine. Von Neumann introduced a machine architecture in which program and data could be intermixed. Practicing programmers know they can always replace code with data or vice versa. It does not make sense to deal with the program and data as if they were different.

In effect, loading a program in the machine selects a terminal submachine consisting of all states that can be reached from the initial state. The software can be viewed as a finite state machine described by two very large tables. This model of software allows us to define what we mean by the number of faults in the software; it is the number of entries in the table that specify behavior that would be considered unacceptable. This fault count has no simple relation to the number of errors made by the programmer or the number of statements that must be corrected to remove the faults. It serves only to help us to determine the number of tests that we need to perform.

Use of hypothesis testing

In most safety-critical applications we do not need to know the actual probability of failure; we need to confirm the failure probability is very likely to be below a specified upper bound. We propose to run random tests on the software, checking the result of each test. Since we are concerned with safety-critical software, if a test fails (i.e., reveals an error in the software), we will change the software in a way that we believe will correct the error. We will again begin random testing. We will continue such tests until we have sufficient data to convince us that the probability of a failure is acceptably low. Because we can execute only a very small fraction of the conceivable tests, we can never be sure that the probability of failure is low enough. We can, however, calculate the probability that a product with unacceptable reliability would have passed the test that we have carried out.

TABLE I. Probability That a System With Failure Probability of .001 Will Pass N Successive Tests

h=1000.	
N	M= (1 - 1/h)^N
500	0.60638
600	0.54865
700	0.49641
800	0.44915
900	0.40639
1000	0.3670
1500	0.22296
2000	0.13520
2500	0.08198
3000	0.04971
3500	0.03014
4000	0.01828
4500	0.01108
4700	0.00907
5000	0.00672

Let us assume the probability of a failure in a test of a program is $1/h$ (i.e., the reliability is $1 - 1/h$). Assuming that N randomly selected tests (chosen, with replacement, from a distribution that corresponds to the actual usage of the program) are performed, the probability there will be no failure encountered during the testing is

$$(1 - 1/h)^N = M. \qquad (1)$$

In other words, if we want the failure probability to be less than $1/h$, and we have run N tests without failure, the probability that an unacceptable product would pass our test is no higher than M. We must continue testing, without failure, until N is large enough to make M acceptably low. We could then make statements like, "the probability that a product with reliability worse than .999 would pass this test is less than one in a hundred." Table I provides some sample values of M for $h = 1000$ and various values of N.

Table I shows that, if our design target was to have the probability of failure be less than 1 in 1000, performing between 4500 and 5000 tests (randomly chosen from the appropriate test case distribution) without failure would mean that the probability of an unacceptable product passing the test was less than 1 in a hundred.

Because the probability of failure in practice is a function of the distribution of cases encountered in practice, the validity of this approach depends on the distribution of cases in the tests being typical of the distribution of cases encountered in practice.

We can consider using the same approach to obtain a measure of the trustworthiness of a program. Let the total number of cases from which we select tests be C. Assume we consider it unacceptable if F of those cases results in faulty behavior; (F might be 1). By substituting F/C for $1/h$ we obtain

$$(1 - F/C)^N = M. \qquad (2)$$

We now assume that we have carried out N randomly selected tests without finding an error. If, during that testing, we had found an error, we would have corrected the problem and started again. We can estimate the value of C, and must determine whether to use $F = 1$ or some higher value. We might pick a higher number if we thought it unlikely that there would be only 1 faulty (state, input) pair. In most computer programs, a programming error would result in many faulty pairs, and calculations using $F = 1$ are unnecessarily pessimistic. After choosing F, we can determine M as above. (F, M) pairs provide a measure of trustworthiness. Note that systems considered trustworthy would have relatively low values of M and F.

As a result of such tests we could make statements like, "The probability that a program with more than five unacceptable cases would pass this test is one in a hundred." Since we are not concerned with the frequency of failure of those cases in practice, the tests should be chosen from a distribution in which all state input combinations are equally likely. Because C is almost always large and F relatively small, it is not practical to evaluate trustworthiness by means of testing. Trustworthiness, in the sense that we have defined it here, must be obtained by means of formal, rigorous inspections.

It is common to try to achieve high reliability by using two or more programs in an arrangement that will be safe if one of their specified subsets fails. For example, one could have two safety systems and make sure that each one could alone take the necessary actions in an emergency. If the system failures are statistically independent, the probability of the joint system failing is the product of the probability of individual failures. Unfortunately, repeated experiments have shown that, even when the programs for the two systems are developed independently, the failures are correlated [6, 7, 8]. As a result, we should evaluate the probability of joint failure experimentally.

The hypothesis testing approach can be applied to the evaluation of the probability of joint failures of two (or more) systems. Both systems must be subjected to the same set of test conditions. Joint failures can be detected. However, because the permitted probability of failures for joint systems is much lower than for single systems, many more tests will be needed. Table II shows some typical values.

In this table, we have been quite vague about the nature of a single test and have focused on how many tests are needed. Next we will discuss what constitutes a test and how to select one or more tests.

Three classes of programs

The simplest class of programs to test comprises

TABLE II. Probability That a System With Failure Probability of .000001 Will Pass N Successive Tests

\multicolumn{2}{c}{$h = 1000000.$}		\multicolumn{2}{c}{$h = 1000000.$}	
N	$M = (1 - 1/h)^N$	N	$M = (1 - 1/h)^N$
1000000.	0.36788	4000000.	0.01832
2000000.	0.13534	4100000.	0.01657
3000000.	0.04979	4200000.	0.01500
4000000.	0.01832	4300000.	0.01357
5000000.	0.00674	4400000.	0.01228
6000000.	0.00248	4500000.	0.01111
7000000.	0.00091	4600000.	0.01005
8000000.	0.00034	4700000.	0.00910
9000000.	0.00012	4800000.	0.00823
10000000.	0.00005	4900000.	0.00745

those that terminate after each use and retain no data from one run to the next. These memoryless batch programs are provided with data, executed, and return an answer that is independent of any data provided in earlier executions.

A second class consists of batch programs that retain data from one run to the next. The behavior of such programs on the nth run can depend on data supplied in any previous run.

A third class contains programs that appear to run continuously. Often these real-time programs are intended to emulate or replace analogue equipment. They consist of one or more processes; some of those processes run periodically, others run sporadically in response to external events. One cannot identify discrete runs, and the behavior at any time may depend on events arbitrarily far in the past.

Reliability estimates for memoryless batch programs: For memoryless batch programs a test consists of a single run using a randomly selected set of input data. If we are concerned with a system required to take action in rare circumstances, and one in which action in other circumstances is inconvenient rather than unsafe, the population of possible test cases should be restricted to those in which the system should take action. It is essential that one know the reliability under those circumstances. Of course, additional tests can be conducted, using other data, to determine the probability of action being taken when no action is required.

Reliability estimates for batch programs with memory: When a batch program has memory, a test consists of a single run. However, a test case is selected by choosing both input data and an internal state. For reliability estimates, the distribution of internal states must match that encountered in practice. It is often more difficult to determine the appropriate distribution of internal states than to find the distribution of inputs. Determining the distribution of internal states requires an understanding of, and experience with, the program.

An alternative to selecting internal states for the test would be to have each test consist of a sequence of executions. The system must be reinitialized before each new sequence. Again, the distribution of these cases must match that found in practice if the reliability estimates are to be meaningful. In addition, it is difficult to determine the length of those sequences. The sequences must be longer than the longest sequence that would occur in actual use. If the sequences are not long enough, the distribution of internal states that occur during the test may be badly skewed. In effect, this means that in actual use, the system must be reinitialized frequently so that an upper bound can be placed on the length of each test.

Reliability estimates for real-time systems: In real-time systems, the concept of a batch run does not apply. Because the real-time system is intended to simulate or replace an analogue system, the concept of an input sequence must be replaced by a multidimensional trajectory. Each such trajectory gives the input values as continuous functions of time. Each test involves a simulation in which the software can sample the inputs for the length of that trajectory.

The question of the length of the trajectory is critical in determining whether or not statistical testing is practical. In many computer systems there are states that can arise only after long periods of time. Reliability estimates derived from tests involving short trajectories will not be valid for systems that have been operating for longer periods. On the other hand, if one selects lengthy trajectories, the testing time required is likely to be impractical.

Statistical testing can be made practical if the system design is such that one can limit the length of the trajectories without invalidating the tests. To do this, one must partition the state. A small amount of the memory is reserved for data that must be retained for arbitrary amounts of time. The remaining data are reinitialized periodically. The length of the period becomes the length of the test trajectory. Testing can then proceed as if the program were a batch program with (memory-state, trajectory) pairs replacing input sequences.

If the long-term memory has a small number of states, it is best to perform statistically significant tests for each of those states. If that is impractical, one must select the states randomly in accordance with a predicted distribution. In many applications, the long-term memory corresponds to operating modes and a valid distribution can be determined.

Picking test cases for safety-critical real-time systems

Particular attention must be paid to trajectory selection if the system is required to act only in rare circumstances. Since the reliability is a function of the input distribution, the trajectories must be selected to provide accurate estimates under the conditions where performance matters. In other words, the population from which trajectories are drawn must include only trajectories in which the system must take action. Similarly,

the states of the long-term memory should be restricted to those in which the system will be critical to safety.

Determining the population of trajectories from which the tests are selected can be the most difficult part of the process. It is important to use one's knowledge of the physical situation to define a set of trajectories that can occur. Tests on impossible trajectories are not likely to lead to accurate reliability estimates. However, there is always the danger that the model used to determine these trajectories overlooks the same situation overlooked by the programmer who introduced a serious bug. It is important that any model used to eliminate *impossible* trajectories be developed independently of the program. Most safety experts would feel more comfortable if, in addition to the tests using trajectories considered possible, some statistical tests were conducted with *crazy* trajectories.

CONCLUSIONS

There is no inherent reason that software cannot be used in certain safety-critical applications, but extreme discipline in design, documentation, testing, and review is needed. It is essential that the operating conditions and requirements be well understood, and fully documented. If these conditions are not met, adequate review and testing are impossible.

The system must be structured in accordance with information hiding to make it easier to understand, review, and repair. The documentation must be complete and precise, making use of mathematical notation rather than natural language. Each stage of the design must be reviewed by independent reviewers with the specialized knowledge needed at that stage. Mathematical verification techniques must be used to make the review systematic and rigorous.

An independent agency must perform statistically valid random testing to provide estimates of the reliability of the system in critical situations. Deep knowledge and experience with the application area will be needed to determine the distribution from which the test cases should be drawn.

The vast literature on random testing is, for the most part, not relevant for safety evaluations. Because we are not interested in estimating the error rates or conducting reliability growth studies, a very simple model suffices. Hypothesis testing will allow us to evaluate the probability that the system meets our requirements. Testing to estimate reliability is only practical if a real-time system has limited long-term memory.

Testing to estimate trustworthiness is rarely practical because the number of tests required is usually quite large. Trustworthiness must be assured by the use of rigorous mathematical techniques in the review process.

The safety and trustworthiness of the system will rest on a tripod made up of testing, mathematical review, and certification of personnel and process. In this article, we have focused on two of those legs, testing and review based on mathematical documentation. The third leg will be the most difficult to implement. While there are authorities that certify professional engineers in other areas, there is no corresponding authority in software engineering. We have found that both classical engineers and computer science graduates are ill-prepared for this type of work. In the long term, those who are concerned about the use of software in safety-critical applications will have to develop appropriate educational programs [15].

Acknowledgments. Conversations with many people have helped to develop these observations. Among them are William Howden, Harlan Mills, Jim Kendall, Nancy Leveson. B. Natvik, and Kurt Asmis. In addition, we are thankful to the anonymous *Communications* referees and the editor for their constructive suggestions.

REFERENCES
1. Britton, K., and Parnas, D. A-7E software module guide. NRL Memo. Rep. 4702, December 1981.
2. Clements, P., Faulk, S., and Parnas, D. Interface specifications for the SCR (A-7E) application data types module. NRL Rep. 8734, August 23, 1983.
3. Currit, P.A., Dyer, M., and Mills, H.D. Certifying the reliability of software. *IEEE Trans. Softw. Eng. SE-12,* 1 (Jan. 1986).
4. Heninger, K. Specifying software requirements for complex systems: New techniques and their applications. *IEEE Trans. Softw. Eng. SE-6,* (Jan. 1980), 2–13.
5. Hester, S.D., Parnas, D.L., and Utter, D.F. Using documentation as a software design medium. *Bell Syst. Tech. J. 60,* 8 (Oct. 1981), 1941–1977.
6. Knight, J.C., and Leveson, N.G. An experimental evaluation of the assumption of independence in multi-version programming. *IEEE Trans. Softw. Eng. SE-12,* 1 (Jan. 1986), 96–109.
7. Knight, J.C., and Leveson, N.G. An empirical study of failure probabilities in multi-version software. Rep.
8. Leveson, N. Software safety: Why, what and how. *ACM Comp. Surveys 18,* 2 (June 1986), 125–163.
9. Mills, H.D. Engineering discipline for software procurement. COMPASS '87—Computer Assurance, June 29–July 3, 1987. Georgetown University, Washington, D.C.
10. Mills, H.D. The new math of computer programming. *Commun. ACM 18,* 1 (Jan. 1975), 43–48.
11. Mills, H.D., Basili, V.R., Gannon, J.D., and Hamlet, R.G. *Principles of Computer Programming—A Mathematical Approach.* Allyn and Bacon, Inc., 1987.
12. Mills, H.D., and Dyer, M. A formal approach to software error removal. *J. Syst. Softw.* (1987).
13. Mills, H.D., Linger, R.C., and Witt, B.I. *Structured Programming: Theory and Practice.* Addison-Wesley, Reading, Mass., 1979.
14. Parker, A., Heninger, K., Parnas, D., and Shore, J. Abstract interface specifications for the A-7E device interface module. NRL Memo. Rep. 4385, November 20, 1980.
15. Parnas, D.L. Education for computing professionals. *IEEE Comp. 23,* 1 (Jan. 1990), 17–22.
16. Parnas, D.L., and Clements, P.C. A rational design process: How and why to fake it. *IEEE Trans. Softw. Eng. SE-12,* 2 (Feb. 1986), 251–257.
17. Parnas, D.L., Heninger, K., Kallander, J., and Shore, J. Software requirements for the A-7E aircraft. NRL Rep. 3876, November 1978.
18. Parnas, D.L., and Wang, Y. The Trace assertion method of module-interface specification. Tech. Rep. 89-261, Queen's University, TRIO (Telecommunications Research Institute of Ontario). October 1989.
19. Parnas, D.L., and Weiss, D.M. Active design reviews: Principles and Practices. In *Proceedings of the 8th International Conference on Software Engineering* (London, August 1985).

An Investigation of the Therac-25 Accidents

Nancy G. Leveson, University of Washington

Clark S. Turner, University of California, Irvine

C omputers are increasingly being introduced into safety-critical systems and, as a consequence, have been involved in accidents. Some of the most widely cited software-related accidents in safety-critical systems involved a computerized radiation therapy machine called the Therac-25. Between June 1985 and January 1987, six known accidents involved massive overdoses by the Therac-25 — with resultant deaths and serious injuries. They have been described as the worst series of radiation accidents in the 35-year history of medical accelerators.[1]

With information for this article taken from publicly available documents, we present a detailed accident investigation of the factors involved in the overdoses and the attempts by the users, manufacturers, and the US and Canadian governments to deal with them. Our goal is to help others learn from this experience, not to criticize the equipment's manufacturer or anyone else. The mistakes that were made are not unique to this manufacturer but are, unfortunately, fairly common in other safety-critical systems. As Frank Houston of the US Food and Drug Administration (FDA) said, "A significant amount of software for life-critical systems comes from small firms, especially in the medical device industry; firms that fit the profile of those resistant to or uninformed of the principles of either system safety or software engineering."[2]

Furthermore, these problems are not limited to the medical industry. It is still a common belief that any good engineer can build software, regardless of whether he or she is trained in state-of-the-art software-engineering procedures. Many companies building safety-critical software are not using proper procedures from a software-engineering and safety-engineering perspective.

Most accidents are system accidents; that is, they stem from complex interactions between various components and activities. To attribute a single cause to an accident is usually a serious mistake. In this article, we hope to demonstrate the complex nature of accidents and the need to investigate all aspects of system development and operation to understand what has happened and to prevent future accidents.

Despite what can be learned from such investigations, fears of potential liability

A thorough account of the Therac-25 medical electron accelerator accidents reveals previously unknown details and suggests ways to reduce risk in the future.

Reprinted from *IEEE Computer*, Vol. 26, No. 7, pp. 18–41, July 1993.

or loss of business make it difficult to find out the details behind serious engineering mistakes. When the equipment is regulated by government agencies, some information may be available. Occasionally, major accidents draw the attention of the US Congress or President and result in formal accident investigations (for instance, the Rogers commission investigation of the Challenger accident and the Kemeny commission investigation of the Three Mile Island incident).

The Therac-25 accidents are the most serious computer-related accidents to date (at least nonmilitary and admitted) and have even drawn the attention of the popular press. (Stories about the Therac-25 have appeared in trade journals, newspapers, *People Magazine*, and on television's *20/20* and *McNeil/ Lehrer News Hour*.) Unfortunately, the previous accounts of the Therac-25 problems have been oversimplified, with misleading omissions.

In an effort to remedy this, we have obtained information from a wide variety of sources, including lawsuits and the US and Canadian government agencies responsible for regulating such equipment. We have tried to be very careful to present only what we could document from original sources, but there is no guarantee that the documentation itself is correct. When possible, we looked for multiple confirming sources for the more important facts.

We have tried not to bias our description of the accidents, but it is difficult not to filter unintentionally what is described. Also, we were unable to investigate firsthand or get information about some aspects of the accidents that may be very relevant. For example, detailed information about the manufacturer's software development, management, and quality control was unavailable. We had to infer most information about these from statements in correspondence or other sources.

As a result, our analysis of the accidents may omit some factors. But the facts available support previous hypotheses about the proper development and use of software to control dangerous processes and suggest hypotheses that need further evaluation. Following our account of the accidents and the responses of the manufacturer, government agencies, and users, we present what we believe are the most compelling lessons to be learned in the context of software engineering, safety engineering, and government and user standards and oversight.

Genesis of the Therac-25

Medical linear accelerators (linacs) accelerate electrons to create high-energy beams that can destroy tumors with minimal impact on the surrounding healthy tissue. Relatively shallow tissue is treated with the accelerated electrons; to reach deeper tissue, the electron beam is converted into X-ray photons.

In the early 1970s, Atomic Energy of Canada Limited (AECL) and a French company called CGR collaborated to build linear accelerators. (AECL is an arms-length entity, called a crown corporation, of the Canadian government. Since the time of the incidents related in this article, AECL Medical, a division of AECL, is in the process of being privatized and is now called Theratronics International Limited. Currently, AECL's primary business is the design and installation of nuclear reactors.) The products of AECL and CGR's cooperation were (1) the Therac-6, a 6 million electron volt (MeV) accelerator capable of producing X rays only and, later, (2) the Therac-20, a 20-MeV dual-mode (X rays or electrons) accelerator. Both were versions of older CGR machines, the Neptune and Sagittaire, respectively, which were augmented with computer control using a DEC PDP 11 minicomputer.

Software functionality was limited in both machines: The computer merely added convenience to the existing hardware, which was capable of standing alone. Industry-standard hardware safety features and interlocks in the underlying machines were retained. We know that some old Therac-6 software routines were used in the Therac-20 and that CGR developed the initial software.

The business relationship between AECL and CGR faltered after the Therac-20 effort. Citing competitive pressures, the two companies did not renew their cooperative agreement when scheduled in 1981. In the mid-1970s, AECL developed a radical new "double-pass" concept for electron acceleration. A double-pass accelerator needs much less space to develop comparable energy levels because it folds the long physical mechanism required to accelerate the electrons, and it is more economic to produce (since it uses a magnetron rather than a klystron as the energy source).

Using this double-pass concept, AECL designed the Therac-25, a dual-mode linear accelerator that can deliver either photons at 25 MeV or electrons at various energy levels (see Figure 1). Compared with the Therac-20, the Therac-25 is notably more compact, more versatile, and arguably easier to use. The higher energy takes advantage of the phenomenon of "depth dose": As

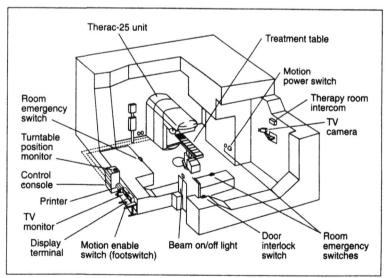

Figure 1. Typical Therac-25 facility.

the energy increases, the depth in the body at which maximum dose buildup occurs also increases, sparing the tissue above the target area. Economic advantages also come into play for the customer, since only one machine is required for both treatment modalities (electrons and photons).

Several features of the Therac-25 are important in understanding the accidents. First, like the Therac-6 and the Therac-20, the Therac-25 is controlled by a PDP 11. However, AECL designed the Therac-25 to take advantage of computer control from the outset; AECL did not build on a stand-alone machine. The Therac-6 and Therac-20 had been designed around machines that already had histories of clinical use without computer control.

In addition, the Therac-25 software has more responsibility for maintaining safety than the software in the previous machines. The Therac-20 has independent protective circuits for monitoring electron-beam scanning, plus mechanical interlocks for policing the machine and ensuring safe operation. The Therac-25 relies more on software for these functions. AECL took advantage of the computer's abilities to control and monitor the hardware and decided not to duplicate all the existing hardware safety mechanisms and interlocks. This approach is becoming more common as companies decide that hardware interlocks and backups are not worth the expense, or they put more faith (perhaps misplaced) on software than on hardware reliability.

Finally, some software for the machines was interrelated or reused. In a letter to a Therac-25 user, the AECL quality assurance manager said, "The same Therac-6 package was used by the AECL software people when they started the Therac-25 software. The Therac-20 and Therac-25 software programs were done independently, starting from a common base." Reuse of Therac-6 design features or modules may explain some of the problematic aspects of the Therac-25 software (see the sidebar "Therac-25 software development and design"). The quality assurance manager was apparently unaware that some Therac-20 routines were also used in the Therac-25; this was discovered after a bug related to one of the Therac-25 accidents was found in the Therac-20 software.

AECL produced the first hardwired prototype of the Therac-25 in 1976, and the completely computerized commercial version was available in late 1982. (The sidebars provide details about the machine's design and controlling software, important in understanding the accidents.)

In March 1983, AECL performed a safety analysis on the Therac-25. This analysis was in the form of a fault tree

Therac-25 software development and design

We know that the software for the Therac-25 was developed by a single person, using PDP 11 assembly language, over a period of several years. The software "evolved" from the Therac-6 software, which was started in 1972. According to a letter from AECL to the FDA, the "program structure and certain subroutines were carried over to the Therac 25 around 1976."

Apparently, very little software documentation was produced during development. In a 1986 internal FDA memo, a reviewer lamented, "Unfortunately, the AECL response also seems to point out an apparent lack of documentation on software specifications and a software test plan."

The manufacturer said that the hardware and software were "tested and exercised separately or together over many years." In his deposition for one of the lawsuits, the quality assurance manager explained that testing was done in two parts. A "small amount" of software testing was done on a simulator, but most testing was done as a system. It appears that unit and software testing was minimal, with most effort directed at the integrated system test. At a Therac-25 user group meeting, the same quality assurance manager said that the Therac-25 software was tested for 2,700 hours. Under questioning by the users, he clarified this as meaning "2,700 hours of use."

The programmer left AECL in 1986. In a lawsuit connected with one of the accidents, the lawyers were unable to obtain information about the programmer from AECL. In the depositions connected with that case, none of the AECL employees questioned could provide any information about his educational background or experience. Although an attempt was made to obtain a deposition from the programmer, the lawsuit was settled before this was accomplished. We have been unable to learn anything about his background.

AECL claims proprietary rights to its software design. However, from voluminous documentation regarding the accidents, the repairs, and the eventual design changes, we can build a rough picture of it.

The software is responsible for monitoring the machine status, accepting input about the treatment desired, and setting the machine up for this treatment. It turns the beam on in response to an operator command (assuming that certain operational checks on the status of the physical machine are satisfied) and also turns the beam off when treatment is completed, when an operator commands it, or when a malfunction is detected. The operator can print out hard-copy versions of the CRT display or machine setup parameters.

The treatment unit has an interlock system designed to remove power to the unit when there is a hardware malfunction. The computer monitors this interlock system and provides diagnostic messages. Depending on the fault, the computer either prevents a treatment from being started or, if the treatment is in progress, creates a pause or a suspension of the treatment.

The manufacturer describes the Therac-25 software as having a stand-alone, real-time treatment operating system. The system is not built using a standard operating system or executive. Rather, the real-time executive was written especially for the Therac-25 and runs on a 32K PDP 11/23. A preemptive scheduler allocates cycles to the critical and noncritical tasks.

The software, written in PDP 11 assembly language, has four major components: stored data, a scheduler, a set of critical and noncritical tasks, and interrupt services. The stored data includes calibration parameters for the accelerator setup as well as patient-treatment data. The interrupt routines include and apparently excluded the software. According to the final report, the analysis made several assumptions:

(1) Programming errors have been reduced by extensive testing on a hardware simulator and under field conditions on teletherapy units. Any residual software errors are not included in the analysis.
(2) Program software does not degrade due to wear, fatigue, or reproduction process.
(3) Computer execution errors are caused by faulty hardware components and by "soft" (random) errors induced by alpha particles and electromagnetic noise.

The fault tree resulting from this analysis does appear to include computer failure, although apparently, judging from these assumptions, it considers only hardware failures. For example, in one OR gate leading to the event of getting the wrong energy, a box contains "Computer selects wrong energy" and a probability of 10^{-11} is assigned to this event.

For "Computer selects wrong mode," a probability of 4×10^{-9} is given. The report provides no justification of either number.

Accident history

Eleven Therac-25s were installed: five in the US and six in Canada. Six accidents involving massive overdoses to patients occurred between 1985 and 1987. The machine was recalled in 1987 for extensive design changes, including hardware safeguards against software errors.

Related problems were found in the Therac-20 software. These were not recognized until after the Therac-25 accidents because the Therac-20 included hardware safety interlocks and thus no injuries resulted.

In this section, we present a chronological account of the accidents and the responses from the manufacturer, government regulatory agencies, and users.

Kennestone Regional Oncology Center, 1985. Details of this accident in Marietta, Georgia, are sketchy since it was never carefully investigated. There was no admission that the injury was caused by the Therac-25 until long after the occurrence, despite claims by the patient that she had been injured during treatment, the obvious and severe radiation burns the patient suffered, and the suspicions of the radiation physicist involved.

After undergoing a lumpectomy to remove a malignant breast tumor, a 61-year-old woman was receiving follow-up radiation treatment to nearby lymph nodes on a Therac-25 at the Kennestone facility in Marietta. The Therac-25 had been operating at Kennestone for about six months; other Therac-25s

---

- a clock interrupt service routine,
- a scanning interrupt service routine,
- traps (for software overflow and computer-hardware-generated interrupts),
- power up (initiated at power up to initialize the system and pass control to the scheduler),
- treatment console screen interrupt handler,
- treatment console keyboard interrupt handler,
- service printer interrupt handler, and
- service keyboard interrupt handler.

The scheduler controls the sequences of all noninterrupt events and coordinates all concurrent processes. Tasks are initiated every 0.1 second, with the critical tasks executed first and the noncritical tasks executed in any remaining cycle time. Critical tasks include the following:

- The treatment monitor (Treat) directs and monitors patient setup and treatment via eight operating phases. These are called as subroutines, depending on the value of the Tphase control variable. Following the execution of a particular subroutine, Treat reschedules itself. Treat interacts with the keyboard processing task, which handles operator console communication. The prescription data is cross-checked and verified by other tasks (for example, the keyboard processor and the parameter setup sensor) that inform the treatment task of the verification status via shared variables.
- The servo task controls gun emission, dose rate (pulse-repetition frequency), symmetry (beam steering), and machine motions. The servo task also sets up the machine parameters and monitors the beam-tilt-error and the flatness-error interlocks.

- The housekeeper task takes care of system-status interlocks and limit checks, and puts appropriate messages on the CRT display. It decodes some information and checks the setup verification.

Noncritical tasks include

- Check sum processor (scheduled to run periodically).
- Treatment console keyboard processor (scheduled to run only if it is called by other tasks or by keyboard interrupts). This task acts as the interface between the software and the operator.
- Treatment console screen processor (run periodically). This task lays out appropriate record formats for either displays or hard copies.
- Service keyboard processor (run on demand). This task arbitrates non-treatment-related communication between the therapy system and the operator.
- Snapshot (run periodically by the scheduler). Snapshot captures preselected parameter values and is called by the treatment task at the end of a treatment.
- Hand-control processor (run periodically).
- Calibration processor. This task is responsible for a package of tasks that let the operator examine and change system setup parameters and interlock limits.

It is clear from the AECL documentation on the modifications that the software allows concurrent access to shared memory, that there is no real synchronization aside from data stored in shared variables, and that the "test" and "set" for such variables are not indivisible operations. Race conditions resulting from this implementation of multitasking played an important part in the accidents.

Major event time line

had been operating, apparently without incident, since 1983.

On June 3, 1985, the patient was set up for a 10-MeV electron treatment to the clavicle area. When the machine turned on, she felt a "tremendous force of heat ... this red-hot sensation." When the technician came in, the patient said, "You burned me." The technician replied that that was not possible. Although there were no marks on the patient at the time, the treatment area felt "warm to the touch."

It is unclear exactly when AECL learned about this incident. Tim Still, the Kennestone physicist, said that he contacted AECL to ask if the Therac-25 could operate in electron mode without scanning to spread the beam. Three days later, the engineers at AECL called the physicist back to explain that improper scanning was not possible.

In an August 19, 1986, letter from AECL to the FDA, the AECL quality assurance manager said, "In March of 1986, AECL received a lawsuit from the patient involved. . . This incident was never reported to AECL prior to this date, although some rather odd questions had been posed by Tim Still, the hospital physicist." The physicist at a hospital in Tyler, Texas, where a later accident occurred, reported, "According to Tim Still, the patient filed suit in October 1985 listing the hospital, manufacturer, and service organization responsible for the machine. AECL was notified informally about the suit by the hospital, and AECL received official notification of a lawsuit in November 1985."

Because of the lawsuit (filed on November 13, 1985), some AECL administrators must have known about the Marietta accident — although no investigation occurred at this time. Further comments by FDA investigators point to the lack of a mechanism in AECL to follow up reports of suspected accidents. The lack of follow-up in this case appears to be evidence of such a problem in the organization.

The patient went home, but shortly afterward she developed a reddening and swelling in the center of the treatment area. Her pain had increased to the point that her shoulder "froze" and she experienced spasms. She was admitted to West Paces Ferry Hospital in Atlanta, but her oncologists continued to send her to Kennestone for Therac-25 treatments. Clinical explanation was sought for the reddening of the skin, which at first her oncologist attributed to her disease or to normal treatment reaction.

About two weeks later, the physicist at Kennestone noticed that the patient had a matching reddening on her back as though a burn had gone through her body, and the swollen area had begun to slough off layers of skin. Her shoulder was immobile, and she was apparently in great pain. It was obvious that she had a radiation burn, but the hospital and her doctors could provide no satisfactory explanation. Shortly afterward, she initiated a lawsuit against the hospital and AECL regarding her injury.

The Kennestone physicist later estimated that she received one or two doses of radiation in the 15,000- to 20,000-rad (radiation absorbed dose) range. He does not believe her injury could have been caused by less than 8,000 rads. Typical single therapeutic doses are in the 200-rad range. Doses of 1,000 rads can be fatal if delivered to the whole body; in fact, the accepted figure for whole-body radiation that will cause death in 50 percent of the cases is 500 rads. The consequences of an overdose to a smaller part of the body depend on the tissue's radiosensitivity. The director of radiation oncology at the Kennestone facility explained their confusion about the accident as due to the fact that they had never seen an overtreatment of that magnitude before.

Eventually, the patient's breast had to be removed because of the radiation burns. She completely lost the use of her shoulder and her arm, and was in constant pain. She had suffered a serious radiation burn, but the manufacturer and operators of the machine refused to believe that it could have been caused by the Therac-25. The treatment prescription printout feature was disabled at the time of the accident, so there was no hard copy of the treatment data. The lawsuit was eventually settled out of court.

From what we can determine, the accident was not reported to the FDA until *after* the later Tyler accidents in 1986 (described in later sections). The reporting regulations for medical device incidents at that time applied only to equipment manufacturers and importers, not users. The regulations required that manufacturers and importers report deaths, serious injuries, or malfunctions that could result in those consequences. Health-care professionals and institutions were not required to report incidents to manufacturers. (The law was amended in 1990 to require health-care facilities to report incidents to the manufacturer and the FDA.) The comptroller general of the US Government Accounting Office, in testimony before Congress on November 6, 1989, expressed great concern about the viability of the incident-reporting regulations in preventing or spotting medical-device problems. According to a GAO study, the FDA knows of less than 1 percent of deaths, serious injuries, or equipment malfunctions that occur in hospitals.[3]

At this point, the other Therac-25 users were unaware that anything untoward had occurred and did not learn about any problems with the machine until after subsequent accidents. Even then, most of their information came through personal communication among themselves.

Ontario Cancer Foundation, 1985. The second in this series of accidents occurred at this Hamilton, Ontario, Canada, clinic about seven weeks after the Kennestone patient was overdosed. At that time, the Therac-25 at the Hamilton clinic had been in use for more than six months. On July 26, 1985, a 40-year-old patient came to the clinic for her 24th Therac-25 treatment for carcinoma of the cervix. The operator activated the machine, but the Therac shut down after five seconds with an "H-tilt" error message. The Therac's dosimetry system display read "no dose" and indicated a "treatment pause."

Since the machine did not suspend and the control display indicated no dose was delivered to the patient, the operator went ahead with a second attempt at treatment by pressing the "P" key (the proceed command), expecting the machine to deliver the proper dose this time. This was standard operating procedure and, as described in the sidebar "The operator interface" on p. 24, Therac-25 operators had become accustomed to frequent malfunctions that had no untoward consequences for the patient. Again, the machine shut down in the same manner. The operator repeated this process four times after the original attempt — the display showing "no dose" delivered to the patient each time. After the fifth pause, the machine went into treatment suspend, and a hos- pital service technician was called. The technician found nothing wrong with the machine. This also was not an unusual scenario, according to a Therac-25 operator.

After the treatment, the patient complained of a burning sensation, described as an "electric tingling shock" to the treatment area in her hip. Six other patients were treated later that day without incident. The patient came back for further treatment on July 29 and complained of burning, hip pain, and excessive swelling in the region of treatment. The machine was taken out of service, as radiation overexposure was suspected. The patient was hospitalized for the condition on July 30. AECL was informed of the apparent radiation injury and sent a service engineer to investigate. The FDA, the then-Canadian Radiation Protection Bureau (CRPB), and the users were informed that there was a problem, although the users claim that they were never informed that a patient injury had occurred. (On April 1, 1986, the CRPB and the Bureau of Medical Devices were merged to form the Bureau of Radiation and Medical Devices or BRMD.) Users were told that they should visually confirm the turntable alignment until further notice (which occurred three months later).

The patient died on November 3, 1985, of an extremely virulent cancer. An autopsy revealed the cause of death as the cancer, but it was noted that had she not died, a total hip replacement would have been necessary as a result of the radiation overexposure. An AECL technician later estimated the patient had received between 13,000 and 17,000 rads.

Manufacturer response. AECL could not reproduce the malfunction that had occurred, but suspected a transient failure in the microswitch used to determine turntable position. During the investigation of the accident, AECL hardwired the error conditions they assumed were necessary for the malfunction and, as a result, found some design weaknesses and potential mechanical problems involving the turntable positioning.

The computer senses and controls turntable position by reading a 3-bit signal about the status of three microswitches in the turntable switch assembly (see the sidebar "Turntable positioning" on p. 25). Essentially, AECL determined that a 1-bit error in the mi-

The operator interface

In the main text, we describe changes made as a result of an FDA recall, and here we describe the operator interface of the software version used during the accidents.

The Therac-25 operator controls the machine with a DEC VT100 terminal. In the general case, the operator positions the patient on the treatment table, manually sets the treatment field sizes and gantry rotation, and attaches accessories to the machine. Leaving the treatment room, the operator returns to the VT100 console to enter the patient identification, treatment prescription (including mode, energy level, dose, dose rate, and time), field sizing, gantry rotation, and accessory data. The system then compares the manually set values with those entered at the console. If they match, a "verified" message is displayed and treatment is permitted. If they do not match, treatment is not allowed to proceed until the mismatch is corrected. Figure A shows the screen layout.

When the system was first built, operators complained that it took too long to enter the treatment plan. In response, the manufacturer modified the software before the first unit was installed so that, instead of reentering the data at the keyboard, operators could use a carriage return to merely copy the treatment site data.[1] A quick series of carriage returns would thus complete data entry. This interface modification was to figure in several accidents.

The Therac-25 could shut down in two ways after it detected an error condition. One was a *treatment suspend*, which required a complete machine reset to restart. The other, not so serious, was a *treatment pause*, which required only a single-key command to restart the machine. If a treatment pause occurred, the operator could press the "P" key to "proceed" and resume treatment quickly and conveniently. The previous treatment parameters remained in effect, and no reset was required. This convenient and simple feature could be invoked a maximum of five times before the machine automatically suspended treatment and required the operator to perform a system reset.

Error messages provided to the operator were cryptic,

and some merely consisted of the word "malfunction" followed by a number from 1 to 64 denoting an analog/digital channel number. According to an FDA memorandum written after one accident

> The operator's manual supplied with the machine does not explain nor even address the malfunction codes. The [Maintenance] Manual lists the various malfunction numbers but gives no explanation. The materials provided give *no* indication that these malfunctions could place a patient at risk.
>
> The program does not advise the operator if a situation exists wherein the ion chambers used to monitor the patient are saturated, thus are beyond the measurement limits of the instrument. This software package does not appear to contain a safety system to prevent parameters being entered and intermixed that would result in excessive radiation being delivered to the patient under treatment.

An operator involved in an overdose accident testified that she had become insensitive to machine malfunctions. Malfunction messages were commonplace — most did not involve patient safety. Service technicians would fix the problems or the hospital physicist would realign the machine and make it operable again. She said, "It was not out of the ordinary for something to stop the machine. . . It would often give a low dose rate in which you would turn the machine back on. . . They would give messages of low dose rate, V-tilt, H-tilt, and other things; I can't remember all the reasons it would stop, but there [were] a lot of them." The operator further testified that during instruction she had been taught that there were "so many safety mechanisms" that she understood it was virtually impossible to overdose a patient.

A radiation therapist at another clinic reported an average of 40 dose-rate malfunctions, attributed to underdoses, occurred on some days.

Reference

1. E. Miller, "The Therac-25 Experience," *Proc. Conf. State Radiation Control Program Directors*, 1987.

PATIENT NAME : TEST				A	1
TREATMENT MODE: FIX	BEAM TYPE: X	ENERGY (KeV):		25	
		ACTUAL	PRESCRIBED		
	UNIT RATE/MINUTE	0	200		
	MONITOR UNITS	50 50	200		
	TIME (MIN)	0.27	1.00		
GANTRY ROTATION (DEG)		0.0	0	VERIFIED	
COLLIMATOR ROTATION (DEG)		359.2	359	VERIFIED	
COLLIMATOR X (CM)		14.2	14.3	VERIFIED	
COLLIMATOR Y (CM)		27.2	27.3	VERIFIED	
WEDGE NUMBER		1	1	VERIFIED	
ACCESSORY NUMBER		0	0	VERIFIED	
DATE : 84-OCT-26	SYSTEM: BEAM READY		OP.MODE: TREAT	AUTO	
TIME : 12:55. 8	TREAT : TREAT PAUSE		X-RAY	173777	
OPR ID: T25VO2-RO3	REASON: OPERATOR		COMMAND:		

Figure A. Operator interface screen layout.

croswitch codes (which could be caused by a single open-circuit fault on the switch lines) could produce an ambiguous position message for the computer.

The problem was exacerbated by the design of the mechanism that extends a plunger to lock the turntable when it is in one of the three cardinal positions:

The plunger could be extended when the turntable was way out of position, thus giving a second false position indication. AECL devised a method to indi-

---

Turntable positioning

The Therac-25 turntable design is important in understanding the accidents. The upper turntable (see Figure B) is a rotating table, as the name implies. The turntable rotates accessory equipment into the beam path to produce two therapeutic modes: electron mode and photon mode. A third position (called the field-light position) involves no beam at all; it facilitates correct positioning of the patient.

Proper operation of the Therac-25 is heavily dependent on the turntable position; the accessories appropriate to each mode are physically attached to the turntable. The turntable position is monitored by three microswitches corresponding to the three cardinal turntable positions: electron beam, X ray, and field light. These microswitches are attached to the turntable and are engaged by hardware stops at the appropriate positions. The position of the turntable, sent to the computer as a 3-bit binary signal, is based on which of the three microswitches are depressed by the hardware stops.

The raw, highly concentrated accelerator beam is dangerous to living tissue. In electron therapy, the computer controls the beam energy (from 5 to 25 MeV) and current while scanning magnets spread the beam to a safe, therapeutic concentration. These scanning magnets are mounted on the turntable and moved into proper position by the computer. Similarly, an ion chamber to measure electrons is mounted on the turntable and also moved into position by the computer. In addition, operator-mounted electron trimmers can be used to shape the beam if necessary.

For X-ray therapy, only one energy level is available: 25 MeV. Much greater electron-beam current is required for photon mode (some 100 times greater than that for electron therapy)[1] to produce comparable output. Such a high dose-rate capability is required because a "beam flattener" is used to produce a uniform treatment field. This flattener, which resembles an inverted ice-cream cone, is a very efficient attenuator. To get a reasonable treatment dose rate out, a very high input dose rate is required. If the machine produces a photon beam with the beam flattener not in position, a high output dose rate results. This is the basic

hazard of dual-mode machines: If the turntable is in the wrong position, the beam flattener will not be in place.

In the Therac-25, the computer is responsible for positioning the turntable (and for checking turntable position) so that a target, flattening filter, and X-ray ion chamber are directly in the beam path. With the target in the beam path, electron bombardment produces X rays. The X-ray beam is shaped by the flattening filter and measured by the X-ray ion chamber.

No accelerator beam is expected in the field-light position. A stainless steel mirror is placed in the beam path and a light simulates the beam. This lets the operator see precisely where the beam will strike the patient and make necessary adjustments before treatment starts. There is no ion chamber in place at this turntable position, since no beam is expected.

Traditionally, electromechanical interlocks have been used on these types of equipment to ensure safety — in this case, to ensure that the turntable and attached equipment are in the correct position when treatment is started. In the Therac-25, software checks were substituted for many traditional hardware interlocks.

Reference

1. J.A. Rawlinson, "Report on the Therac-25," OCTRF/OCI Physicists Meeting, Kingston, Ont., Canada, May 7, 1987.

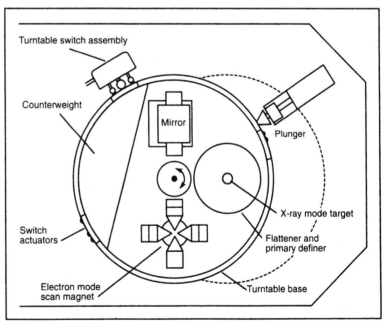

Figure B. Upper turntable assembly.

cate turntable position that tolerated a 1-bit error: The code would still unambiguously reveal correct position with any one microswitch failure.

In addition, AECL altered the software so that the computer checked for "in transit" status of the switches to keep further track of the switch operation and the turntable position, and to give additional assurance that the switches were working and the turntable was moving.

As a result of these improvements, AECL claimed in its report and correspondence with hospitals that "analysis of the hazard rate of the new solution indicates an improvement over the old system by at least five orders of magnitude." A claim that safety had been improved by five orders of magnitude seems exaggerated, especially given that in its final incident report to the FDA, AECL concluded that it "cannot be firm on the exact cause of the accident but can only suspect. . ." This underscores the company's inability to determine the cause of the accident with any certainty. The AECL quality assurance manager testified that AECL could not reproduce the switch malfunction and that testing of the microswitch was "inconclusive." The similarity of the errant behavior and the injuries to patients in this accident and a later one in Yakima, Washington, (attributed to software error) provide good reason to believe that the Hamilton overdose was probably related to software error rather than to a microswitch failure.

Government and user response. The Hamilton accident resulted in a voluntary recall by AECL, and the FDA termed it a Class II recall. Class II means "a situation in which the use of, or exposure to, a violative product may cause temporary or medically reversible adverse health consequences or where the probability of serious adverse health consequences is remote." Four users in the US were advised by a letter from AECL on August 1, 1985, to visually check the ionization chamber to make sure it was in its correct position in the collimator opening before any treatment and to discontinue treatment if they got an H-tilt message with an incorrect dose indicated. The letter did not mention that a patient injury was involved. The FDA audited AECL's subsequent modifications. After the modifications, the users were told that

they could return to normal operating procedures.

As a result of the Hamilton accident, the head of advanced X-ray systems in the CRPB, Gordon Symonds, wrote a report that analyzed the design and performance characteristics of the Therac-25 with respect to radiation safety. Besides citing the flawed microswitch, the report faulted both hardware and software components of the Therac's design. It concluded with a list of four modifications to the Therac-25 necessary for minimum compliance with Canada's Radiation Emitting Devices (RED) Act. The RED law, enacted in 1971, gives government officials power to ensure the safety of radiation-emitting devices.

The modifications recommended in the Symonds report included redesigning the microswitch and changing the way the computer handled malfunction conditions. In particular, treatment was to be terminated in the event of a dose-rate malfunction, giving a treatment "suspend." This would have removed the option to proceed simply by pressing the "P" key. The report also made recommendations regarding collimator test procedures and message and command formats. A November 8, 1985 letter signed by Ernest Létourneau, M.D., director of the CRPB, asked that AECL make changes to the Therac-25 based on the Symonds report "to be in compliance with the RED Act."

Although, as noted above, AECL did make the microswitch changes, it did not comply with the directive to change the malfunction pause behavior into treatment suspends, instead reducing the maximum number of retries from five to three. According to Symonds, the deficiencies outlined in the CRPB letter of November 8 were still pending when subsequent accidents five months later changed the priorities. If these later accidents had not occurred, AECL would have been compelled to comply with the requirements in the letter.

Immediately after the Hamilton accident, the Ontario Cancer Foundation hired an independent consultant to investigate. He concluded in a September 1985 report that an independent system (beside the computer) was needed to verify turntable position and suggested the use of a potentiometer. The CRPB wrote a letter to AECL in November 1985 requesting that AECL install such

an independent upper collimator positioning interlock on the Therac-25. Also, in January 1986, AECL received a letter from the attorney representing the Hamilton clinic. The letter said there had been continuing problems with the turntable, including four incidents at Hamilton, and requested the installation of an independent system (potentiometer) to verify turntable position. AECL did not comply: No independent interlock was installed on the Therac-25s at this time.

Yakima Valley Memorial Hospital, 1985. As with the Kennestone overdose, machine malfunction in this accident in Yakima, Washington, was not acknowledged until after later accidents were understood.

The Therac-25 at Yakima had been modified in September 1985 in response to the overdose at Hamilton. During December 1985, a woman came in for treatment with the Therac-25. She developed erythema (excessive reddening of the skin) in a parallel striped pattern at one port site (her right hip) after one of the treatments. Despite this, she continued to be treated by the Therac-25 because the cause of her reaction was not determined to be abnormal until January or February of 1986. On January 6, 1986, her treatments were completed.

The staff monitored the skin reaction closely and attempted to find possible causes. The open slots in the blocking trays in the Therac-25 could have produced such a striped pattern, but by the time the skin reaction had been determined to be abnormal, the blocking trays had been discarded. The blocking arrangement and tray striping orientation could not be reproduced. A reaction to chemotherapy was ruled out because that should have produced reactions at the other ports and would not have produced stripes. When it was discovered that the woman slept with a heating pad, a possible explanation was offered on the basis of the parallel wires that deliver the heat in such pads. The staff x-rayed the heating pad and discovered that the wire pattern did not correspond to the erythema pattern on the patient's hip.

The hospital staff sent a letter to AECL on January 31, and they also spoke on the phone with the AECL technical support supervisor. On February 24, 1986, the AECL technical support supervisor sent a written response to the director of radiation therapy at Yakima saying, "After careful consideration, we are of the opinion that this damage could not have been produced by any malfunction of the Therac-25 or by any operator error." The letter goes on to support this opinion by listing two pages of technical reasons why an overdose by the Therac-25 was impossible, along with the additional argument that there have "apparently been no other instances of similar damage to this or other patients." The letter ends, "In closing, I wish to advise that this matter has been brought to the attention of our Hazards Committee, as is normal practice."

The hospital staff eventually ascribed the skin/tissue problem to "cause unknown." In a report written on this first Yakima incident after another Yakima overdose a year later (described in a later section), the medical physicist involved wrote

> At that time, we did not believe that [the patient] was overdosed because the manufacturer had installed additional hardware and software safety devices to the accelerator.
>
> In a letter from the manufacturer dated 16-Sep-85, it is stated that "Analysis of the hazard rate resulting from these modifications indicates an improvement of at least five orders of magnitude"! With such an improvement in safety (10,000,000 percent) we did not believe that there could have been any accelerator malfunction. These modifications to the accelerator were completed on 5,6-Sep-85.

Even with fairly sophisticated physics support, the hospital staff, as users, did not have the ability to investigate the possibility of machine malfunction further. They were not aware of any other incidents, and, in fact, were told that there had been none, so there was no reason for them to pursue the matter. However, it seems that the fact that three similar incidents had occurred with this equipment should have triggered some suspicion and investigation by the manufacturer and the appropriate government agencies. This assumes, of course, that these incidents were all reported and known by AECL and by the government regulators. If they were not, then it is appropriate to ask why they were not and how this could be remedied in the future.

About a year later (in February 1987), after the second Yakima overdose led

the hospital staff to suspect that the first injury had been due to a Therac-25 fault, the staff investigated and found that this patient had a chronic skin ulcer, tissue necrosis (death) under the skin, and was in constant pain. This was surgically repaired, skin grafts were made, and the symptoms relieved. The patient is alive today, with minor disability and some scarring related to the overdose. The hospital staff concluded that the dose accidentally delivered to this patient must have been much lower than in the second accident, as the reaction was significantly less intense and necrosis did not develop until six to eight months after exposure. Some other factors related to the place on the body where the overdose occurred also kept her from having more significant problems as a result of the exposure.

East Texas Cancer Center, March 1986. More is known about the Tyler, Texas, accidents than the others because of the diligence of the Tyler hospital physicist, Fritz Hager, without whose efforts the understanding of the software problems might have been delayed even further.

The Therac-25 was at the East Texas Cancer Center (ETCC) for two years before the first serious accident occurred; during that time, more than 500 patients had been treated. On March 21, 1986, a male patient came into ETCC for his ninth treatment on the Therac-25, one of a series prescribed as follow-up to the removal of a tumor from his back.

The patient's treatment was to be a 22-MeV electron-beam treatment of 180 rads over a 10×17-cm field on the upper back and a little to the left of his spine, or a total of 6,000 rads over a period of 6 1/2 weeks. He was taken into the treatment room and placed face down on the treatment table. The operator then left the treatment room, closed the door, and sat at the control terminal.

The operator had held this job for some time, and her typing efficiency had increased with experience. She could quickly enter prescription data and change it conveniently with the Therac's editing features. She entered the patient's prescription data quickly, then noticed that for mode she had typed "x" (for X ray) when she had intended "e" (for electron). This was a common mistake since most treatments involved X rays, and she had become accustomed

to typing this. The mistake was easy to fix; she merely used the cursor up key to edit the mode entry.

Since the other parameters she had entered were correct, she hit the return key several times and left their values unchanged. She reached the bottom of the screen where a message indicated that the parameters had been "verified" and the terminal displayed "beam ready," as expected. She hit the one-key command "B" (for "beam on") to begin the treatment. After a moment, the machine shut down and the console displayed the message "Malfunction 54." The machine also displayed a "treatment pause," indicating a problem of low priority (see the operator interface sidebar). The sheet on the side of the machine explained that this malfunction was a "dose input 2" error. The ETCC did not have any other information available in its instruction manual or other Therac-25 documentation to explain the meaning of Malfunction 54. An AECL technician later testified that "dose input 2" meant that a dose had been delivered that was either too high or too low.

The machine showed a substantial underdose on its dose monitor display: 6 monitor units delivered, whereas the operator had requested 202 monitor units. The operator was accustomed to the quirks of the machine, which would frequently stop or delay treatment. In the past, the only consequences had been inconvenience. She immediately took the normal action when the machine merely paused, which was to hit the "P" key to proceed with the treatment. The machine promptly shut down with the same "Malfunction 54" error and the same underdose shown by the display terminal.

The operator was isolated from the patient, since the machine apparatus was inside a shielded room of its own. The only way the operator could be alerted to patient difficulty was through audio and video monitors. On this day, the video display was unplugged and the audio monitor was broken.

After the first attempt to treat him, the patient said that he felt like he had received an electric shock or that someone had poured hot coffee on his back: He felt a thump and heat and heard a buzzing sound from the equipment. Since this was his ninth treatment, he knew that this was not normal. He began to get up from the treatment table to go for help. It was at this moment that the operator hit the "P" key to proceed with the treatment. The patient said that he felt like his arm was being shocked by electricity and that his hand was leaving his body. He went to the treatment room door and pounded on it. The operator was shocked and immediately opened the door for him. He appeared shaken and upset.

The patient was immediately examined by a physician, who observed intense erythema over the treatment area, but suspected nothing more serious than electric shock. The patient was discharged with instructions to return if he suffered any further reactions. The hospital physicist was called in, and he found the machine calibration within specifications. The meaning of the malfunction message was not understood. The machine was then used to treat patients for the rest of the day.

In actuality, but unknown to anyone at that time, the patient had received a massive overdose, concentrated in the center of the treatment area. After-the-fact simulations of the accident revealed possible doses of 16,500 to 25,000 rads in less than 1 second over an area of about 1 cm.

During the weeks following the accident, the patient continued to have pain in his neck and shoulder. He lost the function of his left arm and had periodic bouts of nausea and vomiting. He was eventually hospitalized for radiation-induced myelitis of the cervical cord causing paralysis of his left arm and both legs, left vocal cord paralysis (which left him unable to speak), neurogenic bowel and bladder, and paralysis of the left diaphragm. He also had a lesion on his left lung and recurrent herpes simplex skin infections. He died from complications of the overdose five months after the accident.

User and manufacturer response. The Therac-25 was shut down for testing the day after this accident. One local AECL engineer and one from the home office in Canada came to ETCC to investigate. They spent a day running the machine through tests but could not reproduce a Malfunction 54. The AECL home office engineer reportedly explained that it was not possible for the Therac-25 to overdose a patient. The ETCC physicist claims that he asked AECL at this time if there were any other reports of radiation overexposure and that the AECL

personnel (including the quality assurance manager) told him that AECL knew of no accidents involving radiation overexposure by the Therac-25. This seems odd since AECL was surely at least aware of the Hamilton accident that had occurred seven months before and the Yakima accident, and, even by its own account, AECL learned of the Georgia lawsuit about this time (the suit had been filed four months earlier). The AECL engineers then suggested that an electrical problem might have caused this accident.

The electric shock theory was checked out thoroughly by an independent engineering firm. The final report indicated that there was no electrical grounding problem in the machine, and it did not appear capable of giving a patient an electrical shock. The ETCC physicist checked the calibration of the Therac-25 and found it to be satisfactory. The center put the machine back into service on April 7, 1986, convinced that it was performing properly.

East Texas Cancer Center, April 1986. Three weeks after the first ETCC accident, on Friday, April 11, 1986, another male patient was scheduled to receive an electron treatment at ETCC for a skin cancer on the side of his face. The prescription was for 10 MeV to an area of approximately 7 × 10 cm. The same technician who had treated the first Tyler accident victim prepared this patient for treatment. Much of what follows is from the deposition of the Tyler Therac-25 operator.

As with her former patient, she entered the prescription data and then noticed an error in the mode. Again she used the cursor up key to change the mode from X ray to electron. After she finished editing, she pressed the return key several times to place the cursor on the bottom of the screen. She saw the "beam ready" message displayed and turned the beam on.

Within a few seconds the machine shut down, making a loud noise audible via the (now working) intercom. The display showed Malfunction 54 again. The operator rushed into the treatment room, hearing her patient moaning for help. The patient began to remove the tape that had held his head in position and said something was wrong. She asked him what he felt, and he replied "fire" on the side of his face. She immediately went to the hospital physicist and told

him that another patient appeared to have been burned. Asked by the physicist to describe what he had experienced, the patient explained that something had hit him on the side of the face, he saw a flash of light, and he heard a sizzling sound reminiscent of frying eggs. He was very agitated and asked, "What happened to me, what happened to me?"

This patient died from the overdose on May 1, 1986, three weeks after the accident. He had disorientation that progressed to coma, fever to 104 degrees Fahrenheit, and neurological damage. Autopsy showed an acute high-dose radiation injury to the right temporal lobe of the brain and the brain stem.

User and manufacturer response. After this second Tyler accident, the ETCC physicist immediately took the machine out of service and called AECL to alert the company to this second apparent overexposure. The Tyler physicist then began his own careful investigation. He worked with the operator, who remembered exactly what she had done on this occasion. After a great deal of effort, they were eventually able to elicit the Malfunction 54 message. They determined that data-entry speed during editing was the key factor in producing the error condition: If the prescription data was edited at a fast pace (as is natural for someone who has repeated the procedure a large number of times), the overdose occurred.

It took some practice before the physicist could repeat the procedure rapidly enough to elicit the Malfunction 54 message at will. Once he could do this, he set about measuring the actual dose delivered under the error condition. He took a measurement of about 804 rads but realized that the ion chamber had become saturated. After making adjustments to extend his measurement ability, he determined that the dose was somewhere over 4,000 rads.

The next day, an engineer from AECL called and said that he could not reproduce the error. After the ETCC physicist explained that the procedure had to be performed quite rapidly, AECL could finally produce a similar malfunction on its own machine. AECL then set up its own set of measurements to test the dosage delivered. Two days after the accident, AECL said they had measured the dosage (at the center of the field) to be 25,000 rads. An AECL engineer explained that the frying sound heard by the patient was the ion chambers being saturated.

In fact, it is not possible to determine the exact dose each of the accident victims received; the total dose delivered during the malfunction conditions was found to vary enormously when different clinics simulated the faults. The number of pulses delivered in the 0.3 second that elapsed before interlock shutoff varied because the software adjusted the start-up pulse-repetition frequency to very different values on different machines. Therefore, there is still some uncertainty as to the doses actually received in the accidents.[1]

In one lawsuit that resulted from the Tyler accidents, the AECL quality control manager testified that a "cursor up" problem had been found in the service mode at the Kennestone clinic and one other clinic in February or March 1985 and also in the summer of 1985. Both times, AECL thought that the software problems had been fixed. There is no way to determine whether there is any relationship between these problems and the Tyler accidents.

Related Therac-20 problems. After the Tyler accidents, Therac-20 users (who had heard informally about the Tyler accidents from Therac-25 users) conducted informal investigations to determine whether the same problem could occur with their machines. As noted earlier, the software for the Therac-25 and Therac-20 both "evolved" from the Therac-6 software. Additional functions had to be added because the Therac-20 (and Therac-25) operates in both X-ray and electron mode, while the Therac-6 has only X-ray mode. The CGR employees modified the software for the Therac-20 to handle the dual modes.

When the Therac-25 development began, AECL engineers adapted the software from the Therac-6, but they also borrowed software routines from the Therac-20 to handle electron mode. The agreements between AECL and CGR gave both companies the right to tap technology used in joint products for their other products.

After the second Tyler accident, a physicist at the University of Chicago Joint Center for Radiation Therapy heard about the Therac-25 software problem and decided to find out whether the same thing could happen with the Therac-20. At first, the physicist was

unable to reproduce the error on his machine, but two months later he found the link.

The Therac-20 at the University of Chicago is used to teach students in a radiation therapy school conducted by the center. The center's physicist, Frank Borger, noticed that whenever a new class of students started using the Therac-20, fuses and breakers on the machine tripped, shutting down the unit. These failures, which had been occurring ever since the center had acquired the machine, might appear three times a week while new students operated the machine and then disappear for months. Borger determined that new students make lots of different types of mistakes and use "creative methods of editing" parameters on the console. Through experimentation, he found that certain editing sequences correlated with blown fuses and determined that the same computer bug (as in the Therac-25 software) was responsible. The physicist notified the FDA, which notified Therac-20 users.[4]

The software error is just a nuisance on the Therac-20 because this machine has independent hardware protective circuits for monitoring the electron-beam scanning. The protective circuits do not allow the beam to turn on, so there is no danger of radiation exposure to a patient. While the Therac-20 relies on mechanical interlocks for monitoring the machine, the Therac-25 relies largely on software.

The software problem. A lesson to be learned from the Therac-25 story is that focusing on particular software bugs is not the way to make a safe system. Virtually all complex software can be made to behave in an unexpected fashion under certain conditions. The basic mistakes here involved poor software-engineering practices and building a machine that relies on the software for safe operation. Furthermore, the particular coding error is not as important as the general unsafe design of the software overall. Examining the part of the code blamed for the Tyler accidents is instructive, however, in showing the overall software design flaws. The following explanation of the problem is from the description AECL provided for the FDA, although we have tried to clarify it somewhat. The description leaves some unanswered questions, but it is the best we can do with the information we have.

As described in the sidebar on Therac-25 software development and design, the treatment monitor task (Treat) controls the various phases of treatment by executing its eight subroutines (see Figure 2). The treatment phase indicator variable (Tphase) is used to determine which subroutine should be executed. Following the execution of a particular subroutine, Treat reschedules itself.

One of Treat's subroutines, called Datent (data entry), communicates with the keyboard handler task (a task that runs concurrently with Treat) via a

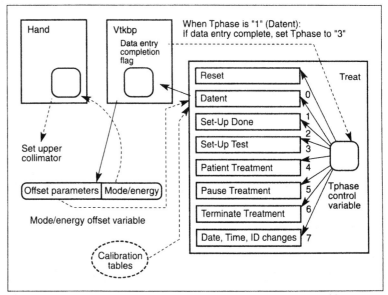

Figure 2. Tasks and subroutines in the code blamed for the Tyler accidents.

211

shared variable (Data-entry completion flag) to determine whether the prescription data has been entered. The keyboard handler recognizes the completion of data entry and changes the Data-entry completion variable to denote this. Once the Data-entry completion variable is set, the Datent subroutine detects the variable's change in status and changes the value of Tphase from 1 (Data Entry) to 3 (Set-Up Test). In this case, the Datent subroutine exits back to the Treat subroutine, which will reschedule itself and begin execution of the Set-Up Test subroutine. If the Data-entry completion variable has not been set, Datent leaves the value of Tphase unchanged and exits back to Treat's main line. Treat will then reschedule it-self, essentially rescheduling the Datent subroutine.

The command line at the lower right corner of the screen is the cursor's normal position when the operator has completed all necessary changes to the prescription. Prescription editing is signified by cursor movement off the command line. As the program was originally designed, the Data-entry completion variable by itself is not sufficient since it does not ensure that the cursor is located on the command line. Under the right circumstances, the data-entry phase can be exited before all edit changes are made on the screen.

The keyboard handler parses the mode and energy level specified by the operator and places an encoded result in another shared variable, the 2-byte mode/energy offset (MEOS) variable. The low-order byte of this variable is used by another task (Hand) to set the collimator/turntable to the proper position for the selected mode/energy. The high-order byte of the MEOS variable is used by Datent to set several operating parameters.

Initially, the data-entry process forces the operator to enter the mode and energy, except when the operator selects the photon mode, in which case the energy defaults to 25 MeV. The operator can later edit the mode and energy

```
Datent:
    if mode/energy specified then
      begin
        calculate table index
        repeat
          fetch parameter
          output parameter
          point to next parameter
        until all parameters set
        call Magnet
        if mode/energy changed then return
      end
    if data entry is complete then set Tphase to 3
    if data entry is not complete then
      if reset command entered then set Tphase to 0
    return

Magnet:
    Set bending magnet flag
    repeat
      Set next magnet
      Call Ptime
      if mode/energy has changed, then exit
    until all magnets are set
    return

Ptime:
    repeat
      if bending magnet flag is set then
        if editing taking place then
          if mode/energy has changed then exit
    until hysteresis delay has expired
    Clear bending magnet flag
    return
```

Figure 3. Datent, Magnet, and Ptime subroutines.

separately. If the keyboard handler sets the data-entry completion variable before the operator changes the data in MEOS, Datent will not detect the changes in MEOS since it has already exited and will not be reentered again. The upper collimator, on the other hand, is set to the position dictated by the low-order byte of MEOS by another concurrently running task (Hand) and can therefore be inconsistent with the parameters set in accordance with the information in the high-order byte of MEOS. The software appears to include no checks to detect such an incompatibility.

The first thing that Datent does when it is entered is to check whether the mode/energy has been set in MEOS. If so, it uses the high-order byte to index into a table of preset operating parameters and places them in the digital-to-analog output table. The contents of

this output table are transferred to the digital-analog converter during the next clock cycle. Once the parameters are all set, Datent calls the subroutine Magnet, which sets the bending magnets. Figure 3 is a simplified pseudocode description of relevant parts of the software.

Setting the bending magnets takes about 8 seconds. Magnet calls a subroutine called Ptime to introduce a time delay. Since several magnets need to be set, Ptime is entered and exited several times. A flag to indicate that bending magnets are being set is initialized upon entry to the Magnet subroutine and cleared at the end of Ptime. Furthermore, Ptime checks a shared variable, set by the keyboard handler, that indicates the presence of any editing requests. If there are edits, then Ptime clears the bending magnet variable and exits to Magnet, which then exits to Datent. But the edit change variable is checked by Ptime only if the bending magnet flag is set. Since Ptime clears it during its first execution, any edits performed during each succeeding pass through Ptime will not be recognized. Thus, an edit change of the mode or energy, although reflected on the operator's screen and the mode/energy offset variable, will not be sensed by Datent so it can index the appropriate calibration tables for the machine parameters.

Recall that the Tyler error occurred when the operator made an entry indicating the mode/energy, went to the command line, then moved the cursor up to change the mode/energy, and returned to the command line all within 8 seconds. Since the magnet setting takes about 8 seconds and Magnet does not recognize edits after the first execution of Ptime, the editing had been completed by the return to Datent, which never detected that it had occurred. Part of the problem was fixed after the accident by clearing the bending-magnet variable at the end of Magnet (after *all* the magnets have been set) instead of at the end of Ptime.

But this was not the only problem.

Upon exit from the Magnet subroutine, the data-entry subroutine (Datent) checks the data-entry completion variable. If it indicates that data entry is complete, Datent sets Tphase to 3 and Datent is not entered again. If it is not set, Datent leaves Tphase unchanged, which means it will eventually be rescheduled. But the data-entry completion variable only indicates that the cursor has been down to the command line, not that it is still there. A potential race condition is set up. To fix this, AECL introduced another shared variable controlled by the keyboard handler task that indicates the cursor is not positioned on the command line. If this variable is set, then prescription entry is still in progress and the value of Tphase is left unchanged.

Government and user response. The FDA does not approve each new medical device on the market: All medical devices go through a classification process that determines the level of FDA approval necessary. Medical accelerators follow a procedure called pre-market notification before commercial distribution. In this process, the firm must establish that the product is substantially equivalent in safety and effectiveness to a product already on the market. If that cannot be done to the FDA's satisfaction, a pre-market approval is required. For the Therac-25, the FDA required only a pre-market notification.

The agency is basically reactive to problems and requires manufacturers to report serious ones. Once a problem is identified in a radiation-emitting product, the FDA must approve the manufacturer's corrective action plan (CAP).

The first reports of the Tyler accidents came to the FDA from the state of Texas health department, and this triggered FDA action. The FDA investigation was well under way when AECL produced a medical device report to discuss the details of the radiation overexposures at Tyler. The FDA declared the Therac-25 defective under the Radiation Control for Health and Safety Act and ordered the firm to notify all purchasers, investigate the problem, determine a solution, and submit a corrective action plan for FDA approval.

The final CAP consisted of more than 20 changes to the system hardware and software, plus modifications to the system documentation and manuals. Some of these changes were unrelated to the specific accidents, but were improvements to the general machine safety. The full implementation of the CAP, including an extensive safety analysis, was not complete until more than two years after the Tyler accidents.

AECL made its accident report to the FDA on April 15, 1986. On that same date, AECL sent a letter to each Therac user recommending a temporary "fix" to the machine that would allow continued clinical use. The letter (shown in its complete form) read as follows:

SUBJECT: CHANGE IN OPERATING PROCEDURES FOR THE THERAC 25 LINEAR ACCELERATOR

Effective immediately, and until further notice, the key used for moving the cursor back through the prescription sequence (i.e., cursor "UP" inscribed with an upward pointing arrow) must not be used for editing or any other purpose.

To avoid accidental use of this key, the key cap must be removed and the switch contacts fixed in the open position with electrical tape or other insulating material. For assistance with the latter you should contact your local AECL service representative.

Disabling this key means that if any prescription data entered is incorrect then [an] "R" reset command must be used and the whole prescription reentered.

For those users of the Multiport option, it also means that editing of dose rate, dose, and time will not be possible between ports.

On May 2, 1986, the FDA declared the Therac defective, demanded a CAP, and required renotification of all the Therac customers. In the letter from the FDA to AECL, the director of compliance, Center for Devices and Radiological Health, wrote

We have reviewed Mr. Downs' April 15 letter to purchasers and have concluded that it does not satisfy the requirements for notification to purchasers of a defect in an electronic product. Specifically, it does not describe the defect nor the hazards associated with it. The letter does not provide any reason for disabling the cursor key and the tone is not commensurate with the urgency for doing so. In fact, the letter implies the inconvenience to operators outweighs the need to disable the key. We request that you immediately renotify purchasers.

AECL promptly made a new notice to users and also requested an extension to produce a CAP. The FDA granted this request.

About this time, the Therac-25 users created a user group and held their first meeting at the annual conference of the American Association of Physicists in Medicine. At the meeting, users discussed the Tyler accident and heard an AECL representative present the company's plans for responding to it. AECL promised to send a letter to all users detailing the CAP.

Several users described additional hardware safety features that they had added to their own machines to provide additional protection. An interlock (that checked gun current values), which the Vancouver clinic had previously added to its Therac-25, was labeled as redundant by AECL. The users disagreed. There were further discussions of poor design and other problems that caused 10- to 30-percent underdosing in both modes.

The meeting notes said

... there was a general complaint by all users present about the lack of information propagation. The users were not happy about receiving incomplete information. The AECL representative countered by stating that AECL does not wish to spread rumors and that AECL has no policy to "keep things quiet." The consensus among the users was that an improvement was necessary.

After the first user group meeting, there were two user group newsletters. The first, dated fall 1986, contained letters from Still, the Kennestone physicist, who complained about what he considered to be eight major problems he had experienced with the Therac-25. These problems included poor screen-refresh subroutines that left trash and erroneous information on the operator console, and some tape-loading problems upon start-up, which he discovered involved the use of "phantom tables" to trigger the interlock system in the event of a load failure instead of using a check sum. He asked the question, "Is programming safety relying too much on the software interlock routines?" The second user group newsletter, in December 1986, further discussed the implications of the "phantom table" parameterization.

AECL produced the first CAP on June 13, 1986. It contained six items:

(1) Fix the software to eliminate the specific behavior leading to the Tyler problem.

(2) Modify the software sample-and-hold circuits to detect one pulse above a nonadjustable threshold. The software

sample-and-hold circuit monitors the magnitude of each pulse from the ion chambers in the beam. Previously, three consecutive high readings were required to shut off the high-voltage circuits, which resulted in a shutdown time of 300 ms. The software modification results in a reading after each pulse, and a shutdown after a single high reading.

(3) Make Malfunctions 1 through 64 result in treatment *suspend* rather than *pause*.

(4) Add a new circuit, which only administrative staff can reset, to shut down the modulator if the sample-and-hold circuits detect a high pulse. This is functionally equivalent to the circuit described in item 2. However, a new circuit board is added that monitors the five sample-and-hold circuits. The new circuit detects ion-chamber signals above a fixed threshold and inhibits the trigger to the modulator after detecting a high pulse. This shuts down the beam independently of the software.

(5) Modify the software to limit editing keys to cursor up, backspace, and return.

(6) Modify the manuals to reflect the changes.

FDA internal memos describe their immediate concerns regarding the CAP. One memo suggests adding an independent circuit that "detects and shuts down the system when inappropriate outputs are detected," warnings about when ion chambers are saturated, and understandable system error messages. Another memo questions "whether all possible hardware options have been investigated by the manufacturer to prevent any future inadvertent high exposure."

On July 23 the FDA officially responded to AECL's CAP submission. They conceptually agreed with the plan's direction but complained about the lack of specific information necessary to evaluate the plan, especially with regard to the software. The FDA requested a detailed description of the software-development procedures and documentation, along with a revised CAP to incluJe revised requirements documents, a detailed description of corrective changes, analysis of the interactions of the modified software with the system, and detailed descriptions of the revised edit modes, the changes made to the software setup table, and the software interlock interactions. The

---

The investigators could not reproduce the fault condition that produced the 1987 Yakima overdose.

FDA also made a very detailed request for a documented test plan.

AECL responded on September 26 with several documents describing the software and its modifications but no test plan. They explained how the Therac-25 software evolved from the Therac-6 software and stated that "no single test plan and report exists for the software since both hardware and software were tested and exercised separately and together over many years." AECL concluded that the current CAP improved "machine safety by many orders of magnitude and virtually eliminates the possibility of lethal doses as delivered in the Tyler incident."

An FDA internal memo dated October 20 commented on these AECL submissions, raising several concerns:

> Unfortunately, the AECL response also seems to point out an apparent lack of documentation on software specifications and a software test plan.
> . . . concerns include the question of previous knowledge of problems by AECL, the apparent paucity of software QA [quality assurance] at the manufacturing facility, and possible warnings and information dissemination to others of the generic type problems.
> . . . As mentioned in my first review, there is some confusion on whether the manufacturer should have been aware of the software problems prior to the [accidental radiation overdoses] in Texas. AECL had received official notification of a lawsuit in November 1985 from a patient claiming accidental over-exposure from a Therac-25 in Marietta, Georgia. . . If knowledge of these software deficiencies were known beforehand, what would be the FDA's posture in this case?
> . . . The materials submitted by the manufacturer have not been in sufficient detail and clarity to ensure an adequate software QA program currently exists. For example, a response has not been provided with respect to the software part of the CAP to the CDRH [FDA Center for Devices and Radiological Health] request for documentation on the revised requirements and specifications for the new software. In addition, an analysis has

not been provided, as requested, on the interaction with other portions of the software to demonstrate the corrected software does not adversely affect other software functions.

> The July 23 letter from the CDRH requested a documented test plan including several specific pieces of information identified in the letter. This request has been ignored up to this point by the manufacturer. Considering the ramifications of the current software problem, changes in software QA attitudes are needed at AECL.

On October 30, the FDA responded to AECL's additional submissions, complaining about the lack of a detailed description of the accident and of sufficient detail in flow diagrams. Many specific questions addressed the vagueness of the AECL response and made it clear that additional CAP work must precede approval.

AECL, in response, created CAP Revision 1 on November 12. This CAP contained 12 new items under "software modifications," all (except for one cosmetic change) designed to eliminate potentially unsafe behavior. The submission also contained other relevant documents including a test plan.

The FDA responded to CAP Revision 1 on December 11. The FDA explained that the software modifications appeared to correct the specific deficiencies discovered as a result of the Tyler accidents. They agreed that the major items listed in CAP Revision 1 would improve the Therac's operation. However, the FDA required AECL to attend to several further system problems before CAP approval. AECL had proposed to retain treatment pause for some dose-rate and beam-tilt malfunctions. Since these are dosimetry system problems, the FDA considered them safety interlocks and believed treatment must be suspended for these malfunctions.

AECL also planned to retain the malfunction codes, but the FDA required better warnings for the operators. Furthermore, AECL had not planned on any quality assurance testing to ensure exact copying of software, but the FDA insisted on it. The FDA further requested assurances that rigorous testing would become a standard part of AECL's software-modification procedures:

> We also expressed our concern that you did not intend to perform the protocol to future modifications to software. We

believe that the rigorous testing must be performed each time a modification is made in order to ensure the modification does not adversely affect the safety of the system.

AECL was also asked to draw up an installation test plan to ensure both hardware and software changes perform as designed when installed.

AECL submitted CAP Revision 2 and supporting documentation on December 22, 1986. They changed the CAP to have dose malfunctions suspend treatment and included a plan for meaningful error messages and highlighted dose error messages. They also expanded diagrams of software modifications and expanded the test plan to cover hardware and software.

On January 26, 1987, AECL sent the FDA their "Component and Installation Test Plan" and explained that their delays were due to the investigation of a new accident on January 17 at Yakima.

Yakima Valley Memorial Hospital, 1987. On Saturday, January 17, 1987, the second patient of the day was to be treated at the Yakima Valley Memorial Hospital for a carcinoma. This patient was to receive two film-verification exposures of 4 and 3 rads, plus a 79-rad photon treatment (for a total exposure of 86 rads).

Film was placed under the patient and 4 rads was administered with the collimator jaws opened to 22 × 18 cm. After the machine paused, the collimator jaws opened to 35 × 35 cm automatically, and the second exposure of 3 rads was administered. The machine paused again.

The operator entered the treatment room to remove the film and verify the patient's precise position. He used the hand control in the treatment room to rotate the turntable to the field-light position, a feature that let him check the machine's alignment with respect to the patient's body to verify proper beam position. The operator then either pressed the set button on the hand control or left the room and typed a set command at the console to return the turntable to the proper position for treatment; there is some confusion as to exactly what transpired. When he left the room, he forgot to remove the film from underneath the patient. The console displayed "beam ready," and the operator hit the "B" key to turn the beam on.

The beam came on but the console displayed no dose or dose rate. After 5 or 6 seconds, the unit shut down with a pause and displayed a message. The message "may have disappeared quickly"; the operator was unclear on this point. However, since the machine merely paused, he was able to push the "P" key to proceed with treatment.

The machine paused again, this time displaying "flatness" on the reason line. The operator heard the patient say something over the intercom, but couldn't understand him. He went into the room to speak with the patient, who reported "feeling a burning sensation" in the chest. The console displayed only the total dose of the two film exposures (7 rads) and nothing more.

Later in the day, the patient developed a skin burn over the entire treatment area. Four days later, the redness took on the striped pattern matching the slots in the blocking tray. The striped pattern was similar to the burn a year earlier at this hospital that had been attributed to "cause unknown."

AECL began an investigation, and users were told to confirm the turntable position visually before turning on the beam. All tests run by the AECL engineers indicated that the machine was working perfectly. From the information gathered to that point, it was suspected that the electron beam had come on when the turntable was in the field-light position. But the investigators could not reproduce the fault condition that produced the overdose.

On the following Thursday, AECL sent an engineer from Ottawa to investigate. The hospital physicist had, in the meantime, run some tests with film. He placed a film in the Therac's beam and ran two exposures of X-ray parameters with the turntable in field-light position. The film appeared to match the film that was left (by mistake) under the patient during the accident.

After a week of checking the hardware, AECL determined that the "incorrect machine operation was probably not caused by hardware alone." After checking the software, AECL discovered a flaw (described in the next section) that could explain the erroneous behavior. The coding problems explaining this accident differ from those associated with the Tyler accidents.

AECL's preliminary dose measurements indicated that the dose delivered under these conditions — that is, when the turntable was in the field-light position — was on the order of 4,000 to 5,000 rads. After two attempts, the patient could have received 8,000 to 10,000 instead of the 86 rads prescribed. AECL again called users on January 26 (nine days after the accident) and gave them detailed instructions on how to avoid this problem. In an FDA internal report on the accident, an AECL quality assurance manager investigating the problem is quoted as saying that the software and hardware changes to be retrofitted following the Tyler accident nine months earlier (but which had not yet been installed) would have prevented the Yakima accident.

The patient died in April from complications related to the overdose. He had been suffering from a terminal form of cancer prior to the radiation overdose, but survivors initiated lawsuits alleging that he died sooner than he would have and endured unnecessary pain and suffering due to the overdose. The suit was settled out of court.

The Yakima software problem. The software problem for the second Yakima accident is fairly well established and different from that implicated in the Tyler accidents. There is no way to determine what particular software design errors were related to the Kennestone, Hamilton, and first Yakima accidents. Given the unsafe programming practices exhibited in the code, it is possible that unknown race conditions or errors could have been responsible. There is speculation, however, that the Hamilton accident was the same as this second Yakima overdose. In a report of a conference call on January 26, 1987, between the AECL quality assurance manager and Ed Miller of the FDA discussing the Yakima accident, Miller notes

> This situation probably occurred in the Hamilton, Ontario, accident a couple of years ago. It was not discovered at that time and the cause was attributed to intermittent interlock failure. The subsequent recall of the multiple microswitch logic network did not really solve the problem.

The second Yakima accident was again attributed to a type of race condition in the software — this one allowed the device to be activated in an error setting (a "failure" of a software interlock). The Tyler accidents were related to prob-

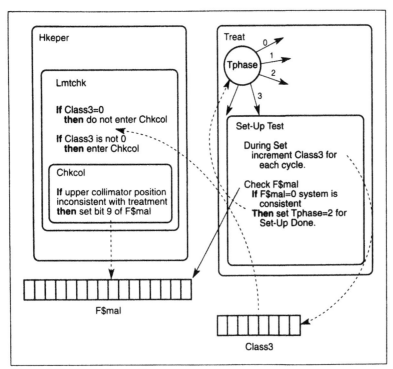

Figure 4. Yakima software flaw.

lems in the data-entry routines that allowed the code to proceed to Set-Up Test before the full prescription had been entered and acted upon. The Yakima accident involves problems encountered later in the logic after the treatment monitor Treat reaches Set-Up Test.

The Therac-25's field-light feature permits very precise positioning of the patient for treatment. The operator can control the Therac-25 right at the treatment site using a small hand control offering certain limited functions for patient setup, including setting gantry, collimator, and table motions.

Normally, the operator enters all the prescription data at the console (outside the treatment room) before the final setup of all machine parameters is completed in the treatment room. This gives rise to an "unverified" condition at the console. The operator then completes the patient setup in the treatment room, and all relevant parameters now "verify." The console displays the message "Press set button" while the turntable is in the field-light position. The operator now presses the set button on the hand control or types "set" at the console. That should set the collimator to the proper position for treatment.

In the software, after the prescription

is entered and verified by the Datent routine, the control variable Tphase is changed so that the Set-Up Test routine is entered (see Figure 4). Every pass through the Set-Up Test routine increments the upper collimator position check, a shared variable called Class3. If Class3 is nonzero, there is an inconsistency and treatment should not proceed. A zero value for Class3 indicates that the relevant parameters are consistent with treatment, and the beam is not inhibited.

After setting the Class3 variable, Set-Up Test next checks for any malfunctions in the system by checking another shared variable (set by a routine that actually handles the interlock checking) called F$mal to see if it has a nonzero value. A nonzero value in F$mal indicates that the machine is not ready for treatment, and the Set-Up Test subroutine is rescheduled. When F$mal is zero (indicating that everything is ready for treatment), the Set-Up Test subroutine sets the Tphase variable equal to 2, which results in next scheduling the Set-Up Done subroutine, and the treatment is allowed to continue.

The actual interlock checking is performed by a concurrent Housekeeper task (Hkeper). The upper collimator

position check is performed by a subroutine of Hkeper called Lmtchk (analog/digital limit checking). Lmtchk first checks the Class3 variable. If Class3 contains a nonzero value, Lmtchk calls the Check Collimator (Chkcol) subroutine. If Class3 contains zero, Chkcol is bypassed and the upper collimator position check is not performed. The Chkcol subroutine sets or resets bit 9 of the F$mal shared variable, depending on the position of the upper collimator (which in turn is checked by the Set-Up Test subroutine of Datent so it can decide whether to reschedule itself or proceed to Set-Up Done).

During machine setup, Set-Up Test will be executed several hundred times since it reschedules itself waiting for other events to occur. In the code, the Class3 variable is incremented by one in each pass through Set-Up Test. Since the Class3 variable is 1 byte, it can only contain a maximum value of 255 decimal. Thus, on every 256th pass through the Set-Up Test code, the variable overflows and has a zero value. That means that on every 256th pass through Set-Up Test, the upper collimator will not be checked and an upper collimator fault will not be detected.

The overexposure occurred when the operator hit the "set" button at the precise moment that Class3 rolled over to zero. Thus Chkcol was not executed, and F$mal was not set to indicate the upper collimator was still in field-light position. The software turned on the full 25 MeV without the target in place and without scanning. A highly concentrated electron beam resulted, which was scattered and deflected by the stainless steel mirror that was in the path.

AECL described the technical "fix" implemented for this software flaw as simple: The program is changed so that the Class3 variable is set to some fixed nonzero value each time through Set-Up Test instead of being incremented.

Manufacturer, government, and user response. On February 3, 1987, after interaction with the FDA and others, including the user group, AECL announced to its customers

- a new software release to correct both the Tyler and Yakima software problems,
- a hardware single-pulse shutdown circuit,

- a turntable potentiometer to independently monitor turntable position, and
- a hardware turntable interlock circuit.

The second item, a hardware single-pulse shutdown circuit, essentially acts as a hardware interlock to prevent overdosing by detecting an unsafe level of radiation and halting beam output after one pulse of high energy and current. This provides an independent safety mechanism to protect against a wide range of potential hardware failures and software errors. The turntable potentiometer was the safety device recommended by several groups, including the CRPB, after the Hamilton accident.

After the second Yakima accident, the FDA became concerned that the use of the Therac-25 during the CAP process, even with AECL's interim operating instructions, involved too much risk to patients. The FDA concluded that the accidents had demonstrated that the software alone cannot be replied upon to assure safe operation of the machine. In a February 18, 1987 internal FDA memorandum, the director of the Division of Radiological Products wrote the following:

It is impossible for CDRH to find all potential failure modes and conditions of the software. AECL has indicated the "simple software fix" will correct the turntable position problem displayed at Yakima. We have not yet had the opportunity to evaluate that modification. Even if it does, based upon past history, I am not convinced that there are not other software glitches that could result in serious injury.

For example, we are aware that AECL issued a user's bulletin January 21 reminding users of the proper procedure to follow if editing of prescription parameter is desired after entering the "B" (beam on) code but before the CR [carriage return] is pressed. It seems that the normal edit keys (down arrow, right arrow, or line feed) will be interpreted as a CR and initiate exposure. One must use either the backspace or left arrow key to edit.

We are also aware that if the dose entered into the prescription tables is below some preset value, the system will default to a phantom table value unbeknownst to the operator. This problem is supposedly being addressed in proposed interim revision 7A, although we are unaware of the details.

We are in the position of saying that the proposed CAP can reasonably be expected to correct the deficiencies for which they were developed (Tyler). We cannot say that we are [reasonably] confident about

the safety of the entire *system* to prevent or minimize exposure from other fault conditions.

On February 6, 1987, Miller of the FDA called Pavel Dvorak of Canada's Health and Welfare to advise him that the FDA would recommend all Therac-25s be shut down until permanent modifications could be made. According to Miller's notes on the phone call, Dvorak agreed and indicated that they would coordinate their actions with the FDA.

On February 10, 1987, the FDA gave a Notice of Adverse Findings to AECL declaring the Therac-25 to be defective under US law. In part, the letter to AECL reads:

In January 1987, CDRH was advised of another accidental radiation occurrence in Yakima, which was attributed to a second software defect related to the "Set" command. In addition, the CDRH has become aware of at least two other software features that provide potential for unnecessary or inadvertent patient exposure. One of these is related to the method of editing the prescription after the "B" command is entered and the other is the calling of phantom tables when low doses are prescribed.

Further review of the circumstances surrounding the accidental radiation occurrences and the potential for other such incidents has led us to conclude that in addition to the items in your proposed corrective action plan, hardware interlocking of the turntable to insure its proper position prior to beam activation appears to be necessary to enhance system safety and to correct the Therac-25 defect. Therefore, the corrective action plan as currently proposed is insufficient and must be amended to include turntable interlocking and corrections for the three software problems mentioned above.

Without these corrections, CDRH has concluded that the consequences of the defects represents a significant potential risk of serious injury even if the Therac-25 is operated in accordance with your interim operating instructions. CDRH, therefore, requests that AECL immediately notify all purchasers and recommend that use of the device on patients for routine therapy be discontinued until such time that an amended corrective action plan approved by CDRH is fully completed. You may also advise purchasers that if the need for an individual patient treatment outweighs the potential risk, then extreme caution and strict adherence to operating safety procedures must be exercised.

At the same time, the Health Protection Branch of the Canadian government instructed AECL to recommend to all users in Canada that they discontinue the operation of the Therac-25

until "the company can complete an exhaustive analysis of the design and operation of the safety systems employed for patient and operator protection." AECL was told that the letter to the users should include information on how the users can operate the equipment safely in the event that they must continue with patient treatment. If AECL could not provide information that would guarantee safe operation of the equipment, AECL was requested to inform the users that they cannot operate the equipment safely. AECL complied by letters dated February 20, 1987, to Therac-25 purchasers. This recommendation to discontinue use of the Therac-25 was to last until August 1987.

On March 5, 1987, AECL issued CAP Revision 3, which was a CAP for both the Tyler and Yakima accidents. It contained a few additions to the Revision 2 modifications, notably

- changes to the software to eliminate the behavior leading to the latest Yakima accident,
- four additional software functional modifications to improve safety, and
- a turntable position interlock in the software.

In their response on April 9, the FDA noted that in the appendix under "turntable position interlock circuit" the descriptions were wrong. AECL had indicated "high" signals where "low" signals were called for and vice versa. The FDA also questioned the reliability of the turntable potentiometer design and asked whether the backspace key could still act as a carriage return in the edit mode. They requested a detailed description of the software portion of the single-pulse shutdown and a block diagram to demonstrate the PRF (pulse repetition frequency) generator, modulator, and associated interlocks.

AECL responded on April 13 with an update on the Therac CAP status and a schedule of the nine action items pressed by the users at a user group meeting in March. This unique and highly productive meeting provided an unusual opportunity to involve the users in the CAP evaluation process. It brought together all concerned parties in one place so that they could decide on and approve a course of action as quickly as possible. The attendees included representatives from the manufacturer (AECL); all users, including their tech-

Safety analysis of the Therac-25

The Therac-25 safety analysis included (1) failure mode and effect analysis, (2) fault-tree analysis, and (3) software examination.

Failure mode and effect analysis. An FMEA describes the associated system response to all failure modes of the individual system components, considered one by one. When software was involved, AECL made no assessment of the "how and why" of software faults and took any combination of software faults as a single event. The latter means that if the software was the initiating event, then no credit was given for the software mitigating the effects. This seems like a reasonable and conservative approach to handling software faults.

Fault-tree analysis. An FMEA identifies single failures leading to Class I hazards. To identify multiple failures and quantify the results, AECL used fault-tree analysis. An FTA starts with a postulated hazard — for example, two of the top events for the Therac-25 are high dose per pulse and illegal gantry motion. The immediate causes for the event are then generated in an AND/OR tree format, using a basic understanding of the machine operation to determine the causes. The tree generation continues until all branches end in "basic events." Operationally, a basic event is sometimes defined as an event that can be quantified (for example, a resistor fails open).

AECL used a "generic failure rate" of 10^{-4} per hour for software events. The company justified this number as based on the historical performance of the Therac-25 software. The final report on the safety analysis said that many fault trees for the Therac-25 have a computer malfunction as a causative event, and the outcome of quantification is therefore dependent on the failure rate chosen for software.

Leaving aside the general question of whether such failure rates are meaningful or measurable for software in general, it seems rather difficult to justify a single figure of this sort for every type of software error or software behavior. It would be equivalent to assigning the same failure rate to every type of failure of a car, no matter what particular failure is considered.

The authors of the safety study did note that despite the uncertainty that software introduces into quantification, fault-tree analysis provides valuable information in showing single and multiple failure paths and the relative importance of different failure mechanisms. This is certainly true.

Software examination. Because of the difficulty of quantifying software behavior, AECL contracted for a detailed code inspection to "obtain more information on which to base decisions." The software functions selected for examination were those related to the Class I software hazards identified in the FMEA: electron-beam scanning, energy selection, beam shutoff, and dose calibration.

The outside consultant who performed the inspection included a detailed examination of each function's implementation, a search for coding errors, and a qualitative assessment of its reliability. The consultant recommended

program changes to correct shortcomings, improve reliability, or improve the software package in a general sense. The final safety report gives no information about whether any particular methodology or tools were used in the software inspection or whether someone just read the code looking for errors.

Conclusions of the safety analysis. The final report summarizes the conclusions of the safety analysis:

> The conclusions of the analysis call for 10 changes to Therac-25 hardware; the most significant of these are interlocks to back up software control of both electron scanning and beam energy selection.
> Although it is not considered necessary or advisable to rewrite the entire Therac-25 software package, considerable effort is being expended to update it. The changes recommended have several distinct objectives: improve the protection it provides against hardware failures; provide additional reliability via cross-checking; and provide a more maintainable source package. Two or three software releases are anticipated before these changes are completed.
> The implementation of these improvements including design and testing for both hardware and software is well under way. All hardware modifications should be completed and installed by mid 1989, with final software updates extending into late 1989 or early 1990.

The recommended hardware changes appear to add protection against software errors, to add extra protection against hardware failures, or to increase safety margins. The software conclusions included the following:

> The software code for Beam Shut-Off, Symmetry Control, and Dose Calibration was found to be straight-forward and no execution path could be found which would cause them to perform incorrectly. A few improvements are being incorporated, but no additional hardware interlocks are required.
> Inspection of the Scanning and Energy Selection functions, which are under software control, showed no improper execution paths; however, software inspection was unable to provide a high level of confidence in their reliability. This was due to the complex nature of the code, the extensive use of variables, and the time limitations of the inspection process. Due to these factors and the possible clinical consequences of a malfunction, computer-independent interlocks are being retrofitted for these two cases.

Given the complex nature of this software design and the basic multitasking design, it is difficult to understand how any part of the code could be labeled "straightforward" or how confidence could be achieved that "no execution paths" exist for particular types of software behavior. However, it does appear that a conservative approach — including computer-independent interlocks — was taken in most cases. Furthermore, few examples of such safety analyses of software exist in the literature. One such software analysis was performed in 1989 on the shutdown software of a nuclear power plant, which was written by a different division of AECL.[1] Much still needs to be learned about how to perform a software-safety analysis.

Reference

1. W.C. Bowman et al., "An Application of Fault Tree Analysis to Safety-Critical Software at Ontario Hydro," *Conf. Probabilistic Safety Assessment and Management*, 1991.

nical and legal staffs; the US FDA; the Canadian BRMD; the Canadian Atomic Energy Control Board; the Province of Ontario; and the Radiation Regulations Committee of the Canadian Association of Physicists.

According to Symonds of the BRMD, this meeting was very important to the resolution of the problems since the regulators, users, and the manufacturer arrived at a consensus in one day.

At this second users meeting, the participants carefully reviewed all the six known major Therac-25 accidents and discussed the elements of the CAP along with possible additional modifications. They came up with a prioritized list of modifications that they wanted included in the CAP and expressed concerns about the lack of independent software evaluation and the lack of a hard-copy audit trail to assist in diagnosing faults.

The AECL representative, who was the quality assurance manager, responded that tests had been done on the CAP changes, but that the tests were not documented, and independent evaluation of the software "might not be possible." He claimed that two outside experts had reviewed the software, but he could not provide their names. In response to user requests for a hard-copy audit trail and access to source code, he explained that memory limitations would not permit including an audit option, and source code would not be made available to users.

On May 1, AECL issued CAP Revision 4 as a result of the FDA comments and users meeting input. The FDA response on May 26 approved the CAP subject to submission of the final test plan results and an independent safety analysis, distribution of the draft revised manual to customers, and completion of the CAP by June 30, 1987. The FDA concluded by rating this a Class I recall: a recall in which there is a reasonable probability that the use of or exposure to a violative product will cause serious adverse health consequences or death.[5]

AECL sent more supporting documentation to the FDA on June 5, 1987, including the CAP test plan, a draft operator's manual, and the draft of the **new safety analysis** (described in the sidebar "Safety analysis of the Therac-25"). The safety analysis revealed four **potentially hazardous subsystems that were not covered by CAP Revision 4:**

(1) electron-beam scanning,
(2) electron-energy selection,
(3) beam shutoff, and
(4) calibration and/or steering.

AECL planned a fifth revision of the CAP to include the testing and safety analysis results.

Referring to the test plan at this, the final stage of the CAP process, an FDA reviewer said

> Amazingly, the test data presented to show that the software changes to handle the edit problems in the Therac-25 are appropriate prove the exact opposite result. A review of the data table in the test results indicates that the final beam type and energy (edit change) [have] no effect on the initial beam type and energy. I can only assume that either the fix is not right or the data was entered incorrectly. The manufacturer should be admonished for this error. Where is the QC [quality control] review for the test program? AECL must: (1) clarify this situation, (2) change the test protocol to prevent this type of error from occurring, and (3) set up appropriate QC control on data review.

A further FDA memo said the AECL quality assurance manager

> . . . could not give an explanation and will check into the circumstances. He subsequently called back and verified that the technician completed the form incorrectly. Correct operation was witnessed by himself and others. They will repeat and send us the correct data sheet.

At the American Association of Physicists in Medicine meeting in July 1987, a third user group meeting was held. The AECL representative gave the status of CAP Revision 5. He explained that the FDA had given verbal approval and he expected full implementation by the end of August 1987. He reviewed and commented on the prioritized concerns of the last meeting. AECL had included in the CAP three of the user-requested hardware changes. Changes to tape-load error messages and check sums on the load data would wait until after the CAP was done.

Two user-requested hardware modifications had not been included in the CAP. One of these, a push-button energy and selection mode switch, AECL would work on after completing the CAP, the quality assurance manager said. The other, a fixed ion chamber with dose/pulse monitoring, was being installed at Yakima, had already been installed by Halifax on their own, and

would be an option for other clinics. Software documentation was described as a lower priority task that needed definition and would not be available to the FDA in any form for more than a year.

On July 6, 1987, AECL sent a letter to all users to inform them of the FDA's verbal approval of the CAP and delineated how AECL would proceed. On July 21, 1987, AECL issued the fifth and final CAP revision. The major features of the final CAP are as follows:

- All interruptions related to the dosimetry system will go to a treatment suspend, not a treatment pause. Operators will not be allowed to restart the machine without reentering all parameters.
- A software single-pulse shutdown will be added.
- An independent hardware single-pulse shutdown will be added.
- Monitoring logic for turntable position will be improved to ensure that the turntable is in one of the three legal positions.
- A potentiometer will be added to the turntable. It will provide a visible signal of position that operators will use to monitor exact turntable location.
- Interlocking with the 270-degree bending magnet will be added to ensure that the target and beam flattener are in position if the X-ray mode is selected.
- Beam on will be prevented if the turntable is in the field-light or an intermediate position.
- Cryptic malfunction messages will be replaced with meaningful messages and highlighted dose-rate messages.
- Editing keys will be limited to cursor up, backspace, and return. All other keys will be inoperative.
- A motion-enable foot switch will be added, which the operator must hold closed during movement of certain parts of the machine to prevent unwanted motions when the operator is not in control (a type of "dead man's switch").
- Twenty-three other changes to the software to improve its operation and reliability, including disabling of unused keys, changing the operation of the set and reset commands, preventing copying of the control program on site, changing the way various detected hardware faults are handled, eliminating errors in the software that were detected during the review process, adding several additional software interlocks, disallowing

changing to the service mode while a treatment is in progress, and adding meaningful error messages.

- The known software problems associated with the Tyler and Yakima accidents will be fixed.
- The manuals will be fixed to reflect the changes.

In a 1987 paper, Miller, director of the Division of Standards Enforcement, CDRH, wrote about the lessons learned from the Therac-25 experiences.[6] The first was the importance of safe versus "user-friendly" operator interfaces — in other words, making the machine as easy as possible to use may conflict with safety goals. The second is the importance of providing fail-safe designs:

> The second lesson is that for complex interrupt-driven software, timing is of critical importance. In both of these situations, operator action within very narrow time-frame windows was necessary for the accidents to occur. It is unlikely that software testing will discover all possible errors that involve operator intervention at precise time frames during software operation. These machines, for example, have been exercised for thousands of hours in the factory and in the hospitals without accident. Therefore, one must provide for prevention of catastrophic results of failures when they do occur.
> I, for one, will not be surprised if other software errors appear with this or other equipment in the future.

Miller concluded the paper with

> FDA has performed extensive review of the Therac-25 software and hardware safety systems. We cannot say with absolute certainty that all software problems that might result in improper dose have been found and eliminated. However, we are confident that the hardware and software safety features recently added will prevent future catastrophic consequences of failure.

Lessons learned

Often, it takes an accident to alert people to the dangers involved in technology. A medical physicist wrote about the Therac-25 accidents:

> In the past decade or two, the medical accelerator "industry" has become perhaps a little complacent about safety. We have assumed that the manufacturers have all kinds of safety design experience since they've been in the business a long time. We know that there are many safety codes,

---

Accidents usually involve a complex web of interacting events with multiple contributing factors.

---

guides, and regulations to guide them and we have been reassured by the hitherto excellent record of these machines. Except for a few incidents in the 1960s (e.g., at Hammersmith, Hamburg) the use of medical accelerators has been remarkably free of serious radiation accidents until now. Perhaps, though, we have been spoiled by this success.[1]

Accidents are seldom simple — they usually involve a complex web of interacting events with multiple contributing technical, human, and organizational factors. One of the serious mistakes that led to the multiple Therac-25 accidents was the tendency to believe that the cause of an accident had been determined (for example, a microswitch failure in the Hamilton accident) without adequate evidence to come to this conclusion and without looking at all possible contributing factors. Another mistake was the assumption that fixing a particular error (eliminating the current software bug) would prevent future accidents. There is always another software bug.

Accidents are often blamed on a single cause like human error. But virtually all factors involved in accidents can be labeled human error, except perhaps for hardware wear-out failures. Even such hardware failures could be attributed to human error (for example, the designer's failure to provide adequate redundancy or the failure of operational personnel to properly maintain or replace parts): Concluding that an accident was the result of human error is not very helpful or meaningful.

It is nearly as useless to ascribe the cause of an accident to a computer error or a software error. Certainly software was involved in the Therac-25 accidents, but it was only one contributing factor. If we assign software error as *the* cause of the Therac-25 accidents, we are forced to conclude that the only way to prevent such accidents in the future is to build perfect software that will never behave

in an unexpected or undesired way under any circumstances (which is clearly impossible) or not to use software at all in these types of systems. Both conclusions are overly pessimistic.

We must approach the problem of accidents in complex systems from a system-engineering point of view and consider all possible contributing factors. For the Therac-25 accidents, contributing factors included

- management inadequacies and lack of procedures for following through on all reported incidents,
- overconfidence in the software and removal of hardware interlocks (making the software into a single point of failure that could lead to an accident),
- presumably less-than-acceptable software-engineering practices, and
- unrealistic risk assessments along with overconfidence in the results of these assessments.

The exact same accident may not happen a second time, but if we examine and try to ameliorate the contributing factors to the accidents we have had, we may be able to prevent different accidents in the future. In the following sections, we present what we feel are important lessons learned from the Therac-25. You may draw different or additional conclusions.

System engineering. A common mistake in engineering, in this case and many others, is to put too much confidence in software. Nonsoftware professionals seem to feel that software will not or cannot fail; this attitude leads to complacency and overreliance on computerized functions. Although software is not subject to random wear-out failures like hardware, software design errors are much harder to find and eliminate. Furthermore, hardware failure modes are generally much more limited, so building protection against them is usually easier. A lesson to be learned from the Therac-25 accidents is not to remove standard hardware interlocks when adding computer control.

Hardware backups, interlocks, and other safety devices are currently being replaced by software in many different types of systems, including commercial aircraft, nuclear power plants, and weapon systems. Where the hardware interlocks are still used, they are often controlled by software. Designing any dangerous system in such a way that one failure can lead to an accident violates basic system-engineering principles. In this respect, software needs to be treated as a single component. Software should not be assigned sole responsibility for safety, and systems should not be designed such that a single software error or software-engineering error can be catastrophic.

A related tendency among engineers is to ignore software. The first safety analysis on the Therac-25 did not include software (although nearly full responsibility for safety rested on the software). When problems started occurring, investigators assumed that hardware was the cause and focused only on the hardware. Investigation of software's possible contribution to an accident should not be the last avenue explored after all other possible explanations are eliminated.

In fact, a software error can always be attributed to a transient hardware failure, since software (in these types of process-control systems) reads and issues commands to actuators. Without a thorough investigation (and without online monitoring or audit trails that save internal state information), it is not possible to determine whether the sensor provided the wrong information, the software provided an incorrect command, or the actuator had a transient failure and did the wrong thing on its own. In the Hamilton accident, a transient microswitch failure was assumed to be the cause, even though the engineers were unable to reproduce the failure or find anything wrong with the microswitch.

Patient reactions were the only real indications of the seriousness of the problems with the Therac-25. There were no independent checks that the software was operating correctly (including software checks). Such verification cannot be assigned to operators without providing them with some means of detecting errors. The Therac-25 software "lied" to the operators, and the machine itself could not detect that a massive overdose had occurred. The Therac-25 ion chambers could not handle the high density of ionization from the unscanned electron beam at high-beam current; they thus became saturated and gave an indication of a low dosage. Engineers need to design for the worst case.

Every company building safety-critical systems should have audit trails and incident-analysis procedures that they apply whenever they find any hint of a problem that might lead to an accident. The first phone call by Still should have led to an extensive investigation of the events at Kennestone. Certainly, learning about the first lawsuit should have triggered an immediate response. Although hazard logging and tracking is required in the standards for safety-critical military projects, it is less common in nonmilitary projects. Every company building hazardous equipment should have hazard logging and tracking as well as incident reporting and analysis as parts of its quality control procedures. Such follow-up and tracking will not only help prevent accidents, but will easily pay for themselves in reduced insurance rates and reasonable settlement of lawsuits when they do occur.

Finally, overreliance on the numerical output of safety analyses is unwise. The arguments over whether very low probabilities are meaningful with respect to safety are too extensive to summarize here. But, at the least, a healthy skepticism is in order. The claim that safety had been increased five orders of magnitude as a result of the microswitch fix after the Hamilton accident seems hard to justify. Perhaps it was based on the probability of failure of the microswitch (typically 10^{-5}) ANDed with the other interlocks. The problem with all such analyses is that they exclude aspects of the problem (in this case, software) that are difficult to quantify but which may have a larger impact on safety than the quantifiable factors that are included.

Although management and regulatory agencies often press engineers to obtain such numbers, engineers should insist that any risk assessment numbers used are in fact meaningful and that statistics of this sort are treated with caution. In our enthusiasm to provide measurements, we should not attempt to measure the unmeasurable. William Ruckelshaus, two-time head of the US Environmental Protection Agency, cautioned that "risk assessment data can be like the captured spy: if you torture it long enough, it will tell you anything you want to know."[7] E.A. Ryder of the British Health and Safety Executive has written that the numbers game in risk assessment "should only be played in private between consenting adults, as it is too easy to be misinterpreted."[8]

Software engineering. The Therac-25 accidents were fairly unique in having software coding errors involved — most computer-related accidents have not involved coding errors but rather errors in the software requirements such as omissions and mishandled environmental conditions and system states. Although using good basic software-engineering practices will not prevent all software errors, it is certainly required as a minimum. Some companies introducing software into their systems for the first time do not take software engineering as seriously as they should. Basic software-engineering principles that apparently were violated with the Therac-25 include:

- Documentation should not be an afterthought.
- Software quality assurance practices and standards should be established.
- Designs should be kept simple.
- Ways to get information about errors — for example, software audit trails — should be designed into the software from the beginning.
- The software should be subjected to extensive testing and formal analysis at the module and software level; system testing alone is not adequate.

In addition, special safety-analysis and design procedures must be incorporated into safety-critical software projects. Safety must be built into software, and, in addition, safety must be assured at the system level despite software errors.[9,10] The Therac-20 contained the same software error implicated in the Tyler deaths, but the machine included hardware interlocks that mitigated its consequences. Protection against software errors can also be built into the software itself.

Furthermore, important lessons about software reuse can be found here. A naive assumption is often made that reusing software or using commercial off-the-shelf software increases safety because the software has been exercised extensively. Reusing software modules does not guarantee safety in the new system to which they are transferred and sometimes leads to awkward and dangerous designs. Safety is a quality of the system in which the software is used; it is not a quality of the software itself. Rewriting the entire software to get a clean and simple design may be safer in many cases.

Taking a couple of programming courses or programming a home computer does not qualify anyone to produce safety-critical software. Although certification of software engineers is not yet required, more events like those associated with the Therac-25 will make such certification inevitable. There is activity in Britain to specify required courses for those working on critical software. Any engineer is not automatically qualified to be a software engineer — an extensive program of study and experience is required. Safety-critical software engineering requires training and experience in addition to that required for noncritical software.

Although the user interface of the Therac-25 has attracted a lot of attention, it was really a side issue in the accidents. Certainly, it could have been improved, like many other aspects of this software. Either software engineers need better training in interface design, or more input is needed from human factors engineers. There also needs to be greater recognition of potential conflicts between user-friendly interfaces and safety. One goal of interface design is to make the interface as easy as possible for the operator to use. But in the Therac-25, some design features (for example, not requiring the operator to reenter patient prescriptions after mistakes) and later changes (allowing a carriage return to indicate that information has been entered correctly) enhanced usability at the expense of safety.

Finally, not only must safety be considered in the initial design of the software and it operator interface, but the reasons for design decisions should be recorded so that decisions are not inadvertently undone in future modifications.

User and government oversight and standards. Once the FDA got involved in the Therac-25, their response was impressive, especially considering how little experience they had with similar problems in computerized medical devices. Since the Therac-25 events, the FDA has moved to improve the reporting system and to augment their procedures and guidelines to include software. The problem of deciding when to forbid the use of medical devices that are also saving lives has no simple an-

swer and involves ethical and political issues that cannot be answered by science or engineering alone. However, at the least, better procedures are certainly required for reporting problems to the FDA and to users.

The issues involved in regulation of risky technology are complex. Overly strict standards can inhibit progress, require techniques behind the state of the art, and transfer responsibility from the manufacturer to the government. The fixing of responsibility requires a delicate balance. Someone must represent the public's needs, which may be subsumed by a company's desire for profits. On the other hand, standards can have the undesirable effect of limiting the safety efforts and investment of companies that feel their legal and moral responsibilities are fulfilled if they follow the standards.

Some of the most effective standards and efforts for safety come from users. Manufacturers have more incentive to satisfy customers than to satisfy government agencies. The American Association of Physicists in Medicine established a task group to work on problems associated with computers in radiation therapy in 1979, long before the Therac-25 problems began. The accidents intensified these efforts, and the association is developing user-written standards. A report by J.A. Rawlinson of the Ontario Cancer Institute attempted to define the physicist's role in assuring adequate safety in medical accelerators:

> We could continue our traditional role, which has been to provide input to the manufacturer on safety issues but to leave the major safety design decisions to the manufacturer. We can provide this input through a number of mechanisms... These include participation in standards organizations such as the IEC [International Electrotechnical Commission], in professional association groups ... and in accelerator user groups such as the Therac-25 user group. It includes also making use of the Problem Reporting Program for Radiation Therapy Devices . . . and it includes consultation in the drafting of the government safety regulations. Each of these if pursued vigorously will go a long way to improving safety. It is debatable however whether these actions would be sufficient to prevent a future series of accidents.
> Perhaps what is needed in addition is a mechanism by which the safety of any new model of accelerator is assessed independently of the manufacturer. This task could be done by the individual physicist at the time of acceptance of a new machine. Indeed many users already

test at least the *operation* of safety interlocks during commissioning. Few however have the time or resources to conduct a comprehensive assessment of safety *design*.

A more effective approach might be to require that prior to the use of a new type of accelerator in a particular jurisdiction, an independent safety analysis is made by a panel (including but not limited to medical physicists). Such a panel could be established within or without a regulatory framework.[1]

It is clear that users need to be involved. It was users who found the problems with the Therac-25 and forced AECL to respond. The process of fixing the Therac-25 was user driven — the manufacturer was slow to respond. The Therac-25 user group meetings were, according to participants, important to the resolution of the problems. But if users are to be involved, then they must be provided with information and the ability to perform this function. Manufacturers need to understand that the adversarial approach and the attempt to keep government agencies and users in the dark about problems will not be to their benefit in the long run.

The US Air Force has one of the most extensive programs to inform users. Contractors who build space systems for the Air Force must provide an Accident Risk Assessment Report (AFAR) to system users and operators that describes the hazardous subsystems and operations associated with that system and its interfaces. The AFAR also comprehensively identifies and evaluates the system's accident risks; provides a means of substantiating compliance with safety requirements; summarizes all system-safety analyses and testing performed on each system and subsystem; and identifies design and operating limits to be imposed on system components to preclude or minimize accidents that could cause injury or damage.

An interesting requirement in the Air Force AFAR is a record of all safety-related failures or accidents associated with system acceptance, test, and checkout, along with an assessment of the impact on flight and ground safety and action taken to prevent recurrence. The AFAR also must address failures, accidents, or incidents from previous missions of this system or other systems using similar hardware. All corrective action taken to prevent recurrence must be documented. The accident and correction history must be updated throughout the life of the system. If any design or operating parameters change after government approval, the AFAR must be updated to include all changes affecting safety.

Unfortunately, the Air Force program is not practical for commercial systems. However, government agencies might require manufacturers to provide similar information to users. If required for everyone, competitive pressures to withhold information might be lessened. Manufacturers might find that providing such information actually increases customer loyalty and confidence. An emphasis on safety can be turned into a competitive advantage.

Most previous accounts of the Therac-25 accidents blamed them on a software error and stopped there. This is not very useful and, in fact, can be misleading and dangerous: If we are to prevent such accidents in the future, we must dig deeper. Most accidents involving complex technology are caused by a combination of organizational, managerial, technical, and, sometimes, sociological or political factors. Preventing accidents requires paying attention to *all* the root causes, not just the precipitating event in a particular circumstance.

Accidents are unlikely to occur in exactly the same way again. If we patch only the symptoms and ignore the deeper underlying causes or we fix only the specific cause of one accident, we are unlikely to prevent or mitigate future accidents. The series of accidents involving the Therac-25 is a good example of exactly this problem: Fixing each individual software flaw as it was found did not solve the device's safety problems. Virtually all complex software will behave in an unexpected or undesired fashion under some conditions — there will always be another bug. Instead, accidents must be understood with respect to the complex factors involved. In addition, changes need to be made to eliminate or reduce the underlying causes and contributing factors that increase the likelihood of accidents or loss resulting from them.

Although these accidents occurred in software controlling medical devices, the lessons apply to all types of systems where computers control dangerous devices. In our experience, the same types of mistakes are being made in nonmedical systems. We must learn from our mistakes so we do not repeat them. ∎

Acknowledgments

Ed Miller of the FDA was especially helpful, both in providing information to be included in this article and in reviewing and commenting on the final version. Gordon Symonds of the Canadian Government Health Protection Branch also reviewed and commented on a draft of the article. Finally, the referees, several of whom were apparently intimately involved in some of the accidents, were also very helpful in providing additional information about the accidents.

References

The information in this article was gathered from official FDA documents and internal memos, lawsuit depositions, letters, and various other sources that are not publicly available. *Computer* does not provide references to documents that are unavailable to the public.

1. J.A. Rawlinson, "Report on the Therac-25," OCTRF/OCI Physicists Meeting, Kingston, Ont., Canada, May 7, 1987.

2. F. Houston, "What Do the Simple Folk Do?: Software Safety in the Cottage Industry," *IEEE Computers in Medicine Conf.*, 1985.

3. C.A. Bowsher, "Medical Devices: The Public Health at Risk," US Gov't Accounting Office Report GAO/T-PEMD-90-2, 046987/139922, 1990.

4. M. Kivel, ed., *Radiological Health Bulletin*, Vol. XX, No. 8, US Federal Food and Drug Administration, Dec. 1986.

5. *Medical Device Recalls, Examination of Selected Cases*, GAO/PEMD-90-6, 1989.

6. E. Miller, "The Therac-25 Experience," *Proc. Conf. State Radiation Control Program Directors*, 1987.

7. W.D. Ruckelshaus, "Risk in a Free Society," *Risk Analysis*, Vol. 4, No. 3, 1984, pp. 157-162.

8. E.A. Ryder, "The Control of Major Hazards: The Advisory Committee's Third and Final Report," *Transcript of Conf. European Major Hazards*, Oyez Scientific and Technical Services and Authors, London, 1984.

9. N.G. Leveson, "Software Safety: Why, What, and How," *ACM Computing Surveys*, Vol. 18, No. 2, June 1986, pp. 25-69.

10. N.G. Leveson, "Software Safety in Embedded Computer Systems," *Comm. ACM*, Feb. 1991, pp. 34-46.

LETTERS TO THE EDITOR

Therac-25 revisited

To the editor:

I am sending this note to thank Nancy G. Leveson and Clark S. Turner for their excellent article on the Therac-25 accidents (*Computer*, July 1993, pp. 18-41).

Preparing this article was a genuine service to the real-time community. For example, I have been using the article in an effort to educate my management about what constitutes adequate qualifications for staff who work on real-time control systems for our chemical plants and refineries.

Norman F. Jerome
Amoco Research Center
Naperville, Illinois

To the editor:

I have a serious question to raise about "An Investigation of the Therac-25 Accidents" by Leveson and Turner:

Where was the doctor?

At several points the authors describe technicians as operating a delicate instrument that exhibited "frequent malfunctions" during routine operation and that issued "malfunction messages" so often that it was standard policy to ignore them. Who was permitted to lay down such a policy?

The combined software and hardware problems are described as having been discovered gradually. Yet why isn't the contribution of medicine recognized? The heroes are said to have been a radiation physicist and a corps of technicians and operating engineers: The impression is of a therapeutic environment in which patients wander into a clinic and pick out a technician just to get a "good dose of radiation treatment." It's not a drug, so why should they need a prescription!

The article suggests that the professional involved, namely the medical doctor prescribing the treatments, did absolutely nothing to discover or prevent the problem. I do not accept this as accurate.

John Michael Williams
Redwood City, California

Authors' reply:

The MD was not involved in the day-to-day operation of the Therac-25; the physicians would write prescriptions for their patients, who would then be scheduled by the hospital for treatment. Obviously, the physicians had to know about the serious results of the accidents, but we could find no information in the boxes of material we received from the FDA and other sources (including two lawsuits for which Nancy Leveson was an expert witness) to indicate any direct involvement of the MDs in finding or resolving the Therac-25 problems. This does not mean that they did nothing, but we could only present what we were able to learn from publicly available documents. We do not mean to imply anything from our omission of information about the doctors' responses except ignorance on our part about them.

To the editor:

I am grateful for the fine analysis of the Therac-25 accidents. At last I'm able to appreciate the vague reports I've heard over the last five years about "software killing patients" under treatment by an "X-ray machine." The agony of the patients injured and killed by the Therac-25 permeates the well-written technical prose.

I'm afraid two other unfortunate impressions reach me: almost criminally bad electromechanical design, and unconscionable clinical usage of the Therac-25.

Safe treatment by the Therac-25 requires the correct mechanical positioning of beam-shaping structures, one for each of the two accelerator modes. If the correct structure is not positioned in the path of the beam, overdosage is likely to occur. I believe it is exceedingly bad design to use an elaborate scheme involving software rather than the simple combination of two cams and two normally open microswitches to interlock the two treatment modes.

Certainly the doctors and other professionals — if not the accelerator technicians — involved in the Therac-25 treatment were remiss in allowing humans to be subjected to an energetic device that issued so many malfunction indications that the operators "became insensitive to machine malfunctions" or that on some days exhibited "40 dose-rate malfunctions." Furthermore, once the suspicion arose that the beam-shaping structures were not properly positioned automatically, it should have been expected of the operators to visually check before beam power was applied.

There isn't space to discuss some of the other design flaws exhibited (consider, for example, an undocumented error message "dose input 2," which means the delivered dose was too high or too low!). And what about the pitiful response of US and Canadian government regulators?

As a programmer, I am critical of any program involving setup followed by actuation that does not *indivisibly* check the setup for consistency, reasonableness, safety, and so forth, immediately before actuation.

The industry's state of the art (and certainly my personal state of the art) in building safe programs is not sufficiently advanced to risk human life. Consequently, I have decided not to write software for high-energy treatment or transportation of humans, or for life support or critical patient monitoring. I would like to correspond with anyone who thinks he or she can responsibly write software when bugs can have lethal consequences.

William E. Drissel
President, CyberScribe Inc.
Grand Prairie, Texas

Authors' reply:

We can only add that the features William Drissel notes, along with other similar problems, are, according to our experience, common in safety-critical software. Perhaps those who write such software should be people exactly like Drissel who appreciate the dangers and are worried about their competence to write the software. Complacency is the most frequent common aspect of major accidents.

To the editor:

I was encouraged to see the issue of software reliability in critical systems brought to the attention of a broad professional audience. However, there is an editorial issue that I feel detracts from the authors' technical credibility.

The editorial point, although minor when compared with the importance of the article's message, is significant for computer professionals dealing with software reliability. The authors use nonstandard terminology in dis-

Reprinted from *IEEE Computer*, Vol. 26, No. 10, pp. 4–5, October 1993.

cussing software faults, failures, and errors. The term "error" is used to refer to faults, the term "fault" is used to refer to failures, and the term "bug" is used in its typically ambiguous way.

IEEE/ANSI Standard 982.2 defines standard terms for discussing software reliability. Researchers working in the software reliability area are undoubtedly aware of this standard. The authors' apparent ignorance of the IEEE standard brings their technical credibility into question. It also reflects poorly on *Computer*'s editorial staff and review process.

Norman Young
Ottawa, Ontario
Canada

Authors' reply:
We are very aware of the standard, but after a great deal of experience in trying to apply these definitions to real software problems, we have found them to be meaningless in practice. This is not the place to go into our objections to the definitions, but we were quite aware that we were not following the IEEE standard. None of the 17 reviewers of the article, most of whom appeared to be software reliability experts, as are the authors, nor any of the hundreds of people who read early versions of the report noted any problem with the terminology or felt that it hindered their understanding.

We have also had enough arguments and communication problems with engineers to recognize the problems that occur when software engineers define terms differently than hardware engineers. To differentiate the type of random, wear-out failures in engineering from design errors of the type that occur in software (and hardware), we use the term "error" to mean a generic design problem with the software. This is also closer to natural language usage, and our goal was communication with a large audience.

We find it indicative of the problems in software engineering and software reliability that lead to accidents such as those described in the article that technical competence is defined as following the definitions of terms in IEEE standards.

To the editor:
"An Investigation of the Therac-25 Accidents" is an excellent example of technical reporting conducted under difficult circumstances due to the legal sensitivities. However, I must comment on the authors' viewpoint for fault analysis and recommendations. The major weakness of the Therac-25

system was not in hardware or software, but in design. The overwhelming, dominant flaw was that the system was not designed to measure radiation dosage throughout the range it was capable of producing. Leveson and Turner write: "The Therac-25 software 'lied' to the operators, and the machine itself could not detect that a massive overdose had occurred. The Therac-25 ion chambers could not handle the high density of ionization from the unscanned electron beam at high beam current; they thus became saturated and gave an indication of low dosage. Engineers need to design for the worst case."

One cannot blame the software for lying if it is accurately reporting the output of the sensors. And the sensors apparently always worked exactly as designed.

If the operators had been informed that they were administering fatal doses of radiation to patients, I very much doubt if they would have repeated the treatments, no matter how simple the command or how mundane the alert. I also believe that the AECL (Atomic Energy of Canada Limited) would have quickly recognized and isolated the software faults if they had been presented with hard physical measurement of the massive dose rates, rather than muddling for almost a year in ambiguous investigations and claiming that overdoses were impossible and no other accidents had occurred previously.

I agree wholeheartedly that "there is always one more bug," especially in systems that deal with concurrent, unsynchronized processes. One cannot disagree that relevant training and experience will reduce the number of programming errors, but they will never be eliminated. Redundant safety systems reduce the number of accidents, but they become prohibitively expensive and frustrate normal operation with false alarms as systems become more complex. The only path to arbitrarily complex reliable systems is through unambiguous detection of errors as they occur. The amount of monitoring information collected from a system will always have to be balanced against the amount of effort required to isolate the fault when an error occurs. However, the absolute minimum monitoring requirement is that it should detect any error that could cause fatal injury. The Therac-25 design failed to meet this minimum requirement.

Thomas D. Gamble
Annandale, Virginia

Authors' reply:
We have to do a lot more than just detect that we have already made a mistake, especially when that mistake is not correctable, such as having given a fatal dose of radiation to a patient. We agree that error checking is important, but it is not the complete answer to preventing accidents: Some errors are not detectable, some are detectable but no recovery path exists at that point, and some are not detectable until after the damage has already been done. There is always a limit (in terms of memory, execution time, etc.,) to how much checking is practical: Checking everything is prohibitively expensive. Accidents usually involve the occurrence of events that everyone thought were impossible before they occur (or they would have taken preventative measures such as putting in checks and interlocks). We said in our article, as the letter writer notes, that they should have designed for the worst case, but a simple message that the worst case has already occurred is not the solution to preventing accidents.

Furthermore, AECL was very much aware that an overdose had occurred after the Hamilton accident (within six weeks of the first overdose), and they even knew that it was caused by an unscanned beam. Yet this did not allow them to "quickly recognize and isolate the software faults" as the letter writer suggests. Knowing that something bad has occurred in a system does not necessarily provide any evidence that software was involved. Hindsight is always perfect, but there are no simple answers to complex problems.

Nancy G. Leveson
University of Washington

Clark S. Turner
University of California, Irvine

Editor: Bertrand Meyer, EiffelSoft, 270 Storke Rd., Ste. 7, Goleta, CA 93117; voice (805) 685-6869; ot-column@eiffel.com

Object Technology

Design by Contract: The Lessons of Ariane

Jean-Marc Jézéquel, IRISA/CNRS
Bertrand Meyer, EiffelSoft

Several contributions to this department have emphasized the importance of *design by contract* in the construction of reliable software. Design by contract, as you will recall, is the principle that interfaces between modules of a software system — especially a mission-critical one — should be governed by precise specifications, similar to contracts between humans or companies. The contracts will cover mutual obligations (*preconditions*), benefits (*postconditions*), and consistency constraints (*invariants*). Together these properties are known as *assertions*, and are directly supported in some design and programming languages.

A recent $500 million software error provides a sobering reminder that this principle is not just a pleasant academic ideal. On June 4, 1996, the maiden flight of the European Ariane 5 launcher crashed, about 40 seconds after takeoff. Media reports indicated that a half-billion dollars was lost—the rocket was uninsured.

The French space agency, CNES (Centre National d'Etudes Spatiales), and the European Space Agency immediately appointed an international inquiry board,

made up of respected experts from major European countries, which produced a report in hardly more than a month. These agencies are to be commended for the speed and openness with which they handled the disaster. The report is available on the Web, in both French and English (http://www.cnes.fr/actualites/news/rapport_501.html).

It is a remarkable document: short, clear, and forceful. The explosion, the report says, is the result of a software error, possibly the costliest in history (at least in dollar terms, since earlier cases have cost lives).

Particularly vexing is the realization that the error came from a piece of the software that was *not* needed. The software involved is part of the Inertial Reference System, for which we will keep the acronym SRI used in the report, if only to avoid the unpleasant connotation that the reverse acronym has for US readers. Before liftoff, certain computations are performed to align the SRI. Normally, these computations should cease at −9 seconds, but because there is a chance that a countdown could be put on hold, the engineers gave themselves some leeway. They reasoned that, because resetting the SRI could take

several hours (at least in earlier versions of Ariane), it was better to let the computation proceed than to stop it and then have to restart it if liftoff was delayed. So the SRI computation continues for 50 seconds after the start of flight mode—well into the flight period. After takeoff, of course, this computation is useless. In the Ariane 5 flight, however, it caused an exception, which was not caught and—boom.

The exception was due to a floating-point error during a conversion from a 64-bit floating-point value, representing the flight's "horizontal bias," to a 16-bit signed integer: In other words, the value that was converted was greater than what can be represented as a 16-bit signed integer. There was no explicit exception handler to catch the exception, so it followed the usual fate of uncaught exceptions and crashed the entire software, hence the onboard computers, hence the mission.

This is the kind of trivial error that we are all familiar with (raise your hand if you have never done anything of this sort), although fortunately the consequences are usually less expensive. How in the world

> **How in the world could such a trivial error have remained undetected and cause a $500 million rocket to blow up?**

can it have remained undetected and produced such a horrendous outcome?

YOU CAN'T BLAME MANAGEMENT

Although something clearly went wrong in the validation and verification process (or we wouldn't have a story to tell), and although the Inquiry Board does make several recommendations to improve the process, it is also clear that systematic documentation, validation, and management procedures were in place.

The software engineering literature has often contended that most software problems are primarily management problems. This is not the case here: the problem was a technical one. (Of course you can always argue that good management will spot technical problems early enough.)

Reprinted from *IEEE Computer*, Vol. 30, No. 1, pp. 129–130, January 1997.

YOU CAN'T BLAME THE LANGUAGE

Ada's exception mechanism has been criticized in the literature, but in this case it could have been used to catch the exception. In fact, the report says:

Not all the conversions were protected because a maximum workload target of 80% had been set for the SRI computer. To determine the vulnerability of unprotected code, an analysis was performed on every operation which could give rise to an ... operand error. This led to protection being added to four of [seven] variables ... in the Ada code. However, three of the variables were left unprotected.

YOU CAN'T BLAME THE DESIGN

Why was the exception not monitored? The analysis revealed that overflow (a horizontal bias not fitting in a 16-bit integer) could not occur. Was the analysis wrong? No! It was right *for the Ariane 4 trajectory*. For Ariane 5, with other trajectory parameters, it did not hold.

YOU CAN'T BLAME THE IMPLEMENTATION

Some may criticize removing the conversion protection to achieve more performance (the 80 percent workload target), but this decision was justified by the theoretical analysis. To engineer is to make compromises. If you have proved that a condition cannot happen, you are entitled not to check for it. If every program checked for all possible and impossible events, no useful instruction would ever get executed!

YOU CAN'T BLAME TESTING

The Inquiry Board recommends better testing procedures, and it also recommends testing the entire system rather than parts of it (in the Ariane 5 case the SRI and the flight software were tested separately). But even if you can test more, you can never test all. Testing, as we all know, can show the presence of errors, not their absence. The only fully realistic test is a launch. And in fact, the launch *was* a test launch, in that it carried no commercial payload, although it was probably not intended to be a $500 million test.

YOU CAN TRY TO BLAME REUSE

The SRI horizontal bias module was indeed reused from 10-year-old software, the software from Ariane 4. But this is not the real story.

BUT YOU REALLY HAVE TO BLAME REUSE *SPECIFICATION*

What was truly unacceptable in this case was the absence of any kind of precise specification associated with this reusable module. The requirement that the horizontal bias should fit on 16 bits was in fact stated in an obscure part of a mission document. But it was nowhere to be found in the code itself!

One of the principles of design by contract, as earlier columns have said, is that *any* software element that has such a fundamental constraint should state it explicitly, as part of a mechanism present in the language. In an Eiffel version, for example, it would be stated as

```
convert (horizontal_bias:
DOUBLE): INTEGER is
require
    horizontal_bias
        <= Maximum_bias
do
    ...
ensure
    ...
end
```

where the precondition (require...) states clearly and precisely what the input must satisfy to be acceptable.

Does this mean that the crash would automatically have been avoided had the mission used a language and method supporting built-in assertions and design by contract? Although it is always risky to draw such after-the-fact conclusions, the answer is probably yes:

- Assertions (preconditions and postconditions in particular) can be automatically turned on during testing, through a simple compiler option. The error might have been caught then.
- Assertions can remain turned on during execution, triggering an exception if violated. Given the performance constraints on such a mission, however, this would probably not have been the case.

- Most important, assertions are a prime component of the software and its automatically produced documentation ("short form" in Eiffel environments). In a project such as Ariane, in which there is so much emphasis on quality control and thorough validation of everything, assertions would have been the quality assurance team's primary focus of attention. Any test team worth its salt would have checked systematically that every call satisfies every precondition. That would have immediately revealed that the Ariane 5 software did not meet the expectation of the Ariane 4 routines that it called.

The Inquiry Board makes several recommendations with respect to software process improvement. Many are justified; some may be overkill; some would be very expensive to put in place. There is a more simple lesson to be learned from this unfortunate event: Reuse without a precise, rigorous specification mechanism is a risk of potentially disastrous proportions.

> **There is a simple lesson here: Reuse without a precise specification mechanism is a disastrous risk.**

It is regrettable that this lesson has not been heeded by such recent designs as IDL (the Interface Definition Language of CORBA)—which is intended to foster large-scale reuse across networks but fails to provide any semantic specification mechanism—Ada 95, or Java. None of these languages has built-in support for design by contract.

Effective reuse requires design by contract. Without a precise specification attached to each reusable component—precondition, postcondition, invariant—no one can trust a supposedly reusable component. Without a specification, it is probably safer to redo than to reuse. ❖

imperial college, london

Ariane 5: Who Dunnit?

A forum for exchanging ideas, philosophy, and experience.

At a 1993 software symposium in inland China, a keynote speaker from the US joked that he had arrived safely because the transportation systems in China "were not yet heavily controlled by software." When disastrous accidents occur, computers are often singled out for blame—sometimes, rightly so. What have we learned from our many expensive lessons? Not much. One lesson is the need for risk management, but as Nuseibeh points out, it is not practiced even in mission critical projects like Ariane 5.
—Tomoo Matsubara

ON 4 JUNE 1996, THE MAIDEN FLIGHT OF the Ariane 5 launcher exploded about 37 seconds after liftoff. Scientists with experiments on board that had taken years to prepare were devastated. For many software engineering researchers, however, the disaster is a case study rich in lessons. To begin learning from this disaster, we need look no further than a report on it issued by an independent inquiry board set up by the French and European Space Agencies.

VARIED VIEWS. Here are some of the interpretations of the report that I have heard.

♦ *What the programmers said:* The disaster is clearly the result of a programming error. An incorrectly handled software exception resulted from a data conversion of a 64-bit floating point to a 16-bit signed integer value. The value of the floating point number that was converted was larger than what could be represented by a 16-bit integer, resulting in an operand error not anticipated by the Ada code. Better programming practice would have prevented this failure from occurring.

♦ *What the designers said:* The disaster is clearly the result of a design error. The system design specification accounted for random hardware failures only, and therefore the exception handling mechanism was unable to recover from a random *software* error. As a result, a correctly functioning processor in the Inertial Reference System (SRI) was shut down, and soon afterwards the backup processor "failed" in the same way. A better design, such as one

that disallowed software exceptions from halting hardware units that were functioning correctly, would have prevented the failure.

The disaster is a case study rich in lessons; we need look no further than the inquiry board's report.

♦ *What the requirements engineers said:* The disaster is clearly the result of incorrect analysis of changing requirements. The requirements for Ariane 5 were different from earlier models of Ariane. However, the rogue piece of alignment code that resulted in the failure of Ariane 5 was not actually needed after liftoff, as it had been on earlier models. It remained operational in Ariane 5 without satisfying any (traceable) requirement. Better requirements analysis and traceability would have prevented this failure from occurring. Software maintenance researchers supported this view. The failure, they claimed, could have been prevented if the adaptive maintenance team had not adopted the approach of "if it ain't broke, don't fix it."

♦ *What the test engineers said:* The disaster is clearly the result of inadequate validation and verification, testing, and review. For example, as the report states, there was no test to verify that the SRI would behave correctly "when being subjected to the countdown and flight time sequence and the trajectory of Ariane 5." This, and many other ground tests that could have been performed by suppliers during acceptance testing or review, would have exposed the failure.

♦ *What the project managers said:* The disaster is clearly the result of ineffective development processes and project management. For example, the review process for Ariane 5 development was inadequate. In reviewing specifications, code, and rationale documents, no participants external to the pro-

Editor:
Tomoo
Matsubara
Matsubara Consulting
1-9-6 Fujimigaoka,
Ninomiya, Naka-gun,
Kanagawa 259-01
Japan
tmatsu@xa2.so-net.or.jp

Reprinted from *IEEE Software,* Vol. 14, No. 3, pp. 15–16, May/June 1997.

ject were involved, and code and its associated documentation were frequently inconsistent. Improved project management processes that facilitate closer engineering cooperation—with "clear-cut authority and responsibility"—would have increased the chances of exposing the failure.

ANOTHER VIEW. All these interpretations are valid. Certainly, a programming error triggered the failure. Certainly, more rigorous design could have prevented such a programming error from occurring. Certainly, better requirements analysis and specification would have made design verification more achievable. And certainly, improved project management could have provided a more effective organizational process that recognized the impact of changing requirements on system functionality and behavior.

I would also add inadequate *risk management* to the preceding list, since it partly explains the original decision not to handle the fatal exception. That decision was the correct one when it was made (when the primary concern was to keep the SRI processor workload below the chosen threshold of 80 percent). Unfortunately, the decision became the wrong one when the requirements changed. So, a requirements conflict—between a requirement for robustness and a requirement for processor load—was resolved one way, but as time passed the original resolution was invalidated (for more on this see my article with Steve Easterbrook, "Using Viewpoints for Inconsistency Management," in *BCS/IEE Software Engineering Journal*, Jan. 1996).

Jean-Marc Jézéquel and Bertrand Meyer suggest that this is a problem of specification reuse, which could have been mitigated through "design by contract" to specify interfaces between modules precisely ("Design by Contract: The Lessons of Ariane," *Computer*, Jan. 1997). I prefer to classify this as a failure of risk management because a risky decision was not reviewed as the project evolved (although, certainly, more precise specifications of affected and reused components could have helped to highlight dependencies and risks). Thus, the key lesson is that risk management

should not be performed at the start of a project and then forgotten; risk can change as requirements change, and in software systems that change, risk is more likely to increase than decrease.

DEBUNKING MYTHS. Over the years, there have been many spectacular failures of safety-critical systems, the technical causes of which have been rigorously analyzed (see, for example, Nancy Leveson's *Safeware:*

> ## Reuse does not necessarily increase safety, as the reuse of the "wrong" piece demonstrated.

System Safety and Computers, Addison-Wesley, 1995). Although the Ariane 5 disaster is generally attributed to software failure, we court danger when we develop unreasonable expectations of software. For example, believing that "computers provide greater reliability than the devices they replace" or that they "reduce risk over mechanical systems" are but two of many myths about software.

Software fails and engineering trade-offs must be made. For example, an unhandled exception forces developers to protect only some variables. Changing software is not easy because doing so can introduce as many errors as changes. Reuse does not necessarily increase system safety, as the reuse of the "wrong" piece of software demonstrated in Ariane 5. Software testing is by its nature partial, because it only flags errors and cannot prove their absence. Conversely, formally verifying an entire software system such as Ariane is typically unfeasible.

Of course, improved fine-grain processes, such as better programming and design techniques, as well as coarse-grain processes, such as better project management, may help prevent such failures from occurring. However, as Anthony Finkelstein and John Dowell point out, for large-scale software systems development, the

complexity of problems and solutions is such that the real reasons for failure are usually *systemic* ("A Comedy of Errors: The London Ambulance Service," *Proc. 8th Int'l Workshop Software Specification and Design*, IEEE Computer Society Press, 1996). That is, it is the combination and interaction of numerous related, overlapping activities and perspectives that result in failure. Clearly, research agendas should recognize the need for sound software engineering principles such as separating concerns (exemplified by object-orientation, multiple views, and component-based development). They must also recognize, however, the importance of relating concerns (exemplified by work on managing interference, interoperability, and coordination). Finally, recognizing that building software systems is an *engineering* process and requires precise specifications and trained engineers is, I believe, an obvious but fundamental first step toward developing safer systems.

Conclusion: Who dunnit? The butler did it. Who discussed it? The researchers. As my colleague Jeff Kramer pointed out, the claims I recount here were made by researchers, rather than practitioners—the latter being much less enthusiastic about accepting blame for the failure!   ◆

A full text of the inquiry board's report, "Ariane 5: Flight 501 Failure," is available at http://www.esrin.esa.it/htdocs/tidc/Press/Press96 /press33.html.

Chapter 7

Whistle Blowing

Never misrepresent or withhold information that is germane to a problem or situation of public concern nor will I allow any such known information to remain unchallenged.
—from the AITP Standards of Conduct
In the work environment the computing professional has the additional obligation to report any signs of systems dangers that might result in serious personal or social damage. If one's superiors do not act to curtail or mitigate such dangers, it may be necessary to "blow the whistle" to help correct the problems or reduce the risk.
—ACM Code of Ethics, explanation of item 1.2
Disclose to appropriate persons or authorities any actual or potential danger to the user, the public, or the environment, that they reasonably believe to be associated with software or related documents.
—IEEE-CS/ACM Software Engineering Code of Ethics, principle 1.4
Accept responsibility in making engineering decisions consistent with the safety, health, and welfare of the public, and disclose promptly factors that might endanger the public or the environment.
—IEEE Code of Ethics, item 1

7.1 WHAT IS "WHISTLE BLOWING"?

IN the "Morality of Whistle Blowing" [3], Sissela Bok defines whistle blowers as "those who . . . make revelations meant to call attention to negligence, abuses or dangers that threaten the public interest. They sound an alarm based on their expertise or inside knowledge, often from within the very organization in which they work. . . . Most [whistle blowers] know that their alarms pose a threat to anyone who benefits from the ongoing practice and that their own careers and livelihood may be at risk." Leon Zelby traces some variation of the phrase "whistle blowing" back to the 1400s, but suggests that modern use became common in the late 1960s [25]. Common examples of whistle blowing are when an employee decides that the company is making an unsafe product, or that tax dollars are being wasted in some fraudulent or flagrant manner.

An important part of the concept of whistle blowing is the degree of involvement on the part of the person doing it. The name "whistle blowing" suggests drawing an analogy to a referee, who blows a whistle to stop the game,

call attention to an illegal action, and assess a penalty. But that analogy would not be entirely correct. The referee is not a member of either team, but an outside person whose specific job is to blow the whistle. A more correct analogy would be a player blowing a whistle to call attention to an illegal action by a member on his team.

In this light, you can see why whistle blowing would be difficult. Most people feel some degree of loyalty to their organization. For its part, the organization generally takes a dim view of anyone who purposefully draws negative attention to some aspect of its operations. Indeed, historically, "whistle blower" has been a rather negative label [3], [25]. However, in the aftermath of the Challenger incident and the passage of federal and state laws to protect whistle blowers, the image of the whistle blower is decidedly more positive. Still, if you plan to blow the whistle on someone, you should do so with the realization that you are likely to face severe personal, professional, and financial stress. In this chapter's case study, for example, the whistle blower at one point arguably had good reason to fear for his life. He also went through some emotionally

DILBERT © UFS

trying years. In the end, however, he received not only vindication in court, but also an award of $11.5 million dollars!

7.2 STAGES OF A WHISTLE-BLOWING INCIDENT

Each whistle-blowing scenario can involve unique concerns and approaches. Also, two different people in the same situation might react somewhat differently without either person being unethical. However, there is some agreement about the general sequence of events and issues that should be considered by the potential whistle blower at each stage [17], [19], [23].

7.2.1 Stage One—Is There a Potential Whistle-Blowing Scenario?

A potential whistle-blowing scenario begins when the following three conditions exist. First, you learn that your organization, or someone in your organization, is pursuing a course of action you believe is ethically wrong. Second, you believe that you know some relevant information that is not generally known. Typically this information is related to your professional expertise, but not always. Third, you believe that if what you know is correct, and if it became widely known and understood, the course of action would be changed.

This description makes it clear that potential whistle-blowing incidents generally don't include things you are merely unhappy about. For example, you may be unhappy when your organization announces the closing of a branch office because it is losing money. True, the closing will mean lost jobs and disruptions in the lives of people who are transferred, but the closing is not inherently unethical. Even if you imparted your special knowledge about the exceedingly high technical quality of the activity at this office, the course of action is not likely to change, since the decision is based on poor economic performance.

At the other extreme are situations that bypass all the intermediate stages presented here and require that you go immediately to an authority outside your organization. For example, if you found that the senior officer in your organization was knowingly engaged in massive fraud against the government, you would probably have no option to address the problem within the organization. The only ethically viable course of action would be to report the problem to the authorities as soon as possible.

To continue through the stages, we need an incident that falls between the extremes: The action being pursued is one you deem unethical, you do know something that is relevant and that should change people's minds, and it appears that the problem can be addressed and remedied within the organization.

7.2.2 Stage Two—Seriousness Test

The immediate question to ask yourself is if the issue is serious enough to merit your concern. Suppose you know that the chosen supplier for computer disks to your organization is financially unstable but has been chosen because it is owned by a friend of one of the officers of the organization. The disks themselves are of reasonable quality and price. Is spending your time and effort on this issue worthwhile? Quite likely not. After all, computer disks are pretty much of a commodity item. If one supplier goes out of business, another one can easily be found. It is not clear that the potential downside in this incident is substantial. Also, the potential downside seems more specific to your organization than to the public as a whole. So in this case, it may be that your effort is better spent on more serious issues.

Most concerns that pass through stage one are likely to fail the seriousness test, but again so that we can keep moving through stages, let us suppose a different scenario. Perhaps you are employed by a company that is supplying a computer system to be used in the real-time control of a new airplane or in a new medical-imaging device. Imagine further that, as a result of your technical specialty, you feel the plan for testing the system is inadequate to discover and correct the type of flaws that are likely to occur. You worry that lives could be lost if you are right. Situations of this type pass almost anyone's seriousness test.

7.2.3 Stage Three—Reality Check

At this point, you have concluded that something must be done. But before you begin to take any action, you should first pause, consider it all again, gather more information, and try to be certain that you are right. Remember, no matter how intelligent and experienced you are, there is always the possibility that your initial impression of the situation is not completely correct.

One way to check your assessment is through discussions with your colleagues. If all your colleagues think the testing plan is great, you should carefully think over how you determined that it was flawed. You need to be certain that you understand your colleagues' reasoning and that you can rationally explain why you reached a different conclusion. In *Controlling Technology: Ethics and the Responsible Engineer* [23], Unger makes essentially the same recommendation:

> The first consideration is to make sure that one's position is valid. This entails a thorough review of the facts, calculations and principles involved. Engineers should listen carefully to opposing arguments. They should understand them well enough to be able to state them to the satisfaction of their proponents.

Being able to summarize the opposing argument to the satisfaction of those who believe it is a good test of your understanding and objectivity. Of course, if you are the only one to reach a certain conclusion, you are not necessarily wrong, but it may be an indication that the situation is not clear enough to justify your doing anything more than simply expressing your reservations and the reasons for them.

At this point, it becomes important to know when to go along with the group and when to postpone consensus by continuing to pursue your objections. There is a cost associated with always being the last to give up on your objections and go along with the group. You will likely find that your colleagues begin to stereotype you as "not a team player." Also, your objections are likely to be taken less seriously because they become expected. On the other hand, if you never speak up, then you may come to be viewed as having nothing to contribute. And, of course, if you do not speak up when you could help save the organization from a disastrous course of action, then you will have failed both yourself and the organization. The ideal is to speak up when you have relevant concerns, be well informed, and have concerns that generally prove serious and valid. This ideal is not easy to attain, but it will greatly enhance your role in any project team.

Continuing with our scenario, suppose your fact-finding and discussions with colleagues substantiate your initial concern. Most of your colleagues are also worried to one degree or another about the adequacy of the testing plan. But no one is quite sure what to do. And, of course, there is at least one vocal colleague who is totally convinced that there is no problem and that talking about it is a waste of time.

7.2.4 Stage Four—Becoming Aware of the Big Picture

You are now reasonably certain that, from the perspective of your position in the organization, there is a problem that needs to be addressed. The next step is to view the problem in a broader setting, beyond your individual perspective. Despite your best intentions, it is almost impossible for you to see the "big picture." An organization of any substantial size is likely to have multiple areas of expertise and levels of management. Final decisions may depend on input from several technical, financial, and marketing experts, as well as an assessment of compatibility with the company's long-term strategic plan. Unless you are near the top of the relevant portion of the management structure, there is no reason that you should already know all of the information that goes into making a final decision. Thus, the next logical step is to acquire more information. Possibly you are unaware of an acceptance-testing step to be performed by the customer. Or maybe you are in the software group and there is a suitable fix to the problem being pursued by the hardware group. It is possible that this information just hasn't gotten back to your group. After you find out enough about the big picture, your concerns may fade. On the other hand, you could become convinced that the big picture does not change anything. When this happens, you have arrived at the beginning of the truly difficult decisions and actions.

7.2.5 Stage Five—Forcing Management Recognition of the Problem

You should start out this stage with the goal of getting the problem remedied from inside the organization and with as few bad feelings as possible. The first step is to make middle management aware of the problem in a clear and positive manner. State the problem succinctly and rationally and avoid finger pointing and placing blame. You might have the concerns brought up more or less naturally during a project-review meeting. Alternatively, you could bring up the concerns in a progress report to the manager. If you can describe the problem clearly to your manager, and possibly even present a viable solution, you may have turned a problem into an "opportunity." People who can spot unanticipated problems and find solutions for them should be, and generally are, valued members of the organization.

The initial attempt to bring up the problem may not be successful. The ideal next step is to have a group of several of the most respected members of the technical team express a common opinion. There is strength in numbers. The same manager who is tempted to ignore or retaliate against an individual should think twice before choosing to antagonize a significant core of the technical staff. If you take this approach, try to make it nonconfrontational. Having the group demand a meeting to say "you are wrong and we are right" should generally be avoided. A better approach is to have each person in the group express some element of concern about the problem in a review meeting. This might give the manager the option of recognizing the problem and deciding to address it without being explicitly pressured. Alternatively, having each person privately and individually express their concern might create the right atmosphere for change. The most effective approach depends on the personalities of the manager and those willing to express the concern.

But what if you are the only one willing to bring up the problem? What if the response from your group is "that's not our problem," or "forget it, our deadline is in two weeks." A negative initial reception does not necessarily mean that the problem has not registered. It may well be that it will be factored into later plans. Your goal then is to find out if the problem is going to be taken seriously or be ignored. This is an especially tricky stage. For a time, there may be a sequence of escalating attempts to get the problem recognized. At some point, the attempts should include getting management to go "on record." This means sending management some form of written notice of the problem and ascertaining that they have responded or clearly chosen not to respond. In "Do's and Don'ts for Whistle Blowers," Peter Raven-Hansen describes some methods likely to generate a response [19]:

> The disclosure's format should force management to go on record about the information. This might be achieved by specifying a reply date, providing an acknowledgment box, or sending copies to other recipients who might expect a response. The oldest response-generating technique in business and the law is simply to write, "I shall assume that you agree with this assessment and with its inclusion in the quarterly report to regulatory agency X unless I hear from you before January 10."

It is at this point that many potential whistle-blowing scenarios become "swallowed whistles." After an initial negative reaction from management, many people rationalize that they have done all that is required in bringing the problem to management's attention. The disaster waiting to happen is then simply a case of "bad management." Neither the *ACM Code of Ethics* nor the *IEEE Code of Ethics* agrees with this limited view of personal responsibility, however. The quotes at the beginning of the chapter state their positions. The *NSPE Code of Ethics* (rule of practice 1a) has a similar position:

> Engineers shall at all times recognize that their primary obligation is to protect the safety, health, property and welfare of the public. If their professional judgment is overruled under circumstances where the safety, health, property or welfare of the public are endangered, they shall notify their employer or client and such other authority as may be appropriate.

From the very beginning of this stage, you should be preparing for the possibility that you will be forced to go outside your organization with your concerns. One aspect of this preparation is the accumulation of supporting documents. As Unger suggests [23],

> Copies of documents such as letters, memorandums, reports, data sheets, program listings, patent applications, and policy statements should be assembled. Notes should be made (with dates and times) regarding key conversations, and a detailed log maintained of all contacts made. . . . A wise precaution would be to keep the file on the dispute at home, rather than at work, to guard against the possibility of suddenly being discharged and denied further access to one's office.

Another aspect is to be thinking about how you might get support from professional societies and whom you might contact should you need legal assistance. A third aspect of this preparation is to be aware that your career path may change abruptly in the near future.

7.2.6 Stage Six—Taking the Problem to Upper Management

When you are thoroughly convinced that the immediate level of management is not going to address the problem, the right thing to do, if it is feasible, is to take your concerns to a higher level. The danger for you in "going over the boss's head" is that this almost certainly puts your job on the line. If the next level of management does not overrule your boss, and you are identified as the one who communicated the problem, then you will likely find yourself fired or at least transferred to an office in the warehouse. Even if the next level of management does overrule your boss, unless that person is replaced as a manager, you may find that a change of jobs or at least a transfer to another group within the organization is the safest thing for your career.

Unger suggests that the upper management person you choose to contact at this stage should fulfill three criteria [23]:

- Have some interest and responsibility in the problem area.
- Be likely to sympathize with the engineer's approach or at least not already be committed to the other side.
- Have enough clout to get something done.

Identifying such a person may require doing some homework to find out people's personalities and predispositions. It is important to communicate effectively with this person from the very beginning. This may mean writing a shorter, more jargon-free, "executive summary" style description of the problem than what you have now. Remember, you are asking this person to step into a potentially unpleasant situation. They will need to see the case as clear and compelling. Be sure to specify the source(s) of the supporting data and facts and avoid name calling and finger pointing.

Another option at this point is to attempt to pass the information up the management ladder anonymously. This approach has its own risks, of course. People generally take anonymous information less seriously simply because it is anonymous. If the information is received positively, then you have foregone the credit for it. Anonymous contacts make it harder for the person receiving the information to interpret it or ask questions about it.

However you choose to deal with this stage, you may quickly reach the point at which you feel you can no longer address the problem within the organization. You are then at the threshold of fully blowing the whistle. Before you cross that threshold, you should try to get advice from people who have been in similar positions, and you should line up good legal representation. Sources for such contacts include colleagues in your own or other organizations, people on the ethics committees of professional organizations, and lawyers who have handled whistle-blowing cases.

Throughout this stage, you should continue compiling documentation about the problem and about any possible retaliation against you for speaking out.

7.2.7 Stage Seven—Going Outside the Organization

Once you have decided that the organization will not address the problem unless there is pressure from the outside, whistle blowing is the only avenue left. The most effective forum and format for the whistle blowing will, of course, depend on the specifics of the situation. However, here are some general issues to consider.

It may be tempting to think of going to reporters and getting lots of publicity. However, professional and governmental regulatory bodies may be a better choice. Reporters will tend to be interested only if they can sell a story. If they can't see how to get a good headline or sound bite, they may conclude that it isn't newsworthy. Unger gives the following advice about the media [23]:

. . . because of the tricky nature of the media, the high degree of uncertainty as to how (or even *if*) they will handle a story, and the fact that they seldom stay with it for any period of time, a direct approach to them should be regarded as a last resort.

Regulatory agencies and legal authorities are a better choice because they may be able to impose fines, close operations, or do other things that get the organization's attention immediately. Also, your elected representatives at the state or federal level may be able to help.

Regardless of where you go to blow the whistle, remember that you are acting as an individual outside the organization not as an employee. In documenting your disclosure, Raven-Hansen suggests the following [19]:

. . . a whistle blower should not make the disclosure on company letter head, or in a manner calculated or likely to make the disclosure seem official. The whistle blower acts on his own in going public and must take pains to stress this fact. He should therefore not make a public disclosure on company time or with company resources.

7.2.8 Stage Eight—Living with the Results

If you have not experienced a change in job status already, you almost certainly will now. The less dramatic change is for the organization to transfer you to a career dead end, in hopes that you will leave on your own. The more direct change is an ultimatum to quit or be fired. As the reprints at the end of this chapter will attest, the whistle blower essentially never continues a happy career in the same organization. Although courts may sometimes order whistle blowers to be reinstated after they have been fired, this is typically something of a hollow victory in that the whistle blower is unlikely to be happy with the old position. Having the old job back may just mean having an income until a new job can be found.

You should of course be concerned for your financial security. Your lawyer can possibly convince your company to smooth the way to finding a position in another company or field. If you are a member of a professional organization, it may help in providing moral and other forms of support. Unger suggests that the presence of IEEE Member Conduct Committee officials at hearings about whistle-blowing incidents has caused companies to settle more readily, and that information assembled in Member Conduct Committee investigations has made some lawsuits by the whistle blower more feasible [23]. Appendix B outlines the procedures of the IEEE Member Conduct Committee. Others are much more pessimistic about the level of support given to whistle blowers by professional organizations and society in general.

In the article "Knowing How to Blow the Whistle," about whistle blowers in high-profile incidents from the late 1970s [17], all the whistle blowers say that they would do it again if they had it to do over. They also offer some words of wisdom for others:

"Document everything you do, thoroughly and completely, and keep a log from the day you begin, listing the moves you make and all the people you contact. I did and that is why I survived."
—*Frank Camps, engineer in the Ford Pinto incident*

"I think speaking out is one hope for the future. If people care about their jobs and their dignity and their country, they may have to speak out. If every person did every small thing possible, perhaps we wouldn't have so many ills in the future."
—*A. Grace Pierce, researcher at Ortho Pharmaceutical in drug-safety incident*

"Do everything you can to avoid it, but I hope that if you had to, you would do the same thing I did. Perhaps I should have done it earlier—it took me 21 months from asking the

company to report the situation to blowing the whistle. And I should have gone out and gotten a lawyer immediately."
—*Morris Baslow, scientist at Skelley Engineers in power-plant pollution incident*

7.3 WHISTLE-BLOWING INCIDENTS

To give you an idea of the importance of whistle blowing to public safety, I have included an article on the Bay Area Rapid Transit whistle-blowing incident. This is probably *the* classic modern case study of whistle blowing [1], [23]. And since it involves concerns about safety-critical software, it is ideal for study here. The whistle blowers in this case received the 1978 Outstanding Service in the Public Interest Award from the IEEE Committee on Social Implications of Technology.

The BART reprint is followed by a more recent article titled "Whistle-Blowing: Not Always a Losing Game." This article gives a brief update on what happened to the whistle blowers in three incidents. Greg Minor, Richard Hubbard, and Dale Bridenbaugh were involved in whistle blowing related to nuclear power plants in 1976. Roger Boisjoly was involved in whistle blowing related to the NASA Challenger space-shuttle explosion in 1986 [2]. Jim Pope was involved in whistle blowing related to Federal Aviation Administration development and acquisition of safety equipment in 1981. The theme of this article is that, while it may require enduring some years of serious personal stress and turmoil, things sometimes turn out well for the whistle blower in the long run.

7.4 LAWS PROTECTING WHISTLE BLOWERS

Whistle blowers in some areas are not without legal support. Both federal and state laws are aimed at protecting those who undertake whistle blowing. However, even with this support, the potential whistle blower must still contemplate a difficult and dangerous path. The details of the case study and the reprinted articles should make this clear.

7.4.1 Federal Law

The primary protection law is the Federal Whistle Blower Protection Act of 1989. I have included a portion of the Act at the end of this chapter. The complete text is rather long and deals with specific revisions of Chapter twelve of title 5 of the *United States Code*. Portions of the revisions deal with the establishment, powers and functions, and various policies and procedures of the Special Counsel. You should, of course, discuss the extent and type of protection provided in the context of any particular incident with a lawyer. The drawback of this law is that it does *not* apply to employees of private companies or state governments. However, employees of private companies may have some degree of protection under other laws, especially if the company is engaged in business regulated

by the federal government, and the whistle blowing is in the form of a report of a violation to a regulatory agency. Employees of state governments may also have protection under state laws.

Another federal law is the False Claims Act, which has been around since 1863. The law allows an individual to file a civil suit against a business that defrauds the federal government. The individual is then eligible to share in a portion of the money recovered. The legal term "qui tam" is used to describe such suits. The False Claims Act had fallen into relative nonuse until 1986, when Congress passed amendments to strengthen the law and make it easier to apply. In 1985, the last year before the amendments to the law, the government recovered roughly $27 million from civil fraud suits. In comparison, roughly $500 million was recovered from over 70 successful suits between 1986 and 1992, with about $250 million coming in 1992 alone [4]. The whistle blowers and their lawyers received more than $70 million of this recovered money.

The False Claims Act states that a whistle blower may receive between 15 and 25% of the recovered funds if the government chooses to participate in the suit. If the government decides not to participate in the suit, the whistle blower may receive between 25 and 30 percent of the recovery, plus legal fees and expenses [14]. As of 1994, the three largest settlements under this Act were

1. $118.8 million from National Health Labs for fraud against Medicare and Medicaid, with whistle blower Jack Dowden receiving $21 million;
2. $48 million from General Electric for fraud in U.S. foreign military sales, with whistle blower Chester Walsh receiving $11.5 million; and
3. $42.5 million from Bicoastal Corporation for fraud against the U.S. Army, Navy and Air Force, with whistle-blower Christopher Urda receiving $7.5 million [18].

Even larger whistle-blower suits, claiming up to one billion dollars in fraud, are working their way through the legal system [7]. To date, about 75 percent of the whistle-blower suits have been against firms in the defense industry, with firms in the health industry being the next most frequent group [14], [7]. Lobbyists and lawyers for both of these industries have challenged the constitutionality of the False Claims Act and lobbied Congress to weaken it [7], [14].

7.4.2 State Laws

Many state governments have passed their own whistle-blower protection acts. I enclose a short description of the Whistle Blower's Act for Florida. (Many other states have passed similar laws.) Compared with the federal law, the Florida law seems stronger, in that it places a burden of proof on the employer and establishes some protection for private-sector whistle blowers as well as state employees. At the same time, it also seems weaker, in that the burden of initiating and pursuing legal action seems shifted more toward the whistle blower. Whistle-blower protection laws at the state level can of course vary greatly among states. Also, interpreting the practical protection afforded in any specific incident should be done with the help of experienced legal counsel.

7.5 CASE STUDY

The case study is of the whistle-blowing incident involving Chester Walsh, General Electric, and the False Claims Act.

7.5.1 The Cast of Characters

General Electric is a huge corporation that deals heavily with both the U.S. and foreign governments, as well as with the general consumer public.

Chester Walsh retired from GE Aircraft Engines in the summer of 1992. At that point, Walsh had worked for General Electric for more than 25 years. He started as a mechanic and rose to the position of manager of a GE aircraft-engineering project in Israel. Walsh worked in Israel for five years, ending in 1989. It is during this period that the interesting part of his story begins.

Herbert Steindler was the manager of international programs for GE's F110 aircraft. Steindler lived in the United States.

George Stringer was the Israel program manager for the F110.

Israeli Brigadier General Rami Dotan was an important representative of the customer, the Israeli government.

Yoram Ingbir was an engineer and a business partner of Dotan's in Israel.

7.5.2 The Sequence of Events

The case involves purchases of GE products by the Israeli government. United States tax dollars and fraud enter the picture because the U.S. Foreign Military Financing Program is being used in the purchases [20]. Essentially, the fraud occurred by GE executives participating with Dotan in the billing for products and services that were never delivered, that were sold at inflated prices, or that were not allowed under the program. Some of the specific incidents mentioned in one report are [20]:

- GE presented paperwork to Israel's Ministry of Defense certifying that the company had built or produced support equipment for the Israeli Air Force. The "equipment" included a $7 million facility for testing the new engines; a $4 million portable test unit, and a $1.2 million high-speed grinder.
- GE used U.S. funds to buy IBM personal computers, which were not eligible for U.S. government funding, from Ingbir at a grossly inflated price. The company then labeled them as ground-support hardware to cor-

respond with fraudulent invoices submitted to the Ministry of Defense. GE was reimbursed $500,000 in U.S. funds.
- GE collected $727,000 for the Hebrew translation of the F110 engine training manual. The manual didn't exist.

In all, the fraud ran to more than $40 million in U.S. military aid. The scheme allowed GE to keep good relations with Dotan, who was their contact to the Israeli government and the authorization for purchases that it could make. And it allowed GE to collect profit on work that was never performed. The scheme allegedly financed, among other things, a $560,000 villa in Tel Aviv for Dotan, a $100,000 personal aircraft for Ingbir and at least $11 million dollars in a Swiss bank account belonging to Steindler and Dotan [20], [16]. Portions of the money were also used for programs inside the Israeli military that did not qualify for U.S. military aid.

Chester Walsh became aware of the ongoing fraud at least as early as 1986, when he realized during a budget meeting that GE had been paid for work that it had not done [12]. Walsh said nothing for years, being afraid that GE would discipline him and cover up the incident if he reported it internally to GE, and/or that he would be in physical danger from Dotan.

GE attorneys would later attempt to make an issue of Chester Walsh not speaking up as soon as he could have, using internal GE channels. The judge in the eventual civil case noted that ". . . another GE employee who raised questions was moved to another project, and General Dotan conspired to have another person kidnapped for asking questions" [11]. (Apparently a rabbi in New York City was paid $50,000 to kidnap and beat up an Israeli national living in the United States [18], [20].)

Chester Walsh quietly compiled documentation of the fraud. He saw a lawyer (using an assumed name) during one of his visits back to the United States. He met with FBI agents in Cincinnati. He smuggled documents out of Israel. He secretly recorded meetings at GE's Evendale, Ohio, facility with those involved in the fraud. Outside of Israel and back in the United States, Chester Walsh filed his lawsuit in November 1990 [24]. Walsh's lawyer was John Philips. Walsh was also supported in his lawsuit by the nonprofit organization Taxpayers Against Fraud, a group founded in part by Philips with funds from previous whistle-blower cases [16]. The government joined Walsh's suit in 1991. This brought a federal investigation and criminal charges. In 1992, GE pled guilty to charges of fraud, money laundering, and corrupt business practices. GE agreed to pay $9.5 million in criminal penalties and $59.5 million in the civil lawsuit. GE was also required to pay $2.3 million in fees and $227,000 in expenses to Walsh's lawyers. United States District Judge Carl Rubin decided that Walsh should receive 22.5 percent of the civil lawsuit amount, or

$13,387,500. (This is within the False Claims Act's allowed range of 15 to 25 percent.)

Walsh split the award with his lawyer and the Taxpayers Against Fraud organization. However, only $2 million was disbursed immediately to Walsh, while GE appealed the size of the judge's award to Walsh. GE, along with some in the Justice Department, made the argument that Walsh should not receive such a large award. They asserted that Walsh let the fraud go on longer than he should have just to let the size of a possible award grow. GE was quoted as saying "Had Chester Walsh dealt honestly with GE, the alleged fraud could have been detected, investigated and reported to the government years earlier, avoiding millions of dollars in damages to the government. These two decisions create a perverse incentive for defense employees to delay reporting wrongdoing while they watch their bounty grow, and for attorneys to counsel their clients to delay reporting. . . ." [16]. Judge Rubin disregarded the GE assertion, commenting that "lawyers are particularly prone to use that argument after the benefits of excellent hindsight" [16].

7.5.3 Conclusions and Questions

Most of the major "bad guys" in this story have received at least some punishment. Israeli authorities discovered in 1989 that Dotan had accepted bribes and kickbacks totaling more than $10 million. (In fact, the Israeli government investigation may have begun before the U.S. government investigation.) Dotan was reduced in rank to private and sentenced to 13 years in an Israeli prison. Steindler was fired by GE in 1991. In addition, "21 other employees were either fired, forced to retire, demoted or fined by the company" [16]. Steindler later pled guilty to charges of wire fraud, conspiracy to defraud the federal government, money laundering, and using the mail to violate an antibribery law [22]. In November 1994, he was sentenced to at least 8 years in prison and fined $1.25 million [18]. A middleman in the scheme, Gary Klein, pled guilty to conspiracy and was sentenced to 18 months in prison.

GE's challenge of the constitutionality of the False Claims Act appears likely to go nowhere. GE was quoted as arguing that "Congress cannot constitutionally deputize private citizen volunteers to prosecute civil claims for the United States government" [4]. However, 16 federal courts have previously ruled that the law *is* constitutional. In addition, according to a brief prepared by U.S. Senate lawyers, "the history of the False Claims Act's qui tam provisions demonstrates both the novelty of the claims that GE presses here and the fact that the qui tam provisions

have not engendered the constitutional concerns that GE perceives."

An interesting sidelight to all of this is how GE itself was treated by the U.S. government: ". . . the Pentagon suspended the company from receiving future government contracts, but lifted the order five days later after a legion of GE lawyers convinced officials that sufficient safeguards were in place to deter and detect fraud by company employees. The lifting of the suspension cleared the way for $1.2 billion in new Pentagon orders. . . ." [16]. Apparently any government threat of a long-term suspension of business with a firm the size of GE is simply unrealistic.

Several aspects of the case bear closer evaluation. One is the implication of the quoted statement by GE when it argued against the size of Walsh's award. The wording "had Chester Walsh dealt honestly with GE" implies that Walsh is dishonest. On the other hand, the wording "the alleged fraud" implies the possibility that there was no fraud. Yet GE had pled guilty! This illustrates the type of treatment that whistle blowers can sometimes expect to receive. Scott Armstrong of Taxpayers Against Fraud labeled GE's assertions as "false and outrageous," commenting that "when questions were raised . . . about the fraud, [GE's] highest executives repeatedly covered up the charges . . . yet the only individual that GE has publicly attacked is Walsh" [16]. After the judge's decision, Walsh himself was quoted as saying, "This has taken quite a toll on my health. Right now, I just want to go somewhere warm and quiet and think about it" [9].

Another point worth examining is why Walsh might not have reported the fraud sooner, using channels within GE. In evaluating the reasonableness of Chester Walsh's fears, consider what you know about the treatment of other whistle blowers. Also consider that more than 20 people inside GE would eventually be implicated either as participants or as people who knew about the fraud and did nothing. In considering the reasonableness of Walsh's fears about Dotan, consider how you would feel about revealing the multimillion dollar fraud of a general in a foreign military while you live and work in that country.

Finally, note the role of Taxpayers Against Fraud. This group undertakes to support selected whistle blowers in pursuing their case under the False Claims Act. Their web address is www.taf.org. Their toll-free phone number is (800) US-FALSE. Their mailing address is

Taxpayers Against Fraud
The False Claims Act Legal Center
1220 19th Street, N. W.
Suite 501
Washington, DC 20036

Points to Remember

- A whistle-blowing incident is probably the most emotionally difficult thing you can experience as a professional.
- Not every incident that should result in whistle blowing does. Sometimes the whistle is "swallowed" rather than blown.
- One rationalization for a swallowed whistle is that the person just won't be able to endure the emotional pressure involved. If you find yourself considering such a line of rationalization, imagine the pressure that you would feel for the rest of your life if you were one who didn't speak up when, for example, the decision to launch the Challenger was made.
- Another rationalization for a "swallowed whistle" is that one person can't make a difference. Of course, the many successful examples of whistle blowing show that this isn't true. But even if a particular incident of whistle blowing is not fully successful, the moral courage shown by one person may be an example to others, and thereby generally raise the frequency of morally correct actions.
- An argument often used against whistle blowing is that it is somehow an act of disloyalty to the organization. This argument presumes that an organization, per se, can be the object of loyalty. Even if you accept this presumption, an organization that has left no alternative but the uncomfortable role of a whistle blower would seem to have already broken the bond of loyalty.
- In some cases, there are federal and state laws meant to provide protection for the whistle blowers.
- If you find yourself in a possible whistle-blowing incident, you should exhaust all internal avenues for addressing the problem and accumulate all documentation possible. If blowing the whistle becomes the only alternative, then you should anticipate a job change and you should get good legal representation.

WORKSHEET—Review of Whistle-Blowing Concepts: Part 1

Read "Whistle-Blowing: Not Always a Losing Game" by Karen Fitzgerald at the end of the chapter. Then answer the following questions.

1. What is "whistle blowing?"

2. What does ". . . whistle blowing violates a prima facie duty to one's employer . . ." mean?

3. Are corporations things that can be the object of loyalty? Why or why not?

4. What was Edward Teller's response to Minor, Hubbard, and Bridenbaugh? How would you characterize this response?

5. Why do you think the FAA converted a job termination into a retirement due to disability?

6. How did Thiokol instruct their employees to respond to the president's commission investigating the Challenger disaster?

WORKSHEET—Review of Whistle-Blowing Concepts: Part 2

1. What is the sequence of stages you should go through before blowing the whistle outside of your organization?

2. What is the False Claims Act and how does it relate to whistle blowing? Why would some large corporations lobby for weakening this law?

3. Who is covered and in what way by the Federal Whistle Blower Protection Act?

4. What is Taxpayers against Fraud?

WORKSHEET—"Final Exam" on Applied Whistle Blowing

Imagine the year is 2015. You have worked for the NCS Company for more than 15 years. NCS is a small company (about 250 employees) that does software subcontracts for larger government contractors. NCS has an outstanding reputation for producing quality software on time.

You are the chief programmer at NCS and have played a major role in its success, although you are not on the corporate management team. The president, all vice presidents, and all other managers at NCS are not technically trained. These managers negotiate almost all contracts and, of course, watch over the company's profit margin very carefully. Although NCS has many other programmers trained in computer science, all are junior employees and most are involved in long-established work on software-maintenance contracts. The only programmers not involved in software maintenance report directly to you.

This month, you are putting the finishing touches on a 550,000-line program for a contractor who is building a large system for the Federal Aviation Agency. Your system obtains readings from a number of different instruments, performs calculations, optionally rereads values from these and other instruments, and provides outputs to several controllers. There were some real-time constraints, but these were not difficult to meet. Although your system was fairly complex, your team finished the project in only 3.5 years. Everyone—NSC management, the FAA contractor, and the FAA representatives—is happy.

Although you knew from the beginning of the project that your programs were part of a new "wind-shear detection and automatic avoidance" system, your requirements documents were very clear and you finished your work without understanding the function of your code in the final system.

You have just learned that your code is the controlling code for the new Boeing 847 jumbo jets. Your programs will essentially detect wind shear in real time, seize control of the plane from the pilot, and automatically control the plane to minimize damage and loss of life. (The new 847 jumbo jets hold 800 passengers when loaded to capacity.) Somehow, this incredibly important, life-dependent system has been created with less attention to absolute program correctness than seems appropriate to you. In fact, you are its creator. Even the testing program adopted seems inadequate for a potentially life-threatening system. You mention this fact to your boss and he says the system works fine, that the FAA is happy, and you should take a well-deserved vacation.

You mention your concern to one of your vice presidents and he says that the NCS subcontract explicitly states that all liability for operation of the system, including your code, will be borne by the FAA contractor and not your company. Legally, you are not responsible. Nevertheless, it is very clear to you that somehow this very important new computer system is about to be installed in potentially very life-threatening circumstances, with too little attention to its reliability. Everyone around you is not technically competent to understand your concern.

Assume that by this time you are married, have four daughters, a house payment, two car payments, an oldest daughter ready to start college, and that you will be eligible for early retirement from your company in only 8 years. Your spouse does not work, and your family is not wealthy.

In one to two pages, describe what you will do.

1. **The Challenger incident.** The Challenger incident is an excellent example for a modern case study. Although the Challenger incident is covered in one of the reprinted articles, the coverage there is quite brief relative to the importance of the incident. A great deal of information relating to the Challenger incident has been published. Boisjoly's personal account appears in *Ethical Issues in Engineering* [2]. Richard Feynman's account of the Challenger inquiry appears in the February 1988 issue of *Physics Today* [8]. Read these and other accounts of the Challenger incident and report on the role of the whistle blowers.

2. **The software-engineering side of the Star Wars project.** David Parnas is a well-known and highly respected professor and senior researcher in software engineering. The Star Wars (or Strategic Defense Initiative) system was proposed by President Reagan as a shield against nuclear attack. The concept was that missiles sent toward targets in the United States would be detected and destroyed before they arrived. In May 1985, Parnas was asked to serve as a member of an advisory panel to SDI that would make recommendations about research and development for the computing-systems side of SDI. At the consulting rate of $1,000 per day (in 1985), this was a plum appointment. However, he soon resigned from the panel and became a firm opponent of SDI [15]. Report on his concerns and the reaction to his whistle blowing.

3. **The Virginia Edgerton case.** Virginia Edgerton was a senior information scientist working for New York City's Criminal Justice Council. She attempted to raise concerns about the combination of two functions on one computer system. One of these functions was the dispatching of police cars to emergencies, which could have been slowed down by the other function. Report on the details of this incident and what happened to Edgerton.

4. **The Pinto case.** The case of the Pinto automobile is an example of a "swallowed whistle" [23]. The Pinto was a popular small car manufactured by Ford. The issue in this case is the safety factor involved in the mounting position for the gas tank and the speed of rear-end collisions that could be withstood without the gas tank exploding. The article by DeGeorge in *Ethical Issues in Engineering* [5] is a good starting point for this case, and contains a number of other references. Report on the particulars of this incident and why it qualifies as a "swallowed whistle."

5. **The Clinch River breeder reactor incident.** The Clinch River breeder reactor was a nuclear-reactor project located near the Clinch River in Tennessee. Demetrios Basdekas is an electrical engineer who worked for the Nuclear Regulatory Committee and was involved with oversight of the Clinch River breeder reactor project. Basdekas's case is unusual in that from his position inside the NRC he was able to speak up about the problems with the Clinch River breeder reactor, which was ultimately canceled, and maintain his career with his employer (apparently happily) [23]. Basdekas received the 1991 Outstanding Service in the Public Interest award from the IEEE Society on Social Implications of Technology [23]. Report on the details of this incident and any possible effects on Basdekas's career.

6. **The Three Mile Island reactor cleanup.** The partial meltdown that occurred at the Three Mile Island nuclear power plant was the worst accident to date in the U.S. nuclear power industry. The cleanup of this accident became, in effect, a major applied research project. Many new special-purpose pieces of equipment were designed and built for the task. Ed Gischel, Rick Parks, and Larry King were engineers on the cleanup project who became concerned that corners were being cut to meet deadlines. *Controlling Technology: Ethics and the Responsible Engineer* [23] provides an overview of this incident and a number of additional references. Report on the details of this incident and the effects on the careers of the whistle blowers.

7. **The Baltimore/Imanishi-Kari research publication case.** David Baltimore is a very senior researcher (at one point being president of Rockefeller University) who coauthored a paper that appeared in the journal *Cell*. Thereza Imanishi-Kari is a relatively junior researcher, who was also a coauthor of the paper. Imanishi-Kari was the hands-on person who reportedly carried out most of the work, while Baltimore's contribution was apparently closer to an administrative authorship. Margaret O'Toole was working as a postdoctoral researcher in the same lab where Imanishi-Kari did the work for the paper. O'Toole became convinced that some of the results reported by Imanishi-Kari were fraudulent, in that the experiments had never been carried out. The story then becomes an interesting one, full of politics and intrigue. A lengthy description of the incident is given in a special issue of *Ethics and Behaviour* [10]. Report on the details of this incident and the effect on O'Toole's career.

8. **The Needlemen research publications case.** Herbert Needleman is a well-known researcher on the effects of lead exposure on children. Needleman's results suggest that lead exposure is harmful to children. Claire Ernhart, Sandra Scarr, and David Geneson are researchers who have questioned some of Needleman's work. A special issue of *Ethics and Behaviour* contains both an article by Ernhart et al. [6] and a response article by Needleman [13]. Both articles give a number of additional references. Report on the details of this incident and the effects on the whistle blowers' careers.

9. **The Breuning scientific fraud case.** Stephen Breuning

is a researcher who was working on the use of drug treatments for mental problems. Robert Sprague is a researcher in related areas who was once a collaborator with Breuning. Sprague became convinced of fraud in Breuning's work and contacted the sponsoring agency, the National Institute of Mental Health. The resulting treatment of Sprague, the whistle blower, by the agency that sponsored the fraudulent work is somewhat amazing. Sprague's own account of this incident also contains a number of additional references [21]. Report on the details of this incident and the effect on Breuning's career.

REFERENCES

[1] R. M. Anderson, *Divided Loyalties: Whistle-Blowing at BART,* Purdue Research Foundation, West Lafayette, IN, 1980.

[2] R. M. Boisjoly, "The Challenger disaster: moral responsibility and the working engineer," Chapter 1, pp. 6–14, in *Ethical Issues in Engineering,* D. Johnson (editor), Prentice-Hall, 1991.

[3] S. Bok, "The morality of whistle blowing," in *Computers, Ethics & Society,* M. D. Ermann, M. B. Williams, and C. Gutierrez (editors), Oxford University Press, New York, 1990.

[4] M. Boyer, "GE fights legality of whistle blower law," *The Cincinnati Enquirer,* November 1, 1993.

[5] Ethical responsibilities of engineers in large organizations: The Pinto Case, Chapter 15, pp. 175–186, in *Ethical Issues in Engineering,* D. Johnson (editor), Prentice-Hall, Englewood Cliffs, NJ, 1991.

[6] C. Ernhart, S. Scarr, and D. Geneson, "On being a whistle blower: The Needleman case," *Ethics and Behaviour,* volume 3, number 1 (1993), pp. 73–94.

[7] A. Epstein, "Companies try to put lid on whistle blowers," *The Tampa Tribune-Times,* February 20, 1994.

[8] R. P. Feynman, "An outsider's inside view of the Challenger inquiry," *Physics Today,* February 1988, pp. 26–37.

[9] W. E. Gibson, "Former GE employee gets reward," *The Tampa Tribune,* December 21, 1994.

[10] S. Lange, "Questions of scientific responsibility: The Baltimore case," *Ethics and Behaviour,* volume 3, number 1 (1993), pp. 3–72.

[11] J. Mintz, "GE whistle blower receives record $13.4 million award," *The Washington Post,* December 5, 1992.

[12] D. Moss, "Whistle blower's windfall: Millions," *USA Today,* July 30, 1992.

[13] H. Needleman, "Reply to Ernhart, Scarr, and Geneson," *Ethics and Behaviour,* volume 3, number 1 (1993), pp. 95–102.

[14] "Whistle blowers live lifestyles of the rich," *The Orlando Sentinel,* February 20, 1994.

[15] D. L. Parnas, "Professional responsibility to blow the whistle on SDI," *Abacus,* Winter 1987, pp. 46–52, Springer-Verlag.

[16] S. Pearlstein and P. Farhi, "GE pleads guilty to fraud in engine sales to Israel," *The Washington Post,* July 23, 1992.

[17] T. S. Perry, "Knowing how to blow the whistle," *IEEE Spectrum,* September 1981, pp. 56–61.

[18] J. R. Philips, personal communication.

[19] P. Raven-Hansen, "Do's and Don'ts for whistle blowers: Planning for trouble," *Technology Review,* May 1980, pp. 34–44.

[20] G. Rhodes, "Phony work, greedy billing ran for years," *The Cincinnati Post,* June 27, 1992.

[21] R. Sprague, "Whistle blowing: A very unpleasant avocation," *Ethics and Behaviour,* special issue on *Whistle Blowing and Scientific Misconduct,* volume 3, number 1 (1993), Lawrence Erlbaum Associates.

[22] Former GE executive from Florida pleads guilty in military aid scheme, *The Tampa Tribune,* Tuesday, July 19, 1994.

[23] S. Unger, *Controlling Technology: Ethics and the Responsible Engineer,* John Wiley & Sons, New York, 1984 (second edition).

[24] S. Wilson, Big suits, *The American Lawyer,* October 1991, p. 24.

[25] L. W. Zelby, "Whistle blowing—somebody has to take a stand," *IEEE Technology and Society Magazine,* September 1989, pp. 4–6.

The case of the three engineers vs. BART

The outcome of a suit brought by three Bay Area Rapid Transit exemployees may set a historic precedent in the public interest

An $885 000 lawsuit was recently filed, and leveled at the Bay Area Rapid Transit (BART) system management, by three of its former engineer-employees. (The trial in Superior Court, Alameda County, Calif., is scheduled to begin on October 25.) This latest in a series of technological and financial troubles—cost overruns caused by inflation, labor stoppages, illegal change orders, erratic appropriations, quality-control deficiencies, etc. (many of which were discussed in the writer's articles in the September, October, and November 1972 issues, and in the March and April 1973 issues of *Spectrum*)—presents potentially the most serious implications to the engineering profession of any of BART's past woes. Although the continued operation and future development of the BART system will remain relatively unaffected by the outcome of this litigation, the dispute that triggered the engineers' suit warrants the attention of every professional engineer because of its grave technical and ethical underpinnings.

As early as 1971, the three BART employees in question became concerned with the design of the system's ATC (automatic train control). As the story unfolded, these engineers' fears eventually became public and all three were fired. The BART management apparently felt that its three critics had jumped the gun, that the bugs in the system were in the process of being worked out, and that the three had been unethical in their release of information. The consequence of the 1972 firing, however, was a flurry of charges and countercharges reaching epic proportions (the three engineers have asserted that BART management has successfully blackballed them in a number of instances).

In an attempt to sort out the issues *Spectrum* has elicited the points of view not only of the three engineers but also of every principal in the case who, mid-way through the litigation process, was willing to speak out.

BART management was not willing. According to a spokesman, its legal department felt compelled not to release any information pending the outcome of the suit. A BART director, William Reedy, concurred in this position. And so did B. R. Stokes, the former BART general manager who resigned last May 24. Now the executive director of the American Transit Association in Washington, D.C., Stokes told *Spectrum* that "in no manner, shape, or form" would he make a statement regarding his side of

the argument. Stokes himself has been named a respondent in the engineers' lawsuit.

One other figure worthy of mention is Vernon Sturgeon, president of California's Public Utilities Commission (PUC). The refusal by the PUC to hire one of the three engineers, following his departure from BART, prompted charges that BART management was successfully blackballing the three. A query to Sturgeon on this matter was diverted to PUC's legal department, which advised that the engineer in question had been passed over only because he lacked the qualifications required for the position for which he had applied.

But while BART, its officers, and the president of PUC had little or nothing to report to *Spectrum*, others did—principally the three engineers themselves, but also: Roy W. Anderson, state director, president, and vice president during 1964–1972 of the Diablo Chapter of the California Society of Professional Engineers; Daniel C. Helix, former mayor of Concord, Calif., and BART board member to whom the three engineers relayed their concerns; Justin Roberts, Pulitzer Prize nominee in journalism and a reporter with the *Contra Costa Times*, Walnut Creek, Calif.; and E. W. Morris (LF), an interested engineer with more than 40 years' experience, and one who has watched BART grow almost from the date of its inception.

The views of these four men—all involved in one way or another with the controversy—will directly follow those of the three principals in the case—Holger Hjortsvang, Max Blankenzee, and Robert Bruder.

The first partisan

Holger Hjortsvang (SM) says that on March 2, 1972, B. R. Stokes, then BART's general manager, summarily fired him and two other employees, accusing all three of disloyalty. According to Hjortsvang, the trio was held responsible for leaking to a local newspaper reports critical

This article is intended to focus on the complexities of ethics and employment practices, not on the technical aspects of the BART system. Nevertheless, the two are related, so that some of BART's history, as it is perceived by those interviewed, is included. Because of the imminent litigation, BART's defense of the charges expressed by the exemployees could not be revealed at this time, but a counterbalancing viewpoint by an experienced engineer is given at the conclusion of the article. (See, also, "Spectral lines," page 45, in this issue.)

Gordon D. Friedlander   Senior Staff Writer

Reprinted from *IEEE Spectrum*, Vol. 11, No. 10, pp. 69–76, October 1974.

Hjortsvang: Had BART been more open-minded, it would have listened to us rather than deprive the public of improvements that could have saved millions of dollars and years of delay.

of BART's management and its handling of the train control contract. But, he goes on to say, that accusation was untrue since the information on which these reports were based was given not to the press, but to BART board member Daniel Helix, and later to computer experts designated by Mr. Helix to evaluate the information in question.

The contact with Helix, says Hjortsvang, was a last-ditch attempt to attract BART management's attention to a situation that, in the opinion of the three engineers, was threatening the successful completion of the system. The worst thing that could happen to their proposals, Hjortsvang says he then felt, would be for Helix to "go public" with them.* When Helix did just that, "BART completely rejected us and our ideas"—this in the words of Hjortsvang, who goes on to suggest that had General Manager Stokes been "more open-minded," he would, nevertheless, have listened to his three engineer-employees rather than deprive the public of improvements that "could have saved millions of dollars and years of delay."

In December 1972, *Spectrum* published a Hjortsvang letter (Forum, pp. 16–17) in which he outlined his criticisms both of BART and of its Westinghouse-designed ATC system. More recently, Hjortsvang testified before the Federal Railroad Commission, the California Public Utilities Commission, the California Senate Public Utilities and Corporations Committee (through Legislative Analyst A. Alan Post who, incidentally, declined to contribute to this article claiming to be a mere spectator and lacking engineering expertise at that), and finally before a "blue ribbon" panel of experts whose views have since been summarized in "A prescription for BART," pp. 40–44 of the April 1973 *Spectrum.*

According to Hjortsvang, today, this last group of experts, who investigated the ATC system early in 1973, only confirmed his observations and those of his disemployed colleagues. Restrictions, he notes, were imposed on BART until it could prove that the most important safety precautions had been incorporated in the control system.

[On August 27, 1974, the Public Utilities Commission gave approval for BART to operate trains in revenue service, commencing September 16, on two routes through the Transbay tube: Fremont to Daly City, and Concord to Daly City. The trains will operate under a computer-augmented block system (CABS-1), with one-station separation between vehicles.]

Hjortsvang's story is as follows:

He joined BART in 1966. At that time, the test-track demonstrations of the WABCO, GRS, General Electric, Westinghouse, and Philco ATC concepts were in their final stages and evaluation reports were being prepared by BART's consultants—Parsons, Brinckerhoff–Tudor–Bechtel (PBTB).

PBTB decided that any of the demonstrated systems would be suitable for the automated, high-density service BART required. Says Hjortsvang, "It is not clear which features in the five systems qualified them, but it is a fact that their relative safety was neither analyzed nor demonstrated. This is remarkable, because safety considerations have been the only reason that automation of mass transit had never been previously attempted."

In August 1966, PBTB issued its specification for the work required to design and provide the ATC system. It was PBTB's intention to give the eventual contractor the opportunity to adopt advanced state-of-the-art methods and designs. Hjortsvang quotes the specification as follows: "The choice of specific methods and equipments that are required shall be at the Contractor's option . . . The Contractor's responsibility shall be to provide a safe, effective, and reliable system which will fulfill the functional requirements." Hjortsvang alleges that the consequence of this freedom was just the opposite of the intent: the purely functional specification was interpreted by the bidders as a license to use the cheapest possible approach to system design.

He goes on to say that the specification was weakened by unrealistic requirements . . . "terms like: 'The major control functions of the system shall be fully automatic . . . with absolute assurance of passenger and train safety, high levels of reliability . . . ,' and 'the control system shall be based on the principles which permit the attainment of fail-safe operation in all known failure modes.' This is specifying Utopia!" Hjortsvang continues: "Fail-safe, as defined in the specifications, is no more meaningful than 'pure water.' How pure is pure, and how safe is safe?"

Hjortsvang feels that the bidders interpreted these safety requirements in terms of their own design principles, perhaps without questioning the applicability of these principles to the exacting demands of fully automatic operation. In the words of this former BART engineer, "by taking fullest advantage of the specification's lack of conciseness, Westinghouse Electric won the contract. They did not offer the innovative system they showed at the test track, but a conventional system based on track signaling and employing multiplexing of the signals to reduce cabling cost."

Accepting the Westinghouse bid was, in the eyes of Mr. Hjortsvang and his colleagues, "an invitation to trouble." They see in the Westinghouse design a series of five deviations from what is generally considered good practice for ATC systems:

1. The time-proven analog signaling technique was re-

---

* Mr. Helix notes that the "computer expert," Edward A. Burfine, was retained by the engineers "prior to my being contacted. It was Burfine's written confirmation of the engineers' allegations which persuaded me to get involved and to continue my investigation." Helix also observes that by taking the matter to the BART board, as the engineers requested, "it automatically became *public,* since the matter was scheduled—through channels—for a hearing by the Engineering Commission. The engineers were alleging problems of *safety,* and I was not going to cover up these charges, once brought to my attention. . . ."

placed by a much more complex digital design, using 100 times more components to accomplish the purpose—to generate a speed analog to apply to the traction in the train. (Digital speed codes have no functional advantage, and are never used in conjunction with track circuits where the steel rails form the conductors. The complexity reduces reliability, and thereby safety.)

2. In conventional systems, a single frequency (the train frequency) is used to carry the signals to the trains. In the Westinghouse design, there were a variety of different frequencies for this purpose. Therefore, the receivers had to have a much wider bandwidth and, consequently, higher sensitivity to noise. This would further decrease reliability.

3. The same frequencies were used for both train detection and speed signaling. (This is contrary to common practice and probably less safe.)

4. Positive speed codes were permitted to flow in unoccupied blocks, violating the safety principle that "stop" should be a normal condition, and "go" be only possible as a result of a definite action.

5. Lower than standard carrier power was used in the track circuits, without proof of adequate signal-to-noise ratio and detection sensitivity.

To Hjortsvang, these deviations made BART's controls inferior to conventional train-control systems. And even if that were not the case, he notes, "the Westinghouse system would not qualify for 'fully automatic operation.' Rail–track signaling is proven as an efficient and safe way to send 'stop' and 'proceed' signals to trains, but there is no evidence that it is safe both to generate the signals automatically and also to have them control the trains without human intervention. A malfunction, or a train-detection failure, could cause an erroneous signal to be generated, with dangerous consequences. On-board equipment failure could likewise result in misinterpretation of received signals." Points out Hjortsvang, an accident (October 2, 1972, Fremont station) caused by on-board equipment failure actually occurred!

"It was later realized," continues Hjortsvang, "that BART's train detection is less reliable than conventional systems, especially if electric power to a train is lost, and various means were proposed to remedy it. None of these proved effective. In an August 1972 report, I indicated that a train's location could be known the instant detection fails, by utilizing logic circuits to retain the latest occupancy indication until the train is detected in the next block. This would make a detection failure inconsequential. It was not until November 1973, before BART (or PBTB) because aware of this. At that time, Hewlett-Packard demonstrated a model of a logical prediction system, based on my suggestion* to the BART board of directors.

---

* Bernard Oliver (F), a vice president of Hewlett-Packard, and a member of the three-man "blue ribbon" panel, states that a panel report of February 5, 1973, recommended logic backups. Furthermore, Dr. Oliver disputes Hjortsvang's statement that "Hewlett-Packard demonstrated a model of a logical prediction system, *based on my [Hjortsvang's] suggestion. . . .*"

They were impressed, and soon instructed BART to have Westinghouse incorporate the measure in the control system."

Belatedly, according to Hjortsvang, it was also realized that BART could not be made fully automatic. In fact, the previously mentioned report by the "blue ribbon" panel states: "We concur with BART's and PBTB's decision that completely automatic control without a train operator is not feasible at the present state of the art. Since an operator is required, he should be able to provide as effective a backup on the automatic system as possible."

Consequently, Hjortsvang feels that PBTB has relieved Westinghouse of its contractual obligation to supply a fully automatic system. "As a result," he says, "we can [now] directly compare BART with numerous other operating systems. Is it as safe, economical, and efficient as the best of them? The fact is: it is not." The former BART employee contends that Westinghouse's money-saving design ideas have backfired in the form of an intolerable number of breakdowns. Circuit adjustments are hypercritical and require frequent attention; and maintenance costs are exorbitant. With the present equipment, he sees it as hopeless to plan on "full operation" with the theoretically possible 50-mi/h (80-km/h) average speed—and headways of 90 seconds—during the peak hours.

"But, I disagree," he says, "with the statement that completely automatic control without a train operator is not feasible. Modern cybernetics prove that any control system can be made as safe and reliable as desired. However, I do agree that it is not feasible for BART." Why? Because, as Hjortsvang sees it, there is a lack of appropriate data channels between trains, and between trains and wayside. The only means of information transfer is the steel rails, which exhibit an extremely narrow bandwidth—thereby limiting the transfer to a few speed commands, plus train detection. Only a very crude control can be effected, Hjortsvang maintains, with only rudimentary closed-loop control.

Since BART, then, must have active train operators, not just train attendants, the question arises: Should the ATC system be "backed up" by train operators, or should BART revert to the classical manual operation, with automatic safety backup? He indicates that there are good psychological reasons for the latter possibility.

"The troubles BART has experienced," says engineer Hjortsvang, "are not the 'usual startup difficulties,' but are traceable to poor design concepts. The process of realizing this, compensating for the weaknesses, and compromising performance to gain acceptable safety, has taken years—and is not yet completed."

The second partisan

Max Blankenzee's input to *Spectrum* provided ten "exhibits"—evidentiary material—in support of the allega-

---

Blankenzee: Throughout my employment with BART, I tried to practice my engineering ethics and integrity by pointing out the system's discrepancies. I received no support from management.

Bruder: An engineer should not have to be either a hero or a martyr to exhibit a sense of ethical responsibility in the public interest.

tions he included in a letter. Spatial constraints preclude publishing the text of these documents; however, a summary of the contents of his letter and "Exhibit One: History of BART Employment" offers a graphic picture of Blankenzee's sentiments.

According to this second former BART engineer (a program analyst, to be precise), less than a year had gone by from the date of his joining BART when numerous "discrepancies" in the planned system began to be apparent. His immediate response was to bring up such problems, both to his manager and to PBTB, the BART consultants, during engineering meetings. The response, according to Blankenzee was no more than "a verbal, sympathetic reply." Referring to his colleagues as well as himself, Blankenzee continues: "Though it was clear to us that BART needed good system engineering, we could not communicate these ideas to our managers. Every time we suggested these things, we were labeled 'troublemakers.'"

What particularly annoys Blankenzee in retrospect, he says, is that his manager, who admitted ignorance concerning computers and computer systems, not only ignored all critical inputs, but insisted on deciding what actions the consulting engineer should take concerning the computers.

Meanwhile, according to the Blankenzee reconstruction of events, Westinghouse's internal control problems "caused them to miss their target date [June 14, 1971]." He further recalls such slippages as having occurred several times previously and notes that PBTB representatives at an engineering meeting claimed they were unable to "get a firm grip" on Westinghouse's progress. Nevertheless, General Manager B. R. Stokes informed the public that the BART system would start service by the beginning of 1972. "Internally," writes Blankenzee, "we knew this was an incorrect date."

As a footnote to this problem of schedule slippages, Blankenzee notes that Westinghouse attempted to conduct static testing of the software with a simulator in August 1971, but the company failed to get "one complete test off the ground until October 18." And six months later, says the former BART employee, there were still some 10 000 man-hours of debugging and error-correcting in the computer system to be done. In fact, a PBTB status report shows that in April 1972 Westinghouse still had problems trying to correct its real-time simulation system.

In the latter months of 1971, Blankenzee and Hjortsvang together attended a seminar in programming development and evaluation of computer systems. The result was that the two became even more convinced that BART needed systems engineering. Blankenzee himself requested a chance to make a presentation to top management—as he puts it: "to let them know the problems we would encounter when we started revenue service." Again, he claims to have been ignored and literally informed that he and his colleagues were considered to be troublemakers.

Then, in late October 1971, Westinghouse completed some static tests of the software. As Blankenzee tells it, "To analyze and evaluate the 'train history' printouts of these tests, I wanted to establish a norm: BART's operating philosophies. When I tried to locate these policies and procedures, I found that they had not yet been developed."

In January 1972, he tried to stop PBTB from running a total acceptance test of the electrification system, reasoning that the individual subsystems had yet to be approved. ("I was told that I was all wet.")

Particularly infuriating to Blankenzee is his recollection that although the manager did investigate his objection—"and found that I was correct"—he still refused to halt the PBTB test. "When I suggested at the subsequent engineering meeting that BART set up a field-test team to monitor all tests conducted by PBTB and Westinghouse, I received complete support from the engineers, but not from my managers. . . ."

Finally, Blankenzee's account begins to climax: "An individual told us that he could put us in contact with the directors to open a line of communication with our top management." One of these BART directors, Daniel Helix, is described by Blankenzee as having been receptive. Consequently, Helix was supplied with backup materials by the three engineers and began to ask questions at the engineering meetings. According to Blankenzee, "the BART staff became worried and changed the issue of 'what is wrong and why is BART completion late?' to 'who are these troublemakers, and let's shut them up.'"

Summing up subsequent events, Blankenzee insists that the issues presented by BART director Helix were "shoved under the rug" by the general manager and the board of directors as a whole. Following a vote of confidence in General Manager Stokes at a crucial meeting, Stokes claimed that nobody would be fired. "At this point," says Blankenzee, "everything backfired, and we were terminated. We were given the choice of resigning or being fired. We would not resign. The reason given for our termination was that we had 'affiliations with Mr. Helix and Mr. Burfine [an outside consultant].'"

Says Max Blankenzee: "I have felt throughout my employment with BART that I tried to practice my engineering ethics and integrity by pointing out the system's discrepancies. I received no support from management; then, in trying to work from the top down, I was fired for my efforts."

The third partisan

Robert Bruder, the third of the trio, views his own role in the BART controversy as less technical than that of his colleagues. While they had the specifics, he felt it his responsibility simply to inform the "proper authorities" that they were "not getting all the facts. . . ."

As Bruder remembers it, "I had made internal attempts to inform my boss that certain events indicated we could not inaugurate service on schedule—although management was telling the public we could." Although Bruder feels that his boss was sympathetic, it soon became apparent that all attempts to alert BART General Manager Stokes "that normal testing of interfaces was not receiving proper attention" were doomed to failure.

"I was ready to give up when Hjortsvang and Blankenzee expressed some of my same concerns. . . ." However, their attempts to alert the BART directors,* who were inexperienced in computer-control system development, only resulted, as Bruder puts it, in a "communications gap." The solution? Bruder recalls that the trio decided to engage a reputable system consultant who could report BART shortcomings, as viewed by the three engineers, to the board of directors in a written report. According to Bruder, two or three of the board members, "especially Mr. Helix," responded positively. In fact, Helix wanted to determine the truth and take any necessary action.

"Meantime," says Bruder, "internally, we were not asked to comment on (nor were we shown) the report . . . ; we were only quizzed on who had 'informed.' "

As Bruder remembers it, all three knew then that if they persisted, their jobs would be in danger. But, in conjunction with Helix, they nevertheless proceeded. Says Bruder, "I informed NSPE representatives at this time that our jobs were in jeopardy . . . These actions, and talking to Mr. Helix, eventually led to my dismissal."

What followed was that the Diablo Chapter of the California Society of Professional Engineers (CSPE), through Gilbert Verdugo and Roy Anderson, attempted to intercede in behalf of the three engineers. But this attempt became highly controversial within the CSPE, especially when it was contended by some members that the society's charter would not permit a direct defense of the dismissed BART employees' cause. A stalemate on CSPE legal aid followed.

for the three engineers to hire an attorney—as well as an attorney for CSPE so we could have legal advice as we moved through some 'sticky ground.' " Furthermore, Anderson contends that neither CSPE nor the Diablo Chapter supported a "citizens' lawsuit." However, the Diablo Chapter and Mr. Roberts did undertake a petition campaign to gain support for a legislative investigation on "The BART Inquiry" report findings that were given to State Senator Nejedly on June 19, 1972.)

In summation, Bruder notes that "the general public never took the matter seriously until a train crashed through the barrier at the Fremont terminal [October 2, 1972]." To bring things up to date, Bruder further points out, "Our cause is in the process of litigation, and it could take another year before a settlement or trial is completed. . . ." Meanwhile, says Bruder, "it is clear to me that the engineering profession needs some kind of 'ombudsman' . . . to protect the individual when situations involving ethics arise. An engineer should not have to be either a hero or a martyr to exhibit a sense of ethical responsibility in the public interest. . . ."

View from the Diablo Chapter, CSPE

Roy W. Anderson served as state director, president, and vice president of the Diablo Chapter of the California Society of Professional Engineers from 1964 to 1972. He was also the first chairman of CSPE's Committee on Transportation Safety. He is presently employed by the National Transportation Safety Board (Washington, D.C.) as its highway and traffic engineer. Anderson submitted a comprehensive report to *Spectrum* based on his detailed familiarity with events occurring during his vice presidency of CSPE and provided his personal professional views on the merits of the issue.

Anderson prefaces his account by noting that the BART system, hailed as the "most advanced transit

---

Helix: Many of the changes the engineers sought are now implemented. The credit for the improvements belongs to them.

Nevertheless, according to Bruder, attempts were made with the initial support of the CSPE (and later, with the support of Justin Roberts, a *Contra Costa Times* reporter) to initiate citizens' lawsuits. These attempts failed, but the efforts on behalf of the engineers drew the attention of state officials and led to investigations by A. Alan Post, the previously mentioned legislative analyst. These investigations culminated in state-sponsored reports that, says Bruder, "verified most of our claims that all was not in order and that remedial actions were needed. However, BART management still denied any out-of-control problems—and time marched on."

(Here it should be mentioned that Roy Anderson asserts "it was never legally proven that the charter prohibited such [funding] action. The Diablo Chapter wanted funds

system in the world" when it opened in 1972, is, because of numerous and serious technical problems, "still functioning [as of March 1974] like railroads of the 1870s." Because of a "faulty train-control system furnished by Westinghouse," he goes on to say, "BART relies on old-fashioned flagmen to prevent collisions. Other problems cause doors to open as trains race down a track, trains speed through stations when programmed to stop, and false detection of 'phantom trains' cause 'real trains' to stop." Further, says Anderson, "transit vehicles are unreliable and 40 percent of the trains placed in service in the morning can be expected to fail during the day. . . ."

Thus, the picture Anderson paints of BART is a severe one. He recalls that it was General Manager Stokes who dictated the firing of the three engineers. "Two of those engineers appeared, one by one, before their supervisors and were given a choice of quitting or being fired. They chose not to resign and were fired. Security guards

---

* Mr. Helix emphasizes that, at this point, he was *not* one of the directors who may have been contacted.

Roberts: Although directors of BART will be listed among the defendants in the suit, individual board members have indicated they will testify in behalf of the engineers and against their own general manager's actions.

escorted them to their desks to pick up their personal possessions and then followed them out the door. The firing of a third engineer occurred the next day. A request for hearing was denied and they left BART without any severance pay."

Anderson also believes that the months following their dismissal were difficult ones for the trio. "One experienced the frustration of several prospective jobs being within his grasp [when] suddenly the offers were withdrawn. In one instance he was told, off the record, that the personnel office received a phone call . . . from BART declaring the engineer was a 'troublemaker.' Another of the trio had his home mortgage foreclosed when he could not find employment."

Why, asks Anderson, were these engineers fired? "Simply, they identified many of the problems that still plague BART today. They became frustrated after trying to convince three levels of supervision that the BART consulting engineering firm and the train-control contractor were not properly addressing and resolving serious problems in the system, and were even denying that serious problems existed. Concerned with obvious future system delays, but [even] more by safety and reliability problems that would endanger the public if the system were put into operation on dates publicly promised by the general manager, they contacted members of the BART board of directors. One member brought the engineers' concerns to the full board (without naming the engineers). The Bay Area press picked up the story from board members and the problem became public knowledge."

As for what followed, Anderson's story parallels that of Hjortsvang, Blankenzee, and Bruder. In strong terms, Anderson offers his judgment of the trio: "The three engineers never sought public exposure of BART's problems, but were sincerely concerned about gaining official recognition of serious problems that existed and which couldn't be lightly dismissed . . . They seemed to be truly shocked that even the board of directors . . . would not seriously consider their concerns. They had proposed to the one director, who acted as their spokesman, that they would come before the full board and testify. They never received that opportunity. . . ."

One who listened

Daniel C. Helix, then mayor of Concord, Calif., is, of course, the BART board member, indicated earlier on, who was sympathetic to the position of the three engineers. Helix has been a BART director since November 1971.

In a phone conversation last May, Helix expressed willingness to cooperate with *Spectrum*'s effort by submitting his viewpoint for publication. However, as we learned belatedly on August 19, he was so involved in a campaign for a seat in the U.S. Congress, BART matters, and his

job as a member of the Concord City Council that he "could not then work in the time for writing the piece."

In his letter, Mr. Helix states: "I have given a deposition to the engineers' attorney and will testify for them in a trial . . . Many of the changes the engineers sought are now implemented. The credit for the improvements belongs to them."

Back in January 4, 1973, at the Contra Costa Mayors' Conference, Helix made a pertinent statement of record, excerpts of which follow:

. . . There are many things of a positive nature that might be said about BART. First and foremost is that BART will be meeting the need for a viable operating mass-transportation system and I will continue to be supportive of the concept and what it will mean for the Bay Area. However, during this past year a number of things have occurred which have not engendered a feeling of confidence toward top management on the BART staff. . . .

In December 1971, there was a collision wherein a moving test train hit a stationary train. At a board meeting, the directors were presented with the final report by the Board of Inquiry [that was] convened and dismissed by the BART general manager [B. R. Stokes]. Some of us . . . had additional questions which had not been presented to the Board of Inquiry and related directly to the possibility of a breakdown of the ATC. The board of directors advised the general manager to reconvene the Board of Inquiry . . . To my knowledge, the Board of Inquiry was never reconvened. . . .

Also in December 1971, the chief engineer of BART [D. G. Hammond], was asked specifically whether or not there were any serious problems with the ATC. He responded that there were a few "bugs" . . . but that there were no serious problems. This statement was made after the September 1971 Battelle Institute Report which pointed out the train-detection problem. . . .

In January 1972, three BART engineers approached me and other directors expressing concern about the reliability of the ATC system and the need to involve lower-echelon staff engineers in the testing phase. They retained an engineering firm which prepared a summary of the ATO problems. The report was rejected out of hand and no action was taken; yet, today, in reading the report, we find many of the concerns expressed by the Battelle Institute, and many of the predictions supported by actual occurrences. The three engineers were summarily fired. . . .

Excerpts from a journalist's notebook

On May 23, 1974, *Spectrum* received an input from Justin Roberts of the *Contra Costa Times*, Walnut Creek, Calif. Roberts has covered the BART story and its ramifications for a number of years. His comments generally tally with

252

the chronology of events already presented by the three engineers and Roy Anderson. To avoid unnecessary repetition and the bela-boring of points already made, some aspects of the case as presented by journalist Roberts will be omitted (though, for continuity's sake, some overlapping of coverage is unavoidable).

To Roberts, "Events have established the three engineers' accuracy in forecasting what has become well known throughout transit and engineering circles." Consequently, the journalist feels that their dismissal raises some serious questions: What are the moral obligations of the engineer to his employer? To the public? And to himself?

But the answers to these questions are complex. Notes Roberts, "In the case of BART, the employer being a public agency, the employer and the public are synonomous—even though BART General Manager Stokes referred to the dismissals as a 'corporate matter.' " Recalling that the case became a cause célèbre within the ranks of the CSPE, he observes that "some members supported the three men, while others chose a more proprietary approach to the events and believed the situation should not have become a public issue. Ultimately, the three engineers joined in retaining a law firm to represent them in a quest for damages, and a suit in their behalf will probably reach the California courts late this year [October 25]."

What is most interesting to Roberts about this chronology is that, as a consequence, "although directors of BART will be listed among the defendants in such a suit, individual board members have indicated they will testify in behalf of the engineers and against their own former general manager's actions [because] they see themselves as representing the public [and] the engineers acted out of concern for the public."

In support of the three engineers' claims, Roberts goes on to point out that the California legislature "has, for the past two years, been showing greater concern over BART failures and has ordered a series of investigations that have substantiated the concerns of Messrs. Bruder, Blankenzee, and Hjortsvang . . . . In the total scope of a $1.7 billion project, [the fate of] three employees seems miniscule in the [overall] picture of the entire BART operation . . . [But] the engineering profession—and every other profession that embraces ethical standards—has also moved ahead, and so has BART which, because of them, has come closer to what the public had expected."

The best defense is . . .

Following this writer's two-part series on BART, published in *Spectrum* last year, E. W. Morris contributed a letter outlining some of his views to "Forum" (June 1973, p. 15). Subsequently, he has supplied the writer with much valuable information updating BART's achievements.

In a letter to Victor Klig, editor of *CSIT* (Committee on Social Implications of Technology) *Newsletter*, Mr. Morris provided a rebuttal to Roy Anderson's article in the June 1974 issue of that publication. Morris updated that letter for this article to reflect his present viewpoint, as follows:

The CSIT Newsletter *indicates an interest in presenting divergent views on a subject. Such apparently is not the case in the presentations of the three engineers released by BART management in March 1972. . . . All CSIT references indicate there is but one side to the story, that of the three former BART engineers . . . No request was made for information on the other side of the story. It is time that readers were given more of the facts.*

As a resident of Contra Costa County since 1958, I have been close to the inspiration and growth of BART almost from the beginning. . . .

I ride BART and talk to many of the passengers who, to date, have helped ring up more than 200 million passenger miles. If you want an enthusiastic report on BART service, ask the riders.

BART and its PBTB consulting design engineers set out on their promise that the public would have the best rapid-transit system that modern technology could provide. It was to be a "design for the future," more versatile and sophisticated than any interurban mass-transit system in the world today. Extensive observations were made of other existing systems. A 4½-mile [7-km] test track was laid for the purpose of field-testing various drive and control systems.

Eighteen months delay in final designs and equipment orders were caused by taxpayers' suits, negotiations with cities about rights-of-way, station locations, and types of construction to be used.

PBTB and BART had planned intensive tests of ten prototype cars, to be followed by six months of testing of the first ten production or revenue cars, before they were placed in revenue service. The design engineers, the manufacturers, and BART's engineering and operating staff . . . needed this time for a "shakedown" of the equipment.

The public, however, was clamoring for service, which they themselves had delayed by [actions previously mentioned]. BART management decided to initiate service on one line with the first production cars, and do the shakedown tests in revenue service . . . (Bear in mind that in 200 million passenger miles to date, there have been no passenger fatalities or serious injuries.)

Had BART been able to make shakedown tests before starting revenue service . . . element failures and design changes would have been discovered. . . .

Morris: The public . . . was clamoring for service which they themselves had delayed. BART management decided to do the shakedown tests in revenue service. Had BART been able to make shadedown tests before . . . , element failures and design changes would have been discovered.

Morris: The three engineers were dismissed, not because they disagreed with management, but because of the way they went around management to serve their position.

As I understand the situation . . . the three engineers were dismissed, not because they disagreed with management but [by] *the way they went around BART management to serve their position. They employed a private consulting engineering firm, spent . . . 24 hours discussing their engineering position with him, and he* [Edward A. Burfine of Backers, Burfine and Associates, Palo Alto] *then presented a report to the BART management. In the meantime, the three engineers had gone around BART management, had reported to* [one] *of the BART Board of Directors, and to the daily press.*

The State Senate Utilities Committee, and PUC, long dissatisfied with BART's "deficit financing" and failure to provide for 1970s-brand inflation, pounced upon the safety features . . . as an entry to becoming involved. Just prior to revenue service in 1972, the State Utilities Committee issued its ultimatum to BART that it would not consider aid in additional funding unless back-up to the Westinghouse ATC system was provided. The ATC had been built to comply with the original consulting and design engineers' specifications. The back-up control selected was one designated by a panel of engineers that included Bernard Oliver, an engineer of established capability . . . In May 1974, Dr. Oliver accused A. Alan Post of misstating the facts of the Oliver recommendations and the reliability of the original ATC system.

BART, on its own, employed TRW, Inc . . . to check and test the system adequacy of the original ATC design. In a report submitted in March 1974, TRW states: "Results of recent BART system tests indicate the extreme unlikeliness of any need for train protection beyond that provided by the existing (original) train-control system, given that the circumstances of the tests are shown to be representative of the general system performance."

The report states further: "Based on that conclusion (the tests to date), the improvement in train protection achieved by the ($1.3 million) SOR back-up system over that offered by the primary (existing original) train-protection functions of the train-control system cannot be shown to be significant."

Where does BART stand today? The Concord line has been operating completely automatic, without telephone dispatching, since March 1974. The Hayward and Richmond lines were put on full automatic control on May 1, 1974. Service through the Transbay tube . . . is scheduled to begin on September 16, 1974, based on 5-minute headway between trains. The goal is to reduce this lead time to 110 seconds at an early date.

. . . BART parking lots are crowded . . . with consideration being given to double-decking in some locations . . . It is a thrill to ride in comfort on this 80 mi/h [130 km/h] system, [to] see the cars stop with doors at prescribed markings on the platforms, and [to] know that you *are riding for less money than the present parallel bus system, and at 20–25 percent of the cost of commuting by automobile. . . .*

In a very recent communication from Mr. Morris to *Spectrum*, he states that "the BART management *did* invite the three engineers to return and discuss [the reasons for their discontent] with them, but they did not take advantage of this invitation . . . ."

He also points out in this letter that the accident in which two test trains collided (see Helix's statement, p. 74) was a "human error," *not* an "automatic control malfunction." Morris also emphasizes that "BART management had to employ and train an entirely new breed of maintenance personnel, since none were available with experience on an entirely new system of automation. . . ." Finally, Morris underscores the fact that he is not a "spokesman" for BART management, PBTB, or the suppliers.

Some reflections in conclusion

There may be objections to this coverage on the grounds that "the case is being tried in the pages of *IEEE Spectrum* instead of in the courts." However, we reject this notion: the case of the three engineers vs. BART *is* newsworthy—and it is of special significance to engineering practitioners. It has been reported and covered at length (if not in depth) in the press, and on radio and television. Admittedly, there are some gaps in our coverage of the story: we regret not having the responses of the BART management, Mr. Stokes, and more of the BART directors; however, we can understand their reasons for not participating in this review. The Alameda County Superior Court's eventual decision (assuming an out-of-court settlement is not reached) could be a benchmark event on the subject of engineering ethics.

More to come

Despite its myriad difficulties, BART represents the first major breakthrough in more than 60 years toward the goal of achieving a sophisticated, safe, and reliable mass rapid-transit system that utilizes the most advanced state-of-the art techniques.

A future article will present (on the basis of first-hand interviews with the equipment suppliers, consultants, and BART management) a comprehensive overview, both retrospective and prospective, of

- The problems that were encountered in the design, testing, shakedown, and initial revenue service.
- How these problems were met, solved, and/or overcome.
- The present status of the ATC as applied to full-service operation (after service through the Transbay tube is inaugurated).
- Plans for the future in increasing peak-hour service, headway reduction, and extension of the system.

Whistle-blowing:
not always a losing game

Five engineers in nuclear power, aerospace, and air-traffic control recount their experiences in following their consciences

Exposing errors or unethical conduct in any occupation is risky, but when engineering judgment is involved, the risks of "blowing the whistle" acquire an added dimension. A technical decision cannot always be categorized as strictly right or wrong— unlike situations in which an organization is falsifying documents or overcharging for a product. Consequently, the engineer must be convinced of being right and then wait, sometimes years and even decades after lives are lost or millions of dollars are spent, to be proved right or wrong. Frequently, the whistle-blower's career is destroyed in the meantime.

In the following cases, which date from the 1970s and 1980s, the whistle-blowers have by now been vindicated to a degree for their actions, though the verdict may not be unanimous. And the careers of the first group may have even benefited by blowing the whistle.

NUCLEAR POWER, FEBRUARY 1976:

Three engineers quit General Electric Co.'s nuclear division to protest alleged inadequate testing and unsafe designs, not only at GE but throughout the nuclear industry.

Though engineers Greg Minor, Richard Hubbard, and Dale Bridenbaugh expected that their decision to resign their jobs might get some attention in the newspapers, they thought it would play itself out in a few days. The day after they quit, however, they realized their lives had irrevocably changed when they were thrust in front of hot lights, cameras, and reporters at a press conference in Los Angeles.

"We're technical people," said Minor. "Our lives changed because we had to become political people—not because we wanted to, but to keep the debate focused on the technical issues."

The three engineers were able to continue practicing engineering and have fared much better than most whistle-blowers. Nine months after resigning from the San Jose, Calif., GE division, they started a successful consulting firm on nuclear power, MHB Technical Associates, also in San Jose.

Each of the GE engineers came independently to his decision to resign, but agreed to do it together publicly in order to have more of an impact on the debate over nuclear power, which at that time was raging in California because of Proposition 15, an initiative requiring that certain safety problems be resolved before more nuclear plants were licensed.

Rude awakenings

With a bachelor's degree in mechanical engineering, Bridenbaugh went to work for GE in 1953 and was a start-up supervisor in 1960 at the world's first commercial boiling-water reactor at Dresden Nuclear Power Station, in Morris, Ill., near Chicago. After the plant had been in operation a short while, Bridenbaugh said failures began occurring that the designers had not foreseen;

Karen Fitzgerald   Associate Editor

pumps stopped working, heat exchangers leaked, and control rods started warping, bending, and cracking. "The reactor began falling apart," he said. "The designers really didn't understand what they were dealing with."

The final straw came when Bridenbaugh, as manager of nuclear reactor performance improvement, reviewed reactor containment response to possible accidents. A computer simulation showed that 19 GE plants in operation in the United States might not survive a serious accident: the release of pressure during an accident would throw up a violent swell of water that the containment could not withstand, possibly resulting in the release of radioactivity into the atmosphere.

Refusing to believe the simulation results, Bridenbaugh's manager wanted to keep the plants operating; he told Bridenbaugh that if they had to shut down, it would be the end of GE's nuclear business. In his last major task at GE, Bridenbaugh and other GE engineers met with the utilities to convince them they had to spend millions of dollars on plant modifications, but the utilities representatives refused, saying that they did not have the authority to make the decision.

Minor began working in GE's San Jose division in 1960. He received a master's in electrical engineering from Stanford University in 1966, and took part in designing the routing of the electrical cabling at the Brown's Ferry plant in Decatur, Ala. It was the first one to incorporate safety requirements increasing the separation of redundant cables. "I thought this was the best plant we had designed," he said.

But the cables were sealed with flammable polyurethane foam, and in 1975 when technicians performed a routine check for air leaks with a candle, the sealant caught fire. Because of about half a dozen mostly human errors, the fire raged for seven hours, damaged 1600 cables, and disabled most of the emergency core-cooling system. The core came close to being uncovered, but the crisis ended when an auxiliary pump was used to dump water into the reactor. "To me it was a disaster," said Minor. "I felt we were very, very lucky we hadn't had a major catastrophe."

Richard Hubbard, who began working for GE in 1960 with a degree in electrical engineering from the University of Arizona, was also disturbed by the Brown's Ferry accident. But as manager of manufacturing quality assurance for the nuclear division, he had already seen what he regarded to be fundamental problems with the company's attitude toward safety. While trying to eliminate a serious vibration in the reactor core, GE engineers stumbled upon a miscalculation in the core-cooling system flow rates and realized that the water would not flood the core as quickly as expected during an accident. When told of the problem, "a GE vice president said, 'It's important when you look under a rock, the angle that you look,'" Hubbard recalled. "He meant to look straight under the rock—don't look around and find other problems."

When the engineers quit, they made a point of not criticizing

Reprinted from *IEEE Spectrum*, Vol. 26, No. 6, pp. 49–52, December 1990.

Engineers Richard Hubbard, Greg Minor, and Dale Bridenbaugh (at right) testify in 1976 on safety problems with nuclear plant designs before the U.S. Congress Joint Committee on Atomic Energy, where they encountered hostility and skepticism. Shown (below) in happier times, Minor, Hubbard, and Bridenbaugh discuss a nuclear plant study at their consulting firm MHB Technical Associates, San Jose, Calif.

any person or the company specifically, but focused on the issue, which for them was that there were fundamental safety problems that the industry and the Nuclear Regulatory Commission (NRC) had not addressed adequately. They felt that there was too much reliance on theoretical models and not enough prototype or field testing. "The rate at which nuclear power was developed outstripped our knowledge and our understanding of the consequences and the side effects," said Minor. "All we were saying was 'Let's slow down and look at the side effects.'"

Testifying in Washington, D.C.

After their resignations, phone calls began flooding in from around the world for interviews and information about nuclear power. The engineers were asked to meet with commissioners of the NRC, who, the engineers believed, seemed more interested in undercutting their position than in understanding the technical reasons for it. Two weeks after resigning, they testified before the Joint Committee on Atomic Energy in Washington, D.C., where they again encountered skepticism and harsh questioning. Physicist Edward Teller and others accused them of being paid by the Soviets to speak against nuclear power.

GE disputed the engineers' views on nuclear power, and today still believes that their resignations were part of a preplanned publicity campaign to influence the Proposition 15 vote. "The resignation letters presented no fresh views or arguments but repeated the emotional claims of an antinuclear group of which they and their families were apparently members," GE spokesman Hugh Hexamer told *Spectrum* in a written statement.

Among their consulting firm's first projects was campaigning for initiatives similar to California's Proposition 15 that were on the ballot in six other states that fall. They also began a safety

assessment of the Diablo Canyon Nuclear Plant in Avila Beach, Calif., for the Center for Law in the Public Interest, which was supporting intervenors in the NRC licensing process.

That year, the Union of Concerned Scientists hired them to write a formal critique of the WASH-1400 risk assessment study, which estimated the probability of a core meltdown. The Swedish Government in 1977 asked them to perform a similar risk assessment for Sweden's nuclear plant at Barsebäck.

In 1978, the firm was asked by movie actor and producer Michael Douglas to devise a technically accurate scenario for a feasible nuclear reactor accident for *The China Syndrome*. For two weeks after it opened, MHB spent most of its time defending the sequence of events portrayed in the movie. After two weeks, the Three Mile Island (TMI) accident occurred in Pennsylvania, with many of the same precursors as the movie's scenario, but it went a step further to a partial core-melt. The press now began asking them to explain what happened at TMI.

The TMI accident gained credibility for MHB's views, and in addition to doing safety studies for intervenors in the licensing for the Shoreham nuclear plant, Brookhaven, N.Y., and others, the firm was hired by state attorneys general and utility regulatory agencies concerned about the economics of nuclear power and the prudence of rate increases.

The firm recently conducted a study of advanced reactors for the Union of Concerned Scientists, putting the engineers in the news again—and back in the position of being pitted against at least some in the nuclear industry. While MHB found that many of the features of the new reactors improved safety considerably, the engineers are concerned that the designs introduced new vulnerabilities not yet adequately explored, and that, despite these weaknesses, the nuclear industry and the Department of Energy are promoting them as inherently safe.

It seems that the three engineers are still blowing the whistle. Undeterred by the difficulties they encountered, they all say they would do it again. "The only regret I have," said Bridenbaugh, "is the hard feelings that developed between the people I worked with for many years who apparently don't understand why I had to do this."

AEROSPACE, JANUARY 1986:

Engineers at Morton Thiokol Inc. warn against the launch of the space shuttle Challenger because low temperatures predicted for the next morning might stiffen O-rings. The launch proceeds as scheduled, and seven astronauts die in an explosion caused by the O-rings' failure to seal rocket booster joints.

Like the GE engineers, mechanical engineer Roger Boisjoly was one of three who spoke out against a management decision at his company, Morton Thiokol Inc. (the aerospace division is now Thiokol Corp.), Brigham City, Utah. However, in his case, Boisjoly found little advantage in numbers. After six years with the company, he lost his job, and despite a 27-year career in the industry, could not find another. His two former colleagues have fared somewhat better—both have retained their jobs at Thiokol, even though apparently derailed from the fast track.

Boisjoly explains the uneven outcome by what transpired in the hearings of the President's commission investigating the shuttle disaster. The company instructed the engineers to give only "yes" and "no" answers and to volunteer nothing. Boisjoly spoke first and "bared all," revealing that the engineers warned that the cold temperatures—a low of 18°F (-8°C)—predicted overnight before the morning launch might render the booster O-rings so stiff that they would be unable to seal the gases properly. He and Thompson presented evidence of a past launch at 53 °F in which one of two redundant joints had not sealed.

Thiokol's upper management initially would not approve a launch below 53 °F, Boisjoly told the commission, but they later buckled under to pressure from the National Aeronautics and Space Administration (NASA), which had already postponed the launch four times. NASA argued that no launch criterion had ever been set for the booster joint temperature. Allan McDonald, the only Thiokol manager at the Kennedy Space Flight Center where the launch took place, fought against the launch to the end.

Although McDonald and engineer Arnold Thompson volunteered information during the commission hearings, Boisjoly believes that their 25 years with the company, compared with his six years, gave them more job security. Furthermore, Boisjoly was singled out for harsh punishment because of his outspokenness, he said. He saw his ultimate transgression as challenging testimony at the commission's public hearing by the company's general manager, who said that no unanimous engineering position against the launch had existed the night before. "That simply was not true," Boisjoly told *Spectrum*. "By telling the commission that, I put myself further and further in the quicksand. When I left that meeting, I knew I was at the top of the hit list."

Growing isolation

Shortly afterward, the company took Boisjoly off the failure investigation team and sent him back to Utah, while Thompson remained on the team in Washington. Boisjoly was assigned to work on the redesign of the booster seal, and although told he was very important to that redesign effort, began to realize he was being left out of meetings. When questioned a couple of months later by the President's Commission looking into whether the Thiokol engineers' jobs had been affected, U. Edwin Garrison, president of Morton Thiokol's aerospace operations, said he had given an official order to isolate Boisjoly in order to minimize friction with NASA.

But Boisjoly believes the real reason was that management did not want a thorough redesign. "I truly believed them when they told us as engineers that we were going to have a clean sheet of paper to redesign these joints, to do the job right." He said he was "devastated" when he realized that management itself had devised a redesign only marginally different from the original in a strategy to fend off outside criticism of the failed design. All management wanted the engineers to do was make the design work, he added. "I really cared about the program," he said. "I had devoted my whole being to doing the best possible job I could do, and when I found this out, it just destroyed me."

Furthermore, he and four other engineers who testified before the commission were feeling heat from co-workers who viewed the group as troublemakers out to hurt the company. Formerly close associates turned away when meeting them in the corridors and would not speak to them.

Boisjoly soon began experiencing stress-induced symptoms, including double vision and pains in his chest and shoulder. After going on sick leave for six months, he was diagnosed in the fall of 1986 as having post-traumatic stress disorder, qualifying for long-term disability benefits. But when the benefits took effect in January 1987, the company terminated his job.

Since that time, Boisjoly has given more than 100 talks on his experience to students, professional societies, and businesses. Anticipating that he might have trouble finding another job, he studied for a professional engineering license so that he could become a consultant. In prior job searches, he had to decide among two or three offers, having had experience at companies including Hamilton Standard Electronics Systems Inc., Atlantic Research Corp., and Rockwell International Corp., but this time he received only one job interview after sending out 150 resumes. In March of last year, he started a consulting business in Mesa, Ariz., to provide expert technical testimony in legal cases.

Although this past year his fees match the salary he received

Engineer Roger Boisjoly works in his office at home where he now does technical consulting for legal cases.

in industry, Boisjoly is bothered by his income's instability. He filed a lawsuit against Morton Thiokol for compensation for "ruining his career," but the case was dismissed by a Federal judge in Utah. "People who are branded whistle-blowers have no rights," Boisjoly said. "The Whistle-blower Protection Act was passed in 1989, but it only deals with Federal employees. I was trying to make the law with my lawsuit."

Arnold Thompson and Allan McDonald are still at Thiokol. Thompson is now working on the manufacturing side of the shuttle program, instead of engineering analysis, and McDonald is off the shuttle program altogether, with the title of vice president of special projects. Thiokol refuses all requests to talk about the Challenger incident. Asked to comment on Boisjoly's case, the company told *Spectrum* in a written statement, "It is our sincere belief that these articles serve no legitimate purpose, and continue to cause unwarranted suffering among our employees, the astronaut families, NASA, and the nation."

AVIATION, MARCH 1981:

A Federal Aviation Administration engineer appears on the television show ''60 Minutes,'' charging that lives have been lost because of the agency's mishandling of collision avoidance system development.

Jim Pope had a clear vision of what he wanted to accomplish when he went to work as a mechanical engineer for the Federal Aviation Administration (FAA) in McLean, Va., in 1966. He had dealt with the agency through its district and regional offices in a five-year stint as chief of aviation safety in Nebraska's Department of Aeronautics in Lincoln in the early 1960s. Afterward, he experienced firsthand what he felt were inefficiencies in the agency's certification process when he started a company to sell a device he invented for preventing wheels-up landings.

"When I tried to get certification for my landing gear control, I found that the FAA officials didn't seem to care about the cash-flow problems that people on the outside were experiencing while waiting for certification," he told *Spectrum*. "I joined the FAA to get that agency moving in a positive direction of service to the aviation community."

But eventually, Pope's mission mushroomed when he concluded that the agency had lost any sense of its original purpose—making flying as safe as possible. The FAA's technical decisions, Pope believes, have needlessly cost the United States 1000 lives in airplane accidents since 1975.

In 1971, after heading R&D efforts at the FAA, Pope became

chief of the industry and government liaison division in the office of general aviation (nonairliner craft). "People in the small business aviation community across the country learned in a hurry that our office—and I in particular—was acting as a catalyst for getting them a timely response," he said. "We got a lot of attention, and we got a lot of things done."

Over the next two years, Pope circulated in meetings among the top leaders of the agency, and began questioning the agency's decisions to spend millions of dollars for R&D on two systems that he felt were unnecessary.

One was a collision avoidance system that would prevent midair crashes through ground radar. In 1972, after two years of work on a system that the agency believed would be on-line in 20 years, the FAA was approached by Honeywell Inc., Minneapolis, Minn., with an airborne collision avoidance system (ACAS), which allowed planes to communicate directly without the ground as go-between. An onboard box would create an egg-shaped envelope of RF energy around each craft, and when two envelopes overlapped, the system would warn the pilots of a potential collision 45 seconds beforehand. If no action was taken 25 seconds from a crash, the system would give complementary commands for evasive action to both pilots.

Congress directed the FAA to evaluate the Honeywell ACAS, as well as two others by RCA Corp. and McDonnell-Douglas Corp. in a four-year, US $12 million program. The conclusion of the study, according to Pope, was that the Honeywell system was the best and the least expensive at US $1000 for small aircraft and US $7000 for airliners, and as stated by an FAA executive committee report of Dec. 16, 1975, that it "meets all the objectives of the agency."

But the FAA told Congress that ACAS caused too many false alarms and that it was concerned about the system's compatibility with the current air-traffic control system. Pope charges that the FAA lied to keep its own development program alive.

"ACAS conflicted with their NIH [not-invented-here] mindset," said Pope. "They wanted control of every airplane from the ground, so they weren't going to certify it."

With the backing of his boss, Pope wrote what he called "hard-hitting" letters to FAA administrator John L. McLucas, trying to convince him of the merits of selecting Honeywell's ACAS. In response to these letters, Pope said, and a run-in with the agency over its microwave landing system (MLS), another technology he said was already available from industry, the next FAA administrator, Langhorne Bond, eliminated the office of general aviation in 1978, fired Pope's boss, who supported Pope's positions, and transferred Pope to the FAA's Seattle office.

The FAA pursued the development of a ground-based system called the discrete address beacon system (DABS), in which air-traffic control would send warnings and evasive action when necessary. The agency also worked on an interim technology it told Congress would be ready in 1978, called the beacon collision avoidance system (BCAS). The active version of BCAS, in which aircraft would have their own receivers so they could interrogate transponders on other aircraft directly, is the basis for the agency's current TCAS (traffic alert and collision avoidance system). Unlike ACAS, BCAS would not allow the two closing craft to

Former Federal Aviation Administration (FAA) aerospace engineer Jim Pope (at right) is writing a book about his experiences at the FAA.

communicate and so each would have to take independent evasive action.

Pope claims that a 1975 study on midair collisions conducted by Mitre Corp. found BCAS to be dangerous, creating interference problems in high-density areas. In a study the next year, Mitre examined the 494 midair collisions that occurred in a prior nine-year period and concluded that improvements in the air-traffic control system could have prevented 118 of them; BCAS would have prevented 120; DABS would have avoided 190; and ACAS came out on top, preventing 228. Nonetheless, problems with DABS moved FAA administrator J. Lynn Helms in 1981 to make the BCAS technology the focus of collision avoidance efforts, though Helms renamed it TCAS, Pope charges, to make it appear to be a new technology. TCAS, which airlines began installing this year, costs about US $150 000 per aircraft.

When Pope was sent to Seattle in 1979, his family remained in McLean, Va., where he had just built a house. After arriving, he found he had little to do, and his boss eventually told him that the job had been fabricated to get him out of FAA headquarters. After a long and fruitless struggle to get reassigned to FAA headquarters, in 1981, Pope went public with his story, appearing on "60 Minutes" and testifying before Congress' Subcommittee on Transportation, Aviation, and Materials.

Pope said the FAA then began a campaign of harassment to build a case for terminating his job. His management reprimanded him for insubordination, failure to carry out orders, and improper use of duty time. When Pope began experiencing stress-related symptoms, including three kidney stone attacks, his doctors recommended that he take sick leave and return to his family in Virginia. A few months later, the agency fired him.

Pope contested his firing as a violation of laws prohibiting retaliation against Federal employees who testify before Congress. In order to prevent a public hearing, Pope believes, the agency converted his termination to retirement due to disability.

FAA associate administrator for regulation and certification Anthony J. Broderick commented on Pope's charges in a written statement to *Spectrum*: "In a perfect world, the [TCAS and MLS] projects may have moved faster and in a direct line from conception to production. But aviation research and development is not filled with black and white choices. . . . Mr. Pope would have your reader believe that the development of the collision avoid-

ance system was victimized by small-minded bureaucrats, and as a result a needed safety innovation was unconsciousably (sic) delayed. To say this, is to be less than accurate. . . ."

In 1985, Pope found employment at NASA's Goddard Space Flight Center in Green Belt, Md., working as an engineer on the Cosmic Background Explorer (COBE) and later the space station. But he left NASA in 1988 after a heart attack. He is now writing a book documenting his experiences at the FAA.

To probe further

A good overview of whistle-blowers in a variety of professions (including discussion of the Boisjoly and Pope cases) is *The Whistleblowers: Exposing Corruption in Government and Industry* by Myron Peretz Glazer and Penina Migdal Glazer, Basic Books Inc., 1989.

For information on the remedies available to government and corporate whistle-blowers, contact Sarah Levitt, intake coordinator at the Government Accountability Project, 25 E Street, N.W., Suite 700, Washington, D.C. 20001; 202-347-0460. ◆

The Federal Whistle Blower Protection Act

The following is the text of the opening sections of Public Law 101-12 of the 101st Congress.

An act to amend title 5, United States Code, to strengthen the protections available to Federal employees against prohibited personnel practices, and for other purposes.

Be it enacted by the Senate and House of Representatives of the United States of America in Congress assembled,

Section 1. Short title.

This act may be cited as the "Whistle Blower Protection Act of 1989."

Section 2. Findings and purpose.

(a) Findings – The Congress finds that –

1. Federal employees who make disclosures described in section 2302(b)(8) of title 5, United States Code, serve the public interest by assisting in the elimination of fraud, waste, abuse, and unnecessary Government expenditures;

2. protecting employees who disclose Government illegality, waste, and corruption is a major step toward more effective civil service; and

3. in passing the Civil Service Reform Act of 1978, Congress established the Office of Special Counsel to protect whistle blowers (those individuals who make disclosures described in such section 2302(b)(8)) from reprisal.

(b) Purpose – The purpose of this Act is to strengthen and improve protection for the rights of Federal employees, to prevent reprisals, and to help eliminate wrongdoing within the Government by –

1. mandating that employees should not suffer adverse consequences as a result of prohibited personnel practices; and

2. establishing –

   (a) that the primary role of the Office of Special Counsel is to protect employees, especially whistle blowers, from prohibited personnel practices;

   (b) that the Office of Special Counsel shall act in the interests of employees who seek assistance from the Office of Special Counsel; and

   (c) that while disciplining those who commit prohibited personnel practices may be used as a means by which to accomplish that goal, the protection of individuals who are the subject of prohibited personnel practices remains the paramount consideration.

Section 3. Merit Systems Protection Board; Office of Special Counsel; Individual Right of Action.

...

The Florida Whistle Blower's Act

This section reprints the text of a short description of the Florida Whistle Blower's Act as published by the Florida Commission on Ethics in *Guide to the Sunshine Amendment and Code of Ethics for Public Officers and Employees*, CE Guide Rev/10-1-93. (Information number: (904) 488-7864.)

> In 1986, the Legislature enacted a Whistle Blower's Act to protect employees of agencies and government contractors from adverse personnel actions in retaliation for disclosing information in a sworn complaint alleging certain types of improper activities on the part of an agency contractor, **or for** participating in an investigation or hearing conducted by an agency.
>
> In 1991, the Legislature revised this law to afford greater protection to these employees by allowing a **written** and **signed** complaint rather than a sworn complaint. Further changes provide that the reporting of a public employer's gross waste of funds is an employee protected action. The most significant revision to the law is the shift to the employer of the burden of proof that an adverse personnel action was not taken in retaliation for the disclosure by an employee of any information pursuant to the Whistle Blower's Act.
>
> This law also creates a private sector Whistle Blower's Act which will prohibit a private employer who employs more than 10 persons from discharging, suspending, demoting, or taking any other adverse personnel action against an employee in retaliation for disclosing, or refusing to participate in, an illegal activity or practice of an employer. As created, the new law provides employee and employer protections, specifies the mechanism by which an employer's violation of law may be reported, and describes remedies that can be imposed by the courts.
>
> Employees who are subject to adverse actions as a result of reporting improper activities or disclosing information under this Act may, after exhausting all contractual or administrative remedies, bring a civil action against their employers in the appropriate court of law. [Sec. 112.3187 and Sec. 112.3188, Florida Statutes]
>
> While this language is contained within the Code of Ethics, the Commission has no jurisdiction or authority to proceed against persons who violate this act in behalf of a person who is being retaliated against. Therefore, a person who has disclosed information alleging improper conduct as described above and who may suffer adverse consequences as a result should consult an attorney for information about his legal rights.

Chapter 8

Intellectual-Property Issues

The Congress shall have the power . . . to promote the progress of science and useful arts by securing for limited times to authors and inventors the exclusive right to their respective writings and discoveries.
—United States Constitution, Article 1, section 8
Not use or take credit for the work of others without specific acknowledgment and authorization.
—*from the* AITP Standards of Conduct
Honor property rights, including copyrights and patents.
Give proper credit for intellectual property.
—ACM Code of Ethics, general moral imperatives 5 and 6
Ensure that there is a fair agreement concerning ownership of any software, processes, research, writing, or other intellectual property . . .
—IEEE-CS/ACM Software Engineering Code of Ethics, principle 5.9

MANY ethical issues arise in the protection of computer-related intellectual property, and it is impossible to do the topic true justice in a short chapter. I have therefore opted to cover only the most fundamental topics—patents, copyrights, and trade secrets—and three controversial topics—reverse engineering, "look and feel" copyright, and software patents. Much of the discussion in this chapter deals with issues of legality as well as issues of ethics. As you might expect, the standard disclaimer applies—none of the material should be interpreted as giving specific legal advice of any type. If you need legal advice about any specific incident, you should consult an attorney with experience in the area.

8.1 PROTECTING THE INTANGIBLE

Something that is "property" is simply "something that can be owned." In its more familiar sense, property is a tangible or physical thing such as a piece of land, a car, or some object. Determining when someone has wrongfully taken another person's property in this sense is fairly clear because a physical object can generally only be in the possession of one person at a time.

The notion of intellectual property does not have such clear distinctions. Intellectual property exists apart from any particular physical realization. Intellectual property can be anything from literary works to industrial processes. In computer science and engineering, things such as hardware design, software, and documentation and educational materials would qualify as intellectual property.

To illustrate the ownership of nonphysical products created through intellectual effort, consider this example. Imagine you have put forth the effort to create a physical product that has some utility to you, say a batch of chocolate-chip cookies. If another person takes the cookies from you and eats them, then the situation is clearly viewed as the other person having "unfairly" taken something of yours.

Now, instead, imagine that the person does not take the cookies, but, without your permission, copies your recipe for making the cookies. You still possess both the cookies and the recipe. So in this particular sense, you have lost nothing. But the other person has gained the ability to make their own cookies. If you had made no substantial effort in developing the recipe, and had intended to use it only to make cookies for yourself, then you might not care about the other person copying the recipe. It would be

DILBERT © UFS

reasonable to conclude that nothing of value had been unfairly taken from you. In fact, it might even seem good that each of you can now make your own cookies.

However, suppose you had invested a great deal of effort developing a unique recipe and you planned to go into business selling the cookies. In this case, something of value *has* been taken from you. The other person has taken away some of your potential to profit from your investment. He can sell the same cookies as you, but without making the same investment. It is reasonable to describe this situation as unfair to you. If you had known the person could copy your recipe as soon as you developed it, you may not have bothered investing the effort to develop it in the first place. In the long run, society would be better off if there was some way to protect you from someone copying your recipe because both of you would then have the incentive to develop new things.

This example underscores that the protection of intellectual property is not really about the protection of the property itself—it really doesn't make sense to talk about an idea being taken away, and who wants a legal system that would allow one person to tell another they can't have a certain idea? What is really being protected in intellectual-property protection is the *opportunity to profit* from the intellectual property.

It is important to realize that this protection of economic opportunity is only a means to an end, and is explicitly **not** the primary purpose of intellectual property law. To be clear about this, return to the quote from the U.S. Constitution at the beginning of the chapter: . . . *to promote the progress of science and useful arts by securing for limited times to authors and inventors the exclusive right. . . .* The constitutional purpose of copyright and patent is to "promote the progress of science and useful arts," and thereby benefit society as a whole. The "securing for limited times to authors and inventors the exclusive right" is simply the means of achieving this goal. The occasional tinkering with the specifics of copyright and patent law is, or at least should be, focused on promoting the progress of science and the useful arts to the benefit of society as a whole. The basis of trade secret protection is

different from that of copyright and patent, and has more to do with enforcing concepts of fairness in business dealings.

8.2 PATENTS

Patents were used in a number of European countries before they were used in America. Also, patents were granted by individual American colonies before the U.S. government was formed. The first U.S. patent law was signed by George Washington in 1790. Since then patent laws have been updated a number of times, and the office in charge of patents has been moved between various departments of the federal government. The U.S. Patent and Trademark Office (USPTO, or just PTO) is currently part of the Department of Commerce.

As is often the case, the laws passed by Congress dealing with patents contain some words that are not given a precise technical definition in the law. The working definition then becomes established as cases are tried in the court system.

8.2.1 What Is Eligible for a Patent?

To be eligible for a patent, an invention must fall within the domain of subject matter for which the law allows patent protection. There are basically four categories of eligible subject matter, as set out in the wording of the patent law:

> . . . any new and useful process, machine, manufacture or composition of matter, or any new and useful improvement thereof . . .

The intent in defining these particular categories of allowed subject matter was to limit patent protection to areas that might be understood as applied technology. Abstract conceptual entities, such as theories, theorems, proofs, and equations, are not eligible subject matter, nor are artistic entities, such as paintings, sculpture, plays and writings. However, these artistic entities may be protected under copyright.

Given that an invention falls into one of the categories of allowed subject matter, it must also satisfy tests of novelty, originality, utility, and nonobviousness. The test of *novelty* requires that the invention be new relative to the "prior art"—all the existing body of technology that could reasonably be known to someone working in the field. An invention cannot pass this novelty test if it is essentially the same as some other previously patented invention, some other invention previously described in a printed publication, or even some other previous invention by someone who made no particular attempt to keep the invention a secret. An invention also cannot pass the novelty test if it has been described in a printed publication or offered for sale more than a year before the date of application for the patent.

The test of *originality* requires that the applicant for the patent be the actual inventor. This is to ensure that a dishonest person cannot unfairly take the credit for another person's invention. Thus, the patent is actually granted in the name of a particular person or persons, although the rights may be assigned to a corporate entity.

The test of *utility* requires that the invention be useful for something. Essentially, this is interpreted to mean that the invention must be able to do what it is claimed to do, what it does must serve some purpose or need, and the purpose or need must not be illegal or immoral. Thus, according to these criteria, a perpetual-motion machine (a machine that, once started, would remain in motion forever without consuming any energy), chemical compounds with no known use, and methods of manufacturing illegal drugs are disallowed.

The test of *nonobviousness* is perhaps the one most open to honest disagreement. The law states that an invention cannot be patented if

> . . . differences between the subject matter sought to be patented and the prior art are such that the subject matter as a whole would have been obvious, at the time that the invention was made, to a person having ordinary skill in the art . . .

Basically, an invention would fail this test if someone with "ordinary" skill in the area and access to all the existing prior art is likely to consider the invention "obvious." Factors that might be offered as evidence of nonobviousness are the degree of distinction that can be drawn between an invention and existing patents in the same area, and documentation of the amount of effort spent by people of ordinary or better skill in developing the invention.

8.2.2 How Is a Patent Obtained?

The inventor must file a patent application with the Patent and Trademark Office. The application must describe exactly what the invention is and how it can be made. This description should be at a level of understandability and detail that a person skilled in the relevant technical area could learn to make the invention from reading the application. The application must set out an argument for how the invention meets all the criteria for the tests outlined above. The application must also spell out what would constitute an infringement of the patent. The application can be lengthy and detailed in both a technical and legal sense and is typically prepared with the help of a lawyer specializing in patent law. However, a lawyer is not required for either the preparation or filing.

At the Patent and Trademark Office, the patent application goes to an examiner, who reads the application to see that all the required elements are present and who searches the prior art to confirm novelty and nonobviousness. The patent examiner may reject the application. If the application is rejected, the applicant is notified in writing of the reasons and has the opportunity to amend the application and request reexamination. After reexamination, the examiner writes a final acceptance or rejection. If the application is rejected again, the applicant may appeal to the PTO's Board of Appeals. The level of appeal after this is the Court of Appeals for the Federal Circuit. Appeals after this level may be made by either side to the U.S. Supreme Court.

In the United States, patents are awarded on the basis of the "date of first invention." This means that if two people are working on the same concept, and both apply for a patent, the patent goes to the one who can prove that they had the important essence of the concept the earliest. For this reason, it is wise to keep good documentation of any research work and when each advance was made. Research and development groups at many companies keep meticulous lab notebooks. On this point of "date of first invention," the United States differs from many other countries, where patents were awarded on a "date of first filing" basis.

The PTO can reexamine a patent at any time. A request for reexamination is typically made by someone who feels that the scope of the patent should be narrowed. A reexamination could be anything from minor narrowing of the patent's scope to disallowing the patent entirely. Since the legislation for the reexamination procedure was enacted in 1980, more than a million patents have been issued, about 3300 reexamination requests have been received, and about 2900 of these have resulted in a reexamination [6], [7].

If it is not already clear from this description, the process of obtaining a patent can easily take several years and cost a good deal of money.

8.2.3 Employee/Employer Patent Rights

Most companies have a standard agreement for their employees on the assignment of patent rights and the split of possible royalties. However, the "standard" arrangement can vary considerably among companies. In general, a company is likely to feel entitled to *all* the rights to any invention an employee makes in the technical area in which they are employed. At the least, the company is likely to expect nonexclusive, royalty-free use of the invention. Only when the invention is made in a technical area outside that in which the person is employed, on the employee's own time, and without company resources can the employee expect to retain full rights to the invention.

8.2.4 Using a Patent

The patent holder has exclusive rights to the patented invention for a period of time. "Patent pending" is often put on a product to inform people that a patent has been applied for but has not yet been granted. There are no legal rights during this stage. The notice is simply a warning that the patent rights are anticipated. To preserve the ability to enforce patent rights, all copies of the patented invention should be marked with the word "patent" and the patent number. If feasible, this should be done both on the invention itself and on the packaging.

The patent holder can grant rights to others to use, make, sell, or import the patented invention in return for payment. The patent holder can also assign all or part of the rights to other parties in return for payment of some type. After the period of the patent, the invention passes into the public domain. The patent period is currently set at 20 years from the time the patent application is filed.

8.2.5 Infringement

Someone who makes, sells, or uses a patented invention without the permission of the patent holder is said to be *infringing* on the patent. The patent holder will normally notify the alleged infringing party that they are believed to be infringing on a patent and demand that they stop ("cease and desist" is the fancy term). If the parties cannot resolve the matter, the patent holder may file suit in a federal district court. To prove infringement, the patent holder must show that (1) there is in fact a patent on the invention, (2) they are the legitimate holder of the patent rights, and (3) what the other person has done constitutes infringement. The first two conditions can be shown by having the letter of patent and being able to show legitimate transfer of title for the patent rights (if such transfer has occurred). Proving the third condition amounts to showing that what the person has made, used, or sold is the equivalent of the patented invention. The patent holder may ask for an award of damages equal to at least what would have been a reasonable royalty for the use, plus interest.

If someone who holds a patent feels that you are infringing on something covered by their patent, you are likely to receive a "cease and desist" letter designed to appear as intimidating as possible. You have several choices, depending on the facts of the situation. If you are infringing on the other person's patent, your realistic choices are to get a license for using the patented technology or to design around it. If you feel certain you are *not* infringing on the

other person's patent, you may want to reply with a simple, clear statement of why you are not infringing. One very effective way of doing this is to point out relevant prior art. The existence of prior art can invalidate a patent, even if the prior art was itself not patented. That is, if prior art that was not previously considered by the patent examiner shows that the invention does not actually pass the tests of novelty and nonobviousness, the patent may be rendered invalid. If the patent is not rendered entirely invalid, then the area of coverage for the patent may be shrunk to only the elements of the invention that still seem novel and nonobvious. This is not unheard-of, since many patents are purposefully written to be too broad and so claim to cover more than they really should. However, also keep in mind that you, as someone expert in the technical area, will likely have a higher standard for "nonobvious" than someone not well-versed in the technology (such as, perhaps, the judge in a patent suit).

8.2.6 Possible Changes to Watch For

The 1994 General Agreement on Tariffs and Trade made a number of changes to bring U.S. intellectual-property law more in line with European and Japanese practice. Before the GATT, the period of a patent in the United States was 17 years from the date of the patent award. The change to 20 years from the date of application filing was made to bring U.S. practice in line with European and Japanese practice. However, there are still some important differences in patent operation between countries. In the United States, patents are not published until they are granted, which can lead to what is sometimes called "submarine patents," patents with a long gap between the date of filing and the date the patent is granted. The analogy to the submarine is that the patent is lurking out there, waiting to torpedo the status quo of business. Gilbert Hyatt's 20-year wait for the award of the microprocessor patent is a good example of a submarine patent (see the Additional Assignment at the end of this chapter). There have been proposals to have patent applications published 18 months after filing. Another point on which U.S. patent law is different from other countries is the use of the "date of first invention" as the criterion for award rather than the "date of first filing." The U.S. Patent and Trademark Office's world wide web site, www.uspto.gov is a good place to check on current details.

8.2.7 Patent Searches Over the Internet

The PTO has a World Wide Web site that you can use to keep abreast of the latest developments in patent law. Also, the office is in the process of translating all its files to digital form (text and images), so that you will be able to use the site to do a patent search as well. The year 2000 is the estimated completion date for having *all* of the patent library on-line, including materials dating back to 1790.

This should be the world's largest electronic technology library. The World Wide Web address for the PTO is http://www.uspto.gov.

8.2.8 Summary

You can view the patent system as a uniform social contract that is worked out between inventors and society. The inventor makes a full disclosure of the workings of the invention and agrees to it becoming public domain after a period of time. In return, society gives the inventor a time-limited legalized monopoly on the use of the invention.

During the time of a patent, others cannot use the same invention that is disclosed in the patent. However, they can use what they may learn from the patent to design other related products that the patent does not cover. In this sense, the patent spurs the progress of technology. Also, since the patent period is limited, the patent holder is hopefully motivated to use some of the profits from the invention to develop new patentable inventions.

That others may gain useful knowledge from the patent application and be motivated to create related products is a motivation for the application to be written as broadly as possible in terms of the technology and uses it covers. This may cause some give and take with the patent examiner during the approval process. It may also leave the patent open for challenges at a later date.

8.3 COPYRIGHTS

Like patent protection, copyright protection exists in federal law, and copyright law has a constitutional basis (see the first quote at the beginning of the chapter). Copyright protection orginally covered books, maps, and charts, but the law was amended to explicitly extend protection to engravings and prints, musical compositions, photographs, motion pictures, sound recordings, and software. The Copyright Office began accepting software for copyright in 1964, but the Computer Software Copyright Act was not passed by Congress until 1980.

Traditionally, patent and copyright have covered complementary areas of subject matter. Patents have covered applied technology as put to use in industry; copyrights have covered creative and artistic works. However, as you will see later in the section on software patents, both patent and copyright law may apply to the protection of software.

8.3.1 What Is Eligible for a Copyright?

Other than falling into an allowed category of subject matter, the primary test for eligibility is orginality. This requires simply that the work be original with the author. There is *no* requirement of novelty, utility, or artistic merit.

An eligible work must be fixed in a tangible medium of expression, from which it can be perceived/experienced/understood by others. However, the law does not require a work to be "published" in the sense of there being a number of physical copies available for sale or use—copyright of "unpublished" work is explicitly allowed.

An important point about copyright is that it protects the *expression* of an idea rather than the idea itself. Someone who examines the copyrighted work and understands the idea is not prohibited from using the idea, only that particular expression of the idea. Consider, for example, someone who reads a program. If they then write their own program with the same expression of the algorithm, this would be a violation of copyright. On the other hand, if the person uses a different algorithm to accomplish the same purpose, or even uses the same algorithm but with a substantially different coding, there is no violation.

8.3.2 How Is a Copyright Obtained?

In principle, an eligible work has copyright protection the moment it is fixed in some tangible medium. All published versions of the work should carry a clearly visible copyright notice that consists of the word "copyright" or the copyright symbol ©, the year of first publication, and the author's name. For software, the copyright notice should appear on (1) the packaging, (2) the diskette or CD on which the software is distributed, (3) as a part of the program listing in both source and object code, and (4) during program execution as part of either an initial or a continuous display.

It is *not* a requirement that the eligible work be registered with the Copyright Office. However, it may be in your best interest to do so anyway because you then have added protection against infringement. For example, if the copyright notice is omitted from copies of the work and the work is not registered with the Copyright Office, the copyright may become invalid. Also, a person who infringes a copyright by copying a work that lacks a copyright notice may be found not liable for any damages. Thus, the best course of action to ensure maximum copyright protection is to be sure a copyright notice appears on all copies of the work *and* register the work with the Copyright Office. Registration of a copyrighted work is relatively easy and inexpensive. It involves paying a small registration fee, filing a Copyright Office Form TX, and sending the appropriate copy or copies of the work to fulfill the deposit requirement. Registration may be done at any time during the period of the copyright.

8.3.3 Using a Copyright

For personal authorship, copyright protection extends for the life of the author plus 50 years. For authorship by an employee of a business as part of their job, the work is considered a "work for hire" and is protected for 75 years from first publication or 100 years from creation, whichever expires first. The copyright owner has the right to control the creation of direct copies of the work, creation of derivative versions of the work, distribution of copies of the work, and public performances or display of the work. The control over public performance and display of the work is perhaps most relevant to works such as plays, movies, and graphical art. Similar to a patent holder, a copyright holder generally exchanges some or all of these rights in return for royalties.

Control over distribution of a work is generally meant to give a copyright holder the control necessary for sale, rental, lease, or lending of their work. However, the "first sale rule" generally gives the copyright holder control over distribution only of the *first* sale of a copyrighted work. If you sell a copy of your copyrighted work to another party, that person cannot make copies of the purchased copy without violating the copyright, but can generally resell, rent, lease, or lend the copy purchased. Exceptions to this rule have been made for the rental of sound recordings and software. Under the Software Rental Amendments Act of 1990, someone who purchases copyrighted software and rents it to others *is* in violation of copyright. These exceptions came about because the business of software and sound-recording rentals made unauthorized copying so easy that it resulted in a substantial loss in sales to the copyright holders.

Copyright protects against someone making a literal exact copy of something, of course, but it also protects against copying in translation between languages (such as creating a French translation of a work written in German, or a C version of a Pascal program) or conversion from one medium to another (such as creating an electronic version of a book published in paper). These would be simple derivative works.

However, remember that copyright protects the *expression* of an idea not the idea itself, so someone could decide to remake a movie with the same basic plot but change some of the characters and the time and place of the story and probably not be infringing the copyright on the original movie. In the same way, someone could study a program to learn how it worked, create a substantially different expression of the same algorithm, and be performing legitimate reverse engineering, which would not violate the copyright. From a traditional view, this would provide only weak protection for software. However, when copyright protection is applied to the "look and feel" of software, there is, in fact, much greater protection, as we will see later in this chapter.

Another area of potential problems in applying copyrights is "work for hire." The first reprint in this chapter, "Copyright and Work Made for Hire," describes how copyright law deals with this type of work. The problem arises when one person hires a second person to create a product that is copyrightable—who, then, should the copyright belong to? The courts have developed some guidelines for such cases, which the article describes.

8.3.4 *Infringement*

The process of claiming infringement against a copyright is similar to that of claiming infringement against a patent. The copyright holder must show that they actually hold a valid copyright on the work, typically by showing the registration certificate for the copyright and the chain of transfer of the rights. The copyright holder must also prove that the alleged infringer has copied their work. To prove copying took place, the copyright holder can either provide direct evidence (e.g., produce someone who saw the copying occur) or argue that the situation meets criteria of access and substantial similarity. To satisfy the *criterion of access,* the copyright holder must show that the alleged infringer had access to the copyrighted work, or show that the work was so generally well-known and available that it is reasonable to believe the alleged infringer had access. To satisfy the *criterion of substantial similarity,* the copyright holder must compare their work with the work that allegedly violates the copyright. Factors such as the existence and nature of any dissimilar material will be important. The presence of similar "errors" or "accidents" in the works increases the credibility of a copying claim. If the degree of similarity makes it seem clear that a direct copy was made, it may not be necessary to show access.

Moreover, even showing access and substantial similarity does not automatically mean that a court would rule that the work was copied. For example, if there was a relatively low degree of orginality in the copyrighted work to begin with, and the degree of similarity is not indicative of a direct copy, the possibility of independent creation must be seriously considered. Independent creation does not constitute an infringement of copyright. In this respect, a copyright differs fundamentally from a patent, which does *not* allow independent creation as a defense against an infringement claim.

Thus, there are several strategies for a defendant in a copyright suit. He could argue that

- the copyright is not valid, perhaps by showing that the copyright holder in fact copied the work from someone else,
- he had never seen the copyrighted work and so could not have copied it,
- the degree of similarity is not substantial,
- the work should be considered an independent creation in spite of possible access and some degree of similarity, or
- only limited and *fair use* was made of the copyrighted work (see the next section).

The copyright holder may ask for compensation on the basis of an estimate of lost revenue, the defendant's profit, or damage to the market caused by the defendant's activity. Alternatively, the copyright holder may simply ask for statutory damages, which are at the discretion of the court within the range fixed by law. Asking for statutory damages is simpler, but the limit on the amount that may be requested might be too low in many commercial situations. For willful infringement, there may be additional criminal penalties in the form of fines or a prison sentence.

8.3.5 Fair Use of Copyrighted Material

The concept of fair use provides for some limits on copyright protection so as to advance the larger intent of copyright—the creation and dissemination of works that enhance the public's access to knowledge. Specified categories of activity in which fair use may occur include the use of a copyrighted work for news reporting, commentary, criticism, research, scholarship, and teaching. In general, the limits of fair use are more liberal for

- noncommercial/educational applications than for commercial ones,
- use from a factual work than an artistic work,
- use from a published work than an unpublished work,
- use from an out-of-print work than one that is in print,
- use of lesser and less important parts of a work, and
- uses that have less detrimental effect on the work's economic value.

A typical example of fair use of copyrighted material is the use of a short quotation from a copyrighted work in a set of class notes.

Information that is in digital form, and is thus easy to reuse and manipulate, raises a number of interesting questions about what constitutes fair use. Paula Samuelson addresses this issue in depth [21], [22].

8.3.6 Changes to Watch For

Like the patent system, the copyright system is not perfect and has changed over time. For example, copyright was once available only for published works, and copyright protection was once available for 28 years plus a possible renewal for another 28 years. So, like the patent, copyright as a specific legal concept is something that has evolved and can be expected to continue to evolve.

8.3.7 Software Piracy

Software piracy is simply the illegal copying of software. It warrants a separate section in this chapter because it has become a pervasive ethical and legal problem. The estimated magnitude of economic loss due to software piracy is huge. Estimates of losses to the personal-computer software industry in the United States run as high as $3 billion a year, and estimates of losses in Europe run as high as $5.3 billion a year [34]. Estimates of global losses to the software industry run as high as $39 billion a year [5]. Even allowing for these estimates to be high by a substantial amount, the losses are huge. These losses represent an effective transfer of investment away from the software industry and into the areas in which the piracy occurs. In this sense, the software industry is not receiving full value for the products it creates, so there may be fewer jobs and less investment in future products than if the normal price were paid for all software products.

Under current U.S. law, you are subject to prosecution for a *felony* if you make 10 or more illicit copies of copyrighted works, with the sum of the values of the works totaling $2,500 or more, in any six-month period. Conviction on a first offense can result in a fine of up to $250,000 and a jail sentence of up to five years. Even for lesser instances of willful copyright infringement for private financial use, the misdemeanor criminal penalty can be as much as a fine of $25,000 and a jail sentence of one year. Additional financial liability may arise from a civil suit for infringement of copyright. A civil suit may ask for actual damages or for statutory damages up to $100,000 per infringement.

In the United States, there were orginally two organizations that worked against software piracy, the Business Software Alliance, and the Software Publishers Association. These are now merged into one organization, the Software and Information Industry Association. Their web site is www.siia.net. The SIIA fights software piracy on a variety of fronts, including educational efforts, pursuit of legal cases against pirates and lobbying Congress for laws more favorable to software copyright holders. Some of the worksheets at the end of this chapter will point you to studying the SIIA's antipiracy efforts more carefully.

The Berne Convention for the Protection of Literary and Artistic Works is the primary international copyright treaty, providing reciprocal copyright protection with a number of countries. However, the global, multicultural aspects of software piracy are very difficult to understand, assess, and react to. This is due to the widely varying ethical and legal standards among cultures, as well as to sharp differences between lesser developed and more developed countries. Some lesser developed countries may argue that accepting the concepts of intellectual-property protection supported by more developed nations will help to perpetuate their lesser developed status. Even in some "industrialized" countries, it may not be against the law to make copies of software for personal, noncommercial use.

8.3.8 Plagiarism

Plagiarism is the taking of the ideas, writings, drawings, words, or other similar intellectual property created by others and presenting it as your own. It is generally not a legal issue, like copyright infringement, but it is an ethical one. For example, you can reuse writings in the public domain without worrying about the legal problem of infringing a copyright, but presenting them as your own without proper credit to their true orgin is an act of plagiarism. And plagiarism is always unethical.

There is also *self-plagiarism,* when you reuse your own words from a previous publication in a newer publication without bothering to reference the older one. This might seem innocent enough, since the words are yours both times, but if you reuse any substantial amount of text, it is proper to credit the orginal publication. Also, when you publish something, you typically sign a copyright release to the publishing company. In this case, the self-plagiarism affects your ability to ethically sign the copyright release for the newer publication. Both Harold Stone and Paula Samuelson describe aspects of an author's responsibilities to avoid plagiarism [20], [32].

8.3.9 Summary

Like the patent system, the copyright system can be viewed as a uniform social contract worked out between authors and society. The author receives some protection of the ability to profit from his work for a period of time, and society receives the benefit of the work, which eventually passes into the public domain. From the relative length of time of copyright and patent protection, it seems that patent holders are expected on average to be able to gain sufficient profit in a shorter time than are copyright holders.

8.4 TRADE SECRETS

A trade secret is something that a person wishes to keep secret to maintain the health of their business. Trade-secret status is an alternative to the use of patent or copyright. When making something known to the public would work against being able to exploit its economic potential—even if it had patent or copyright protection—making it a trade secret may be an appropriate alternative.

Trade-secret protection is not governed by federal law, so laws about the protection of trade secrets may vary across jurisdictions. This can complicate trade-secrecy protection for companies operating in multiple jurisdictions.

8.4.1 What Is Eligible to Be a Trade Secret?

In general, something qualifies as a trade secret if all of the following are true:

- You took serious steps to maintain its secrecy.
- It represents some economic value to you in conducting your business.
- It has required some effort or cost to develop.
- It has some degree of novelty.

In principle, almost any apparatus, formula, or compilation of information that is of some value in conducting a business can qualify as a trade secret. Some commonly cited examples of trade secrets are the formula for a soft drink, a list of customers, and a business plan for new products.

8.4.2 Using a Trade Secret

A trade secret is kept secret by (1) not revealing it to anyone unless it is necessary to do so to conduct business, and (2) when it is necessary to reveal the secret, making it clear that the information is considered secret and is to be kept confidential. This might be done by having the person to whom it is revealed sign some type of "nondisclosure agreement" that states that the person is not allowed to reveal or use the trade secret outside this specific business transaction. In some cases, you may need to maintain a list of all the people to whom the trade secret has been revealed.

There is no time limit on how long something may be a trade secret. In this respect, trade secrecy is quite different from a patent or copyright. Frederick and Snoeyenbos [9] cite the example of the Zildjian family's trade-secret metallurgical process for producing cymbals. The material properties of the cymbals apparently give them unique musical qualities. The family discovered the metallurgical process in Turkey in 1623 and have maintained its trade-secret status to the present day, with their business now located in Massachusetts.

Trade secrecy protects you only from someone unfairly taking and using the information. For example, someone cannot sneak into your place of business and steal a copy of some trade-secret information. Nor can someone given the trade-secret information under a nondisclosure agreement give or sell it to another person. Finally, an employee cannot take trade-secret information with them to use when they leave your business to work for a competitor.

However, trade secrecy does *not* protect you from someone independently developing the same information or purposefully reverse-engineering the information. So, for example, there is no protection from someone buying a bottle of your soft drink made with a trade-secret formula and analyzing it to discover the chemical composition. In this sense, trade-secret protection is very unlike patent protection, in which you would be protected even against someone who independently discovered the same invention. It is also in a way less shielding than a copyright, in which you would not be protected from truly independent creation of the same expression, but you *would* be protected from a derivative work.

Trade-secret status also does not protect against an employee who leaves to go to another company and takes with them some level of general understanding, knowledge, or skill related to previous work. It can sometimes be very difficult to prove that an employee has taken trade-secret knowledge to use in a job with a competing company. Partly for these reasons, an employer may ask you to sign an agreement stating that, after leaving this job, you will not work for a directly competing business for some period of time (a "no compete" agreement). A written employment agreement may also include prohibitions against soliciting customers for a new company you might join and against soliciting employees of your former company to join your new company. A no-compete clause in an employment contract will generally be enforceable only if it can be considered a "reasonable" restriction. An example of a reasonable restriction is a prohibition against taking a position with essentially identical responsibilities working on an essentially identical product with a new company that has offices within a certain distance of the current company for a period of a few years.

Trade-secrecy protection for computer software is often done by licensing the customer to use the software, rather than actually selling the software, and having a nondisclosure clause as part of the license agreement.

Although it may no longer be true, at one time trade-secret status was the favored method for protecting software. A 1980 monograph, *Legal Protection for Computer Programs,* at one point states that ". . . more has been written about copyrights and patents for software, but an examination of industry practices reveals that trade secret is utilized far more frequently than the other forms for protecting computer programs" [10]. This quote underlines how concepts and practices of software protection have changed over the years.

8.4.3 Infringement

If someone does unfairly take a trade secret from you, you may seek some remedy in civil court. You will generally need to show that there was a trade secret, that the person has taken it from you and used it, and that the person should have known that confidentiality was expected. You may ask for damages and/or an injunction against the use of the trade secret by the other party. Depending on the particular nature of the trade secret and how it was taken, there may also be the possibility of criminal charges.

8.4.4 Summary

Trade secrecy is unlike a patent or copyright in that you cannot view it as a social contract between inventor and society for the long-term benefit of society. The basis of trade secrecy seems to stem more from supporting concepts of fairness and honesty in the conduct of business.

8.5 Reverse Engineering

The practice of *reverse engineering* has a long tradition in engineering. The idea is to take something apart to educate yourself about how it works so that you can use your improved level of general knowledge to create better things yourself. Reverse engineering in itself is generally not viewed as either unethical or illegal, providing you do in fact make an honest effort at understanding the disassembled object and then also honestly use the knowledge you

gained. This is the positive sense of reverse engineering, in which incremental improvement of technology occurs and all involved are rewarded for honest effort. What is unethical, and quite possibly also illegal, is to simply make a straightforward copy of a competitor's product with little or no changes or improvement, possibly without even understanding exactly how it is made or why it works.

Examples of reverse engineering in computer science and engineering are easy to come by. The second reprint in this chapter. "Reverse-Engineering Someone Else's Software: Is It Legal?" describes a number of cases. One often cited example is the BIOS (basic I/O system) of the IBM personal computer. Many companies made small (and maybe not so small) fortunes by reverse-engineering the BIOS. The BIOS is essentially just a set of control routines that are located at specific addresses in ROM and used by the operating system and possibly other software. Producing an equivalent of the BIOS is a necessary step in producing a machine that runs the same software as an IBM PC. A reverse-engineering team might set about creating a functional equivalent of the BIOS by examining a list of memory locations that the program control can branch to, a specification of what can be assumed about the contents of the processor registers, and a specification of what must be accomplished before returning control. They can gather all this information from the IBM technical manuals. The team would then attempt to create the specified function within the specified constraints. The team might never be allowed to see the actual IBM BIOS, for fear that seeing it would bias them toward using a similar implementation and increase the chances of copyright violation. If their company was being extra careful to guard against possible copyright violations, another group that was allowed to look at the actual IBM BIOS might compare it with the reverse-engineered solution and send the reverse-engineering team back to work if some of the control routines accidentally turned out to be too similar.

Reverse engineering is also commonly applied to hardware products, particularly the design of computer chips. The Semiconductor Chip Protection Act of 1984 provides for a chip manufacturer to register a chip design with the Copyright Office. The design is then protected for a period of 10 years from the date of registration or 10 years from the date the chip was first made commercially available, whichever is later. The Semiconductor Chip Protection Act makes it clear that copying all or part of a chip to analyze its layout is legal. However, this is to *understand the layout,* not to manufacture and market another version of the original chip design. A new chip that is legitimately reverse-engineered should include some element of new design and should not be substantially identical to the first chip. In addition, a team should keep records during the reverse-engineering process that make it clear how much time and effort they invested in the process. A good example of a reverse-engineering case is summarized by Rauch [16]. In *Brooktree* v. *AMD,* Brooktree sued AMD for copying two of its ramdac chips (a ramdac is a RAM and digital-to-analog converter on one chip, which is used to generate signals for display devices). There were a number of substantial similarities between the static RAM cell in the two chip designs. The AMD engineer was not able to convincingly answer questions about the similarity of the designs. AMD was, however, able to present substantial documentation of the effort put into reverse-engineering the design. In this case the degree of similarity of the two designs outweighed the documentation of effort, and the jury decided in Brooktree's favor. AMD ended up paying $28 million to Brooktree.

8.6 The "Look and Feel" Copyright Controversy

The term "look and feel" refers to the user interface of a software product. Part of the "look" of a software product is the design of the menus and graphics it uses in communicating with the user. Part of the "feel" is the set of inputs the user can give and the action each input causes. The overall "look and feel" then refers to the style of the interactions that take place between the user and the program. Certainly the Apple McIntosh was responsible for popularizing a certain style of look and feel for using a personal computer. The concept of one product having "keystroke compatibility" with some original product indicates that there was at least some distinctive "feel" to the previous product. And the concept of a "clone" product is specifically that it look and act like the original.

8.6.1 Where Does the Controversy Come From?

The Copyright Office has accepted programs for copyright since 1964. From this time until perhaps the mid-1980s, the entire computer industry shared the same clear concept of copyright protection for software. This period includes revisions to the copyright law passed by Congress in 1976 and 1980. The concept of copyright with respect to a software product was that it protected against copying the source code or object code, but did not protect against someone studying the program to understand how it works and then developing a product that uses similar means to solve the same problem. This notion of creating a work-alike program extended to having a similar user interface.

To drive home the point about just how pervasive and clear this concept of copyright protection was, consider the following quotes. A 1980 manual on the subject of marketing software discusses copyright, patent, and trade secret and includes the statement that [13]:

> Copyrights applied to computer programs are practically meaningless, since a program can easily be modified to circumvent any copyright.

A 1980 monograph on legal protection for software contains the statement [10]:

> Anyone may create a program similar to or even identical to a copyrighted program without infringing the first programmer's copyright if there was no copying of the protected program. In other words, copyright law does not prohibit the independent creation of a program similar to or identical to a copyrighted program.

As recently as 1985, a monograph on computer ethics could include the clear statement that "copyright . . . only protects the source program and the object program" and not contain any mention of the look and feel [15]. You can imagine how surprised people were when told that this view of software copyright protection was wrong! Actually, this view is not so much wrong as it is incomplete. Everyone still agrees that copyright does protect against copying the source or object code, but now some court decisions suggest that the copyright of a program also protects against copying the distinctive elements of the look and feel in a software product.

How could an entire industry have not realized for more than two decades that copyright might apply to the look and feel of software? It could be that the common informal understanding of copyright as it applies to books would lead people to focus on copyright protecting against copying source code. Since the object code is a "direct" translation of the source code, the extension to protection of the object code is automatic. The analogy to books suggests that, just as copyright does not protect against another author copying the basic plot, it does not protect against another programmer copying the basic idea embodied in your software. The common understanding of reverse engineering would contribute to the acceptance of this view.

Perhaps it was only as people began to make analogies to the copyright protection of audiovisual works that things began to change. The concept of look and feel copyright for programs may have had its start in a case filed by Atari in 1982 [18]. This case involved a clone of Atari's Pac-Man program. The clone was called K.C. Munchkin and it had mazes and gobbled up dots in a manner similar to Pac-Man, although the particular design of the mazes, and the sounds and colors used were different. The court case was decided in Atari's favor. Now it becomes possible to see some of the incompleteness in drawing a software-protection analogy to books. It is correct that copyright does not protect one author from another author copying their plot. However, if you were to write a novel about a brave, witty, womanizing British spy named James Bond, Agent 007, and one of his battles against Spectre to save the world, you should rightly expect that someone may take legal interest in your work! Almost anyone would understand this as infringing on the look and feel of the James Bond novels. So an appropriate deeper level of analogy between software and books might actually be that copyright offers protection against a software product that performs essentially the same functions when you click the mouse on essentially the same distinctive icons.

The look and feel controversy moved into high gear with a court case filed in early 1987 by Lotus Development Corporation against Paperback Software. Lotus claimed that Paperback Software's VP-Planner infringed on their product, 1-2-3. The claim was not that the source or object code of the two programs was similar enough to be a problem, but rather that the VP-Planner used the same command names, keystroke sequences, and screen layout as 1-2-3. Lotus was effectively claiming that the protected "expression" of their product was not just the static source code listing but also the dynamics of the way it presented itself to the user. The federal court decision in favor of Lotus came in June 1990. The presiding judge, Judge Keeton, wrote a 110-page opinion to explain his decision. At least one commentator has been quite harsh on Judge Keeton. Pamela Samuelson, a law professor who contributes regularly to *Communications of the ACM,* wrote [27]:

> . . . I have read Judge Keeton's opinion carefully and I have worked very hard to figure out what it means. I would tell you what it means if I could figure it out, but I cannot. And neither can anyone else.

Her reasoning is that the decision does not make it clear what would and would not constitute infringement on look and feel. Lotus picked an extreme example of a clone product to tackle in this suit. Would it have been okay if VP-Planner had not copied *all* of 1-2-3's structure? Could they have used all the same commands but presented them in a different order? Could they have included a facility that allowed the end user to customize the commands to be the same as those of 1-2-3?

There was a brief frenzy of concern immediately after Keeton's decision [30], [27]. Perhaps the most forcefully presented set of arguments against look and feel copyright are those in "Viewpoint: Against User Interface Copyright," by Richard Stallman and Simson Garfinkel [30]. This article is worth reading as an exercise in critical thinking. One of their arguments not to have look and feel (user-interface) copyrights is "User interface developers as a group do not seem to want user interface copyright" [30]. The background for this argument is that, in surveys conducted at professional meetings in areas related to user-interface development, most respondents oppose the concept of interface copyright [26]. The authors continue to argue that to the extent that user-interface copyright is meant to help the people who create the interface, this might be taken as evidence that these people do not want this particular type of "help." This is perhaps the least valid of the arguments made against look and feel copyright. For one thing, it asks you to accept that copyright is primarily to help those whose products are copyrighted. As this chapter has (hopefully) made clear, this is plainly wrong.

The purpose of copyright is ". . . to promote the progress of science and the useful arts. . . ." The argument also asks you to accept that the opinion of the interest group most directly affected by something should be the ruling factor in whether it is a valid concept! The question is not whether something is best for one group, but whether it is best for the whole of society. Valid arguments against user-interface copyright must be in one of two classes. The first is that user-interface copyright would not promote "the progress of science and the useful arts." The second is that user-interface copyright would conflict with other legal rights.

In spite of some initial fears, it now appears that program look and feel will have relatively narrow coverage [4], [18], [23], [26], [24]. In a 1992 decision in *Computer Associates* v. *Altai,* a stringent test emerged for determining infringement on look and feel [23], [4]. Joseph Costello describes the three-step test of "abstraction, filtration, and comparison" as follows [4]:

> In abstraction, the allegedly infringed program is dissected into its structural parts. In filtration, each part is examined to identify and eliminate unprotected material. In comparison, the remaining kernels of creative expression are compared with the structure of the allegedly infringing program to disclose if there is substantial similarity.

A test of this type would potentially allow even a perfect clone of a user interface to be noninfringing. This could happen if, for example, the expressions of the original interface's individual elements were substantially merged with their function, or if they were the equivalent of "standard plot devices." The concepts of "merger" and "standard plot devices" are well established in copyright law, and limit the extent of coverage [24]. Recall that copyright protects the expression of an idea, not the idea itself. To the extent that expression and idea are necessarily merged, the expression cannot be protected. Also, the interface equivalent of a "standard plot device"(e.g., boy meets girl, they fall in love, get married, and live happily ever after) in literature would not have copyright protection.

8.6.2 Summary

In summary, some level of copyright protection is available for the look and feel of a program. Relative to the traditional view of copyright protection for software, the existence of any coverage at all for look and feel is something of a shock to the industry. However, relative to the fears immediately after the *Lotus* v. *Paperback Software* suit, the coverage provided for look and feel is at least "narrow." The final resolution of exactly how much of the look and feel of a program is covered may come only with additional future lawsuits. In the meantime, the remaining confusion represents an uncertainty and associated costs for the software industry.

The phrase "software patent" as it is commonly being used is a little too vague and generic for our purposes. Instead, we need to focus on three categories of things that "software patent" might refer to:

- A larger process or machine that contains some element of what people in the computing industry would recognize as control software. There might be some computer calculations involved in an automated process for curing rubber, for example.
- A process that takes place entirely within the framework of a computer system. For example, the Unix operating system might be considered a process or an abstract machine.
- A "pure algorithm," that is, an algorithm irrespective of any implementation within a computer framework. An algorithm for converting binary-coded-decimal numbers to an equivalent binary representation is a possible example here.

These three categories are not totally distinct, but an analysis to distinguish among them may help clarify some issues.

8.7.1 Where Does the Controversy Come From?

In software patents, as in interface copyright, the controversy comes from the perception that the "rules of the game" have undergone an abrupt and unexpected change. Patent law had a long and well-developed history before computers existed. At that time, the meaning of the word "process" in the clause ". . . any new and useful process, machine, manufacture or composition of matter . . ." was clearly understood to refer to some industrial process. The meaning of "process" as it is commonly understood in computer science and engineering today was not known to most people at that time. Given the established interpretation of "process," and given that things such as mathematical equations were firmly understood to be outside the realm of what can be patented, it seems natural that the computer industry would initially have understood that software systems and algorithms are not patentable. However, at least three factors work to blur this understanding:

- You can draw appealing analogies between the older concept of "process" as the transformation of physical raw material into a final product and the newer concept of "process" as the transformation of raw data into useful information. To the extent that the new meaning of "process" is seen as a natural extension of its earlier meaning, the idea of patent protection for software systems and algorithms begins to seem plausible.
- It is hard to cleanly divide hardware and software. The existence of the term "firmware" is evidence that the line is a blur even to the computer science and engineering professional. To the extent that something can be seen as an element of hardware, it would tend to fall into the category of "machine" in the clause ". . . any new and useful process, machine, manufacture or composition of matter. . . ." Thus to the extent that the word "machine" takes on a broader meaning, which includes some overlap with software systems and algorithms, again the idea of patent protection for software begins to seem plausible. In fact, the Court of Appeals for the Federal Circuit appears to have found this analogy of software to the creation of a new machine plausible [3].
- Hardware and software are often embedded in a machine or larger industrial process. If a manual (noncomputerized) version of some process would be patentable, it seems reasonable the patent protection should be available to an automated (computerized) version of the process. However, as the embedded computer-control portion becomes a larger part of the whole process, we are again led toward considering patent protection for software systems and algorithms.

Given the above interpretation, we should not be surprised to find out that U.S. Supreme Court decisions made early in the computer era indicate that software systems and algorithms are not patentable, but that this conclusion is being chipped away. One Supreme Court decision often referred to as supporting the notion that algorithms are not patentable is the *Gottschalk* v. *Benson* case of 1972 [8], [28]. In this case, Gottschalk is the commissioner of patents and Benson is an employee of Bell Laboratories. Benson had developed an algorithm to convert BCD numbers into their pure binary equivalent. The U.S. Patent and Trademark Office originally rejected the application for patent, the appellate court ruled against the PTO, and the Supreme Court reversed the appellate court decision. The essence of the decision seems to revolve around the conclusion that the algorithm is similar to a "mathematical equation," "law of nature," or "scientific principle"—elements of pure knowledge (as opposed to a specific application of knowledge) that are not patentable. However, it seems that today the PTO will issue patents for things that many people might characterize as pure algorithms [8], [14]. One article published in 1992 [29] asserts that the PTO had by then granted at least 2000 "software patents." Many of these may be in the less worrisome category of control software within an industrial process, but at least some are of a more controversial nature. It is, of course, part of our patent system that these patents may be challenged in court and the rules of the game will not emerge until there is a substantial enough body of court rulings to provide a consistent interpretation of the law. While a clearer picture does seem to be emerging [14], [8], there is still some degree of confusion.

There are many outspoken professionals on either side of the software-patent issue, arguing from backgrounds in computer science and engineering, law, economics, or public policy. A long series of opinions and responses has recently run in the form of articles and letters to the editor in *Communications of the ACM* [12], [11], [17], [25], [29]. In the next sections, I summarize and comment on some of the arguments made both against and for.

8.7.2 Arguments against Software Patents

Stallman and Garfinkel are also the authors of the article that kicked off a *Communications of the ACM* debate over software patents [29]. This article makes a number of claims and complaints about the use of software patents. I have distilled what appear to be the main points of the article and provided an explanation and rebuttal.

- The Patent and Trademark Office's level of competence in computer science and engineering is low.
- Patents are granted for techniques that are "too obvious to publish."

The argument is that patent examiners are not well prepared to evaluate software patent applications for reasonable standards of novelty, originality, and nonobviousness. Thus, too many patents are granted that should not be granted. These patents could later be challenged and found invalid through the courts, but such an approach can be costly and time consuming. This seems an unfair burden, especially on small software companies.

8.7.2.1 Rebuttal. A possible response is that the U.S. Patent and Trademark Office is not expected to always make perfect decisions in any area of technology, which is why we have a procedure for challenging them through the court system. The less strict the PTO is in approving patents, the greater the effort that must be exerted through the court system to separate valid and invalid patents. The stricter the PTO is, the smaller the effort. Even if we agree that the standards for approving patents are too low, it does not at all follow that there is no software invention that should be patented. The obvious possibility is simply to reform the PTO procedures to employ people with greater expertise, who would apply stricter standards.

- Software technology is different in a fundamental and relevant way.

Basic components of software (sequence, decision structures, iteration structures, . . .) are idealized intellectual things. This being the case, the cost of designing and building a software system with a given number of components is generally much less than that of designing and building a hardware system with the same number of components. The likelihood of patent infringement is somehow related to the number of components needed to construct a system. Because the cost involved in building a hardware system is so much greater, the expense of licensing and dealing with patent infringement is not as important. However, for software, the relative expense of dealing with patent issues is much larger and would effectively inhibit software development.

8.7.2.2 Rebuttal. This line of argument seems to assert that if, in some particular technology area, the cost of dealing with the patent system becomes some appreciable fraction of the cost of creating a product, then patent protection should not apply to that technology area. Seen this way, the argument doesn't make much sense. A possible answer is to raise the price of products according to the cost of licensing multiple patents.

- Patent infringement is difficult to anticipate and avoid.
- Patent licensing will make some software products unprofitable.

Any large software product is by definition composed of a number of smaller modules, algorithms, and techniques. Each module, algorithm, or technique is potentially similar to something that someone has already patented. Conducting a patent search to determine what patents your product will potentially infringe could be expensive. Further, the results of a patent search are not perfectly reliable. Thus, the existence of patents in the software industry will raise the cost of doing business. The cost of some products that require multiple licenses may be pushed up to the point at which they are no longer profitable.

8.7.2.3 Rebuttal. These points are similar in nature to the previous point. The existence of software patents would tend to work to raise the costs of doing business in the software industry, leading to higher prices for products. But this is not a problem unique to software technology. And it is not necessarily a rational argument for or against software patents. The real question is whether "the progress of science and the useful arts" is better served by having or not having software patents.

- Independent reinvention is common in software development.

The argument here is that good programmers are continually reinventing algorithms that could potentially infringe on some patent.

8.7.2.4 Rebuttal. If the patent system were operating correctly, this should not be a serious problem. Something that passes the novelty and nonobviousness tests should, by definition, not be something that many programmers are continually reinventing independently. Thus, this argument seems to be just a restatement of the need for the PTO to apply a stricter standard in the nonobviousness test.

- Software patents continue a mistaken emphasis on inventions rather than products.

The argument here is that in software ". . . success depends primarily on getting the details right. And that is most of the work in developing any useful software system. Inventions are a comparatively unimportant part of the job" [29].

8.7.2.5 Rebuttal. Whether or not inventions are a "comparatively unimportant part of the job" of producing software products is not really relevant. And because no person can make money from inventions (patents) unless someone makes products based on those inventions, it is hard to see where there is misplaced emphasis.

- Patents do not solve any problems in the software industry.

The assertion here is that software patents would do nothing to help the industry, so ". . . software patents are not urgently needed by anyone but patent lawyers" [29].

8.7.2.6 Rebuttal. To the extent that this assertion is true, it would be a powerful argument against software patents. However, the article does not offer reasonable proof that this assertion is true. Consider just one specific counterexample. Most people would accept the assertion that new releases of software products generally have too many bugs. Part of the reason for this is that firms do not feel they can afford more expensive design, testing, and debugging procedures. If the firms that existed were able to accumulate larger amounts of capital, they might be able to afford more expensive development techniques that would yield higher quality software. Whether a company would in fact invest the extra capital in this way is, of course, another question.

8.7.3 Arguments for Software Patents

Paul Heckel wrote an article [12] responding to the Stallman and Garfinkel article against software patents. (I recommend both these articles to those who are convinced that all articles in professional journals are dull!) Heckel presents points that he asserts represent "the consensus of informed opinion on software patents." Again, I summarize the main points, explain them (when they aren't obvious), and offer a rebuttal.

- Patents have served to promote innovation in nonsoftware areas, particularly in small- and medium-sized companies.

Patents are generally accepted as "promoting the progress of science and the useful arts" throughout a range of technology areas. Arguments against software patents must be either arguments against patents in general, in which case they are going against centuries of accepted wisdom and suggesting foundational change to our economic system, or arguments against *software* patents specifically, in which case they have the burden of explaining how the software

industry is different in some relevant way from other industries.

8.7.3.1 Rebuttal. This point is true, but does not directly address the issue of whether the software industry is somehow different from other industries.

- Patent law has evolved to address concerns about software patents.

The assertion is that the patent system is a well-developed system, including ". . . patent lawyers, case law examples of valid and invalid, infringed and not infringed patents, and books and articles explaining patents to both lawyers and non-lawyers."

8.7.3.2 Rebuttal. This seems to be true *only of technology areas other than software!* The simple existence of the sequence of articles and responses debating the pros and cons of software patents [12], [11], [17], [25], [29] totally undermines this assertion as it relates to software patents.

- Patents are not perfect.

No system devised by humans will be truly perfect, and so if we insist on perfection as the standard then we effectively avoid making a rational argument. So the fact that software patents are not a perfect mechanism is not a serious argument against their existence either.

8.7.3.3 Rebuttal. This point is certainly true. However, the fact that software patents are not a perfect mechanism is also hardly an argument *for* their existence.

- Software is not inherently different from other technology areas with respect to the way that innovation and/or patents work.

8.7.3.4 Rebuttal. This point actually has two parts. First, it maintains that software is not inherently different from other technology areas that have a history of accepted use of patent protection. In terms of its degree of abstraction from any physical realization, it seems unquestionable that software is fundamentally different from any other technology covered by patent protection. The next question is whether or not this difference is relevant to the way that patents work. You could answer in terms of either the economics of the software industry or conflict with other legal principles. The article does not, in my opinion, make a convincing case that the difference is unimportant with respect to all elements of how patents work.

- "A nonprofit Marxist economic system is not optimal in promoting innovation in software."

8.7.3.5 Rebuttal. The wording chosen for this point seems to imply that anyone who is against software patents must be a Marxist. Much of Heckel's discussion of this point degenerates into personal comments about one of the authors of the other article. Even leaving these problems aside, substitute the phrase "A nonprofit Marxist economic system" for "Patents" in Heckel's own third point and it is clear that this point is not in and of itself, a rational argument for or against anything.

- Software may have unique problems, but so does every area of technology.

8.7.3.6 Rebuttal. This point is almost certainly true. However, this point in and of itself is again not a rational argument for or against software patents. The question is what are the specific unique problems of the software industry and how do these relate to the patent system in particular and intellectual-property protection in general.

- "Legally, software is patentable and it will remain so."
- "Whether or not one agrees that software patents are beneficial, patents are here to stay and so we should plan to work with them."
- "The practical effect of continuing to spread misinformation on software patents will be to hurt small developers and U.S. competitiveness alike."

8.7.3.7 Rebuttal. These points are not rational arguments for why software should be patentable. They seem to be nothing more than unilateral attempts to declare that the whole controversy is over and a certain side has won. The "will remain so" and "here to stay" claims require some ability to predict the future. The implied decision about what is "misinformation" and what isn't certainly prejudges the issue. Certainly spreading misinformation is bad—*regardless of which side it supports!*

- "In considering the issues, we should deal with real examples of real patents and where possible, real infringement where facts for both sides are fairly stated."

8.7.3.8 Rebuttal. This point is certainly true, though it seems that people on each side of the issue have routinely ignored it.

Heckel also seems to make an argument that patent rights are "inherent" and guaranteed by the constitution in the same sense that "all men are endowed by their creator with certain inalienable rights." This argument is a bit fanciful. It rests on interpreting the word "rights" as used in the phrase "certain inalienable rights" and in the phrase "right to their respective writings and discoveries" as referring to the same thing, and it ignores the clear statement of purpose in the phrase ". . . to promote the progress of science and the useful arts. . . ."

8.7.4 Summary

At this point, after reviewing the arguments made in the two articles, you would be entirely justified if you find yourself thoroughly confused. To try to clarify a framework for your own reasoning about software patents, I offer my own attempt to concisely summarize the main facts:

- Most people seem to accept that an industrial process that is patentable without automation is also patentable with it. This type of software patent is relatively uncontroversial.
- At one time, the software industry widely and clearly understood that a software system or an algorithm, in and of itself, was not patentable. It is the use of patents for software systems and algorithms that is most controversial.
- Some "inventions" that most would agree are software systems or algorithms are currently being granted patents by the U.S. Patent and Trademark Office. No person can honestly say with complete certainty if all these patents will withstand court challenges.
- If software systems and algorithms survive as eligible subject matter for a patent, they would be the most abstract technology covered by patents. They would also be unique in being potentially covered by both a copyright and patent.
- The only relevant arguments in the debate over whether patent protection should extend to software systems and algorithms are those that argue whether or not this would better "promote the progress of science and the useful arts."
- Large portions of the debate over whether patent protection should extend to software systems and algorithms have been irrelevant and conducted in a self-interested and mean-spirited manner that should be embarrassing to any professional in the field.

In coming to a rational opinion, we should focus on whether "the progress of science and the useful arts" is best served by having or not having patent protection for software systems and algorithms. The main issues to consider appear to be:

Would patent protection for software systems and algorithms cause research and innovation that would not otherwise occur? Patent protection always gives some element of additional economic reward to specific developments. Such an additional reward may stimulate research and innovation that would not otherwise occur. It may also *not* stimulate it. Much depends on the nature of the technology and the market. This could be a subject for lengthy and detailed economic studies, but it is unlikely that they would result in precise and reliable characterizations of the economic effects of software patents.

What are the relative costs of having patents for software algorithms versus not having them? The focus of the preceding issue was the effects of software patents on "the progress of science and the useful arts" in the software industry itself. There is, of course, the wider focus of how a change in the software industry might affect other industries. A change in the oil industry, in the form of sharp increases in oil prices, has had a ripple effect, extending to almost all other sectors of the economy—it has even been blamed for initiating recessions.

Within the software industry, software patents would raise costs, raise prices, eliminate the more marginal firms and products, and concentrate greater return to a smaller number of firms. Those outside the software industry would probably be affected most by the higher prices for software. In principle, the prices for some software products that companies in other industries need to conduct business could increase so much that the companies would go out of business. However, the cost of software is generally not a significant fraction of the expense of doing business in most other industries.

On the basis of this very high level (and admittedly subjective) analysis, we could form the tentative conclusion that costs to other industries (society as a whole) of having patent protection in the software industry do not seem serious enough to argue against software patents.

Would software/algorithm patents conflict with other legal rights? Neither Stallman and Garfinkel nor Heckel addresses this point. Whenever introduction of some new legal right is proposed, it is important to know whether and how it might conflict with other existing rights. One area of concern in legal rights (although it is not strictly a conflict) is the need for both software patents and user-interface copyrights. User-interface copyright says that you cannot use the same interface design as someone else, even if the implementation is entirely different. A software patent would say that you cannot use an essentially equivalent implementation. So the two protections would be to some degree complementary in what aspects of a software product they cover. But are both needed? The argument for user-interface copyright is based on the cost of the user interface being a significant portion of the cost of developing a software product and that with no protection, the interface would be cheaper to copy than it was to develop. This argument should now seem fairly dubious. The argument for patenting implemented software systems seems more plausible. Thus, you could tentatively conclude that patent coverage for the implementation of software systems removes, or at least further weakens, the argument for user-interface copyright.

Another area of concern is what exactly would be meant by patent coverage for pure algorithms. If software patents are eventually accepted in their fullest possible sense, they would cover algorithms independent of their function as part of any particular hardware or software implementation. But where exactly would the line be drawn? Would it infringe on a patented algorithm to execute it manually, with a pencil and paper? Would stepping through it in your head be an infringement? Once these problems are considered, it seems that patent protection for algorithms would have to be limited to their execution by computer systems. Any larger protection would begin to encroach

on freedom of thought! But if algorithms are covered only in their execution by computers, there may not be much incremental protection beyond having a patent for an implemented software system.

On the basis of this analysis, I offer the following conclusions:

- Patent protection should be allowed for implemented software systems.
- Patent protection should not be allowed for pure algorithms.
- User-interface copyright should not be allowed.

I recognize that a reasonable person could think through the same framework, evaluate the basic concerns differently, and reach a different set of conclusions. Also, it is worth noting that there is another possible solution to the protection of software. The U.S. Congress could enact sui generis ("of its own kind") legislation to create a form of protection different from either copyright or patent. Some academics have advocated this possibility, but it does not appear that it will be considered in the near future [26].

8.8 CASE STUDY

The dominant theme in this incident of software piracy is violation of intellectual property rights [1], [2]. Related secondary themes are greed and whistle blowing.

8.8.1 The Cast of Characters

The Software Publishers Association is a trade group for the software industry, whose main purpose is to discourage software piracy. (The SPA is now a part of the SIIA; see www.siia.net for more about the SIIA.)

Vicon Industries Inc. is a manufacturing firm that makes components for closed-circuit TV systems. Vicon is based in Melville, New York, and employs about 300 persons.

Autodesk Inc. makes the popular AutoCAD software package, which sold for about $3,500 per copy at the time of this incident (1994).

Cadam Inc., a subsidiary of IBM, makes the software package Master Designer, which sold for about $16,000 per copy at the time of this incident.

The whistle blower is an anonymous former employee of Vicon Industries.

8.8.2 The Sequence of Events

Vicon Industries purchased one properly licensed copy of AutoCAD and Master Designer. The license allowed the company to use one copy on one machine. Vicon also bought another software product designed to allow the user to circumvent copy-protection mechanisms built into software packages. Vicon management then instructed an employee (the eventual "whistle blower") to make copies of AutoCAD and Master Designer for use on Vicon's personal computers. This employee later left Vicon and after leaving apparently blew the whistle to SPA through their toll-free hotline (1-800-388-7478).

The SPA went to the U.S. District Court on behalf of Autodesk, Cadam, and other software companies. They obtained an ex parte writ of seizure and a temporary restraining order. Federal marshals and SPA attorneys "raided" Vicon. The raid consisted of searching the personal computers at Vicon for copies of the software packages in question. SPA has developed a special software tool to help search the hard disk for copies of software packages. The raiders found five copies of AutoCAD and six copies of Master Designer. SPA announced plans to file a civil suit against Vicon for $400,000.

8.8.3 Conclusions and Questions

Vicon management is easy to identify as the "bad guy" in this story. They clearly set out to violate copyright laws, and they instructed an employee to carry out an illegal action. The raid, the civil suit, and the resulting publicity would seem to be a substantial penalty for Vicon.

Less is known about the motivation and intent of the whistle blower. Was the whistle blower a person who was so uncomfortable with being instructed to violate copyright laws that they found another job and then blew the whistle? Or did the whistle blower willingly participate in the copyright violations, and, after being fired for an unrelated reason, decide to blow the whistle in retaliation? The Vicon officials are guilty in either case, but the whistle blower may be seen as more or less noble, depending on the circumstances.

Finally, what about SPA policies and actions? There is no question that the software companies' rights were being violated. But SPA has consciously chosen a policy of "making an example" of some companies in hopes of scaring a larger number of companies into compliance. An SPA lawyer was quoted as stating, "We expect this action will persuade other companies to establish procedures necessary to ensure that the software they use is properly licensed [2]. Is this the most fair and effective method of increasing compliance with copyright laws?

Points to Remember

- It is both illegal and unethical to knowingly infringe on what you understand to be a valid patent.
- It is unethical to make claims in a patent application when you know there is prior art that would invalidate the claim.
- It is unethical to use what you know to be false claims of patent infringement in an attempt to intimidate competitors.
- It is both unethical and illegal to knowingly infringe on a valid copyright. This includes making copies of copyrighted software products.
- It is unethical to appropriate other people's ideas and present them as your own.
- It is unethical and illegal to hire someone away from another firm with the specific intent of having them bring some trade-secret knowledge with them.
- It is unethical and illegal to violate a valid nondisclosure or "no compete" agreement.
- It is unethical to attempt to use unreasonable clauses in a "no compete" agreement.

WORKSHEET—Review of Intellectual-Property Concepts: Part 1

1. Describe what is required for something to receive patent protection.

2. Describe what is required for something to receive copyright protection.

3. Describe what is required for something to receive trade-secret protection.

4. Which means—trade secret, copyright, or patent—is generally the best way to protect software-related intellectual property? Why?

5. Which means—trade secret, copyright, or patent—is generally the best way to protect hardware-related intellectual property? Why?

WORKSHEET—Review of Intellectual-Property Concepts: Part 2

1. What is the essential difference between what constitutes infringement of a copyright versus infringement of a patent.

2. Describe what is meant by "prior art."

3. Describe what is meant by "fair use."

4. Describe what is meant by a "no compete agreement."

5. Define what is meant by "reverse engineering."

6. Define what is meant by "work made for hire."

WORKSHEET—"Copyright and Work Made for Hire"

Read the reprinted article "Copyright and Work Made For Hire," by John P. Costello, and answer the following questions.

1. What is the general effect of the "work made for hire" doctrine in terms of who owns the copyright?

2. What terms are **not** defined in the Copyright Act, giving rise to confusion about copyright ownership in work made for hire?

3. Briefly explain the "manner and means" criteria for determining copyright ownership.

4. Based on the *Aymes* v. *Borelli* decision, what are the two most important factors in determining if software is work made for hire?

5. What is the easiest way to avoid disagreements in the area of work made for hire?

WORKSHEET—"Reverse-Engineering Someone Else's Software: Is It Legal?"

Read the reprinted article "Reverse-Engineering Someone Else's Software: Is It Legal?" by Pamela Samuelson and answer the following questions.

1. Briefly explain the "black box" concept in reverse engineering of software.

2. Under the "strict constructionist" view, what are the two main reasons that reverse engineering of copyrighted software must be illegal?

3. Under what scenario(s) would copying a program to reverse engineer and modify it most likely be legal?

4. What are the two important lessons that Samuelson points to in the Sony Betamax case?

5. What is the legal way to acquire a trade secret?

6. What is Samuelson's point about copyright, utilitarian works, and reverse engineering of software?

WORKSHEET—"Does the Patent Office Respect the Software Community?"

Aharonian argues that the sheer number of software patents—20,000 per year—suggests that the patent office is failing to follow appropriate standards for patentability. Is this argument convincing? Why or why not?

1. What three factors does Aharonian suggest cause the PTO to issue so many software patents?

2. Why is it a concern that half of software patents issued cite no prior art?

3. What is Aharonian's opinion of the 1989 quote ". . . many of the software patents which are granted today will ultimately be held to be invalid . . . ?"

4. What is the level of experience of most software patent examiners in the PTO?

5. Who does Aharonian cite as surprisingly in the top five software patent companies in 1998? What does he suggest about the validity of their patents?

6. Explain how you would recommend to "fix" the problems in the software patent area.

WORKSHEET—SIIA Antipiracy Efforts: Part 1

Browse the SIIA web site (www.siia.net) pages on antipiracy and answer the following questions.

1. What is the SIIA?

2. What legal rights does the owner of a copyright have?

3. What does it mean to infringe a copyright?

4. Summarize in premise-conclusion from the argument for why "everyone benefits from a healthy computer software industry." What problems, if any, do you see with the argument?

5. When you purchase software, what rights to make copies do you automatically have independent of the license agreement?

6. What properties of software make it especially prone to copyright violation?

7. What is the maximum penalty for a criminal conviction for copyright infringement?

8. What is the purpose of the Software Rental Amendments Act of 1990?

9. How valid is the analogy between software and textbooks?

WORKSHEET—SIIA Antipiracy Efforts: Part 2

The SIIA "raids" on commercial companies are reasonably well known, but efforts targeted at individuals may be less well known. Browse the SIIA news release archive for the August 20, 1999 release on the software piracy conviction of Jeffrey Levy.

1. What is the "No Electronic Theft" law, when did it take effect, and what was the "LaMacchia loophole?"

2. Who is Jeffrey Levy? (age, occupation, etc.)

3. What was Levy convicted of doing?

4. What is the maximum penalty Levy could receive for his conviction?

5. What does SIIA claim is the estimated economic loss due to "traditional business software piracy?" What questions would you ask about how this figure is estimated?

6. How is an "Internet pirate" different than a traditional business software pirate? What kind of person does the SIIA suggest often runs an Internet pirate site?

7. What penalty do you think Levy should receive for his crime? Look further through the SIIA press release archive—what penalty did he receive?

1. **Credit for inventing the microprocessor.** In 1990, some 20 years after an original filing, patent 4,942,516 was awarded to Gilbert Hyatt for inventing the microprocessor. Five years later, after a special hearing, the Patent Office invalidated Hyatt's patent! Most textbooks credit Ted Hoff of Intel Corporation with inventing the microprocessor. Gary Kildall and a team at Texas Instruments team also made important contributions to developing microprocessor technology. What are the relevant contributions of the players in this story? Why was credit given to Hyatt 20 years after the fact? And then withdrawn? Do you agree with the (apparent) outcome of this story?

2. **Reexamination of the Compton multimedia patent.** An example sometimes cited to show how badly the patent procedure works with respect to software inventions is the Compton multimedia patent. However, this patent was in fact reexamined by the U.S. Patent and Trademark Office after complaints from the software industry [6], [7]. Report on this patent—what it first covered, why it was reexamined, and what it covered after reexamination.

3. **The E-data patent dispute.** In 1985 a patent was awarded to Charles Freeny. The patent right eventually came to be owned by E-data Corporation. E-data claimed that this patent gave them rights to basic elements of electronic commerce, and sent letters to a number of companies asserting rights and demanding royalties. Report on the claims made in the original patent, the claims asserted by E-data and the eventual resolution of this incident.

4. **The Church of Scientology versus X.** The Church of Scientology has frequently asserted intellectual property claims against people that distribute Church of Scientology materials on the Internet (e.g., Dennis Elrich). The resulting controversy has become the subject of news articles and even a book. Report on the specifics of the claims made by the church and the defenses raised by their critics.

5. **The Vermont Microsystems versus Autodesk trade secret dispute.** Vermont Microsystems was a small company that made products that work with other products sold by the much larger company Autodesk. A key employee at Vermont Microsystems left to join Autodesk. Autodesk then came out with their own version of the product sold by Vermont Microsystems. This led to a trial in which Autodesk was convicted of misappropriating trade secrets. Report on the specifics of the incident and the effect on Vermont Microsystems.

6. **Disputes over ownership of domain names.** The reprint "Trademarks and potholes on the superhighway" addresses the problem of disputed ownership of domain names such as www.amazon.com. Report on this problem in general, and on the current legal status of the problems of linking and framing specifically.

7. **Copyright infringement on chip designs.** In December 1993, a federal court decision allowed Intel Corporation to proceed with copyright infringement suits against Advanced Micro Devices. Intel alleged that AMD infringed on an Intel copyright in copying Intel's 386 microprocessor designs and is asking $600 million in damages. Find out what you can about the current status or settlement of the suit. What were the basic arguments made by each side? How was the copying alleged to have occurred? If the suit is over, what was the result and do you think it was fair? If the suit is not over, who do you think will win and why?

8. **Reconsidering a point in the ACM Code of Ethics.** Eight persons, including four winners of the ACM Turing Award, wrote a letter to the editor of *Communications of the ACM* [31], in which they questioned general moral imperative 5 of the *ACM Code of Ethics,* which states, "Honor property rights including copyrights and patents." What are the arguments made in this letter? What response was made to them? Can you design a better wording for the imperative in question?

9. **Patent infringement suits between Microsoft and Stac Electronics.** Microsoft and Stac Electronics filed a claim and counterclaim over patent infringement in suits that were settled in early 1994. Stac was awarded $120 million from Microsoft, and Microsoft was awarded $13.6 million from Stac [33]. Report on the specifics of the claim and counterclaim and your impression of their validity.

REFERENCES

[1] J. Bernstein, "Feds find illegal software in raid," *Newsday*, Friday, October 30, 1992.

[2] "SPA Raids Long Island Firm," *Business Wire*, Thursday, October 29, 1992.

[3] B. Carlson, "Patents for software, U.S. court says *yes*," *Computer*, September 1994, p. 92.

[4] J. P. Costello, "Trend is toward less copyright protection," *IEEE Software*, September 1993, pp. 92–93.

[5] J. Cox, "U.S. loses ground in crackdown," *USA Today*, March 8, 1993.

[6] I. H. Donner, "Is the patent office correctly examining computer-related patents?" Part 2, *Computer*, January 1995, pp. 93–94.

[7] I. H. Donner, "Is the patent office correctly examining computer-related patents?" Part 1, *Computer*, December 1994, pp. 78–79.

[8] S. Donovan, "Patent, copyright and trade secret protection for software," *IEEE Potentials*, August/September 1994, pp. 20–24.

[9] R. E. Frederick and M. Snoeyenbos, Trade secrets, patents and morality in *Ethical Issues in Engineering*, D. G. Johnson, editor, Prentice-Hall, pp. 291–297.

[10] L. N. Gasaway and M. Murphy, *Legal protection for computer programs*. CAUSE Publications, Boulder, Colorado, 1980.

[11] P. Heckel, E. R. Yoches, "ACM Forum: Patent war continues," *Communications of the ACM*, November 1992, pp. 20–22, 111.

[12] P. Heckel, "Debunking the software patent myths," *Communications of the ACM*, June 1992, pp. 121–140.

[13] B. K. Korites, *Free-Lance Software Marketing*, Kern Publications, 1980.

[14] J. S. Iandiorio, "Software protection under patent and copyright," *IEEE Technology and Society Magazine*, September 1988, pp. 9–10.

[15] D. G. Johnson, *Computer Ethics*, Prentice-Hall, Englewood Cliffs, NJ, 1985.

[16] J. G. Rauch, "The law on reverse engineering," *IEEE Spectrum*, August 1993, pp. 47–48.

[17] D. M. Ritchie, E. Ve'tillard, B. E. Hayden, S. L. Sanders, R. Stallman, and S. Garfinkel, "ACM Forum: The continued debate on software patents," *Communications of the ACM*, June 1992, pp. 13–16.

[18] W. L. Rosch, "The look and feel issue: the copyright law on trial," Chapter 24 in *Computers, Ethics and Society*, M. D. Ermann, M. B. Williams and C. Gutierrez (editors), Oxford University Press, New York, 1990.

[19] F. Ruiz, "Company going after AutoCAD software pirates in the bay area," *The Tampa Tribune*, June 1, 1992.

[20] P. Samuelson, "Self plagiarism or fair use?" *Communications of the ACM*, August 1994, pp. 21–25.

[21] P. Samuelson, "Copyright's fair use doctrine and digital data," *Communications of the ACM*, January 1994, pp. 21–27.

[22] P. Samuelson, "Computer programs and copyright's fair use doctrine," *Communications of the ACM*, September 1993, pp. 19–25.

[23] P. Samuelson, "The ups and downs of look and feel," *Communications of the ACM*, April 1993, pp. 29–35.

[24] P. Samuelson, "Updating the copyright look and feel lawsuits," *Communications of the ACM*, September 1992, pp. 25–31.

[25] P. Samuelson, J. Stern, J. P. Kesselman, C. T. Mathews, and R. Hill, "ACM Forum: Once again, patents," *Communications of the ACM*, October 1992, pp. 15–19.

[26] P. Samuelson, M. Denber, and R. J. Glushko, "Developments on the intellectual property front," *Communications of the ACM*, June 1992, pp. 33–39.

[27] P. Samuelson, "How to interpret the Lotus decision (and how not to)," *Communications of the ACM*, November 1990, pp. 27–33.

[28] P. Samuelson, "Should algorithms be patented?" *Communications of the ACM*, August 1990, pp. 23–27.

[29] R. Stallman and S. Garfinkel, "Viewpoint: Against software patents," *Communications of the ACM*, January 1992, pp. 17–22, 121.

[30] R. Stallman and S. Garfinkel, "Viewpoint: Against user interface copyright," *Communications of the ACM*, November 1990, pp. 15–18.

[31] G. L. Steele, D. Hillis, R. Stallman, G. J. Sussman, M. Minsky, J. McCarthy, J. Backus, and F. J. Corbato, "Code of ethics reconsidered," *Communications of the ACM*, July 1993, pp. 17–18.

[32] H. S. Stone, "Copyrights and author responsibilities," *Computer*, December 1992, pp. 46–51.

[33] "Microsoft found guilty," *The Tampa Tribune*, February 24, 1994.

[34] S. P. Weisband and S. E. Goodman, "International software piracy," *Computer*, November 1992, pp. 87–90.

John P. Costello, Attorney at Law

COPYRIGHT AND WORK MADE FOR HIRE

Legal and policy aspects of information-technology use and development.

UNDOUBTEDLY THE MOST IMPORTANT and powerful legal right you can have as a program writer is to own the copyright to your software. You then have the right to license and market the product and prevent others from making copies. If you have written the program without being hired to do so, you can claim the copyright, usually without complications. The courts have established that programs are no different from any other literary creation. You may claim a copyright just as an author may claim a copyright to a story. Moreover, you don't have to register the copyright; it is automatically in effect when you create the program.

But what if you have been hired by someone to write a program? Do you own it or does the party who hired you?

WORK-FOR-HIRE DOCTRINE.

The answer lies in an analysis of the work-made-for-hire doctrine in copyright law. The law maintains that when the program is created by a person employed by another party, the program is considered work made for hire, and the party for whom the work was prepared is the author and has the copyright. This is generally the case unless the parties involved have a written agreement to the contrary.

The law defines a work made for hire as one prepared by an employee within the scope of employment or a specially ordered work for use in a collective work that the parties agree shall be considered work made for hire. But although the definition seems simple enough, it is often difficult to determine when a developer is working as an employee and when he is an independent contractor.

If the program was developed as part of an employee's work for a software developer, the copyright obviously belongs to the employer. But, unfortunately, a variety of business and employment relationships can lead to the development of copyrighted programs. An additional complication is that the Copyright Act does not

> **IF SOMEONE HIRES YOU TO WRITE A PROGRAM, DO YOU OWN IT OR DOES THE PARTY WHO HIRED YOU?**

define "employee" or "employment," making the distinction between employee and independent contractor somewhat fuzzy.

Also, under certain circumstances, the two parties can be joint authors of a work and thus coowners of the copyright.

DETERMINING FACTORS. The landmark case in establishing factors for determining if a work falls under the work-made-for-hire doctrine is *Community for Creative Nonviolence* v. *Reid*. Before this 1989 US Supreme Court case, the courts looked almost exclusively at whether or not the hiring party had the right to control or actually wielded control over the creation of a work. The more control the hiring party had, the greater the likelihood that he would be awarded the copyright.

Reid involved ownership to a sculpture commissioned by an advocacy organization for the homeless. The organization had conceived a rather detailed plan for a sculpture to depict a Nativity scene, substituting homeless people for the traditional holy family. The group gave the sculptor explicit instructions about how the figures were to appear. The sculptor donated his services, the organization paid for the materials, and no one mentioned ownership or copyright.

After the sculpture was completed and initially displayed, a dispute arose between the advocacy group and the sculptor over a tour for the work. Both the organization and the sculptor claimed copyright to the sculpture and filed competing copyright registrations. A lawsuit ensued.

The advocacy group argued that since they controlled the creation of the work and contributed many of the critical ideas, the copyright belonged to them. The court rejected this simplistic analysis. Instead, it ruled that the advocacy group was entitled to the copyright as work made for hire only if it controlled the

Editor: George Trubow
John Marshall Law School
315 S. Plymoth Ct.
Chicago, IL 60604

Reprinted from *IEEE Software*, Vol. 11, No. 3, pp. 93–94, May 1994.

"manner and means" by which the sculpture was created.

The decision was based on a number of factors, including

- skill required,
- source of instruments and tools,
- location of work,
- if the hiring party could assign additional projects to the hired party;
- length of relationship between the parties,
- extent of discretion by the hired party over when and how long to work,
- the hired party's role in hiring and paying assistants,
- if the work was part of the regular business of the hiring party,
- method of payment, and
- tax treatment of the hired party.

Weighing these factors, the court found that the sculpture was not work made for hire. Although the advocacy group exercised close control over the project's details, nearly all the factors weighed in favor of the sculptor. He was a skilled artist who supplied the tools and studio, and he decided when and how long to work. In addition, the group had retained him for only a short period and paid him a flat fee without furnishing traditional kinds of employee benefits.

Thus, the court found that the sculptor had a valid copyright in the work, although it did not resolve if the group and the sculptor were joint authors and coowners of the copyright.

RECENT CASES. Two recent court decisions have addressed this issue and provided some guidance on how *Reid*'s factors affect the software copyrights. The more significant is the 1992 case *Aymes v. Bonelli*. Clifford Aymes was hired by Jonathan Bonelli to create a program to handle records for Bonelli's swimming pool. Bonelli was not a programmer and therefore Aymes had considerable freedom in developing the program. He generally worked on the premises, but was not always paid by the hour, received no health benefits, and was compensated under an IRS 1099 form. Inevitably, the parties had a falling out and, without an agreement

on who owned the copyright of the program, a lawsuit ensued.

The court ruling was significant. It ruled that the factors identified in *Reid* for determining if a hired party is an employee are not equally important. It found the skill required, employee benefits provided, the tax treatment of the hired party, and the ability of the hiring party to assign other projects to the hired party to be particularly significant. Other factors, such as whether the work was part of Bonelli's regular business, the location of the work, and the source of the equipment were found to be less important.

Although Bonelli had the right to control much of Aymes' work and assigned other projects to him, the skill level required to create the program, the failure of Bonelli to extend traditional employee benefits, and his tax treatment of Aymes weighed heavily in Aymes' favor. Ultimately, this upset Bonelli's copyright claim and the court ruled in favor of Aymes.

Aymes is significant because, although the court considered each factor identified in *Reid*, it ultimately determined that the skill required to create the program and the employee benefits and tax treatment given by the hiring party were the most important factors in determining if a program is work made for hire.

In an earlier case, *MacLean Associates v. William. M. Mercer-Meidinger-Hansen*, a different federal appellate court also looked to the programmer's skill and his degree of independence from the hiring party in analyzing copyright ownership under the work-made-for-hire doctrine.

PLAN AHEAD. Many programs are developed without any thought to who owns the copyright until after the work is finished. By then it may be too late to settle the issue amicably. If the program is good enough,

THE EASIEST WAY TO AVOID PROBLEMS IS TO OBTAIN A WRITTEN AGREEMENT BEFORE WORK BEGINS.

both the hiring party and the hired party will claim the rights and only lengthy and costly litigation will decide the issue.

The easiest way to avoid a problem is to settle it before the work begins, through a written agreement. If your employer is to have the copyright, the agreement should state that the program is considered work made for hire, and the employer owns all rights in the copyright.

If you, as the hired party, are to have the copyright, the agreement should state that the program is not work made for hire, is created by you in your capacity as an independent contractor, and that you own the copyright. To be on the safe side, you should also register the copyright with the US Copyright Office in Washington, DC, as should your employer if he is entitled to the copyright.

If you do not have a written agreement and litigation ensues, you and the hiring party must submit to a detailed examination of your relationship to determine copyright ownership. The issue will be if the hiring party controlled the "manner and means" of the program creation as determined by an analysis of the *Reid* factors. The less the relationship resembles the traditional employer-employee pattern, the more likely the decision will be in your favor.

The courts have recognized that the skill required to create a program helps establish you as an independent contractor. Also, if you do not receive traditional employee benefits (vacation time, unemployment, and health insurance), use your own equipment, and set your own work schedule, the court is likely to rule that the work is *not* made for hire, and the copyright will be yours. ◆

John Costello's address is 45 Glen ellyn Way, Rochester, NY 14614

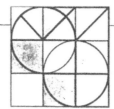

Reverse-Engineering Someone Else's Software: Is It Legal?

Pamela Samuelson, University of Pittsburgh

Does reverse-engineering software infringe intellectual-property law? While opinion is divided, courts seem to be saying it's legal if you take no actual, protected expression.

Lawyers disagree about whether it is legal to use the sophisticated reengineering technology now in existence (and being developed) to reverse-engineer programs developed by other firms. The benefits of the reengineering technology all but ensure that the law will not ban the technology outright, just as videotape recorders could not be banned from the market merely because the machines could be used to make unauthorized copies of copyrighted movies (even though two movie studios once sought such a ban against them).

Because so much of the valuable software available in today's market is copyrighted, copyright law has become the main battleground of the legal debate over whether reengineering technology can be used to reverse-engineer other firms' programs.

The technicality on which this legal debate hangs is whether it infringes the other firm's copyright if you make unauthorized copies of a copyrighted program, either in the course of analyzing it or to analyze it. Some lawyers believe it does infringe the copyright.[1,2] Other lawyers do not.[3,4]

While there are conflicting judicial decisions on the legality of reverse engineering under copyright law (see the box on p. 92), the trend in US case law is toward finding copyright infringement only where the reverse engineer has developed a competing program that is substantially similar *in expression* to the copyrighted program whose code was analyzed.

This trend is not surprising if you understand the traditional principles of copyright law and doctrines of other intellectual-property laws like patents about reverse-engineering activity.

Defining terms

Technologists may find a sharp contrast between their own perspectives on whether such conduct is or should be legal and the perspectives of lawyers. For

Reprinted from *IEEE Software*, Vol. 7, No. 1, pp. 90–96, January 1990.

lawyers, such questions must be asked in the context of an existing legal framework — a framework in which technological issues may have little or no relevance.

Definitions. Even how technologists and lawyers define the term "reverse engineering" may differ. From a technologist's standpoint, reverse engineering is generally understood as the act of creating a set of functional specifications for a system by someone other than the original designer based on an analysis of an existing system and its component parts.[5] In the case of software, you can reverse-engineer it through a variety of means.

For intellectual-property lawyers, software reverse engineering has two meanings, both of which differ from the technological meaning, but only one of which is troublesome under the law.

There is general agreement among lawyers that studying a copyrighted program through extensive black-box testing of its operations under many conditions and inferring its logic by analyzing its output is legal conduct and does not infringe the copyright[2,6] (unless there is a valid contractual agreement to the contrary).

The debate over the legality of reverse engineering of software concerns whether you can go inside the black box to study the code. More concretely, the legal question is whether you infringe a copyright when you copy a copyrighted program to study it (for example, making a core dump of the code) or when you run the code through a disassembler, decompiler, or other program that makes copies of the code so you can effectively recreate an equivalent of the source or assembly code.

(It would take another article to explore in detail yet another legal debate affecting the legality of going inside the black box to reverse-engineer software: whether shrink-wrap or other software licenses, insofar as they prohibit decompilation or other forms of reverse engineering, are valid and enforceable as a matter of contract law. However, the Fifth Circuit Court of Appeals recently struck down parts of a Louisiana statute that tried to validate software-licensing restrictions on backup copying, reverse engineering, and modifications. In the court's view, the Louisiana law conflicted with federal copyright law, which gives purchasers the right to do such things with their software. In view of this ruling, it is doubtful whether shrink-

---

From a technologist's standpoint, reverse engineering is generally understood as the act of creating a set of functional specifications for a system by someone other than the original designer based on an analysis of an existing system.

---

wrap or other licenses for mass-marketed software that prohibit making copies of programs for reverse-engineering are enforceable contracts.)

Interpreting the law. The lawyers who argue that reverse-engineering copyrighted software is (and should be) illegal believe that such conduct violates not just one law, but two laws: It is both an infringement of copyright (because of the unauthorized copying of the program that must be done to analyze its contents) and a misappropriation of trade secrets (because copyright infringement is an improper way to obtain trade secrets). Because this view relies on a narrow reading of the copyright statute, I call it the strict-constructionist view.

Lawyers who believe that reverse engineering does not violate either law take a more pragmatic view, arguing that any copying of the code during reverse engineering is an incidental part of this process and not the sort of copying with which copyright law is really concerned. Because reverse engineering is generally considered a legal way to take trade secrets in other engineering disciplines, the pragmatists think it should be considered as an appropriate competitive conduct in software as well.

Strict-constructionist theory

The strict-constructionist theory, which holds that reverse-engineering copyrighted software — whether by core dump, disassembly, decompilation, or other such process — is always illegal, relies on a strict reading of the US copyright statute. This statute gives copyright owners the exclusive right to copy or authorize the copying of their works.

For software, there is a special provision giving owners of copies of copyrighted programs the right to make copies as backups and as an essential step in executing the program. The strict-constructionist theory holds that if you copy a program to reverse-engineer it, you have gone beyond the two copying privileges in this special statutory provision and thus have infringed the copyright.

Fair use. Some people argue that such copying is permitted by the copyright law's fair-use doctrine. The fair-use doctrine lets people other than the copyright owner copy a protected work (or, more often, parts of it) for purposes and to an extent that won't significantly interfere with the rights of the copyright owner. The copyright statute lists a set of factors to be considered in determining whether a use is fair or unfair, including

- the defendant's purpose in using the protected work,
- the nature of the copyrighted work,
- the amount and substantiality of what is taken, and
- the potential for harm to the market for the protected work.

For example, fair-use doctrine would let you copy or quote from part of this article (with credit to the source) but not copy the entire article for distribution or sale.

But the strict constructionists argue that copying software to reverse-engineer it cannot be a fair use of the copyright because people who do this generally have a commercial motivation and are seeking to misappropriate trade secrets. Moreover, reverse engineers copy the whole of the work, not just some little piece of it. There is clear harm to the software developer's market arising from the reverse engineering. All these factors weigh heavily against a fair-use

defense, in the eyes of strict constructionists.

Trade secrets. If a court agreed with the assumption that copying a program in the course of reverse-engineering it is an improper way to extract trade secrets, it could find that the reverse engineer misappropriated the original developer's trade secrets. If the strict-constructionist theory is correct, the only legal way to learn what trade secrets copyrighted soft-

Reverse-engineering case law

There have been several judicial decisions on whether making copies of programs for reverse engineering constitutes copyright infringement. The case law is conflicting, although the two cases in which judges ruled that such copying *was* infringement involved other infringing and otherwise inequitable conduct. The more recent cases have found infringement only when the results of the reverse-engineering process have been used to create a program with substantially similar expression to the protected program that had been analyzed.

MAI v. Hubco. In one case, Hubco obtained copies of the different versions of MAI's software (apparently in a legal manner) and made printouts of the 1's and 0's representing its machine-readable form. By comparing the printouts, Hubco was able to discern where the software's governors were located in the cheaper versions and what the pattern of 1's and 0's had to look like for the governors to be removed. Hubco then began contacting MAI's customers and asked those who had acquired the cheaper version whether they'd like to hire Hubco to "fix" MAI's software so it would work as if they'd purchased the more expensive version. Hubco eventually developed a program to automate this enhancement of the MAI software.

MAI sued Hubco for infringement of its copyright of operating-system software and for misappropriation of the trade secrets in the software. Although the judge ruled that Hubco had not stolen any trade secrets from MAI because it had deciphered them through reverse engineering, the judge issued a preliminary injunction against Hubco's use of its program and its on-site visits to customers of MAI to remove the governors.

The noncontroversial part of the judge's ruling in the Hubco case was the finding of infringement based on Hubco's preparation of its upgrade program, which included within it a copy of the MAI program. The more controversial part of the Idaho federal court's 1983 ruling was the injunction against on-site visits, which was based on a finding of copyright infringement because of the printouts Hubco had made of the upgraded versions of the MAI program. Hubco brought these printouts to MAI customers' places of business and used them as a basis for making changes in the MAI software. (The judge did not rule that it was infringement for Hubco to make changes to the software for MAI customers, but only to copy the program to learn where the governors were.)

SAS Institute v. S&H Computer Systems. Two years after Hubco,

a Tennessee federal court decided another case, SAS Institute v. S&H Computer Systems, that involved the copying of a program for reverse-engineering purposes. SAS successfully charged the developer of a competitive statistical-analysis program with copyright infringement and trade-secret misappropriation. S&H had acquired a copy of the source and object code of the SAS software by a license agreement with the intent of studying it so S&H could make a similar program to run on a different kind of computer than that on which SAS ran.

Although the finding of copyright infringement rested heavily on similarities between the two programs (some for source-code listings and some for the code's structural aspects), the fact that S&H had made unauthorized copies of both the source and object code so it could study it was also ruled to be copyright infringement, as well as a breach of a licensing agreement that S&H had signed.

Disassembly decisions. Later that same year, another judicial decision was rendered in a software copyright case where competitive software had been developed in part by disassembling the plaintiffs' programs. Notwithstanding the rulings in the Hubco and SAS cases, the judges in the E.F. Johnson. v. Uniden case (decided in Minnesota) ruled that disassembly — said to be a common industry practice — alone was not copyright infringement. Rather, copyright infringement had to be based on similarities in the programs produced after disassembly, the judge ruled.

The judge ruled that Uniden had infringed the copyright because the two programs were more similar in details of their implementation than was explainable by the need to be compatible with the radio-system software produced by Johnson.

NEC v. Intel. The most recent copyright case involving reverse engineering is NEC v. Intel , decided in a federal court in California in February 1989. Although NEC personnel admittedly had disassembled the Intel 8086/8088 microcode, Intel mainly relied on similarities in the microcode that NEC developed for a competitive product (not the disassembling) for its copyright-infringement claim. The clean-room process NEC had set up to separate the analysis of the Intel microcode from the development of NEC's functionally equivalent microcode was an important factor in persuading the judge that the similarities in the two sets of microcode resulted from constraints imposed by hardware, architecture, and specifications, and therefore did not infringe the Intel copyright.

ware might contain would be by testing the software and treating it as if it were a black box. (The law generally lets people try to reverse-engineer a product sold in the market to discern its producer's trade secrets (see the box on pp. 94-95), as long as no improper methods are used.)

The strict constructionists argue that there needs to be a strong rule against copying software for reverse engineering because the software industry is economically a very fragile industry whose costly and valuable innovations can too easily be pirated. Among the most valuable parts of software products are the algorithms, concepts, and techniques embedded in the software — parts not traditionally covered by copyright that thus must be protected as trade secrets.

The competitive edge these valuable secrets provide should, in the view of the strict constructionists, be maintained and respected by copyright law. Other firms are always free to write competitive software. There is then no need to reverse-engineer to develop a competitive product.

To the extent that a strict rule against reverse engineering might clamp a lid on competition in the modification and enhancement of software, the strict constructionists would say this is appropriate, since copyright gives software developers the exclusive right to control the making of derivative works. Unlike the semiconductor-chip industry, which actively sought a reverse-engineering privilege when a new law was created to protect chip designs, the software industry, they would argue, has not clamored for a reverse-engineering right, which is why there is no such provision in the copyright statute.

Pragmatist theory

It is a curious feature of programs, unlike other copyrighted works, that they do not directly reveal their contents to users. One reason the strict-constructionist theory of illegality is so hard for traditional copyright lawyers to accept is that it would mean that the weight of the copyright law could be brought to bear against someone who purchased a copy of a copyrighted work and tried to figure out what it "says."

In another article,[7] I have argued at length that — consistent with the histori-

cal purposes of copyright and patent law — disclosure of a program's contents ought to be *required* to obtain copyright protection. Although copyright law does not now require disclosure of program contents, it would be an aberration from copyright tradition to say that someone can be penalized by copyright law for seeking to obtain disclosure on one's own by reverse engineering.

Fair use. Lawyers who do not adhere to the strict-constructionist theory of copying for reverse engineering take a very dif-

---

The competitive edge these valuable secrets provide should, in the view of the strict constructionists, be maintained and respected by copyright law. Other firms are always free to write competitive software, they argue.

---

ferent view of the fair-use privilege. For one thing, they say that it is in the nature of machine-readable programs to have to be copied to be read and studied.[6] For another, they do not regard copying a program to reverse-engineer it as directly affecting the copyright owner's economic interest any differently than does copying it for backup. Such copying does not, for example, displace a sale that might otherwise come to the copyright owner — the reverse engineer, like the person making a backup, has already bought the program.

The pragmatists regard the strict constructionists' argument as similar to one unsuccessfully raised by the two movie studios who sued Sony for contributing to copyright infringement because Sony knew that its customers could use Betamax videotape machines to make unauthorized copies of the studios' movies. The studios argued these copies were in-

fringing copies, even if the copies were made only so viewers could watch the movies at more convenient times than they were broadcast (called "time-shifting").

In the Sony case, the US Supreme Court ruled that it *was* a fair use for owners of videotape recorders to use their machines to copy the whole of a copyrighted movie shown on television for time-shifting. It also ruled that, because Sony's machines were capable of *non*infringing uses, Sony could not be held liable for contributory copyright infringement — even though Sony knew that some of its customers might make infringing copies of protected works. The Sony decision forecloses the theory that the mere copying of the program is enough to negate a fair-use defense.

Another factor affecting the fair-use theorists' judgment about reverse-engineering programs is that it often requires exceedingly tedious, time-consuming, and concentration-intensive activity. Reverse-engineering machine-readable code is not unlike trying to break the "code" of Egyptian hieroglyphics or Sumerian cuneiform. Indeed, it can be more difficult than either of these, for there are only two elements — 1's and 0's — to be read, and the same sequence appearing at one place in the code may mean something entirely different than the same sequence later on.

Moreover, many software developers encrypt parts of their code to make it more difficult to read. Reading code — assuming it can be done at all — would seem to be conduct that traditional copyright law would not envision as an infringing activity. Even with the aid of reengineering technology that may considerably ease the task of deciphering the code, reverse engineering is a far cry from the straight piracy that virtually everyone in the industry would agree is illegal — and rightly so.

Trade secrets. It is not so much the copying of the code that is of concern to the software developer who wants to make reverse engineering illegal but more the reading of the code that, once deciphered, will let the reader discern the trade secrets that might be embedded in it. If its code can be read and if its trade secrets can be discovered, the developer is in danger of losing its trade secrets.

But, as with the copying issue, it is not really the reading itself but what the reader does thereafter that has a potential for a destructive effect on the trade-secret owner's economic interest.

What you may do

There are many things you can do with the knowledge obtained from reverse-engineering another firm's program.

Making modifications. One reason you may reverse-engineer software is to be able to modify the software, perhaps fixing a bug, perhaps enhancing it so the software can better perform the function for which it was obtained, and perhaps even to remarket a customized version of it. Of course, the developer of the original software may perceive that it has a significant interest in controlling who modifies its software and how the software is modified.

Because a copyright gives its owner a right to control the making of derivative works, the strict constructionists read the copyright statute as giving its owner the right to control all modifications. They also rely on a narrow reading of a special statutory provision that lets people who buy software make some modifications to it.

One judge has ruled that this provision permits only modifications that are necessary to let the software be executed. Another judge has interpreted it more broadly to allow modifications that make the software more usable for the purposes for which it was acquired.

It is consistent with the legislative history of this provision and with copyright tradition to permit users to make copies of programs to reverse-engineer them, to fix bugs, and to enhance them to make them more usable.[8]

Developing similar software. Apart from modifying the software, another thing you could do with the results of reverse engineering would be to develop another piece of software that is similar but not identical to the one that was reverse-engineered. As with modifications, some

Different laws and reverse engineering

Before the legal debate over the legality of software reverse engineering, the legality of reverse engineering had come up in several other contexts.

Trade-secret law. Trade-secret law was the first intellectual-property law to develop a rule about the legality of reverse engineering. Owners of trade secrets have the right to be protected against misappropriation of their trade secrets. The two most commonly recognized ways to misappropriate such secrets are either by breach of a confidential relationship that arose when the owners disclosed the secret in confidence to another or by use of improper means (like industrial espionage or bribery) to obtain the trade secret.

Trade-secret law has traditionally *not* protected any property interest as such in a trade secret, just the right to be free from unwarranted interference with confidential relationships and use of improper means to get the secret. Because of this, someone who can learn another's trade secret by reverse engineering — working backward from the final product to analyze how or of what the product was made — acquires the trade secret *legally*.

Competitors, then, have the "right" to use reverse engineering to obtain trade secrets. It is in the public interest for competitors to have such a right — even if it means that the successful reverse engineer may be able to take a free ride on the research and development efforts of the innovator firm. Reverse engineering may well lead to further innovation by the firm that does the reverse engineering or to expanded production of and lower prices for the desired product.

Reverse engineering is considered to be a good thing under trade-secret law, even if it has the potential to harm some economic interests of the trade-secret owner.

Patent law. Reverse engineering has generally not arisen as a problem area in patent law for the simple reason that patent law has always required that an inventor reveal a considerable amount of detail about the invention to get a patent. Patent applications must contain "a written description of the invention, and of the *manner and process of making* and using *it*, in such full, clear, concise, and exact terms as to enable any person skilled in the art to which it pertains, or with which it is most nearly connected, to make and use the same," according to the patent law (emphasis added).

Someone obtaining a patent must also "set forth the *best mode* contemplated by the inventor of carrying out the invention," the law says (emphasis added). (Failure to abide by these disclosure requirements can be grounds for not issuing the patent, for invalidating any patent mistakenly issued, and for denying relief in a later trade-secret lawsuit about things that should have been disclosed in the patent application.)

When a patent is issued, this disclosed information is printed as part of the patent. During the life of the patent, anyone is free to read and learn from the patent; what is forbidden is only making, using, or selling the invention during the 17 years the patent lasts.

If it does become necessary to try to make another person's invention to evaluate how it works or to understand the scientific principles underlying it, patent law leaves some room for a person to make the invention for "experimental purposes" without infringing the patent. It is only making or using the invention for its intended end use that infringes the patent.

The experimental-use doctrine is, then, a kind of doctrinal cousin to trade secret's reverse-engineering rule in that it too serves as a public-policy limitation on the scope of rights of the holder of an intellectual-property interest.

American copyright law. Until software came along, reverse engineering had never arisen as a problem area for copyright law. There are several reasons for this.

First, until the admission of machine-readable software to the copyright realm, all copyrighted works revealed their contents, either directly (like a book) or indirectly (like sound recordings when played). You never had to reverse-engineer a copyrighted work to find out what it "said."

Although copyright law never formally required disclosure as patent law has done, this may be because — until software — there was never a need to do so, since disclosure traditionally happened as a matter of course when the work was published. It is unquestionably a fundamental purpose of US copyright law to promote dissemination of knowledge.

Second, "reverse engineering" is a term that describes conduct about utilitarian things. (It makes sense to talk about reverse-engineering a carburetor, but not a poem.) Until software was made copyrightable, copyrights did not protect utilitarian works. Works that have a utility beyond merely conveying information or displaying an appearance have been considered utilitarian and, because of this, have traditionally been *excluded* from copyright. Yet it is only utilitarian works that you would try to reverse-engineer.

Third, until software, copyright law gave only the most limited protection to engineering designs. Reverse engineering, as the term itself implies, is an engineering enterprise, a search for the underlying technical ideas, techniques, or designs of a work, perhaps to make a competitive product.

In the US, engineering drawings, because they are drawings, are protectible under the copyright statute. But the copyright on an engineering drawing does not give rise to an exclusive right to make the engineered product depicted in the drawing nor to an exclusive right to make other drawings of the engineered product. No matter how much effort went into developing the engineering design itself, and no matter how detailed its content, that *design* was not protected by the copyright. Indeed, traditional copyright law considered the engineering design to be in the public domain. To protect the design, you must patent it.

British copyright law. Until 1988, the rule about copyright protection for engineering designs was different in the UK than in the US.

This difference is illustrated by a case decided in 1986 involving a dispute between British Leyland and Armstrong, a firm that manufactured an exhaust system that could be installed as a replacement part in British Leyland cars. British Leyland copyrighted a set of engineering drawings of, among other things, the exhaust system of its automobiles. These drawings depicted the configuration of the exhaust system and its various intersection coordinates. Armstrong did not have or have access to the British Leyland drawings, but it did have an opportunity to inspect a British Leyland exhaust system.

From its examination of this system, Armstrong made its own drawings of the British Leyland exhaust system and subsequently made and sold exhaust systems of the same basic design as the British Leyland system — without, of course, paying British Leyland any royalty. British Leyland sued Armstrong for copyright infringement of the engineering drawings — and won, despite the fact that Armstrong had reverse-engineered the system, not copied any of British Leyland's drawings.

This result is the reverse of what a US court would reach if presented with the same or a similar situation. US copyright has always assumed that unless a utilitarian work, like an exhaust system, was patented, it was in the best interest of the public in a competitive economy for such works to be freely copied by competitors.

The UK has just recently adopted a new intellectual-property law that changed copyright law to overturn the result in the British Leyland case and to adopt a copyright rule similar to the US rule for engineering drawings.

US semiconductor-chip law. Before the passage in 1984 of the Semiconductor Chip Protection Act, some chip manufacturers had copyrighted technical drawings of the layouts of their chip products and then argued that the mask works and finished chip products were covered by the copyright in the technical drawings or were separately copyrightable derivative works.

The US Copyright Office, although it accepted registration of the technical drawings, denied registration to the mask works and finished products on the ground that these were utilitarian works not qualified for copyright protection.

Unsatisfied with this, some chip firms went to Congress to get protection for their chip designs. Although some thought was given to amending the copyright statute to protect chip designs, Congress eventually decided to create a new intellectual-property law to protect chip designs. (Some have argued that software too needs a special-purpose statute of this sort because its utilitarian character makes copyright such an awkward law to apply to programs.)

Industry proponents of chip-protection legislation insisted that it was only the exact copyists of their layouts against whom they sought protection, not those who might copy the chip design to reverse-engineer it. Reverse engineering was said to be a common practice in the chip industry and was believed by those who testified about it to be a positive form of competition. There was considerable discussion in the chip community about whether copying for reverse engineering would be considered a fair use if the chip-protection provisions were put in the copyright system or whether a special provision authorizing reverse engineering ought to be made a part of the statute. The industry strongly desired a reverse-engineering privilege.

Responding to this concern, Congress eventually adopted a special reverse-engineering privilege in the chip law. This provision lets competitors not only copy a protected mask work to study the concepts or techniques embodied in the mask work or in the chip's circuitry, logic flow, or organization but also to incorporate results of this study and analysis in a competitive chip product as long as the latter is itself an original work and not substantially identical to the protected mask work that had been studied.

of those who reverse-engineer for this purpose will pose no threat to the market for the original software. If, however, the reverse engineer develops a competing software product, the copyright owner of the original software has more reason to be concerned about the effect on the market for its original software.

There are, of course, many things a reverse engineer might appropriate if he could decode another firm's code, not all of which would necessarily interfere with the copyright owner's legitimate interests.

If, for example, the reverse engineer took only ideas, algorithms, techniques, logic, and functional elements from the original software and incorporated these into a new piece of software, no infringing derivative software would have been created, at least under traditional copyright theory, because no protectible expression would have been taken from the protected work.

Making compatible products. Another reason to reverse-engineer software is to discover how the program's interfaces are constructed so you can develop programs that will be compatible with that program. Although whether copyrights can be infringed based on interface similarities needed to achieve compatibility is itself a hotly contested issue in copyright law, the better view seems to be that similarities of this sort are not infringing.[6]

As an aid to proving that you took only ideas, functional specifications, or the like from the program under study, it may help to have a clean-room procedure, where one team works on reverse-engineering the code and a second team works from the functional specifications derived from the code and reimplements them.

But a clean-room procedure is not necessary to prove that you didn't infringe the copyright. What is necessary is to show that you took no protected expression.

Certainly, taking the literal expression used by the original programmer, or making only minor variations (such as in the naming of variables) would be an infringement, even though much work might have gone into this effort. Sometimes even plagiarism is hard work, but that doesn't mean it isn't plagiarism! In such a situation, it is not the reverse engineering per se that would support the copyright-infringement charge but the making of an infringing work.[9]

Describing the software's workings. Apart from modifying and developing a new program, yet another category of things you might do with the results of reverse engineering would be to disclose the results to other people, for example, by publishing an article about them. This would destroy the trade secret, unquestionably injuring the economic interest of the trade-secret owner. Yet it is doubtful that copyright law — which is aimed at *promoting* the dissemination of knowledge — should be used to vindicate this kind of trade-secret interest.

The policy reasons that support permitting reverse engineering of all other kinds of trade secrets ought to come into play when judging the reverse engineering of software trade secrets. Software developers have not yet made the case that they should be given special privileges not granted to other trade-secret owners.

Are strict rules enforceable? But perhaps the best reason not to have a strict rule against reverse engineering is because such a rule would likely be unenforceable. Software reverse engineering by competitors, would-be competitors, customers, and computer scientists is widespread and considered by many to be perfectly legal behavior.

Many would say that the reverse engineering of software has contributed to more rapid growth in the software industry and to the increased competition in product development and refinement than would have occurred in an environment in which software reverse engineering was illegal.

To persuade those who hold such views that a strict rule against any reverse engineering must now be respected would probably be impossible. To even try to enforce it might backfire, for those who stop respecting copyright principles based on what is widely perceived to be an overly strict rule may tend to stop respecting other rules of copyright as well.

One important lesson of the Sony Betamax case is that copyright owners are not entitled to control every economic benefit that the public might derive from their works. Another important lesson of the Sony case is that copyright law should take into account the interests of the public in the use and availability of new technologies. A reasonable balance between the public's right and the innovator's right must be maintained. Software owners should not be able to get special privileges under the copyright law simply because it would strengthen their market position.

The strict-constructionist view of copyright law that holds that reverse engineering is always illegal confuses means with ends. Reverse engineering is a set of methods and tools that may enable a software designer to create new and better programs. But whether copyrights are infringed by reverse engineering must depend on the programs that ultimately result, not on the incidental copying that is required to use the reverse-engineering methods and tools. ◆

Acknowledgments

I thank Elliot Chikofsky, the anonymous reviewers of this article, and my husband, Robert J. Glushko, for their helpful suggestions about how the article might be improved. I also thank the faculty and students of the Computer Science Dept. at Carnegie Mellon University for their enlightening comments on this subject when I presented an earlier version of this article at a programming-systems seminar series a few years ago.

References

1. A.R. Grogan, "Decompilation and Disassembly: Undoing Software Protection," *Computer Lawyer*, Feb. 1984, pp. 1-11.

2. D. Davidson, "Common Law, Uncommon Software," *Univ. of Pittsburgh Law Review*, Summer 1986, pp. 1,037-1,117.

3. R.S. Laurie and S.M. Everett, "Protection of Trade Secrets In Object-Form Software: The Case for Reverse Engineering," *Computer Lawyer*, July 1984, pp. 1-11.

4. Committee on Computer Law, "Reverse Engineering and Intellectual-Property Law," *Record Assn. the Bar of the City of New York*, March 1989, pp. 132-158.

5. M.G. Rekoff, "On Reverse Engineering," *IEEE Trans. Systems, Man, and Cybernetics*, March-April 1985, pp. 244-252.

6. Center for Law, Science, and Technology, "Last Frontier Conference Report on Copyright Protection of Computer Software," *Jurimetrics J.*, Winter 1989.

7. P. Samuelson, "Contu Revisited: The Case against Copyright Protection for Computer Programs in Machine-Readable Form," *Duke Law J.*, Oct. 1984, pp. 663-752.

8. P. Samuelson, "Modifying Copyrighted Software: Adjusting Copyright Doctrine to Accommodate a Technology," *Jurimetrics J.*, Winter 1988, pp. 179-221.

9 B. Kocher, "President's Letter: Reverse Engineering," *Comm. ACM*, April 1989, p. 419.

Address questions to Samuelson at Law School, Gambrell Hall, Emory University, Atlanta, GA 30322.

Gregory Aharonian

S o f t L a w

Does the Patent Office Respect the Software Community?

How much brilliant innovation is there in the software industry? I mean the type of development you might read about in a new IEEE or ACM article or conference paper that causes you to think, "That's cool!" Probably not much considering software development is more evolutionary than revolutionary, with people constantly sharing ideas and techniques. The steady and collaborative development of Linux and the efforts of the Free Software Foundation typify such development in the Internet era. Isn't the Internet just an evolution of videotex, albeit with better interfaces and communications protocols? Isn't C++ and Java object-oriented programming just a gradual evolution of Lisp, Smalltalk, and Simula from the 1980s?

If this is true, software programmers should view the tally of US software patents issued during the last few years with great concern, and some outrage. The number has steadily increased from 1,300 in 1990 to 22,500 in 1999 (estimated).

The US Patent and Trademark Office (PTO) is now issuing about 20,000 new software patents every year—a tenfold increase in the last six years. I would point you to an Internet FAQ for more information, but I can't because I might be inducing you to infringe a patent—US Patent No. 5,842,221 entitled, "Dynamic Frequently Asked Questions (FAQ) System." Patents are supposed to be limited to inventions that are both novel (no one has ever made the invention the same way before) and not obvious. "A claimed invention is unpatentable if the differences between it and the prior art are such that the subject matter as a whole would have been obvious at the time the invention was made to a person having ordinary skill in the art." (In re Dembiczak, 50 USPQ 2d 1614, Fed. Cir. 1999) Considering these inexplicable numbers, the IEEE, the

ACM, and similar organizations should ask the PTO on what basis it thinks there are 20,000 novel and not obvious software inventions each year.

The Japanese and European patent offices are demonstrating the same problems, but there are a few well-known reasons why the PTO issues so many patents:

♦ the indifference to prior art,
♦ the flood of patent applications, and
♦ the patent examiners' assembly-line working conditions.

PRIOR ART

One of the weaknesses of the current patent system is the absence of any searching requirements for patent applicants to prove their inventions are novel and not obvious. Prior to filing a patent application, an applicant is under no obligation to go to a library or access online databases to find prior art. Patent examiners are expected to issue a patent only if an invention is novel and not obvious. Both the PTO and patent lawyers know examiners don't have enough time, money, or resources to search thoroughly, especially for software applications.

In the last 20 years, more than 700,000 patents have been issued for electronics inventions, such as hardware, software, circuits, optics, and communications. Of these, approximately 80 percent have barely cited a single IEEE, ACM, or SPIE conference paper, journal article, or book. In other words, the PTO has concluded that the inventions were novel and not obvious by examining prior issued patents while largely ignoring all other published literature. Ironically, this literature is searched during expen-

EDITOR: Larry Graham • Christensen O'Connor Johnson & Kindness • graham@cojk.com

Reprinted from *IEEE Software*, Vol. 16, No. 4, pp. 87–89, July/August 1999.

sive litigation and successfully used to invalidate software patents. Tolerance of this evaluation system for this long reflects contempt for both the technology and those who develop it.

In part, patent examiners fail to cite nonpatent prior art because they do not have access to an adequate library or database of nonpatent materials. Regardless of the reasons, we should question the validity of many patents considering the dearth of materials cited. Some patent applications don't even cite prior patents. For example, U.S. Patent No. 5,796,943, recently issued for a smart card, cites no prior art at all. As late as May 1999, half of the software patents issued cited no nonpatent prior art.

The patent system should pay more attention to nonpatent prior art.

A 1988 COMPCON paper (R. Laurie, "The Patent/Copyright Interface for Software Protection," *Proc. Int'l COMPCON*, IEEE Computer Soc. Press,1989, pp. 370–375) by a software patent lawyer outlined the same issue a decade ago.

The percentage of software written today that would satisfy the obviousness requirement is probably in the 5 to 10 percent range. The question of obvious-ness is necessarily a case by case inquiry. Moreover, because the Patent Office has a limited collection of prior art, many of the software patents which are granted will ultimately be held to be invalid in litigation based on prior publications, foreign patents, or commercial uses which were not available to the Patent Office.

Apparently, little has changed in the last 10 years.

FLOOD OF PATENT APPLICATIONS

A second reason for the large number of software patents being issued is that the PTO is simply overwhelmed with patent applications. The PTO issues patents for about half of the applications it receives. Therefore, a tenfold increase in the output of software patents means the number of patent applications has also increased about tenfold in the last six years, a rate much higher than the increase in PTO personnel. The high turnover among patent examiners has compounded this problem. A favorable high-tech job market also makes it difficult for the PTO to hire and retain qualified examiners—approximately 66 percent of the current software patent examiners only have a bachelor's degree and a few years of industry experience.

Where is this flood of patent applications coming from? Surprisingly, many of the companies filing software patent applications are not considered traditional software companies. Based on a sample of 3,300 software patents from 1998, IBM, Motorola, Fujitsu, and Canon were in the top five. These are large, well-established companies with a long history of developing and patenting hardware and software. They use these patent portfolios to extract hundreds of millions of dollars in royalties and control the marketplace, even though the validity of many of their patents is questionable.

Many companies with ample resources to seek out quality patents choose not to. Recently, this has led to an interesting example of game theory and cooperation, because other companies have decided that if they can't beat the larger corporations by reforming the software patent examination process, then they should join in by filing their own growing sets of patent applications. Much like the larger corporations, they use the impotence of the current patent laws to ignore prior art. Companies that spend $10,000 to $20,000 to obtain a patent should not find it an undue burden to spend 10 percent more to sufficiently search for prior art to ensure higher quality.

ASSEMBLY-LINE PATENT EXAMINATION

These problems are compounded by the harried conditions under which patent examiners must analyze patent applications. A software patent examiner at the PTO sent me a private e-mail message to explain the environment:

One of the reasons so many [bad] software patents are issued is that examiners are forced to do so. The PTO's production system [that] discourages continued searches is a really big problem for 2 reasons: upon first amendment, PTO management's strong encouragement to either issue or make final (do not continue searching) and, in effect, actually taking away counts for finding new art with which to make a rejection (for continuing to search). Why? We not only get no points for non-final rejections, but a non-final rejection also takes much longer to finally go to a count (abandonment or issue). So if they rewrite their claims to get around our first action, they usually win, especially if they throw in additional claims to drag things out. Thus, we might throw a couple of good punches, but essentially we always are forced to quit the fight in the first round. And applicants know this.

These ingredients combine in a recipe for explosive growth in software patents. The result is patents of dubious validity. Some PTO patents are actually silly, such as US Patent No. 5,491,779, issued in February 1996 for three-dimensional pie charts, and US Patent No. 5,764,906, issued in June 1998 for mapping phrases to URL addresses.

WHAT SHOULD BE DONE?

I think it is reasonable to conclude that the quality of issued patents is suffering. However, this is a dilemma for organizations like the IEEE. Many IEEE members belong to large companies, where patent quality is less important than the patent portfolio size. Other IEEE members are independent or work for small companies, where patent quality is very important in order to be taken seriously in the marketplace. Any reform that the IEEE supports will face conflicting interests. For IEEE members in the US, I encourage you to get involved with the IEEE-USA's Intellectual Property Committee, http://www.ieeeusa.org/committees/IPC/ to voice your opinion. There should also be more contact between the IEEE and ACM and the software committees of the American Bar Association and American Intellectual Property Law Association.

As a matter of professional pride, software developers should demand the patent system to respect and pay more attention to nonpatent prior art, including the many conferences, journals, books, and Web sites. The members of professional organizations have worked together to provide forums to discuss, share, and advance software technology. Issuing patents without referring to this substantial body of nonpatent prior art reflects a lack of respect that should not be tolerated. ❖

Larry Graham

EDITOR: Larry Graham • Black Lowe & Graham • graham@blacklaw.com

Trademarks and Potholes on the Superhighway

Practically overnight, the Internet has become a major commercial channel. Those of you who buy groceries at HomeGrocer.com, health care items at drugstore.com, and books at Amazon.com are sure to agree. The numbers confirm that commerce is booming on the Web. With hundreds of billions of dollars changing hands, the World Wide Web might just as well be called the Wild Wild West as far as trademarks are concerned. Although disorder and uncertainty were hallmarks of the Web only a few years ago, there is now a substantial and growing body of law that provides ample guidance for the proper use of trademarks on the Internet.

DOMAIN NAMES

Like miners scrambling to stake a claim in a gold rush, thousands of companies and individuals have registered domain names because of their potential resale value, rather than for commercial or personal use. These speculative registrants are often referred to as cyber squatters or cyber pirates. Numerous well-known corporations have been the target of such opportunistic domain-name registration, including Porsche, Panavision, Toys "R" Us, Nintendo, Paccar, 3M, Hasbro, and countless others.

Many early domain-name disputes involved open and intentional piracy. For example, the test preparation company Princeton Review registered kaplan.com, posted disparaging messages about its competitor's service, and praised those of the Princeton Review. Consumers were naturally surprised to see such content on a site they assumed was affiliated with Kaplan. When confronted by Kaplan, Princeton Review offered to give up the name for a case of beer; Kaplan soberly refused. The parties eventually settled when an arbitrator convinced Princeton Review to give up the name.

Well-known companies that have chosen to take such cases to the courts have been predictably successful. There are few cases in which a company that owns a well-known trademark has failed to gain control of a domain name. Some recent domain-name disputes, however, have been more difficult to resolve. For example, some opportunists have capitalized on common misspellings and typographical errors. One organization registered numerous domain names corresponding to well-known companies (such as altabista.com, microsuft.com, and nentendo.com), many of which are or have been linked to an adult content site. Others have registered domain names that incorporate www, presuming that users will sometimes leave out the "dot" between www and the second level domain. The US District Court for the District of Virginia recently disapproved of such activity, barring a cyber pirate's use of wwwpainewebber.com. Still others have added an appendix or a suffix to a well-known trademark (for example, porschecars.com). Although the suffix and appendix cases must be decided on a case-by-case basis, it is often easy to tell when someone misappropriates a well-known trademark.

Not all domain-name disputes involve pirating or misappropriation. Trademark law recognizes that consumers can distinguish between companies using similar marks in different industries. The US Patent and Trademark Office routinely grants trademarks even when others have registered the same one when it believes there will be no consumer confusion. But when one company is the first to register the "dot com" domain name, others using the same mark may turn to the courts to get the domain name for themselves. For example, Ty Inc., the maker of Beanie Babies, owns a trademark registration for the word Ty superimposed on a

Reprinted from *IEEE Software*, Vol. 16, No. 5, pp. 19–21, September/October 1999.

299

heart. Another individual registered ty.com, apparently as a tribute to his son, Ty, and used it in his software business. Ty Inc. tried, but failed, to obtain the domain name through Network Solutions Inc., the company in charge of domain-name distribution in 1996. When the dispute was brought before the US District Court for the Northern District of California, it concluded that the numerous other uses of the Ty trademark weighed against any like-

Incorporating a well-known trademark into a domain name is a bold and improper move.

lihood of confusion. In fact, Ty Inc. argued as much when the Trademark Office originally rejected its trademark application. As a general rule, if the trademark is not well-known and consumers are not likely to get confused, the first to register the domain name will likely be allowed to keep it.

METATAGS AND HIDDEN TEXT

Increasingly, people seem to recognize that incorporating a well-known trademark into a domain name is a bold and improper move. Moreover, it might not be the best way to draw customers. While some users might take a stab at a URL by typing in a well-known company name or trademark and adding .com, most are likely to try a search engine first. Accordingly, an effective way to draw consumers to a site is to use metatags and text read by search engines.

Companies have sometimes used competitors' metatags in their sites, only to be admonished by the courts. The only likely exception to the metatag rule is where the use is accurate, descriptive, and does not create a false association. For example, a former Playboy Playmate of the Year was allowed to use the Playboy and Playmate trademarks as metatags in her site.

Likewise, the use of hidden text should be avoided. There are many examples of the hidden text device, many of which are related to adult content sites. For example, some Web pages have added the word "Playboy" a few hundred times in a color that matches the background. Users looking for a Playboy site with a search engine will see such sites and likely assume that they are official or affil-

iated Playboy sites. As with metatags, courts have consistently frowned on using others' trademarks in hidden text.

LINKING

Although most metatag, hidden-text, and domain-name registration cases are fairly easy to resolve, others are not so simple. Linking presents one question that is still open for debate. Even though some companies might not want to be linked to other sites, few, if any, have complained about homepage links. Instead, the linking disputes arise when users are linked to pages within another site, bypassing the homepage altogether. Ticketmaster objected to this link type used by Microsoft's http://sidewalk.com site; the complaint eventually led to litigation. Ticketmaster alleged that Microsoft's site led consumers to internal Ticketmaster pages, bypassing the Ticketmaster homepage that contained advertising and other information Ticketmaster wanted consumers to see. Because Microsoft and Ticketmaster recently settled their dispute, the legality of these links remains uncertain.

FRAMING

Another type of linking that might be inappropriate is framing. In some instances, frame-based sites link to other sites while retaining the original frames and placing the linked content inside the viewing window. This sort of linking creates two primary problems. First, it potentially creates the impression that the two sites are affiliated, even though they are not. Second, the original frames might block advertising or other information on the linked site. In the only case of this type to reach the courts so far, The Washington Post sued Total News. Although the parties settled before the court rendered a decision, it seems likely that The Washington Post would have prevailed.

KEYWORDS AND SEARCH ENGINES

A new flavor of search engine targeting that has arisen lately is the purchase of well-known trademarks for use as keywords. America Online and some other Internet service providers use keywords that enable users to quickly find targeted Web pages. Similarly, search engines frequently sell the rights to keywords so that when a user enters the keyword as a search term a tailored banner ad appears on the screen. Obviously, certain keywords are more valuable than others. By acquiring a good keyword, such as your primary competitor's trademark, you can attract many more consumers to your site. Because many consumers know that banner ads are tailored to searches, they might assume that the products in the ad are associated with the keyword. There might be cause for legal action when there is no such association. Although there are presently no court decisions addressing the matter, the issue is analogous to metatags and will likely be treated similarly.

NONCOMMERCIAL USES

Based on the cases mentioned above, we can see that the courts have broadly enforced trademark rights on the Web, but these rights take a backseat when the trademark is used noncommercially. In several cases, trademark owners have unsuccessfully tried to obtain or block the use of domain names used in a noncommercial way. For example, a California court concluded that the domain name ballysucks.com did not infringe or dilute Bally's trademarks. When a Web site like ballysucks.com is used noncommercially, the courts will be reluctant to transfer a domain name to a complaining trademark owner.

The Network Solutions Inc. domain-name dispute policy, however, is not concerned with whether or not the use is commercial. NSI's policy seeks to define bright or easily distinguishable lines as much as possible, and the commercial use question is often debatable. Under NSI's policy, the party with either the earliest domain-

name registration date or effective federal trademark registration date will be given the domain name. In other words, first come, first served. Those who dislike NSI's policy are free to take their cases to court. However, that option is expensive, so it isn't a viable route for everyone.

Fortunately, help is on the way. Although there have been numerous proposals over the past few years, the World Intellectual Property Organization recently issued its final report on domain names and related intellectual-property issues (http://wipo2.wipo.int/process/eng/processhome.html). The report addresses many of the shortcomings of the present registration and dispute resolution procedures, suggesting changes in both. Although there is a strong suggestion that disputes should be resolved outside the courts, parties will always have that option. In any event, the WIPO will resolve most of the future disputes in a manner consistent with the court decisions thus far. With the court decisions to date and the likely adoption of most or all of the WIPO report, the end of the Wild Wild West on the World Wide Web might be at hand. ❖

Chapter 9

Environmental and Health Concerns

To the best of my ability, insure that the products of my work are used in a socially responsible way.
         —from the AITP Standards of Conduct

Manage personnel and resources to design and build information systems that enhance the quality of working life.
         —ACM Code of Ethics, organizational leadership imperative 2

Approve software only if they have a well-founded belief that it is safe, meets specifications, passes appropriate tests, and does not diminish quality of life, diminish privacy or harm the environment. The ultimate effect of the work should be to the public good.
         —IEEE-CS/ACM Software Engineering Code of Ethics, principle 1.3

Improve understanding of technology; its appropriate application, and potential consequences.
         —IEEE Code of Ethics, item 5

9.1 INTRODUCTION

THE computing industry is no different from any other industry when it comes to being responsible for preserving the environment and protecting the health of those who both use and manufacture computers. The computing industry is large and far-reaching, so ignoring environmental or health concerns could do much more damage to society in general than industries that are perhaps not so pervasive. There is no way to do this immense area justice in only one chapter, but I have tried to select articles that represent the major environment and health problems: manufacturing of computer products, the day-to-day use of computer products, and the conservation of natural resources.

Because the computing industry is relatively young, many issues are just now being recognized and dealt with. In some areas, such as ergonomic design of displays and introduction of "clean" manufacturing processes, improvement is fairly rapid. In others, such as possible radiation effects due to computing equipment, there is still debate over whether a problem actually exists.

9.2 MANUFACTURING

The first reprint in this group, "Cleaning Up," looks at some of the environmental and health concerns related to chip manufacturing. A number of steps in chip fabrication use potentially dangerous chemicals, gases, and solvents. The article mentions studies funded by DEC and IBM that cite higher miscarriage rates for pregnant women working in particular processes in chip fabrication. The good side of this story is that the studies were funded by the companies involved and that policies were put in place to transfer the affected employees to another area of the company. The article also makes it clear that the economics of "clean" processes are often better than those of the processes that they replace. However, the current introduction of clean processes does nothing to solve the problem of past pollution. The article points out that as a result of the lack of knowledge and sound environmental practices in the past, California's Silicon Valley has more federal Superfund sites than any other area of its size in the nation. (The Superfund is a federal program to provide the resources

303

DILBERT © UFS

to clean up the most serious toxic waste sites around the country.)

The second reprint in this group, "Recipe for Recycling," focuses on the idea that the best time to consider how to dispose of a product is when it is designed. Designs that reduce the variety of materials used and make disassembly easier will enhance recycling efforts.

9.3 DAY-TO-DAY USE

There are many possible health hazards in using computers. Two that have received substantial publicity are repetitive stress injury to the wrist and emissions from video display terminals. The reprints address problems stemming from VDTs. The case study and item 1 of this chapter's additional assignments address a form of RSI, carpal tunnel syndrome. Item 4 of the additional assignments invites you to research the incidence and effects of eye strain.

There are two reprints in this group. The first is a short point–counterpoint on safety standards for video displays. The "point" author concludes that "any frequency magnetic field exposure near video display units is biologically insignificant." The "counterpoint" author responds that there is no basis for some of the assertions made in the "point" article and that the models used there are not relevant to the effects being considered. The tone of the point–counterpoint clearly shows that this is a controversial topic. The second reprint is a short summary of a study of the health effects of electromagnetic fields (EMF) completed by the National Research Council. This overview emphasizes the uncertainty attached to interpreting the experimental and statistical data in this area.

9.4 RESOURCE CONSERVATION

The last two reprints deal with the supply of natural resources. This topic tends to be highly controversial, with highly vocal advocates on each side. The article, "Running Out of Resources," argues that "today, most applied economics is aimed at supporting an unachievable model: unlimited growth" and that "the world's critical resources,

all of them, are being exhausted." At least 44 readers sent in responses to this article, which are summarized in the next article. The viewpoints expressed in the responses run from "the most important article yet published in *Spectrum* . . . alerts us to the coming economic crisis" to "Larsen's article . . . is so incredibly shortsighted as to stagger belief." Any article that discusses economics, growth, and natural resources is, of course, destined to be controversial. Whatever the conclusion of such an article, many people will feel that their personal philosophy, religion, politics, or economics is being attacked. Regardless of where your knee-jerk reaction takes you, the fact is that issues of resource use are already affecting the computer industry. For example, as another article in *IEEE Spectrum* points out [4], one reason "green" processes are needed in chip fabrication is that the old nongreen processes have contaminated water sources. Consumption or pollution of natural resources will always have economic effects—the more extreme the consumption or pollution, the more detrimental the effects.

9.5 CASE STUDY

Potential health problems related to long periods of computer use include carpal-tunnel syndrome, eye strain, headaches, and back strain. [3], [5], [11]. Carpal tunnel syndrome is a potentially painful and disabling form of repetitive stress injury, which in extreme cases may require surgery. It appears that, in at least some people, the stress to the wrists during long periods of keyboard and mouse use may be a contributing factor in the onset of CTS. Methods of avoiding CTS include the use of wrist pads, special gloves, and specially designed keyboards that reduce stress on the wrists, and mouse pens. Compaq, Apple, and IBM have been sued by computer users over repetitive stress injury. In the first suit against Compaq, Compaq won. The case study is the suit against Apple and IBM.

9.5.1 The Cast of Characters

Apple is the well-known maker of personal computers and workstations.

IBM is the well-known maker of a variety of computer systems.

Nancy Urbanski is 30 years old, a mother of two, and an employee at the local high school in Eagan, Minnesota.

9.5.2 The Sequence of Events

As part of her job at the local high school, Urbanski worked with Apple and IBM personal computers from 1989 to 1991. She apparently developed CTS around 1991. It was claimed that even tasks such as brushing her hair or opening jars would cause her pain. The high school apparently could not change her job to one that would allow her to avoid tasks requiring hand strength. As a result, she was laid off from her job in 1993.

Urbanski sued both Apple and IBM, claiming that use of their computer keyboards had caused her injuries and that they should have used a different keyboard design or warned users of the danger.

Apple settled out of court for the ever-popular "undisclosed amount." IBM went ahead with the case to receive the jury's verdict. Urbanski's lawyers introduced evidence of CTS cases that occurred in IBM employees and of actions that IBM had taken to address the problem. IBM's lawyers asserted that there was no scientific link between keyboard design and keyboard injuries, that injuries are related to a variety of person-specific factors, and argued that "Urbanski was a disgruntled employee" whose injuries "were actually attributable to a 1988 automobile accident or her hobby of playing volleyball" [9].

In March 1995, the jury ruled that IBM was not liable for Urbanski's injuries.

9.5.3 Conclusions and Questions

Should it be the case that someone (employer, computer maker, . . .) must be responsible when an employee is affected by CTS? How important is the fact that someone plays a sport like volleyball or has been in an automobile accident? How important is the fact that the computer company had taken steps to help its own employees avoid CTS?

Points to Remember

- Chip manufacturing involves a number of potentially dangerous chemicals. While there was little knowledge about the effects of these chemicals in the early days, there is greater knowledge and concern today.
- Greater attention is now being given to how computer products are disposed of. This has given rise to an emphasis on designs that reduce the variety of materials used and make disassembly easier.
- The use or pollution of natural resources does have associated costs. It is quite possible that when the big picture is considered, "green" processes may have an economic advantage over nongreen processes.
- Carpal-tunnel syndrome is of increasing concern among computer users, if only because of recent publicity.

WORKSHEET—Review of Health and Environment Issues

1. List some of the toxic chemicals used in chip fabrication.

2. List some of the potential pollutants that are part of the typical personal computer.

3. Summarize the arguments for and against the existence of dangers from the emissions of video display terminals.

4. Summarize the arguments for and against this statement: "The world's critical resources, all of them, are being exhausted."

1. **Carpal-Tunnel Syndrome.** Carpal-tunnel syndrome was the subject of the case study in this chapter. Look into CTS in more detail to find out how often it is occurring in different types of occupations, and how businesses and health-insurance plans are treating it in terms of a work-related disability.

2. **The Limits To Growth.** *The Limits To Growth* was first published in 1972 and caused quite a stir at the time [8]. It used computer-simulation models to predict what would happen to the world's population and resources under different scenarios. Read the book carefully and evaluate its predictions and methodology.

3. **Water pollution related to chip fabrication.** The problem of water pollution from chemicals used in chip fabrication was touched on in the first article in this chapter (see also [4]). Since the chip-fabrication industry first started in the Silicon Valley, a great deal has been learned about such problems. Report on the water-pollution problems experienced in the Silicon Valley and what has been done in other areas of the country to avoid repeating these problems.

4. **Eye strain related to computer use.** Report on the rate of occurrence, severity of, and treatment of incidences of eye strain among computer users.

5. **The controversy over electromagnetic fields.** The possible relationship between cancer and electromagnetic fields is one of great controversy and emotional debate. Some references dealing with the topic are [1], [2], [6], [7], [10], [12]. Report on the claims that are made both for and against electromagnetic fields causing cancer and on the evidence that exists for the claims.

REFERENCES

[1] E. Adair, "Nurturing electrophobia," *IEEE Spectrum,* August 1990, pp. 11–14.

[2] J. R. Ashley, "Electric and magnetic fields: The perceived public risks," *IEEE SouthCon '94,* pp. 463–467.

[3] J. Baird, "New laser used to treat carpal tunnel syndrome," *The Tampa Tribune-Times,* January 23, 1994.

[4] D. Bendz, "Green Products for Green Profits," *IEEE Spectrum,* September 1993, pp. 63–66.

[5] A. Dunkin, "Making your office human-friendly," *Business Week,* August 20, 1990, pp. 100–101.

[6] K. Fitzgerald, I. Nair, and G. Morgan, "Electromagnetic fields: The jury's still out," *IEEE Spectrum,* August 1990, pp. 22–35.

[7] K. B. Maracas, "Electric & magnetic fields," *IEEE Potentials,* April 1994, pp. 22–25.

[8] D. H. Meadows, D. L. Meadows, J. Randers, and W. W. Behrens, *The Limits to Growth* (Second Edition), Signet Books, 1975.

[9] "IBM cleared by jury in stress injury case," *New York Times report, The Tampa Tribune,* March 9, 1995.

[10] T. S. Perry, "Today's view of magnetic fields," *IEEE Spectrum,* December 1994, pp. 14–23.

[11] D. Sellers, *Zap! How your computer can hurt you.* IEEE Computer Society Press, Piscataway, NJ, 1994.

[12] G. Taubes, "Fields of fear," *The Atlantic Monthly,* November 1994, pp. 94–108.

Cleaning up

Electronics manufacturers are rethinking their processes to remove toxic threats to workers' health and the environment

 Dec. 3 announcement only intensified an already ongoing storm of activity at many electronics companies. Design and manufacturing engineers, managers, and corporate health and safety specialists were not decking the halls with holiday cheer, however. Instead, in particular in the semiconductor area, they were planning their responses to the finding.

The toxicity of yet another process involved in manufacturing electronic goods had just been confirmed. Ethylene-based glycol ethers, used in the manufacture of integrated circuits, had been implicated as a cause of miscarriages by researchers at the University of California at Davis, after a US $3.8 million, four-year study.

Several California environmental groups immediately began pressuring companies to phase out the substances, and threatened consumer boycotts of products manufactured with them. Until then, the electronics industry had been in a self-congratulatory mood, having mostly succeeded in ridding processes of chlorofluorocarbons (CFCs). CFC, also called Freon, depletes the ozone shield in the upper atmosphere that protects the earth and its inhabitants from excessive amounts of ultraviolet light.

Unwanted side effects from electronics manufacturing are not merely a concern of the present. They stretch back into the past and forward into the future. Past toxic leaks burden many older electronics companies with a clean-up task that could last for decades. Today about 150 toxic leaks are being monitored in Silicon Valley alone. Design of future processes will require vigilance to steer them clear of new toxic problems. To do so, companies are integrating a Design for the Environment approach throughout their operations.

Nor are today's problems confined to glycol ethers and CFCs. Metals and gases

Tekla S. Perry   Senior Editor

now used in electronics processes could also cause harm, and the industry is trying to decrease the risks involved. Overall, the electronics industry is now convinced that the clean way is the best way—not least because it can cost far less.

Photoresist at fault

Take the ethylene glycol ethers that caused the December uproar. They are a class of chemical compounds that thin the photoresist used in IC manufacture. The photoresist is spread on silicon wafers and exposed to ultraviolet light shone through a patterned mask. The unwanted material is then etched away, leaving part of a circuit pattern. The photoresist must be applied evenly to the entire wafer, and this evenness is ensured by the glycol ether.

The ethylene glycol ethers became popular in the mid-'70s. At first they were thought to be the "safety solvents," because earlier solvents had been highly flammable, said Angela Boggs, director of corporate health, safety, and environmental affairs at M/A-COM Inc., Wakefield, Mass., and a specialist in glycol ethers and their alternatives. Due to certain solvency properties, including evaporation rate and water miscibility, glycol ethers were found to be ideal solvents for casting positive photoresists.

But soon it was the ethylene glycol ethers' turn to be suspect. In the late '70s and early '80s, animal studies suggested that lengthy exposure to these substances caused still births, birth defects, and other reproductive

> **Miscarriage rates were 20–40 % higher for chip fabrication workers**

problems in both females and males. In 1982 the Semiconductor Industry Association (SIA), San Jose, Calif., alerted its members to these toxic effects. The companies responded by ensuring that ventilation kept workers' exposure to vapors below 5 parts per million (now the Federal standard, which was much higher back then) and that production procedures minimized skin contact.

But few chip manufacturers immediately began introducing alternative substances. "Photoresist suppliers have been making alternative photoresists for years," Boggs told

IEEE Spectrum, "but the user community is reluctant to make changes, and that is realistic. There are a lot of variables in the process, and if you have a system that works, you don't want to tinker with it."

The first major switch began in 1983 at the Digital Equipment Corp. in Hudson, Mass. A pregnant worker in a semiconductor fabrication facility contacted the company's environmental health and safety manager, James Stewart. She was concerned, she said, because her co-workers seemed to be having a great many miscarriages. Stewart told *Spectrum* that he found nothing in the available internal and external medical data to prove or disprove her fears. The company then contracted with the University of Massachusetts to study Digital's fabrication workers. Eighteen months and $450 000 later, the researchers raised concerns that these women might indeed be at a significantly higher risk of miscarriage than those in other departments. (The study was too small to pin the blame on photoresist processes or ethylene glycol ethers, just on fabrication work in general.)

Digital passed the findings on to its employees and to other semiconductor companies. It encouraged workers who were pregnant or planning a pregnancy to transfer out of fabrication at full salary and status. (Several other companies have instituted similar policies in the years since the DEC study.)

In hope of more specific results, studies of larger populations were begun in 1988 by the SIA and by IBM Corp. Big Blue contracted for its fab workers to be studied by Johns Hopkins University, Baltimore, Md. Preliminary results, announced in October 1992, indicated twice the normal rate of miscarriages for the small population of fabrication workers involved in two specific processes—chemical mixing and photoresist application.

The SIA contracted with the University of California at Davis for the work that led to the Dec. 3 announcement. Some 15 000 workers at 14 companies were sampled. The finding: that miscarriage rates were 20–40 percent higher among workers in chip fabrication.

The SIA study concluded that semiconductor fabrication in general and, considering the animal tests, probably ethylene glycol ethers in particular, posed reproductive hazards, even at exposures an order of magnitude below the 5-ppm Federal standard. It inferred that significant exposure is occur-

Reprinted from *IEEE Spectrum*, Vol. 30, No. 2, pp. 20–26, February 1993.

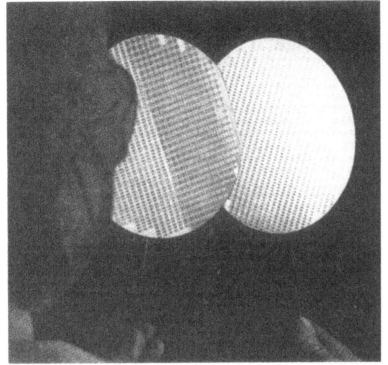

[1] *Photolithography is the process of developing circuit patterns on semiconductor wafers, as shown. But some types of the photosensitive material spread on each wafer contain a class of chemicals called ethylene glycol ethers. Recent studies have demonstrated that pregnant women who work with these chemicals in photolithography are at a high risk of miscarrying.*

chips have to undergo reliability tests in customer systems before the new process is qualified. And if the resist selected does not work, all the parts made with it are thrown away, and the entire drill begins again.

OTHER OPTIONS. Of the three alternatives to ethylene glycol ethers found to date, one is quite similar to them chemically, the others, quite different. Propylene glycol monomethyl ether acetate has only a slightly different atomic structure that appears to be metabolized differently in animals. Ethyl-3-ethoxypropionate is derived from propionic acid, similar to acetic acid. Ethyl lactate is a derivative of a lactic acid produced in mammals during normal respiration.

"These three substances have been studied [in animals] and have demonstrably less toxicity than ethylene glycol ethers. [Propylene glycol] seems somewhat less toxic than ethoxypropionate; ethyl lactate has not been studied as heavily as the others, so we have less data to look at," said Boggs at M/A-COM. But these known replacements are not always satisfactory substitutes so research continues.

The SIA has called for a joint effort by the Semiconductor Research Corp., Research Triangle Park, N.C., and Sematech, Austin, Texas, to find other replacements. In the interim, ethylene glycol ether use will be minimized. Sematech is also working with the Massachusetts Institute of Technology in Cambridge to redesign the nozzle that dispenses the solvent to spray less of it. With some older application methods, all but 3 percent of the photoresist applied runs

ring either through nonrespiratory routes during maintenance or when cleaning spills, or that the minute amounts released in the air are still too high.

PHASE-OUT. Before its study was completed, DEC began phasing in substitutes for ethylene glycol ethers and by early 1990 had eliminated them from semiconductor production. In their place, DEC uses propylene-based glycol ethers, one of three currently available alternatives, and continues to "look aggressively" for a viable alternative solvent for use in manufacturing disk drives, according to a company spokesman.

Some other IC makers also moved to eliminate ethylene glycol ethers in the late '80s. Since 1989, IBM has halved its use of them. Cypress Semiconductor Corp. has gotten rid of 70 percent of the ethylene glycol ethers used in its San Jose facility.

For the companies that acted early, the transition away from ethylene glycol ethers meant little downtime or loss of revenue. Said the DEC spokesman: "Since we phased in new processes over six years, disruption to business was relatively little." And few companies, after the 1986 DEC release, have designed the substances into new production processes.

But replacing ethylene glycol ethers in existing processes is another matter. It is like switching from silicon to gallium arsenide, chief executive officer T.J. Rodgers of Cypress Semiconductor told *Spectrum*. "Photographic emulsion forms every wire, every transistor, and every insulator on a chip. It has to maintain 0.6-micron images with high integrity. We put it on a wafer some 20

times." The switch, Rodgers said, involves doing half of a production run with a new resist, comparing the yields with those for the former resist, changing the formulation, and trying again. Once yields are satisfactory, the

Some chemical emissions in Silicon Valley, 1987–91*

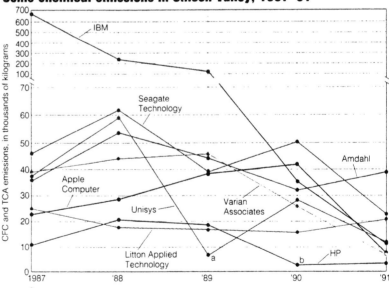

* Chlorofluorocarbons and 111–trichloroethane
a The sale of Unisys' Santa Clara Peripherals Division was announced by the company in December 1989
b HP moved manufacturing from Sunnyvale to Roseville, Calif., in 1990

[2] *In 1990, the Silicon Valley Toxics Coalition identified the local divisions of 12 companies as the area's "top ozone eaters," or top emitters of chlorofluorocarbons and 1,1,1 trichloroethane. Many in that group, including these eight electronics companies, have succeeded in reducing their emissions, according to data from the California Environmental Protection Agency.*

off the semiconductor wafer or evaporates.

Meanwhile, some health specialists harbor a rarely discussed fear: that glycol ethers are not the only reproductive hazards.

Said Stewart, initiator of the DEC study and now director of environmental health and safety at Harvard University in Cambridge, Mass.: "The miscarriages are not just in the photo and masking areas, they are in other fab areas as well. It could mean that factors other than glycol ethers might be responsible." The Davis researchers agree and are currently discussing possible follow-up studies with the SIA.

Ozone-eating CFCs

The electronics industry has proven that when it goes all out, it can find environmentally safe alternatives to process chemicals—and, as what follows shows, the alternatives may be more effective than the toxic substances they replace. The best example is the ozone-eating CFCs.

CFCs had several uses in electronics manufacturing. They degreased and dried components before labeling or assembly. They were used for precision cleaning, of everything from disk drive heads to the outside of communications satellites, to remove contaminants that might affect reliability or that might cause the system to degrade prematurely.

But by far the largest use in the electronics industry was for defluxing: removing flux residue from printed-circuit boards after components were soldered in place. "Flux" is applied after components are inserted in a board, but before their connections are wave-soldered to the board by passing it over a wave of liquid solder. Typically a derivative of pine resin, flux acts as a deoxidizer, ensuring better adhesion between the solder and the components. But resin fluxes may eat away at the board and the components, causing metal changes resulting in short circuits; so for the sake of long-term reliability, they must be removed. CFCs seemed ideal for the job: they stripped the resin cleanly, harmed neither the board nor components, and evaporated quickly, drying out the entire board, down to the tiniest spaces between components.

Like ethylene glycol ethers, the electronics industry turned to CFCs as a safety solvent. They replaced trichloroethylene (TCE), a chemical that had been determined in the mid-'70s to be a potential human carcinogen. Recalled Ralph Ponce de Leon, vice president of supply and environmental affairs at Motorola Inc., Schaumburg, Ill., "In the '70s, the friendly chemical companies came around and said you need a replacement for TCE and we have one; we have Freon. It's so safe, people can bathe in it." (Freon's ozone-depleting properties were suspected at that time. It had been banned for use in aerosols but not in other applications.)

OUT OF THIS WORLD. The electronics industry embraced CFCs because they had a number of desirable attributes—they are safe, economical, and pure.

Concern about the ozone-damage done by CFCs ballooned in 1985, when a hole in the ozone layer was discovered over Antarctica. In response, representatives of 23 countries gathered in Montreal in 1987 and agreed to cut CFC usage in half by 1999.

In the mid-'80s, the quantity of CFCs being released by just Silicon Valley companies was surprising. In 1987, the first year that companies were required to report publicly the volumes of chemicals being discharged into the environment, CFC releases by IBM Corp.'s San Jose facility alone were nearly 700 000 kg [see graph, p. 21], the second-largest individual plant release of CFCs in the United States. At that time, the electronics industry consumed only about 20 percent of all CFCs used (refrigeration, air conditioning, auto painting, and printing are among the other applications).

As more and more data about the growing hole in the ozone layer became available, CFC's D-Day was moved up. It is now the end of 1995. The civilian electronics industry will probably meet or beat that date, thanks to its development of highly successful CFC alternatives.

A Federal law passed in 1990 gave the electronics industry's efforts in this area an extra sense of urgency. It requires that, as of May 15 of this year, all products manufactured with ozone-depleting chemicals be conspicuously labeled: "Warning: Manufactured with (name of substance), a substance which harms public health and the environ-

[3] At Hughes Aircraft Co.[top], electronic circuit cards pass through a new lemon-juice foaming flux solution, called HF-1189, that can be cleaned off with water instead of depleting chlorofluorocarbons. At IBM Corp. [bottom], assembled circuit boards go t a water cleaning process in a machine that behaves like a powerful dishwasher.

ment by destroying ozone in the upper atmosphere." No company wants such a stigma on its products.

At first, some industry leaders had been apprehensive. In 1989, Japan's Ministry of International Trade and Industry (MITI) argued that CFCs were vital to the electronics industry and it would be wrong to curtail their use unilaterally. But today Japan is keeping pace with the rest of the world's electronics industry in CFC elimination. Many of the world's electronics firms had virtually stopped using CFCs by the end of 1992. For example, their use by DEC's semiconductor operations dropped from 24 000 kg in 1989 to 0 in 1992, while companywide use is down 85 percent from 1989. Intel, one of the first major companies to go public with a CFC-elimination goal, had pledged to be CFC-free by the end of 1992; the company said it achieved 99 percent of its target.

FRUITS AND FLUXES. Replacements for CFCs have been found to be plentiful. Nevertheless, "it has been impossible to find a drop-in replacement" for them, said Douglas Heden, product manager for printed-circuit materials, Dupont Electronics, Wilmington, Del., which had been a major supplier of CFCs to the electronics industry. "That has been a frustrating experience."

By and large, two approaches have been developed in eliminating the use of CFCs in cleaning flux residue from PC boards. Both depart from standard resin flux formulations. One approach relies on organic fluxes that can be cleaned with water, called aqueous technology; another uses low-solids fluxes that need not be cleaned off at all, called no-clean technology.

The inspiration for one early organic flux was the kitchen. At Hughes Aircraft Co. in Fullerton, Calif., in 1989, a production engineer in a circuit-board facility, Ray Turner, was reprimanded when a lid on a tank of CFCs was left open. Annoyed, he decided he could eliminate such problems by eliminating CFCs. He chose to search for an organic flux, one that could be washed away with water, as food residue is washed from the dishes at home. He began the search in his kitchen, testing vinegar, then lemon rind, then lemon juice. He found that lemon juice made an excellent soldering bond and was soluble in water.

Originally called Turner's Crazy Flux, then renamed HF-1189 (Hughes Flux November 1989), the formula required little retooling of the production line, merely the addition of a dishwasher. The company has been phasing the new flux into its operations. Besides being cheaper and more environmentally friendly, the substance is a more active flux than the resin flux it replaced. Soldering is faster, so the speed of the assembly line can be increased, so exposure of components to the heat of the solder bath is less, so that system reliability increases.

Other companies—like AT&T and DEC—have developed processes that use aqueous cleaning and are offering their technology to the rest of the industry. Several water-soluble fluxes are commercially available.

For companies that are still using resin-based fluxes, there is the semi-aqueous cleaning process—non-CFC solvents used with water. Some are based on terpene, which can be made from substances in citrus fruits or trees. Like turpentine, they can clean off resin residue. AT&T, for one, has developed a process using a a terpene ex-

Lemon juice made an excellent solder bond

tracted from orange rind by Petrofirm Inc., Fernandina Beach, Fla.

Other semi-aqueous processes depend on petroleum products. "The petroleum-based hydrocarbon can be refined to do what we want, to be more stable over time. Fruit extracts smell, they turn rancid. Nature only gives you what nature wants," said Dupont's Heden.

Terpene and hydrocarbon-based solvents can only be an interim solution, however, because they do release volatile organic compounds (VOCs) into the air. VOCs pollute the air at ground level and are already being controlled in some cities.

NO-CLEAN PROCESSES. In the long run, the industry is expected to move to processes that require no cleaning at all. Said M/A-COM's Boggs: "Ultimately, we have to ask ourselves why we clean. We have to get our process engineers thinking about how we can make the product differently, with the same quality and reliability, without cleaning."

The first company to put a no-clean process into wide use was Northern Telecom Ltd., based in Mississauga, Ont., Canada. It got a head start because of the efforts of a group at its Research Triangle Park, N.C., facility. Three manufacturing engineers with an environmental bent fell to talking about their company's use of CFCs and how the chemicals could be eliminated. They concluded that the most obvious solution was simply not to clean. They began testing various flux formulations to find one that would not require cleaning but still be effective.

From 1985 through 1987, before much of the electronics industry was worrying about CFCs, this group tested 200 different flux formulations, recalled Dennis Brown, manager of advanced engineering and one of the trio. They finally found one that would work, a mixture of 2 percent synthetic solids and 98 percent alcohol. But to use it they needed a new application method—instead of passing the circuit board through foaming

flux, this formulation had to be blown on the circuit boards [Fig. 3]. They purchased such a spray fluxer and modified it.

(AT&T, which initiated research into alternatives in the early '80s, also has developed a low-solids fluxer; the device sprays flux coatings onto boards, leaving little flux residue, so that some systems can be assembled without a cleaning step. Tokyo's NEC Corp. has a similar device.)

When Northern Telecom began a corporate-wide search for CFC replacements in 1988, the trio was ready with its no-clean solution. The company tested aqueous cleaning in one facility and the use of an inert gas, which stops additional oxides from forming during soldering, in another. (Fujitsu Ltd. of Tokyo is using a no-clean flux soldered in an inert atmosphere, and other companies are experimenting with similar techniques, although this option is fairly expensive.) In 1991 Northern Telecom agreed that no-clean was best.

Apple Computer Inc., Santa Clara, Calif., is another early convert to no-clean processes. Between 1989 and mid-'90 the company implemented one with the manufacture of its Macintosh Portable. By mid-'91, Apple had moved from CFC usage to no-clean processes in its assembly lines worldwide.

COSTS AND BENEFITS. Developing CFC alternatives has not been cheap. AT&T, which began its efforts in the mid-'80s, has spent some $25 million on the project.

IBM in 1990 congressional testimony estimated that CFC elimination from its operations would require $140 million for R&D and $70 million for capital costs. But CFC elimination has turned out to have an up side for the companies as well as the environment. The substitutes are not only cheaper (IBM estimates CFC replacements and heavy metals recovery led to $10 million savings in 1990), but they are improving yields.

"Everyone was going about saying I hope we can find something as good as Freon, and we found something better than Freon, which was a surprise," M/A-COM's Boggs told *Spectrum*.

Military contractors have been lagging behind commercial manufacturers in switching to water-based or no-clean processes. They face a physical and a bureaucratic problem. Military components are designed to survive in harsh environments, and therefore must be cleaned to tighter tolerances to reduce the chance of system degradation. Second, an estimated 7000 military specifications call for CFC-113; replacing it in the process requires renegotiating contracts on a case-by-case basis, and then only after extensive testing of parts made from the new process.

So far, a few substitutes have been approved for use in certain contracts, including Hughes' Crazy Flux and a mild solution of adipic acid (an ingredient in commercial gelatin desserts) developed by Sandia National Laboratories, New Mexico.

For CFCs in uses other than PC board

cleaning, the industry has found a variety of replacements. Instead of marking parts with ink, which required a degreasing step with CFCs to prevent the ink from smearing, companies like NEC and Advanced Micro Devices Inc., Sunnyvale, Calif., are switching to laser marking.

For precision cleaning, systems based on surfactants (soap) and water are so far best. At IBM Corp. in San Jose, disk drive heads are now cleaned in a system that agitates soapy water with ultrasonics; then they are rinsed with water only, and dried with hot air. The most difficult part of the process to design was the drying. The company had to redesign some parts and put new coatings on others before they would dry without oxidizing. Tokyo-based Fujitsu Ltd. is also cleaning its hard disk components with soap, water, and ultrasonics, but uses a pressurized atmosphere to vaporize water, followed by vacuum drying. The company said this method removes 10 times as much dust as CFCs.

Companies are still searching for CFC substitutes in specialized applications. For example, Lockheed Missiles & Space Co., Sunnyvale, Calif., is experimenting with cleaning surfaces with blasts of frozen carbon dioxide pellets (dry ice), to avoid having to dry wet areas. Sematech is working on a similar process. Cypress has instituted a plasma-cleaning process that cleanses parts with oxygen; AT&T is testing a similar process for cleaning hybrid ICs. Tokyo's Toshiba Corp. has recently installed a system that shoots water and foam at its liquid-crystal substrates.

TCA, another ozone eater

CFCs are not the only chemical used in the electronics industry that depletes the ozone; 1,1,1 trichloroethane (TCA), also called methyl chloroform, was brought in as a replacement for TCE in the '60s. It is somewhat less hazardous to the ozone but still is classed as a depleter and is scheduled to be eliminated by the end of 1995. Companies that continue to use TCA as a solvent will also be subject to the May labeling requirement.

TCA is used in much smaller quantities than CFCs by electronics companies and only in specialized applications. Some who work with the chemical see it as more difficult to replace than CFC. Said Gary Kern, manager of corporate environmental affairs at Varian Associates Inc., Palo Alto, Calif.: "We still use TCA for degreasing of certain parts. We just haven't found the right substitute for all applications yet."

At Hewlett-Packard Co., TCA is still employed on thin-film ICs used in microwave instruments, which require a high level of cleanliness because of their small geometries. But the company's goal is to eliminate TCA use by May 1993. For some applications, reluctance to move away from TCA may be similar to the initial resistance some companies faced in attempting to replace

ethylene glycol ethers and CFCs.

Cypress CEO Rodgers said he has tolerated no such resistance. He told *Spectrum*, "As soon as I found out in 1985 that TCA was no good, I told the people running the assembly operation, where it was used for degreasing parts [before marking], that they would get no more TCA. We had a two-to-three-week supply in house. They wailed that it wasn't possible. I said we aren't buying any more, we are getting off the stuff cold turkey. The vice president came in and told me he couldn't run his operation without TCA. I told him, 'Well, the next vice president will probably figure out a way.' They found a new process in a week."

What Cypress moved into was plasma cleaning, which had been used in wafer

> 'It's always economically favorable to do the clean thing'

cleaning, but not for assembly. It was fairly expensive, as the machines ran $150 000 each; so more recently the company changed cleaning technologies again, to gas torches. The parts are sped through the flame and the grease is burned off.

At AT&T, TCA is used in the manufacture of multichip modules. There it acts as a photographic developer, dissolving a polymer applied to the modules that has been photographically imaged to create circuit patterns. After much testing, AT&T found two existing materials for which it developed new processes that work as well as TCA-based processes. They are glycol ethers and n-butyl butyrate, a substance that occurs naturally in cantaloupes, other melons, peaches, and plums but is formulated chemically by Dow Chemical Co. AT&T picked butyl butyrate as it is nontoxic and biodegradable and it led to improved yields—it causes less swelling in the polymer and therefore circuits are more clearly defined.

So far, no one has had much success in replacing TCA in one application: it is injected in diffusion furnaces to grow oxides on silicon wafers, producing better oxides than the acid alone. For this use, TCA is purchased in sealed ampules and is virtually consumed by the process with no atmospheric impact. All the same, Sematech is investigating alternatives, according to Phyllis Pei, environmental safety and health manager. However, she told *Spectrum* that the alternatives so far are not ideal. "They are much more flammable, and when used in furnaces, that is a serious consideration."

Intel has tested a different form of chlorine that it will use in its new Santa Clara facility when manufacturing begins this year. The company is evaluating another chemical substitute for TCA in older wafer fabri-

cation operations and told *Spectrum* that it intended to begin retrofitting those facilities early this year.

Not for public consumption

Some are concerned about other aspects of electronics manufacturing, including the unavoidable use of heavy metals and toxic gases. Chromium, copper, and nickel are used to plate aerospace and electronic components and create electrical connections on circuit boards and ICs. Arsine, phosphine, diborane (gaseous arsenic), phosphorus, and boron give silicon wafers their electrical properties.

Dissolved metals are picked up by cleaning solutions when the electronic parts are washed. If discharged into the sewer system, they end up in nearby bodies of water. For Silicon Valley, that has been the South San Francisco Bay, a Federally designated toxic hot spot where the metals may endanger fish, birds, marine mammals—and people who eat fish from the bay.

Even before this prompted new clean-up action in 1990, many large electronics companies had already instituted systems to remove heavy metals from waste water before discharging it into the sewage system. Some of the mechanisms are simple—like holding a component above the chemical rinse bath and letting it drip-dry before moving to a water rinse, or using evaporation, distillation, or membrane osmosis to separate water from residual metals. Others are more complex: NEC has developed a magnetic method of waste water treatment using ferrite. The current move from chemical to aqueous PC board cleaning increases this concern because it adds a new source of water that picks up excess metals.

According to Greg Karras, staff scientist, Citizens for a Better Environment, San Francisco, smaller companies that supply some of the large manufacturers are the biggest offenders. His organization is negotiating with city governments to help small companies financially with process changes, reasoning that in the long run it will save the cities on sewage treatment costs.

The arsine, phosphine, and diborane gases used in the semiconductor industry can all be fatal if inhaled. That leads some environmentalists and the public to picture an accident causing a toxic cloud to descend on a heavily populated neighborhood, dropping residents dead in their tracks.

The companies said that this scenario is ridiculous. "I think the dangers of gaseous sources are overhyped," Rodgers told *Spectrum*. "They plain aren't that dangerous." Safeguards in place—like isolated storage facilities and high-powered ventilation systems—certainly limit the danger. Some cities are also mandating additional safety devices, like monitors and automatic shut-off valves, which began to come into use in the '70s.

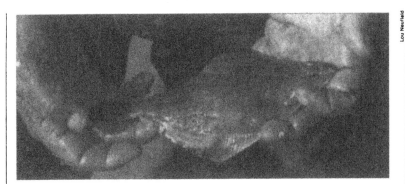

[4] This fish, its skin spotted with ugly tumors, was caught in the South San Francisco Bay in 1990, near the waste water outfalls of the sewage plants that serve Silicon Valley. Heavy metals, discharged from electronics and other manufacturing facilities, are among the pollutants in the San Francisco Bay.

Replacing a volatile gas with a less volatile solid of course lessens the risk of a toxic cloud, no matter how slim. Sematech has demonstrated processes that use solid arsenic, and Intel has completely switched to solid arsenic in its processes, sharing its technology industrywide.

TOXIC SHOCK. Until 1982, Rodgers said, electronics executives had their blinders on and rarely considered the environmental consequences of their processes. Yet today, the industry overall is in favor of expelling toxic chemicals from their processes wherever possible. "If you look at the total cost of having a dangerous chemical in the plant—training people to handle it, creating a safe storage facility, disposing of it—it's always economically favorable to do the clean thing," Cypress CEO Rodgers said.

In January 1982, the San Jose *Mercury News* reported that an underground storage tank at Fairchild Semiconductor Corp.'s San Jose plant had leaked solvents into a nearby well. The regional water quality control board investigated 80 other electronics manufacturing facilities, and found leaks in 85 percent of the underground tanks checked. Today, 150 toxic sites in Silicon Valley are being monitored and about one in five sites are so devastating as to be part of the national Superfund program [see map, at right]. Most are in the process of being cleaned up. The companies had followed the storage guidelines of fire and building codes of the time; but the codes were not good enough.

Rodgers recalled that his then-employer, Advanced Micro Devices, was among the companies declared a Superfund site. "I was shocked; everyone was. We had all considered the chip industry to be superclean, all been proud of our smokeless chimneys, clean green lawns, and nice-looking buildings. The leaking solvents problem sur-

prised everyone in the Valley." Indeed, the problem is international in scope.

The U.S. companies affected have been working on cleaning up these sites for years now, and the work will go on for decades. What's involved, by and large, is pumping out the ground water, purifying it through evaporation, activated-carbon filtering, or other methods, then returning it to the underground aquifer if appropriate. In some cases, the soil must also be dug up and the chemicals vacuumed out. Nor do these mechanisms deal with all the contaminants—better clean-up technologies are on the drawing board or being used in a limited way, including degrading the chemicals by means

of ultraviolet radiation, electron beam accelerators, and the use of bacteria. The job is not cheap: IBM's San Jose toxic plume alone is expected to cost over $100 million to clean up.

The electrical equipment industry is dealing with a similar problem—polychlorinated biphenyls, or PCBs, were banned for use in manufacturing in 1979; research identified them as the cause of birth defects and other health problems and as a potential carcinogen, and Congress legislated a phase-out schedule for electrical network components containing the chemical. PCBs had been in use since the '30s in the manufacture of insulators and capacitors. Westinghouse Corp. alone will be spending an estimated $1 billion to clean PCBs out of the ground at its Bloomington, Ind., capacitor plant, and is being sued by former workers.

Environmental designs

With costs like these, it is no surprise that companies today are making serious efforts to prevent environmental damage. These efforts are spreading beyond production processes to the environmental impact of electronic products throughout their lives. To inculcate an awareness of the environment into their entire operations, electronics companies are implementing programs that go under a variety of names, the most common being "Design for the Environment." These programs offer resources to help design engineers look at the environmental im-

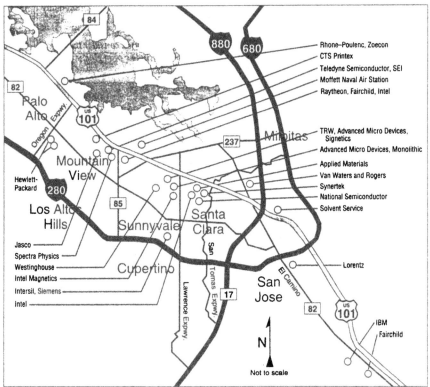

[5] California's Silicon Valley has more Federal Superfund sites than any other area of its size in the nation, plus many other toxic sites that are being monitored by state and regional agencies.

pact of their choices of processes and materials for everything from printed-circuit boards, to plastic housings, to the box the final system is shipped in.

NEC was a pioneer in the field. In 1969, its then chairman Koji Kobayashi announced a plan to set up organizations for environmental control, including an environmental research group, the Resource and Environmental Protection Research Laboratories. An environmental program has been in operation there since 1973. In the United States AT&T Bell Laboratories has had an environmental R&D organization for years.

In 1991 and 1992, numerous other companies instituted some form of design for environment program. Some, like Toshiba's, are part of corporate affairs, where they help decide overall corporate strategies. Others, like Apple's, are part of the engineering divisions, and act as resources for design engineers throughout the company.

Design changes made so far, besides transitioning from toxics in production processes, are quite varied. They include making products easier to disassemble into recyclable components; labeling parts as recyclable or hazardous; using single-resin plastics, which are more easily reused; instituting programs to recover and reuse toner cartridges from laser printers; and making sure any lead in circuit boards is fully encased in plastic so it does not leach out in landfills.

Governments worldwide are spurring on these activities. Japan enacted a law in October of 1991 that encourages manufacturers to design products for recycling. And MITI has instituted a 10 percent tax credit for companies that invest in environmentally clean technologies, and itself is spending some $60 million to develop environmentally friendly manufacturing technology.

In Europe, laws have begun to be enacted that require companies to take cradle-to-grave responsibility for the products they make. As of Jan. 1, 1994, a German take-back law goes into effect for all electronic products. Other European countries are expected to follow suit.

The U.S. EPA has launched the "Energy Star" program, a voluntary effort that encourages companies to reduce the power consumption of computer systems. Industry organizations are getting into the act as well. The Microelectronics & Computer Technology Corp. (MCC), in Austin, Texas, is completing an extensive project to assess the life cycle of a computer workstation. A summary report was to be released in January, with the final version being published in the spring. One preliminary recommendation is to establish a neutral organization similar to Underwriters Laboratories to evaluate products as "environmentally clean."

U.S. environmentalists are placing their hopes on Sematech, which teams the nation's semiconductor companies with semiconductor manufacturing equipment makers and therefore, they feel, is in a better position to address environmental issues across the board. Congress seems to agree, mandating in October 1992 that Sematech dedicate $10 million in 1993—10 percent of its Federal appropriation—to "the development of a pollution-preventing environmentally safe microchip manufacturing process."

Design for the Environment is expected to be a major competitive thrust for electronics companies in the '90s, much as Design for Quality was a competitive thrust in the '80s. Said Diana J. Bendz, director of integrated safety technology for IBM's corporate worldwide manufacturing and development organization, in Purchase, N.Y., addressing an IEEE satellite videoconference last year: "Environmental considerations must become part of the requirements of our jobs. It's everybody's business—educators, product designers, process designers, environmental engineers, managers, and researchers."

TO PROBE FURTHER. The IEEE will hold its first International Symposium on Electronics and the Environment on May 10-12 in Arlington, Va. This international conference will include a half-day tutorial on fundamentals of Design for the Environment; plenary sessions will address international environmental regulations, legislation, public opinion trends, and environmental marketing. For additional information, contact the IEEE Conference Registrar, IEEE Technical Activities, 445 Hoes Lane, Box 1331, Piscataway, N.J. 08855-1331; 908-562-3878.

The IEEE's 1992 satellite videoconference, "Environmental Issues and Impact to Engineers," is available on a three-hour videotape; call 800-678-IEEE; fax, 908-981-9667; outside the United States, 908-981-0060. Price is US $495 to members, $795 list.

"The Legacy of High Tech Development: The Toxic Lifecycle of Computer Manufacturing" explains in lay terms how toxic substances are used in electronics processes as well as their varied health and environmental effects. Its authors are Ted Smith and Phil Woodward, and it was published in January 1992 by the Silicon Valley Toxics Coalition, National Toxics Campaign Fund, and Campaign for Responsible Technology. It is available for $10 from the Silicon Valley Toxics Coalition, 760 North First St., San Jose, Calif. 95112; 408-287-6707.

"Coming clean: industrial solvents and the ozone layer" reports on the use of solvents in the electronics and other industries and on efforts at replacing them. The publication is obtainable from the Friends of the Earth, 26-28 Underwood St., London N17JQ, Great Britain; (44+1) 490 1555; fax, (44+1) 490 0881. Angela Boggs discusses photoresist solvents in "A comparative risk assessment of casting solvents for positive photoresist," in the *Applied Industrial Hygiene Journal*, April 1989, pp. 81-87.

"The Not-So-Clean Business of Making Chips" (Joseph Ladou, *Technology Review*, Vol. 87, May/June 1984, pp. 22-36) describes many of the hazards of the semiconductor manufacturing process, particularly the risks to worker health. For the report, "Lifecycle Environmental Assessment of a Computer Workstation," contact Microelectronics & Computer Technology Corp. (MCC) in Austin, Texas, at 512-343-0978 after April; cost is $40, prepaid. ◆

[6] In designing products with the environment in mind, engineers must consider the recyclability of components. This IBM PS/2 Model 40 is made up of a single type of plastic for simpler recycling, and the system snaps together for easy disassembly.

Recipe for recycling

Recycling goes beyond the recovery of precious metals to the reuse of plastics, resale of components, and even the reprocessing of glass

Consumer electronic and computer products bubble to the surface and disappear more quickly than most manufactured items. Design cycles are short; obsolence comes soon; and the secondhand market is small, since most consumers want only the latest and greatest. Yesterday's models typically end up first on a closet shelf, then in a landfill. There's the rub. Increasingly, such cavalier disposal of bulky devices that often contain toxic elements is being recognized as a problem.

But there is an alternative.

A market already exists globally for a certain amount of electronic equipment at the end of its useful life—anything that is refurbishable or has salvageable components. Parts supply and service organizations often use refurbished components.

Still, the fraction of equipment and components "recycled" along these routes is rather small, especially in terms of weight and volume. Of the average mixed batch of equipment sent for recycling, only 5–15 percent by weight can be re-marketed. Furthermore, the refurbishable and recovered items will in the end fail irrevocably, at which time they must be disposed of or recycled from scratch.

Quite often, older electronic equipment in general and computers in particular have contained enough precious metals to make recovery of certain items a profitable enterprise. A typical computer contains gold, silver, palladium, and platinum, while a telephone, according to British Telecom, has the same metal content minus the platinum. However, as levels of integration have risen and competitive pressures, too, precious metals are finding their way into electronic equipment in ever smaller quantities—to wit, the use of copper instead of gold for electrical contacts. The reduction has already af-

fected many of the smaller recyclers, who cannot glean a profit from printed-circuit boards containing only 150–450 grams of gold per ton versus the 400–1400 grams per ton of older equipment.

While these types of activities certainly retrieve the most valuable components and materials, the fraction those represent of the entire equipment stream is still rather small; so to date, discarded electronic equipment has mostly ended up in landfills. In fact, the infrastructure needed for full electronic equipment recycling is only just emerging.

INTEGRATED RECYCLING. The complete recycling of electrical and electronic equipment will in the future probably be handled by independent recyclers who become specialized in understanding the varieties of discarded

On their arrival at the recycler, discarded electronic products are broken down into their component elements. Those of value are recovered for reuse or resale.

equipment. They will plan the logistics of recovering any assemblies, components, and materials of value, and will develop the technologies necessary to extract them in a way that is economical and environmentally sound. The actual recycling activities will also probably take place in central locations, if for no other reason than the substantial costs of moving material and equipment.

The integrated recycling approach ranks the means of disposal in order of feasibility: refurbishing; or equipment brokering, possibly to underdeveloped countries; component recovery; or full material recycling.

Equipment that qualifies for refurbishing has mostly been discarded because of obsolescence or minor damage. The markets for used equipment will not tolerate much

added cost, but the suppliers of used functioning equipment may expect some type of payment. While this activity usually accounts for only a small part of the total discarded equipment, it is well worthwhile. Next, once the equipment is recovered, refurbished, and certified as operational, it must be brokered. The brokering activity is still evolving globally, but has become a reasonably reliable marketplace for some used equipment.

For items of equipment that are not repairable or for which no market exists, the recovery of components may be warranted. Again, market value is balanced against cost of recovery in determining which devices will be recovered from what equipment. The ICs in newer equipment, for example, including processors, dynamic RAMs, and erasable programmable ROMs, can be removed for sale and reused in toys or control equipment. Obsolete electronic parts may be valuable as replacement parts, but some are worth more when recycled for their precious metals. Both equipment and component recovery require an extensive understanding of an ever-changing market. To be successful, the marketing of equipment and components must in addition be done in volume, for only a consistent presence in the marketplace will guarantee reasonable returns.

DUST TO DUST. The last process, full material recycling, has been the missing piece of the puzzle. For economic and environmental viability, it must combine the appropriate process technology (which should be under continuous development) with the optimization of logistical, marketing, and accounting systems; with sufficient economies of scale; and with market creation activities.

The materials frequently extracted from electronic products include aluminum, copper, steel, plastic, and glass. Aluminum may have pieces of steel attached to it in the form of screws, inserts, or brackets. When the mix is processed in a furnace, the steel is left behind, and the aluminum will go to a secondary melting operation. The material can be used for an aluminum-based product, depending on its alloying requirements.

Copper is processed in the same way as aluminum. It is well suited to being returned to its original use with no loss of properties. Copper from cable can become cable again, just as the laminate from circuit-board assemblies can resurrect as laminate.

Michael B. Biddle   Mann USA
Ray Mann   Mann Organisation

Reprinted from *IEEE Spectrum*, Vol. 31, No. 8, pp. 22–24, February 1993.

Steel is probably the most forgiving of the materials. Many grades are used throughout manufacturing—one grade in car bodies and perhaps another in computer parts. Yet whatever the grade, so similar is the material base that almost all steel scrap streams can contribute to virgin stock manufacturing.

Glass is mainly found in cathode-ray tubes (CRTs). In some recycling operations, it is recovered by dismantling. In others, it is "landfilled" as a whole assembly, used as road-fill, incinerated, or employed as a fuel and material additive in cement kiln processes. In recovery operations, the tubes are sent through proprietary processes to separate and clean the glasses, which have many specific formulations. Some of the glass may be good enough to make new CRTs, while less suitable glass can be used in ceramic insulation or in containers for nuclear waste that utilize the glass's lead content.

Finally, plastics are extracted in hunks by dismantling their host equipment, and then are passed through proprietary identification, separating, and cleaning processes. The flakes of specific plastics thus generated can be remolded into parts similar to the original ones, always provided the sorting process can distinguish among different formulations of incompatible plastics.

Recycled plastics have two obstacles to their reuse. They must often meet strict color matching requirements from manufacturers, and if reclaimed from older electronics, they may contain flame retardants or other additives now being phased out. In the latter case, reuse may even be forbidden. If so, the plastic must be landfilled or incinerated—exactly the opposite of what the public and legislators want to befall these additives. A better alternative is to continue recycling these materials with virgin stocks to dilute the additive content.

Currently, only the most valuable plastics are being recovered from electronics streams. Polycarbonate, for example, which is used in housings and covers, yields a high enough return to make recycling worthwhile, particularly if it is clear. And a few years ago Digital Equipment Corp. and General Electric Plastics announced a program that recycled phenylene oxide into roofing shingles. Most other plastics have not been considered worth their recovery costs, which include dismantling, removing paint or other coatings, and identifying the types of plastic.

The few examples of full material recycling that do exist involve very narrowly defined streams, like telephones. Here, recovery systems were developed and have been tolerably successful because the equipment was traditionally leased and returned in large quantities, a practice that created both the required volumes and the need. The narrowly defined material stream, consisting mostly of one plastic, acrylonitrile butadiene styrene (ABS), also eased recycling.

Apart from telephones, it is rare for large quantities of similar electronic products to be returned through well-established channels. Complete recycling of other types requires a fully integrated approach, one that can generate enough volume to create markets for the motley materials found in electronic equipment. Nonferrous and ferrous metals, for example, can each be sold as composite mixtures, but only at low prices.

FULL CIRCLE. Truly integrated recycling includes the equipment manufacturer, who can play a big part in market development for the recycled materials. Some companies have already recognized the possibilities by mandating recycled-content products. In fact, one of the first closed-loop examples of plastics recycling from durable goods has already occurred in the computer industry. In Britain, IBM Corp. is using plastics from its own discarded keyboards for its new keyboards. It teamed up with its material supplier (GEON) and its recycler (Mann Organisation) in a program to produce high-quality and lower-cost products using post-consumer recycled plastics. It has been demonstrated that 100 percent of post-consumer plastic, polyvinyl chloride (PVC) in this case, can be reused in new parts.

The general approach to hierarchical integrated recycling can be seen in the case studies shown. (Many aspects of the very few integrated systems for electronics recycling in operation today are considered proprietary, but even a cursory overview should suffice to outline the general lines of attack.)

Hierarchical recycling first requires that efficient and organized assessments be made of all incoming equipment. Moreover, because the discards flow in from many sources, the recycler's auditing and accounting systems are a critical part of system and quality control. (The economies of scale vital to the success of an integrated recycler hinge on having customers by the score—the Mann Organisation has almost 100 in the United Kingdom alone.) The incoming equipment, components, and materials are therefore separately credited to the appropriate customers' accounts before being pooled for marketing.

A database is used to log in refurbishable equipment, which is immediately channeled either to the direct brokering activity or to the refurbishing area. The remainder of the equipment—the larger volume—is sent to the initial disassembly area.

Disassembly area employs manual labor,

An IBM keyboard manufactured from post-consumer plastic emerges from a closed-loop recycling system under the scrutiny of chief executive officer Ray Mann of the Mann Organisation and plastic department supervisor Aileen Lear.

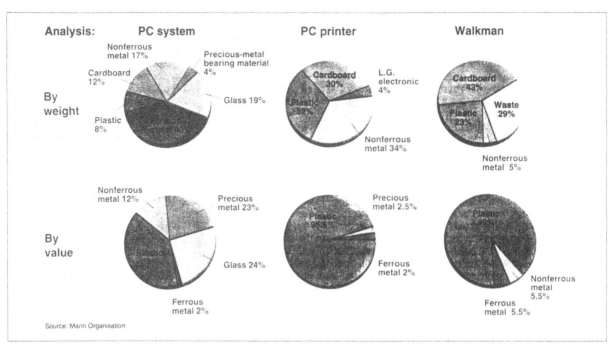

Analysis:	PC system	PC printer	Walkman
By weight	Nonferrous metal 17% · Cardboard 12% · Plastic 8% · Precious-metal bearing material 4% · Glass 19%	Cardboard 30% · Plastic 32% · L.G. electronic 4% · Nonferrous metal 34%	Cardboard 43% · Plastic 23% · Waste 29% · Nonferrous metal 5%
By value	Nonferrous metal 12% · Precious metal 23% · Glass 24% · Ferrous metal 2%	Plastic 93.5% · Precious metal 2.5% · Ferrous metal 2%	Plastic · Nonferrous metal 5.5% · Ferrous metal 5.5%

Source: Mann Organisation

In hierarchical integrated recycling, discarded electronic products are assessed for their diverse material content, which may include precious metals, ferrous and nonferrous metals, cardboard, and plastics. After the item is dismantled and any salvageable components are removed, the different substances can be separately recovered and sold for reuse. The pie charts show the breakdown of the materials used to make three typical electronic products; the personal computer system includes the cathode-ray tube (CRT) in its monitor. CRTs are composed of a variety of special glasses, some of them including lead, and have become possible to recycle into new CRTs only recently, with the development of new processes.

not to break apart the equipment, but to disassemble it neatly and efficiently. Operators are encouraged to suggest improvements because their hands-on experience is a fertile source of development ideas. Disassembly contributes also to environmental design. Because those doing it deal with so many types of equipment, they soon learn what sorts of design practices are most conducive to reverse-manufacturing activities.

Somewhat redundantly, the electronics and materials industries are busy funding design-for-disassembly (or recyclability) projects. Meanwhile the integrated recycler has already compiled much practical knowledge of potential use in electronic equipment design, and this know-how is readily available, particularly to those using the one-stop recycling service. A case in point is the misguided use of clips rather than screws to hold housings together. Well-meaning designers have popularized this practice on the grounds that clips are easier to dismantle, whereas often it is actually harder to pry apart clips than to remove screws with an air-powered tool.

Materials suppliers, manufacturers, recyclers, and others have come up with a number of design guidelines for recycling. Designers should avoid molded-in inserts, paint and metallic coatings, adhesive labels, and potentially hazardous materials. Colors could instead be molded in, and labels could be molded in or mechanically attached. Nor should different kinds of plastic be bonded or firmly attached together or too many ma-

Cathode-ray tubes are dismantled for recycling after the specific types of glass used in them have been identified.

terials be used in the same assembly.

Engineers who break these rules make the recycler's job more difficult, but not impossible. Means of liberating molded-in inserts have been demonstrated and methods of getting rid of coatings exist, but they cost in both economic and environmental terms.

TO PROBE FURTHER. Numerous publications dwell on the importance of considering environmental issues. One of the better books, *Beyond the Limits*, discusses a model that a team of respected scientists and economists developed to describe the impact of continued growth and consumption rates and predicts possible scenarios.

A British journal, *Long Range Planning* (Pergamon Press, Oxford), published an issue in August 1992 that dealt with "Strategic Management of the Environment" and included an article on the recycling of end-of-life electronic equipment:

"Successful Recycling Through Value-Chain Collaboration," by R. Roy and R. C. Whelan.

More information on recycling plastics from electronic equipment appears in papers presented at the 1992 and 1994 Structural Plastics Technical conferences held by the Society for Plastics Industry and printed in the conference proceedings. The first is "The Challenges Associated with Recycling Plastics from Durable Goods," by Michael Biddle and Robert Christy, and the second is "A Mechanical Recycling Process for the Recovery of Plastics from End-of-Life Computer and Business Equipment," by Biddle and Michael M. Fisher. ◆

STANDARDS

Editor: Norman F. Schneidewind, Naval Postgraduate School, Code AS/Ss, Monterey, CA 93943, fax (408) 646-3407
e-mail 0422p@cc.nps.navy.mil

Point/Counterpoint

Safety standards for CRT visual display units

Editor's note: The alleged health hazards of prolonged exposure to computer monitors has engendered much discussion in the industry and in legislative bodies. The articles below represent the viewpoints of J. Robert Ashley, a microwave researcher working on ELF (extremely low frequency) standards, and Fletcher J. Buckley, whose article in the April 1990 issue of Computer *introduced this topic. The authors' opinions do not necessarily represent the views of the IEEE, the IEEE Computer Society, or* Computer *magazine. The editor welcomes submission of additional news and contrasting views for publication in this department.*

 Point

J. Robert Ashley*
IEEE Standards Co-
ordinating Committee
28 and IEEE-USA
Committee on Man
and Radiation

Over the past decade, concern for occupational health of computer data-entry operators has focused on possible effects of electrical quantities. Cathode ray tube (CRT) visual display units (VDUs), also called video display terminals (VDTs), have been questioned.

The peer-reviewed literature through 1989 is evaluated in a 1990 IEEE-USA Entity Position Statement developed by the IEEE-USA Committee on Man and Radiation (COMAR).[1] Epidemiologists have conducted studies on computer data-

---

* Readers can contact Ashley at 2523 Lake Ellen Ln., Tampa, FL 33618, e-mail j.ashley.

entry operators who use VDUs. As pointed out by COMAR, these studies taken as a whole have not found statistically significant health effects that can be attributed to magnetic, electric, or electromagnetic fields.[1] Television receivers use the same CRT electronics; thus, questions about health hazards apply just as much to TVs.

Sapashe and Ashley discuss the electrical measurements required to quantify exposure.[2] The measured VDU fringing magnetic fields for ELF vertical deflection and the very low frequency (VLF) horizontal deflection are incapable of biological effects on human tissue.[2] A suitable method for measuring the AC electric field near the CRT face plate has not been published.

My crude and uncalibrated measurements for the VLF range are of the order of 1/10 kilovolt per meter for VDUs and perhaps 2/10 kV/m for 25-inch color TVs. Similar estimates for the ELF range are 1/3 kV/m for VDUs and 1/2 kV/m for newer TVs with polarized power plugs.

Older TVs in the US can apply the 120-volt, 60-hertz line voltage to the CRT screen to add another 1/2 kV/m at 60 Hz. In terms of measured expo-

sure, the electric field for older TVs has the largest magnitude.

As with all appliances, the magnitudes are significant only within a meter of the center of the appliance. The magnitudes are such that both peak exposure (such as the electric field terminating on a hand as it tunes a TV) and some kind of average (such as along the torso of a VDU operator) must be considered in computing the interaction with human tissue.

No research has been published on lab-tissue studies of VDU electric fields. Difficulties in distinguishing between electric and magnetic fields near VDUs would arise during laboratory animal studies. Thus, we must rely on theoretical physics in estimating safe exposure limits. My current knowledge of the problem indicates that only the ELF electric field near TVs has sufficient magnitude to cause concern about health effects.

Comparison not justified. Some notions about VDUs[3] reported in the trade press are based on unjustified comparison with power-frequency epidemiology studies.[2] My recent discov-

Reprinted from *IEEE Computer*, Vol. 25, No. 9, pp. 68 & 70, September 1992.

eries about the magnitude of electric fields near TVs add another confounder to the epidemiology difficulties: How can one find a control population not exposed to TV fields?

The safety of many uses of electrical energy is addressed in ANSI/IEEE Standard C95.1-1991,[4] which was released in the spring of 1992. As applied to VDUs such as TVs and computer, or workstation, monitors, there are clear guidelines for the VLF region above 3 kHz. Thus, VLF fringing electric and magnetic fields related to the horizontal deflection system and high-voltage power supply are now limited by the guidelines of C95.1-1991.

No IEEE consensus position exists regarding power frequency (50 or 60 Hz) or ELF (3 to 3,000 Hz) electrical safety. A subcommittee of Standards Coordinating Committee 28 was activated in November 1991 to address this region in a new standard. The subcommittee informally expects it will take five years to produce a consensus agreement needed for a true IEEE standard.

In the meantime, I have used theory to extrapolate C95.1-1991 guidelines to the ELF region. Theory would allow increases in the limits in going from VLF to ELF; consequently, my very conservative extrapolation of the VLF limits to ELF is to use the same limits.

Therefore, the current state of knowledge of the biological effects — good or bad — of magnetic intensity, electric potential gradient, or electromagnetic field strength suggests common ELF and VLF maximum permissible exposure (MPE) limits as follows:

- Magnetic intensity: 163 amperes per meter
- Magnetic flux density: 205,000 nanotesla (2,050 milligauss)
- Electric potential gradient: 614 volts per meter
- Induced current: 450 × frequency milliamperes (f in MHz)
- Electromagnetic field strength: Not specified below 100 MHz.

The electromagnetic field strength is not specified below 100 MHz because the wavelength is long enough so that a valid measurement requires measurement of both electric and magnetic fields. Thus, the specification of magnetic intensity and electric potential gradient below 100 MHz is sufficient.

The increased cancer risk associated with ELF electromagnetic fields is about the same as the risk of solar radiation burns from nude moon bathing.

Practically speaking, 765-kV power lines do not radiate biologically significant electromagnetic traveling waves away from transmission lines. Obviously, true ELF or VLF electromagnetic fields near any electrical appliance have no biological effect, good or bad, on nearby people using the appliance.

Older television receivers — primarily those with vacuum-tube electronics — do not meet a portion of the extrapolated MPEs above. Depending on the direction of insertion of the power plug in the US, the CRT face plate or screen can be at either 0 volts or 120 volts at 60 Hz, with respect to ground. Properly measured, the electric potential gradient a few centimeters from the screen exceeds the above limit. Since this is a 60-Hz electric field, experience from the IEEE Power Engineering Society and the Florida Department of Environmental Regulation is worth examining.

Long-standing concern. The safety of high-voltage power lines, particularly for utility workers who repair the lines and control the growth of vegetation on cleared rights-of-way, has been of concern to the IEEE and its forerunners, the American Institute of Electrical Engineers and the Institute of Radio Engineers, from the early days of US electrification. The biological research before 1985 centered on the electric field safety question. The results of all those years of extensive research by engineers and life scientists is distilled into the *National Electrical Safety Code*.[5] The electrical field limit is indirectly specified in terms of vertical clearance rules for overhead power lines.

The utility-regulating agencies of several states have expanded the ANSI C2-1990 vertical clearance rules to include an exposure limit for electric fields. The Florida Electric and Magnetic Fields Rule developed by the Department of Environmental

Regulation is typical.[6] The highest limit listed is 10 kV on the right-of-way for 500-kV power lines. The lowest electric field limit given is 2 kV/m at the edge of any new power line right-of-way. These limits are based on perception of the electric fields and the potential for electrical shock.

ANSI/IEEE 644-1987 adequately discusses the measurement of the quantities related to power frequency safety limits.[7] The electric field measurement methods it discusses are of doubtful use for appliances because the electric field varies so rapidly over the dimensions of the instrument. Also, the instrument significantly perturbs the electric field being measured.

Conclusions. In terms of measured quantities and our knowledge of biological interactions, only the ELF electric fields near VDUs (especially older TVs) have the possibility of a significant biological effect on human tissue. The only comparable exposure to ELF electric fields is near other appliances and transmission power lines. Any frequency magnetic field exposure near VDUs is biologically insignificant. The increased cancer risk associated with ELF electromagnetic fields is about the same as the risk of solar radiation burns from engaging in nude moon bathing.

References

1. *Biological Effects of Electric and Magnetic Fields from Video Display Terminals*, IEEE-USA Entity Position Statement, Aug 13, 1990.

2. D. Sapashe and J.R. Ashley, "Video Display Terminal Fringing Magnetic Field Measurements," *IEEE Trans. Instrumentation and Measurement*, Vol. 41, No. 3, Apr. 1992, pp. 178-184.

3. P. Brodeur, "The Magnetic Field Menace," *MacWorld*, July 1990, pp. 136-145.

4. *IEEE Standard Safety Levels with Respect to Human Exposure to Radio Frequency Electromagnetic Fields, 3 kHz to 300 GHz*, ANSI/IEEE C95.1-1991, IEEE, New York, Apr. 27, 1992.

5. *Nat'l Electrical Safety Code*, ANSI/IEEE C2-1990, IEEE, New York, Aug. 1, 1989.

6. Florida Electric and Magnetic Fields Rule, Florida Administrative Code, Chapter 17-274.

7. *IEEE Standard Procedures for Measurement of Power-Frequency Electric and Magnetic Fields from AC Power Lines*, ANSI/IEEE 644-1987, IEEE, New York, Mar. 16, 1987.

Research council reviews EMF

The National Research Council (NRC) in October completed a three-year review of some 500 studies related to the health effects of electromagnetic fields (EMF). It concluded, among other things, that there exist:

• A robust statistical link between childhood leukemia and wire-code ratings (which researchers use to relate the distance of a home from electric power distribution lines, their size, and current capacity to levels of EMF in the home).

• No link between the incidence of childhood leukemia and present-day measurements of electromagnetic fields in a home.

• A moderately consistent, statistically significant association of leukemia and brain cancer with indirect measurements of occupational exposure to magnetic fields.

• No biologically plausible, proven explanation linking exposure to electromagnetic fields to an adverse effect in animals or humans.

• No convincing evidence that exposure to 60-Hz electric and magnetic fields causes cancer in animals.

• Convincing evidence that low-frequency pulsed magnetic fields greater than 5 gauss are associated with bone-healing responses in animals.

• Some laboratory evidence that animals treated with carcinogens show a positive relationship between intense magnetic-field exposure and the incidence of breast cancer.

These are not necessarily contradictory findings. Perhaps some factor independent of power distribution lines but statistically associated with their presence contributes to childhood leukemia. Suppose, say, a certain species of owl that prefers to nest near large power poles carries a virus that triggers leukemia. However, most of the obvious of suspects, like the age of homes, the socioeconomic status of residents, and air pollution, have been investigated already and have not been found to change the study results.

As for the animal and tissue research, the report noted that it contains much unconfirmed or controversial data, and the studies to date have failed to identify a mechanism by which electromagnetic fields may act on the body.

How all this is to be interpreted is a matter of individual judgment. While the NRC committee's 16 members agreed to the report as written, how it was presented to the press proved a matter of some dispute. The official press release of Oct. 31 highlighted the fact that "no clear, convincing evidence exists to show that residential exposures to electric and magnetic fields are a threat to human health."

But a separate press release, issued the same day by the Bioelectromagnetics Society on behalf of three members of the committee, stated that the report's most important aspect "is that it establishes that even under the strictest possible standards of proof, there is a reliable, though low, statistical association between power lines and at least one form of cancer." It cautioned "against taking the attitude that a lack of confirmed proof at this point in the study of EMF effects mean that the question can be ignored."

In fact, committee members had diverse opinions. Chairman Charles F. Stevens told *IEEE Spectrum*, "If you were to ask them now if, when we know everything, EMFs are a health hazard, you would find a spectrum of opinion ranging from yes, probably, to no, certainly not."

What next? The report suggested several areas where further research might prove useful. "It is quite likely," it said, "that, at least in the near term, only further epidemiological research can more strongly implicate or exonerate magnetic fields." A look at exposures in day-care centers or schools, and a study of children with high exposure to sources other than outdoor distribution lines might be fruitful, it indicated.

Refinements in field measurement are also called for, it said. For example, instrumentation is needed that can measure changes in magnetic-field strength on the order of every 0.1 second, rather than today's once every few seconds. A standard method of measuring transient currents should also be developed, the report indicated. How grounding system currents vary as a function of distance from substations also would be useful to interpret the wire-code based studies, it stated.

In the biological arena, the NRC report suggested several promising avenues of research, including clarifying the mechanisms by which field exposure helps bone healing, investigating the reported effects of fields on gene expression, rigorously investigating the development of mammary tumors in animals exposed to magnetic fields, and studying why electromagnetic fields seem to affect the levels of the hormone melatonin in animals (an effect not reproduced in humans). —*Tekla S. Perry*

Reprinted from *IEEE Spectrum*, Vol. 34, No. 1, p. 98, January 1997.

Running out of resources

As economic challenges confront the entire world, the IEEE has a unique opportunity to help on both local and global levels

lthough many people reject the idea, humanity's future will be largely shaped by the zero-sum nature (at best) of the world economy. Since that economy is rooted in the continued exploitation of resources that are both finite and nonrenewable, any time one individual or group gets more of something, some other individual or group must necessarily get less: hence the term *zero sum*.

Supply-side economists scoff at this notion, maintaining that the economic pie can be made to grow indefinitely through human ingenuity and effort. According to them, everyone on earth can aspire to increasing material wealth and prosperity.

One reason that the zero-sum nature of the world economy is not evident to some skeptics is that the developed nations have gotten where they are by ignoring it—by exploiting cheaply available natural resources as if they were inexhaustible. Unfortunately, the developing nations will not be able to follow that example. As the cheap resources disappear, growth cannot continue in the same way, and the pie could shrink drastically—especially on a per capita basis.

Why is it appropriate to discuss this matter in the flagship publication of the IEEE? Because the Institute, through its constitution, has charged itself with a noble goal—namely, to promote understanding of the influence of technology on the public welfare of the entire world.

That goal has never been more apposite. It makes clear the proposition that the Institute's view of the implications of technology, as well as its benefits, cannot be confined to a narrow scope based on any country's national interest, but must represent the IEEE global constituency.

DISTURBING EVIDENCE. Of all nations, the United States is probably the most competent at wresting economic gain from the

Raymond S. Larsen   ASA Instruments Inc.

environment. Yet, even here, the timber industry is dying as the prime old-growth forests are running out and raw logs are exported to be milled overseas; the fishing industry on both East and West coasts has been devastated by dredge-net fleets from around the world; and farmlands in the heartland are being drained of their natural riches, with the result that crops increasingly depend on expensive chemical fertilizers.

In consequence, prices have climbed so high that the large middle class now requires two wage earners to support the same family that was easily supported by one wage earner in the '50s. If that is what is happening in the most technologically advanced country in the world, the implications for the less advanced are grim indeed.

John G. Clark, in his 1990 book, *The Political Economy of World Energy*, shows that in 1987 the United States consumed a total of 10 436 petajoules of energy [see figure]. (A petajoule—10^{15} joules—is the energy content of approximately 175 000 barrels of oil.) Although the detailed patterns of energy consumption vary from region to region around the world, two facts are undeniable: the bulk of the world's energy comes from irreplaceable fossil fuels, and growth in the less developed areas is proceeding at a greater relative pace than in

> Today, most applied economics is aimed at supporting an unachievable model: unlimited growth

the more industrialized regions.

Clearly, as underdeveloped countries begin to expand their economies, the rate of consumption worldwide will accelerate. What is needed are substitutes for the rapidly disappearing fossil fuels, which currently supply a full 90 percent of our total energy needs.

The most suitable substitute would be nuclear power were it not for its high cost and unresolved waste management problems. Others, like solar, geothermal, wind, and hydroelectric power, cannot even meet the bulk of present needs, let alone those of the future.

Comments are invited

The editors of *IEEE Spectrum* recognize that some of the ideas in this article may be controversial, but feel that the subject is of critical importance. We are publishing it, therefore, in the hope of stimulating an exchange of ideas on the several topics discussed by the author. Readers are encouraged to send their comments to Michael J. Riezenman, Senior Editor, at *IEEE Spectrum*, 345 East 47th St., New York, NY 10017. Alternatively, responses may be transmitted to the *Spectrum* electronic bulletin board at 212-705-7308 (1200-N-8-1) or faxed to 212-705-7453.

Perhaps the brightest hope for the future is fusion electric power generation, with its relative absence of harmful radiation waste products. However, the technology is proving to be very difficult to exploit. Though great strides have been made, researchers have been unable to sustain a fusion reaction, let alone build a practical generator.

The IEEE's present position paper on fusion energy supports a government goal for a demonstration of practical power production by the year 2025, and the first commercially viable on-line plant by the year 2040. During those 50 years, energy efficiency to extend the use of natural resources is expected to become ever more critical, especially for home and for automobiles.

WATER CRISES. Water, too, can be added to the list of depletables, along with oil, gas, and coal, which have been exploited at low cost in the past to support economic growth. In her article last year in *World Magazine*, Diane Ward shows how much of the fresh water consumed by mankind throughout the world is provided by deep aquifers [see To probe further, p. 45].

One vital aquifer runs under parts of the Sahara desert. Another, the Ogallala, runs under eight thirsty states in the U.S. Southwest, and waters one-fifth of the irrigated cropland in the United States.

These aquifers have been charged over hundreds and even thousands of years by river and stream seepage and by rainfall. Not only are the aquifers being depleted by excessive pumping ("water ranching" has become a big business in the Southwest United States), but their sources, such as the Colorado River system, have been exploited to the point where their ability to replenish the aquifers has been seriously compromised.

Reprinted from *IEEE Spectrum*, Vol. 30, No. 7, pp. 43–45, July 1993.

Patterns of energy consumption in four industrialized regions

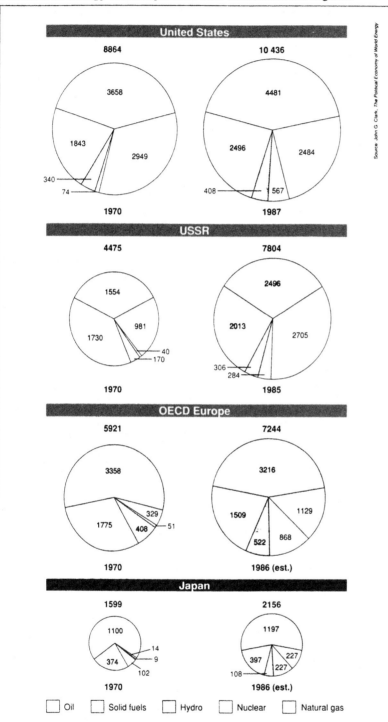

Source: John G. Clark, *The Political Economy of World Energy*

Consumption of fossil fuels [shown in these pie charts in petajoules] is increasing. Although these fuels form a smaller fraction of the energy pies now than in the past, the pies are getting larger. Note that energy consumption is increasing fastest in the least developed areas. The Soviet Union's consumption grew by 74 percent over the studied period, while that of the United States went up by only 18 percent. The figures for Japan and the European member nations of the Organization for Economic Cooperation and Development increased by 35 and 22 percent, respectively. Those numbers suggest that global consumption will accelerate rapidly as the Third World becomes more industrialized. (A petajoule—10^15 joules—is the energy contained in approximately 175 000 barrels of oil.)

A side effect of depletion is the inevitable collapse of the mined-out aquifers, destroying them top-down forever for future generations, as well as damaging the surface extensively.

Obviously, fresh water can be extracted from the oceans, but only at a high cost in capital equipment and energy. Large population centers in most countries of the world will face increasing or even critical shortages in the near future. In several areas, the cost of water is about to soar.

TECHNOLOGY TO THE RESCUE? Notwithstanding these shortages, technology proponents are predicting that science will come to the rescue. They are confident that substitutes will be found for the exhaustible natural resources: artificial fibers for cotton to make clothing, the paperless society to save the trees, and solar-powered vehicles and fusion-generated electricity to circumvent depletion of fossil fuels and the attendant pollution. To do any good, these advances have to begin now; yet they remain as concepts and research projects, some of which predictably will not succeed.

Unfortunately, technology, which drives the world economy, has no ethics of its own. Moreover, it is incapable of transcending the very laws that govern it, most obviously the second law of thermodynamics, which in effect states that everything comes at a cost.

Worse yet, thanks to technology, humanity is able to exploit the irreplaceable at an ever-faster pace, creating temporary wealth for a privileged few among the world's people. Instant worldwide communications, the facsimile machine, and that latest scourge of the superhighways—the car phone—are all aimed at getting an even faster jump on competitors, thus further accelerating the depletion of natural resources.

In the short run, the illusion of creating something out of nothing at no cost holds up just fine. All participants can prosper as long as the forests hold out, the fish still run, the oil still flows, the gold is still mined, the ground is still rich, the water does not run out, and the air remains clean.

But this approach just taps a long list of finite—not infinite—resources. All the resources to be tapped may not have been discovered yet. Some may even be manufactured artificially in the future, at the expense of, at a minimum, energy. But the underlying fact remains: *the world's critical resources, all of them, are being exhausted.*

Over the long term, the evidence suggests that the world economy is inevitably a negative-sum game—that is, real global wealth will decline, forcing growing economic disparity among nations, as well as among citizens within a nation. Until strong evidence to the contrary emerges—possibly, but improbably, in the form of major scientific breakthroughs—it will be prudent to calculate the sums very carefully. Within the IEEE, it behooves us as technologists to apply our best intellects to the technical issues and our best social instincts toward planning our future. And as purveyors of technology, we should recognize our responsibilities toward global humanity.

Technology will have an even greater effect on our future than it has had on our past. Properly applied, it can help enormously toward developing ways to live in a negative-sum world. Misapplied, it can hasten a global crisis. But in either case, it cannot change the sign of the equation.

THE TECHNOLOGISTS' BURDEN. At the core of any economic debate lies technology—what it can do, and what it cannot; both its promises and its limits must be recognized. Technologists are needed in the core debate, but they must be armed with much more than just technical knowledge and personal opinion. And they must contribute as a group, rather than as hired guns to support one preconceived political view or another.

We technologists in the IEEE and elsewhere need to acquaint ourselves with both the economic discussion and the political tools used in attempts to manage economics on behalf of the nation. This will be a drastic change, but a necessary one, for a group that traditionally lets economists and politicians do its thinking in these areas.

Today, most applied economics is aimed at supporting an unachievable economic model: unlimited growth. Also, economists ultimately work for others whose agenda is to do the best they can for their constituents. This is interpreted to mean more material wealth for all the people within a nation. But it is impossible to have more for all, even within a nation, let alone among nations. Therefore, the need to face reality, and to insist that our planners do so, is paramount.

Another need is to focus on transnational economic models because without them the solutions reached will be nonsensical. Rich nations will be reluctant to do this, but unless they do, the model is doomed to failure. Also, more than ever, we need to question the moral and ethical implications of technical-economic decisions as they affect others worldwide. This is perhaps not much different in principle from examining those decisions within a nation, but it is much more challenging.

If the world economy is really a zero-sum or negative-sum proposition, there is no longer an *us* and a *them*; there is only *us*.

IEEE'S ROLE. As a transnational organization, the IEEE has a tremendously diverse constituency, encompassing a wide range of social and economic structures. It should call upon its members to contribute toward debate, the development of a consensus, public and self-education, and future planning. To be effective, it needs to create both an internal structure and external relationships that reflect its transnational character.

The Institute must become informed in both economics and politics, so that it can become a useful part of the interdisciplinary team required to address these broad problems. No longer is it enough to explain technological tradeoffs to decision-makers and then retreat to the comfort of the laboratory. The decision-makers must be held accountable to the public interest. The IEEE must be not just an observer or a lobbyist, but a partner in leadership as well.

Within the framework of addressing global issues vital to the future of humankind, the engineering and scientific entrepreneurial communities need to be challenged. We must learn how to participate and how to use the tools of both technology and politics to do so; but we also need to rise

> The IEEE must be not just an observer or a lobbyist, but a partner in leadership as well

above regional or national politics.

Building a consensus among ourselves is necessary, but at the same time we have to expand our horizons as part of a team dedicated to solving global problems. Not only must we explain the technology-cost tradeoffs of a traditional growth-economy model, but we should point out the technological, societal, and ecological cost tradeoffs of zero-sum or negative-sum models, which more accurately represent the future.

These are issues that every IEEE member, and every aspiring IEEE member, should be called upon to consider. The Institute has a challenging role to play in making this happen. Along with our continuing emphasis on education and professionalism, these global issues should be our dominant theme for the future.

TO PROBE FURTHER. For an excellent review of the various factors contributing to the world's economic problems and proposed solutions, including the role of technology, three books by economist Lester Thurow of the Massachusetts Institute of Technology are recommended: *The Zero-Sum Society* (Viking Penguin, New York, 1981), *The Zero-Sum Solution* (Touchstone, New York, 1986), and *Head to Head: The Coming Economic Battle Among Japan, Europe, and America* (William Morrow & Co., New York, 1992).

John G. Clark gives a good overview of the development of the modern energy mix, and the political-economic reasons driving the choices that have been made, in *The Political Economy of World Energy: A Twentieth Century Perspective* (University of North Carolina Press, Chapel Hill, 1990).

Bernard L. Cohen's defense of nuclear power's relative safety, "Reducing the Hazards of Nuclear Power: Insanity in Action," is to be found in the July 1987 issue of *Physics and Society*, pp. 2–4.

The IEEE positions on various energy issues can be obtained from IEEE-United States Activities, Energy Policy Committee, Washington, DC; 202-785-0017.

Diane Ward's article "Water's Worth" appeared in *World Magazine*, Vol. 26, no. 2, pp. 20–35, published by KPMG Peat Marwick, New York, 1992.

A collection of discussions on sustainable societies can be found in *Preparing for a Sustainable Society*, Proceedings of the Interdisciplinary Conference, Ryerson Polytechnical Institute, Toronto, June 21–22, 1991. Conference co-sponsors included the IEEE Society on Social Implications of Technology and the IEEE Toronto Section.

For an overview of the planet's ecological crises, see Vice President Al Gore's highly readable book, *Earth in the Balance: Healing the Global Environment* (Houghton Mifflin Co., Boston, 1992). Some people regard Gore as an alarmist, but his warnings are mild compared with the apocalyptic outlook of Herbert Gruhl, whose book *Ein Planet Wird Geplündert* is available only in German (Fischer Taschenbuch, Frankfurt am Main, 1992; U.S. residents will probably prefer to obtain it from Albert J. Phiebig Books, White Plains, NY). A translation of the short essay "Mankind is at an End," which appeared in *Der Spiegel*, no. 113, 1992, is available from the author.

A classic paper, "World Population Growth and Related Technical Problems," by Arthur L. Austin and John W. Brewer, discusses the global ecological effects of the population explosion. It appeared in *IEEE Spectrum*, December 1970, pp. 43–54.

For a sociologist's view of the role of associations in a democratic society, see Robert N. Bellah et al., *Habits of the Heart: Individualism and Commitment in American Life* (Harper Collins Publishers Inc., New York, 1986). The title comes from an expression used by Alexis de Tocqueville in *Democracy in America*, his classic commentary on the developing U.S. society. ◆

A second look at . . .

...running out of resources

Last July, IEEE Spectrum published an article entitled "Running out of resources" [pp. 43–45], in which author Raymond S. Larsen voiced his concern about the accelerating pace at which the earth's resources are being consumed. More specifically, he pointed out that IEEE members, if only because of our Constitution, have a special obligation to consider the effects of technology on our environment, and to air their concerns for the public good.

Because of the possibly controversial nature of some of Larsen's ideas, the editors of Spectrum *explicitly invited comments on the article. And we received a fair number. By regular mail, e-mail, and fax, some 44 readers from around the world have shared their thoughts with us. This is a summary of their responses.*

Overall, we would categorize 28 of the responses as agreeing with Larsen, and 16 as disagreeing. But those numbers may be misleading since not everyone who agreed with him agreed with everything he said, and some who disagreed with his analysis nevertheless found themselves in substantial accord with one or more of his conclusions.

As editors, we were pleased to learn that 15 of the responders explicitly stated that they felt it was appropriate for *Spectrum* to address such issues, and said that they looked forward to more articles on related topics. One reader, George D. Hathaway of Toronto, went so far as to claim that the piece was "...the most important article yet published in *Spectrum*...."

Eleanor V. Goodall of Enschede, the Netherlands, was happy that the IEEE chose to publish the article. "Those who are familiar with the possibilities and limitations of technology must not only share their knowledge but also educate themselves about other, nontechnological, approaches to solving the problem of diminishing resources," she said.

On the other side of the fence, Douglas J. Hackenbruch of Trinity, NC, urged us to stick to engineering. "You only have so much energy and talent. Don't waste it on the unscientific social sciences," he said.

Bertil Ohlsson of Västerås, Sweden, found it "...difficult *not* to agree with his [Larsen's] analysis...but I still cannot support his view that IEEE should become what he calls 'a partner in leadership.' The reason is simply that this would transform IEEE into a sort of transnational political party." To do so, Ohlsson felt, would be to jeopardize the Institute's position as a "respected organization and a powerful base for promoting an understanding of technology."

Virgil I. Johannes of Holmdel, NJ, went further and protested "formally and forcefully" against the article. He felt that, since *Spectrum* published it, "...I think you have an obligation to solicit and publish an equal length article...presenting the case for economic growth, human resourcefulness, the market system, and freedom." We agree, and hope to publish such an article in the near future.

MARKET FORCES. So much for counting noses. What were some of the substantive points made by our correspondents? On the con side, the most common comment was a statement of belief that the operation of the marketplace would deal with matters adequately. As W. Alan Burris of Pittsford, NY, put it, "[Julian] Simon points out that if natural resources are becoming scarcer, then resource prices such as the price per pound of copper, should be rising in constant dollars. Yet for decades and centuries, the prices of natural resources have declined, and known reserves have increased. Known reserves of fossil fuels are sufficient for hundreds of years at present rates of consumption, and discovery and extraction methods are constantly improved. And there seems to be an unlimited supply of Malthusian-type doomsday prophets."

Stephen Fleming of Franklin, TN, would agree. He found Larsen's piece "so incredi-

> *'In the most important article yet published in* Spectrum...*, Raymond Larsen alerts us to the coming resource crises...'*

bly shortsighted as to stagger belief." Its main thesis—that one man's gain is another's loss—he called "demonstrably false." In support of his position, he said, "After the Arab oil crunch, we were told that we had as little as 50 years of petroleum left; today, we have 500 years of proven reserves."

POPULATION PROBLEM. Among those who agreed with Larsen, the most common feeling expressed was gratitude for broaching the subject and opening it up for debate. Dave Collins of Pleasantville, NY, for example, said that "As an IEEE member, I am proud of you for stepping up to the challenge of addressing these critical issues, and I hope to see more on this in future issues of *Spectrum*." But he felt that the article had one serious omission: "[Larsen] does not even mention the engine that is driving the need for unlimited growth: unlimited population growth. As long as there is no accepted cap on world population, there can be no cap on resource utilization."

Collins was not alone in his assessment. Emil C. Evancich of Carmel, IN, considered overpopulation to be "the most serious problem the world faces." And P. Paxton Marshall of Charlottesville, VA, opined, "He [Larsen] may not be right on every point, but bold and even speculative assertions are needed to counteract the conspiracy of silence on long-term resource and population issues."

Some who agreed with Larsen's statement of the problem considered that he nevertheless had too pessimistic an outlook. Others found him too optimistic. Sid Deutsch of Tampa, FL, for example, doubts that Americans have the will to change their wasteful ways.

"Regretfully, I for one do not believe that people will pay much attention to Larsen and the other prophets of doom," Deutsch wrote. "Anybody who travels knows that gasoline abroad typically costs $4 a gallon, while in the United States we pay close to $1 a gallon, yet it is political suicide to vote for a substantial gasoline tax increase.... 'Tis the nature of the beast to drink and be merry, without an effective global plan for the future because, in the end, it will all be gone anyway when the sun blows up."

James Mathieu of Danvers, MA, who considers Larsen's article "a religious attempt to influence technology," would seem to agree. He believes that "mankind does not have either the capacity or will to save the earth's natural resources."

Several readers wrote in with detailed—sometimes exceedingly detailed—plans for solving the resource problem. David R. Criswell of Houston, TX, for example, told us about a lunar solar power system in which sunlight impinging on the moon would be converted to microwaves and then beamed to earth.

At another technological extreme, Tan Kuan Soon of Singapore sent in a very detailed analysis of a scheme in which electricity would be generated by animal power. The plan, which would be most appropriate in third-world countries, has the advantage of raising food and producing power at the same time.

Such plans deserve more space than we are able to give them in this follow-up arti-

Reprinted from *IEEE Spectrum*, Vol. 30, No. 11, pp. 11–13, November 1993.

A second look

cle; we hope to treat them at greater length in the future.

R.S. Larsen responds: I can understand why members who expect only technical and engineering topics to be covered in *Spectrum* reacted negatively to one that cannot be considered with scientific rigor. But I believe that bringing up the issues—even if my arguments were imperfect—was valuable.

The main questions I wanted to open for discussion were whether there are inherent natural limits to economic growth, and whether the IEEE should be more active in looking at how its technology affects those limitations. That said, let me respond briefly to some of the readers who disagreed with me.

Stephen Fleming simply states that everything I say is wrong, everybody knows it except me, and we have gone

'Raymond Larsen's article in the July issue is so incredibly shortsighted as to stagger belief'

from a 50-year to a 500-year oil reserve since the 1973 oil crisis. I don't know where he found those figures, but they do not tally with any I have seen. For example, a recent study by the World Energy Council, a nongovernmental organization representing more than 100 countries, said that reserves of oil and gas will start to run dry by the middle of the next century, according to the *Financial Times* of Sept. 15, 1993.

Furthermore, the World Bank's *World Development Report 1992* concludes that "All told, fossil fuel resources are probably sufficient to meet world energy demands for the next century, perhaps longer." Since more than half of those fossil fuel resources are coal, the two reports appear to be in substantial agreement: the world of today has about a 50-year reserve of oil and gas.

And finally, John G. Clark, in his book *The Political Economy of World Energy*, states that oil consumption from 1973 through 1987 averaged about 2.8 teragrams annually (Table 7.4, p. 246). After the considerable additional exploration that followed the 1973 crisis, total global reserves were estimated (in 1986) to be 100 Tg—less than a 50-year supply (p. 323). All the new discoveries made between 1973 and 1986 increased the world supply by only 5–10 percent. Moreover, the new oil will cost more to produce because it is located in more hostile areas.

Fleming has a simple solution—find

more of everything, in outer space if necessary. The question he fails to consider is: will the growing world economy and an increasing global population force a crisis before this becomes feasible? Contrary to Fleming's belief, world hunger is not just the occasional famines we read about in our newspapers, but a much more insidious and pervasive problem.

Marvin King and W. Alan Burris state that if materials are or come to be in short supply, prices will be bid up, and we will be motivated to find substitutes. That is what I thought was supposed to happen, too. But when it comes to oil, things clearly do not work that way, and that is what worries me.

To quote Clark again, "During the course of my research, I learned that political explanations are more useful than economic in understanding energy transactions. Prices of energy are constantly manipulated by companies and/or governments to achieve institutional goals, and have little to do with the actual cost of anything." He cites the 1989 Exxon Valdez affair, which affected only Exxon's supplies—and those only marginally—but became the excuse for all companies to raise oil prices all over the United States. Later that month, "...Exxon blamed American motorists and [OPEC] for the sudden rise in price."

It does not necessarily follow, as my critics seem to believe, that since prices have not been bid up, resources are not in danger. At least in the critical case of fossil fuel energy, this view can be challenged.

James O. Hill wonders at my lukewarm support of nuclear energy. I believe that increased nuclear energy generation will be needed and there are signs it is already taking place. Hill makes a valid point that nuclear power generation has been held to a higher standard of waste management than other industries, but that, of course, is for good reason.

James Brandt accuses me of misappropriating Lester Thurow. I cited Thurow not to support my theories, but because he discusses an aspect of zero sum—that of the distribution of wealth at a given point in time. Clearly, economies have grown, and equally clearly, the cost of raw ingredients is a minor part of the equation, with the one important exception of energy. My contention is that growth will continue as long as we remain able to fuel it. At some point it will level off and then decline as competition for energy and global population growth combine to increase the pressure on the nonrenewables. I cited Thurow because he has written well about many of the same issues that concern me. *[Editor's note: Thurow was given an opportunity to review Larsen's manuscript, but declined, explaining that he was too busy to do so.]*

Richard Plourde believes that none of these problems will become an issue for

millions of years. I would be most delighted if that were true. Plourde thinks I am advocating a regimented approach to problem solving. I am not. But neither do I have a blind faith that all will be well by and by.

In November 1992, a group of 1575 scientists, including 99 Nobel laureates, issued the statement, "World Scientists Warning to Humanity," which addressed a wide range of issues, including the environment, energy, global population growth, poverty, women's equality, and war. "No more than a few decades remain before the chance to avert the threats we now confront will be lost and the prospects for humanity immeasurably diminished....Pressures from unrestrained population growth...can overwhelm any efforts to achieve a sustainable future."

Henry Kendall, chairman of the Union of Concerned Scientists, noted that "This kind of consensus is truly unprecedented. There is an exceptional degree of agreement within the international scientific community that natural systems can no longer absorb the burden of current human practices" (AP, Nov. 18, 1992).

Claude L. Emmerich believes that recycling will solve all problems. I agree that recycling can solve many problems, and is a key to future sustainability. But some things—oil, for example—really do get used up, once and for all. And having unlimited energy in the universe is very different from being able to tap into it at an acceptable cost and risk. Nuclear energy, for example, may prove to be too expensive, too risky, or quite possibly both.

Finally, Douglas J. Hackenbruch advocates that the IEEE keep its nose to the grindstone of technology and leave these issues to nonscientists. To whom, I would ask? To politicians, most of whom are trained as attorneys, and whose overwhelming agenda is to be re-elected? To economists, who rarely agree with each other, and whose record leaves much to be desired? To corporate leaders, who seem obsessed with the short-term goal of returning "bottom-line" results, and who increasingly view employees as a commodity to be exploited and then disposed of?

If we do not cultivate a healthy dissatisfaction with the status quo, we will go nowhere. Some say we should become involved with the issues, but only as individuals. I disagree. The responses to this article have shown enormous disagreement on such basic facts as the extent of global oil reserves. If we speak out individually without first resolving such basic discrepancies among ourselves, we will only cause more confusion. A planned effort, intended not to introduce regimented thinking but to establish a body of facts that we all can share, is what I advocate.

Michael J. Riezenman   Senior Editor

Chapter 10

Striving for Fairness

10.1 Introduction

ONE common generally accepted definition of fairness is "equality of opportunity." A system that presents equality of opportunity to all individuals would be blind to any factor not directly related to an individual's performance. However, although it is typically easy to agree on general principles of fairness in the abstract, it is often nearly impossible to reach the same level of consensus on how to *apply* these principles.

In recognition of that struggle, I have tried to establish a framework for considering issues of fairness and discrimination that (hopefully) supports a high level of consensus. Within that framework, I consider both issues in the large—how society has come to view fairness and discrimination—and issues in the small—what individuals can do to foster the concepts of fairness and nondiscrimination. I urge you to become familiar with the federal laws that govern behavior in this important area. The last two reprints of the chapter describe the equal opportunity laws and the Family and Medical Leave Act. The essence of the equal opportunity laws will seem familiar to most of you, but the Family and Medical Leave Act is relatively new and still not widely understood [19]. Basically, it requires companies that employ 50 or more people to allow an employee to take up to 12 weeks of *unpaid* leave per year for allowed reasons. To be eligible, the person must have been an employee for at least one year and worked at least 1250 hours in the previous 12 months. Allowed reasons for leave include personal or family medical problems. Family is defined to include parents, children, and spouse. It does not include the spouse's parents or "domestic partners."

10.2 A Brief Historical Perspective

The history of U.S. society may seem to be an odd topic for a book on ethics. However, to understand current issues of social controversy, it is helpful to view them in the historical context of their origin. Many students studying computing at the college level have received their early education outside the United States and so are not familiar at all with U.S. history. Even students who have had their precollege education in the United States may be a bit rusty on the details. Such details put the diversity inherent in the United States into a more meaningful perspective.

What is now the United States of America began as a group of colonies of the British Empire. As you might expect given this beginning, the positions of power in the early United States were mostly occupied by people of western European descent. The population also consisted of Native Americans and people from Africa, most of whom–but not all–had been imported to work as slaves. As individual state governments were created, all but South Carolina and Georgia prohibited the import of slaves. Massachusetts went further and outlawed the ownership of slaves. Women in New Jersey had the right to vote, though only temporarily as it turned out. Tax-supported churches in New York and the Southern states were done away with, and religious freedom generally increased, relative to that in many European countries. The early United States had many social problems clearly visible to us today, but for its time, it was literally a revolutionary place. It offered, at least to its white male citizens, much greater freedom and social mobility than the "old" society.

The Declaration of Independence announced to the world that the new United States was to be considered independent from England. An early section of the Declaration of Independence contains the following sentence, which should be familiar to most U.S. citizens:

> We hold these truths to be self-evident, that all men are created equal; that they are endowed by their Creator with certain unalienable rights; that among these, are life, liberty and the pursuit of happiness.

United States history demonstrates a continual broadening of this ideal to include all people. The truth, and difficulty, of this should be evident in the sequence of events outlined below.

The Thirteenth Amendment to the Constitution, adopted in 1865, states

> Neither slavery nor involuntary servitude, except as punishment for crime whereof the party shall have been duly convicted, shall exist within the United States, or any place subject to their jurisdiction.

The passing of an amendment to the Constitution is of course not immediately reflected in the hearts and minds of all people. One history text describes the situation as follows [5]:

> . . . Northern opinion was aroused by the so-called Black Codes, which the Southern legislatures adopted during the sessions of 1865–66. These measures were the South's solution for the problem of the free Negro laborer, and they were also the South's substitute for slavery as a white-supremacy device. They all authorized local officials to apprehend unemployed Negroes, fine them for vagrancy, and hire them out to employers to satisfy the fine. . . . In April (1866) Congress struck at the Black Codes by passing the Civil Rights Bill, which made United States citizens of Negroes and empowered the Federal government to intervene in state affairs when necessary for protecting the rights of its citizens. . . .

The Fifteenth Amendment to the Constitution, adopted in 1870, states

> The right of the citizens to vote shall not be denied or abridged by the United States or by any State on account of race, color, or previous condition of servitude.

However, poll taxes, literacy tests, and other qualifications were used to create barriers to voter registration. The 1960s saw another major push on the front of voting rights. There is still a great deal of ongoing debate in this area. However, the debate now is not so much about personal voting rights as the results, or lack of results, for groups of people.

In 1896, the U.S. Supreme Court ruled, in the case of *Plessy* v. *Ferguson,* that a state could enforce segregation in facilities if the facilities were equal. This is the origin of the "separate but equal" doctrine that held until overturned in 1954. This doctrine allowed state-enforced separation of public facilities and accommodations (such as schools, restaurants, hotels, and public water fountains).

The Nineteenth Amendment to the Constitution, adopted in 1920, states

> The right of the citizens of the United States to vote shall not be denied or abridged by the United States or by any State on account of sex.

In 1954, in the case of *Brown* v. *Board of Education of Topeka,* the Supreme Court ruled that "equal protection of the laws" did *not* allow "separate but equal." To quote from the unanimous opinion of the court, "We conclude that in the field of public education the doctrine of 'separate but equal' has no place. Separate educational facilities are inherently unequal."

The Twenty-fourth Amendment to the Constitution, adopted in 1964, states

> The right of the citizens of the United States to vote in any primary or other election for President or Vice President, for electors for President or Vice President, or for Senator or Representative in Congress, shall not be denied or abridged by the United States or by any State by reason of failure to pay any poll tax or any other tax.

Congress also passed the Civil Rights Act of 1964, which strengthened voting rights, expedited desegregation of schools, and prohibited discrimination in public facilities and private employment. This was the core of the "civil rights movement" of the time. Bus boycotts and lunch-counter sit-ins became tools of the movement. A "bus boycott" meant not riding the buses in a system that made people of your race sit in the back of the bus or give up their seat to people of a different race. A "lunch-counter sit-in" meant taking a seat at a place where meals were served, though not to people of your race, and refusing to leave.

What should you take away from this short historical

DILBERT © UFS

review? First, equality of opportunity is meant to apply to all persons, regardless of race, religion, sex, or disability. This is the common moral and ethical view in our society and is supported by the legal system. Second, it should be clear that the concept of equality of opportunity has broadened over time. The society and its legal system at one time explicitly enforced open and blatant discrimination against women and minorities. Progress toward the goal of equal opportunity for all citizens should be clear. However, different people may reasonably have different perspectives on the pace and the techniques used to achieve progress. For example, to a 20 year old, the Civil Rights Act of 1964 may seem like remote history. To a 50 year old, it is almost certainly a vividly remembered part of personal experience. Neither person could hope to truly understand the other's perception. Similarly, it is important to keep in mind that many U.S. citizens have only recently come here and may feel (with justification) that arguments about historical discrimination or advantage are irrelevant to them.

10.3 UNDERREPRESENTATION

The computing professional may be tempted to imagine that problems of harassment and discrimination occur only in "other areas" of society. This is of course wrong. Such problems arise in all areas of our society. In some ways, the most difficult problems are those that arise when there is no identifiable explicit discrimination even though there are clear indications that not all types of people are represented in a certain area of opportunity. This sort of situation is typically described with the relatively neutral term "underrepresentation."

10.3.1 Among PhDs in Computing

As an example of how underrepresentation can occur in all areas of society, I present some statistics on the production and employment of PhDs in computer science and computer engineering. Examining this particular group is illuminating for several reasons. First, these people

staff the research labs in industry and the faculty positions in colleges and universities, and so are in positions of influence. Also, the median income and career expectations of this group are well above those for our society as a whole. Finally, this group is one that a substantial number of today's undergraduates in computing will eventually join.

In 1970, Orrin Taulbee started a survey of PhD-granting departments of computer science and computer engineering in the United States and Canada to determine basic facts about PhD production and employment. The statistics presented are from the 1990–91 *Taulbee Survey Report* [11]. For that year, the respondents included all 137 of the departments that grant PhDs in computer science in the United States and Canada and 29 of the 31 departments that grant PhDs in computer engineering.

Figure 10.1 summarizes the gender and minority status of people earning PhDs in computer science from 1970 through 1990–91. As the figure shows, those earning PhDs in computer science increased from 112 in 1970 to 862 in 1990–91. The number of women earning a PhD in computer science increased from 1 in 1970 to 113 in 1990–91, going from 1% of the total in 1970 to 13% of the total in 1990–91. Thus, both in absolute numbers and as a percentage of the whole, the participation of women increased. The number of African Americans increased from 1 in 1970 to 7 in 1990–91, representing 1% of the total each time. There was no separate category for Hispanics until the 1984–85 version of the survey. (There is still no tracking of other minority groups.) The number of Hispanics increased from 7 in 1984–85 to 19 in 1990–91, representing 2% of the total each time. It is clear that women, African Americans, and Hispanics are underrepresented in terms of percentages of those earning PhDs in computer science relative to percentages of the general population.

Figure 10.2 summarizes the gender and minority status of people employed as members of the faculty in the departments participating in the survey. The numbers are further broken down by faculty rank. There are basically just three ranks for faculty. The initial position is assistant professor. After five to eight years, a person can earn a promotion to associate professor. After another five or

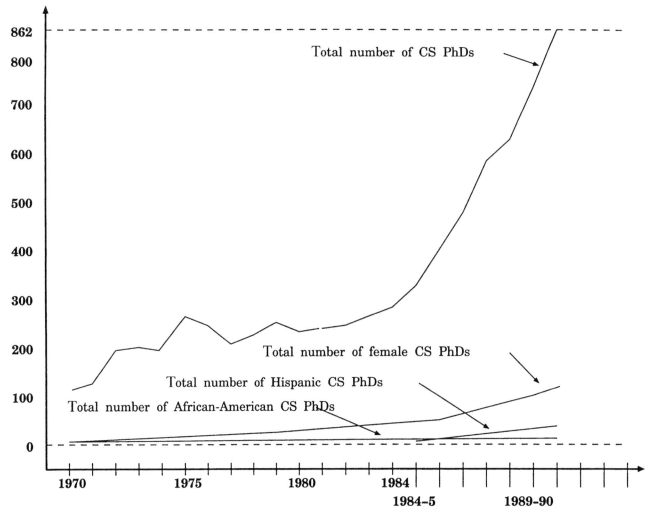

Fig. 10.1 Gender and minority status of people earning computer science PhDs.

more years, that person may earn a promotion to full professor. Thus, someone employed as a full professor will normally be at least 10 years beyond the completion of their PhD.

As a warning about how much care and thought must be given to arrive at a rationally supported analysis of such figures, consider the following quote from the survey:

> For women, however, the numbers are depressing in another way. At the assistant professor level, the numbers are reasonable in that the percentage of women (10 percent) is close to the percentage in PhD production (10–14 percent since 1973 and 13 percent this year). At the full professor level, however, the percentage of women falls drastically to 5 percent, indicating poor retention of women in academia over the years.

This quote asserts that the numbers show "poor retention" of women in academic careers. Poor retention would mean that women who start out in the academic career path do not stay in academic careers as frequently as men. Putting on your best critical-thinking hat, ask yourself if the num-

bers in fact support this conclusion. Let's assume that an average age for completing a PhD might be between 25 and 30 years of age (take 27.5). Also assume that a person might then work for 35 to 40 years (take 37.5). And assume that it would take roughly 10 years to advance to the rank of full professor. Now, the people who were full professors in 1990–91 would have completed their PhD in 1980–81 or earlier. The expected percentage of women who are full professors would then be the weighted sum of the percentage of women CS&E PhD recipients in the 27 or 28 years previous to that. Note that data exist for only the previous 10 years, which makes any further analysis open to some question. If we look at the numbers that do exist, from 1970 through 1980, there were 150 women out of 2264 PhD recipients, or about 6.5%. Since the trend indicates smaller percentages of women in the earlier years, 6.5% would probably be an overestimate for the total period. Thus, there appears to be no support in the actual numbers for a conclusion that women drop out of academic careers more frequently than men. Note that this does not mean

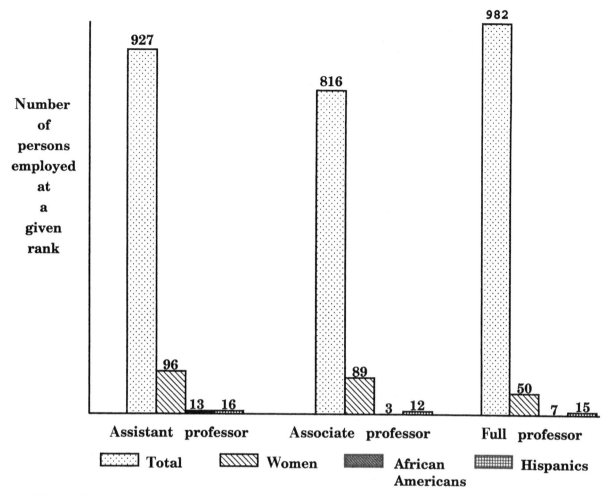

Fig. 10.2 Gender and minority status of faculty members.

that the conclusion is false, only that the survey numbers do not provide good evidence of it being true.

10.3.2 What Do These Numbers Mean?

The Taulbee survey makes it clear that substantial underrepresentation exists for women, African Americans and Hispanics. The important questions to ask are:

- Why should such underrepresentation exist?
- Why is underrepresentation changing (or not changing) at the current pace?
- Should anything be done about the situation?
- If something should be done, what is likely to be effective?

Also, even though I use the example of computer science and engineering, essentially the same situation exists in all areas of science and engineering and in our society as a whole.

10.3.2.1 Why should underrepresentation exist? Why is there underrepresentation of women and minorities? One

possible response to this question is simply that women and minorities choose to pursue advanced study in computing proportionately less often. However, this is something of a nonanswer, in that it simply begs the question of why this pattern of choices exists.

Actually, there is no one easy answer. Focusing on underrepresentation at the faculty level does not go deep enough. Underrepresentation at the faculty level cannot easily change because of the underrepresentation at the PhD student level, which cannot easily change because of underrepresentation among undergraduate students, which cannot easily change because of the underrepresentation in preparatory courses at the high-school level, and so on. As an example, consider that African Americans and Hispanics make up about 6 percent of college seniors graduating with engineering degrees [10], yet they make up about 30 percent of the population at large. Thus, even if literally *all* minority graduating seniors went on to receive PhDs, there would still be substantial underrepresentation. In other words, nothing that affects people after the high-school level can make a significant change in the big picture. So the more important question to ask is, "What causes women and minorities at the high-school (or lower) level to begin making choices that lead away from the opportunity to pursue advanced study in computer science and engineering?

It seems that the answer must be rooted in some complicated mixture of social culture and family structure. One possibility is that science and engineering have been populated primarily with white males, which meant that there was a low proportion of women and minorities in the field to serve as role models for later students. It could be that women and minority students may not fully realize that this field is a viable option. Instead, they may gravitate toward fields where they more frequently see examples of successful professional women and minorities. Fortunately, women's attitudes about career choice are changing. A 1993 study of nearly a quarter million freshman at 427 colleges and universities indicated that 66 percent of female freshmen planned to earn advanced degrees, as opposed to 63 percent of male freshmen. This represents a tripling of the percentage of females with this ambition over similar statistics from 25 years ago [30].

A factor in underrepresentation that is specific to women is having children. The years women would typically spend working toward a PhD and be in the early stages of their career are the same years they would typically begin child bearing and child rearing. Most career tracks in academia and industry are still not well adapted to give women the freedom to both work and devote time to starting a family.

A factor in underrepresentation that applies most heavily to minority students is income level. Proportionately more minority families have lower income levels, possibly due in large part to history. Families who are less well off financially may tend to view beginning any career earlier as a more viable option than investing extra years in education to begin a different kind of career later.

Finally, in spite of what we might wish, some individuals in our society and in our profession still actively work to impede the progress of women and minorities. The number of such persons is hopefully small and rapidly decreasing, but there is no reason to believe that it is yet zero.

All these factors contribute to underrepresentation. Others have published an extended discussion of these and related issues [3], [6], [7], [9], [10], [17], [20], [22], [37]. The Ada Project is a resource for information about women in computing. You can find out more about it on the World Wide Web at http://www.cs.yale.edu/HTML/YALE/CS/HyPlans/tap/tap.html.

10.3.2.2 Will Underrepresentation Change? To the extent that the present reality is simply the result of people freely making natural choices, the pace of change will follow the natural change in people and society. But note that the notion of "freely" here is open to question. Many of the factors that seem to be influencing decisions are the result of history that the individual could not control. This would seem to mean the representation of women in computer science and engineering might continue to increase slowly over a relatively long period, and that the representation of minorities would increase even more slowly, if at all.

Given the complexity of the answer to the "why" question, it would seem that speeding the natural pace of change would require an equally complex approach. To the extent that government programs are involved, a complex approach might well translate into high cost, bureaucracy, and inflexibility. So it is useful to consider carefully why we might want to speed the natural pace of change. What problems does the current situation cause and what benefits might result from faster change?

One answer to that is, "There is strength in diversity." The people who make up a business, academic, government, or social organization are in some sense like an "investment" that the organization has made in its future. Different economic conditions at different times relatively favor different types of investments. An investment portfolio that consists entirely of one type of asset is more easily wiped out than a diversified portfolio. By analogy, an organization faces different demands at different times, and a diversified human resource may allow it to better adapt. The first reprint in this chapter, "Diversity in the High-Tech Workplace," underlines these points [7].

Different analogies to make the same point can be found in sports teams. A "7-footer" is generally considered a great asset on a basketball team, but you never see a team composed only of 7-footers. They may do great when the ball is already near the basket, but they typically aren't much help in getting the basketball up the court. Similarly, a business needs different skills in people who play different roles in the business. People generally have no problem grasping this principle in the context of needing different skills in sales staff versus assembly line versus accounting staff. But the principle is more difficult to grasp in the context of gender, race, and ethnicity. To make the point more clearly, consider the (possibly apocryphal) story of General Motors introducing its Nova automobile in the Mexican market. The name of the automobile sounds like the Spanish for "doesn't go." Thus, the sales for the automobile "didn't go" until the name was changed. The situation would have had little chance of happening had there been a Hispanic senior manager somewhere on the scene.

More generally, whenever an activity of an organization may be viewed differently by people of different gender, race, or ethnic background, that organization is better off if diverse people participate in the decision-making process. The concept of looking at the diversity of the individuals who make up an organization as one of the attributes of the organization is a recent phenomenon. It may be an outgrowth of both the continuing emphasis on equality of opportunity in our society and the pressures of businesses competing increasingly on a worldwide, rather than a United States-only, basis.

Another benefit of changing underrepresentation is

global competiveness. Historically, the level of participation in advanced study in science and engineering has been highest in the white-male portion of the population, lower in the female portion of the population, and lower still in the minority portion of the population. Each group's level of participation has remained relatively constant over time, except for a noticeable spike around the time of the Russian launch of the Sputnik satellite, and perhaps with a slow increase in the level of participation of women and minorities. Population-trend projections indicate that the percentage of women and minorities in the work force is increasing and the percentage of white males is decreasing. These trends should not seem surprising. While women are staying at a constant 50 percent of the population, more women are entering the work force than in the past. Minority groups are projected to simply make up a larger percentage of the total population because of differences in immigration and birth rates. The implication of these trends is that unless there is some change, our society is destined to have a smaller fraction of people with advanced training in science and engineering. This arouses concern over the ability of U.S. industry to compete in the increasingly global high-technology markets. Decline of the human infrastructure in science and engineering could lead to a decline of U.S. high technology and so possibly to a decline in the overall U.S. economy. In one sense, the greatest potential for altering the trends would lie in the faster growing population groups that have had low participation rates, women and minorities.

A third argument for greater diversity is that there is stability through inclusion. The stability of any society relies on the majority of its citizens feeling that it is in their interest to work within the system. When a substantial segment of a society believes that it is isolated and discriminated against by the system, and that there is no hope for change, it is natural for that segment to consider alternatives. A case in point is the American Revolution. It is not necessary that this belief of isolation and discrimination be correct or rational; it merely has to exist and to affect peoples' decisions. This argument leads to the conclusion that, in the long run, society as a whole would be better off if we make sure that no substantial segment comes to such a belief.

10.3.3 Summary

The computing profession is affected by many of the same problems that occur in our society at large. You as an individual can speed the pace of change simply by being aware of the issues and problems, and supporting what you feel are the right solutions. The root problem is *not* simply that someone has counted groups of people and noted that the numbers are out of balance. The numbers, as well as the desire to count such numbers, are only symptoms of a more complex problem. The root problem is really the lack of trust among people that made it necessary to do the counting in the first place. The real solution lies in an increase in trust among people to the point that counting the numbers no longer seems necessary.

10.4 DEALING WITH DISCRIMINATION

Almost all forms of bias, discrimination, and harassment stem from dealing with people as members of a stereotyped group rather than as individuals. Thus, one general way of avoiding bias in your treatment of others is to be aware of stereotypes that occur in your thinking and to be sure that you look beyond those stereotypes when you deal with another person.

10.4.1 Sexual Harassment

The stereotypical incident of sexual harassment is a male in some position of authority pressuring a female into submitting to sexual favors. But we have already agreed to avoid stereotypes, so a more encompassing general definition of sexual harassment is

> Person A is guilty of sexual harassment with respect to person B whenever (1) some interaction between them has an element of sex-based content, and (2) a reasonable person would say that person A should have known that person B would be offended by the interaction.

Note that harassment can happen in either direction between a male and a female or between two males or two females. The government received 1070 sexual harassment complaints in 1993, with nearly 1 in 10 filed by men [2]. The government does not keep track of whether the harassment was heterosexual or homosexual in nature. However, there have been news stories of a variety of same-sex harassment complaints. In one case, three women at a computer sales company filed discrimination complaints, ". . . saying that they were forced from their jobs . . . because they complained about harassment from office manager Isabel Arango." The alleged harassment consisted of ". . . repeated remarks about their breasts, photographs of nude women, loud and lewd telephone conversations with a girlfriend" [23].

Another important element of the definition of harassment is that the person doing the harassing does *not* have to have the conscious intention of harassing the other person. The harasser may honestly think that they were "just joking around," or that it was just their way of "paying the person a compliment." However, if a reasonable person observing the incident would say that the harasser should have known it would be taken as hostile, intimidating, or offensive, then it is harassment.

This standard is obviously a little vague, especially because it relies on some hypothetical "reasonable person" as an observer. Different people observing the same incident may have different conclusions. For this reason, the roles of those in an allegedly harassing incident bear closer scrutiny. There are three roles in such an incident: harassee, harasser, and innocent bystander.

10.4.1.1 What to Do As a Harassee. The first rule for someone who feels that they are the target of sexual harassment is to inform the person that you consider this to be harassment and that they should not repeat the same or a similar behavior. Make a note of the time, place, and wording of what you tell them. If the behavior is repeated, the next step is to notify the harasser's manager and/or the human resources officer. You might also ask colleagues how they would view the incident. If you have doubts about whether the incident really was harrassment, you might want to discuss it with colleagues *before* you decide whether to say anything to the harasser. This way, if it was an innocent misunderstanding, you might save yourself an embarrassing moment. On the other hand, even if it was a clear incident of harassment and you have already said something to the person, talking with others may help you gauge how much effort to put into your complaint. If the person has a reputation of being a problem, you may want to notify their manager and/or the human resources officer regardless of whether the behavior is repeated.

10.4.1.2 What to Do if You Are Accused of Harassing. If someone complains that you have harassed them, you can do any number of things, depending on the situation. If you had no intention of harassing anyone, you should apologize very politely for any misunderstanding you may have caused and thank the person for alerting you to your unintentionally offending behavior. You should do this even if you feel that the person's reading of your actions is unreasonable. You should also make sure that someone else knows you made this response. After all, if the person is being unreasonable or irrational, part of your response must be aimed at protecting yourself because even claims of harassment that are shown to be false can damage your career. If you feel that the person is looking to find harassment where none exists, try to limit your future interactions with the person to occasions when other people are around.

You may also realize, after the person says something to you, that a reasonable person *could* have taken your actions as harassment. In this case, you should be sincerely thankful to the person. They have pointed out something that could be a limiting factor in your career advancement in time for you to do something about it. If you are not quite certain how to alter your behavior, check with the human resources office to find out if they offer seminars on how to deal effectively with people.

10.4.1.3 What to Do As an Observer. If you happen to be a manager and observe an incident of harassment between employees, the following advice taken from an article in *Fortune* may help [8] (the article assumes that a "him" is doing the harassing):

Talk to him, of course. If that doesn't work, and odds are it won't, turn him in to the human resources person in charge of these matters. And do it pronto. Otherwise you could be liable along with your employer.

More than a third of the Fortune 500 companies have been sued for sexual harassment, many of them more than once. Harassment suits sometimes also name as defendants managers who knew about the harassment but did nothing. So it is important not to ignore the incident. You should do the following:

• Meet with and talk to the person.
• Document the meeting.
• Point the person to books or seminars that might help them.
• Consider meeting with the person who has been harassed to let them know that you do not condone the incident and that you have taken the normal first step in responding to such incidents. This may help keep the person from feeling isolated and angry toward the company in general.

One sexual-harrassment case that received wide news coverage in 1993 is the suit filed by Teresa Harris against her former employer Charles Hardy, of Forklift Systems, Inc. Hardy was apparently a stereotypical male chauvinist pig, being credited with remarks such as "you're a woman, what do you know" and "let's go over to the Holiday Inn and negotiate your raise" [13]. A federal judge found that Hardy's behavior was crude and vulgar and that a reasonable woman would have been offended, but found that Harris had not suffered psychological harm and dismissed the complaint. The dismissal was upheld on first appeal. However, the U.S. Supreme Court ruled that employees are not required to prove psychological harm and sent the case back to the Sixth U.S. Circuit Court of Appeals. This ruling by the Supreme Court effectively expanded the legal definition of sexual harassment.

10.4.2 Racial Discrimination

The experience of many people who are not members of any traditional minority is that discrimination doesn't exist at any significant level. Of course, since these people would generally not be the target of discrimination, their personal experience may be misleading. There can be little question that discrimination based on race still occurs at a significant level in our society. Those who doubt that should consider the lawsuits against the Denny's restaurant chain that were settled in 1994 [16]. One of the incidents involved six African-American and 15 Caucasian U.S. Secret Service agents who were guarding President Clinton and went into a Denny's in Maryland. The Causcasian agents were served and even got second and third helpings while the African-American agents waited more than hour without being served. Thus, it is important to admit that racial bias does exist and does need to be dealt with. On the other hand, not everything negative that happens to a member of a minority group is necessarily racially motivated.

Returning to the Harris and Hardy sexual harassment case, suppose a manager was known to say, "You're an African American, what do you know." Actually this sort of explicit racial harassment seems to be relatively infrequent (compared with explicit sexual-harassment incidents), perhaps because almost no one fails to immediately recognize it, understand that it is unacceptable, and agree that corrective measures are needed, the sooner the better. When it does occur, it should be handled in much the same way as sexual harassment.

However, explicit harassment is only a fraction of the racial discrimination that goes on. Other forms can be much more subtle. The only clue to the possible existence of discrimination may be the lack of people of a certain race in a particular area of an organization. There are situations in which, over time, the percentage of minorities holding jobs at a certain level remains significantly below the percentage of minorities in the pool of qualified candidates. The larger the gap in the percentages and the longer the situation persists, the stronger the suspicion that some form of racial bias is operating. The individuals responsible may feel certain that they are not racist or discriminatory, and yet still act on the basis of stereotypes that lead to a racially biased result. The only way to deal with such situations seems to be to monitor the percentages of minorities in different subgroups and to educate people about the negative effects of acting on the basis of false stereotypes. Unfortunately, the monitoring mechanisms our society has introduced (like affirmative action programs) have generated great controversy and misunderstanding. Monitoring the racial composition of groups is the exact opposite of what a color-blind society should be doing. And the numbers that are generated by such monitoring are, of course, subject to self-interested misuse and exploitation.

Columnist William Raspberry has summarized the situation as follows [21]. The two main arguments advanced by critics of affirmative action are (1) it leads to lower standards, and (2) it encourages reverse discrimination. Supporters of affirmative action reply that a color-blind society is, of course, the goal, but that even very recent history suggests that only the most naive person could believe that a color-blind society could be attempted today without a continuance of severe discrimination. In other words, a period of enforced preferences is required as a transition between the explicitly racist society of the recent past and a time when a color-blind society can be trusted to be a fair society. The obvious question then becomes: "How long does the period of enforced preferences continue?" or "How does affirmative action end?" His answer is that affirmative action can end ". . . when people really come to believe not that the numbers are perfect but that the system is open. It will end when we can, with confidence, simply stop counting and turn our attention to more important things."

10.4.3 Other Forms of Bias

Other common forms of bias include that against immigrants, the elderly, and the disabled. There is also a growing area of bias, reverse discrimination. Although I do not cover these in detail here, none of them are any less serious than sexual harassment or bias against gender or race. There is simply not enough space here to catalog and describe all of the many forms of bias, and they are not much different in concept, or in treatment methods than other biases already covered.

10.4.3.1 Against Immigrants. Bias against people who immigrate to the United States is not limited to our own time. In speaking about German immigrants, Benjamin Franklin said "instead of learning our language, we must learn theirs, or live as if in a foreign country" [32]. Today, approximately 8 percent of the people living in the United States are foreign born. This is proportionally fewer than in previous times. In 1960, the figure was 6 percent. In 1920, it was 13 percent [32]. However, current immigrants come from different places than in previous times. Currently, approximately four out of five immigrants are from either Latin America or Asia [32]. Bias against immigrants to the United States is a serious current problem, with some immigrants feeling that they are being made a scapegoat for society's problems [26].

10.4.3.2 Against Age. Age bias is a concept that probably seems odd to the typical college student. However, it is something that the computing industry takes quite seriously. There is even a federal law, the Age Discrimination in Employment Act, to protect persons 40 years or older. At the end of this chapter is text from *Information for the Private Sector and State and Local Governments,* a brochure produced by the Equal Employment Opportunity Commission. The brochure contains an overview of this law.

10.4.3.3 Against the Disabled. The 1992 Americans with Disabilities Act is meant to protect the disabled from bias. The text from the EEOC brochure also summarizes this law. Employers are prohibited from discriminating against workers with disabilities, provided that the worker is qualified to perform the job properly. The law has made the process of interviewing job applicants a delicate process. Interviewers can ask about disabilities that would affect the ability to meet a specific job requirement, but not about disabilities in general. The more visible meaning of this law has been reasonable accommodation of those with some physical disability that does not interfere with the requirements of a particular job. However, the act also protects those with mental disabilities. Since the implementation of the Americans with Disabilities Act, the number of complaints pending with the EEOC has reached an all-time high, with complaints about disability-related discrimination increasing the fastest [12].

10.4.3.4 Reverse Discrimination. Reverse discrimination occurs when someone who is from a group that has traditionally benefitted from discrimination is discriminated against in favor of a person who is from a group that has traditionally suffered from discrimination. The U.S. Supreme Court has held that taking race or sex into account when making affirmative action decisions is legal so long as it is *not the sole or primary factor.* Incidents of reverse discrimination that are grounds for legal action seem to occur most often when well-meaning but short-sighted administrators get overly caught up in wanting to be able to claim that they have done something about (traditional) discrimination. The landmark case in this area was brought by Allan Bakke against the University of California at Davis Medical School in 1978. The U.S. Supreme Court found that Bakke had been the victim of reverse discrimination in being denied admission to medical school.

Reverse-discrimination suits are becoming increasingly common. In one case [24], a Caucasian female was hired by the University of South Florida at the same time and in the same area as an African-American male. After several years, the Caucasian female found that she had been hired at a salary more than $10,000 less than that of the African-American male. The jury awarded her nearly $400,000 in lost wages and compensation for emotional suffering. (If the jury is right, then they would seem to have "solved" the problem by forcing the university to overpay two people rather than one!)

10.5 Case Study

This case shows just how much a company can stand to lose in a sexual-harassment suit. It also illustrates that the responsibility for preventing such incidents belongs to all persons of authority in the organization.

10.5.1 The Cast of Characters

Baker & McKenzie is a very large and well-known law firm on the west coast. Martin Greenstein is a lawyer who was a partner at the firm of Baker & McKenzie. Rena

Weeks is a 40-year-old woman who worked as a secretary at Baker & McKenzie.

10.5.2 The Sequence of Events

Rena Weeks worked at Baker & McKenzie for about three months in 1991. After leaving the firm, she filed suit against Martin Greenstein and Baker & McKenzie. Martin Greenstein was apparently out of control in terms of sexual harrassment in the workplace. The allegations made by Weeks against Greenstein included that Greenstein ". . . dumped candies in a breast pocket of her blouse, groped her breast, pressed against her from behind, and pulled her arms back "to see which one is bigger." More than a half dozen other women testified about offensive conduct that Greenstein had committed toward them, dating back as far as 1988. Greenstein acknowledged offensive conduct toward two other secretaries, but denied the charges by Weeks.

In August and September 1994, a jury found that Greenstein had sexually harassed Weeks and that Baker & McKenzie had "failed to take sufficient action to prevent it and showed a conscious disregard for Weeks' rights" [29]. Weeks was awarded $50,000 in general damages, plus another $6,900,000 in punitive damages from the law firm, and another $225,000 in punitive damages from Greenstein. The $6,900,000 award against the firm was later reduced to $3,800,000 [27].

10.5.3 Conclusions and Questions

Even with the award against the firm being cut nearly in half, it still seems a tremendous cost to the firm. This was essentially a penalty against the firm for allowing Greenstein to behave so far outside accepted norms. It is effectively a cost due to poor management of personnel by those in charge of the firm. Does the award seem "fair?" Does it seem likely to change the firm's practices in terms of personnel management?

Does the award against Greenstein seem likely to change his behavior? Should there have been an educational aspect to the judgment against him (such as going to counseling sessions of some type)?

Points to Remember

- The evaluation of issues surrounding harassment and discrimination is made more complex by the historical context of our society.
- Diversity of human resources can be an important positive attribute of an organization.
- Discrimination and harassment are both unethical and illegal.
- The definition of sexual harassment does not require that the harasser be proven to have conscious intent to harm the harassee.
- Federal laws exist to cover a variety of situations related to discrimination and harassment.

WORKSHEET—Sexual Harassment on Computer Networks

1. Give a brief definition of what constitutes sexual harassment.

2. Is anything fundamentally different about the problems of sexual harassment in an environment with computers and networks compared with a noncomputer environment? Explain.

3. Have you ever witnessed any form of computer-facilitated harassment? If so, what was it? Why do you think it was done? What do you think the punishment should have been?

4. Should there be any limit to the images that someone can use as a background display on their computer in the workplace? Explain.

5. Should there be legal limits on what can be sent to another person via e-mail? Explain.

6. What would constitute "electronic stalking?"

WORKSHEET—Review of Age Bias/ADEA Law

1. What is age bias?

2. One assertion is that when layoffs are necessary, older workers may be laid off before younger workers, because older workers tend to have higher salaries and so laying them off saves the company more money. Does this constitute age bias? Why or why not?

3. Is it ethical to offer a severance package that includes an agreement not to sue over the termination?

4. Give an example of something you think definitely constitutes ". . . arbitrary age bias in hiring, firing, promotions, . . ."

5. Why do you think the Age Discrimination in Employment Act of 1967 protects only people age 40 or older?

WORKSHEET—Improving Your Vocabulary

Briefly define the following phrases in the context of U.S. society and use the term in a sentence that shows you understand the meaning of the term.

Civil rights

Melting pot

Multicultural

Salad bowl

Balkanize

Misogyny

Bigotry

Glass ceiling

Xenophobia

Demagogue

Set aside

Race norming

1. **Street harassment.** The term "street harassment" refers to inappropriate comments made to women walking down the street. A *Harvard Law Review* article has suggested that street harassment be made a crime [1]. This proposal would seem to ignore some important first amendment considerations. As one columnist said, "the answer lies somewhere between legal measures and referring the problem to Miss Manners. Consciousness-raising and social pressures by women and civilized men can change a cultural climate to be less tolerant of street harassment—and eventually convince silly, immature men that it isn't cute or funny to be obnoxious" [1]. Report on the phenomena of street harassment and measures that have been taken to combat it.

2. **The Night Trap video game.** Many retailers have removed Night Trap from their shelves because the game featured "scantily clad sorority sisters" and a gang of "hooded killers" who "used a neck-drilling device to drain the blood of the women characters" [31]. The game's maker, Sega, had labeled the game as not appropriate for children under 17. Certainly stores must make decisions on a regular basis about which products to carry. Did stores do the right thing in dropping this video game? What are the effects of such a decision on the store? its customers? video-game makers? society in general?

3. **Pornography on the Internet.** The Lawrence Livermore National Laboratory discovered that someone (apparently an employee) had set up one of their systems to act as a file server for some hardcore pornography [33]. Carnegie Mellon University made a decision to block student access to bulletin boards that provide pornographic images [28]. Find out what you can about these and other similar incidents, and about what an organization can do to detect this type of computer use.

4. **Scholarships restricted by race.** At one time, many colleges and universities would have turned down scholarship programs that were restricted on the basis of race. Such programs have become quite common. According to a Government Accounting Office study using a random sample of 300 four-year undergraduate and graduate schools for the 1991–92 academic year, 4 percent of undergraduate scholarship dollars are awarded on the basis of race [14]. The predominate source of such scholarships is government programs aimed at minorities. However, private sources have endowed "Caucasians-only" scholarship programs [15]. Also, a federal appeals court has ruled against a University of Maryland scholarship program that was restricted to African Americans [36]. Report on the recent history of scholarship programs restricted by race and the scholarships of this type that may exist at your institution.

5. **Race and ethnicity categories used by the government.** In the summer of 1994, the federal government began to look at the set of categories used to monitor race and ethnicity. The Office of Management and Budget conducted public hearings on race and ethnic standards for federal statistics and administrative reporting" [18]. Some feel that the set of categories currently used is too restrictive and that additional categories are needed—a "multiracial" category for children of biracial marriages, a "Middle Eastern" category for those from the Middle East, a "native Hawaiian" category and a split of the "Hispanic" category into as many as seven categories. Look into the OMB conclusions at the end of their public hearings and report on what you find out. You might also compare the race and ethnicity categories used in the United States with those used by other countries.

6. **Possible bias in the National Merit Scholarships.** The Educational Testing Service and the College Entrance Examination Board are involved in the testing process that leads to the National Merit Scholarships. Several groups have asserted that the selection process is biased against women. The main support for this is that women tend to get slightly better grades than men in high school and college, yet represent only about 35 percent of the National Merit Scholarship semifinalists [25]. Look into this problem and report on the ways in which a standardized test might tend to be biased for or against particular groups. As one of your conclusions, try to define as specifically as you can what it is you believe standardized tests such as the Scholastic Aptitude Test actually measure.

7. **Coed versus single-sex colleges.** Single-sex colleges were once much more numerous in the United States than they are currently [35]. Report on the number and type of single-sex colleges that remain in the United States, as well as the pros and cons of attending such an institution.

8. **National Association for the Advancement of White People.** The National Association for the Advancement of White People obviously takes the form of its name from the National Association for the Advancement of Colored People. One of the officials in the NAAWP is Dan Daniels [4]. Report on the stated aims of the NAAWP and on the background and beliefs of Dan Daniels. Contrast the origin and goals of the NAAWP to those of the NAACP.

9. **Ratings of top companies for working mothers.** *Working Mother* magazine publishes an annual "top 10" list of companies whose policies are favorable to working

mothers. The 1994 list includes AT&T, IBM, and Xerox [34]. Report on the criteria that go into the ranking and the variability of the rankings from year to year.

10. **The Ada Project.** The Ada Project (TAP) is described as "tapping Internet resources for women in computer science." The World Wide Web address for this site is

http://www/cs.yale.edu/HTML/YALE/CS/HyPlans/tap/tap.html

Look into what information is available through this resource, how the resource is supported, who uses it and how much, and whether it is viewed as successful.

REFERENCES

[1] J. Beck, "Catcalls offend, but should they be a crime?" *The Tampa Tribune*, March 13, 1993.

[2] S. Cohen, "More men claiming sex harassment," *The Tampa Tribune*, January 24, 1994.

[3] "Special issue on women in computing," *Communications of the ACM*, January 1995.

[4] G. Coryell, "Former sheriff starts chapter for whites only," *The Tampa Tribune*, August 31, 1994.

[5] R. N. Current, T. H. Williams and F. Freidel, *The Essentials of American History*. Alfred A. Knopf, New York 1972.

[6] N. DiTomaso, G. F. Farris, and R. Cordero, "Degrees and diversity at work," *IEEE Spectrum*, April 1994, pp. 38–42.

[7] N. DiTomaso and G. F. Farris, "Diversity in the High-Tech Workplace," *IEEE Spectrum*, June 1992, pp. 20–32.

[8] A. N. Fisher, "Sexual harassment: What to do," *Fortune*, August 23, 1993, pp. 84–88.

[9] K. Frenkel, "Women & computing," *Communications of the ACM*, November 1990, pp. 34–46.

[10] E. W. Gordon, "Educating more minority engineers," *Technology Review*, July 1988, pp. 69–73.

[11] D. Gries and D. Marsh, "The 1990-91 Taulbee Survey Report," *Computer*, November 1992, pp. 69–75.

[12] A. Grimes, "Reinvigorating the fight against discrimination," *The Washington Post*, October 27, 1994.

[13] G. Klein, "Court expands sex harassment definition," *The Tampa Tribune*, November 10, 1993.

[14] L. L. Knutson, "Scholarships based on race have value, study says," *The Seattle Post-Intelligencer*, January 15, 1994.

[15] Charles Krauthammer, "Grants by race illustrate demise of colorblindness," *The Tampa Tribune*, September 27, 1992.

[16] J. Lawlor, "Denny's settles bias case," *USA Today*, May 25, 1994.

[17] N. G. Leveson, "Women treated differently in CS department," *Computing Research News*, January 1991, p. 13.

[18] D. Murdock, "New pigeonholes would create more barriers to unity," *The Tampa Tribune*, July 7, 1994.

[19] *New York Times* Report," Final rules give clearer picture of unpaid family, medical leave," *The Tampa Tribune*, February 6, 1995.

[20] A. Pearl, M. E. Pollack, E. Riskin, B. Thomas, E. Wolf, and A. Wu, "Becoming a computer scientist," *Communications of the ACM*, November 1990, pp. 47–57.

[21] W. Raspberry, "Diversity: When enough is enough," *The Tampa Tribune*, February 11, 1994.

[22] M. Sadker and D. Sadker, *Failing at fairness. Failing at fairness: How our schools cheat girls*, Simon & Schuster, New York, 1995.

[23] D. Solov, "Three women file same-sex harassment complaint," *The Tampa Tribune*, February 24, 1994.

[24] D. Sommer, "Professor wins race bias suit," *The Tampa Tribune*, June 3, 1993.

[25] "Girls get only a third of National Merit Scholarships," *The St. Petersburg Times*, May 26, 1993.

[26] C. L. Tien, "America's scapegoats," *Newsweek*, October 31, 1994.

[27] "Secretary accepts reduced award," *The Tampa Tribune*, December 13, 1994.

[28] "School presses delete key on computer porn photos," *The Tampa Tribune*, November 22, 1994.

[29] "Harrassment case nets woman cash," *The Tampa Tribune*, September 2, 1994.

[30] "Women now top men in college goals," *The Tampa Tribune*, January 24, 1994.

[31] "Controversial video game removed by retailer," *The Tampa Tribune*, December 17, 1993.

[32] "Masses huddle to block immigrants," *The Tampa Tribune*, July 25, 1993.

[33] "Porn pirates and software smugglers," *Time*, July 25, 1994.

[34] R. Trigaux, "Family policies earn praise from companies," *The St. Petersburg Times*, September 13, 1994.

[35] R. Vigoda, "Women's colleges filling classrooms," *The Tampa Tribune-Times*, September 11, 1994.

[36] G. F. Will, "A step toward colorblind public policy," *The Tampa Tribune*, November 3, 1994.

[37] C. M. Yentsch and C. J. Sindermann, *The Woman Scientist*. Plenum Press New York, 1992.

DIVERSITY IN THE HIGH-TECH WORKPLACE

Reprinted from *IEEE Spectrum*, Vol. 29, No. 6, pp. 20–32, June 1992.

he number of people who enter the U.S. workforce each year is steadily declining, a reflection of the declining birthrate. At the same time, the proportions of women, blacks, Hispanics, American Indians, and the foreign-born are growing. Between 1985 and 2000, native-born white men will constitute only 15 percent of the increase in the number of workers, the Hudson Institute predicted in its classic 1987 study, *Workforce 2000: Work and Workers for the 21st Century*. Women—white, nonwhite, and foreign-born—will constitute 64 percent of the increase, and native-born nonwhite and immigrant men will account for the balance.

The changing character of the workforce presents a major challenge to high-technology industry, which depends so strongly on people and ideas. With a smaller pool of talent to draw from, industry must cultivate new sources of engineers and scientists, in addition to the white men who have formed the backbone of the workforce.

The shift in the makeup of workers will also present important opportunities for women and minorities—provided that they are well-qualified for jobs that are becoming increasingly demanding. "Overall, the skill mix of the economy will be moving rapidly upscale," the Hudson Institute forecast, "with most new jobs demanding more education and higher levels of language, math, and reasoning skills."

Many U.S. corporations, large and small, are responding to these demographic trends by doing more than just passively accepting diversity; rather, they are positively embracing it. Their premise is that encouraging the best and the brightest, regardless of race, color, sex, religion, national origin, age, sexual orientation, or disability, gives them a competitive edge. The more diverse their talent, they believe, the more access they will have to creativity, ingenuity, and innovative ideas in a world where corporate success increasingly depends on such intellectual commodities.

The new corporate attitude differs strongly from earlier policies of equal opportunity and affirmative action. In the past, women and minorities were often hired into responsible jobs and simply left to languish in an unfamiliar environment. Companies sometimes played a quota game, happy that they could claim increasing numbers of women and minorities on their payroll, but giving only lip service to high-minded ideals. Diversity policies, in contrast, actively nurture nontraditional employees; companies now want them to succeed and to stay.

To speak of encouraging diversity in a period of widespread corporate downsizing may seem incongruous. Yet the facts remain that the workforce is being replenished at a decreasing rate and that high-technology companies need a continuing supply of talent as economic equilibrium returns.

In this special report, *IEEE Spectrum* asked experts from industry to examine aspects of the new workforce and the diversity it embodies. A pioneer in the field offers advice based on first-hand experience in implementing a diversity program. A diversity manager describes how affinity groups can help a diverse workforce work better together, a training expert shows how engineers can adapt to new cultures, and a human-resources professional presents a plan for helping diverse people prepare for greater responsibility.

We also asked management researchers to share their findings about job performance in diverse, highly technical work environments. They report revealing differences between the work experiences of U.S.-born white men and others.

And from four nontraditional engineers—a black, a Hispanic, a native American, and an Asian woman—we solicited firsthand accounts of their careers: why they chose engineering, their experiences at school and on the job, and the special qualities they feel they bring to the profession.

While the United States may be only beginning to encourage diversity, its successful application is not new. As one example, we examine diversity in microcosm in the city-state of Singapore.

—*George F. Watson, Senior Editor*

Diversity and performance in R&D

Women, with or without Ph.D.s, tend to rate themselves lower than men on innovativeness

New hires in U.S. R&D laboratories since the mid-1970s have changed from being almost exclusively U.S.-born men to being predominantly, in some companies, U.S.-born women or foreign-born scientists and engineers. At the same time, the proportion of native-born minorities has increased to a small extent.

These new entrants find themselves in work environments where most of the managers are U.S.-born white men. And they are finding that their work styles, communication patterns, and personal needs do not always match those of the people who evaluate their performance.

To understand these and other issues, we are surveying scientists and engineers in R&D jobs in major industrial companies ["Surveying diversity," p. 22]. Our purpose is to determine whether a gap does

Nancy DiTomaso and George F. Farris
Rutgers University

exist between native-born white men and others and, if so, to gauge its extent and implications. And indeed, we are finding differences, both predictable and unpredictable, between the work experiences of native-born white men and the rest.

These differences make it important to understand now the issues confronting R&D managers. Most of what is known about managing R&D comes from studies of U.S.-born white men, yet our research shows the pathway to success may not be the same for others.

LEADING THE WAY. For companies that depend on innovation for their survival, these issues are fundamental. Whether good ideas get developed or squelched, whether people can build on each other's contributions (absolutely essential in today's R&D), and whether companies can keep good people depends on learning to manage diversity.

And for R&D to work well with other parts of the company, the differences within it and between it and the rest of the company must be bridged. Perhaps R&D is where these problems and opportunities can first be productively addressed. Perhaps R&D will lead the way for the rest of the corporate world.

Our study is continuing, but we can report on our findings on performance, teamwork, and leadership. Because the number of U.S.-born blacks and Hispanics in our sample is small, we can as yet form some conclusions only about women (mostly U.S.-born) and the foreign-born (mostly male).

THE BOTTOM LINE. Performance—how much of a contribution an individual is making—is the bottom line in R&D, as it is elsewhere in a company. We used four measures of performance, both self-assessment and managers' ratings: innovativeness (increas-

ing knowledge through lines of R&D that are useful and new); usefulness (helping the organization carry out its responsibilities); promotability (readiness for advancement into management should an opening occur); and cooperativeness (effectiveness in working with others). We asked respondents and their managers to indicate, on a 100-point scale, what proportion of people the respondent "stands above." (The survey also includes self-reports on patents and publications. These correlate modestly with performance measures for U.S.-born white males, but not for foreign-born of either sex and only slightly for U.S.-born women.)

The foreign-born rate themselves higher than the U.S.-born on innovativeness, usefulness, and cooperativeness, but no differently on promotability [Fig. 1]. Their managers rate the foreign-born as no better than the U.S.-born on the first three dimensions and as lower on promotability. Interestingly, it makes no difference how long a foreign-born respondent has resided in the United States; manager ratings and self-ratings followed the same trend.

Of course, not all foreign-born are the same. We have to wait until our sample sizes are larger before we can comment on their differences. But we can say that males from Europe, Canada, and Australia (whom we call "Europeans") seem to rate themselves much as U.S.-born white males do.

Those from Asia, Southeast Asia, Africa, and Latin America (whom we call "non-Europeans") tend to rate themselves higher than U.S.-born white males and European males. Despite the differences among the non-Europeans, they tend to be more alike in their responses than they are like the Europeans. We do not have a large enough sample of foreign-born females to draw firm conclusions about them.

DOCTORATE HELPS WOMEN. Unlike the foreign-born males, women respondents rate themselves lower on innovativeness, usefulness, and promotability, but higher on cooperativeness [Fig. 2]. Managers also rate women as lower on innovativeness but as no different from men on usefulness, promotability, and, it turns out, cooperativeness.

When these differences are broken down further, the managers' lower rating for women in innovativeness applies only to those without a Ph.D.; women Ph.D.s are rated like men on all dimensions. Interestingly, women Ph.D.s are just as likely as non-Ph.D.s to rate themselves lower than men.

That even non-Ph.D. women are rated lower on innovativeness by their managers must be interpreted with caution because our study also shows that women have less opportunity to be innovative. For example, they are given less responsibility than men for initiating new activities and less freedom to work in their own way.

Surprisingly, on the measures of innovativeness and usefulness, the self-ratings of U.S.-born white men coincide almost identically with the ratings of their managers,

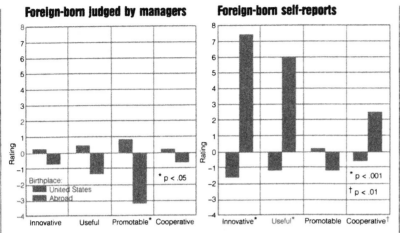

Foreign-born judged by managers

Rating

Birthplace:
■ United States
■ Abroad

* p < .05

Innovative Useful Promotable* Cooperative

Foreign-born self-reports

Rating

* p < .001

† p < .01

Innovative* Useful* Promotable Cooperative†

*[1] Foreign-born scientists and engineers tend to rate themselves more highly on innovativeness, usefulness, and cooperativeness than their managers do. Performance values here and in Fig. 2 are deviations from the mean of all responses, adjusted for seniority, level of education, and gender. The term p is the probability that a result is due to chance; p = .01 means that there is no more than 1 chance in 100 that a difference as large as the one shown is a chance finding. * and † mark all statistically significant results.*

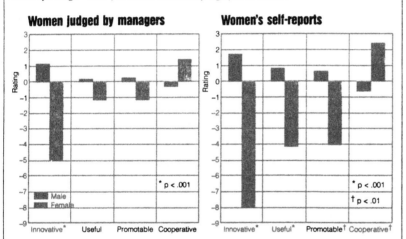

Women judged by managers

Rating

■ Male
■ Female

* p < .001

Innovative* Useful Promotable Cooperative

Women's self-reports

Rating

* p < .001

† p < .01

Innovative* Useful* Promotable† Cooperative†

[2] Women scientists and engineers give themselves low ratings on innovativeness, usefulness, and promotability, and their managers tend to agree with them on innovativeness. If only Ph.D.s are considered, managers rate women like men (not shown here), although women with Ph.D.s still rate themselves low.

perhaps because they understand the culture around them and can easily interpret any feedback on how they are faring on the job. Of course, such insight may be aided by the fact that their managers are, for the most part, drawn from the same group as themselves.

In contrast, the non-European males not only rate themselves higher than do the U.S.-born, but also rate themselves much higher than do their managers.

Should we assume from the high self-ratings of non-European males and the low self-ratings of women (lower even than their managers) that neither non-European men nor women are attuned to the signals they are getting from those around them, or perhaps are not getting any signals at all?

PLAYING INTO STEREOTYPES. Besides uneven understanding of feedback, there may be other explanations for the discrepancies in assessment of performance. Both women and non-European men may be playing into the stereotypes about themselves, because the stereotypes may be reinforced by the ways in which they approach their work.

The fact that women are under-represented in technical fields, for example, may contribute to stereotypical attitudes. It is undoubtedly difficult for those women who persist in getting technical training and who enter technical fields to have confidence that they are as good as the men around them. Otherwise, there would be more women, they may reason.

Further, research on performance appraisal indicates that, in jobs where the outcome measures are ambiguous, women do tend to rate themselves lower than men, while in positions where performance is easily measured,

women rate themselves the same as men.

For the foreign-born—especially Asians and Southeast Asians—the opposite is true. Partly because U.S. immigration laws restrict legal entry and extended stays to those with "critical" work skills that are not otherwise available in the U.S. population, there is a bias in favor of foreign applicants in science and engineering fields. Thus, they tend to be overrepresented in such occupations, and perhaps need to believe themselves to be better than the U.S.-born.

Moreover, the foreign-born in our study place greater emphasis on their work; they are more involved, less concerned about spending time with their families, and attach more importance to success on the job. Therefore, they may have a higher investment in believing they are making a contribution.

ARE MANAGERS BIASED? While recognizing these factors, we cannot dismiss the possibility of bias in the managers' ratings. If so, they are biased in favor of women and against the non-Europeans. Given that most women in our sample are themselves U.S.-born and white, it may be that managers understand their contributions better, but are less able to communicate with and evaluate the non-Europeans with whom they work.

On the other hand, if the managers' ratings are *not* biased, it is heartening to see that they differentiate less by demography than some might expect. Possibly, too, managers' ratings do not reflect their true feelings, but, even so, they could not easily manipulate the rankings. They were asked to rate individuals, while our measures are aggregated by subgroups of hundreds of people.

Clearly, managers need to examine their ratings for traces of bias attributable to cultural differences. Biased or not, managers must focus more attention on the kind of feedback they give, and probably on how they give it. They need to pay more attention to how the "rules of the game" are communicated and whether everyone in the game understands how to play.

PREVENTING FRUSTRATION. If a large and growing proportion of the labor force in R&D believe they are not getting rewarded for the contributions they believe they are making, they are likely to become frustrated. Frus-

It is difficult for women who persist in getting technical training to believe they are as good as men

As newcomers are promoted, a white male may wonder how he is being viewed

tration, in turn, often leads to poorer performance, a less productive work environment, and higher turnover.

Our study shows that the foreign-born, both Europeans and non-Europeans, are less likely to be satisfied than the U.S.-born with life in the United States, and they are more likely to say they would consider working abroad, either for their current or a different company. Non-Europeans are also more likely to want to start their own businesses than are the U.S.-born.

For women, their underestimation of their contributions is equally problematic. If women are more tentative about their contributions and less confident about what they have to offer, then they surely are not as likely to offer their opinions, to challenge those they think are on the wrong track, or to make suggestions about new directions.

Such speculation about the effects for both women and foreign-born scientists and engineers is consistent with what we have found for teamwork. There is no such thing these days as the isolated inventor. Problems are too complex and solutions too interdisciplinary for people to work alone.

In our measures of how well people work together, we are finding that women and foreign-born males differ in many respects from their U.S.-born male colleagues. (Again, non-European men are similar to each other, while European men are more similar to U.S.-born white men. U.S.-born women and foreign-born women are not as similar on the teamwork measures as they are on performance measures.)

A key indicator of teamwork is networking; generally, the larger one's network within R&D, the better one performs. We measured the size of a network as the number of people a subject talked to about work in a given time period. We find that the foreign-born talk to fewer people within their own laboratories than do the U.S.-born, though their networks are just as extensive outside the lab, both inside and outside the company.

Women resemble men in their lab and intracompany networks, but they talk to fewer people outside the company. While it is not clear which kind of network is most important for long-term career prospects, managers tend to rate those with large lab networks most highly.

We also evaluated teamwork by asking respondents about the level of cooperation they receive, both within R&D and across functions. The foreign-born respond like U.S.-born males on these measures, although they are less likely to work with other functions. Women report getting more cooperation than men from other functions such as marketing and manufacturing; in fact, they say this cooperation is greater than that from their own colleagues in R&D.

We probed further into cooperation by asking people about the characteristics of their own work group. Like the U.S.-born men, foreign-born men responded favorably about group cooperation and, on some questions, even more favorably. For example, they see greater similarity of work styles than U.S.-born men do.

Women, however, are less favorable. They report less confidence and trust within their group, less mutual support, less enthusiasm, less similarity in work styles, less comfort with the decision-making process, and less equality. They are less likely than men to agree with the direction of the group, to say that they themselves can influence the group, and to feel a part of the group.

The message therefore is mixed. The foreign-born generally get cooperation and feel quite comfortable in their groups, but they talk to fewer people in their laboratory about their work. Women talk to people in the lab, but seem to feel less fully accepted in their group. If interactions with others are limited, neither women nor the foreign-born are as likely to contribute fully—or to have their contributions fully recognized.

EVALUATING LEADERS. In all of this, the managers are the unknown quantity. We did not ask managers for self-evaluations or ask their superiors for appraisals. It would surely be interesting to correlate this kind of information with the results of our survey, and perhaps that will be possible in the future. But we did ask their subordinates to address the question of leadership.

In our focus groups before the survey, we heard again and again how important leadership is to subordinates; success in R&D *depended* on the manager—that is, the first-line supervisor—people told us. A good manager can help a scientist or engineer get ahead by giving highly visible assignments, smoothing interactions with others so that the job is easier to do, and offering coaching.

Women are more likely than men to get coaching and to have access to mentors and social networks, we found, contrary to the findings of most mentoring studies. The foreign-born are less likely to report having such access. Generally, however, the foreign-born respond favorably about their leaders, sometimes more favorably than U.S.-born men.

Women rate their supervisors lower than men on such issues as getting people to

work together, letting people know where they stand, being sensitive to differences among people, and minimizing hassles with the staff. But women's opinions are just as favorable as men's on the ability of their supervisors to communicate goals, define problems, get resources, and motivate commitment, among other things.

BRIDGING GAPS. An encouraging aspect of our findings is that there is not more overt evidence of discrimination or exclusion for ''new'' groups in R&D on the part of either supervisors or colleagues. Differences seem to have more to do with culture than with competence and contribution. In other words, there may be avenues toward bridging gaps and managing diversity. But change will not occur without concerted steps toward a better mutual understanding and esteem for the differences that will persist.

We need to understand more the differences among the foreign-born and among women as groups, the sources of misperception and misunderstanding of contributions, the work dynamics that make some feel a part of the group and others excluded, and where managers can make a difference.

In most cases, U.S.-born white men have an edge over other groups in terms of integration into the work group, interaction with managers, and benefiting from the rewards of their jobs. Such distinctions cannot continue, however, as women and the foreign-born become more numerous in R&D. And as these newcomers get promoted into management, there may be questions as well about how they view incoming U.S.-born white males.

ABOUT THE AUTHORS. Nancy DiTomaso is associate professor of organization management in the Graduate School of Management at Rutgers University, Newark, N.J. She does research and consulting on the management of diversity and change, minorities and women in management, and politics and decision-making in organizations.

George Farris (EM) is acting dean and professor of organization management at Rutgers' Graduate School of Management, where he also directs the Technology Management Research Center. He is a member of the editorial board of the *IEEE Transactions on Engineering Management*.

Commitment from the top makes it work

David Barclay
Vice President, Diversity
Hughes Aircraft Co.

Like any major aerospace company, Hughes Aircraft Co. has had affirmative action programs for about 20 years. But our emphasis on workforce diversity began in 1987, when the Hudson Institute released *Workforce 2000*, with its predictions of a huge influx of women and minorities into the workforce of the next century.

Hughes's management took that forecast very seriously. At the same time, the company was worried that the United States was not producing sufficient numbers of engineers and scientists. These concerns motivated Malcolm Currie, our former chairman and chief executive officer, to commit himself and the company to achieving diversity in our workforce.

To achieve our goal, we developed a variety of strategies. One was to establish employee networking organizations so that people with common interests could communicate with each other and with management, and management could communicate with them. Through such communication, of course, we wanted to create an environment that would encourage and value diversity. Currently, our employee network organizations are composed of women, Asians, blacks, Hispanics, and employees with disabilities.

We also set up a program of planned mentoring where experienced, respected managers were matched with promising new employees and asked to counsel and guide them. Mentoring has always existed on a spontaneous, informal basis at Hughes, but we wanted to institutionalize it, to give it explicit support and encouragement with the goal of developing women and minorities for positions of greater responsibility.

A third strategy was to expand our efforts to ensure a steady flow of qualified prospective employees through the educational "pipeline." Within a few years, the average high-school class in Los Angeles will be 50 percent Hispanic, 13 percent black, and 7 percent Asian—and the dropout rate is already 50 percent. To encourage high schoolers, and those from underrepresented groups in particular, to stay in school and study science and engineering, we began working on several projects.

One was the sponsorship of the Youth Motivation Task Force, a group of several hundred employees who visit junior and senior high schools to encourage students to consider a technical education. We also set up the Hughes Galaxy Institute for Education, which designs innovative and exciting curricula for kindergarten through fifth-grade students by using communication satellites, television, and interactive technology.

Accept and value diversity

The National Society of Black Engineers—or NSBE—has had a major influence on my life. It is the organization that first introduced me to engineering when I was in high school in Chicago. And today I'm still active in it; I currently serve as NSBE's national chairperson emeritus.

My initial meeting with the group happened when my chemistry teacher at Mendell High School arranged for us seniors to visit Northwestern University. There, the NSBE chapter members, all engineering students themselves, told us about their course work and their career prospects.

I was impressed by their enthusiasm for the school, for the curriculum, and for the NSBE as an organization. They were certainly strong role models, and I came away feeling that going to college would be a good experience and that I would have ample opportunity to apply my learning afterward.

I went on to get my B.S. in electrical engineering at the Illinois Institute of Technology on an AT&T Bell Laboratories scholarship; it wouldn't have been possible without that financing. Then I went to the Georgia Institute of Technology for my EE master's.

At graduation, Bell Labs offered me a job at Indian Hill, in Naperville, Ill., and I spent several satisfying years there as a member of the technical staff working on the 5ESS electronic switch project. This led to work on real-time network software, and I collaborated with operating company engineers on developing intelligent networks.

An offer to join Pacific Bell grew out of these contacts. I joined the company in 1987 and am now director of the Information Technology Engineering Consulting Group in San Ramon, Calif. Our role in this group is to support the regional business units of Pacific Bell by conducting information technology studies and developing specifications for new technology strategies. We also develop new product concepts.

Sometimes people ask me what it's like to be a black engineer in a predominantly white profession; how do I cope? Initially, it was something of a challenge. I had to make the transition from a university setting to a work environment, and I had to adjust to a bicultural experience—one culture by day and another at night. But I soon found that there is a

sense of support in an engineering environment, that engineers tend to work together.

My personal experience has been positive, not only as an engineer but also as a manager. I think this is partly because I value diversity. While at Bell Labs, I experienced a powerful revelation; my work there exposed me to diverse cultures, many from outside the United States, that I simply did not know about when I was growing up. I came to appreciate how these differing perspectives helped us solve problems faster and more effectively.

Of course, I've heard stories of frustration from black professionals at other corporations—complaints about dull jobs, lack of acceptance, and the inability to get ahead. My perception of why blacks, Asians, Hispanics, and females run into such problems is that management is ineffective in addressing issues, relying on negative stereotypes rather than positively valuing diversity. If managers were more effective in coaching and mentoring, employees would have more opportunities that would lead to equitable career development, independent of the individual's background.

Something we all have to guard against is thinking in terms of stereotypes. The cover story in the winter issue of The Bridge sticks in my mind; the NSBE sends the magazine to precollege students to excite them about engineering and encourage them to enter the profession. "Racial harmony begins with you," the cover blurb said. The article, "Stereotypes: The Beginnings of Prejudice," drove home the idea that stereotypes not only divide people, but, worse than that, they create a mindset that hinders progress for all.

This idea can be developed even further in an industrial setting. How often one hears marketing people criticizing the engineers, the engineers criticizing the lab, and buyers criticizing suppliers. The criticism always invokes stereotypes like the "over-aggressive" sales rep, the "nerdy" engineer, the "ivory tower" researcher, or the "unscrupulous" vendor. My belief is that in the '90s, U.S. industry will have to face the challenge of fostering teamwork and cooperation. The best way to do this is to accept and value diversity among people and among functional organizations.　　　　*—Louis S. Hureston*

348

Besides these ongoing efforts, today we also support the California Academy of Mathematics and Science, a unique high school intended to increase the number of women and minorities interested in pursuing math, science, and engineering.

We participate, too, in several other precollege education ventures. For example, our desire to make a measurable difference in kindergarten through twelfth-grade education has led to the Hughes K-12 collaborative partnerships with schools throughout southern California.

We have developed partnerships with historically black colleges and universities and other minority institutions. We also contribute hundreds of thousands of dollars every year in grants and scholarships to minority engineering programs.

How well have we succeeded in attaining our goal of diversity? We don't know yet; obviously, we need some kind of measurement

system, and we are now defining what the measures should be. By one standard, the ethnic, gender, and racial mix of employees, we've certainly made progress. Women constitute 36 percent of our workforce, and minorities, 33 percent. These percentages are much larger than they were 10 years ago, and we've achieved them despite a truly difficult economy and continued downsizing.

Diversity, however, is not a replacement for equal employment opportunity or affirmative action; it is an extension. The complexity of these programs goes far beyond bottom-line numbers, though numerical goals are clearly an effective measurement tool.

It will take time to answer such questions as: are the numbers distributed among all levels of management and responsibility? How harmoniously and creatively do diverse elements work together? Do we evaluate performance in ways that let us draw on the

special strengths of employees with different cultural backgrounds? Acting on these answers will also take time, but we knew at the outset we were in this for the long haul.

To any company, large or small, that contemplates implementing a diversity program, I would offer one key recommendation: make sure top management is fully committed to diversity and will take a leadership role in implementing it. No company, regardless of its size, can be successful in this area unless executive management states emphatically its commitment to change and to a workforce diversity program.

A case in point is Malcolm Currie's address to the first joint meeting of Hughes employees' networking organizations in Los Angeles on Aug. 8, 1990. Currie reminded everyone that Hughes's products, as marvelous as they are, are transitory. ''Our real strength, our competitive edge, and what we

The Individual is important

Engineering was an easy choice for me. I liked science, I wanted a professional career, and I knew that engineering promised a good income after only a few years of study—less than for medicine or law. Also, the title "engineer" carries a lot of prestige in Latin America, more than it does in the United States.

My high school years were spent in Caguas, Puerto Rico, where I was born. When it came time to pick an engineering school, I opted for the Florida Institute of Technology (FIT) in Melbourne mainly because it had a four-year BSEE program and a strong electronics orientation. The University of Puer-

to Rico, on the other hand, had a five-year program and emphasized power.

FIT also offered a Ph.D. program, which I figured would be an advantage if I decided to go into graduate school. As it turned out, I did stay at FIT on a teaching assistantship and eventually got my doctorate on a Ford Foundation fellowship.

I started at FIT in 1970. It was a painful transition for me. I had to adapt to a new language, a new culture, and a different climate. Northerners may think central Florida is balmy, but we never had to worry about frost harming the citrus crop in Puerto Rico, as people do in Melbourne.

Language was certainly a challenge because I had to become fluent in English fast. On the island, I had gotten only a smattering of English, just like kids who study a foreign language in the States. I had learned the King's English pronunciation in school, but when I first heard people speaking in Florida, I thought, "What are they saying?" They skipped so many syllables that their words were unintelligible to me. (We do the same thing in Spanish, of course.)

What made the language barrier more serious was that it could have had an impact on my grades. I remember one quiz in physics that had a problem focusing on a freight train's caboose and when the caboose might be hit by another train. I didn't know what a caboose was, but I figured it must be an important part of the train and therefore either at the beginning or the end.

So I answered the problem in two ways: one, assuming the caboose was at the beginning of the train, and the other, at the end. The professor was impressed that I had analyzed the problem so thoroughly. Little did he know that I had improvised

to come up with an answer and not lose credit.

Cultural adaptation was also tough. Everybody complains about college cafeteria food, but I saw foods at FIT that I didn't even recognize. Other students would say, "Well, it tastes different at home," but I didn't even have that reference.

More seriously, the biggest shock was going from a close-knit Hispanic community to the individualistic American culture. I had thrust myself into a very competitive environment where the emphasis was on the individual rather than on the team or the group.

But all of my adapting, thriving, and surviving, I think, helped me later in my career as an engineer and a manager. Today I speak (and think) English as easily as I do Spanish, and I understand American individualism. However, I haven't forgotten that I come from a culture that believes in working together as a team and is more interested in winning the game than in the individual scores.

That trait has influenced my professional life. As an engineering manager, I have been able to build teams more effectively than some of my colleagues. For me it comes naturally; I would not do it any other way.

After graduation, I accepted employment with AT&T Bell Laboratories in Naperville, Ill., near Chicago. I've been working in switching ever since, first in design and now as switch product manager for the international 5ESS switch. My group advises marketing, sales, and customers; we're the ones who know our products best.

In working as a manager, my assignment most recently has been in the Central and South American markets. Since I know the language, the culture, and the technology, it has been fairly easy for me to access the highest levels of telephone companies and ministries. When special attention is shown, the customer feels, "I really do matter; I'm not just an account, just a number of telephone lines, just a $20 million proposal. I'm an individual to AT&T."

Another managerial plus, I think, is the ability to accept more than one view, more than one language,

349

will do in the future lies in the minds of our people," he said.

And he continued, pointedly, "This is why the release of human possibilities of all our people must be our highest and never-ending activity. It must be worked at and cultivated. And it's important that all levels of supervision and management understand this." It was important that Hughes not concentrate on numbers alone, he said. It was time to go beyond affirmative action; it was not enough to simply affirm the notion of equality of opportunity.

Once this commitment is established, the first thing a company should do to implement a diversity program is to develop a mission statement and objectives so that all employees have a clear vision of where they are going. To determine where improvements need to be made, a company must also collect data internally.

Many other activities should follow. Examples are: setting up awareness training for management people; identifying specific processes that affect career growth and development and evaluating their effectiveness; and developing measurement tools and management accountability systems.

Some further advice is: use a variety of media to get the message across—and to receive messages. At Hughes, we report on diversity efforts and results in *Hughesnews*, our employee newspaper. We also produce videotapes that address various issues in a diverse workplace, and our executives meet with small groups of employees to learn their feelings and perceptions. And we take full advantage of the two-way communication that our employee network groups provide.

The greatest asset our company has is the talent and energy of its employees. We recognize the need to use and develop the skills of all employees, while helping them achieve their career goals on an equal basis according to their contributions and performance. We believe that a diverse workforce helps us meet our business objectives and increase our productivity. To us, commitment to diversity is a fundamental management philosophy that is an integral part of the company's overall operating strategy.

---

more than one culture, and more than one way of solving a problem. This flexibility gives a person a definite edge over those who do things in a monolithic way. In my own case, having accepted a second culture—Anglo-American—I found it easier to accept a third—Asian.

The experience learned in adapting to a new culture also makes adapting to new technology easier. I think that has helped me stay current and will allow me to avoid the fate of succumbing to technological obsolescence.

Another advantage I have had that has helped me as a manager is my Hispanic background. Before discussing any business, Hispanics ask, "How are you?," and they really want to know. And the next question almost immediately is, "How is your family?" Hispanics are sincerely concerned about the welfare of a colleague's family—healthwise and otherwise. Only then are they ready to conduct serious business.

But those preliminaries make good business sense. An engineer who is preoccupied with family worries is not going to work as productively as he or she otherwise would. That's why I spend time with my team as often as I can and try to develop personal relationships with them. Often, I can help them adjust their work schedules so that they can tend to pressing problems or illness at home. "What are you doing here?," I said to one worried parent. "Why aren't you home taking care of your sick children?"

On the subject of diversity in general, I think we are extremely lucky in the United States to have such varied people resources. With 25 million Hispanics, we are the fifth largest Spanish-speaking country in the world.

If we develop a proportional number of Hispanic engineers and managers, we can relate to technological markets in Mexico and Central and South America. Similarly, black engineers can help us relate to the vast potential markets in Africa, and Asian engineers can help to make us more effective in the Pacific Rim and India.   —*Manuel Figueroa (M)*

Forums for diversity

Ethel Batten
Head, Diversity Department
AT&T Bell Laboratories

Here at AT&T Bell Laboratories, our technical staff has nearly reached the level of demographics predicted by the Hudson Institute report *Workforce 2000*. Our engineers and scientists are from everywhere in the world.

You can walk throughout the halls and see different cultures represented by various forms of dress. You will also see people with physical disabilities. Why is that? Because through our recruiting process, we look for the best and the brightest, regardless of race, lifestyle, or physical challenges.

However, most of the diversity is not yet at the executive or managerial level. And that can be a problem: if managers don't feel comfortable with the differences among the technical staff, then even subconsciously they tend to hire and give opportunities only to people like themselves.

I am not speaking about only traditional white males. We have some groups headed by Asians that have a dominant Asian composition, where the white male in the group is the outsider. Or a young department head may be looking for workers who are "innovative" or "creative" or who have "young blood," and older employees may not be selected for that group, which then

In high schools in Los Angeles, the dropout rate is already 50 percent

loses out on their experience and wisdom.

From the company's viewpoint, diversity is an issue of quality: using all your resources—especially people—to their full potential, including all their unique and different points of view and skills.

Moreover, people are more productive if they're comfortable at work—if they feel they can be open and honest. One example of such candor is sexual orientation. It's natural that on Monday a colleague might ask me: "What did you do this weekend?" I might say: "My husband and I planted bulbs." But what about the gay person? He or she might say: "My friend and I saw a play," and avoid mentioning the friend's gender to fit in with heterosexual expectations.

This person, if not comfortable with colleagues, may be the one who always comes alone to the company picnic, who has no pictures in the office, and who is always busy when invited with family to dinner. Colleagues, in turn, feel the distance and treat the gay person like a loner.

Thus he or she becomes the outsider. And that can translate into fewer opportunities in the person's career—because a lot of work gets done at the lunch table and at social or informal settings.

Keep in mind, merit in work is sometimes a result not only of competence, but also of opportunity. If this person has fewer opportunities and promotions, then the company loses out on the full use of his or her talents. Some of this we find out during exit interviews. But it's more important that we get driving instructions while we're driving, not after a collision. I want people to tell me how they feel while they're still here.

Another area where the company gains a competitive advantage from a diverse workforce is customer service. As companies become more global, their customer base is becoming more diverse. If we can utilize the skills, backgrounds, language, and culture of the people in the company, we can better meet the needs of the customers.

For example, after the dissolution of the Soviet Union, AT&T was looking immediately toward proposing some communications systems in Ukraine. We had a number of people from Ukraine here at Bell Labs, and they became advisors to the marketing or-

350

ganization. Even here at home, AT&T has begun to see real gains in sending Hispanic sales people into Hispanic neighborhoods.

People with differences want to be asked for their views because their cultures are important to them. We have to be conscious of differences in our planning. To cite an instance, we don't want to schedule a major meeting or company picnic on Chinese New Year or on Yom Kippur or on Hindu New Year, any more than we do on Christmas.

All of our survival depends on managing relationships: at work that means relationships with our bosses, our subordinates, and our colleagues. Feeling comfortable with differences in people comes only through understanding them. We're encouraging that understanding in two ways: by soliciting the views of diverse groups for strategic planning and corporate policy, and by supporting certain extracurricular cultural events to help everyone appreciate and value the differences between people.

The oldest, largest, and probably most influential diverse group here is the Black Technical Managers, which includes techni-

Managers are inclined to hire and promote those in their own image

cal supervisors, department heads, directors, and executive directors throughout the technical organization. Its counterpart, representing the nontechnical managers, is the Black Administrative Managers.

Another group is the Asian-Americans for Affirmative Action, representing the Asian and Pacific Island populations of Bell Labs. Our Hispanic group is the Bell Labs chapter of the national organization Hispa, and the Native American Club represents the American Indians in all of AT&T. Also active is a group called League (Lesbian and Gay United Employees). Although League was formed at Bell Labs, it has now become a nationwide organization and held its first national conference this past February in Florida.

Among Bell Labs' disabled employees, the hearing-impaired subgroup is especially busy. This year we're having workshops for managers who have hearing-impaired employees, teaching them how to deal with the deaf culture. We're also holding workshops for hearing-impaired employees to help them get the most out of being a corporate citizen and working here. On staff we also

Raising the gross national spirit

Many native Americans entering an engineering college or university today find themselves in a disquieting situation on two fronts. First, their technical background is likely to be inadequate owing to poor preparation in Government-run reservation schools or in many inner-city schools. Second, there are significant differences in the value systems of the indigenous cooperative culture and the western competitive culture.

As a Hopi removed one generation from Government schools, I was fortunate enough to receive adequate technical preparation for my undergraduate work in the late 1950s. I earned a B.S. in mechanical engineering from California State Polytechnic University (1961) and an M.S. in mechanical/control systems engineering from the University of Southern California (1966).

Nonetheless, I was still disquieted by the gap in the value systems—a gap that still exists today. The difficulty arises not, as past U.S. government policy has assumed, because native peoples do not have the intellectual capacity or cognitive ability to learn. It emerges because, at the root, native peoples have

a life ethic that differs from today's competitive western world. That ethic emphasizes family, knowledge of tradition and self, understanding of the individual's relationship with the Creator and the land, sharing with others, and the wise use of resources. Fundamentally, our people still believe they are keepers of the land, stewards for generations, not exploiters of resources for short-term gain.

Only very recently—in the 1970s—did the Federal government adopt a policy of self-determination for native peoples rather than relying on paternalism and cultural absorption. Among other things, self-determination, which we had adopted for ourselves generations earlier, means governing our own destiny, including developing the physical and personal infrastructure of the tribes. Such development has created needs for leaders, engineers, scientists, doctors, lawyers, and businesspeople.

In the past two decades, native Americans have begun to focus on creating the infrastructure to encourage and train young people for entering

professions—like engineering and science—that were seldom considered or encouraged by the culture of Federal government schools. But the highly specialized and secular European style of education used in teaching these professions is different from the more holistic and spiritually conscious native American cultures.

As a native American, a Hopi, I take a holistic approach to life. Our ancestors did not set boundaries separating traditional forms of engineering, science, art, and the spiritual Creator-centered life. Even today I find myself freely shifting back and forth among these areas.

For the first 10 years after receiving my degrees, I was an engineering specialist and a project engineer at Litton Guidance and Control Systems in Woodland Hills, Calif. There, I designed and developed inertial measurement units and star trackers for military and intercontinental commercial aircraft.

The next 18 years, I worked on creating and managing the Environmental Department at the Salt River Project, a power and water utility serving Phoenix, Ariz. The emphasis there was placed on sensitivity to the environment and to people when siting large coal-fired power plants, railroads, dams, and other projects.

During this time, however, I was also highly influenced by my aunt Elizabeth White, who taught me the philosophy and art of making pottery. In 1990, I left industry to pursue an artistic career and community service. Now I provide technical and political assistance to my Hopi tribe on coal mining and mineral resources.

I have also helped to set up two groups that are aimed at helping young native Americans find their way in technical fields while retaining their cultural traditions. One, which I co-founded in 1977, is the American Indian Science and Engineering Society (Aises). Now based in Boulder, Colo., the 2000-member society is dedicated to increasing the number of American Indians in science and engineering and to developing Indian leaders.

Aises has mentorship programs, interactive tutoring, several hundred annual scholarships, and 81 student chapters in the United States and Canada. Although the students in Aises represent 250 tradi-

have two sign-language interpreters, one in Indian Hill and one in South Jersey. And this year one of the things we are enhancing is the access and mobility needs of our wheelchair-bound employees.

We encourage all these groups to be aware of one another by holding Diversity Day at the various Bell Labs sites. The groups all come together and set up tables with brochures. Highlighting the day is a meeting in the auditorium to talk about diversity, legislation, and other work-related issues.

One reason for such get-togethers is that many of the issues these employees face are generic to all. Thus, we are planning to set up a permanent intercouncil of the different groups. From that, we hope to learn what issues need to be addressed by train-

ing and education to get people away from doing unproductive things. After all, bigotry, chauvinism, and racism are all unproductive.

In addition, Bell Labs encourages the observation of various cultural activities, which can range from serious to lighthearted. Usually they're held during lunchtime. For example, during Women's History Month, we had a couple of female Nobel Prize winners come in as speakers. During Black History Month, our opening keynote address was given by William H. Gray III, president and chief executive officer of the United Negro College Fund Inc. We also had a display of attire for African women and a concert by the Harlem Boys' Choir. And during Asian Heritage Month, we had art work displayed and performances by Asian

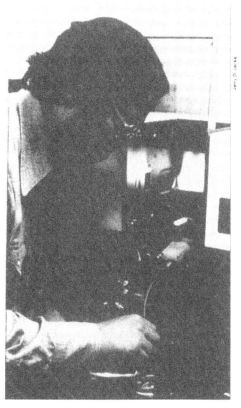

tional tribes, they have a common spiritual tie and a tradition of honoring one another. Supported by the Indian community, by donations from corporations and foundations, and by grants from Government agencies, including the National Science Foundation, Aises works to give young people the opportunity to lead major projects.

The society originally started as a college-level organization to encourage native Americans to enter technical careers. But we've found that even high school is often too late: young people gain or lose their academic motivation around age 12 or 13. So now we're looking at ways to open up the pipeline by reaching students as young as those in grammar school (and their parents as well).

Through Aises, we're also working with young people to show them they do not have to lose their In-

dian heritage to enter the professional world. On the contrary, there is much value their holistic background can bring to engineering and science.

To encourage such thinking, every November since 1979, Aises has held a three-day national conference; 1991's had more than 3000 attendees and over 100 exhibitors. Unlike most technical society meetings today, the hallmark of Aises meetings is prayer and blessings, part of our ancient traditions.

Our students have called for additional orientation in their cultural values or traditions while learning technical fields. One organization that can meet that call is the Institute of American Indian Arts, which a number of us founded in 1988 in Santa Fe, N. M. At present the institute is a two-year accredited college with about 50 faculty and staff and more than 250 students. It teaches all the arts, computer graphics, and film-making, and is opening a new museum in downtown Santa Fe this June.

Now being planned is a campus on a 140-acre site in Santa Fe, with a first-phase vision of a four-year college or university for 1000 students, with integrated studies of architecture, science, the environment, business, and liberal arts.

Eventually, the Institute's emphasis will be on providing national and international students with a holistic education, focusing on ways to meet the vision of renewal and rebirth for all native peoples of North, Central, and South America. Its aim will be to revitalize and honor each tradition and language, and to emphasize the wholeness of the family, the sanctity of all living things, and the healing of the earth.

At Aises's annual meeting last year, our young people affirmed their greater concern for North America's gross national spirit rather than for its gross national product.

Both Aises and IAIA give us new hope because they represent not only technical grounding but also the rebirth and continuation of our past civilization, even in today's materialistic and energy-consuming Western civilization. Our traditional value system helps keep people whole. And it's one that I expect our young people will apply in the workplace and in their positions of leadership.

—*Alfred H. Qöyawayma (M)*

marking exercise. Visiting five different companies, we looked at what they do in this business and how they do it and compared it to what we're doing here.

More commonly, people call us wanting to know how our groups got started, how are they funded, and how Bell Labs works with them. Also, I conduct workshops during the fall and spring at historically black colleges and colleges that have a lot of women students. I also work with high schools and inner-city groups such as Inroads and Aspira. From these activities, I see what is going on in many places.

The best signal I get from this work is that companies are beginning to see diversity as a business issue, not just a moral issue. Being a second-class nation is not what any of them want. We want to be No. 1. We want everybody to be utilized. That means we have to understand what issues impact everybody.

Making engineers feel at home

Sharon Richards
Intercultural Program Manager
Intel Corp.

Intel Corp.'s intercultural training for employees goes back to 1983, when a group of senior managers saw a need to support foreign-born engineers—primarily Asians at that time—by helping them understand and adapt to U.S. culture. The senior managers instituted our "Multicultural Integration Workshop," a one-day session where newly hired professionals get together with managers to identify the cross-cultural issues in the workplace that affect them directly. The managers strive to provide the newcomers with role models and help them with career planning. Perhaps most importantly, the workshop gives these employees an informal environment for meeting people and making contacts.

Still the keystone of our intercultural program, the workshop is now augmented by courses on American business culture, accent improvement, speaking under pressure, American idioms and vocabulary in the workplace, and technical and business writing.

The accent improvement course, for example, recognizes that foreign-born employees often have a good command of English vocabulary and structure but find that colleagues have trouble understanding them. Participants practice the sounds, rhythm, stress, and intonation of American English. We promise students that they will speak more clearly and confidently in person and over the phone. We follow up with a maintenance program in which students practice prepared presentations and extemporaneous speech; the maintenance course can be taken several times.

dancers.

All the functions put on by these diverse groups are funded by Bell Labs. The groups apply for funding from my diversity department, listing and describing what they plan to do during the year and how much money they want. We on the committee look at the funding request and either grant it, trim it, or do what is needed.

Awareness training programs are also in place to educate employees to recognize and respect the value of human differences. Some of these programs include workshops like "Gay and Lesbian Issues in the Workplace," "Women and Men in the Work Environment," "Managing Diversity," and "Minority Workshops for Asians/Blacks/Hispanics in the Corporate Environment."

To better understand how effectively Bell

Labs uses minorities, women, and people with disabilities, we have started a program of utilization analysis to compare work experiences in hiring, promotions, salaries, and performance reviews.

The success of all these programs is measured through questionnaires, asking employees and customers their reactions about the value of the activity and whether or not it will enhance our ability to value diversity. Thus we can summarize the data at the end of the year and provide the technical organization with some kind of metrics about how it was received, which ones had the greatest impact, and whether we should do it again next year.

We also communicate with people in equivalent positions at other companies. Just recently, we finished a competitive bench-

Speaking out runs counter to many Asians' cultural norms; it is considered boastful

We also coach foreign-born professionals in making effective oral presentations, as well as in writing with clarity and precision. Our idioms and vocabulary course introduces 200 common American idioms; we teach techniques for vocabulary building, read the news together for current usage, and present phrases for speaking smoothly.

Foreign-born professionals have joined in these courses enthusiastically, and we in the program are hard-pressed to keep up with the demand for them.

At the same time, the program has expanded in another direction: helping U.S.-born engineers understand and adapt to other cultures. One aim is to enable them to work effectively and productively in our U.S. facilities with people from diverse backgrounds, and in our international sites as well. We want them to be aware of and sensitive to local customs, courtesies, and business practices.

In an intensive all-day session, for example, managers learn how people from four different cultures approach problem-solving, conflicts, work relationships, time management, and information exchange. They hear their fellow employees' views about what it's like to work at Intel and what it's like to be foreign-born in an American work environment.

A topic that is cited often is speaking up, which is regarded as countercultural by many people who come from Asian cultures. It's seen as boastful bragging, tooting your own horn. Yet, for all of us, accomplishments and achievements need to be known in the workplace; that's critical to success in the work environment. It's also no less important for the company to have the benefit of our ideas, even if they seem to contradict or compete with those of others. So we try to develop practical techniques of communication whereby frank discussion is encouraged and diffidence is overcome for the sake of solving common problems.

Another session, "Managing in a Cultural Environment," gives the managers firsthand experience and suggests strategies for building a multicultural team. Managers get feedback from our "Multicultural Integration Course," too, when appropriate, as to how they can best support and guide those who report to them.

But a bigger aim of the program derives from Intel's international presence and involvement in joint ventures around the world that deal with customers and suppliers abroad. To expand our management competency globally, we offer culture-specific training classes for engineers who are on assignment to—or who interface frequently with—Japan, Korea, Taiwan, Malaysia, the Philippines, Ireland, and Israel. Another group called "inpatriates"—employees from international sites who are on assignment in the United States—are also given both intercultural and country-specific training as part of their relocation.

For example, "Intel-Ireland Interface" is an eight-hour session in which participants learn about U.S. and Irish cultural differences and how they affect business communication styles and practices. Another, "Japanese Culture/Language," comes in three segments that, combined, give 132 hours of training in such practical activities as making appointments, describing events, and requesting items and services. Along with that, students learn about Japanese values, norms, and communication style.

In all our training, we point out that our goal is to help participants acquire insights and skills that can enhance their professional development, and that we're not encouraging them to give up their core values or their cultural heritage. Inpatriates often ask me, "Do I have to give up who I am to be successful in the American environment?" Not at all.

What we do recommend is that people—both expatriates and inpatriates—acquire a repertoire of skills that will help them to work in multiple environments. In our classes, we refer to that battery of skills as "style switching." On a rainy day, for instance, you put on a raincoat, but that doesn't mean you wear it all day long. We wear our most comfortable jeans and T-shirts to a picnic; we wear more formal clothes to a graduation dinner.

I think the most valued part of our training is presenting to the students successful men and women who represent diversity. They talk about their career paths, their accomplishments, and the hurdles they cleared. They convey their own personal perspective and the message that, at Intel, you can take initiative; you can make things happen.

Single-minded striving

My father always wanted each of his daughters to become a professional—a doctor, a lawyer, or an engineer. I was supposed to become an engineer—and I did. In Vietnam, where my family comes from, engineering is regarded as one of the most prestigious professions—more so than it is here in the United States.

My family left Vietnam in April 1975, when the Thieu government was falling and the Viet Cong were taking over in the south. My mother brought me, my four sisters, and my brother to the United States with exactly US $100, while my father stayed behind to try to secure at least some of our savings. We had to get out fast, but our money was tied up in the bank. He wasn't able to rejoin us for another two years, and he could bring nothing with him.

My mother settled us in Houston, Texas, and we proceeded to acclimate ourselves, enrolling in the local schools. I went down one grade, but after a year in sixth grade at Gordon Elementary School, I skipped the next three grades. I graduated from Alief Hastings High School in 1979 as class valedictorian—not bad for a 16-year-old girl who spoke no English four years earlier.

Even though my parents encouraged me to study engineering, I considered studying mathematics in college. I loved math in high school and got good grades in trigonometry and calculus. But when I thought carefully about it, I realized that engineering offered a more financially rewarding career—one that would be profitable sooner than mathematics would be. I'll never get rich in engineering, but it does provide a good income. One of my goals, too, was to help my parents as soon as possible.

After I received my BSME from the University of Texas in Austin in 1982, Texas Instruments Inc.

offered me a job in Houston. I was eager to work in Houston because I would be close to my family. At the same time, at 19, I wanted to be independent and rented my own apartment in the neighborhood.

My first assignment at TI was working on defect analysis of manufacturing software for dynamic RAMs. At that time, a 64M-bit memory was state of the art; I worked on schematic verification to ensure an error-free manufacturing tape.

Two years later, I joined the 1M-bit dynamic RAM project. While our supervisor was in Japan working with TI's wafer fab there, I coordinated the team effort in Houston. Later I myself spent nine months in Japan, interfacing with the wafer fab and debugging the chip through several revisions.

In the meantime, I was also taking night courses at the University of Houston, where I received my MBA in 1989.

My work at TI continued to focus on enhanced versions of the 1M-bit dynamic RAM. At one point, I gave design tutorials to engineers at TI sites in Japan, Singapore, and Italy.

Starting in 1989, I led a small team to study the feasibility of manufacturing TI's first biCMOS 4M-bit dynamic RAM. This was to be a superfast chip, with an access time of 35 ns. We evaluated market demand, the progress of competitors, and resource requirements. Then we actually designed the chip, drew up a proposal, and presented it to top management.

Currently I am section design manager for 16M-bit-wide input/output dynamic RAM devices. These are application-specific memories, and so far we've designed a device with over 200 possible options.

A team of nine engineers now reports to me. We work closely with the manufacturing people, with

353

Preparing for responsibility

Thomas J. Smith
Director, Human Resources
Computer Sciences Corp.
Integrated Systems Division

Computer Sciences Corp. (CSC) manufactures no equipment—only ideas. In the Integrated Systems Division, we integrate large systems, mostly for the U.S. government. Our products are complete "megasystems," with all the hardware, software, communications, training, and initial operation and maintenance that go with them. We choose from a variety of hardware and software suppliers to obtain the best solution for a system problem.

To develop our megasystems and put them together, we need many systems engineers, programmers, and communications experts; about 80 percent of the division's staff is highly technical.

Our technical people have such titles as systems analyst, systems engineer, computer scientist, network engineer, office automation specialist, telecommunications programmer, and scientific real-time programmer. They are educated in computer science, mathematics, electrical engineering, physics, and related fields.

We also need managers—people who can coordinate and direct the work of these professionals. In fact, much of our future growth will depend on the success of managers. We found that, as we captured new business, the same names kept coming up time after time as candidates for the project managers' positions. This meant we were continually placing a heavy burden on the same people—and were not developing new people for new business.

To remedy that practice, our division president, Gary Bard, conceived the idea of placing deputy managers under a project manager. The deputies would assist the project manager and accept gradually increasing responsibility. In a year or two, they would be ready to manage a product of their own.

Now, every year we select about seven middle-level managers who show promise. We put them on a fast track and make sure they have frequent contact with the division president and various vice presidents, all people whom they would ordinarily be unlikely to meet. The intent is to encourage middle-level managers and vice presidents to develop mutual trust as the middle-level people mature in responsibility.

Our experience with this program has shown that several advantages accrue from it. First, it provides a route for women and minorities to advance. Our technical staff now consists of about one-third women and 12 percent minorities. We expect the proportions of both groups to grow as *Workforce 2000* predictions materialize, and we want our management as well as our staff to reflect that makeup.

Second, it signals the rest of the workforce that their contributions are equally important and they are not forgotten. When all employees see that selections are based on demonstrated skills and abilities, management will establish credentials for fairness.

Third, we believe that the deputy manager policy will reduce turnover, which can be high in our business. Our employees' skills tend to be highly portable; they can pick up and move almost anywhere they choose, especially in good economic times. We want to retain our good people, and we believe that by showing opportunity for advancement and offering visible recognition, we can do that. We want to show that, even though people may not be immediately promoted, we are concerned about them, their progress, and their future.

Fourth, and most important from a business standpoint, CSC is developing a cadre of experienced, skilled, highly motivated managers drawn from the best that diversity has to offer. When a suitable project comes in, they can take charge immediately—and so far, about a dozen people have done so with outstanding results.

marketing and product engineering, and sometimes with the customers directly. When a problem crops up, we determine whether it's in the process or in the design.

I feel that I have a good relationship with my team and that we work reasonably well together. If I have a complaint, it's that they are too tall! I have a hard time keeping up with them when we walk along the hall, and I certainly couldn't join them in an impromptu baseball game. But my small stature doesn't stop me from joining them in a local pub occasionally to celebrate an accomplishment—or to commiserate over a problem that seems intractable.

I know that I work too hard. I used to work till I dropped, almost. I could work through the night; when I'm working on a problem, I get hooked on it. People have told me I'm "uptight," but I care about my work and I expect the same level of care in others.

These days, I'm trying to be more relaxed. But even when I go home, say at nine or ten o'clock at night, I sometimes feel guilty. Dinner is ready, everything is in order, and my husband has been waiting for me. On the way home, I will often stop for some Hagen-Dasz as a little peace offering. It's easier for a man; he might work that late and not feel guilty because it's traditional for him to put in long hours.

My husband is understanding about it, of course. He is an engineer, too, and he kids me, "If I worked as hard at my company as you do at yours, I'd be a vice president!" We want to start our own family soon, and then I *know* I'll have to limit my work more strictly. —*Duy-Loan T. Le (M)*

TO PROBE FURTHER. *Workforce 2000: Work and Workers for the Twenty-First Century,* by William B. Johnston and Arnold H. Packer (Hudson Institute, 1987), examines the forces shaping the U.S. economy, proposes three scenarios for turn-of-the-century economics, and predicts the demographics of the workforce of the future. It can be ordered from the institute, Box 26-919, Indianapolis, Ind. 46226; 317-545-1000.

Donna E. Thompson and Nancy DiTomaso survey the problems of minorities in management and suggest solutions in *Ensuring Minority Success in Corporate Management* (Plenum Press, New York, 1988).

DiTomaso, George F. Farris, and George C. Gordon give early results of their diversity research in "Managing Diversity in R&D Groups," *Research-Technology Management,* January–February 1991, published by the Industrial Research Institute, Washington, D.C.

The Second Annual Diversity Conference, May 27-29, 1992, Washington, D.C., offered

Singapore: diversity in microcosm

Perhaps no country has a greater racial and cultural diversity in its population than Singapore. Yet with a per capita gross national product of US $13 600—larger than that of many European countries—the small city-state enjoys a prosperity neck and neck with Hong Kong's and exceeded only by Japan's and Brunei's in Asia. Its peoples work together for their common good, encouraged and closely controlled by the Government. Its efficient roads, port, and telecommunications are famous.

Of its 2.7 million citizens and permanent residents, 77 percent are ethnic Chinese, 14 percent are Ma-

Multiracial, polyglot, multireligious—Singapore accepts diversity as a way of life

lays, and 7 percent are Indians (including Pakistanis, Bangladeshis, and Sri Lankans). The balance consists of Eurasians (largely descendants of Portuguese colonials), Arabs, Armenians, and Jews.

To these must be added more than 300 000 temporary residents: North Americans, Europeans, and Japanese from the multinational companies whose investments fuel the island's economy; "guest workers" admitted from Malaysia, the Philippines, Thailand, and other countries as construction and factory workers and domestics; and foreign students, many of them attending Singapore's cosmopolitan

Institute of Southeast Asian Studies.

These residents—along with 5 million foreign tourists a year, ships' crews and passengers in the busiest port in the world, and those in transit at Changi Airport—make up a polyglot lot.

To communicate, these Singaporeans can choose from not one, but four official languages: Malay, Mandarin Chinese, Tamil, and English. Other Chinese dialects spoken are Hokkien, Teochew, Cantonese, Hakka, Hainanese, and Foochow. Indian languages, besides Tamil, include Telegu, Malayalam, Punjabi, Hindi, and Bengali.

English is the medium of instruction in schools and the language of administration, courts, and big business. English is also a *lingua franca* for hundreds of thousands of people who otherwise simply could not talk with each other. Almost half the population speak at least two languages.

Over eight religions are practiced. Most Singaporeans—59 percent—embrace Buddhism, Taoism, and/or Confucianism. Islam, Christianity, and Hinduism together account for another 32 percent, while Sikhism and Judaism account for a significant minority.

In managing this vast diversity, the Singapore Government actively promotes a common Singaporean national identity while recognizing the importance of its people's ethnic roots. Underscoring that recognition, the Government maintains official links with ethnic group representatives. For example, the Islamic Religious Council advises the Government on matters affecting Muslim citizens and administers the mosque-building program and the disbursement of financial assistance to poor Muslims. Similarly, the Hindu Advisory Board provides a link to the Hindu community.

Groups are accorded special treatment, as the Government deems appropriate. For example, marriages (and divorces) between Singaporean Muslims are carried out according to Muslim law, and

so are any inheritance settlements.

Traditionally women in Singapore have worked in lower-level clerical and routine operator jobs in electronics and textile factories. Their salaries have consistently been lower than men's in the private sector, although the Government operates on an equal-pay-for-equal-work basis. Indeed, the Civil Service is one of the major employers of women; more than half its personnel are female.

Women's status in industry may be changing. In keeping with the Government's swing in emphasis to R&D from low-skill, labor-intensive manufacturing, increasing numbers of women are being trained in such technical skills as programming and computer science. Women make up 15 percent of the electrical engineering class at the National University of Singapore.

Indian Singaporeans seem to share less, proportionately, in the country's technological jobs than does the Chinese majority. This underrepresentation may be traced to poor preparation for high-tech careers. In 1989, for example, only 62 percent of 12-year-old Indians passed the national examination in mathematics, compared to 88 percent of Chinese of the same age. The Government exhorts Indian parents to cut back on their children's household chores and television watching in favor of more homework.

The Government is officially committed to diversity. "Tolerance is crucial when peoples of many races, languages, cultures, and religions live together," Lee Kuan Yew, when prime minister, told a gathering of Sikhs. "Singaporeans have by and large accepted diversity as an unchangeable fact of life," he said.

The Singaporean Government is known as a strict one that regulates many aspects of its people's lives, all for what is seen as the greater good of the community. This interventionism is being relaxed, albeit slowly, by a new administration under Lee's successor, Goh Chok Tong. —G.F.W.

---

panels and workshops on such wide-ranging topics as breaking the "glass ceiling," handling white male backlash, and developing conflict resolution skills. For information, contact the National Diversity Conference, Box 978, Danville Square Station, Danville, Calif. 94526-9922; 510-831-0272.

Several engineering organizations provide guidance to members of groups under-represented in the profession. Among them:
• American Indian Science and Engineering Society (Aises), 1630 30th St., Suite 301, Boulder, Colo. 80301; 303-492-8658.
• National Action Council for Minorities in Engineering (Nacme), 3 W. 35th St., New York, N.Y. 10001-2281; 212-279-2626.
• National Society of Black Engineers (NSBE), 1454 Duke St., Alexandria, Va. 22314; 703-549-2351.
• Society of Hispanic Professional Engineers (SHPE), 500 E. Olympic Blvd., Suite 306, Los Angeles, Calif. 90022; 213-725-3970.
• Society of Women Engineers (SWE), 345 E. 47th St., New York, N.Y. 10017;

212-705-7855.

American Demographics, a Dow Jones & Co. publication, covers changing population patterns. A booklet analyzing the 1990 U.S. census results, "American Diversity," is available. Contact the publisher at 127 W. State St., Ithaca, N.Y.; 800-828-1133.

Human Resource Management magazine (John Wiley, New York) frequently addresses diversity issues that affect personnel professionals. See the June 1990 compilation of articles on diversity in the workplace.

The American Society for Engineering Education, Washington, D.C., publishes *ASEE Prism* in which a frequent topic is encouraging diversity in education. See, for example, "The Missing Piece," September 1991, for an analysis of the complex issues underlying efforts to attract and retain women in engineering schools.

For more on diversity in Singapore, see *Singapore Facts and Pictures 1991*, a compendium of useful information and history, published by the Ministry of Information and

the Arts, 460 Alexandra Rd., PSA Building, Singapore 1511; (65) 270 7988. For insight into the challenges Singapore faces, see *Dragons in Distress* by Walden Bello and Stephanie Rosenfeld (Institute for Food and Development Policy, San Francisco, 1990).

ACKNOWLEDGMENTS. Many people cooperated with the *Spectrum* staff on this report. Special thanks go to Michele Bourdon, Intel Corp.; Alok Chakrabarti, New Jersey Institute of Technology; Margarita Colmanares, U.S. Board of Education; Richard Dore, Hughes Aircraft Co.; Robert Ford, AT&T Bell Laboratories; Iris Chin Choo Geddis, Singapore Mission to the United Nations; Dundar Kocaoglu, Portland State University; Debra LaFountaine, American Indian Science and Engineering Society; Ah-Choy Lieu, National University of Singapore; William Pinkston III, National Society of Black Engineers; Betty Prince, Texas Instruments Inc.; Walter Robb, General Electric R&D Center; and Michael F. Wolff, contributing editor. ◆

Reprint: Excerpt from
"Information for the Private Sector and State and Local Governments" produced by the Equal Employment Opportunity Commission.

[The text of the laws discussed in this brochure is contained in another brochure, *Laws enforced by the EEOC*, available from the EEOC.]

THE EQUAL EMPLOYMENT OPPORTUNITY COMMISSION (EEOC)

The U.S. Equal Employment Opportunity Commission (EEOC) was created by Congress and enforces Title VII of the Civil Rights Act of 1964, which prohibits employment discrimination based on race, color, religion, sex or national origin.

Since 1979, EEOC also has enforced: the Age Discrimination in Employment Act of 1967, which protects employees 40 years of age or older; the Equal Pay Act of 1963, which protects men and women who perform substantially equal work in the same establishment from sex-based wage discrimination; and Section 501 of the Rehabilitation Act of 1973, which prohibits federal sector discrimination against persons with disabilities.

On July 26, 1992, EEOC began enforcing the Americans with Disabilities Act, which prohibits discrimination against individuals in the private sector, and in state and local governments based on disability. EEOC is also responsible for enforcing any subsequent changes to the above statutes.

EEOC provides oversight and coordination of all federal regulations, practices and policies affecting equal employment opportunity.

THE COMMISSION

EEOC has five Commissioners and a General Counsel appointed by the President and confirmed by the Senate. Commissioners are appointed for five-year, staggered terms. The term of the General Counsel is four years. The President designates a Chairman and a Vice Chairman. The Chairman is the chief executive officer of the Commission. The five-member Commission makes equal employment opportunity policy and approves all litigation. The General Counsel is responsible for conducting EEOC enforcement litigation.

WORK OF THE COMMISSION

EEOC staff receives and investigates employment discrimination charges against private employers and state and local governments. If the investigation shows reasonable cause to believe that discrimination occurred, the Commission will begin conciliation efforts. If conciliation fails, the charge will be considered for litigation. The Commission's policy is to seek full and effective relief for each and every victim of employment discrimination, whether sought in court or in conciliation agreements before litigation, and to provide remedies designed to correct the discrimination and prevent its recurrence. The Justice Department is the only federal agency that may sue a state or local government for a violation of Title VII or the ADA. EEOC may sue a state or local government for violations of the ADEA or EPA. If the Commission decides not to litigate a charge, a notice of the right to file a private suit in federal district court will be given to the charging party. At the charging party's request, a notice of right to sue also will be issued at any time after the expiration of 180 days from the date the charge was filed.

Reprinted from *Ethics and Computing, Living Responsibly in a Computerized World*, K. Bowyer, pp. 365–373, IEEE. U.S. Government work not protected by U.S. Copyright.

EEOC'S MISSION

The mission of the Commission is to ensure equality of opportunity by vigorously enforcing federal laws prohibiting employment discrimination through investigation, conciliation, litigation, coordination, education and technical assistance.

COMMISSION MEETINGS

In accordance with the Government in the Sunshine Act, meetings of the Commission are open to the public. However, all or part of a meeting may be closed for consideration of matters exempted under the Sunshine Act, such as recommendations for litigation, litigation strategy and other specified matters. For information about Commission meetings, call 202-663-4070 (voice) or 202-663-4018 (TDD). Agenda items for Commission meetings are announced in the Federal Register one week in advance of the meeting.

HEADQUARTERS OFFICES AND THEIR FUNCTIONS

Communications and Legislative Affairs: Serves as the Commission's primary external communications link with the news media, the U.S. Congress, constituency groups, and the public, and conducts internal communications.

Equal Employment Opportunity: Develops policies and implements approved affirmative employment programs to ensure equal employment opportunity within EEOC and executes procedures for prompt and fair resolution of EEO complaints.

General Counsel: Recommends and conducts all EEOC litigation in class, systemic and individual cases of discrimination and subpoena enforcement actions. Presents the Commission's views as *amicus curiae* in cases which the Commission is not a party.

Inspector General: Conducts internal and external investigations and audits related to the programs and operation of the Commission.

Legal Counsel: Serves as principal advisor to the Commission on non-enforcement litigation matters and represents the Commission in defensive litigation and administrative hearings. Prepares Commission decisions on charges involving issues for which there is no precedent, develops all policy guidance for Commission consideration and carries out the Commission's leadership and coordination role for the federal government's EEO programs.

Writes regulations, conducts outreach and education efforts, and coordinates all federal issuances affecting equal employment opportunity.

Management: Overseas administrative, financial, personnel and management support services. Develops and administers the Commission's budget.

Program Operations: Manages, directs and coordinates field office operations and systemic investigations. Implements the Commission's state and local charge deferral and contracting program and conducts the national EEO survey report program.

Federal Operations: Develops policy guidance for federal agency affirmative action programs and provides guidance and a hearings program for federal discrimination complaints. Decides or recommends decisions to the Commission on appeals from federal agency decisions on EEO complaints or negotiated bargaining agreement grievances where allegations of discrimination are raised and on petitions for review of Merit Systems Protection Board decisions involving allegations of discrimination.

TITLE VII
Employment discrimination based on race, color, religion, sex or national origin is prohibited by Title VII of the Civil Rights Act of 1964.

Title VII covers private employers, state and local governments, and educational institutions that have 15 or more employees. The federal government, private and public employment agencies, labor organizations, and joint labor-management committees for apprenticeship and training also must abide by law.

It is illegal under Title VII to discriminate in:

- Hiring and firing;
- Compensation, assignment or classification of employees;
- Transfer, promotion, layoff or recall;
- Job advertisements;
- Recruitment;
- Testing;
- Use of company facilities;
- Training and apprenticeship programs;
- Fringe benefits;
- Pay, retirement plans and disability leave; or
- Other terms and conditions of employment.

Under the law, pregnancy, childbirth and related medical conditions must be treated the same as any other non-pregnancy-related illness or disability.

Title VII prohibits retaliation against a person who files a charge of discrimination, participates in an investigation or opposes an unlawful employment practice.

Employment agencies may not discriminate in receiving, classifying or referring applications for employment or in their job advertisements.

Labor unions may not discriminate in: accepting applications for membership; classifying members; referrals; training and apprenticeship programs; and in advertising for jobs. It is illegal for a labor union to cause or try to cause an employer to discriminate. It is also illegal for an employer to cause or try to cause a union to discriminate.

The Immigration Reform and Control Act of 1986 requires employers to be able to prove that all employees hired after November 6, 1986, are legally authorized to work in the United States. However, an employer who requests employment verification only from individuals of a particular national origin, or individuals who appear to be or sound foreign, may have violated both the

Immigration Act and Title VII.

Citizenship requirements, preferences or rules requiring employees to be fluent in English or speak only English at work may be unlawful if they disproportionately exclude individuals of a particular national origin and are not justified by business necessity. For further information about employment rights and responsibilities under the Immigration Reform and Control Act, call the Office of Special Counsel for Immigration-Related Unfair Employment Practices toll free at 1-800-255-7688 (voice) or 1-800-237-2515 (TDD).

THE AMERICANS WITH DISABILITIES ACT (ADA)

Title I of the Americans with Disabilities Act of 1990, which took effect July 26, 1994, prohibits private employers and state and local governments with 15 or more employees, employment agencies, and labor unions from discriminating against qualified individuals with disabilities in job application procedures, hiring, firing, advancement, compensation, fringe benefits, job training, and other terms, conditions and privileges of employment. An individual with a disability is a person who:

- Has a physical or mental impairment that substantially limits one or more major life activities:
- Has a record of such an impairment; or
- Is regarded as having such an impairment.

A qualified employee or applicant with a disability is an individual who satisfies skill, experience, education, and other job-related requirements of the position held or desired, and who, with or without reasonable accommodation, can perform the essential functions of that position.

Reasonable accommodation may include, but is not limited to:

- Making existing facilities used by employees readily accessible to and usable by persons with disabilities:
- Job restructuring, modification of work schedules, reassignment to a vacant position; or
- Acquiring or modifying equipment or devices, adjusting or modifying examinations, training materials, or policies, and providing qualified readers or interpreters.

An employer is required to make a reasonable accommodation in order to provide an equal employment opportunity to a qualified applicant or employee with a disability, unless this would impose an "undue hardship" on the operation of the employer's business. Undue hardship is defined as an action requiring significant difficulty or expense when considered in light of factors such as a business' size, financial resources and the nature and structure of its operation.

An employer is not required to lower quality or production standards to make an accommodation. Nor is an employer generally obligated to provide personal use items such as eyeglasses or hearing aids.

Before a job offer is made, employers may not ask job applicants about the existence, nature or severity of a disability. Applicants may be asked about their ability to perform specific job functions. A job offer may be conditioned on the results of a medical examination, but only if the examination is required for all entering employees in the same job category. Medical examinations of current employees must be job-related and consistent with the employer's business needs.

Employees and applicants currently engaging in the illegal use of drugs are not covered by the ADA, when an employer acts on the basis of such use. Test for illegal use of drugs are not subject to the ADA's restrictions on medical examinations. Employers may hold individuals who are illegally using drugs, and alcoholics, to the same performance standards as other employees.

EQUAL PAY ACT (EPA)

THE EQUAL PAY ACT prohibits employers from discriminating between men and women on the basis of sex in the payment of wages where they perform substantially equal work under similar working conditions in the same establishment. The law also prohibits employers from reducing the wages of either sex to comply with the law.

A violation may exist where a different wage is paid to a predecessor or successor employee of the opposite sex. Labor organizations may not cause employers to violate the law.

Retaliation against a person who files a charge of equal pay discrimination, participates in an investigation or opposes an unlawful employment practice also is illegal.

The law protects virtually all private employees, including executive, administrative, professional and outside sales employees who are exempt from minimum wage and overtime laws. Most federal, state and local government workers are also covered.

The law does not apply to pay differences based on factors other than sex, such as seniority, merit or systems that determine wages based upon the quantity or quality of items produced or processed.

Many EPA violations may be violations of Title VII or the Civil Rights Act of 1964, which also prohibits sex-based wage discrimination. Such charges may be filed under both statutes.

AGE DISCRIMINATION IN EMPLOYMENT ACT (ADEA)

Persons 40 years of age or older are protected by the Age Discrimination in Employment Act of 1967. The law prohibits age discrimination in hiring, discharge, pay, promotions and other terms and conditions of employment.

Retaliation against a person who files a charge of age discrimination, participates in an investigation or opposes an unlawful practice also is illegal.

The law applies to private employers of 20 or more workers, federal, state and local governments, employment agencies and labor organizations with 25 or more members. Labor organizations that operate a hiring hall or office that recruits potential employees or obtains job opportunities also must abide by the law.

It shall be unlawful to cease or reduce the rate of pension benefit accruals or allocations because of age for employees who have at least one hour of service in pension plan years beginning on or after January 1, 1988. Limitations on the amount of benefits, years of service or years of participation may be permissible, if the limits are imposed without regard to age.

The Older Workers Benefit Protection Act (OWBPA) was enacted on October 16, 1990, effective generally on April 15, 1991. There are delayed effective dates for certain collectively bargained plans and certain state and local government employers. OWBPA makes clear that employee benefits and benefit plans are subject to the ADEA. The Act codifies EEOC regulations addressing employee benefits and states that the employer has the burden of proving the lawfulness of certain benefits-related actions. New provisions were enacted affecting early retirement incentive plans and permitting certain offsets against severance payments and long-term disability. Title II of OWBPA sets out minimum criteria that must be satisfied before a waiver of any ADEA right or claim will considered a "knowing and voluntary" waiver.

State and local governments may make age-based hiring and retirement decisions for firefighters and law enforcement offers if the particular age limitation was in effect on March 3, 1983, and the action taken is pursuant to a *bona fide* hiring or retirement plan that is not subterfuge to evade the purposes of the Act. The section in question is scheduled to expire on December 31, 1993.

Institutions of higher education may involuntarily retire an employee at age 70 who is serving under a contract of unlimited tenure or a similar arrangement. The section in question is scheduled to expire on December 31, 1993.

The ADEA does not prohibit the compulsory retirement of certain *bona fide* executives or high policymaking personnel as discussed in section 12(c)(1) of the Act.

HOW TO FILE A CHARGE

If you believe you have been discriminated against by an employer, labor union or employment agency when applying for a job or while on the job because of race, color, sex, religion, national origin, age, or disability, you may file a charge of discrimination with the U.S. Equal Employment Opportunity Commission. Charges may be filed in person, by mail or by telephone by contacting the nearest EEOC office. If there is not an EEOC office in the immediate area, call toll free 800-669-4000 (voice) or 800-800-3302 (TDD) for more information. To avoid delay, call or write beforehand if you need special assistance, such as an interpreter, to file a charge.

There are strict time frames in which charges of employment discrimination must be filed. To preserve the ability of EEOC to act on your behalf and to protect your right to file a private lawsuit, adhere to the following guidelines when filing a charge.

Title VII charges must be file with EEOC within 180 days of the alleged discriminatory act. In states or localities where there is an antidiscrimination law and an agency authorized to grant or seek relief, a charge must be presented to that state or local agency. In such jurisdictions, you may file charges with EEOC within 300 days of the discriminatory act, or 30 days after receiving notice that the state of local agency has terminated its processing of the charge, whichever is earlier. It is best to contact EEOC promptly when discrimination is suspected. When charges or complaints are filed beyond these time frames, the private right of action may be unavailable.

EEOC may file a lawsuit if it finds reasonable cause to believe that discrimination occurred and conciliation efforts fail. An individual may file a private suit within 90 days of receiving a notice of right-to-sue from EEOC.

Americans with Disabilities Act (ADA) enforcement procedures and time line requirements are the same as those for Title VII charges.

Age Discrimination in Employment Act (ADEA) charges may be filed by or on behalf of an aggrieved person. If a charge is filed on behalf of another, the aggrieved individual's identity may be kept confidential. Individuals who are aware of practices that may involve age discrimination, but who do not wish to file a charge, may bring the matter to EEOC's attention by filing a complaint. If a complaint is filed, the identity of the complainant ordinarily will not be disclosed without prior written consent. A complaint does not preserve the right to file a private suit. However, if a charge is filed, the charging party's name will be given to the employer.

ADEA charges must be filed with EEOC within 180 days of the alleged discriminatory act. In states where there is a law prohibiting age discrimination in employment or authorizing a state agency to grant or seek relief, a proceeding must be commenced with the state agency as a prerequisite to private suit. In such jurisdictions, a charge may be filed with EEOC within 300 days of the discriminatory act, or 30 days after receiving notice that the state terminated its processing of the charge, whichever is earlier. When charges or complaints are filed beyond these time frames, the private right of action may be unavailable.

Persons who file timely charges of age discrimination or who are the beneficiaries of timely filed charges, may file suit against the respondent named in the charge within 90 days of receipt of notice that the Commission has dismissed or otherwise terminated proceedings. EEOC is also empowered to file suit to remedy violations of the Act.

Equal Pay Act (EPA) - Individuals are not required to file an EPA charge with EEOC before filing a private lawsuit. However, some cases of wage discrimination also may be violations of Title VII. Charges may be filed concurrently under both laws. If an EPA charge is filed with EEOC, the procedure for filing is the same as for charges brought under Title VII.

An EPA lawsuit must be filed within two years (or three years for willful violations) of the discriminatory act, which in most cases will be a payment of a discriminatorily lower wage. Filing a charge with the EEOC will not stop the running of the two-year (or three-year) period for filing a lawsuit.

If a complaint is filed under EPA, the identity of the complainant will not be disclosed. However, if a charge is filed under both Title VII and EPA, the charging party's name will be given to the employer.

If EEOC finds reasonable cause to believe that discrimination occurred and conciliation efforts fail, EEOC may file a lawsuit on behalf of the victim in federal district court. Should EEOC take action first, a private lawsuit may not be filed.

GENERAL PROCEDURES

1. EEOC interviews the potential charging party to obtain as much information as possible about the alleged discrimination. If all legal jurisdictional requirements are met, a charge is properly drafted and the investigative procedure is explained to the charging party.

2. EEOC notifies the employer about the charge. In investigating the charge to determine if discrimination occurred, EEOC requests information from the employer that addresses the

issues directly affecting the charging party as well as other potentially aggrieved persons. Any witnesses who have direct knowledge of the alleged discriminatory act will be interviewed. If the evidence shows there is no reasonable cause to believe discrimination occurred, the charging party and the employer will be notified. The charging party may exercise the right to bring private court action.

3. If the evidence shows there is reasonable cause to believe discrimination occurred, EEOC conciliates or attempts to persuade the employer to voluntarily eliminate and remedy the discrimination, following the standards of EEOC's Policy on Remedies and Relief for Individual Cases of Unlawful Discrimination. Remedies may include reinstatement of an aggrieved person to the job he or she would have had but for the discrimination, backpay, restoration of lost benefits and damages to compensate for actual monetary loss. Limited monetary damages may also be available to compensate for future monetary loss, mental anguish or pain and suffering, and to penalize a respondent who acted with malice or reckless indifference. The employer may also be required to post a notice in the workplace advising employees that it has complied with orders to remedy the discrimination.

4. EEOC considers the case for litigation if conciliation fails. If litigation is approved by the Commission, EEOC will file a lawsuit in federal district court on behalf of the charging party(ies). Charging parties may initiate private civil action on their own in lieu of EEOC litigation.

STATE AND LOCAL FAIR EMPLOYMENT PRACTICE AGENCIES (FEPAs)

Under Title VII and ADA, EEOC must defer charges of discrimination to state or local Fair Employment Practice Agencies. The charge may be processed initially by either EEOC or the state or local agency, where a worksharing agreement so specifies.

LITIGATION

Most charges are conciliated or settled, making a court trial unnecessary. EEOC's Statement of Enforcement Policy commits the agency to consider for litigation each case in which reasonable cause has been found and conciliation has failed. If EEOC decides not to litigate a case, a notice of right to sue is issued, permitting the charging party to take the case to court if he or she chooses.

RELIEF

The Commission's policy is to seek full and effective relief for each and every victim of employment discrimination, whether it is sought in court or in conciliation agreements reached before litigation.

In general, relief that may be sought includes:

- Backpay (all);
- Hiring, promotion, reinstatement, benefit restoration, front pay and other affirmative relief (Title, VII, ADA, ADEA);
- Actual pecuniary loss other than backpay (Title VII, ADA);
- Liquidated damages (ADEA, EPA);
- Compensatory damages for future monetary losses and mental anguish (Title VII, ADA);
- Punitive damages when employer acts with malice or reckless disregard for federally protected rights (Title VII, ADA);

363

- Posting a notice to all employees advising them of their rights under the laws EEOC enforces and their right to be free from retaliation (all);

- Corrective or preventative actions taken to cure the source of the identified discrimination and minimize the chance of its recurrence (all);

- Reasonable accommodation (ADA); or

- Stopping the specific discriminatory practices involved in the case (all).

EEOC OFFICES

EEOC has 23 district, 1 field, 17 area and 9 local offices. District offices are full service units which investigate charges and systemic cases and conduct litigation. Area offices investigate charges, including charges for potential litigation. Local offices investigate charges but forward cases to district offices for litigation development. The field office investigates charges and systemic cases and conducts litigation. It reports directly to Headquarters.

[listing of office locations omitted from reprint]

ADDITIONAL INFORMATION

If you need further information, you may call EEOC toll free on 1-800-669-EEOC. The TDD number is 1-800-800-3302. For calls from the Washington, DC, metropolitan area, dial (202) 663-4900. The TDD local number is (202) 663-4494.

The information contained in this brochure is intended as a general overview and does not carry the force of legal opinion.

This brochure is available, upon request, in large print, Braille or on tape by writing to the Office of Equal Employment Opportunity, EEOC, 1801 L St., NW, Washington, DC 20507.

Material contained in the publication is in the public domain and may be reproduced, fully or partially, without the permission of the federal government.

The text of these laws is contained in the booklet "Laws Enforced by the EEOC," available by writing the Office of Communications and Legislative Affairs, EEOC, 1801 L St., NW, Washington, DC 20507.

Reprint: Excerpt from
"Your Rights Under the Family and Medical Leave Act of 1993," produced by the US Department of Labor

FMLA requires covered employers to provide up to 12 weeks of unpaid, job-protected leave to "eligible" employees for certain family and medical reasons. Employees are eligible if they have worked for a covered employer for at least one year, and for 1,250 hours over the previous 12 months, and if there are at least 50 employees within 75 miles.

Reasons For Taking Leave:
Unpaid leave must be granted for <u>any</u> of the following reasons:

- to care for the employee's child after birth, or placement for adoption or foster care;
- to care for the employee's spouse, son or daughter, or parent, who has a serious health condition; or
- for a serious health condition that makes the employee unable to perform the employee's job.

At the employee's or employer's option, certain kinds of <u>paid</u> leave may be substituted for unpaid leave.

Advance Notice And Medical Certification:
The employee may be required to provide advance leave notice and medical certification. Taking of leave may be denied if requirements are not met.

- The employee ordinarily must provide 30 days advance notice when the leave is "foreseeable."
- An employer may require medical certification to support a request for leave because of a serious health condition, and may require second or third opinions (at the expense of the employer) and a fitness for duty report to return to work.

Job Benefits And Protection:

- For the duration of the FMLA leave, the employer must maintain the employee's health coverage under any "group health plan."
- Upon return from the FMLA leave, most employees must be restored to their original or equivalent positions with equivalent pay, benefits, and other employment terms.
- The use of FMLA leave cannot result in the loss of any employment benefit that accrues prior to the start of an employee's leave.

Unlawful Acts By Employers:
FMLA makes it unlawful for any employer to:

- interfere with, restrain, or deny the exercise of any right provided under the FMLA;
- discharge or discriminate against any person for opposing any practice made unlawful by FMLA or for involvement in any proceeding under or relating to FMLA.

Enforcement:

- The U.S. Department of Labor is authorized to investigate and resolve complaints of violations.
- An eligible employee may bring civil action against an employer for violations.

FMLA does not effect any Federal or State law prohibiting discrimination, or supersede any State or Local law or collective bargaining agreement which provides greater family or medical leave rights.

Chapter 11

Managing Your Career

. . . the most important element in job satisfaction is the opportunity to be creative.
—"How Engineers See Themselves," IEEE Spectrum, *April 1993*
Having a failure does not mean that you are a failure. You are a failure only when you give up or do not learn from the experience.
—"Risking Your Way to the Top," Graduating Engineer, *March 1994*
Maintaining high quality in an affluent society is perhaps one of the most difficult problems that human beings have ever confronted.
–*Kaneyuki Kurokawa,* Fujitsu Corporation's director of research

11.1 INTRODUCTION

AS you may have noticed in the case studies and other incidents covered so far, the way in which you choose to conduct your professional life can greatly influence your level of satisfaction with, and success in, life in general. Whistle blowers, for example, often must give up their current career path to act in a highly ethical manner, yet most would do the same thing if they had the opportunity. On the other side, those who lowered their ethical standards for the most part paid some penalty. Of course, this is not true in every case, but generally there is a connection between how you live and how successful you are in your career. Thus, "managing your career" means moving beyond purely professional aspects, such as job interviews and promotions, and examining elements of your personal life as well.

So what is the key to maximizing your satisfaction level? I believe it is no more complicated than taking responsibility for your professional and personal development and striving for the highest ethical standards possible. At first glance, the two requirements don't seem to be related at all, but one is actually a prerequisite for the other—in taking responsibility for yourself, you take the first step toward living ethically.

Unfortunately, there are many roadblocks to taking that first step—far too many to mention specifically here. I

have, however, seen some common threads that allow me to *loosely* categorize roadblocks into three areas: perceived societal pressures, addictive behaviors, and corporate "politics."

11.2 PERCEIVED SOCIETAL PRESSURES

How society feels about something can often dictate how an individual will feel about it. Even those who go out of their way to take the opposite path have been influenced (albeit negatively) by how society as a whole deals with an issue. Thus, anyone preparing to spend the rest of their life in society must be prepared to recognize the trends that can subtly shape how people behave. One unavoidable trend is the emphasis on affluence. The general perception appears to be that becoming and staying affluent is to be desired above all things. Indeed, it seems that more opportunities are offered to and more respect is afforded those who make (and spend) a lot of money. Likewise, those who appear not to be affluent or care about becoming affluent are often given fewer opportunities and treated with less respect. This emphasis on affluence can subtly affect behavior. For example, some people find it too embarrassing to enter a mall without being dressed a certain way that will place them in the near-affluent if not affluent category.

This belief in those who "have" and those who "have not" leads many to select a career path that will guarantee entrance into the world of the "haves." That path often leads to the computing disciplines because of the belief that knowing about computers gives you a certain edge in obtaining and holding a lucrative career. This may be true, but if this is the only reason you choose a computing career, there may be a cost later on in life. Indeed, there is perhaps a wider gap between earning a living (in terms of "making money") and being *satisfied with* earning a living than most people might suspect.

Hopefully you have chosen to study computing at least in part because this type of activity brings you some level of enjoyment. If you have chosen computing solely because there are seemingly more job opportunities or higher salaries, you may be headed for a career dead end: The longer you work, the more your future is determined by your current path. If you don't enjoy what you are doing, you typically won't excel in it, and you will languish in a kind of middle ground—neither very good (which is exciting and ultimately satisfying), nor very bad (which often forces a change to something better that may lead to satisfaction).

Another subtle influence of affluence is complacency and its by-products: less drive to be original and a lower commitment to quality. As Kim Woo-Choong, founder of the South Korean Daewoo Industrial Group, now a $25 billion company, puts it [6],

> Overconsumption becomes a bad habit. People fall prey to the temptations of laziness and extravagance at the expense of diligence and frugality. Instead of accumulating small amounts through healthy efforts, they look for windfalls. All of this leads to the corruption and decay of human nature and eventually of a people and a nation.

We have only to reflect on the popularity of lotteries and sweepstakes to see that there is a sad element of truth to this quote. (As an interesting rhetorical exercise, listen carefully to U.S. corporate leaders and see if they don't voice similar sentiments.)

The first reprint at the end of this chapter, "Quality and Innovation," amplifies this point. It is the text of a speech given by the director of research for Fujitsu Corporation, Kaneyuki Kurowaka. The quote at the beginning of this chapter is taken from this speech. Kurokawa relates three brief anecdotes about major figures in Japanese industry and then discusses the problem involved in managing for quality and innovation. The anecdotes about Japanese industrial leaders make some interesting points. The first point is especially relevant to the subtleties of affluence, since profit is often the sole motive.

- Profit should not be viewed as an end, but rather as a means to better serve customers.
- A good manager should be able to communicate with engineers in their own language.
- It is dangerous for managers to delegate to others the development of things that they (the managers) do not understand.

His insights about quality, division of labor, graceful growth, effective manpower, and probability of success are also important.

11.3 ADDICTIVE BEHAVIORS

A variety of addictive behaviors can be destructive to both your personal life and your professional career. Drugs, alcohol, and gambling are some of the most common debilitating addictions. There is no space to treat any of these in great depth here, but it is important to at least touch on the topic of substance abuse.

Substance abuse is a serious manifestation of not being able to take responsibility for your professional and personal development. Although we can make some important distinctions between the use of alcohol and, say, cocaine, the overuse of any form of intoxicant is a self-destructive behavior and is a clear sign that you are abdicating responsibility, even though you may think it is temporary. It should also be clear that using any form of intoxicant to any degree that affects performance in the workplace is an ethical issue. It is typically also a legal issue. In fact, the federal government recognized this issue as important enough to warrant regulatory action. In 1986, they passed the Drug-Free Workplace Act, which pertains to any entity performing substantial business with the federal government. The Act requires such an entity to

- have a drug-free workplace policy,
- be sure that employees are informed about the policy,
- notify the contracting agency if an employee is convicted of a drug violation occurring in the workplace, and
- have a plan for dealing with employees convicted of a drug violation occurring in the workplace.

The text of this law may be a little dry to read straight through, but to get the details of exactly what these points cover, you should read the excerpt of the Act at the end of this chapter. This is not a matter only for contractors of the federal government either. Three quarters of all large companies require drug tests for screening job applicants and one third use random drug tests to check for drug use by current employees [4]. Approximately 30 percent of companies that do test employees automatically dismiss those who test positive. Other companies refer employees who test positive (the first time) to treatment programs.

Many organizations exist to help those whose lives have been affected by drug and alcohol abuse. Some of the more well-known organizations are Alcoholics Anonymous, Al-Anon Family Groups, Adult Children of Alcoholics, and Narcotics Anonymous. National toll-free hotlines exist for cocaine and drug abuse, (800) 262-2463, and alcohol abuse, (800) 992-9239.

11.4 CORPORATE POLITICS

Corporate politics is a catch-all phrase that has been used to connote everything from daily communication with co-workers to disagreements with a specific individual, usually a direct manager. Some people seem to blame all their misfortunes on the political atmosphere of a company, generally meaning one or two individuals in middle or upper management. Although this is certainly possible, especially in small companies, where individuals wear more hats and thus have more freedom to exercise their likes and dislikes, it is often the case that poor communication and attitudes contribute as much to an individual's downfall as a corporate environment.

A variety of behaviors can erode your professional and personal life. Mild examples are pessimism, egocentricity (always talking about only yourself), or overt and frequent criticism (in the guise of "telling it like it is"). These types of problems can reduce your ability to communicate effectively with others and reduce your value as a member of a team. Fortunately, there are many self-help books for these tendencies. Dale Carnegie's *How to Win Friends and Influence People* [1] is a classic in this area.

Another impediment to communication—and one that is very subtle—is sexism. Consider the following quote, which is suggesting that you should attempt to give credit where due by attaching the originator's name to an idea [2]:

> . . . the "Harris Matrix," the "Jones Algorithm," "Janet's Chart," or the "Levin Technique". . .

A reviewer of this book pointed out that using this collection of naming conventions when Janet is the only female in the group might be taken as sexist and demeaning. In other words, why use Janet's first name instead of her last unless it was to emphasize her gender? Someone might argue that hardly anyone would notice such a thing, let alone take offense, but I believe this argument would just enforce the point that sexist language can be very subtle. The proponent of such an argument may very well, although unintentionally, be building a communication barrier with another member of the group.

I have included several articles that address how to handle yourself in a corporate environment. You may be tempted to skip the first, "Dos and Dont's for Young EEs," thinking it is not really specific to computing disciplines. Don't be put off by the title. The points apply to anyone starting out in any area of the computing industry.

Indeed, many jobs today may just as easily be filled by an electrical engineer, a computer engineer, or a computer scientist. The article describes how to have "product-oriented" focus, learn the "big picture" of how your company operates, and work well with others. You should take special note of the comments about developing your communication skills, continuing your education, and becoming the "local expert" on something of value to the company.

The next reprint, "Taking Charge of Your Promotion," is similar in spirit to the dos and don'ts article, but has a different perspective. The first article speaks from a more technical point of view than the second. Consequently, the advice given is different in some details, such as studying for advanced degrees. Also note the advice given about deciding what level of the career ladder is right for you. There is good wisdom in what it says. Higher levels of the career ladder do generally require greater sacrifices in your personal life. You will be better able to live with the trade-off if it is one you make consciously.

Points to Remember

- Continuing professional success will likely require effective self-discipline in your personal life.
- Successful management for quality and innovation is a difficult task, requiring balanced attention to many competing factors.
- A drug- and alcohol-free workplace is generally the ethically correct environment. Drug-free environments are also in keeping with the federal Drug Free Workplace Act.
- Many problems in the workplace can be attributed to poor communication or ineffective resolution of personality differences.
- Maintaining and improving your value to your company requires some explicit planning on your part and some investment in continuing your education and improving your skills.

WORKSHEET—The Social Responsibility of Business

Milton Friedman is a Nobel-prize-winning economist who wrote an article, "The Social Responsibility of Business Is to Increase Its Profits," which ran in *The New York Times Magazine* September 13, 1970, and is reprinted in Deborah Johnson's book *Ethical Issues in Engineering*. Read his article, think it over carefully, and answer the following questions.

1. What is the essence of his argument against a business having a social responsibility?

2. Friedman states that "in an ideal free market resting on private property, no individual can coerce any other, all cooperation is voluntary, all parties to such cooperation benefit or they need not participate." To what extent do you believe that today's U.S. economy is an "ideal free market resting on private property?"

3. At another point Friedman states ". . . there is one and only one social responsibility of business—to use its resources and engage in activities designed to increase its profits so long as it stays within the rules of the game, which is to say, engages in open and free competition without deception or fraud." Is this statement correct or incorrect and why?

4. The quality of life in U.S. society can be adequately measured by the summation of the profit and loss statements of all the businesses in the United States. Is this correct or incorrect and why?

WORKSHEET—Ethics of Computer Use on the Job

The question of whether or not computer games should be used by employees, or even be available on company computers, is sometimes controversial. Imagine that you, as the vice president in charge of computer operations, are writing a background paper to your CEO on this topic. The CEO feels that some policy should be announced to all employees but is uncertain about what would be best for the company. This is your chance to demonstrate your insight into problems that go beyond the strictly technical domain and show that you have the people skills needed to move up to the next level in the company.

A typical, but not absolutely required, organization of your paper might be:

1. Introduction/Problem Definition

2. Arguments against Recreational Use of Computers

3. Arguments for Recreational Use of Computers

4. Conclusions and Recommendation

You might consider at least the material in the various professional codes of ethics in writing your paper. You might also want to use Nexis or some other source to find out more about what has happened in other companies. And of course you want to recommend a solution that is both technically feasible and acceptable to the employees of the company.

Try to stress *content* rather than length in preparing your paper. The paper should reflect (1) opinions or conclusions regarding the subject of the assignment that are reasonably supported by the background materials and clearly expressed.

WORKSHEET—Prioritizing Concerns about Ethical Problems

1. What are the three most important ethical problems that confront you as a student pursuing your education?

2. What are the three most important ethical problems that you expect to confront as a professional in your career?

3. What are the three most important ethical problems that confront our society in general?

4. After completing this worksheet, compare it with your responses to the same questions on the worksheet in Chapter 1.

1. **The "Mythical Man-Month."** Fred Brooks was a manager with IBM when the System 360 was developed. His book, *The Mythical Man-Month,* relates lessons learned about the management of software development. Compare Brooks's ideas about the difficulty of managing teams of people with Kurokawa's ideas about "effective manpower."

2. **Link between cerebral hemorrhage and cocaine use.** Neurosurgeon Douglas Chyatte has suggested that cocaine use may result in an increased likelihood of cerebral hemorrhage. Report on this and other adverse health effects linked to cocaine use.

3. **The "How Engineers View Themselves" survey.** *IEEE Spectrum* has at least twice published articles based on the results of surveys of how engineers view their profession. (e. g., see [5].) Report on the results of the most recent survey of this type and the trends of how things appear to be changing over time.

4. **The IEEE "Professional Practices" Guidelines.** The *IEEE* publishes a pamphlet titled "Professional Practices for Engineers, Scientists and Their Employers." Report on the concept of complementary employee–employer responsibilities as expressed in this pamphlet.

REFERENCES

[1] D. Carnegie, *How to Win Friends and Influence People.* Simon and Schuster, New York 1936.

[2] C. A. Fowler, "Dos and don'ts for young EEs," *IEEE Spectrum,* October 1993, pp. 59–61.

[3] J. Matson, "Risking your way to the top," *Graduating Engineer,* March 1994, pp. 34–36.

[4] M. Odum, "Drug testing of employees is on the rise," *The Tampa Tribune,* November 3, 1993.

[5] H. Woolf, "How engineers see themselves," *IEEE Spectrum,* April 1993, pp. 24–28.

[6] K. Woo-Choong, "Every street is paved with gold," *Success,* October 1992, pp. 62–64.

Quality and Innovation

Dr. Kaneyuki Kurokawa

First I would like to talk about three gentlemen who were leaders in the Japanese electronics industry.

Konosuke Matsushita

The management guru in the US may be Peter Drucker, who is a writer, commentator, journalist, and of course a professor. He wrote a number of influential books on management and served many large companies in the US as a consultant. But he is not a manager himself.

Druckers's counterpart in Japan, our management guru, is in my opinion, *Konosuke Matsushita*. Matsushita was not a consultant. He was the founder of Matsushita Electric Co. He wrote more than a dozen books on various topics related to management, but not necessarily on management per se. His books are collections of his talks given to his employees at one time or another. Nevertheless, I think he was a great teacher of management, not in the classroom, but in the marketplace. Most Japanese executives in the electronic consumer products business learned lessons through their competition with Matsushita.

Matsushita did not finish his elementary school education because of his family's financial difficulties. He became an apprentice at a bicycle shop in Osaka at the age of ten. When he was 24 years old in 1918 he started Matsushita Electric with his wife and his brother-in-law and no other employees. He made and peddled small items such as bike lights and flashlights with some innovations of his own.

His operation was small but his mission was big: the modernization of Japan through electricity.

As his company grew, he did two important things. One was changing his employees' attitude towards profit and the other was the establishment of a dealer network.

70 years ago, average Japanese people had only a vague idea about profit. Profit was something the crooked gained by cheating. So, people had a guilty conscience about making profit.

Matsushita told his employees many times that he was serving customers to help improve their living standards. When customers appreciated the value of his service, they allowed him some profit so that he could continue and expand his operation to further satisfy customer needs. Profit is not an end, it is a means to serve customers. His employees' attitude improved.

Next, he reasoned that to accomplish modernization of Japan through electricity, he had to reach customers all over Japan. To do so, he established a network of dealers throughout Japan, a new concept in the 1930's. Because of his large, nation-wide dealer network, each lot size of his products became double or triple that of his competitors. As a result, he could make the price of his product 10 to 20% lower than others.

Long before the Boston Consultant Group popularized the concept of the experience curve, Matsushita gave his competitors an important lesson, *Economies of Scale*. To serve customers better, lot size becomes an important factor if other factors are equal.

Our recent export boom seems to be a manifestation of how well Japanese executives learned his lesson, although an excessive trade imbalance is something to be frowned upon and is now being reduced.

Kanjiro Okada, Fujitsu

Kanjiro Okada was made President of Fujitsu in 1959 when he was 68 years old. He came to Fujitsu from a chemical company and his educational background was in economics.

After a year or so at Fujitsu, he realized he could not communicate with engineers so he began to read *Fundamentals of Electronics Engineering*. To learn from the book, he made a notebook that is still displayed in a room set aside in his honor at Fujitsu Kawasaki Laboratories. In the notebook, alternating current theory, Fourier series expansion, and Biot-Savart's Law are all neatly

Dr. Kaneyuki Kurokawa is Director of Research for Fujitsu Corporation. This is the text of the plenary address he presented at the 1990 IEEE International Conference on Robotics and Automation.

Dr. Kurokawa first presents the stories of three leaders in Japanese electronics industry which provide insight into the differences and similarities in management in the US and Japan. Then, the paper discusses five topics: quality, excessive division of labor, graceful growth, effective manpower for a breakthrough and the probability of success in technology transfer. Through these discussions, it will become clear that quality, innovation, and breakthrough each requires different management approaches.

Reprinted from *IEEE Robotics and Automation Newsletter*, Vol. 4, No. 3, pp. 14–19, Summer 1990.

illustrated by his drawings together with his own explanations.

After he finished this undergraduate textbook he began to read a graduate school textbook on transistor theory. Apparently, it was difficult for him. He got up a 4 o'clock every morning to spend an hour and a half for reading. He read the first 50 pages or so, but he could not understand it at all. So, he read that portion of the book about 40 times. He described his difficulty in reading this book as being similar to chewing grains of sand in his mouth.

After much repetition, however, he felt he had become slightly familiar with the terminology. He asked an engineer at Fujitsu to explain the book to him. The engineer was happy to serve as a tutor to the company president and told his colleagues what he was doing.

Suddenly, Okada had five volunteer tutors. They made hand drawings and everything else to teach their president. Although he did not pretend he had mastered transistor theory, Okada could now communicate with engineers in their own language.

Kouji Kobayashi, NEC

Kouji Kobayashi is the honorary chairman of NEC. Fujitsu people do not like him because he is such a strong competitor of Fujitsu. However, I think we have to learn from him because he made NEC one of the largest communication equipment companies in the world.

A little more than ten years ago, one of the largest revolutions in the history of electronics industry, the microprocessor revolution, swept through Japan. With it, almost everything analog became digital and software became an important discipline. This revolution was comparable to the one caused by the conversion from vacuum tubes to transistors.

Most executives in other companies in Japan said they did not understand software and therefore they delegated the responsibility of software development to their subordinates. Delegating to others the development of something one does not understand is a dangerous proposition.

Kobayashi decided that he did not understand software and therefore he had to learn. I think he was President of NEC at that time and he invited all of his VP's regardless of their professions to join him to receive lessons on personal computers.

He hired two *female instructors from the outside*, although there were a number of programmers and some experts on personal computers inside his company. He and all of his VP's began to receive lessons on a personal computer, everything from keyboard operation to programming. The lessons lasted several months.

However, as soon as the lessons started, managers in NEC began to receive all kinds of questions about personal computers from their VP's. Managers found they could not give satisfactory answers to seemingly trivial questions their VP's asked. So, managers got together and hired instructors. It is my understanding that the fees were paid from their own pockets, and lessons were given on weekends. At one time, three to four hundred managers joined.

Within one year or so, computer illiteracy was virtually wiped out from all of NEC. This may have some bearing on the fact that NEC presently enjoys the largest share of the Japanese personal computer market.

Although I have presented the stories of three top executives, you may have noticed that their primary concern was average managers and employees. In fact, if you compare newspapers and magazines in the two countries, you may notice that Japan is a society of the middle 80% of the population while the US is a society of the top 10% and bottom 10%. So, in his numerous books,

Matsushita emphasizes the importance of effort. His argument is: *try hard enough, then result follows*.

Peter Drucker emphasizes result. His argument is: *only results counts*.

Both arguments are appropriate since their readers are different. In the US, who reads books? The top 10%. In Japan who reads books? The middle 80%. The top 10% play golf. Well, I have said one sentence too many, so let me change my subject.

Quality

Now I would like to present some of my own thoughts on quality and innovation. First let me discuss *quality*. The quality of products depends on the attitudes of a large number of people, people in the laboratory, people in the factory, people in the sales office, people in the shipping department and, of course, customers.

Delegating to others the development of something one does not understand is a dangerous proposition.

The attitude of a large number of people, say 100 or 200 million, is difficult to manage. A drastic change in the environment seems to be necessary for its improvement. As some of you may recall, *Made in Japan* was known as the label of shabby products, which easily broke or malfunctioned.

In my opinion, this has changed primarily because of the hardship the Japanese people experienced after World War II. Japan was literally burned down in the War. The gross national product per capita plunged 50% and it took more than 10 years for it to recover to the previous level. What this really meant to individuals is that all essentials for their lives became scarce. Food was rationed, but it was below subsistence level and

378

malnutrition was common. Since food was so precious at that time, after 45 years, I still feel guilty when some food served has to be left over.

In order to avoid mass starvation, the Japanese worked hard for high quality. It was the only choice they had. The situation had improved slightly after ten years, but the hard work continued. *Thirty years later, Japanese products became competitive for the first time in the world marketplace.*

Note that US products were of supreme quality in the 1960's, which was about *30 years after* the Great Depression. Thirty years is the necessary time for a young generation who suffered from a hardship not under their control to reach the prime of their lives.

> **In order to avoid mass starvation, the Japanese worked hard for high quality. It was the only choice they had.**

Now, having passed through the 30 years, Japan entered into a new era. A significant fraction of students in engineering schools in Japan no longer consider manufacturing as an attractive job. They seek employment at banks and brokerage houses. At the same time, Japanese quality has started to show signs of decline.

During one month in the beginning of this year, four large Japanese consumer electronics companies, Toshiba, Pioneer, Matsushita and Sony announced the recall of their TV sets because of a possible fire hazard. I hope this is not a harbinger of what may follow.

However, maintaining high quality in an affluent society is perhaps one of the most difficult problems human beings have ever confronted. Competition among companies cer-

tainly helps. To promote fair competition among companies and to foster high regard for quality among average people Quality Olympic Games or Nobel Prize for Quality may be desired.

The only other solution I can imagine is a hardship similar to the one we experience after the War. However, this kind of hardship is not possible or desirable. So without a solid proposal, I would like to change my subject to innovation.

Division of Labor

At the turn of this century, most innovations were done by individuals. Innovation here refers to the process of bringing any new technological idea into practical use. Innovation differs from invention in its effect on society. The effect of invention is felt by specialists, while an innovation affects people's daily lives.

When Thomas Edison demonstrated the first incandescent lamp in his laboratory, it was an invention. When Edison formed a company to distribute electricity and people started to use electric lamps instead of gas lights, it was an innovation.

With this definition of innovation, individual innovators perform four distinct functions in sequence: *research, development, manufacturing and marketing* as shown in Figure 1.

> **Thirty years is the necessary time for a young generation who suffered from a hardship not under their control to reach the prime of their lives.**

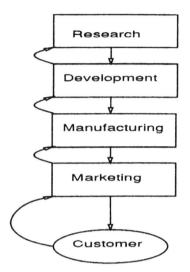

Figure 1.
Innovation Process

In the middle of this century, however, large companies started to play the role of innovators. *Innovation was institutionalized.*

Institutionalized innovators thought that the same four functions were necessary for innovation. And they decided to perform these four functions by division of labor. Some people were assigned to research, some people to development, some other people to manufacturing and the remainder to marketing. This was OK while companies were small.

Unfortunately, this division of labor is against human nature and it is susceptible to NIH *(Not Invented Here)* syndrome As companies grew

> **A significant fraction of students in engineering schools in Japan no longer consider manufacturing as an attractive job. They seek employment at banks and brokerage houses.**

379

bigger and as the division of labor became more distinct, most institutionalized innovators began to fail in innovations. The problem of technology transfer from one group to the next became insurmountable. This happened in the US and this happened in Japan.

An example may be the failure in semiconductor memory chip innovation in large US corporations such as GE, RCA, Westinghouse, and Sylvania.

Manufacturing became the weakest link in the chain of the innovation process. The strength of a chain is determined by its weakest link, and these companies could not prosper in the memory chip business in spite of the fact that each of these companies had a number of excellent researchers in its laboratories.

The concept of division of labor needs careful handling. If it is misused what can be done becomes impossible. The misuse of division of labor becomes fatal in R&D management.

Let me present a simple thought experiment. Suppose I would like to make as large a sound as possible by clapping hands, and suppose I give a right hand to one person and a left hand to another person to study carefully. When both hands are given to

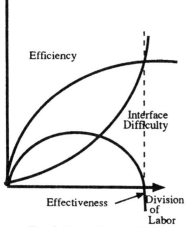

Fig. 2 The effect of division of labor

one person, he will experiment clapping hands and sooner or later he will get a result.

Figure 2 shows why excessive division of labor is harmful. As division of labor becomes more distinct, efficiency increases, but interface difficulty increases faster and effectiveness starts to decline and eventually becomes negative.

Fujitsu's organization is illustrated in Figure 3.

Research and development are in one group. Fujitsu Laboratories. Manufacturing divisions have strong development capabilities, so they are essentially development and manufacturing groups.

People are transferred with the technology from one group to another and many people in marketing have experience in development and/or manufacturing. Information flows in all directions as indicated by the arrows. Even in the R&D group, we have direct contact with customers.

I would like to keep research and development in one group, although this is against the present trend in Japan

Graceful Growth

So far I have discussed the division of labor which is related to technology transfer. Another concept institutionalized innovators have to take into careful consideration is graceful growth.

An individual innovator cannot expect a large sum of money for his or her development; early entrance of the invention into the marketplace is always taken for granted. This is not the case for the institutionalized innovator, but the innovator has to be doubly careful. Before an institutionalized innovator brings the invention into full-scale development, the innovator should ask this question. *Can the system or device grow gracefully in the marketplace?*

To answer this seemingly innocent question, one has to consider

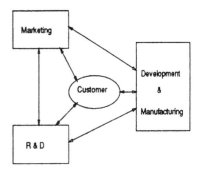

Fig. 3. Information flow for innovation

two different aspects of the question. The first aspect is that the invention must have at least one very strong point that more than compensates for all its weak points.

The second aspect is that after the entrance into the marketplace, the invention should anticipate successively wider applications guided by the feedback from the marketplace. Early entrance into the marketplace is almost mandatory for any technology that grows big.

An excellent example of graceful growth is transistor technology. On the other hand, IBM's Josephson Junction, Bell's Picturephone and RCA's Video Disc are examples of technology that could not grow gracefully in the marketplace. Too many "best sellers in the lab" have flopped in the marketplace.

When a new transistor, HEMT, was invented in our laboratory in 1980, we wanted to make HEMT LSI's for computer applications. After all, Fujitsu is a computer maker. Nevertheless, we took the concept of graceful growth seriously.

In order to get into the marketplace and to receive feedback from there as soon as possible, we assigned a few people to the development of discrete devices for microwave applications. This was in addition to the main LSI development group.

Five years later, the HEMT discrete device was used in the radio telescope of Nobeyama Observatory of Tokyo University, and a new interstellar molecule was discovered. Two more years later, a new market for HEMT was opened up unexpectedly. Satellite broadcasting began and the demand for low noise microwave amplifiers skyrocketed to reduce the size of receiving dish antennas. The mass production of HEMT discrete devices began. HEMT was accepted by the marketplace.

We are now pretty sure that HEMT has at least one strong point: low noise at microwave frequencies, and hence high-speed operation. We still have two or three more years to go before HEMT is used in real computers.

However, our engineers are all in high spirits, and our top executive officers no longer express doubts. Although I know the HEMT project still needs careful management, I can now express cautious optimism, thanks to our application of the concept of graceful growth. The early entrance of HEMT into the marketplace helped to reduce an anxiety from which otherwise everybody involved might have struggled.

Effective Manpower

Now, I would like to discuss the effective manpower for achieving a breakthrough, such as an invention or a discovery. HEMT was invented by one person, Mimura, and the first working model was constructed by just two persons. Hiyamizu grew the crystal and Mimura performed all the necessary processing and tests.

How many cooks are too many?

An invention is rarely made by a committee. It is usually made by a small number of dedicated people. Why? Because too many cooks spoil the broth. Now the question is, how many cooks are too many?

In an exploratory study, many ideas seemingly trivial or ridiculous have to be tried out in succession.

The outcome is uncertain although it be comes obvious by hindsight.

In this kind of situation, the very possibility of being laughed at or criticized prevents ideas in their embryonic stage from coming out in consciousness. Thus the involvement of a large number of people becomes harmful rather than helpful.

To explain how many cooks are really too many, let n be the number of people involved and q be the probability of two persons cooperating wholeheartedly without criticizing the apparent triviality or absurdity of any idea.

If a pair of persons among n cannot cooperate wholeheartedly, then ideas in their embryonic stage are killed. The number of pairs among n is given by $n(n-1)/2$.

So the expected value of manpower effectively used in the formation of a new idea, or the effective manpower in short, is given by n times q to the $n(n-1)/2$ power.

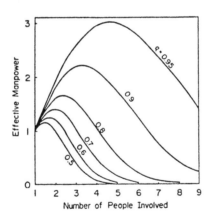

Fig. 4 Effective manpower vs. the number of people involved

Figure 4 shows the effective manpower vs. the number of people involved. If q is 80%, no more than 2 persons should be involved. If q is 90%, no more than 3 persons should be involved.

One may well realize how difficult it is for two persons to cooperate

wholeheartedly 90% of the time. Then, the maximum numbers of people for an important invention may be 3. Managers must be careful not to intervene in the process of achieving a breakthrough by trying to give helping hands.

Probability of Success

Finally, I would like to discuss the probability of success in technology transfer. From my own experiences in R&D , I have realized that successful technology transfer does not take place unless all the people involved think in the same way simultaneously.

Suppose the probability of one person concurring with his subordinate is p and the probability of one person and his counterpart in another group have the right chemistry is q.

Then the probability of a successful transfer is given by

$$p^{m-1+n}q^n$$

where m is the number of ranks in the hierarchy of the transferring group and n is the number of ranks in the hierarchy of the receiving group, as illustrated in Figure 5.

Suppose p is a very reasonable 80% and q is 60% and $m=7$ and $n=4$. Then the probability of success is 1.4%, a frightening number. If one more transfer is required, then a factor of $p^n q^n$ has to be multiplied and the result becomes 0.074% .

This explains very well why a large institution is almost always a poor innovator. The role of managers is, then, to increase p and q and effectively decrease m.

A method used to decrease effective m is *management by walking*

If a pair of persons cannot cooperate wholeheartedly, then ideas in their embryonic stage are killed

---

around. Managers walk around the labs and chat with researchers at their own workbenches. This creates casual but valuable interaction between managers and researchers. Sony's Walkman and HP's calculators are two well-known results of this doctrine.

Stick to the knitting is an effective way to increase p and q. Examples of not sticking to the knitting are abundant: for example, Exxon's attempt into Electronics, TI's digital watch, and GE's coal mining. As you know they all gave up their attempts. Fujitsu did not stick to the knitting when Okada was president. However Okada learned to communicate with engineers, reducing effective m. And that is why Fujitsu is a computer company today.

Conclusion

In summary, I have presented the stories of three leaders in the Japanese electronics industry. Then I discussed five topics: quality, excessive division of labor, graceful growth, effective manpower for a breakthrough, and the probability of success in technology. I hope the stories of these three gentlemen gave some insight into the differences and similarities in the two countries and the five topics clarified the following: Quality, innovation and breakthrough each require entirely different approaches in management.

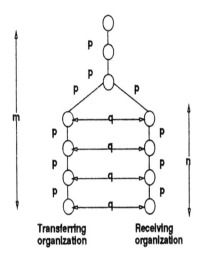

Figure 5 The effect of hierarchy on technology transfer

*DO*s and *DON'T*s for young EEs

Subtitled 'Advice I wish I'd had when I started,' this article by a long-time engineer presents a road map for moving ahead

During a long and unillustrious career, I've accumulated a few "rules" on what a young, or perhaps more accurately, a starting, EE should and should not do on the job. A few came naturally to me, some were picked up by observing others, but most were learned the hard way. None were taught when I went to school.

I wish I could say I eventually practiced all of them myself. The list is not meant to be comprehensive but rather emphasizes certain points that have not been discussed much, and that might be useful. I assume, though, that anyone going into an EE career should really start somewhere in design—of systems, logic, integrated circuits, analog circuitry, of just about anything. It's important to get the experience of doing the calculations and then creating something that's going to be reduced to practice.

GENERALLY SPEAKING. First, some general rules:

1. DO relate what you are doing to the overall system or project objective. Make it your business to understand how your part of a project fits into the system being designed, and what mission or objective that system is trying to accomplish. Putting it another way, try to understand the big picture.

There are two reasons for doing this. It makes your job more interesting and exciting and it may suggest a simpler, better approach to your part of the work than the one someone has laid on you. There are hundreds of cases where someone completed the assigned part of a larger system and, after learning the overall objective, pointed out a much better way to

Charles A. Fowler
C. A. Fowler Associates

accomplish the same objective.

If the people around you are too busy, try asking the boss at lunchtime to tell you "a little more" about how you fit into the overall program. And almost always there are pages and pages that have been written on the subject. Ask to see the technical proposal your company made or the progress reports on the program.

Thus, *DON'T* be afraid to challenge the planned way of doing something or to propose a new way. Of course, you need to be able to do this with forethought and a little diplomacy. You don't want to risk becoming a constant irritant.

2. DO think "cost." Someone said that the difference between science, where discovery is so important, and engineering, where a product is of prime importance, is cost. (Cost is important in science, too, but it's a secondary consideration.) So try to estimate the cost of each project, each design, and each deliverable item.

Start out by finding how much *you* cost: your salary and the "fringes." By the way, the fringes—holidays, vacation, health insurance, education, retirement, and so on—frequently amount to another 30–40 percent of your salary. Then add in other overhead costs like light, heat, and real estate taxes plus the G&A (the general and administrative costs for "those guys in corporate") and even some profit, we hope.

DO find out how much the things you use cost. What did your organization pay for that sampling oscilloscope? How much for the new workstation? How much for that software package? Keep a notebook and create your own cost database. Get acquainted with your employer's cost database. (They sure better have one!)

There are three ways of making an early cost estimate for your project:

Make it your business to understand how your part of a project fits into the system being designed.

• The *bottom-up* approach, based upon a detailed estimate of the design, fabrication, and materials costs of each item in the system.
• The *comparison* approach, based upon the known costs of similar previous efforts. For example, the new system consists of a transmitter that has about twice the complexity of the one used on project A, an antenna about one-and-a-half times the challenge of the one on project B, a software package with about half (watch out!) the code on project C, and so on.
• The *rule-of-thumb* approach, based upon experience over a number of jobs and companies on cost per pound, per printed-circuit card, per line of code, and so on.

The comparison approach supplemented by some rule-of-thumb checks is usually the most accurate and takes the least time for an estimate early on. I've never seen anything yet that couldn't be broken down so as to relate a large part of it to projects that had already been done. That even goes for projects you believe you'll be starting from scratch. It can even apply to integration of an entirely new system. So *DO* get familiar with cost results on prior jobs and start creating some rules of thumb of your own.

3. DO think manufacturing. We've all read about the differences between the United States and Japan in emphasizing the manufacturability of items. Most of my generation grew up in an era where the entire focus was on R&D. Designs were just about thrown over the wall to manufacturing. The prestige and the good salaries went to the R&D staff.

It was later on that we R&D types came to realize that the really tough jobs were tackled by the manufacturing staff and the company profits depended largely on them. Today's concurrent engineering approach for designs scheduled to be manufactured ensures the proper emphasis.

4. I used to say DON'T put anything on a computer until you can describe the system and outline the objective on the back of an envelope or on the blackboard, including a first-order calculation of the expected results. Engineers today who use the computer as both a blackboard (BB) and the back of an envelope (BoE) are ad-

Reprinted from *IEEE Spectrum*, Vol. 30, No. 10, pp. 59–61, October 1993.

monished to *stick* to the BB or BoE phase until the system design has been described, the objective has been defined, and the first-order calculation of performance has been carried out.

5. DO *go way out of your way to give credit to others for their ideas and contributions*. It's the right, ethical, professional, and, in some cases, legally required thing to do. In describing your own work, give credit to each person or organization whose work you are drawing on. Your listeners or readers will be more comfortable and impressed knowing you have explored the field.

They will also assume that the work not credited to others is yours. In contrast, if you do not credit others, and they are aware of this work, your own contributions will be suspect. Further, the persons receiving the credit will respect you and be more likely to share their other new thoughts with you.

Within a group, such behavior is often crucial to effective cooperation. Nothing can turn a colleague off more than your picking up his or her idea and acting like it's yours. To give emphasis and add a bit of fun, identify a particularly original idea with the originator's name: the "Harris Matrix," the

Think manufacturing; the days when R&D threw a design "over the wall" are long gone.

"Jones Algorithm," "Janet's Chart," or the "Levin Technique."

CLIMBING THE LADDER. Now, for some items related to career growth:

1. *Technology proceeds at a furious pace in practically every field, but especially so in electronics, where the half life is about five years, 10 at the outside.* Think of that; half of what you know now won't be applicable in five to 10 years! The good news, I suppose, is that half of what you forgot won't be needed either. Therefore, *DO* keep learning. Go to school to take technical courses. The degree is not as important as the knowledge (except perhaps on a résumé). *DO* join your technical society, the IEEE and its relevant professional specialty sections.

2. *Closely related to this schooling is:* DON'T *even think of taking business courses, let alone going for an MBA, for a long while.* Some companies won't (I believe none should) pay for such courses until the engineer has been out of school for five years or more. I believe you're better off gaining knowledge about costs and marketing concerning the system you're working on. Save those night courses for improving your ability in technical areas. Management and business courses are

more appropriate later on. *DO* remember you are in a business and your bosses must also make business, and not just technical, decisions.

3. DO *read technical articles and books, use the library, and attend technical meetings.* Set up a requirement of reading at least one technical paper a week. Select difficult ones. If you don't understand the paper, ask a more senior person within your organization. Don't give up.

If you want to go all the way, follow the advice J. Presper Eckert Jr. (of Eckert-Mauchly and Univac computer fame) gave to a then still-young Bernard Gordon (founder and chief executive officer of the innovative Analogic Corp.). As Gordon related it:

"I remember his [Eckert] saying to me: 'When you go home tonight, your wife is going to want you to mow the grass. Don't do it. Hire somebody else to cut the grass who is a grass cutter, and you study and design for the company.' And Eckert also said: 'This effort will come back to you many times in the future.'

"I never did cut the grass and always felt as a result of his direction that it was my mother-in-law's job to take out the garbage and not mine! In any event, I have always spent continuously over the last 35 years two hours a day studying at home or at the MIT [Massachusetts Institute of Technology] library or elsewhere...every day."

Far be it from me to take issue with two U.S. engineering heroes, but I must note that many creative ideas have come while doing "idiot" (rote) work like mowing the lawn or weeding the garden. I can't, however, think of any professional career-advancing reason for taking out the garbage voluntarily.

4. DO *learn to express yourself clearly in speech and writing.* This ain't exactly an area engineers are known for. During the late '60s and early '70s, in an attempt to improve writing skills, many companies as well as the Federal government gave employees copies of *The Elements of Style* by William Strunk Jr. and E.B. White. I have no special expertise in this area (as you may readily conclude from reading these opinions of mine), but I believe there's no

better book to help you with your writing skills except, of course, *Modern English Usage* by H.W. Fowler (as you may guess, no relation).

5. DO *write papers.* It's hard and takes time and discipline, but it's important for you and your profession. If you've got something important to report but have trouble putting together a professional paper, here's a time-proven forcing function: submit an abstract for a paper or talk; make it sound good; if it's accepted, then you're stuck with doing it; and you'd better do it right!

6. DO *become the "local" expert in some area, even if it's a fairly narrow one.* Your colleagues will look up to you. Do this in addition to your normal duties. Take that extra time and put in that extra effort to know more about some (hot) subject than anyone else in your surroundings.

But don't cling to one area for too long. The world keeps moving and you should always consider making your next move into another area of expertise.

7. DON'T *let yourself be led off into the fringes of engineering—into the "-ilities" or into engineering administration.* Manufacturability, reliability, and maintainability are, of course, important, but you should consider them in the context of your main role as a design engineer. Such areas on their own tend to be fads that get worn out in a few years. Most important, when times get tough, these areas are the most vulnerable. Further, if you find that's your bent, there's always time for such moves later on.

8. DON'T *be in a hurry to become a supervisor; there's plenty of time for that, too.* Stay on the design side of things for a good long time. If you're especially good at it, you may choose to stay there indefinitely and follow a career path open in many companies with dual management and engineering ladders.

If and when you do move into supervision, you'll spend a significant amount of your time on non-engineering problems and the amount will keep increasing as your supervisory duties increase. Even so, it is most important that you keep current with the technology—at least to the degree needed to perform as a technical manager. This is difficult.

ON THE JOB ITSELF. Now for some *DO*s and *DON'T*s on the job.

1. DO *plan and schedule your work.* Make a detailed plan of all you must do to finish the job you have been assigned. Then work against that plan. As someone said: "Plan the work, then work the plan."

A good plan has some "binary" (it's either completed or it isn't; DON'T hedge with "it's essentially complete") accomplishment for every week, at most for every two weeks; that is, use "footstones" instead of milestones.

If you have something to complete in five to 10 days, you can tell at the end of the first or second day if you're on schedule. If you have something to be accomplished in 30 days, you won't know for almost a week if you're on schedule or not, and that's too late.

A principal reason software programs have had more than their share of troubles over the years was that the *hardware* supervisors didn't know how to make the detailed plans with meaningful footstones, and there were no experienced software managers.

Make your own plan, but review it with your boss. Creating a meaningful, detailed plan is difficult and learning to do so is essential to becoming a good engineer. A corollary is *never* (well, hardly ever) go to work in the morning and have to ask yourself, "What do I do today?"

2. DO *calculate.* The difference between engineering and arm-waving is numbers. Whenever you, or anybody else, have what looks like a great idea, put numbers in it. If you can't reduce it to numbers, then it's arm-waving.

3. DO *document your design.* Write it down. For a long time I've had this rule: if I can't put it in writing, I don't understand it. Recently, I've learned some professions go even further. In his most interesting book and a fun read on computers and hackers, *The Cuckoo's Egg,* author Cliff Stoll quotes the Astronomer's Rule of Thumb: "If you didn't write it down, it didn't happen."

After you've written it down, try this: delete all adjectives (larger, smaller, faster, lighter, heavier, and so on) and substitute numbers. This will probably ruin your day but it will improve your writing and your grasp. A special request: please don't do it to my writing, especially to this article.

4. DON'T *be afraid to ask questions that show your ignorance.* Most of the time, after you've asked, someone will say, *sotto voce,* "God, I was hoping someone would ask that."

5. DO see your boss regularly. It's not only his or her job but your job to make this happen. When you do, *DON'T* go in to pass the time of day; take a set of technical or cost or operational questions to review.

6. DO *track your costs—for the design effort, for purchases, and for manufacturing the product.* Work hand in glove with manufacturing.

7. DO *perform early tests on your part of the project.* There is a fundamental law: if there are no problems, the tests won't take long; if there are problems, you'll thank

Get out into the field with an early model of your equipment. The experience may surprise you.

your lucky stars you found out about them early on!

8. DO *understand the environment.* Visit the environmental test lab; learn about humidity, temperature, shake, rattle, and roll, and that combination of everything, shipping.

9. DO *make every effort to go into the field with an early model of your equipment.* Don't wait to be asked; volunteer. One of the greatest learning experiences an engineer can have is seeing and living with his or her product being subjected to the test of doing something useful. This interaction, involvement with the user, is, in most instances, the critical test for a systems designer. So *DO* try to understand the user and his or her needs.

My impression (probably like yours) of most U.S. cars, for example, is that the designers never took trips in them. The glove compartment will hardly hold the registration, let alone a flashlight and a decent set of maps. And there is no place for a pad to write on, or for an umbrella, an atlas, and so forth.

As I look back on these words, I find my depiction of an engineer's life may sound austere, demanding, and not much fun. It is, to be sure, demanding, but my experience over the years says that EEs (like blondes?) do have more fun. Further, it has been my observation that the groups that are the most creative, that have the high morale, drive, and curiosity that go with technical innovation, also have lots of parties. In fact, they seem to go to great lengths to concoct reasons for getting together in an informal, friendly climate. Loud singing seems to be a key ingredient of such gatherings.

And, as Shakespeare said, this above all: when a project has problems (and all challenging, worthwhile programs have problems), when the chips are down, it is *not* the vice presidents, the managers, the administrators, the marketeers, the "ilities" guys, or the consultants who are asked to fix things; it is the hardware and software design engineers who must face the problems, prepare the fixes, and make the system work. *That* is where the action is.

There aren't many experiences in life more exhilarating than those where *you, the designer,* are making things come together to provide something new, something different, something better. That's what engineering is all about.

Others may make higher salaries, but as my old friend, colleague, and guru Eugene Fubini (a former assistant secretary of defense in the mid-sixties and a widely recognized expert on military matters) has pointed out, "Real compensation equals salary plus psychic income." And there is a lot of psychic income to be had out there and some pretty good salaries, too. Electrical engineering is a great field to be in, both for the engineer and for mankind.

TO PROBE FURTHER. For Bernard Gordon's remarks, and the insights of other engineers back at almost the beginning, see *Computer engineering attitudes from Eckert-Mauchly to Analogic* (The Computer Museum, Boston, 1984). A version of this article first appeared in last June's *Aerospace and Electronic Systems* magazine (pp. 50–53) published by the IEEE's Aerospace and Electronic Systems Society. ◆

Your colleagues will look up to you if you become the local expert on one thing or another.

Taking charge of your promotion

How to steer your career toward the goals you want is outlined in this article, the first in a series on advancing your career that deals with topics they don't teach in school

Are you in control of your career? Many engineers who think they are, in fact are not. They go to work each day assuming that the big raise and promotion are just around the corner. When nothing happens, they're bewildered.

"I deserved it," they complain. "Why does everyone else get promoted? Why am I still waiting?" The answer is simple: they left their promotion up to chance.

Never leave your promotion up to chance. Controlling your career takes planning, hard work, and the ability to turn circumstances to your advantage. Knowing everything it takes to get promoted in your company and constantly working toward that goal is essential to steady advancement. It will certainly mean faster raises and promotions.

Several factors could be limiting your career growth. Key among them are obsolescence, your personality, your level of education, your supervisor, and maybe even the structure of your company or department.

Ask yourself these questions:
• Were your last pay increase and/or your performance rating lower than you expected?
• Do you feel your hard work often goes unrewarded? Does it seem other people are always getting awards or recognition?
• Have you ever been passed over for a promotion and really don't understand why?
• Are you stuck in a dead-end, thankless job?

The more times you've said "yes," the stronger the indication that you are not in control. A "yes" to the final question merely emphasizes this fact. Waiting to discuss your career plans until your job review with your supervisor leaves it much too late.

John A. Hoschette   Loral Infrared and Imaging Systems

Adapted from Chapters 1 and 2 of Career Advancement and Survival for Engineers *by John A. Hoschette (with permission, John Wiley & Sons Inc. [800-225-5945], 1994, 200 pp., $39.95 cloth, $15.95 paper).*

Career planning and preparation should take place long before you enter your supervisor's office. You must be aware of the dynamics within your company and use them to your benefit. Convincing the supervisor that you deserve a promotion should be the last thing on your agenda, not the first.

Do you need to be in control at all times? Yes! Yes! Yes! If you are not planning the next step in your career, you are out of control. Worse yet, you are letting others control your advancement. Failing to take charge and plan is not the way to a successful career. To succeed you must know what to do, when and how—in short, how to play the game.

KNOW THE RULES. Your fellow employees may have some rules of thumb to suggest: flatter the boss; it's who you know that counts; work overtime and be a hero, and so on. But, these are guesses at best. To get ahead you must know how the promotion game is played at your company and how to score points.

Let's assume you are the key player of the team—everyone is counting on you. It is the second period of the third quarter, the teams have lined up, and the goalie is calling the play. On the previous play the putt was good for 3 points, but the right wing was penalized when 5th base was stolen. They have the option to bowl for a strike or fast pitch for a slam dunk. What do you recommend?

Everything sounds somewhat familiar, right? But as you really don't know the rules or how points are scored, your chances of making the right decisions are small.

Moving up in your career is similar. You are the key player in this game of doing a good job, flattering your supervisor, and working hard. But will all these things lead to advancement? More than likely, they won't.

The bottom line is this: if you don't understand how your company plays the career advancement game, you cannot expect to get ahead. So learn the game and how your company keeps score, and start calling the plays that will score your career advancement. There's no time like the present. Remember, your next promotion may be a year or more away from the time you start planning.

GETTING STARTED. As the first step, determine your company's structure. If necessary, sit down with your supervisor or someone senior in the company and map it out.

In point of fact, you should be aware of several structures. Probably the most familiar is the hierarchy of the engineering levels in the company. But just as important is the task and reporting structure, of which there are generally two types. One is product oriented and the other is function oriented. Within these structures, hidden career barriers often exist of which you must be aware.

The career path at most engineering companies begins with nonsupervisory engineers at the bottom [Fig. 1]. As many as four or five engineering levels may intervene before the staff or supervisory level is reached.

In the lower engineering levels [E1 and E2 of Fig. 1], you are expected to be a good team player and learn from your seniors—

Reprinted from *IEEE Spectrum*, Vol. 31, No. 11, pp. 96–99, October 1999.

the old pros. You may be able to do your assignments in as little as a day or two, usually by yourself or with the help of another person. As you rise in the middle levels [senior and principal engineer], you start to lead small teams of two or three people to accomplish specific objectives. Assignments may last weeks or months. You are responsible primarily for technical work.

In the upper engineering levels [E4 and E5 of Fig. 1], you direct large teams of engineers with various backgrounds. Objectives are seldom well defined, and it is up to you to plan things out. Along with providing the team's technical direction, you must maintain schedule and cost controls. You need good interpersonal skills to ensure that work is being done by other people rather than by yourself.

ARE YOU A TECHIE? At the staff level, several career choices must be made. Typically there are four paths upward. At larger companies, the very technically oriented ladder is the fellows ladder [Fig. 1, far left]. In less formal organizations, they are the "senior scientist" types. They are usually Ph.D.s often recognized for their speciality both in and out of the company. The stereotype is of a silver-haired figure in a messy office hung with patents, plaques, and awards.

Usually they are interested in only one thing—science! They may deal only with technical issues and avoid managerial or cost issues. Learn who they are in your company. They know thousands of technical shortcuts and can usually get you out of a jam if you don't understand something.

A word of caution, though. Fellows have seen practically everything and are thorough. Don't shoot from the hip around them. Be precise. Associating with fellows can accelerate your career if they are well respected—or dead-end it quickly if they are labeled as eccentric professors.

STAFF LADDER. Another ladder is staff engineering [second from left in Fig. 1]. These people mostly have a master's degree and deal with putting systems together. The staff engineers work with system-type problems such as the overall performance of a product. In the case of a car, this may include aerodynamic shaping, motor efficiency, weight, and speed, whereas a fellow may deal only with one specialized characteristic of the product—for example, the performance of the spark plug.

Staff engineers, like fellows, concentrate mainly on technical issues but also often advise management on schedule and cost issues as well as technical matters. Highly analytical, they are responsible for how things are coming together technically. They generally have the best computers in the group. Their office walls sport collections of flow charts and graphs showing tradeoff studies. If you try to get an answer out of them, they invariably qualify it with the phrase "That depends upon...."

Another word of warning. Staff engi-

neers are big picture people, who want to know what all the causes and effects are. So if you go to them with only the small picture, they may quickly tag you as not understanding the problem and incompetent—not what you want your boss to hear. As with the fellows, be prepared if you plan on interfacing with them.

RUNNING A PROGRAM. A third career ladder is program management. Typically, these managers run programs or projects and are responsible for cost and schedule performance, not the technical side. They organize teams of engineers to get the job done on time at the cost they quoted. Generally, they are the primary interface with the customer.

The program managers control the funding for programs and have little to do with personnel and salary administration (raises). Quite the reverse—they discount personnel problems and often the company will pay them a bonus if the project is brought in on time and within cost.

A third cautionary word: program managers are not interested in excuses but in getting the job done, so you may find that they can be abrasive at times. They can do a lot to help you get your raise, or prevent it.

Last but not least, there is the management career ladder. Profits and personnel are these people's responsibility. They hand out the raises, promotions, and demo-

tions. They make most of their decisions based on profitability. Their philosophy is "if we can make money, let's do it; if not, stop doing it!" I've seen great engineering projects suddenly halted because they were not making money for the company. This is usually the tallest ladder of the company with the highest salaries.

As you move up the ranks, you will have to decide which ladder is right for you. If you like technical work, prepare yourself by taking more technical courses. If you prefer management, take more business courses.

Also, since each successive level becomes more demanding, you must decide what level is right for you. If your family is important to you, being vice president may not be for you, as the job usually infringes on family life. In short, how high you decide to climb is strictly a personal decision as to how much responsibility you care to accept.

Nonetheless, you can have a very successful career without becoming president of the company. Your success need not be measured in terms of titles, power, and profits. If you remain technical, it can be measured in terms of breakthroughs, papers published, patents, and technical awards.

The crucial point here is that you must define what success means to you, whether it is getting to the senior level or becoming a supervisor or simply doing the best possi-

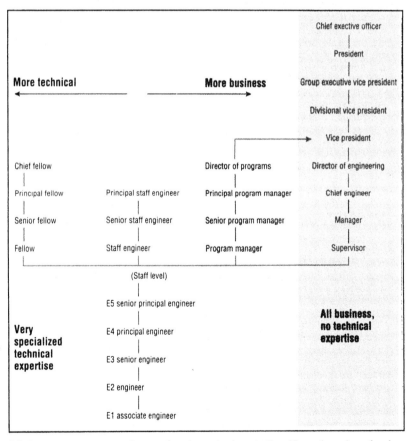

[1] *Your career may move along engineering or business paths with varying mixes of each.*

ble job. Not everyone wants to become vice president of the company. But everyone should define what success means to them.

FRONT-LINE SUPERVISOR. Which level is the toughest? In my opinion, it is the first-line supervisor. All the great ideas generated by the president of the company on how to run the organization must be implemented at this level. The first-line supervisor follows policies on vacations, health care, drug testing, expense reports, employee training, security, raises and promotions, and project successes and failures, personnel problems, and department budgeting, to name just a few.

Put simply, first-line supervisors are caught in a vise between all of the directives from management above and all of the employee problems below. They must do everything and it all has to be done now. They are frequently so overloaded with work that a good many quit and return to the technical ladder or else end up divorced. It is an extremely stressful and time-consuming position.

Make your supervisor your friend, not your enemy. The last thing they need is you running into their office whenever there's a problem. When you go in to talk to your supervisor, remember they probably have a thousand concerns on their mind.

Depending on the company, of course, between the lowest level and the top there can be as many as 12 levels, though recent downsizing is paring such numbers down. If you got a promotion every three years (and this is considered fast), it would take you 36 years. Clearly, every promotion must count. But at a major corporation, the president is usually 1 of, maybe, 40 000 people. At those odds, you are unlikely to become president.

At most companies, top-level executives are expected to have a broad background and understand all aspects of the business. For this reason, most of them will have worked on a variety of career paths before they make it to the top.

THE TOP LOT. Invisible barriers exist all along the ladders. One that spans everything is the higher-degree barrier. Consider the pyramid structure of a company with the chief executive officer (CEO) at the top and the workers at the bottom. From informal surveys of fairly large engineering organizations, I judge that below the first-line supervisor, about 80 percent of the people have bachelor's degrees, about 15 percent have master's, and about 5 percent have doctoral degrees.

Between the first-line supervisor and the director, a mere 10 percent have bachelor's degrees, about 40 percent have master's degrees, and 50 percent are doctors. Between director and CEO, about 60 percent have doctoral degrees and 40 percent have master's degrees. In fact, a director or vice president may well have degrees in more than one area: a doctorate in engineering along with a master's in business. In my survey, I found no one at these rar-

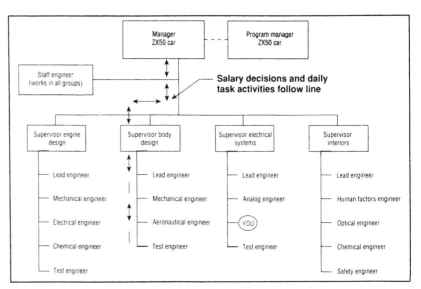

[2] A product-oriented organization melds people with varying backgrounds on a single program.

efied levels with only a bachelor's degree.

So the message is clear: to become an upper-level manager, you need an advanced degree. Survey your own company. Find out how common advanced degrees are in your organization and which type of advanced degree virtually ensures getting ahead. If you are a mechanical engineer at an electronics company and all upper-level managers are electrical engineers, or if you are a programmer in a chemical company and all the advanced degrees are chemical, you can readily infer the promotion policies being followed.

In any case, do find out what types of degrees people have. There is nothing more flattering to a vice president than being asked about his or her background during a company party. They will immediately tell you everything they have accomplished. This is your opportunity. Ask what they would recommend for a younger employee. With any luck, you'll hear about shortcuts you need to know and hidden criteria for promoting.

PRODUCT ORIENTATION. Be aware of other organizational structures at your company in addition to the engineering ladder. These structures define the employees' roles and responsibilities, as well as the manner in which engineering tasks are accomplished. At most companies, engineers are organized into either product-oriented or functional-matrix structures.

In a product-oriented organization everyone works on the same product. Often the entire department is responsible for getting the product out the door. Everyone reports to a single top-level manager.

For example, in the organization for the ZX50 car [Fig. 2], the departmental manager has four subsystem departments reporting to him. The engine department is responsible for designing and testing engines, the body-design department for the exterior body, and so on.

Those who report to the department manager are often the program manager and one or two staff engineers. The program manager determines what is to be worked on, and the engineering department finds the best technical approach. The work to be done is planned by the two managers together. A plus about this type of setup is that your work direction and salary review often come through your supervisor; one person, then, tells you what to do and hands out the raises.

Although in agreement as to the outcome, the program manager and engineering department manager may not see eye to eye. The first wants the fastest job done and the second wants the best engineering job—seldom identical goals.

A product-oriented organization offers several advantages. First, the organization gets to build the entire product, and seeing it all come together provides a real sense of accomplishment. If the product is a huge success, management knows whom to reward. Second, everyone reports through the same chain and decisions are more easily made.

OTHER PERSPECTIVES. Third, if the people you work with have very different backgrounds from you, dealing with them will broaden your own background. And since staffs now tend to be lean, you might be the only one in the group with your type of background—an excellent position, since there is no competition. Another advantage: if you have the same background as your supervisor or manager, they can understand your work more easily. Managers tend to promote people with backgrounds similar to their own. The rationale is: it worked for me and I am successful, so why not continue the trend? But if, say, you are a chemical engineer and your boss is an electrical one, she may not appreciate the great job you are doing.

Naturally, a product-oriented organiza-

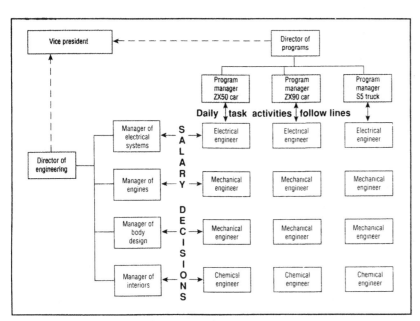

[3] *Large companies may group engineers with similar skills in a functional-matrix organization.*

tion has disadvantages. If the product runs into trouble (because of poor planning or performance), you will be branded as coming from a failed program. Also, when product development ends, there is no place for you to go unless a new product is waiting in the wings. Finally, working on a product all too easily creates engineers who know everything about one little thing—not the best situation if you plan on running the organization some day.

MATRIX OF FUNCTIONS. In a functional-matrix organization, the company is grouped around functions. Members of a group generally have the same background but may not work on the same product.

The left-hand column of the matrix in Fig. 3 identifies departments by function. The top row identifies the projects within the company. In the example, three types of vehicles are produced: the ZX50 and ZX90 cars and the S5 truck. The top row identifies the program manager(s) responsible for getting work done.

Large companies find this organization efficient in running their business. People are grouped according to their skills; and they can be moved quickly on and off programs. Usually the supervisor determines salary increases and the program manager determines the work to be done.

This kind of organization can help your career in several ways. First, your colleagues have your sort of background, so someone who has faced something similar could help you if you get stuck on a problem. Second, you may work on more than one product at a time—a real plus if one of the products is pure tedium. Third, in a functional-matrix organization, you can quickly move from one product to another as the products come and go.

The functional-matrix organization, naturally, also has its down side. By and large, work direction comes from your program manager and technical direction from your supervisor—a tricky situation when the two disagree. Following your supervisor's direction may upset the program manager enough even to kick you off the product. Following your program manager's direction may upset your supervisor, who, of course, directly controls your salary.

You have two masters to please—and to get that raise, you must keep both happy. When it comes to a raise, the ultimate decision is up to your department supervisor, but you had better make sure the program manager agrees with him about your worth. It doesn't hurt to ask each of them how you're doing. It's better to find out before rather than after raises are given out, while you can still do something about it.

Another disadvantage of the functional-matrix organization is also one of its advantages—everyone in your group has a similar background and it's tough to stand out in a crowd. You must find ways to be different.

Few companies are organized strictly in either a product-oriented or a functional-matrix fashion. Rather, they are a mix of both. No one type of organization is better for your career than the other, but you need to recognize the differences and that what works in one may not work in another.

Find out how your company is organized and who determines your salary. You could be working hard to impress someone with no involvement in your raise. Make sure you report your progress at regular intervals to the person who does control it.

Recent engineering school graduates tend to come into a company believing that someone is looking out for them. They go

off into a corner, do a great job, and expect their boss will reward them when they are finished. Remember, only you are looking out for you. So spend time each week with your supervisor. Let your boss know the problems you are solving. Ask for feedback on your performance. No one enjoys hearing criticism, but it's the only way you will be sure of turning things around.

HOMEWORK. Getting ahead also requires doing some homework—or more precisely, some on-the-job assignments:

• Map out the engineering ladder at your company. A good place to start is with your boss. Inquire about the levels of responsibility, next ask to see an organization chart and where you fit in.

• If possible, obtain a description of each level. Larger companies at one time or another have written this down. Smaller companies are less formal, a state of affairs that may give the engineer greater freedom to perform tasks at all levels, but which may also lead to misunderstandings between employee and supervisor. So a job description may be more important at a small company than at a large one.

• Study the description for your current level and judge how you measure up. To get promoted, remember, you must be sure you are fulfilling each and every requirement. Next, study the level above yours and see how you and it compare.

• Find out how your company is organized—with a product-oriented or a functional-matrix organization, or a combination? Who reports to whom? Can you identify all the levels and who is at each level between you and the vice president? If you can you're in great shape! But if you don't know who they are, how can you expect them to know you and promote you?

• The final homework assignment is to determine the career path you want. How high up the ladder do you want to go? How much time will it take? What must you do to reach your goal?

TO PROBE FURTHER. Author Hoschette is scheduled to speak at a meeting next April of the Boston Section. Contact Barbara Roberts for the time and location at 617-271-2772; e-mail, broberts@mitre.org.

IEEE-U.S. Activities' Career Maintenance committee sponsors three career workshops geared toward helping engineers deal with change in their careers. Contact Scott Grayson, 202-785-0017; e-mail, s.grayson@ieee.org. ◆

The Drug-Free Workplace Act

Subtitle D – Drug-Free Workplace Act of 1988
Sec. 5151. Short Title
   This subtitle may be cited as the "Drug-Free Workplace Act of 1988."
Sec. 5152. Drug-Free Workplace Requirements For Federal Contractors.
(A) Drug-Free Workplace Requirement. –

1. Requirement for persons other than individuals. No person, other than an individual, shall be considered a responsible source, under the meaning such term as defined in section 4(8) of the Office of Federal Procurement Policy Act (41 U.S.C. 403(8)), for the purposes of being awarded a contract for the procurement of any property or services of a value of $25,000 or more from any Federal agency unless such person has certified to the contracting agency that it will provide a drug-free workplace by –

   (a) publishing a statement notifying employees that the unlawful manufacture,

   distribution, dispensation, possession, or use of a controlled substance is prohibited in the person's workplace and specifying the actions that will be taken against employees for violations of such prohibition;

   (b) establishing a drug-free awareness program to inform employees about

      i. the dangers of drug abuse in the workplace;
      ii. the person's policy of maintaining a drug-free workplace;
      iii. any available drug counseling, rehabilitation, and employee assistance programs; and
      iv. the penalties that may be imposed upon employees for drug abuse violations;

   (c) making it a requirement that each employee to be engaged in the performance of such contract be given a copy of the statement required by subparagraph (a);

   (d) notifying the employee in the statement required by subparagraph (a), that as a condition of employment on such contract, the employee will

      i. abide by the terms of the statement; and
      ii. notify the employer of any criminal drug statute conviction for a violation occurring in the workplace no later than 5 days after such conviction;

   (e) notifying the contracting agency within 10 days after receiving notice under subparagraph (d)(ii) from an employee or otherwise receiving actual notice of such conviction;

   (f) imposing a sanction on, or requiring the satisfactory participation in a drug abuse assistance or rehabilitation program by, any employee who is so convicted, as required by section 5154; and

   (g) making a good faith effort to continue to maintain a drug-free workplace through implementation of sub-paragraphs (a), (b), (c), (d), (e), and (f).

2. Requirement For Individuals. – No Federal agency shall enter into a contract with an individual unless such contract includes a certification by the individual that the individual will not engage in the unlawful manufacture, distribution, dispensation, possession, or use of a controlled substance in the performance of the contract.

(B) Suspension, Termination, or Debarment of the Contractor. –

1. Grounds For Suspension, Termination, or Debarment. Each contract awarded by a Federal agency shall be subject to suspension of payments under the contract or termination of the contract, or both, and the contractor thereunder or the individual who entered the contract with the Federal agency, as applicable, shall be subject to suspension or debarment in accordance with the requirements of this section if the head of the agency determines that –

   (a) the contractor or individual has made a false certification under subsection (A);
   (b) the contractor violates such certification by failing to carry out the requirements of subparagraph (a), (b), (c), (d), (e), or (f) of subsection (A)(1); or
   (c) such a number of employees of such contractor have been convicted of violations of criminal drug statutes for violations occurring in the workplace as to indicate that the contractor has failed to make a good faith effort to provide a drug-free workplace as required by subsection (A).

2. Conduct of Suspension, Termination, and Debarment Proceedings.

   (a) If a contracting officer determines, in writing, that cause for suspension of payments, termination, or suspension or debarment exists, an appropriate action shall be initiated by contracting officer of the agency, to be conducted by the agency concerned in accordance with the Federal Acquisition Regulation and applicable agency procedures.
   (b) The Federal Acquisition Regulation shall be revised to include rules for conducting suspension and debarment proceedings under this subsection, including rules providing notice, opportunity to respond in writing or in person, and such other procedures as may be necessary to provide a full and fair proceeding to a contractor or individual in such proceeding.

3. Effect of Debarment. – Upon issuance of any final decision under this subsection requiring debarment

   of a contractor or individual, such contractor or individual shall be ineligible for award of any contract by any Federal agency, and for participation in any future procurement by any Federal agency, for a period specified in the decision, not to exceed 5 years.

Sec. 5153. Drug-Free Workplace Requirements For Federal Grant Recipients.
[This section parallels section 5152, with wording appropriate to grant recipients.]

Sec. 5154 Employee Sanctions and Remedies
A grantee or contractor shall, within 30 days after receiving notice from an employee of a conviction pursuant to section 5152 (A)(1)(d)(ii) or 5153 (A)(1)(d)(ii) –

1. take appropriate personnel action against such employee up to an including termination; or
2. require such employee to satisfactorily participate in a drug abuse assistance or rehabilitation program approved for such purposes by a Federal, State, or local health, law enforcement, or other appropriate agency.

Sec. 5155 Waiver.

1. In General. – A termination, suspension of payments, or suspension or debarment under this subtitle may be waived by the head of an agency with respect to a particular contract or grant if –

(a) in the case of a waiver with respect to a contract, the head of the agency determines under section 5152 (B)(1), after the issuance of a final determination under such section, that suspension of payments, or termination of the contract, or suspension or debarment of the contractor, or refusal to permit a person to be treated as a responsible source for a contract, as the case may be, would severely disrupt the operation of such agency to detriment of the Federal Government or the general public; or

(b) in the case of a waiver with respect to a grant, the head of the agency determines that suspension of payments, termination of the grant, or suspension of debarment of the grantee would not be in public interest.

2. Exclusive Authority. – The authority of the head of an agency under this section to waive termination, suspension, or debarment shall not be delegated.

Sec. 5156 Regulations.

Not later than 90 days after the date of enactment of this subtitle, the governmentwide regulations governing actions under this subtitle shall be issued pursuant to the Office of Federal Procurement Policy Act (41 U.S.C. 401 et seq.).

Sec. 5157 Definitions.

For the purposes of this subtitle –

1. the term "drug-free workplace" means a site for the performance of work done in connection with a specific grant or contract described in section 5152 or 5153 of an entity at which employees of such entity are prohibited from engaging in the unlawful manufacture, distribution, dispensation, possession, or use of a controlled substance in accordance with the requirements of this Act;

2. the term "employee" means the employee of a grantee or contractor directly engaged in the performance of work pursuant to the provisions of the grant or contract described in section 5152 or 5153;

3. the term "controlled substance" means a controlled substance in schedules I through V of section 202 of the Controlled Substances Act (21 U.S.C. 812);

4. the term "conviction" means a finding of guilt (including a plea of nolo contendere) or imposition of sentence, or both, by any judicial body charged with the responsibility to determine violations of the Federal or State criminal drug statutes;

5. the term "criminal drug statute" means a criminal statute involving the manufacture, distribution, dispensation, use, or possession of any controlled substance;

6. the term "grantee" means the department, division, or other unit of a person responsible for the performance under the grant;

7. the term "contractor" means the department, division, or other unit of a person responsible for the performance under the contract; and

8. the term "Federal agency" means an agency as that term is defined in section 552(f) of title 5, United States Code.

Appendix A

Notes for the Instructor

This appendix contains notes for possible use by an instructor teaching a course based on this text.

A.1 CONTENT OVERVIEW

I had two goals in mind when I created the material for this text. The first is to make students aware of ethical considerations and encourage their commitment to ethical behavior. The second is to enhance their communication skills, both written and oral. The material is suitable for a course that might be offered in any of several academic departments concerned with computing: Information Systems, Computer Science, Computer Engineering, or Electrical Engineering. There is easily more than enough material to fill a typical one-semester, three-credit-hour course. A "road map" of suggested coverage for such a course appears in Figure A.1. The book could just as easily support a one-credit-hour seminar, focusing on selected topics.

Some may question why there is a chapter on critical-thinking skills or why it appears so early in the text. In fact, I did not include this topic in the course in the first few semesters that I taught it at the University of South Florida. However, I quickly realized that some explicit coverage of critical-thinking skills in the context of ethics and computing could greatly improve the students' abilities to analyze the material covered. For that reason, I recommend the critical-thinking skills chapter as a "must cover."

I also recommend the chapter on the codes of ethics as a "must cover." It is important that students know that there are standards of ethical conduct endorsed by the professional societies in computing. It is also important that studies are introduced to issues surrounding licensing of software engineers.

Cracking and computer security is a traditional core area in any ethics and computing course. The same is true of Encryption and Law Enforcement—although the content in this area is possibly the most rapidly changing. Only a

few years ago the proposed "Escrowed Encryption Standard" was the focus of this area, but this has now become more of a historical note. Public policy in this area is still evolving, and it is important that students be aware of the issues involved.

The chapters on safety-critical systems, whistle blowing, and intellectual-property issues are also recommended. The amount of material in these chapters may make it difficult to cover each chapter in its entirety. Depending on time constraints and your desired emphasis, you may want to cover only selected portions of some of these chapters.

The chapter on environmental and health concerns covers some larger environmental concerns relevant to the computing industry and to society as a whole. My goal was to have students realize that computer-system design must take into account not only performance and other user requirements, but also the consumption of resources and the long-term effects on health and well-being. While each chapter is important, recognizing that not all instructors will have time to cover the whole book, this is one chapter that might be considered optional.

The chapter on striving for fairness will no doubt be controversial with some students and even some faculty. However, this material is central to the ethical treatment of others, both in the workplace and in society. It is sure to generate some excellent discussion about ethical issues, and it offers opportunities for students to exercise their critical-thinking skills. Many instructors pressed for time will want to consider this chapter as optional. However, I recommend they carefully evaluate the importance of the various topics in this chapter against those they do find time to cover.

The chapter on managing your career provides some

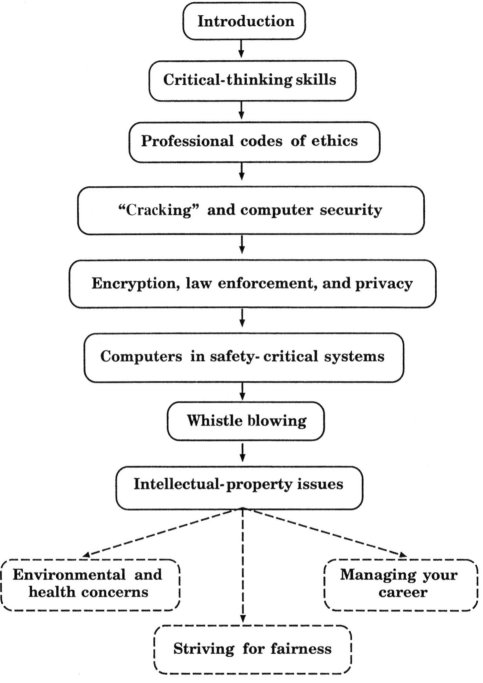

Figure A.1 A road map for using this text. Bold lines indicate strongly recommended coverage at some level. Dashed lines indicate topics for optional coverage.

advice on how to approach the task of planning for a successful career. Instructors who cannot cover all of this chapter may still want to devote a few minutes to the section on the Drug-Free Workplace Act.

A.2 IMPROVING STUDENTS' WRITING SKILLS

As I mentioned earlier, my secondary goal in creating this text was to enhance communication skills, both written and oral. To that end, I have provided many opportunities for students to practice writing, and suggest that you make writing assignments an integral part of the course. One element of negative stereotyping of people in technical disciplines is that they have poor writing skills. Whether bad writing is in fact more common in technical disciplines is subject to debate. But it should be clear that writing well about technical subject matter is just plain different in some important ways from writing well on a nontechnical topic. Consider just one example of how this is true. In creative writing courses, people are typically told not to reuse a word or sentence structure so as not to give a repetitive or boring feeling to the prose. However, in technical writing this rule can lead to disaster. Once a technical term is introduced to describe some object or effect in a piece of technical writing, you absolutely do not want to use any other term to describe the same object or effect. To do so would only result in confusion. Also, in technical writing, simple sentence structure works best because the reader must concentrate on absorbing the meaning behind the sentence. A discussion of statistical testing methods, for example, would suffer horribly from poetic license. Also, the precision, or degree of specificity you desire to achieve in technical writing is fundamentally different than that in creative writing. So it is natural and necessary that technical writing be more obviously uniform than creative writing. Technical writing needs a well-defined framework and uniformity so that the meaning can come forth uninterrupted by unusual words or strange constructions. This does not mean that technical writing must be dull and boring. But it does mean that greater care and attention are required to craft technical writing that is both clear and interesting. You might find it useful to take some time early in the course to explicitly address the goals and standards for the writing assignments and to give hints on how students can improve their writing skills.

To assist you in this part of the instruction, I have summarized common problems that occur in technical writing, and the types of tools and habits that students should develop to support their technical writing efforts, such as a checklist for proofreading and revising first drafts. Finally, I include a reprint of "Good Writing," by Professor Marc Raibert of the Massachusetts Institute of Technology, which hopefully will motivate students to be interested in producing good technical writing.

A.2.1 Common Problems Found in Technical Writing

I synthesized the following list of common problems from a discussion with students in one of my classes at the University of South Florida. You can probably think of things you have read that exhibit each of these problems. Consider how you would get the students to recognize that the problem is present, how they would correct the problem, and how they can work to prevent the problem from recurring.

A.2.1.1 Failing to Provide the "Big Picture" Early Enough. Readers need some idea of why they should read your paper and how the parts of it will fit together so that they can be motivated to read further. The first outline of the "big picture" should be given in the introduction. After that, the transitions between major sections of the paper should serve to reconnect to the big picture and suggest how the pieces of the puzzle are coming together.

A.2.1.2 Failing to Provide or Specify the Foundation to

Understand the Material. If a document presumes that the reader has a certain level of background in a certain area, it can be useful to state this. An example might be: "This technical report assumes that you have read or have access to a copy of Technical Report N-1 on Definition of Terms for the International Whatsit Standard." If all the reader needs is some brief summary of other material, you could provide it in an appendix to the document. You often see these sorts of things in textbooks—a statement in the preface about the nature of the intended audience and some appendices in the back that summarize needed mathematics.

A.2.1.3 Using Acronyms and Technical Phrases Without Defining Them. There are several elements to this problem. One is simply the use of "established" acronyms. Whenever you use an acronym that you are not absolutely certain will be familiar to every reader, you should spell it out at the first use.

Also, don't presume that everyone has your interpretation of a common term. Many standards are the result of months of effort spent trying to define terms and develop taxonomies. When in doubt, define the scope of a common term like "verification" with a sentence like "Here, 'verification' is meant to include x, y, and z." Your readers will thank you for being specific. Another is the tendency by some authors to define a dozen or so of their own acronyms in each paper. In general, avoid this tendency. The world has enough acronyms already. If it isn't being used as an acronym by someone else (excluding your colleagues or office mates), think hard about whether it needs to be in your writing. Also, when you present a new term that you want the reader to remember, it helps to put it in bold or italic type. Depending on the level of jargon used and the intended audience, you may want to include a glossary in the back.

A.2.1.4 Having too Few (or no) Examples. Using examples helps make abstract discussions more concrete and shows how ideas and methods might be applied in practice.

A.2.1.5 Having too Few (or no) Graphics. Diagrams, pictures, and tables serve a purpose similar to that of examples. They reinforce ideas and clarify certain points. We all know that one picture can take the place of "a thousand" words.

A.2.1.6 Including too Much Theory or Discussion with too Little Application. This point is related to several of the earlier points. Readers' interest in your paper will wane if they can't see what reading it will do for them. Keeping the reader's interest can be as simple as adding an example of an application that would benefit from the technique, describing a hypothetical implementation, or providing a conceptual ("cloud diagram") figure that shows how the technique would fit into a larger body of techniques.

A.2.1.7 Failing to Present the Material Logically and Coherently. This problem can occur in the organization of the entire paper (macro level) or an individual paragraph (micro level). At the macro level, it probably points to the paper being poorly organized from the start. If you look at the set of section and subsection headings as an outline of the content, the flow should seem natural and coherent. If the basic organization is sound, you need worry only that your individual paragraphs work to reconnect each chapter to the big picture. At the micro level, it points to poor reasoning. The remedy is to revise the paragraph until it does in fact support the conclusion or point made in the closing sentence, or in some cases, opening sentence—such as when you are proving a theorem. One of the main reasons writers end up with a lack of coherence is that they tend to try to include everything about a topic in the interest of being precise. Ask yourself at each step, "Does the reader have to know this to understand the points being made, and does this sentence fit in the chosen focus?"

A.2.1.8 Writing in a Way that Is Just Plain Boring to Read. There is no need to strive for stiff formality in a technical paper. Even the federal government has issued a "plain English" mandate that asks its contractors to write in the active voice instead of the passive voice: "The team tested system x," instead of "System x was tested by the team," or even worse, "System x was tested." If you are wondering whether or not your writing is stilted, ask yourself if you would explain it the same way to someone in conversation. If so, you are on the right track, and you may need only a few adjustments. If not, try explaining it to someone and note what changes in your speech. Of course, you wouldn't write pauses, such as "uh" or "um," but watch for structural changes in your oral explanation.

A.2.1.9 Having No Substance. This is perhaps the most damaging complaint of all to hear about your writing. There are two possibilities. If there really *isn't* much substance, maybe you have nothing to write about, and your remedy should be to try to get more substance. If the substance is there, you must work harder at making its presence known. The problem could be that the sentences are too long and convoluted to the point that the reader has given up trying to figure out your points. Try simplifying your writing by shortening the sentences and making it clear who is doing what when.

A.2.2 Habits and Tools to Support Good Writing

One element of being able to write well is to use good tools and to develop good habits. Corey and Rhodes suggest six steps for accomplishing this [1]:

1. **Acquire your own small library.** You should of course have a dictionary at hand when you are writing. You may also want to have a thesaurus (dictionary of antonyms and synonyms), an "elements of good grammar" book, and a "how to" book specific to technical writing. Many good texts are available in each of these categories, and it is well worth a visit to your favorite bookstore to look over several alternatives for each and select ones that suit your taste.

2. **Don't let your ego hurt your writing.** Don't be afraid of, or be resentful toward, feedback on the quality of your writing. Getting the opinion of others is an important step in improving your writing. Also, don't try to write in a style that is "not you." That is, don't attempt to write in a style you are not comfortable with or use unfamiliar words.

3. **Know your writing weaknesses.** As you get experience and feedback on your writing, you should be able to identify tendencies and habits that you need to work to improve. Perhaps you tend to write sentences that are too long, overuse the passive voice, have subject–verb mismatches, or suffer from other writing problems. You should have a mental list of these things and actively look for them as you proofread your writing.

4. **Don't overestimate the background of your audience.** Do not be afraid that you will insult your audience by being "too introductory" or "not technical enough." And do not take the attitude that a certain level of obscurity in your writing is somehow necessary to impress your audience. If you do, the only impression you are likely to leave is that of a person who can't communicate well.

5. **Use the document-creation tools available on your computer.** You should certainly have a spell-checking utility, and you should have a utility that will allow you to produce graphics. You may even want to use a tool to check grammar in your writing, although such tools are not terribly sophisticated.

6. **Seek out more experience and feedback.** For most people, writing becomes easier to do and with better results, as they practice and gain experience. As one article on writing says, "Everything engineers can learn about correct, effective writing is useless if they avoid writing opportunities" [2].

A.2.3 A Checklist for Proofreading and Revising Your Writing

"Good writers count on being able to revise several drafts, because they know the writing process is messy" [2]. Revising the current draft of a paper into a better draft involves reading the current draft critically, recognizing problems in it, and rewriting the paper to fix the problems. The following checklist for reading your paper is suggested in a monograph on how to improve writing skills [3]. If you do not use an explicit written checklist such as this, you should at least keep a mental checklist as you proofread your writing.

1. **The thesis:** Can you underline it? Is it expressed clearly and specifically?

2. **The paragraphs:** Does each develop one main idea? Do they develop the ideas adequately and coherently?

3. **Evidence:** Are your examples sufficient to support your ideas? (Here, for technical writing, the appropriate wording of the question might be, are your data, experiments, and results sufficient to support your conclusions? If not, there are just two alternatives: revise your claims for your work and revise or extend your work so that it does support the claims you want to make.)

4. **Definition:** Have you identified the key terms in your paper and defined them adequately?

5. **Sentences:** Do the sentences express your main ideas concisely and effectively?

6. **Transitions:** Do the transitions work well to tie one part of the paper to another?

7. **Word choice:** Do the words you use in your paper aptly and precisely express your meaning? Have you used specialized or technical words correctly?

8. **Errors of structure and usage:** Can you spot any major errors (such as fragments, run-on sentences, agreement errors), particularly the problems specific to your writing style?

9. **Audience:** In your own judgment, does the writing as a whole make the most effective appeal it can to the readership for which it is intended?

Once you have completed your own proofreading and revision, you should get feedback from others. If you are not writing in your native language, get feedback from at least one person who is a native speaker of that language.

REFERENCES

[1] J. R. Corey and G. Rhodes, "Write on the money," *Graduating Engineer,* March 1994, pp. 43–45.

[2] W. W. Dorman and J. M. Pruett, "Engineering better writers: Why and how engineers can teach writing," *Engineering Education,* April 1985, pp. 656–658.

[3] A. Moss and C. Holder, *Improving student writing.* Kendall-Hunt, Dubuque, IA, 1988.

"Good Writing," Marc Raibert, Boston Dynamics
January 1985; revised January 1995

It is important that you produce good writing for technical reports and research papers. Good writing will permit your readers to concentrate on your ideas, and may help you to give the impression that you know what you are talking (writing) about. I am not going to define good writing, but will assume that you know good writing when you see it. Instead, I will concentrate on giving you some tips that will help you to produce good writing.

My formula for good writing is simple: once you decide that you *want* to produce good writing and that you *can* produce good writing, then all that remains is to write bad stuff, and to revise the bad stuff until it is good. So we start with two top-level tips for good writing:

- *You must want to produce good writing.*

- *You must believe you can produce good writing.*

My first point is that you can produce good writing only if you want to. It takes lots of hard work, and an unfortunate fact of life is that for most people, it will always take lots of hard work. Your writing will get better with experience and confidence, but it will probably not get much easier. Because good writing requires hard work, your motivation is a key factor – you must want your writing to be good if you are to spend the time and effort required to make it good. So my first point is that good writing starts with your desire to produce good writing.

My second point is that you must believe that you can do it. If you don't have the confidence that you can hammer out a good result, you may rely too heavily on someone else's help, or worse, settle for mediocre results. Almost all documents containing good writing go through initial and intermediate phases, when they are mostly bad.[1] Confidence in the ultimate outcome of your efforts will be essential if you are to keep plugging away at draft after draft in order to convert the bad stuff into good stuff. So even though it won't be easy, you need to have confidence that you can do it.

You have good reason to be confident. Almost anyone who makes it to graduate school (and certainly everyone else) can learn to communicate clearly through the written word. No matter how bad your writing is today, you can make it substantially better.

Now that you are committed and confident, here are some tips that will help you to write the good stuff:

Good Writing is Bad Writing That Was Rewritten.
Almost all good writing starts out bad. Rather than leave it bad, the good writer rewrites and refines it until it is good, or even very good. This process may take several passes over the same words, sentences, and paragraphs, but a dozen or so passes is typical. This observation, that good writing starts out bad, is important because it has two implications. The first implication is that when you start a new paper or report, there is nothing wrong with using bad writing. Your goal when you start is to get your ideas down on paper in any form you can. Incomplete sentences, streams of consciousness, lists of ideas, and outlines are all good ways to get started. These methods will help you to figure out what you want to say, which is the main purpose of this phase in writing. You don't have to worry about the writing being bad, because you will revise it later.

The second implication of the idea that good writing starts out bad, is that you will revise the bad stuff until it is good. Unfortunately for most of us, our first exposure to writing was for

---

[1]I admit it. There are a few jerks out there who write perfect stuff the first time, and who don't have to work hard to make their writing good. But I'm assuming that you are not one of those irritating individuals.

grammar school term papers or essays. I don't know about you, but I always did those things the night before they were due, and rarely read them once they were written, let alone revised them. My job was to write, my teacher's job was to read, and no one revised. Once you get the idea that you will keep working on a paper, writing and rewriting it, until all the writing is good, the rest is relatively easy. Here's what you should do during all that revising:

- Scrutinize each paragraph and revise it until it is a good one. Topic sentences are particularly helpful and important. Try to have one main idea for each paragraph. Paragraphs are good when they say what you want to say, and when all the sentences hang together harmoniously. When you are reading and rewriting your paragraphs, read them out loud occasionally to get a feel for their rhythm.

- Scrutinize the glue between your paragraphs. Make sure that your paragraphs fit together nicely. Does each paragraph follow from the last and set up the next?

- Scrutinize each sentence and rewrite it until it is a good one.[2] I assume you can tell a good sentence when you hear one, so read your stuff out loud to test it on your ear.

That's all there is to it. Write down everything you want to say. Then grovel over it until it is good. Here are a few other tips that might help.

Spill the Beans Fast.

Unlike murder mysteries that keep the reader from knowing *whodunit* until the very end, a research paper should reveal whodunit and whodunwhat as soon as possible. You should summarize your whole story at the very beginning of your paper, without holding anything back. Not only should you describe what you set out to do, but you should also tell your reader what you found out. You should put your best stuff up front, in the title if possible.

Now this tip about spilling the beans fast makes real sense. Assuming that you are writing the paper because you did something very clever and you want everyone to know about it, then you might as well start letting them know at the beginning of your paper. Most folks aren't going to hang around to read the whole thing anyway, so you have your best shot at revealing how devilishly ingenious you are if you do it right away:

- Spill the beans in the title,

- Spill the beans in the abstract,

- Spill the beans in the introduction, and

- Spill the beans in the body.

When you are spilling the beans at the beginning of your paper, don't just *refer* to your results, *give* your results. Use simple summaries of your most important points. For instance:

Wrong way: In this paper I will give you my formula for good writing.

---

[2] I said I wouldn't give details of what makes good writing good, but I can't resist saying a few things. Of course, the grammar must be perfect. Avoid run-on sentences. I get particularly annoyed by sentences that use words with unclear antecedent. For instance, there might be three "it"s in one sentence, each referring to something different. Instead of using the word "it", substitute exactly the same words that were used to name "it" in the first place. There is nothing wrong with repeating the same phrase several times in one sentence or a paragraph to improve the clarity. For some reason we are taught to randomly vary wording to avoid repetition. This practice makes binding antecedents much harder. Another pitfall is to write "*the* whatsit," when no whatsits have yet been mentioned.

Right way: My formula for good writing is simple – once you decide that you *want* to produce good writing and that you *can* produce good writing, then all that remains is to write bad stuff, and to revise the bad stuff until it is good.

I find it useful to spill the beans at the end of the introduction. This is a good place for bean spilling because the introduction has provided the reader with the background needed to understand the message, and because a simple statement of the message at this point improves the transition from introductory stuff to the main exposition. If you do a good job of spilling the beans in the introduction, then the introduction stands on its own, summarizing the entire paper.

Don't Get Attached to Your Prose.

Suppose you've worked very hard on a sentence that was giving you trouble. Not only did you fix the problem, but you made the sentence into the best sentence you've ever written, probably the best sentence anyone has ever written in the entire state of Pennsylvania, a real prize-winner. It has a melodious ring and mellifluous rhythm that will make you famous. Unfortunately, after some other revisions to your paper and some more thinking, you find that your prize-winning masterpiece doesn't say quite what you intended to say, or that it is part of a paragraph that must now be eliminated for some other reason. What to do? (Multiple choice:)

- Maybe if you move the sentence to another paragraph you can make it sound true and keep it.

- Who cares what the paper says anyway. If it sounds good, go ahead and use it.

- Give up this year's prize for great literature and flush the damn thing.

I've used all three methods, but only the last one really works. So here's a technique that will help you to discard a good sentence or paragraph that doesn't really belong in your paper: Create a special file called PRIZE_WINNING_STUFF.TXT. Move all deleted text to this file. Should you find a new home for your special sentence later, either in this paper or some other paper, you are assured that it will still be in good health, available for resurrection at an instant's notice. I find that using a *refuse file* for all the well-written text that I don't need permits me to get on with the task of telling my story, without worrying too much about losing potentially valuable intermediate results. By the way, I've often been surprised at how positively mediocre a prize-winning sentence can sound when read a year later.

Just as you can get attached to your prose, you may get attached to a clever idea or argument that does not really fit in the paper. My advice is the same: flush.

Getting Unstuck.

There usually comes a point in writing a paper when you get stuck. You try generating several descriptions or statements, but nothing you write seems to work. Getting stuck is frequently an indication that you don't have a clear idea of what you want to say, or you don't fully understand some of the things you planned to explain. This is normal – it takes more understanding to explain clearly what you did, than it took to do it.

When you are stuck, try making a list of the points you want to make. An outline can be very useful when you're stuck, especially if you have already begun to write text. You may find that you can write good paragraphs that clearly express parts of your story, but you still have trouble with the overall organization of your paper. For instance, after

generating several pages of text you read them to find that they ramble and repeat, and that parts of your story are missing. You can't figure out what you are trying to say. At this point you should make a new outline and reorganize using the following procedure:

1. Write down the topic of each paragraph you have written, in a two or three word phrase.

2. Shuffle and organize the topics into a coherent outline, adding or deleting topics as necessary.

3. Rearrange the paragraphs of text according to the organization of the revised outline. You may need to add new text for new topics.

4. Go back to paragraph and sentence refinement.

This procedure will often help you to figure out what you've done, what is missing, and what needs to be done to get back on the right track. Occasionally, you may even try this on a sentence-by-sentence basis.

One way to get stuck writing is to lose track of where you are and get lost. I get lost when I've written a lot of text but the organization of the paper has not yet gelled. A way to get unstuck in this case is to line up all the pages of your paper face up on a big table or the floor, so you can see the whole paper at once. This will help you see the overall organization and the balance among the various sections. You will also see the arrangement of figures and their proximity to the sections of text. I find looking at the whole paper at once provides me with a map of the paper that says "You Are Here."[3]

Another means of getting unstuck is to keep at it. I frequently get stuck during the first three or four days of a new writing project, presumably because I still don't know what I want to say and because I have not yet abandoned some of the more exciting half-baked topics I had in mind. I find, however, that my productivity eventually improves if I keep working on the project, day after day. I seem to lose ground in terms of productivity when I skip writing days.

An important step in producing good writing is to get feedback from a friend or colleague about your work. I have two more tips for this aspect of good writing: you should husband your readers and trust them.

---

[3]It may be possible to carry this technique too far: I have a friend who photocopied all 554 pages of her Ph.D thesis at 1/4 scale, hoping for an organizational overview.

Husband Your Readers.

Serious review of your writing by someone other than yourself is an essential ingredient in making your writing clear and good. However, readers who will carefully review your work are a precious resource that you must conserve. It is difficult to get someone to read your stuff carefully even once, and you probably have only a very few friends who are devoted enough (or demented enough) to do it twice. Most readers are only effective for one reading anyway, because they know too much about what you are going to say by the time they attempt a second pass.

Ideally, you shouldn't show your paper to anyone until you've written all the sections and fixed every problem you know about. Every sentence should have good grammar. Include all the figures, at least in sketch form. Circulate a draft to just one or two people at a time. It is unpleasant to go to work when everyone in your building is hiding from you because they haven't gotten around to looking at today's draft of your paper yet. The basic idea is that you as the writer should do whatever hard work you can do in preparing your paper. Don't waste your readers on obvious grammar and typo problems. Your readers should be saved for the special task of giving you a fresh perspective on what you have written, and for revealing what is not clear.

There is an important exception to this rule. You may find it useful to get help with the overall organization of your paper in the early stages of its development. The purpose of this sort of review is to focus on the broad thrusts and concepts in your technical exposition, rather than on the details or wording. The best source of this kind of feedback is someone with a broad and mature view of your research area.

Trust Your Readers.

When you get comments back from your readers, trust what they tell you. If they get confused at a particular point, don't argue with them, explaining why what you wrote is actually clear, and they just didn't get it. Rewrite that part to overcome whatever confused them. You'll be surprised to find that more than one reader will get stuck at the very same place in your paper, even if you have an argument of why what you wrote is perfectly clear. When a reader marks a word or sentence in your paper, they are telling you *something is wrong here*. It is not necessary that you take the specific remedial advice the reader offers. Their suggested fix may be good, or you may be able to generate a better one.

The urge to ignore many of your reader's corrections will be strong. Just as you were reluctant to discard prize-winning sentences, changes that accommodate your readers comments may disrupt text that you were happy with, or even downright proud of. However, tough toenails: you must make the changes. Afterward you can go back and repair your desecrated text.

That's all there is to it. Now you can produce good writing. My main points are:

- *You must want to produce good writing.*

- *You must have confidence that you can produce good writing.*

- *Good writing is bad writing that was rewritten.*

- *Spill the beans fast.*

- *Don't get attached to your prose.*

- *Outlining helps to get unstuck.*

- *Husband your readers.*

- *Trust your readers.*

Appendix B

Codes of Ethics

THIS appendix contains reprints of the ACM code of ethics, the IEEE code of ethics, the joint IEEE Computer Society/ACM code of ethics for software engineers, and the NSPE code of ethics.

The text of the ACM code comes from the electronic copy of the ACM bylaws available by ftp from acm.org in May 1995.

The IEEE publishes the *IEEE Policy and Procedures Manual,* of which section 7.8 contains the *IEEE Code of Ethics.* The IEEE code itself is quite short, and so I have opted to include portions of Sections 7.6 through 7.12 as well to give you a better feel for how the IEEE emphasizes different issues. Sections 7.6 and 7.7 outline concerns for "protection of the public" and "professional welfare of members," respectively. Section 7.9 describes IEEE policy for taking official positions on "matters of ethical principle." Section 7.10 states the policy for dealing with alleged infractions of the code of ethics and the policy for supporting members placed in jeopardy by adhering to the code of ethics. Section 7.11 expands on the policy for dealing with alleged infractions of the code. It outlines "procedures for use by the Member Conduct Committee," a body that carries out investigations of alleged infractions. Finally, Section 7.12 expands on the policy for dealing with requests for support from members who feel in jeopardy as a result of following the code of ethics. It outlines the procedures for the Member Conduct Committee to follow in processing such requests.

The text of the joint IEEE-CS/ACM Software Engineering Code of Ethics is version 5.2, as approved by the IEEE Computer Society and the ACM in late 1998. At the time of this writing, the revised code had not been printed in *CACM* or *Computer,* and the text was taken from the web site www-cs.etsu.edu/seeri.

The text of the NSPE code comes from NSPE Publication 1102, January 1987.

THE ACM CODE OF ETHICS

Preamble. Commitment to ethical professional conduct is expected of every member (voting members, associate members, and student members) of the Association for Computing Machinery (ACM).

This Code, consisting of 24 imperatives formulated as statements of personal responsibility, identifies the elements of such a commitment. It contains many, but not all, issues professionals are likely to face. Section 1 outlines fundamental ethical considerations, while Section 2 addresses additional, more specific considerations of professional conduct. Statements in Section 3 pertain more specifically to individuals who have a leadership role, whether in the workplace or in a volunteer capacity such as with organizations like ACM. Principles involving compliance with this Code are given in Section 4.

The Code shall be supplemented by a set of Guidelines, which provide explanation to assist members in dealing with the various issues contained in the Code. It is expected that the Guidelines will be changed more frequently than the Code.

The Code and its supplemented Guidelines are intended to serve as a basis for ethical decision making in the conduct of professional work. Secondarily, they may serve as a basis for judging the merit of a formal complaint pertaining to violation of professional ethical standards.

It should be noted that although computing is not mentioned in the imperatives of section 1.0, the Code is concerned with how these fundamental imperatives apply to one's conduct as a computing professional. These imperatives are expressed in a general form to emphasize that ethical principles which apply to computer ethics are derived from more general ethical principles.

It is understood that some words and phrases in a code of ethics are subject to varying interpretations, and that any ethical principle may conflict with other ethical principles in specific situations. Questions related to ethical conflicts can best be answered by thoughtful consideration of fundamental principles, rather than reliance on detailed regulations.

1. General Moral Imperatives. As an ACM member I will . . .

   1.1 Contribute to society and human well-being.
   This principle concerning the quality of life of all people affirms an obligation to protect fundamental human rights and to respect the diversity of all cultures. An essential aim of computing professionals is to minimize negative consequences of computing systems, including threats to health and safety. When designing or implementing systems, computing professionals must attempt to ensure that the products of their efforts will be used in socially responsible ways, will meet social needs, and will avoid harmful effects to health and welfare.

   In addition to a safe social environment, human well-being includes a safe natural environment. Therefore, computing professionals who design and develop systems must be alert to, and make others aware of, any potential damage to the local or global environment.

   1.2 Avoid harm to others.
   "Harm" means injury or negative consequences, such as undesirable loss of information, loss of property, property damage, or unwanted environmental impacts. This principle prohibits use of computing technology in ways that result in harm to any of the following: users, the general public, employees, employers. Harmful actions include intentional destruction or modification of files and programs leading to serious loss of resources or unnecessary expenditure of human resources such as the time and effort required to purge systems of "computer viruses."

   Well-intended actions, including those that accomplish assigned duties, may lead to harm unexpectedly. In such an event the responsible person or persons are obligated to undo or mitigate the negative consequences as much as possible. One way to avoid unintentional harm is to carefully consider potential impacts on all those affected by decisions made during design and implementation.

   To minimize the possibility of indirectly harming others, computing professionals must minimize malfunctions by following generally accepted standards for system design and testing. Furthermore, it is often necessary to assess the social consequences of systems to project the likelihood of any serious harm to others. If system features are misrepresented to users, coworkers, or supervisors, the individual computing professional is responsible for any resulting injury.

   In the work environment the computing professional has the additional obligation to report any signs of system dangers that might result in serious personal or social damage. If one's superiors do not act to curtail or mitigate such dangers, it may be necessary to "blow the whistle" to help correct the problem or reduce the risk. However, capricious or misguided reporting of violations can, itself, be harmful. Before reporting violations, all relevant aspects of the incident must be thoroughly assessed. In particular, the assessment of risk and responsibility must be credible. It is suggested that advice be sought from other computing professionals. See principle 2.5 regarding thorough evaluations.

   1.3 Be honest and trustworthy.
   Honesty is an essential component of trust. Without trust an organization cannot function effectively. The honest computing professional will not make deliberately false or deceptive claims about a system or system design, but will instead provide full disclosure of all pertinent system limitations and problems.

   A computer professional has a duty to be honest about his or her own qualifications, and about any circumstances that might lead to conflicts of interest. Membership in volunteer organizations such as ACM may at times place individuals in situations where their statements or actions could be interpreted as carrying the "weight" of a larger group of professionals. An ACM member will exercise care to not misrepresent ACM or positions and policies of ACM or any ACM units.

   1.4 Be fair and take action not to discriminate.
   The values of equality, tolerance, respect for others, and the principles of equal justice govern this imperative. Discrimination on the basis of race, sex, religion, age, disability, national origin, or other such factors is an explicit violation of ACM policy and will not be tolerated.

   Inequities between different groups of people may result from the use or misuse of information and technology. In a fair society, all individuals would have equal opportunity to participate in, or benefit from, the use of computer resources regardless of race, sex, religion, age, disability, national origin or other such similar factors. However, these ideals do not justify unauthorized use of computer resources nor do they provide an adequate basis for violation of any other ethical imperatives of this code.

1.5 Honor property rights including copyrights and patents.

Violation of copyrights, patents, trade secrets and the terms of license agreements is prohibited by law in most circumstances. Even when software is not so protected, such violations are contrary to professional behavior. Copies of software should be made only with proper authorization. Unauthorized duplication of materials must not be condoned.

1.6 Give proper credit for intellectual property.

Computing professionals are obligated to protect the integrity of intellectual property. Specifically, one must not take credit for others' ideas or work, even in cases where the work has not been explicitly protected by copyright, patent, etc.

1.7 Respect the privacy of others.

Computing and communication technology enables the collection and exchange of personal information on a scale unprecedented in the history of civilization. Thus there is increased potential for violating the privacy of individuals and groups. It is the responsibility of professionals to maintain the privacy and integrity of data describing individuals. This includes taking precautions to ensure the accuracy of data, as well as protecting it from unauthorized access or accidental disclosure to inappropriate individuals. Furthermore, procedures must be established to allow individuals to review their records and correct inaccuracies.

This imperative implies that only the necessary amount of personal information be collected in a system, that retention and disposal periods for that information be clearly defined and enforced, and that personal information gathered for a specific purpose not be used for other purposes without consent of the individual(s). These principles apply to electronic communications, including electronic mail, and prohibit procedures that capture or monitor electronic user data, including messages, without the permission of users or bona fide authorization related to system operation and maintenance. User data observed during the normal duties of system operation and maintenance must be treated with strictest confidentiality, except in cases where it is evidence for the violation of law, organizational regulations, or this Code. In these cases, the nature or contents of that information must be disclosed only to proper authorities. (See 1.9)

1.8 Honor confidentiality.

The principle of honesty extends to issues of confidentiality of information whenever one has made an explicit promise to honor confidentiality or, implicitly, when private information not directly related to the performance of one's duties becomes available. The ethical concern is to respect all obligations of confidentiality to employers, clients, and users unless discharged from such obligations by requirements of the law or other principles of this Code.

2. More Specific Professional Responsibilities. As an ACM computing professional I will . . .

2.1 Strive to achieve the highest quality in both the process and products of professional work.

Excellence is perhaps the most important obligation of a professional. The computing professional must strive to achieve quality and to be cognizant of the serious negative consequences that may result from poor quality in a system.

2.2 Acquire and maintain professional competence.

Excellence depends on individuals who take responsibility for acquiring and maintaining professional competence. A professional must participate in setting standards for appropriate levels of competence, and strive to achieve those standards. Upgrading technical knowledge and competence can be achieved in several ways: doing independent study; attending seminars, conferences, or courses; and being involved in professional organizations.

2.3 Know and respect existing laws pertaining to professional work.

ACM members must obey existing local, state, province, national, and international laws unless there is a compelling ethical basis not to do so. Policies and procedures of the organizations in which one participates must also be obeyed. But compliance must be balanced with the recognition that sometimes existing laws and rules may be immoral or inappropriate and, therefore, must be challenged. Violation of a law or regulation may be ethical when that law or rule has inadequate moral basis or when it conflicts with another law judged to be more important. If one decides to violate a law or rule because it is viewed as unethical, or for any other reason, one must fully accept responsibility for one's actions and for the consequences.

2.4 Accept and provide appropriate professional review.

Quality professional work, especially in the computing profession, depends on professional reviewing and critiquing. Whenever appropriate, individual members should seek and utilize peer review as well as provide critical review of the work of others.

2.5 Give comprehensive and thorough evaluations of computer systems and their impacts, including analysis of possible risks.

Computer professionals must strive to be perceptive, thorough, and objective when evaluating, recommending, and presenting system descriptions and alternatives. Computer professionals are in a position of special trust, and therefore have a special responsibility to provide objective, credible evaluations to employers, clients, users, and the public. When providing evaluations the professional must also identify any relevant conflicts of interest, as stated in imperative 1.3.

As noted in the discussion of principle 1.2 on avoiding harm, any signs of danger from systems must be reported to those who have opportunity and/or responsibility to resolve them. See the guidelines for imperative 1.2 for more details concerning harm, including the reporting of professional violations.

2.6 Honor contracts, agreements, and assigned responsibilities.

Honoring one's commitments is a matter of integrity and honesty. For the computer professional this includes ensuring that system elements perform as intended. Also, when one contracts for work with another party, one has an obligation to keep that party properly informed about progress toward completing that work.

A computing professional has a responsibility to request a change in any assignment that he or she feels cannot be completed as defined. Only after serious consideration and with full disclosure of risks and concerns to the employer or client, should one accept the assignment. The major underlying principle here is the obligation to accept personal accountability for professional work. On some occasions other ethical principles may take greater priority.

A judgment that a specific assignment should not be performed may not be accepted. Having clearly identified one's concerns and reasons for that judgment, but failing to procure a change in that assignment, one may yet be obligated, by contract or by law, to proceed as directed. The computing professional's ethical judgment should be the final guide in deciding whether or not to proceed. Regardless of the decision, one must accept the responsibility for the consequences.

However, performing assignments "against one's own judgment" does not relieve the professional of responsibility for any negative consequences.

2.7 Improve public understanding of computing and its consequences.

Computing professionals have a responsibility to share technical knowledge with the public by encouraging understanding of computing, including the impacts of computer systems and their limitations. This imperative implies an obligation to counter any false views related to computing.

2.8 Access computing and communication resources only when authorized to do so. Theft or destruction of tangible and electronic property is prohibited by imperative 1.2—"Avoid harm to others." Trespassing and unauthorized use of a computer or com-

munication system is addressed by this imperative. Trespassing includes accessing communication networks and computer systems, or accounts and/or files associated with those systems, without explicit authorization to do so. Individuals and organizations have the right to restrict access to their systems so long as they do not violate the discrimination principle (see 1.4). No one should enter or use another's computer system, software, or data files without permission. One must always have appropriate approval before using system resources, including communication ports, file space, other system peripherals, and computer time.

3. Organizational Leadership Imperatives. As an ACM member and an organizational leader, I will . . .

Background Note: This section draws extensively from the draft *IFIP Code of Ethics,* especially its sections on organizational ethics and international concerns. The ethical obligations of organizations tend to be neglected in most codes of professional conduct, perhaps because these codes are written from the perspective of the individual member. This dilemma is addressed by stating these imperatives from the perspective of the organizational leader. In this context, "leader" is viewed as any organizational member who has leadership or educational responsibilities. These imperatives generally may apply to organizations as well as their leaders. In this context, "organizations" are corporations, government agencies, and other "employers," as well as volunteer professional organizations.

3.1 Articulate social responsibilities of members of an organizational unit and encourage full acceptance of those responsibilities.

Because organizations of all kinds have impacts on the public, they must accept responsibilities to society. Organizational procedures and attitudes oriented toward quality and the welfare of society will reduce harm to members of the public, thereby serving public interest and fulfilling social responsibility. Therefore, organizational leaders must encourage full participation in meeting social responsibilities as well as quality performance.

3.2 Manage personnel and resources to design and build information systems that enhance the quality, effectiveness and dignity of working life.

Organizational leaders are responsible for ensuring that computer systems enhance, not degrade, the quality of working life. When implementing a computer system, organizations must consider the personal and professional development, physical safety, and human dignity of all workers. Appropriate human-computer ergonomic standards should be considered in system design and in the workplace.

3.3 Acknowledge and support proper and authorized

uses of an organization's computing and communications resources.

Because computer systems can become tools to harm as well as to benefit an organization, the leadership has the responsibility to clearly define appropriate and inappropriate uses of organizational computing resources. While the number and scope of such rules should be minimal, they should be fully enforced when established.

3.4 Ensure that users and those who will be affected by a system have their needs clearly articulated during the assessment and design of requirements. Later the system must be validated to meet requirements.

Current system users, potential users and other persons whose lives may be affected by a system must have their needs assessed and incorporated in the statement of requirements. System validation should ensure compliance with those requirements.

3.5 Articulate and support policies that protect the dignity of users and others affected by a computing system.

Designing or implementing systems that deliberately or inadvertently demean individuals or groups is ethically unacceptable. Computer professionals who are in decision making positions should verify that systems are designed and implemented to protect personal privacy and enhance personal dignity.

3.6 Create opportunities for members of the organization to learn the principles and limitations of computer systems.

This complements the imperative on public understanding (2.7). Educational opportunities are essential to facilitate optimal participation of all organizational members. Opportunities must be available to all members to help them improve their knowledge and skills in computing, including courses that familiarize them with the consequences and limitations of particular types of systems. In particular, professionals must be made aware of the dangers of building systems around oversimplified models, the improbability of anticipating and designing for every possible operating condition, and other issues related to the complexity of this profession.

4. Compliance with the Code. As an ACM member, I will . . .

4.1 Uphold and promote the principles of this code.

The future of the computing profession depends on both technical and ethical excellence. Not only is it important for ACM computing professionals to adhere to the principles expressed in this Code, each member should encourage and support adherence by other members.

4.2 Treat violations of this code as inconsistent with membership in the ACM.

Adherence of professionals to a code of ethics is largely a voluntary matter. However, if a member does not follow this code by engaging in gross misconduct, membership in ACM may be terminated.

This Code and the supplemental Guidelines were developed by the Task Force for the Revision of the ACM Code of Ethics and Professional Conduct: Ronald E. Anderson, Chair, Gerald Engel, Donald Gotterbarn, Grace C. Hertlein, Alex Hoffman, Bruce Jawer, Deborah G. Johnson, Doris K. Lidtke, Joyce Currie Little, Dianne Martin, Donn B. Parker, Judith A. Perrolle, and Richard S. Rosenberg. The Task Force was organized by ACM/SIGCAS and funding was provided by the ACM SIG Discretionary Fund. This Code and the supplemental Guidelines were adopted by the ACM Council on October 16, 1992.

Excerpt from the <u>IEEE Policies & Procedures Manual</u>

Section 7.6—Protection of the Public

The IEEE recognizes the obligation of the profession to protect the health, welfare and safety of the public. Where legislation, regulations, codes, or customs impact on electrical and electronics engineering, the Institute shall interface whenever and wherever appropriate with legislative and regulatory bodies. In particular, legislation may include the establishment of qualifications of engineers and the registration and/or licensure of engineers. In furtherance of this policy, the IEEE:

A. Offers advice and assistance to legislative and regulatory entities;

B. Encourages the establishment of uniform law as being in the public interest;

C. Recommends that there be a minimum of restrictions of a legal nature in the functioning of qualified engineers;

D. Offers advice and assistance to Boards of Engineering Examiners and similar agencies;

E. Recommends that, upon request, committees of IEEE members cooperate with appropriate agencies in the development of sound registration examinations which will adequately protect the public interest.

Section 7.7—Professional Welfare of Members

The IEEE is concerned with the professional welfare of its members. The administrative, geographical and technical units are encouraged to pursue appropriate activities in this area, such as the following:

A. Organizing or sponsoring career development seminars for members.

B. Organizing or sponsoring educational activities which upgrade the skills of members.

C. Publishing information on existing legislation or proposed legislation which may affect the professional welfare of IEEE members.

D. Arranging for group insurance plans which benefit members, provided these do not duplicate other plans sponsored by the IEEE and provided the IEEE unit does not benefit financially from such plans. Prior to establishment of an insurance plan by an organizational unit, legal approval must be sought through Headquarters and the plan referred to the Executive Committee for authorization.

Section 7.8—IEEE Code of Ethics

We, the members of the IEEE, in recognition of the importance of our technologies in affecting the quality of life throughout the world, and in accepting a personal obligation to our profession, its members and the community we serve, do hereby commit ourselves to conduct of the highest ethical and professional manner and agree:

1. to accept responsibility in making engineering decisions consistent with the safety, health, and welfare of the public, and to disclose promptly factors that might endanger the public or the environment;

2. to avoid real or perceived conflicts of interest whenever possible, and to disclose them to affected parties when they do exist;

3. to be honest and realistic in stating claims or estimates based on available data;

4. to reject bribery in all of its froms;

5. to improve understanding of technology; its appropriate application, and potential consequences;

6. to maintain and improve our technical competence and to undertake technological tasks for others only if qualified by training or experience, or after full disclosure of pertinent limitations;

7. to seek, accept, and offer honest criticism of technical work, to acknowledge and correct errors, and to credit properly the contributions of others;

8. to treat fairly all persons regardless of such factors as race, religion, gender, disability, age, or national origin;

9. to avoid injuring others, their property, reputation, or employment by false or malicious action;

10. to assist colleagues and co-workers in their professional development and to support them in following this code of ethics.

Section 7.9—Matters of Ethical Principle

A. The Executive Committee is empowered by the Board of Directors to enter an amicus curiae[1] brief in any court in the U.S.A. or in cooperation with cognizant national societies in other countries where a member of the profession is involved as a consequence of his taking a position on a matter of ethical principle.

B. The Executive Committee is empowered to publicize actions described in paragraph A in any fashion deemed suitable and appropriate.

C. It is Institute policy that the IEEE will not, as to disputed facts, intervene or take an adversary position on

---

[1]*Amicus curiae* means "friend of the court." An *amicus curiae* brief would be filed by a person of organization that is neither the plaintiff nor the defendant, but that might have some special knowledge or interest in the issues at hand.

behalf of or against any member involved in a matter of ethical principle.

D. It is Institute policy that changes to the IEEE Code of Ethics will be made only after the following conditions are met:

1. Proposed changes shall have been published in THE INSTITUTE at least three months in advance of final consideration by the Board of Directors, with a request for comments, and

2. RAB, TAB and USAB shall have the opportunity to discuss proposed changes prior to final action by the Board of Directors, and

3. A two-thirds affirmative vote shall be required by the Board of Directors for changes to be made.

Section 7.10—IEEE Involvement in Matters of Ethical Conduct

A. Infractions of the Institute's Code of Ethics by members, when reported to and investigated and evaluated by the Board of Directors, or its designated representative, are subject to appropriate action by the Institute's Board of Directors on the basis of procedures established by that body.

B. Members who are placed in jeopardy as a consequence of adherence to the Institute's Code of Ethics may be offered assistance, provided that in the opinion of the Board of Directors or its designated representative such assistance is warranted.

Section 7.11—Procedures for Use by Member Conduct Committee

Part A—The Complaint

1. Submission of Complaint. The Member Conduct Committee shall receive and consider only those complaints which are delivered by certified mail to IEEE, 345 East 47th Street, New York, NY 10017. Complaints should be addressed to the attention of Chairman, Member Conduct Committee, and should be sent in triplicate.

2. Form and Contents of Complaint. The complaint shall be in the form of an affidavit, typewritten, notarized, and signed by a member of IEEE in good standing as permitted in Bylaw 112.2. The complaint shall include:
   (a) the name and address of the IEEE member(s) whose conduct is the subject of the complaint;
   (b) a statement which sets forth with reasonable specificity the alleged conduct of the IEEE member(s) which is alleged to constitute a material violation of the Constitution, Bylaws, or Code of Ethics of IEEE or conduct which is seriously prejudicial to IEEE;
   (c) the specific provisions of any documents described in Part A.2(b) which the conduct alleged is thought to violate or contravene;

(d) the name and address of the person(s) believed by the complainant to have knowledge pertaining to the subject of the complaint;

(e) the identification and location of any documentation or materials upon which the complaint in whole or part, is based; the complaint may be accompanied by any materials or documentation which are thought to be relevant to the Committee's consideration and review;

(f) a statement declaring that the person submitting the complaint will be present at any hearing at which the complaint is considered upon the written request of either the Member Conduct Committee or the IEEE member charged in the complaint.

3. Acknowledgment: Copies and Distribution. The Member Conduct Committee Chairman shall acknowledge receipt of the complaint by letter to the complainant(s). Concurrently the Chairman shall transmit copies of the complaint to the Committee members. No other distribution or duplication of the complaint shall be made, except (1) the Committee may furnish a copy to IEEE counsel in connection with a request for legal advice relating to the complaint, (2) the Committee may furnish a copy to a third party during the course of its preliminary investigation, subject to the limitation of disclosure set forth in Part B.1(c), and (3) if a proceeding is instituted against a member, the Committee shall furnish a copy of the complaint to such member as provided in Part C.3(b).

4. Timeliness of Complaint. No complaint submitted pursuant to Part A.1 shall be accepted or considered by the Member Conduct Committee if based upon conduct alleged to have occurred more than two years prior to the date on which the notarized complaint is received. Such complaints shall be returned by the Chairman, without distribution or copying, to the IEEE member submitting the complaint.

Part B—Review of the Complaint

1. Preliminary Investigation of Complaint
   (a) The Member Conduct Committee shall have a maximum of one hundred and twenty days, from the date the Chairman acknowledges receipt of the complaint, to consider the complaint, assemble information relevant to the complaint, and investigate and prepare the Report on Preliminary Investigation.
   (b) During the period of its investigation, the Member Conduct Committee, acting on its own behalf or through ad hoc committees appointed by and under the direction of the Chairman of the Member Conduct Committee, may seek relevant information from IEEE employees, members and others as may be appropriate to the nature and contents of the complaint. Such relevant information as may be obtained shall be reduced to writing and included

in the file or records maintained by the Chairman of the Member Conduct Committee pertaining to the specific complaint under review.

(c) During the Committee's investigation, the contents of the complaint, identity of the persons involved and the scope of the Committee's inquiry shall remain undisclosed to the extent practicable, consistent with the need for information and expeditious review. If the identity of any person complained against is disclosed pursuant to this Part B.1(c), the person or entity to whom such disclosure was made shall be notified of the complaint's final disposition.

Part C. Initiation of Proceedings Against IEEE Member

1. Requisite Findings. The Member Conduct Committee must determine whether a reasonable basis exists for believing that:

(a) the facts alleged in the complaint, if proven, constitute cause for expulsion, suspension, or censure of the member(s) charged; and

(b) the facts alleged in the complaint can be proven.

These findings shall be made in writing by the Committee, dated and signed by its members. These findings shall be the Committee's "Report on Preliminary Investigation" and shall be distributed pursuant to Part C.2(b) or Part C.3.

. . .

Part D—Hearing Board; Procedures

1. Selection and Composition.
. . .

2. Term of Hearing Board Members.
. . .

3. Procedure at the Hearing.

(a) The Hearing Board Chairman shall convene the session to consider the presentment by the Committee and the submission(s) by the member(s) charged. The session shall be in confidence and shall commence at the date and time specified in the notice. A Hearing Board setup should be used with separate table for the complainant and the accused each facing the table for the Hearing Board. A sound recording shall be made of the hearing. The sound recording and any written material submitted during the proceeding shall be retained by the Chairman until final action on the case is taken by the Hearing Board. Thereupon, all recording and written materials presented to the Hearing Board shall be filed with the Secretary of the Board of Directors.

(b) The Hearing Board Chairman shall be the final authority in any matters relating to procedures and administrative functions pertaining to the conduct of the hearing. The hearing shall include:

i. Opening instructions by and at the discretion of the Hearing Board Chairman;

ii. Opening statements by the Member Conduct Committee and the member charged;

iii. Presentation of evidence by the Member Conduct Committee;

iv. Cross-examination by the member charged;

v. Presentation of evidence by the member charged;

vi. Cross-examination by the Member Conduct Committee;

vii. Closing statements by the Member Conduct Committee and the member charged; and

viii. Conclusion/adjournment by the Hearing Board Chairman.

Part E—Deliberation and Findings by Hearing Board

. . .

Part F—Board of Directors; Sanction, Publication

1. Sanction by Board of Directors
. . .

2. Final Action by the Board of Directors (On Review of Hearing Board Decision).
. . .

3. Publication of Final Action by Board

(a) The Board at its discretion may notify the membership of IEEE of its final action and the final action by the Hearing Board.

(b) Any such publication or notice to the IEEE membership shall be issued through the office of the General Manager of IEEE.

Section 7.12—Ethical Support

Part A—Submission of Requests for Support, Inquiries and Information

1. All requests for support regarding circumstances of employment or professional activities as may be affected by IEEE member adherence to the Code of Ethics shall be sent to the Chairman, IEEE Member Conduct Committee, IEEE, 345 East 47th Street, New York, NY 10017 by certified mail.

2. Information which any member wishes to bring to the attention of, or inquiries for which a response is sought from IEEE shall be submitted in the same manner but need not be notarized or sent by certified mail. Information and inquiries shall be reviewed by the Member Conduct Committee and forwarded, with or without comment or recommendation, to the Executive Committee for consideration and action as may be appropriate.

Part B—Form and Contents of the Request for Support

The request for support shall be in the form of an affidavit, typewritten, notarized and signed by the member who must be in good standing at the time of submission. The Request for Support shall include:

412

1. The name(s), position(s) or title(s) and address(es) and telephone numbers (where available) of the employer or others who are believed to have knowledge pertaining to the subject of the Request;

2. The issue, incident(s), or the matter of ethical principle which the IEEE member believes is involved together with the specific provisions of the Code of Ethics deemed relevant or considered by the member to have precipitated the condition(s) of jeopardy.

3. Documents, statements and any other evidence to be considered as supporting the Request. The identification and location of any other documents and material relevant to the Request but not provided in the submission.

4. A full description of the circumstances, events and facts which relate to the ethical matter for which IEEE support is sought.

Part C—Procedure on Receipt of Request for Support

The Chairman of the Member Conduct Committee shall:

1. Review the Notarized Request for Support, inquiry or matter of information to ascertain that the incident or event involved occurred no longer than two years prior to receipt thereof. Should the interval exceed two years, all material shall be returned to the IEEE member without duplication or distribution, noting this limitation.

2. If the incident occurred within the two year limitation period, then promptly acknowledge Receipt of the Request, Inquiry or information.
Transmit copies of the Request, Inquiry or information to Committee members, ensuring that no other distribution or duplication of the material is made, except to provide IEEE counsel with relevant documents, etc. in connection with a request for legal advice.

3. Take steps to consider the Request for Support, Inquiry or information submitted, assemble information, provide for Committee evaluation and prepare a Report on Preliminary Investigation within a period of one hundred twenty days from acknowledgment of receipt of the Request, Inquiry or information. In those instances where investigative difficulties preclude completion within this limitation, the Executive Committee may grant extension upon request.

4. Ensure, during the period of its investigation, that the Member Conduct Committee, acting on its own behalf or through ad hoc Committees appointed by the Member Conduct Committee Chairman, seek relevant information from IEEE members, employees and others as may be appropriate to the nature and contents of the Request for Support, Inquiry or information. Such information as may be obtained shall be reduced to writing and included in the file or records of the Chairman

of the Member Conduct Committee of the case under review.

5. During the course of the investigation ensure that the contents of the Request, identity of persons involved and the scope of the inquiry shall remain undisclosed by the Member Conduct Committee to the extent practicable, consistent with the need to secure valid information and conduct an expeditious review.

Part D—Responsibilities of the Member Conduct Committee

1. If in the course of its investigation and review the Committee deems it appropriate to contact persons or entities outside the membership of IEEE or the employer concerned, the Committee shall:
   (a) obtain from the requesting IEEE member a letter of waiver; and
   (b) send to the employer(s) concerned a letter disclaiming any and all purpose or intent to engage in collective bargaining on behalf of the IEEE member with respect to such matters as salaries, wages, benefits, and working conditions, customarily dealt with by labor unions.

2. The Member Conduct Committee, upon concluding its investigation, shall prepare a Report on Preliminary Investigation which shall include findings, conclusions and recommendations based on relevant information and technical and professional opinions.

3. If the request is deemed to be meritorious, the Committee shall submit to the Executive Committee the request and its Report on Preliminary Investigation upon conclusion of its review of the request together with any matters or information related thereto.

4. If the Request for Support is deemed to be without merit, the Member Conduct Committee Chairman shall notify the requesting member by certified mail of the action to terminate and shall include a copy of the Report on Preliminary Investigation.

5. If new or additional information considered material is received within ten business days following service of notice by the Chairman of the Member Conduct Committee, the Committee may reconsider and revise its findings. If the prior findings are affirmed, no further consideration shall be granted and the requesting member so notified. Subsequent submission of a Request or Inquiry bearing on the same or substantially similar incident or issue may result in the Committee declining further consideration.

THE SOFTWARE ENGINEERING CODE OF ETHICS
AND PROFESSIONAL PRACTICE

Version 5.2, as recommended by the IEEE-CS/ACM Joint Task Force on Software Engineering Ethics and Professional Practices and jointly approved by the ACM and the IEEE-CS as the standard for teaching and practicing software engineering.

Short Version

Preamble. The short version of the code summarizes aspirations at a high level of abstraction. The clauses that are included in the full version give examples and details of how these aspirations change the way we act as software engineering professionals. Without the aspirations, the details can become legalistic and tedious; without the details, the aspirations can become high sounding but empty; together, the aspirations and the details form a cohesive code.

Software engineers shall commit themselves to making the analysis, specification, design, development, testing and maintenance of software a beneficial and respected profession. In accordance with their commitment to the health, safety and welfare of the public, software engineers shall adhere to the following Eight Principles:

1. **Public**—Software engineers shall act consistently with the public interest.
2. **Client and employer**—Software engineers shall act in a manner that is in the best interests of their client and employer, consistent with the public interest.
3. **Product**—Software engineers shall ensure that their products and related modifications meet the highest professional standards possible.
4. **Judgment**—Software engineers shall maintain integrity and independence in their professional judgment.
5. **Management**—Software engineering managers and leaders shall subscribe to and promote an ethical approach to the management of software development and maintenance.
6. **Profession**—Software engineers shall advance the integrity and reputation of the profession consistent with the public interest.
7. **Colleagues**—Software engineers shall be fair to and supportive of their colleagues.
8. **Self**—Software engineers shall participate in lifelong learning regarding the practice of their profession and shall promote an ethical approach to the practice of the profession.

Full Version

Preamble. Computers have a central and growing role in commerce, industry, government, medicine, education, entertainment and society at large. Software engineers are those who contribute by direct participation or by teaching, to the analysis, specification, design, development, certification, maintenance and testing of software systems. Because of their roles in developing software systems, software engineers have significant opportunities to do good or cause harm, to enable others to do good or cause harm, or to influence others to do good or cause harm. To ensure, as much as possible, that their efforts will be used for good, software engineers must commit themselves to making software engineering a beneficial and respected profession. In accordance with that commitment, software engineers shall adhere to the following Code of Ethics and Professional Practice.

The Code contains eight Principles related to the behavior of and decisions made by professional software engineers, including practitioners, educators, managers, supervisors and policy makers, as well as trainees and students of the profession. The Principles identify the ethically responsible relationships in which individuals, groups, and organizations participate and the primary obligations within these relationships. The Clauses of each Principle are illustrations of some of the obligations included in these relationships. These obligations are founded in the software engineer's humanity, in special care owed to people affected by the work of software engineers, and in the unique elements of the practice of software engineering. The Code prescribes these as obligations of anyone claiming to be or aspiring to be a software engineer.

It is not intended that the individual parts of the Code be used in isolation to justify errors of omission or commission. The list of Principles and Clauses is not exhaustive. The Clauses should not be read as separating the acceptable from the unacceptable in professional conduct in all practical situations. The Code is not a simple ethical algorithm that generates ethical decisions. In some situations, standards may be in tension with each other or with standards from other sources. These situations require the software engineer to use ethical judgment to act in a manner which is most consistent with the spirit of the Code of Ethics and Professional Practice, given the circumstances.

Ethical tensions can best be addressed by thoughtful consideration of fundamental principles, rather than blind reliance on detailed regulations. These Principles should influence software engineers to consider broadly who is affected by their work; to examine if they and their colleagues are treating other human beings with due respect; to consider how the public, if reasonably well informed, would view their decisions; to analyze how the least empowered will be affected by their decisions; and to consider whether their acts would be judged worthy of the ideal professional working as a software engineer. In all these judgments concern for the health, safety and welfare of the public is primary; that is, the "Public Interest" is central to this Code.

The dynamic and demanding context of software engineering requires a code that is adaptable and relevant to new situations as they occur. However, even in this generality, the Code provides support for software engineers and managers of software engineers who need to take positive action in a specific case by documenting the ethical stance of the profession. The Code provides an ethical foundation to which individuals within teams and the team as a whole can appeal. The Code helps to define those actions that are ethically improper to request of a software engineer or teams of software engineers.

The Code is not simply for adjudicating the nature of questionable acts; it also has an important educational function. As this Code expresses the consensus of the profession on ethical issues, it is a means to educate both the public and aspiring professionals about the ethical obligations of all software engineers.

Principles

Principle 1—Public.
Software engineers shall act consistently with the public interest. In particular, software engineers shall, as appropriate:

1.01. Accept full responsibility for their own work.

1.02. Moderate the interests of the software engineer, the employer, the client and the users with the public good.

1.03. Approve software only if they have a well-founded belief that it is safe, meets specifications, passes appropriate tests, and does not diminish quality of life, diminish privacy or harm the environment. The ultimate effect of the work should be to the public good.

1.04. Disclose to appropriate persons or authorities any actual or potential danger to the user, the public, or the environment, that they reasonably believe to be associated with software or related documents.

1.05. Cooperate in efforts to address matters of grave public concern caused by software, its installation, maintenance, support or documentation.

1.06. Be fair and avoid deception in all statements, particularly public ones, concerning software or related documents, methods and tools.

1.07. Consider issues of physical disabilities, allocation of resources, economic disadvantage and other factors that can diminish access to the benefits of software.

1.08. Be encouraged to volunteer professional skills to good causes and to contribute to public education concerning the discipline.

Principle 2—Client and employer.
Software engineers shall act in a manner that is in the best interests of their client and employer, consistent with the public interest. In particular, software engineers shall, as appropriate:

2.01. Provide service in their areas of competence, being honest and forthright about any limitations of their experience and education.

2.02. Not knowingly use software that is obtained or retained either illegally or unethically.

2.03. Use the property of a client or employer only in ways properly authorized, and with the client's or employer's knowledge and consent.

2.04. Ensure that any document upon which they rely has been approved, when required, by someone authorized to approve it.

2.05. Keep private any confidential information gained in their professional work, where such confidentiality is consistent with the public interest and consistent with the law.

2.06. Identify, document, collect evidence and report to the client or the employer promptly if, in their opinion, a project is likely to fail, to prove too expensive, to violate intellectual property law, or otherwise to be problematic.

2.07. Identify, document, and report significant issues of social concern, of which they are aware, in software or related documents, to the employer or the client.

2.08. Accept no outside work detrimental to the work they perform for their primary employer.

2.09. Promote no interest adverse to their employer or client, unless a higher ethical concern is being compromised; in that case, inform the employer or another appropriate authority of the ethical concern.

Principle 3—Product.
Software engineers shall ensure that their products and related modifications meet the highest professional standards possible. In particular, software engineers shall, as appropriate:

3.01. Strive for high quality, acceptable cost, and a reasonable schedule, ensuring significant tradeoffs are clear to and accepted by the employer and the client, and are available for consideration by the user and the public.

3.02. Ensure proper and achievable goals and objectives for any project on which they work or propose.

3.03. Identify, define and address ethical, economic, cultural, legal and environmental issues related to work projects.

3.04. Ensure that they are qualified for any project on which they work or propose to work, by an appropriate combination of education, training, and experience.

3.05. Ensure that an appropriate method is used for any project on which they work or propose to work.

3.06. Work to follow professional standards, when available, that are most appropriate for the task at hand, departing from these only when ethically or technically justified.

3.07. Strive to fully understand the specifications for software on which they work.

3.08. Ensure that specifications for software on which they work have been well documented, satisfy the users requirements and have the appropriate approvals.

3.09. Ensure realistic quantitative estimates of cost, scheduling, personnel, quality and outcomes on any project on which they work or propose to work and provide an uncertainty assessment of these estimates.

3.10. Ensure adequate testing, debugging, and review of software and related documents on which they work.

3.11. Ensure adequate documentation, including significant problems discovered and solutions adopted, for any project on which they work.

3.12. Work to develop software and related documents that respect the privacy of those who will be affected by that software.

3.13. Be careful to use only accurate data derived by ethical and lawful means, and use it only in ways properly authorized.

3.14. Maintain the integrity of data, being sensitive to outdated or flawed occurrences.

3.15. Treat all forms of software maintenance with the same professionalism as new development.

Principle 4—Judgment.
Software engineers shall maintain integrity and independence in their professional judgment. In particular, software engineers shall, as appropriate:

4.01. Temper all technical judgments by the need to support and maintain human values.

4.02. Only endorse documents either prepared under their supervision or within their areas of competence and with which they are in agreement.

4.03. Maintain professional objectivity with respect to any software or related documents they are asked to evaluate.

4.04. Not engage in deceptive financial practices such as bribery, double billing, or other improper financial practices.

4.05. Disclose to all concerned parties those conflicts of interest that cannot reasonably be avoided or escaped.

4.06. Refuse to participate, as members or advisors, in a private, governmental or professional body concerned with software related issues, in which they, their employers or their clients have undisclosed potential conflicts of interest.

Principle 5—Management.
Software engineering managers and leaders shall subscribe to and promote an ethical approach to the management of software development and maintenance. In particular, those managing or leading software engineers shall, as appropriate:

5.01. Ensure good management for any project on which they work, including effective procedures for promotion of quality and reduction of risk.

5.02. Ensure that software engineers are informed of standards before being held to them.

5.03. Ensure that software engineers know the employer's policies and procedures for protecting passwords, files and information that is confidential to the employer or confidential to others.

5.04. Assign work only after taking into account appropriate contributions of education and experience tempered with a desire to further that education and experience.

5.05. Ensure realistic quantitative estimates of cost, scheduling, personnel, quality and outcomes on any project on which they work or propose to work, and provide an uncertainty assessment of these estimates.

5.06. Attract potential software engineers only by full and accurate description of the conditions of employment.

5.07. Offer fair and just remuneration.

5.08. Not unjustly prevent someone from taking a position for which that person is suitably qualified.

5.09. Ensure that there is a fair agreement concerning ownership of any software, processes, research, writing, or other intellectual property to which a software engineer has contributed.

5.10. Provide for due process in hearing charges of violation of an employer's policy or of this Code.

5.11. Not ask a software engineer to do anything inconsistent with this Code.

5.12. Not punish anyone for expressing ethical concerns about a project.

Principle 6—Profession.
Software engineers shall advance the integrity and reputation of the profession consistent with the public interest. In particular, software engineers shall, as appropriate:

6.01. Help develop an organizational environment favorable to acting ethically.

6.02. Promote public knowledge of software engineering.

6.03. Extend software engineering knowledge by appropriate participation in professional organizations, meetings and publications.

6.04. Support, as members of a profession, other software engineers striving to follow this Code.

6.05. Not promote their own interest at the expense of the profession, client or employer.

6.06. Obey all laws governing their work, unless, in exceptional circumstances, such compliance is inconsistent with the public interest.

6.07. Be accurate in stating the characteristics of software on which they work, avoiding not only false claims but also claims that might reasonably be supposed to be speculative, vacuous, deceptive, misleading, or doubtful.

6.08. Take responsibility for detecting, correcting, and reporting errors in software and associated documents on which they work.

6.09. Ensure that clients, employers, and supervisors know of the software engineer's commitment to this Code of ethics, and the subsequent ramifications of such commitment.

6.10. Avoid associations with businesses and organizations which are in conflict with this code.

6.11. Recognize that violations of this Code are inconsistent with being a professional software engineer.

6.12. Express concerns to the people involved when significant violations of this Code are detected unless this is impossible, counterproductive, or dangerous.

6.13. Report significant violations of this Code to appropriate authorities when it is clear that consultation with people involved in these significant violations is impossible, counterproductive or dangerous.

Principle 7—Colleagues.
Software engineers shall be fair to and supportive of their colleagues. In particular, software engineers shall, as appropriate:

7.01. Encourage colleagues to adhere to this Code.

7.02. Assist colleagues in professional development.

7.03. Credit fully the work of others and refrain from taking undue credit.

7.04. Review the work of others in an objective, candid, and properly-documented way.

7.05. Give a fair hearing to the opinions, concerns, or complaints of a colleague.

7.06. Assist colleagues in being fully aware of current standard work practices including policies and procedures for protecting passwords, files and other confidential information, and security measures in general.

7.07. Not unfairly intervene in the career of any colleague; however, concern for the employer, the client or public interest may compel software engineers, in good faith, to question the competence of a colleague.

7.08. In situations outside of their own areas of competence, call upon the opinions of other professionals who have competence in that area.

Principle 8—Self.
Software engineers shall participate in lifelong learning regarding the practice of their profession and shall promote an ethical approach to the practice of the profession. In particular, software engineers shall continually endeavor to:

8.01. Further their knowledge of developments in the analysis, specification, design, development, maintenance and testing of software and related documents, together with the management of the development process.

8.02. Improve their ability to create safe, reliable, and useful quality software at reasonable cost and within a reasonable time.

8.03. Improve their ability to produce accurate, informative, and well-written documentation.

8.04. Improve their understanding of the software and related documents on which they work and of the environment in which they will be used.

8.05. Improve their knowledge of relevant standards and the law governing the software and related documents on which they work.

8.06. Improve their knowledge of this Code, its interpretation, and its application to their work.

8.07. Not give unfair treatment to anyone because of any irrelevant prejudices.

8.08. Not influence others to undertake any action that involves a breach of this Code.

8.09. Recognize that personal violations of this Code are inconsistent with being a professional software engineer.

This Code was developed by the IEEE-CS/ACM joint task force on Software Engineering Ethics and Professional Practices (SEEPP). Executive Committee: Donald Gotterbarn (Chair), Keith Miller and Simon Rogerson. Members: Steve Barber, Peter Barnes, Ilene Burnstein, Michael Davis, Amr El-Kadi, N. Ben Fairweather, Milton Fulghum, N. Jayaram, Tom Jewett, Mark Kanko, Ernie Kallman, Duncan Langford, Joyce Currie Little, Ed Mechler, Manuel J. Norman, Douglas Phillips, Peter Ron Prinzivalli, Patrick Sullivan, John Weckert, Vivian Weil, S. Weisband and Laurie Honour Werth.

The NSPE Code of Ethics

Preamble. Engineering is an important and learned profession. The members of the profession recognize that their work has a direct and vital impact on the quality of life of all people. Accordingly, the services provided by engineers require honesty, impartiality, fairness and equity, and must be dedicated to the protection of the public health, safety and welfare. In the practice of their profession, engineers must perform under a standard of professional behavior which requires adherence to the highest principles of ethical conduct on behalf of the public, clients, employers and the profession.

NSPE Code of Ethics—I. Fundamental Canons
Engineers, in the fulfillment of their professional duties, shall:

1. Hold paramount the safety, health and welfare of the public in the performance of their professional duties.
2. Perform services only in areas of their competence.

417

3. Issue public statements only in an objective and truthful manner.
4. Act in professional matters for each employer or client as faithful agents or trustees.
5. Avoid deceptive acts in the solicitation of professional employment.

NSPE Code of Ethics—II. Rules of Practice

1. Engineers shall hold paramount the safety, health and welfare of the public in the performance of their professional duties.
   (a) Engineers shall at all times recognize that their primary obligation is to protect the safety, health, property and welfare of the public. If their professional judgment is overruled under circumstances where the safety, health, property or welfare of the public are endangered, they shall notify their employer or client and such other authority as may be appropriate.
   (b) Engineers shall approve only those engineering documents which are safe for public health, property and welfare in conformity with accepted standards.
   (c) Engineers shall not reveal facts, data or information obtained in a professional capacity without the prior consent of the client or employer except as authorized or required by law or this Code.
   (d) Engineers shall not permit the use of their name or firm name nor associate in business ventures with any person or firm which they have reason to believe is engaging in fraudulent or dishonest business or professional practices.
   (e) Engineers having knowledge of any alleged violation of this Code shall cooperate with the proper authorities in furnishing such information or assistance as may be required.
2. Engineers shall perform services only in the areas of their competence:
   (a) Engineers shall undertake assignments only when qualified by education or experience in the specific technical fields involved.
   (b) Engineers shall not affix their signatures to any plans or documents dealing with subject matter in which they lack competence, nor to any plan or document not prepared under their direction and control.
   (c) Engineers may accept assignments and assume responsibility for coordination of an entire project and sign and seal the engineering documents for the entire project, provided that each technical segment is signed and sealed only by the qualified engineers who prepared the segment.
3. Engineers shall issue public statements only in an objective and truthful manner.

(a) Engineers shall be objective and truthful in professional reports, statements or testimony. They shall include all relevant and pertinent information in such reports, statements or testimony.
(b) Engineers may express publicly a professional opinion on technical subjects only when that opinion is founded upon adequate knowledge of the facts and competence in the subject matter.
(c) Engineers shall issue no statements, criticisms or arguments on technical matters which are inspired or paid for by interested parties, unless they have prefaced their comments by explicitly identifying the interested parties on whose behalf they are speaking, and by revealing the existence of any interest the engineers may have in the matters.

4. Engineers shall act in professional matters for each employer or client as faithful agents or trustees.
   (a) Engineers shall disclose all known or potential conflicts of interest to their employers or clients by promptly informing them of any business association, interest, or other circumstances which could influence or appear to influence their judgment or the quality of their services.
   (b) Engineers shall not accept compensation, financial or otherwise, from more than one party for services on the same project, or for services pertaining to the same project, unless the circumstances are fully disclosed to, and agreed to by, all interested parties.
   (c) Engineers shall not solicit or accept financial or other valuable consideration, directly or indirectly, from contractors, their agents, or other parties in connection with work for employers of clients for which they are responsible.
   (d) Engineers in public service as members, advisors or employees of a governmental body or department shall not participate in decisions with respect to professional services solicited or provided by them or their organizations in private or public engineering practice.
   (e) Engineers shall not solicit or accept a professional contract from a governmental body on which a principal or officer of their organization serves as a member.
5. Engineers shall avoid deceptive acts in the solicitation of professional employment.
   (a) Engineers shall not falsify or permit misrepresentation of their, or their associates', academic or professional qualifications. They shall not misrepresent or exaggerate their degree of responsibility in or for the subject matter of prior assignments. Brochure or other presentations incident to the solicitation of employment shall not misrepresent pertinent facts concerning employers, employees, associates, joint venturers or past accomplishments with the intent and purpose of enhancing their qualifications and their work.

(b) Engineers shall not offer, give, solicit or receive, either directly or indirectly, any political contribution in an amount intended to influence the award of a contract by public authority, or which may be reasonably construed by the public of having the effect or intent to influence the award of a contract. They shall not offer any gift, or other valuable consideration in order to secure work. They shall not pay a commission, percentage or brokerage fee in order to secure work except to a bona fide employee or bona fide established commercial or marketing agencies retained by them.

NSPE Code of Ethics—III. Professional Obligations

1. Engineers shall be guided in all their professional relations by the highest standards of integrity.
   (a) Engineers shall admit and accept their own errors when proven wrong and refrain from distorting or altering the facts in an attempt to justify their decisions.
   (b) Engineers shall advise their clients or employers when they believe a project will not be successful.
   (c) Engineers shall not accept outside employment to the detriment of their regular work or interest. Before accepting any outside employment, they will notify their employers.
   (d) Engineers shall not attempt to attract an engineer from another employer by false or misleading pretenses.
   (e) Engineers shall not actively participate in strikes, picket lines, or other collective coercive action.
   (f) Engineers shall avoid any act tending to promote their own interest at the expense of the dignity and integrity of the profession.

2. Engineers shall at all times strive to serve the public interest.
   (a) Engineers shall seek opportunities to be of constructive service in civic affairs and work for the advancement of the safety, health and well-being of their community.
   (b) Engineers shall not complete, sign, or seal plans and/or specifications that are not of a design safe to the public health and welfare and in conformity with accepted engineering standards. If the client or employer insists on such unprofessional conduct, they shall notify the proper authorities and withdraw from further service on the project.
   (c) Engineers shall endeavor to extend public knowledge and appreciation of engineering and its achievements and to protect the engineering profession from misrepresentation and misunderstanding.

3. Engineers shall avoid all conduct or practice which is likely to discredit the profession or deceive the public.
   (a) Engineers shall avoid the use of statements containing a material misrepresentation of fact or omitting a material fact necessary to keep statements from being misleading or intended or likely to create an unjustified expectation; statements containing prediction of future success; statements containing an opinion as to the quality of the Engineers' services; or statements intended or likely to attract clients by the use of showmanship, puffery, or self-laudation, including the use of slogans, jingles, or sensational language or format.
   (b) Consistent with the foregoing, Engineers may advertise for recruitment of personnel.
   (c) Consistent with the foregoing, Engineers may prepare articles for the lay or technical press, but such articles shall not imply credit to the author for work performed by others.

4. Engineers shall not disclose confidential information concerning the business affairs or technical processes of any present or former client or employer without his consent.
   (a) Engineers in the employ of others shall not without the consent of all interested parties enter promotional efforts or negotiations for work or make arrangements for other employment as a principal or to practice in connection with a specific project for which the Engineer has gained particular and specialized knowledge.
   (b) Engineers shall not, without the consent of all interested parties, participate in or represent an adversary interest in connection with a specific project or proceeding in which the Engineer has gained particular specialized knowledge on behalf of a former client or employer.

5. Engineers shall not be influenced in their professional duties by conflicting interests.
   (a) Engineers shall not accept financial or other considerations, including free engineering designs, from material or equipment suppliers for specifying their product.
   (b) Engineers shall not accept commissions or allowances, directly or indirectly, from contractors or other parties dealing with clients or employers of the Engineer in connection with work for which the Engineer is responsible.

6. Engineers shall uphold the principle of appropriate and adequate compensation for those engaged in engineering work.
   (a) Engineers shall not accept remuneration from either an employee or employment agency for giving employment.
   (b) Engineers, when employing other engineers, shall offer a salary according to professional qualifications.

7. Engineers shall not attempt to obtain employment or advancement or professional engagements by untruth-

fully criticizing other engineers, or by other improper or questionable methods.

(a) Engineers shall not request, propose, or accept a professional commission on a contingent basis under circumstances in which their professional judgment may be compromised.

(b) Engineers in salaried positions shall accept part-time engineering work only to the extent consistent with policies of the employer and in accordance with ethical consideration.

(c) Engineers shall not use equipment, supplies, laboratory, or office facilities of an employer to carry on outside private practice without consent.

8. Engineers shall not attempt to injure, maliciously or falsely, directly or indirectly, the professional reputation, prospects, practice or employment of other engineers, nor untruthfully criticize other engineers' work. Engineers who believe others are guilty of unethical or illegal practice shall present such information to the proper authority for action.

(a) Engineers in private practice shall not review the work of another engineer for the same client, except with the knowledge of such engineer, or unless the connection of such engineer with the work has been terminated.

(b) Engineers in governmental, industrial or educational employ are entitled to review and evaluate the work of other engineers when so required by their employment duties.

(c) Engineers in sales or industrial employ are entitled to make engineering comparisons of represented products with products of other suppliers.

9. Engineers shall accept responsibility for their professional activities; provided, however, that Engineers may seek indemnification for professional services arising out of their practice for other than gross negligence, where the Engineer's interests cannot otherwise be protected.

(a) Engineers shall conform with state registration laws in the practice of engineering.

(b) Engineers shall not use association with a nonengineer, a corporation, or partnership, as a "cloak" for unethical acts, but must accept personal responsibility for all professional acts.

10. Engineers shall give credit for engineering work to those to whom credit is due, and will recognize the proprietary interests of others.

(a) Engineers shall, whenever possible, name the person or persons who may be individually responsible for designs, inventions, writings, or other accomplishments.

(b) Engineers using designs supplied by a client recognize that the designs remain the property of the client and may not be duplicated by the Engineer for others without express permission.

(c) Engineers, before undertaking work for others in connection with which the Engineer may make improvements, plans, designs, inventions, or other records which may justify copyrights or patents, should enter into a positive agreement regarding ownership.

(d) Engineers' designs, data, records, and notes referring exclusively to an employer's work are the employer's property.

11. Engineers shall cooperate in extending the effectiveness of the profession by interchanging information and experience with other engineers and students, and will endeavor to provide opportunity for the professional development and advancement of engineers under their supervision.

(a) Engineers shall encourage engineering employees' efforts to improve their education.

(b) Engineers shall encourage engineering employees to attend and present papers at professional and technical society meetings.

(c) Engineers shall urge engineering employees to become registered at the earliest possible date.

(d) Engineers shall assign a professional engineer duties of a nature to utilize full training and experience, insofar as possible, and delegate lesser functions to subprofessionals or to technicians.

(e) Engineers shall provide a prospective engineering employee with complete information on working conditions and proposed status of employment, and after employment will keep employees informed of any changes.

"By order of the United States District Court for the District of Columbia, former Section 11(c) of the NSPE Code of Ethics prohibiting competitive bidding, and all policy statements, opinions, rulings or other guidelines interpreting its scope, have been rescinded as unlawfully interfering with the legal right of engineers, protected under the antitrust laws, to provide price information to prospective clients; accordingly, nothing contained in the NSPE Code of Ethics, policy statements, opinions, rulings or other guidelines prohibits the submission of price quotations or competitive bids for engineering services at any time or in any amount."

Statement by NSPE Executive Committee

In order to correct misunderstandings which have been indicated in some instances since the issuance of the Supreme Court decision and the entry of the Final Judgment, it is noted that in its decision of April 25, 1978, the Supreme Court of the United States declared: "The Sherman Act does not require competitive bidding."

It is further noted that as made clear in the Supreme Court decision:

1. Engineers and firms may individually refuse to bid for engineering services:

2. Clients are not required to seek bids for engineering services.

3. Federal, state, and local laws governing procedures to procure engineering services are not affected, and remain in full force and effect.

4. State societies and local chapters are free to actively and aggressively seek legislation for professional selection and negotiation procedures by public agencies.

5. State registration board rules of professional conduct, including rules prohibiting competitive bidding for engineering services, are not affected and remain in full force and effect. State registration boards with authority to adopt rules of professional conduct may adopt rules governing procedures to obtain engineering services.

6. As noted by the Supreme Court, "nothing in the judgment prevents NSPE and its members from attempting to influence governmental action. . . ."

Note: In regard to the question of the application of the Code to corporations vis-a-vis real persons, business form or type should not negate nor influence conformance of individuals to the Code. The Code deals with professional services, which services must be performed by real persons. Real persons in turn establish and implement policies within business structures. The Code is clearly written to apply to the Engineer and it is incumbent on a member of the NSPE to endeavor to live up to its provisions. This applies to all sections of the code.

Appendix C

Pointers to Additional Resources

- **The Ada Project (TAP)**
  The Ada Project (TAP) is described as "tapping Internet resources for women in computer science."

  http://www.mills.edu/ACAD_INFO/MCS/TAP/tap.html

- **Alcohol abuse**
  Santa Barbara County Alcohol and Drug Program online information service; starting points for general resources for this problem.

  http://www.silcom.com/~sbadp/

- **American Indian Science and Engineering Society (AISES)**

  http://www.aises.org

- **Association for Computing Machinery (ACM)**

  http://www.acm.org

- **Association of Information Technology Professionals (AITP)**

  http://www.aitp.org

  AITP
  315 South Northwest Highway, Suite 200
  Park Ridge, IL 60068-4278
  phone: 800.224.9371
  e-mail: aitp_hq@aitp.org

- **Computer Crime Directory**
  "The police officer's internet directory"

  http://www.officer.com/c_crimes.htm

- **Computer Emergency Response Team (CERT)**
  The organization to help with computer security on the Internet.

  http://www.cert.org

- **Computer Professionals for Social Responsibility (CPSR)**
  "A non-profit, public interest organization concerned with the effects of computers on society."

  http://www.cpsr.org/

- **Computing Research Association**
  Association of organizations of computing professionals; publishes the *Computing Research News* newsletter.

  http://www.cra.org

- **Electronic Frontier Foundation (EFF)**
  "A non-profit civil liberties public interest organization working to protect freedom of expression, privacy, and access to online resources and information."

  http://www.eff.org

- **Electronic Privacy Information Center (EPIC)**
  "A public interest research center to focus public attention on emerging civil liberties issues."

  http://www.epic.org

- **Equal Employment Opportunity Commission (EEOC)**

  http://www.eeoc.gov/

  toll-free number outside Washington, DC, area:
  (800) 669-EEOC
  TDD number outside Washington, DC, area:
  (800) 800-3302
  in Washington, DC, metropolitan area: (202) 663-4900
  TDD local number: (202) 663-4494

- **"Firewalls" mailing list**
  A mailing list for discussion of "firewall" systems for network security.
  To subscribe, send e-mail to majordomo@great-circle.com with "subscribe firewalls" in the body of the message.

- **Forum of Incident Response and Security Teams**
  "A coalition which brings together a variety of computer security incident response teams from government, commercial and academic organizations."

  http://www.first.org/

- **The "GNU's Not UNIX" ("free software") project**
  Recommended browsing—the source of the "open source" philosophy before the term existed.

  http://www.gnu.org/

- **Institute of Electrical and Electronics Engineers (IEEE)**

  http://www.ieee.org/

- **Internet Free Expression Alliance**
  "Works to ensure the continuation of the Internet as a forum for open, diverse and unimpeded expression and to maintain the vital role the Internet plays in providing an efficient and democratic means of distributing information around the world . . . ."

  http://www.ifea.net/

- **IEEE Society on Social Implications of Technology (SSIT)**

  http://www4.ncsu.edu/unity/users/j/jherkert/index.html

- **League for Programming Freedom**
  "The League for Programming Freedom is an organization that opposes software patents and user interface copyrights."

  http://lpf.ai.mit.edu/

- **National Action Council for Minorities in Engineering (NACME)**

  fttp://www.nacme.org/

- **National Society for Black Engineers (NSBE)**

  http://www.nsbe.org/

- **Online Ethics Center for Engineering–Ethics Help-Line**

  http://onlineethics.org/helpline/

- **RSA Data Security, Inc.**

  http://www.rsa.com

- **Society of Hispanic Professional Engineers (SHPE)**

  http://www.shpe.org/

- **Society of Women Engineers (SWE)**

  http://www.swe.org/

- **Software and Information Industry Assocation (SIIA)**

  http://www.siia.net

- **Special Counsel for Immigration-Related Unfair Employment Practices**
  toll-free number: (800) 255-7688
  TDD: (800) 237-2515

- **Taxpayers Against Fraud**
  An organization to aid whistle blowers in pursuing legal options under the False Claims Act.

  http://www.taf.org/

- **US House of Representatives**

  http://thomas.loc.gov

- **US Patent and Trademark Office**

  http://www.uspto.gov

INDEX

About the Editor

Kevin W. Bowyer is the author of the "Your Call" ethics and computing column that appears in *Computer* magazine. His columns on ethics and computing topics have also appeared in the IEEE Computer Society student newsletter, *Looking Forward.* Professor Bowyer led NSF-sponsored workshops for college and university faculty on "Teaching Ethics and Computing" in 1998 and 1999. Currently, Professor Bowyer is teaching in the Department of Computer Science and Engineering at the University of South Florida (USF).

Professor Bowyer received the B.S. from George Mason University and the Ph.D. from Duke University. Before joining USF, he was a member of the Computer Science faculty of Duke University and a member of the faculty of the Institute for Informatics at the Swiss Federal Technical Institute in Zurich. His current research interests are image understanding, pattern recognition, and medical image analysis. His research work in these areas has been supported by the National Science Foundation, the Air Force Office of Scientific Research, the Army Medical Research and Materiel Command, the National Aeronautics and Space Administration, and other sponsors.

Professor Bowyer received an Outstanding Undergraduate Teaching Award from the USF College of Engineering in 1991 and Teaching Incentive Program awards in 1994 and in 1997. Currently, he is serving as editor in chief of *IEEE Transactions on Pattern Analysis and Machine Intelligence,* and is a member of the editorial boards of *Computer Vision and Image Understanding, Image and Vision Computing, Machine Vision & Applications,* and the *International Journal of Pattern Recognition and Artificial Intelligence.* He served as general chair for the 1994 IEEE Computer Vision and Pattern Recognition Conference, and as chair of the IEEE Computer Society Technical Committee on Pattern Analysis and Machine Intelligence during 1995–1997. Professor Bowyer was elected as a Fellow of the IEEE in 1997.

Professor Bowyer's e-mail address is kwb@csee.usf.edu.

CPSIA information can be obtained
at www.ICGtesting.com
Printed in the USA
BVOW05s2339131216

470715BV00004B/45/P